MOON

HANDBOOKS

CHARLESTON & SAVANNAH

IM MOREKIS

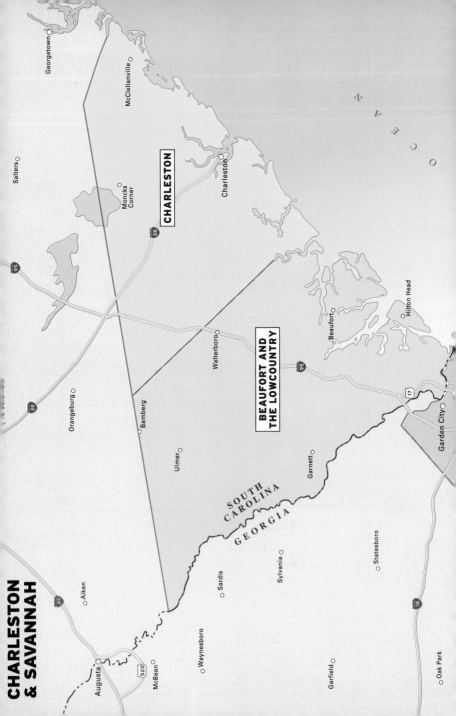

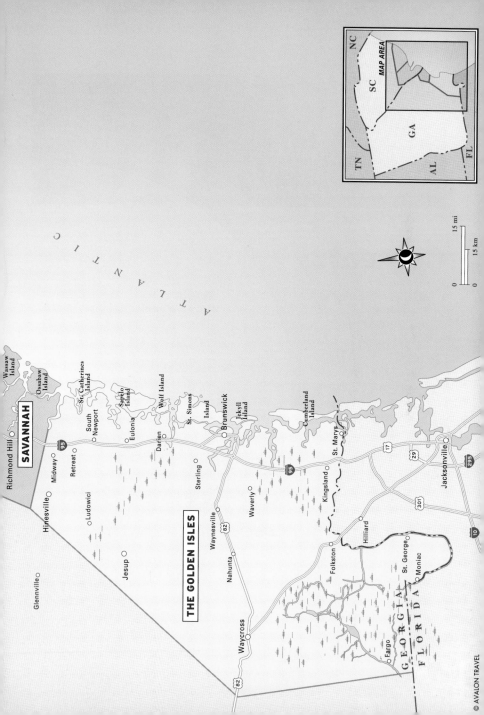

Contents

► **Discover Charleston &
Savannah** **6**
  Planning Your Trip 8
  Explore Charleston & Savannah. . 11
  • The Best of Charleston and
    Savannah 11
  • Southern Cooking: High-Style
    and Home-Style. 12
  • Literary Larks. 15
  • African American Heritage 16
  • Civil War History 18
  • Seaside Romance 20
  • Kayakers' Paradise 22

► **Charleston** **25**
  Sights. 32
  Entertainment and Events. 73
  Shopping. 85
  Sports and Recreation. 91
  Accommodations 97
  Food. 102
  Information and Services 114
  Getting There and Around. 115
  Greater Charleston. 117

► **Beaufort and
the Lowcountry** **127**
  Beaufort 131
  Hilton Head Island. 156

► **Savannah** **178**
  Sights. 185
  Entertainment and Events. 226
  Shopping. 236
  Sports and Recreation. 240
  Accommodations 245
  Food. 250
  Information and Services 260
  Getting There and Around. 262
  Outside Savannah. 264

► **The Golden Isles** **271**
  Brunswick and Glynn County 275
  Jekyll Island 285
  St. Simons Island. 294
  Darien and McIntosh County. 304
  Cumberland Island and St. Marys. . 310
  The Okefenokee Swamp 315

▶ **Background**.................. **321**
 The Land...................... 321
 Flora and Fauna................ 330
 History........................ 337
 Government and Economy 354
 People and Culture 357

▶ **Essentials** **364**
 Getting There and Around....... 364
 Recreation 366
 Tips for Travelers 369
 Health and Safety 371
 Information and Services 374

▶ **Resources** **377**
 Suggested Reading............. 377
 Internet Resources 379

▶ **Index**........................ **381**

▶ **Map Index** **391**

Discover Charleston & Savannah

Y ou can stand on the Battery in Charleston, feeling the salty breeze on your face, and easily imagine yourself in a throng of boisterous Charlestonians that fateful evening in 1861, gossiping of how the Yankees would be taught a lesson they'd never forget. Or you can walk the squares of Savannah and imagine yourself in cotton's heyday, walking from your townhouse through the squares to the river, seeing a forest of masts rise into view as the tall ships take on their precious cargo.

But contrary to stereotype, history is not all that's here. The Lowcountry and the Georgia coast comprise the largest contiguous salt marsh in the world and one of the most unique ecosystems on the planet. Kayakers are at home paddling in the blackwater of the ACE Basin or the vast Okefenokee Swamp. Sun-worshippers and beachcombers are often amazed at the underrated quality of the area's expansive, serene strands.

And then there are the people. It's one of the enduring ironies of America that deep in the heart of our most conservative region lie some of our most fun-loving cities. New Orleans heads the list of course, but Charleston and Savannah are hard on its heels. It's not just the fabled Southern hospitality, it's a joie de vivre born out of great weather and proximity to the ever-invigorating, all-encompassing water of the rivers, marshes, and ocean.

History, nature, good times — it's all there, but there's another

special ingredient that has inspired generations of writers to rise to the challenge of putting this area's many intangibles into words. Simply put, there's something about this region that cries out to have its story told.

You feel it when you canoe down the Altamaha River and come across a wooden sluice gate from an old rice paddy. You feel it when you pick up an oyster shell from an ancient Native American shell midden on Skidaway Island. You feel it when you walk from the heat of Charleston's Old City Market — a scene complete with fan-waving and basketweaving that wouldn't be out of place 200 years ago — into an air-conditioned, ultramodern café on King Street that wouldn't be out of place in Manhattan or Milan.

Ancient philosophies tell us that everything in the universe moves to a particular rhythm. That might be the "it" factor that compels so many to come to Charleston and Savannah again and again and inspires so many artists and writers. To put it in musical terms, Charleston and Savannah have found their groove.

Planning Your Trip

▶ WHERE TO GO

Charleston

One of America's oldest cities and an early national center of arts and culture, Charleston's legendary taste for the high life is matched by its forward-thinking outlook. The birthplace of the Civil War is not just a city of museums resting on its historic laurels. Situated on a hallowed spit of land known as "the peninsula," the Holy City is now a vibrant, creative hub of the New South.

Beaufort and the Lowcountry

The Lowcountry's mossy, laidback pace belies its former status as the heart of American plantation culture and the original cradle of secession. Today it is a mix of history (Beaufort and Bluffton), natural beauty (the ACE Basin), resort development (Hilton Head), military bases (Parris Island), and relaxed beaches (Edisto and Hunting Islands).

Savannah

Surprisingly cosmopolitan for a Deep South city, Savannah's quirky hedonism permeates any visit. The brainchild of General James Oglethorpe, the city's layout is studied even today as a masterpiece of urban design. Whether you're admiring an antebellum home from the cotton era or enjoying the sea breeze and a cocktail out on Tybee Island, a sense of fun imbues all parts of life here.

The Golden Isles

Georgia's Golden Isles are home to a third of the East Coast's salt marsh, and their natural beauty is a testament to the Gilded Age millionaires who kept the area largely undeveloped over the years. Even today, this region evokes a timeless mystique redolent of Spanish missions, Native American shell ring ceremonies, insular-but-friendly shrimping communities, and lonely English outposts.

Savannah's Forsyth Park Fountain

▶ WHEN TO GO

Springtime is for lovers, and it's no coincidence that springtime is the time when most love affairs with the region begin. Unless you have severe pollen allergies—not a trivial concern given the literal explosion of plant life at this time—you should try to experience this area at its peak of natural beauty during the magical period from mid-March to mid-May. Not surprisingly, lodging is the most expensive and most difficult to secure at that time.

The hardest time to get a room in Charleston is during Spoleto from Memorial Day through mid-June. Hilton Head's busiest time is during the Verizon Heritage golf tournament in mid-April. Savannah's tricky time of year is the St. Patrick's Day celebration, a multiday event clustering around March 17. While last-minute cancellations are always possible, the only real guarantee is to secure reservations as far in advance as possible (a full year in advance is not unusual for these peak times).

Activity here slows down noticeably in July and August. But overall, summertime in the South gets a bad rap, and is often not appreciably worse than summers north of the Mason–Dixon Line.

My favorite time of year on the southeastern coast is the middle of November, when the tourist crush noticeably subsides with the onset of the holidays. Not only are the days delightful and the nights crisp (but not frigid), but you can get a room at a good price.

IF YOU HAVE...

- **THREE DAYS:** Charleston, Beaufort, and Savannah.
- **FIVE DAYS:** Add Edisto Island, Hunting Island, Bluffton, and Hilton Head Island.
- **ONE WEEK:** Add the ACE Basin, Jekyll Island, and St. Simons Island.
- **TEN DAYS:** Add Cumberland Island and the Okefenokee Swamp.

Camellias bring brightness to the wintertime.

► BEFORE YOU GO

Walking is the best way to find the quiet joys of the area.

Getting There and Around

The most centrally located airport is Savannah/ Hilton Head International Airport; it's about 20 minutes from downtown Savannah, a half-hour from Hilton Head Island, and less than two hours from Charleston.

Less convenient to the rest of the region because of its location well north of the city is Charleston International Airport, about 20 miles north of Charleston, a 30-minute drive, minimum, from town. It's two hours from Charleston to Savannah, making the Charleston Airport at least 2.5 hours from Savannah.

Some travelers are using Jacksonville International Airport, about 20 miles north of Jacksonville, Florida. While it's a two-hour drive from Savannah, this airport's proximity to the attractions south of Savannah makes it attractive for some visitors, who can often find a good deal and make it worthwhile to make the drive.

I-95 is the dominant north–south interstate highway in the region, with the east–west interstates of I-16 and I-26 serving Savannah and Charleston, respectively.

The ideal way to get the full experience is to stay awhile in one or both cities, relying mostly on your own two feet for transportation, and visit outlying areas in your personal vehicle or a rental car. Outside the two main urban areas, public transportation is slim to none, so a vehicle is mandatory.

What to Take

Unless you're coming in the winter to take advantage of lower rates or to enjoy the seasonal cheer, there's no need for a heavy jacket. A sweater or windbreaker will do fine for chillier days. Also note that the ocean and the larger rivers can generate some surprisingly crisp breezes, even on what otherwise might be a warm day.

Because of the area's temperate climate, perspiration is likely to be a constant travel companion; pack accordingly. Whatever you wear, stay with natural fabrics such as cotton. The humidity and generally warm weather combine for a miserable experience with polyester and other synthetic fabrics.

Unless you're coming in the hottest days of summer or the coldest part of winter—both unlikely scenarios—plan on a trip to a drugstore or supermarket to buy some bug spray or Skin-So-Soft, an Avon product that also keeps away the gnats.

Explore Charleston & Savannah

▶ THE BEST OF CHARLESTON AND SAVANNAH

One of the South's most popular parlor games is comparing Charleston and Savannah, alike in so many ways but so different in others. The usual line is, "In Charleston they ask you what your mother's maiden name is, and in Savannah they ask what you're drinking." But the truth is that Savannah can be just as obsessed with arcane genealogy, and anyone who's ever spent a weekend night in downtown Charleston knows that city is no stranger to a carousing good time. Both cities share an abiding respect for social manners and mores, for history, for making money, and for good food and strong drink. They do differ in outlook: Charleston has one well-shod foot firmly in the global future, whereas Savannah tends to be more insular. The difference is also one of scale: Savannah's downtown is bigger and has more room to breathe and stretch

out, whereas Charleston's charms are more compact and serendipitous in nature. This "Best of" tour will allow you to come to your own conclusions. You'll also have an opportunity to factor in the unique charms of the South Carolina Lowcountry—once a hotbed of secession, now home to some of America's most patriotic citizens—and the scenic, enchanting Golden Isles of Georgia, one of the world's great natural playgrounds.

Day 1

Begin your journey in Charleston, the Holy City, named so not for any particular piety but for the number of steeples in its skyline. Avoid the rush to immerse yourself in the history all around you. First, feel the pulse of the city by going to its bustling heart, Marion Square. Maybe do a little shopping on King Street and at Old City Market

the legendary Jekyll Island Club

SOUTHERN COOKING: HIGH-STYLE AND HOME-STYLE

Food is one of the great delights of the Charleston and Savannah area – seafood, to be sure, from fresh shrimp to fish to crab cakes to oysters. But there's also barbecue galore, and a multicultural bonanza of worldly flavors. Here are some of the highlights of the area restaurant scene:

SEAFOOD

The best seafood places in the area depend on fresh, locally harvested fish and shellfish.

- Barbara Jean's, St. Simons Island (Golden Isles)
- Bowens Island Restaurant, Charleston
- COAST Bar and Grill, Charleston
- The Crab Shack, Tybee Island (Savannah)
- 11th Street Dockside, Port Royal (Lowcountry)
- Hymans Half Shell, Charleston
- Mistral, Charleston
- Mudcat Charlie's, Darien (Golden Isles)
- Red Fish, Hilton Head Island (Lowcountry)
- Saltus River Grill, Beaufort
- Speed's Kitchen, Shellman Bluff (Golden Isles)

NEW SOUTHERN

The area is home to some adventurous chefs offering an updated take on Lowcountry classics.

- Charleston Grill, Charleston
- Elizabeth on 37th, Savannah
- J. Mac's Island Restaurant, St. Simons Island (Golden Isles)
- McCrady's, Charleston
- Sapphire Grill, Savannah
- Slightly North of Broad, Charleston
- Tristan, Charleston

CLASSIC SOUTHERN

Here are your best bets for fine old-school Southern cooking, both high-style and home-style:

- Gullah Grub, St. Helena Island (Lowcountry)
- Jestine's Kitchen, Charleston
- Mom & Nikki's, Savannah
- Mrs. Wilkes's Dining Room, Savannah
- Peninsula Grill, Charleston
- See Wee Restaurant, Charleston

BARBECUE

The pleasures of the pig are never far away in this region. Here are the best coastal 'cue joints:

- Angel's BBQ, Savannah
- Bessinger's, Charleston
- Fiery Ron's Home Team, Charleston
- Georgia Pig, Brunswick
- Po-Pig's BBQ, Edisto Island (Charleston)
- Wall's BBQ, Savannah

Hymans Half Shell oyster bar

afterward. Take a sunset stroll around the Battery and admire Rainbow Row before diving right into a great meal at one of the city's fine restaurants.

Day 2

Today you put your historian's hat on and visit one of Charleston's great house museums, such as the Aiken-Rhett House or the Edmonston-Alston House. Have a hearty Southern-style lunch, then take an afternoon trip to Fort Sumter. After another fantastic Charleston dinner, take a carriage ride through the French Quarter to close the evening.

Day 3

After a hearty breakfast, head over the Ashley River to gorgeous Middleton Place, where you'll tour the gardens. Then stop at nearby Drayton Hall and see one of the oldest and best-preserved plantation homes in the nation. Head on into Beaufort and spend the afternoon around the beautifully preserved historic district.

Day 4

Check out early and go over the bridge to St. Helena Island and visit historic Penn Center. From there drive on to nearby Hunting Island State Park, where you can climb the lighthouse and enjoy the beach. On the way to Savannah, make an afternoon stop in Old Bluffton to shop for art, see the beautiful Church of the Cross on the May River, and have a light dinner. Check into a cute B&B in Savannah and relax for the night, maybe stopping in a pub for a pint or two.

Day 5

Hit downtown Savannah hard today, starting with a walk down River Street. Then enjoy the aesthetic charms of the two adjacent art museums, one traditional and

Tybee Lighthouse

one very modern, comprising the Telfair Museum of Art. Tour the exquisite Owens-Thomas House Museum and then take a walk through the squares, visiting the Cathedral of St. John the Baptist in Lafayette Square and the Mercer-Williams House on Monterey Square.

Day 6

On your way out to Tybee Island, stop for a walk through amazing Bonaventure Cemetery and pay your respects to native son Johnny Mercer. Then hit scenic and historically important Fort Pulaski National Monument. Scoot on into Tybee and take a climb to the top of the Tybee Lighthouse before dinner.

the tabby ruins of the Horton House on Jekyll Island

Day 7

Drive down scenic Highway 17 through the Altamaha River estuary and stop by historic Hofwyn-Broadfield Plantation, one of the most authentic glimpses at an old rice plantation you'll find. Head on into Brunswick's Old Town Historic District and have a leisurely walk around, maybe picking up a barbecue sandwich. Go over the causeway and enjoy the afternoon at The Village on St. Simons Island.

Day 8

This morning head to the Jekyll Island Historic District. Tour the grounds and have a lunch at any of the great restaurants on-site. Rent a bike and pedal up to the Clam Creek Picnic Area, checking out the Horton House Ruins along the way. Ride on the sand to Driftwood Beach and relax awhile.

Day 9

This morning drive to St. Marys and have a walk around the cute little downtown area before heading out on the ferry to Cumberland Island National Seashore for a full day of biking or hiking the many trails among the ruins and dunes.

Day 10

Make the drive into Folkston on to the Suwanee Canal Recreation Area at Okefenokee National Wildlife Refuge. Take a guided tour up and down the blackwater canal, or walk the trails out to the swamp's prairie vistas and drink in this unique natural beauty.

Cathedral of St. John the Baptist

historic Bonaventure Cemetery

intersection of King and Queen Streets

LITERARY LARKS

The area from Charleston down to Glynn County, Georgia, has hosted some of America's most beloved literary figures, each indelibly influenced in some way by the charms and mystique of the area itself. Here are some literary highlights of the area, with an eye toward soaking in the aspects of the South Carolina and Georgia coast that had such an impact on these authors' work.

- **Dorothea Benton Frank:** Fans can have a seafood lunch in Mount Pleasant outside Charleston on Shem Creek, namesake for her novel of the same name. Afterwards you can head over to the beach on nearby Sullivan's Island, namesake of Frank's novel *Sullivan's Island* and the place of her birth. Edgar Allen Poe was inspired to write *The Gold Bug* by his stay on Sullivan's Island during a stint in the Army.

- **Fanny Kemble:** A couple of miles south is Butler Island Plantation, where English actress Fanny Kemble, married to the owner, was moved to write *Journal of Residence on a Georgia Plantation,* one of the first anti-slavery books.

- **Flannery O'Connor:** In Savannah, visit the Flannery O'Connor Childhood Home and tour her church, the Cathedral of St. John the Baptist.

- **John Berendt:** Devotees of *Midnight in the Garden of Good and Evil* will enjoy the Mercer-Williams House, Club One, and Bonaventure Cemetery, which is also the final resting place of two of Savannah's most beloved native writers, Oscar-winning lyricist Johnny Mercer and Pulitzer-winning author Conrad Aiken.

- **Melissa Faye Green:** Darien, Georgia, is where Melissa Faye Green set her best-seller *Praying for Sheetrock.*

- **Pat Conroy:** Connoisseurs can visit Charleston's The Citadel, setting for *The Lords of Discipline;* Daufuskie Island, setting of *The Water is Wide;* and Beaufort, where he grew up. Conroy's dad Donald, the "Great Santini" himself, is buried in Beaufort National Cemetery.

- **Pogo:** For fans of the classic comic strip "Pogo," there's Okefenokee Swamp!

the Mercer-Williams House on Monterey Square

► AFRICAN AMERICAN HERITAGE

The cities and Sea Islands of the Lowcountry and Georgia coast are integral to a full understanding of the experience of African Americans in the South. More than that, they are living legacies, with a thriving culture whose roots can be traced directly back to West Africa. This tour not only hits the entirely unique Gullah/Geechee highlights, such as Daufuskie, St. Helena, and Sapelo Islands, but also the lesser-known historic aspects within cities such as Charleston, Beaufort, and Savannah.

Day 1

Begin your trip in Charleston with a busy day on foot. Shop in Old City Market; it never hosted a slave auction, but during its heyday, it was home to a number of African American entrepreneurs and vendors. Don't forget to walk by Cabbage Row, inspiration for "Catfish Row" of the African American–themed George Gershwin opera *Porgy and Bess.* Visit the newly opened Old Slave Mart and learn more about the Middle Passage and how Charleston's black population overcame the legacy of slavery. Spend the rest of the afternoon browsing through the research library at the Avery Research Center, one of the main repositories of Gullah and Lowcountry African American culture and history.

Day 2

Early this morning you take the ferry out to Fort Sumter, where the Civil War began. From the fort you can see nearby, undeveloped Morris Island, scene of the 1863 Battle of Battery Wagner, featuring the first all-black regiment in the U.S. Army, the 54th Massachusetts, whose gallant tale was recounted in the film *Glory.* Visit the nearby wrought-iron garden of the noted black Charleston artisan Phillip Simmons. After lunch take a guided African American history tour of downtown Charleston

Charleston's Old City Market

Penn Center on St. Helena Island

or tour the Aiken-Rhett House, with its excellently and respectfully preserved aspects of the African American servants who made the historic property run.

Day 3

Leave Charleston and cross the Ashley River for a trip to the National Trust–owned Drayton Hall; take the guided tour and pay respects at the African American cemetery. Then make the one-hour drive down to Beaufort. While walking around the scenic historic district, make sure to visit the Smalls House, home of the African American Civil War hero Robert Smalls, as well as his burial site at the Tabernacle Baptist Church. Drive by the Berners Barnwell Sams House to see where Harriet Tubman worked as a nurse and helped ferry slaves to freedom on the Underground Railroad. Visit Beaufort National Cemetery and see the memorial to the African American troops of the 54th and 55th Regiments of the U.S. Army in the Civil War.

Day 4

Make the short drive over the Beaufort River to St. Helena Island and spend the morning on the scenic campus of the Penn Center, a key clearinghouse for study and celebration of Gullah culture and the site of activism by Martin Luther King, Jr. in the 1960s. Head on into Hilton Head, stop by the Coastal Discovery Museum and take an African American heritage tour, visiting the site of Mitchelville, the first community of freed slaves in the United States.

Day 5

Drive an hour into Savannah and check out the African American Memorial statue on River Street. Head over to the former center of black life in Savannah, Martin Luther King Jr. Boulevard (once West Broad Street), and see the Ralph Mark Gilbert Civil Rights Museum and then the First African Baptist Church in City Market, the oldest black congregation in North America. Then visit the Second African Baptist Church,

CIVIL WAR HISTORY

This area is well known for its role in the Civil War. Throughout the region there are plenty of military history sights that highlight the Civil War era.

- In Charleston, go to **The Citadel** and enjoy the colorful weekly parade of cadets, the fabled "Thin Grey Line," at 3 P.M. most Fridays.

- Take the ferry out to **Fort Sumter,** where the Civil War began, as well as **Fort Moultrie,** which hosted a young Edgar Allen Poe in the years prior to the war.

- See the newly raised **CSS *Hunley*** at the decommissioned Navy Yard (only open Fridays and Saturdays).

- Visit historic **Drayton Hall,** America's oldest standing plantation home, saved from the torch only because Union troops thought it might have been used to quarantine smallpox victims.

- In Savannah, stop at the **Green-Meldrim House** where General Sherman made his headquarters.

- Visit **Fort Pulaski,** which a young Lieutenant Robert E. Lee helped to build.

- Stop by **Fort McAllister,** overrun by Union troops in 1864.

a peek inside the barracks at The Citadel

Robert Smalls Memorial · Gullah art at Red Piano Too · River Street and the Savannah River

where Sherman announced the famous "40 Acres and a Mule" field order. Close by is the Beach Institute, a repository of African American art, culture, and history. If you have time, check out the restored schoolroom at Massie School, Savannah's first African American school, and the Carnegie Library, Savannah's first black library, where future Supreme Court Justice Clarence Thomas once studied.

Day 6

You'll take the ferry from River Street for an entire day on Daufuskie Island, perhaps the best example of living Gullah culture in the world today. Take a guided tour of the entire island, including the famous Field School of Pat Conroy's *The Water is Wide,* and enjoy the glorious beach before taking the ferry back to Savannah for the night.

Day 7

On the way out of Savannah visit Laurel Grove South, a historic African American cemetery with stirring memorials to some of Savannah's most notable black figures. Jump on I-95 and head down to Darien. Take the ferry from nearby little Meridian out to Sapelo Island, taking a guided day tour of the island and its rich Gullah/Geechee history, including the community of Hog Hammock.

Drayton Hall is the nation's oldest surviving plantation home.

► SEASIDE ROMANCE

This is a no-brainer, because we're dealing with one of the most romantic areas on earth. Spanish moss, friendly beaches, sunsets over the water, sultry weather, moonlit carriage rides—what more could you ask for? The Lowcountry and Georgia coast pretty much wrote the book on romantic getaways for couples. Because the whole idea of a romantic getaway is to avoid too much stress and travel fatigue, here are two separate, short strategies—one oriented toward Charleston and the South Carolina Lowcountry, the other toward Savannah and Georgia's colonial coast. Or if you prefer, you can easily combine both trips into one longer one.

Lowcountry

DAY 1

Today you arrive at one of Charleston's most evocative historic B&Bs, such as the John Rutledge House or Two Meeting Street. Enjoy the sunset on a leisurely early evening stroll around the Battery before taking a cute pedicab ride a few blocks to your romantic Italian dinner on Lower King at Ile Cortile de Re. If you've got some walk left in you, mosey on up to Upper King for a nightcap at one of its hip cafés, and maybe get a little dancing in.

DAY 2

Enjoy the morning at your leisure before your next adventure, browsing the shops of world-famous King Street. End up near Marion Square and have a light lunch, maybe followed by a sweet treat at Cupcake. After dropping off your new purchases at your B&B, rest awhile before going on a ultra-romantic French Quarter carriage ride or maybe a sunset boat tour around Charleston Harbor. Have a fantastic French dinner at La Fourchette or mussels and music at Mistral. Then cuddle together in the bracing night air off the Cooper River on one of the swings at Waterfront Park.

the gorgeous historic gardens of Middleton Place Plantation

the expanse of Hunting Island State Park

DAY 3

Check out this morning and you're off to West Ashley to soak in the beauty of Middleton Place Plantation and its amazing landscaped gardens and beautiful Butterfly Lakes. Drive to Beaufort and have a tasty lunch at the upscale Saltus River Grill on the scenic waterfront. After enjoying Beaufort's quiet, friendly charms, drive onto your stay for the night, nearby Hunting Island State Park. You'll camp for the night in a cozy tent, or if it's the off-season—a great time for couples to visit—you can rent one of the 1930s-era cabins for two nights. (Cabin rentals require a week minimum during the high season.)

DAY 4

Hunting Island is a shell-collector's paradise, so take your morning coffee onto the beach and comb for shells together. Then it's time for a drive over to the secluded yet visitor-friendly Pinckney Island National Wildlife Refuge just outside Hilton Head. If you're ready for some civilization, head into Harbour Town for a bite at the marina. In any case, before spending your final night back at Hunting Island, be sure to stop by Old Town Bluffton and browse the funky art galleries before taking in the quiet views of the May River from grounds of Christ Church high on the bluff that gave the town its name. Before leaving Bluffton, have a tasty dinner at Pepper's Porch and a nightcap at the "Back Bar."

Georgia Coast

DAY 1

After your arrival in Savannah, begin with a leisurely walk through the squares of the Historic District. Avoid the lines at Lady & Sons and instead share a late lunch at quiet little Firefly Café on Troup Square. Check into your romantic B&B, such as the Foley House Inn in the heart of downtown. Tonight take in a show at the Lucas Theatre, a short walk away. Afterwards, walk down Broughton Street and have a late bite at the swank bar of *Il Pasticcio* or a Parisian-style dinner at Bistro

KAYAKERS' PARADISE

The area's rich matrix of criss-crossing tidal creeks, wide alluvial rivers, and exotic blackwater rivers is tailor-made for a special experience out on the water. This isn't a thrill-seeker's water odyssey, but rather a contemplative, almost primordial place teeming with wildlife, both indigenous and migratory.

CHARLESTON

Cape Romaine National Wildlife Refuge: Bull Island and Capers Island are highlights of this largely maritime preserve north of town, which comprises 66,000 acres of kayaking opportunities.

Crab Bank Heritage Preserve: This little 22-acre spot in Charleston Harbor is a hot bird-watching area, accessible to the public below the high water tidal line October 16–March 14.

BEAUFORT AND THE LOWCOUNTRY

ACE Basin: Comprising the estuaries of the Ashepoo, Combahee, and Edisto Rivers (the latter being the largest and most traveled), this is the most satisfying endeavor in the area for committed kayakers. Public landings and guided tours abound for trips on these nearly pristine blackwater runs.

More casual kayakers will enjoy putting in near Beaufort on the **Beaufort River, Factory Creek,** and **Port Royal Sound,** and on **Broad Creek** and **Skull Creek** on Hilton Head Island.

SAVANNAH

Little Tybee Island: This completely undeveloped island is a short run across the Back River from Tybee Island proper. You can do some wilderness camping there, too.

Skidaway Narrows: This route takes you by the grounds of the Skidaway Island State Park and often features dolphin. Look for the osprey nests on the channel markers.

Ebenezer Creek: This peaceful and sublime blackwater creek west of Savannah has some amazing cypress stands and old rice plantation artifacts.

THE GOLDEN ISLES

St. Simons Island: This barrier island is the focus of kayak activity down the Georgia coast. Tour operators based here can also take you on guided kayak trips to other nearby barrier islands accessible only by water, including Sapelo and Cumberland Islands.

Altamaha River: A run down this hybrid blackwater river, Georgia's largest, takes you by what were once some of America's largest rice plantations.

an old sluice gate at a rice paddy at Magnolia Plantation

relaxing Pinckney Island National Wildlife Refuge

Savannah near City Market. Up for a crazy night of dancing? Club One's the ticket.

DAY 2

Enjoy a relaxed breakfast and mosey on down to Forsyth Park and soak in its open greenspace. Pick up a few healthy goods at nearby Brighter Day Natural Foods and get in the car and go have a picnic at moss-draped, poignant Bonaventure Cemetery (yes, this cemetery can actually be quite romantic). Continue on to the scenic drive out to Tybee Island. Once on Tybee, kayaking couples can make the run across the Back River to secluded, undeveloped Little Tybee Island for a truly intimate nature experience. Or just take your time and walk along the beach until sunset. Have a quiet, classy dinner at the Hunter House before retiring back to the mainland for the evening, perhaps with a downscale nightcap at the always-fun Pinkie Masters or Hang Fire.

DAY 3

After breakfast, check out and take the scenic drive down the coast to Jekyll Island. Loll around on Driftwood Beach before checking into the Jekyll Island Club Hotel for a luxurious night in a suite that once may have hosted a famous millionaire. Rent a bike and criss-cross the whole island in the late afternoon, coming back to the Club to enjoy a romantic dinner by the fireplace at the Courtyard at Crane on the grounds.

DAY 4

Get up bright and early and drive down to St. Marys to take the ferry to Cumberland Island National Seashore, surely one of the most romantic locations on earth. Rent a bike on arrival and take your time pedaling among the ruins of the old mansions, making sure to visit the chapel at First African Baptist Church, site of the wedding of John F. Kennedy Jr. and Carolyn Bessette. Before you board the ferry to conclude your journey, maybe you'll get lucky and encounter some of the island's famous wild horses, a fitting symbol of passion and romance.

CHARLESTON

Charleston, South Carolina, boasts so many American "firsts" that it's almost a cliché to point them out: first museum, first theater, first public library, first municipal college, first golf club, first historic preservation ordinance—the list goes on and on.

But for the majority of visitors, the most important Charleston "first" is its perennial ranking at the top of the late Marjabelle Young Stewart's annual list for "Most Mannerly City in America." (Charleston has won the award so many times that Stewart's successor at the Charleston School of Protocol and Etiquette, Cindy Grosso, has retired the city from competition.) This is a city that takes civic harmony so seriously that it boasts the country's only "Livability Court," a binding legal proceeding that meets regularly to enforce local quality-of-life ordinances.

Everyone who spends time in Charleston comes away with a story to tell about the locals' courtesy and hospitality, and I'm sure you'll be no exception. Mine came while walking through the French Quarter admiring a certain handsome old single house on Church Street, one of the few that survived the fire of 1775. To my surprise, the lady chatting with a friend nearby turned out to be the homeowner. Noticing my interest in her house, she invited me in, a total stranger, to check out the progress of her renovation.

To some eyes, Charleston's hospitable nature has bordered on licentiousness, and from its earliest days the city gained a reputation for indulging in all kinds of vice. (The city's nickname, "The Holy City," derives from its abundance of church steeples rather than any excess

HIGHLIGHTS

The Battery: Tranquil surroundings combine with beautiful views of Charleston Harbor, key historical points in the Civil War, and amazing mansions (page 32).

Rainbow Row: Painted in warm pastels, these old merchant homes near the cobblestoned waterfront take you on a serene journey to Charleston's antebellum heyday (page 37).

Fort Sumter: Taking the ferry to this historic place where the Civil War began also features some gorgeous views along the way (page 45).

St. Philip's Episcopal Church: A sublimely beautiful sanctuary and two historic graveyards, all in the heart of the evocative French Quarter (page 46).

Old City Market: Equal parts history and kitsch combine to make this a fun stop in the heart of the tourist district (page 51).

Aiken-Rhett House: There are certainly more ostentatious house museums in Charleston, but none that provide such a virtually intact glimpse into real antebellum life (page 54).

Drayton Hall: Charleston's oldest surviving plantation home and one of America's best examples of professional historic preservation (page 58).

Middleton Place: Quite simply one of the world's most beautifully landscaped gardens – and the first in North America (page 61).

CSS *Hunley:* Newly ensconced for public viewing in its special preservation tank, the first submarine to sink a ship in battle is a moving example of bravery and sacrifice (page 64).

Edisto Beach State Park: A mecca for shell collectors and one of the most gorgeous beaches on the East Coast (page 117).

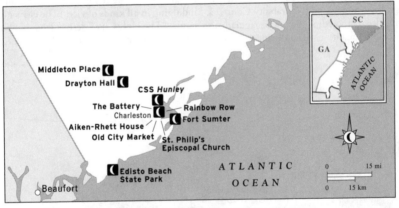

LOOK FOR **(** TO FIND RECOMMENDED SIGHTS, ACTIVITIES, DINING, AND LODGING.

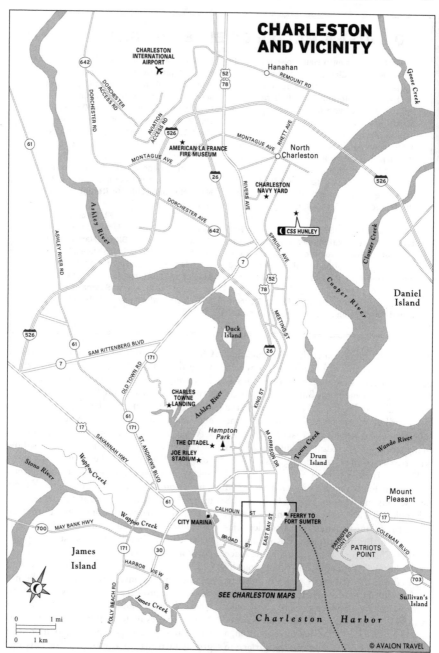

CHARLESTON AND VICINITY

CHARLESTON INTERNATIONAL AIRPORT

Hanahan

REMOUNT RD

DORCHESTER ACCESS RD

DORCHESTER RD

AVIATION ACCESS RD

MONTAGUE AVE

AMERICAN LA FRANCE FIRE MUSEUM

MONTAGUE AVE

RHETT AVE

North Charleston

RIVERS AVE

CHARLESTON NAVY YARD

DORCHESTER AVE

SPRUILL AVE

CSS HUNLEY

Ashley River

ASHLEY RIVER RD

MEETING ST

Cooper River

Clouter Creek

Goose Creek

Daniel Island

Duck Island

SAM RITTENBERG BLVD

OLD TOWN RD

CHARLES TOWNE LANDING

Ashley River

KING ST

M ORRISON DR

Town Creek

Wando River

ST. ANDREWS BLVD

SAVANNAH HWY

Hampton Park

THE CITADEL

JOE RILEY STADIUM

Drum Island

Mount Pleasant

Stono River

Wappoo Creek

MAY BANK HWY

Wappoo Creek

CALHOUN ST

EAST BAY ST

CITY MARINA

FERRY TO FORT SUMTER

PATRIOTS POINT RD

COLEMAN BLVD

PATRIOTS POINT

James Island

HARBOR VIEW RD

FOLLY BEACH RD

BROAD ST

James Creek

SEE CHARLESTON MAPS

Sullivan's Island

Charleston Harbor

0   1 mi

0   1 km

© AVALON TRAVEL

NOT JUST A MATTER OF BLUE AND GRAY

While this area is most well known for its role in the Civil War – Charleston's as the instigator of the conflict, and Savannah's as the terminus of Sherman's notorious "March to the Sea" – this is a drastic oversimplification. Although South Carolina was the "cradle of secession," it also lost more men in the fight for American independence than any other colony, including Massachusetts. Here are some military history highlights from other eras:

In Charleston, go to **The Citadel** and enjoy the colorful weekly parade of cadets, the fabled "Thin Grey Line," at 3 P.M. most Fridays. In Mount Pleasant eat lunch in the mess hall of the USS *Yorktown* at the **Patriot's Point Naval Museum.** Visit historic **Middleton Place,** home of one of the signers of the Declaration of Independence and where some scenes from Mel Gibson's *The Patriot* were filmed.

On Parris Island tour the **Marine Recruit Depot Parris Island** and see one of the oldest European archaeological sites in the United States, **Charlesfort.**

In Savannah, head to **Battlefield Park** and see the replicated British redoubt marking the failed Siege of Savannah. Visit **Old Fort Jackson,** an 1812-era installation on the Savannah River. Tour the **Mighty Eighth Air Force Museum,** which honors the contributions of the Eighth Air Force, founded in Savannah in 1942.

In Darien, Georgia, is **Fort King George,** first English outpost in Georgia. Nearby is **Harris Neck National Wildlife Refuge,** formerly a World War II airfield.

On St. Simons Island is **Ft. Frederica,** a tabby fort built by General James Oglethorpe, and the nearby **Battle of Bloody Marsh** site, where Oglethorpe ended the Spanish threat to Georgia.

While the big U.S. Navy Trident sub base at Kings Bay, Georgia, is not open to the public, check out the **St. Marys Submarine Museum** in St. Marys, which pays tribute to the "Silent Service."

---

of piety.) The old drinking clubs are gone, and the yearly bacchanal of Race Week—in which personal fortunes were won or lost in seconds—is but a distant memory. But that hedonistic legacy is alive and well today in Charleston; the city is full of lovers of strong drink and some serious foodies, with every weekend night (and many weeknights) finding downtown packed with partiers, diners, and show-goers.

Don't mistake the Holy City's charm and joie de vivre for weakness, however. That would be a serious mistake, for within Charleston's velvet glove has always been an iron fist. This is where the colonists scored their first clear victory over the British during the Revolution (yet another Charleston "first"). This is the place where the Civil War began, and which stoically endured one of the longest sieges in modern warfare during that conflict. This is the city that survived the East Coast's worst earthquake in 1886 and one of its worst hurricanes a century later. Despite its fun-loving reputation, a martial spirit is never far from the surface in Charleston, from the Citadel military college along the Ashley River, to the aircraft carrier *Yorktown* moored at Patriots Point across the harbor, to the cannonballs and mortars that children climb on at the Battery—even to the occasional tour guide in Confederate garb.

What may surprise you the most about this incredibly historic city is how *alive* it is, how young in spirit despite the length of its chronology. Not content to look backward in time, Charleston attracts some of the nation's most talented young professionals and entrepreneurs. Artists from all over the world continue to flock here, lured as always not only by the beauty and gentle climate, but the city's longstanding support for and keen enjoyment of the arts.

Despite Charleston's often-deserved reputation for conservatism, some of the nation's most progressive activity is going here, from the renovation of the old Navy Yard in North Charleston (currently the nation's largest urban redevelopment project), to impressive green start-ups, to any number of cutting-edge, sustainable residential developments. Charleston's a leader in conservation as well, with groups like the Lowcountry Open Land Trust and the Coastal Conservation League setting an example for the entire Southeast in how to bring environmental organizations and the business community together to preserve the area's beauty and ecosystem.

While many visitors come to see the Charleston of Rhett Butler and Pat Conroy— finding it and then some, of course—they leave impressed by the diversity of Charlestonian life. It's a surprisingly cosmopolitan mix of students, professionals, and longtime inhabitants—who discuss the finer points of Civil War history as if it were last year, party on Saturday night like there's no tomorrow, and go to church on Sunday morning dressed in their finest.

But don't be deceived by these history-minded people. Under the carefully honed tradition and the ever-present ancestor worship, Charleston possesses a vitality of vision that is irrepressibly practical and forward-looking.

HISTORY

Unlike so many of England's colonies in America that were based on freedom from religious persecution, Carolina was strictly a commercial venture from the beginning. The tenure of the Lords Proprietors—the eight English aristocrats who literally owned the colony—began in 1670 when the aptly named ship *Carolina* finished its journey to Albemarle Creek on the west bank of the Ashley River.

Those first colonists would set up a small fortification called Charles Town, named for Charles II, the first monarch of the Restoration. In a year they'd be joined by the first colonists from the prosperous and overcrowded British colony of Barbados, who brought a unique Caribbean sensibility that exists in Charleston to this day.

Finding the first Charles Town unhealthy, not very fertile, and vulnerable to attack from Native Americans and the Spanish, they moved over to the peninsula and down to "Oyster Point," what Charlestonians now call White Point Gardens. Just above Oyster Point they

set up a walled town, bounded by modern-day Water Street to the south (then a marshy creek, as the name indicates), Meeting Street to the west, Cumberland Street to the north, and the Cooper River on the east.

Growing prosperous as a trading center for fur and other goods from the great American interior, Charles Town really came into its own after two nearly concurrent events in the early 1700s: the decisive victory of a combined force of Carolinians and Native American allies against the fierce Yemassee tribe, and the final eradication of the ominous pirate threat in the deaths of Blackbeard and Stede Bonnet. Flushed with a new spirit of independence, Charles Town threw off the control of the anemic, disengaged Lords Proprietors, tore down the old defensive walls, and was reborn as simply Charlestown—outward-looking, expansive, and increasingly cosmopolitan.

With safety from hostile incursion came the time of the great rice and indigo plantations. Springing up all along the Ashley River soon after the introduction of the crops, they turned the labor and expertise of imported Africans into enormous profit for their owners. However, the planters much preferred the pleasures and sea breezes of Charlestown, and gradually their summer homes became their year-round residences.

It was during this Colonial era that the indelible marks of Charlestonian character were stamped: a hedonistic aristocracy combining a love of carousing with a love of the arts; a code of chivalry meant both to reflect a genteel spirit and reinforce the social order; and, ominously, an ever-increasing reliance on slave labor.

As the storm clouds of civil war gathered in the early 1800s, the majority of Charleston's population was of African descent, and the city was the main importation point for the transatlantic slave trade to the United States. The worst fears of white Charlestonians seemed confirmed during the alleged plot by slave leader Denmark Vesey in the early 1820s to start a rebellion. The Lowcountry's reliance on slave labor put it front and center in the coming national confrontation over abolition, which came to a head literally and figuratively in the bombardment of Fort Sumter in Charleston Harbor in April 1861.

By war's end, not only did the city lay in ruins—mostly from a disastrous fire in 1861, as well as from a 545-day Union siege—so did its way of life. Pillaged and burned by northern troops and freed slaves, the great plantations along the Ashley became the sites of the first strip mining in America, as poverty-stricken owners scraped away the layer of phosphate under the topsoil to sell—perhaps with a certain poetic justice—as fertilizer.

The Holy City didn't really wake up until the great "Charleston Renaissance" of the 1920s and '30s, when the city rediscovered art, literature, and music in the form of jazz and the world-famous Charleston dance.

This also was the time that the world rediscovered Charleston. In the 1920s, George Gershwin read local author Dubose Heyward's novel *Porgy* and decided to write a score around the story. Along with lyrics by Ira Gershwin, the three men's collaboration became the first American opera, *Porgy and Bess,* which debuted in New York in 1935. It was also during this time that a new appreciation for Charleston's history sprang up, as the local Preservation Society spearheaded the nation's first historic preservation ordinance.

World War II brought the same economic boom that came to much of the South in those times, most notably with an expansion of the Navy Yard and the addition of an Air Force base. By the 1950s, the automobile suburb and a thirst for "progress" claimed so many historic buildings that the inevitable backlash came with the formation of the Historic Charleston Foundation, which continues to lead the fight to keep intact the Holy City's architectural legacy.

Civil rights began coming to Charleston in earnest with a landmark suit to integrate the Charleston Municipal Golf Course, an effort which concluded in 1960 when Mayor Palmer Gaillard chose not to fight with what was clearly a losing legal hand. The mostly nonviolent resolution of years of Jim Crow continued, as a series of lunch counter sit-ins and lawsuits went on peacefully.

The biggest battle, however, would be the 100-day strike in 1969 against the Medical University of South Carolina, then, as now, a large employer of African Americans. The strike brought national attention to Charleston's civil rights struggle and ensured that the sacrifices of previous generations would not be in vain.

Charleston's next great renaissance—still ongoing today—came with the redevelopment of downtown and the fostering of the tourism industry under the 30-year-plus tenure of Mayor Joe Riley, during which so much of the current, visitor-friendly infrastructure became part of daily life here. Today, Charleston is completing the transition away from a military and manufacturing base and attracting professionals and artists to town.

PLANNING YOUR TIME

Even if you're just going to confine yourself to the peninsula, I cannot imagine spending less than two nights there. You'll want at least half a day for shopping on King Street and a full day for seeing various attractions and museums. Keep in mind that one of Charleston's key sights, Fort Sumter, will take almost half a day to see once you factor in ticketing and boarding time for the ferry out to the fort and back; plan accordingly.

If you have a rental car, there are several great places to visit off the peninsula—especially the plantations along the Ashley. None are very far away and navigation in Charleston is a snap. The farthest site from downtown should take no more than 30 minutes, and because the plantations are roughly adjacent, you can visit all of them in a single day if you get an early start.

While a good time is never far away in Charleston, keep in mind that this is the South and Sundays can get pretty slow. While the finely honed tourist infrastructure here means that there will always be something to do, the selection of open shops and restaurants dwindles on Sundays, though most other attractions keep working hours.

But for those of us who love the old city, there's nothing like a Sunday morning in Charleston—church bells ringing, families on their way to worship, a beguiling slowness in the air, perhaps spiced with the anticipation of a particular Charleston specialty—a hearty and delicious Sunday brunch.

Technically speaking, there are two high seasons in Charleston: mid-March through the first half of June, which of course includes Spoleto USA; and mid-September through the end of November. For practical purposes, however, many places are opting to consider the high season February–November.

The real issue for most visitors boils down to two questions: How much do you want to spend on accommodations, and in which part of town do you want to stay? Lodging is generally not cheap in Charleston, but because the price differential is not that much between staying on the peninsula and staying on the outskirts, I recommend the peninsula. You'll pay more, but not *that* much more, with the bonus of probably being able to walk to most places you want to see—which, after all, is the best way to enjoy the city.

ORIENTATION

Charleston occupies a peninsula bordered by the Ashley River to the west and the Cooper River to the east, which "come together to form the Atlantic Ocean," according to the haughty phrase once taught to generations of Charleston schoolchildren. Though the lower tip of the peninsula actually points closer to southeast, that direction is regarded locally as due south, and anything towards the top of the peninsula is considered due north. It's technically incorrect, but there's no use fighting it.

The peninsula is ringed by islands which have become more and more important and populated as suburbs. Clockwise from the top of the peninsula they are: Daniel Island, Mount Pleasant, Isle of Palms, Sullivan's Island, Morris Island, Folly Island, and James Island. The resort island of Kiawah and the much less-developed Edisto Island are farther south down the coast.

North Charleston is not only a separate municipality to the north of Charleston on the peninsula, it's also a different state of mind. A sprawling combination of malls, light industry, and lower-income housing, it's known as an area of high crime and poverty, though that's gradually changing.

While Charlestonians would scoff, the truth is that Charleston proper, the "Holy City" itself, has a surprising amount in common with Manhattan. Both are on long spits of land situated roughly north/south. Both were settled originally at the lower end in walled fortifications—Charleston's walls came down in 1718, while Manhattan still has its Wall Street as a reminder. Both cityscapes rely on age-old north/south streets that run nearly the whole length—Charleston's King and Meeting Streets, with only a block between them, and Manhattan's Broadway and Fifth Avenue. And like Manhattan, Charleston also has its own "Museum Mile" just off of a major greenspace, in Charleston's case up near Marion Square—though certainly its offerings are not as expansive as those a short walk from New York's Central Park.

Unfortunately, also like Manhattan, parking is at a premium in downtown Charleston. Luckily the city has many reasonably priced parking garages, which I heartily recommend that you use. But cars should only be used when you have to. Charleston is best enjoyed on foot, both because of its small size and the cozy, meandering nature of its old streets, designed not for cars and tour buses but for boots, horseshoes, and carriage wheels.

Charleston performs a kind of magic with time and space, its compact, walkable scale paradoxically making the city a world unto itself. A new surprise awaits you around every corner of the downtown area. A few short blocks from Meeting Street and its constant bustle of hotel staff preparing for the evening's banquets, you follow narrow streets curling through the old French Quarter until you find yourself at an old cemetery. In a flash you go from new to old as you read the names and dates on the worn tombstones, imagining what life was like in former days. Then you catch a whiff of fresh bread from a nearby artisan bakery, drawing you back into the new again. That's the magic of Charleston.

You'll see on your walks that Charleston is made up of many small neighborhoods, many of them quite old. The boundaries between them are confusing, so your best bet is to simply look at the street signs (signage in general is excellent in Charleston). If you're in a historic neighborhood, such as the French Quarter or Ansonborough, a smaller sign above the street name will indicate that.

Other key terms you'll undoubtedly hear are "the Crosstown," the portion of U.S. Highway 17 that goes across the peninsula; "Savannah Highway," the portion of Highway 17 that traverses "West Ashley," which is the suburb across the Ashley River; "East Cooper," the area across the Cooper River including Mount Pleasant, Isle of Palms, and Daniel and Sullivan's Islands; and "the Neck," up where the peninsula narrows. These are the terms that locals use, and hence what you'll see in this book.

Sights

Though most key sights in Charleston do indeed have some tie to the city's rich history, house museums are only a subset of the attractions here. Charleston's sights are excellently integrated into its overall built environment, and often the enjoyment of nearby gardens or a lapping river is part of the fun.

© JIM MOREKIS

the Battery and White Point Gardens

SOUTH OF BROAD

As one of the oldest streets in Charleston, the east–west thoroughfare of Broad Street is not only a physical landmark, it's a mental one as well. The first area of the Charleston peninsula to be settled, the area south of Broad Street—often shortened to the mischievous acronym "SOB" by local wags—features older homes, meandering streets (much of them built on "made land" filling in former wharfs), and a distinctly genteel, laid-back feel.

As you'd expect, it also features more affluent residents, sometimes irreverently referred to as "SOB Snobs." This heavily residential area has no nightlife to speak of and gets almost eerily quiet after hours, but rest assured that plenty of people live here. While I highly recommend just wandering among these narrow streets and marveling at the lovingly restored old homes, keep in mind that almost everything down here is in private hands. Don't wander into a garden or take photos inside a window unless you're invited to do so (and given Charleston's legendary hospitality, that can happen).

◀ The Battery

For many, the Battery (East Battery Street and Murray Boulevard, 843/724-7321, 24 hrs., free) is the single most iconic Charleston spot, drenched in history and boasting gorgeous

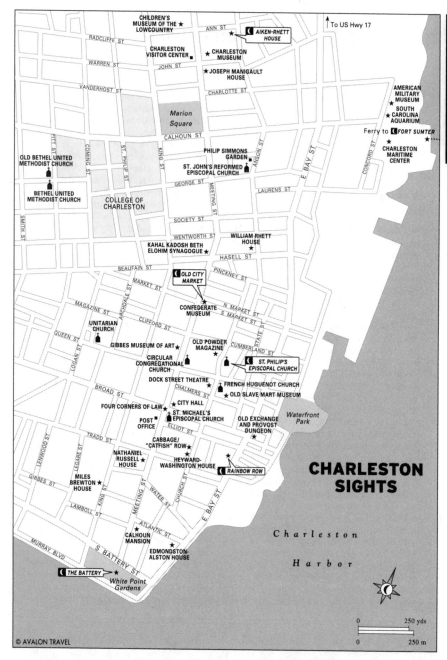

CHARLESTON SIGHTS

© AVALON TRAVEL

KNOW YOUR CHARLESTON HOUSES

As architects and historic preservationists have long known, Charleston's homes boast not only a long pedigree, but quite an interesting and unique one as well. Here are some key terms you should be familiar with:

Single House: A direct legacy of the early Barbadian planters among the very first settlers here, the Charleston single house is named for the fact that it's a single room wide – the better to fit deep, narrow downtown lots. The phrase refers to layout, not style, which can range from Georgian to Federal to Greek Revival, or even a combination. Furnished with full-length piazzas on the south side to take advantage of southerly breezes, the single house is perhaps America's first sustainable house design. The house sits lengthwise on the lot, with the main entrance on the side of the house. This of course means that the "backyard" is actually the side yard. Entry from the street is by a gate on one end of the lower piazza. A typical single house has three floors: a ground floor for business; a main floor for entertaining, living, and dining; and a top floor for sleeping. You can find them everywhere, but Church Street has some great examples, including 90, 92, and 94 Church Street, and the oldest single house in town, the 1720 Robert Brewton House (71 Church St.).

Double House: Two rooms' wide with a central hallway and a porched facade facing the street. Double houses often had separate carriage houses, the top floor of which was often reserved for servants' quarters. The Aiken-Rhett and Heyward-Washington houses are good examples of this more affluent, ostentatious design.

Piazza: The long porch or veranda of a single house, usually one for each floor and with southern exposure so that prevailing winds can sweep the length of the house. The roof of the piazza shades the windows on that side of the house. Room doors are also on the piazza side so that they can be left open if need be. The typical dearth of windows on the north side exemplifies the so-called "northside manner," protecting the privacy of the house next door. Another Caribbean trait via Barbados, piazzas sometimes feature balconies on top.

Charleston Green: This distinctively Charlestonian color – an extremely dark green that looks pitch black in low light or at a casual glance – has its roots in the penurious aftermath of the Civil War. The federal government distributed thousands of gallons of surplus black paint to contribute to reconstruction of the shell-and-fire-ravaged peninsula, but Charlestonians were too proud (not to mention too tasteful) to use it as is. So they added the tiniest bit of yellow to each gallon, producing the distinctive, historic color we now know as Charleston Green.

Earthquake Bolt: Structural damage after the 1886 earthquake was so extensive that many buildings were retrofitted with one or more long iron rods from wall to wall to keep the house stable. After installation the rod is then capped at both ends by a "gib plate," which is often disguised with a decorative element such as a lion's head, an S or X shape, or other design. Opinion among preservationists and engineers differs as to the efficacy of the bolts. Earthquake bolts can be seen all over town, but notable examples are at 235 Meeting Street, 198 East Bay Street, 407 King Street, 51 East Battery (rare star design), and 190 East. Bay Street (unusual for an X and an S plate on the same building).

Joggling Board: This long (10-15 ft.), flexible plank of cypress, palm, or pine with a handle at each end served various recreational purposes for early Charlestonians depending on their age. As babies, they might be gently bounced to sleep. As small children, they might use it as a trampoline. Later, it was a method of courtship, whereby a couple would start out at opposite ends and bounce up and down until they met in

© JIM MOREKIS

a great example of a single house in the French Quarter

the middle. Painted black or Charleston Green, joggling boards have made quite a comeback as decorative furnishings at many local homes.

Carolopolis Award: For over 50 years, the Preservation Society of Charleston has handed out these little black badges, to be mounted near the doorway of the winning home, to local homeowners who have renovated historic properties downtown. "Carolopolis" is the Latinized name of the city, "Condita A.D. 1670" is the Latin word for founding with the date of Charleston's inception, and the other date on the award refers to the award was given. Don't try counting them; well over 1,000 Carolopolis Awards have been given out since the Preservation Society came up with the idea in 1953.

Ironwork: Before the mid-19th century, wrought iron was a widely used ornament in Charleston, with the oldest surviving ex-

amples going back to the Revolutionary War period. Charleston's best-known blacksmith, Philip Simmons, has made a life's work of continuing the ancient craft of working in wrought iron, and his masterpieces are visible throughout the city, most notably at the Philip Simmons Garden (91 Anson St.), a specially commissioned gate for the Visitors Center (375 Meeting St.), and the Philip Simmons Children's Garden at Josiah Smith Tennent House at the corner of Blake and East Bay Sreets. Mass-produced cast iron became more common after the mid-1800s. *Chevaux-de-frise,* an early security device of sorts, comprises an iron bar on top of a wall, through which project some particularly menacing iron spikes. *Chevaux-de-frise* became popular after the Denmark Vesey slave revolt conspiracy of 1822. The best existing example is on the perimeter wall of the Miles Brewton House (27 King St).

views in all directions. A look to the south gives you the sweeping expanse of the Cooper River, with views of Fort Sumter, Castle Pinckney, Sullivan's Island, and off to the north the old carrier *Yorktown* moored at Mount Pleasant. A look to landward gives you a view of the adjoining, peaceful **White Point Gardens,** the sumptuous mansions of the Battery, and a beguiling peek behind them into some of the oldest neighborhoods in Charleston.

But if you had been one of the first European visitors to this tip of the peninsula about 400 years ago, you'd have seen how it got its first name, Oyster Point: This entire area was once home to an enormous outcropping of oysters. Their shells glistened bright white in the harsh Southern sun as a ship approached from seaward, hence its second name, White Point. Though the oysters are long gone and much of the area you're walking on is actually reclaimed marsh, the Battery and White Point Gardens are still a balm for the soul.

Once the bustling (and sometimes seedy) heart of Charleston's maritime activity, the Battery was where pirate Stede Bonnet and 21 of his men were hanged in 1718. As you might imagine, the area got its name for hosting cannon during the War of 1812, with the current distinctive seawall structure built in the 1850s.

Contrary to popular opinion, no guns fired from here on Fort Sumter at the beginning of the Civil War, as they would have been out of range. However, many thankfully inoperable cannon, mortars, and piles of shot still reside here, much to the delight of boys of all ages.

This is where Charlestonians gathered in a giddy, party-like atmosphere to watch the shelling of Fort Sumter in 1861, blissfully ignorant of the horrors to come. A short time later the North would return the favor, as the Battery and all of Charleston up to Broad Street would bear the brunt of shelling during the long siege of the city (the rest was just out of reach of Union guns).

But now, the Battery is a place to relax, not fight. The relaxation starts with the fact that there's usually plenty of free parking all along Battery Street. A promenade all around the periphery is a great place to stroll or jog. Add the calming, almost constant sea breeze and the meditative influence of the wide, blue Cooper River, and you'll see why this land's end—once so martial in nature—is now a favorite place for after-church family gatherings, tourists, lovestruck couples, and weddings (about 200 a year at the gazebo in White Point Gardens).

Still, military history is never far away in Charleston, and one of the chief landmarks at the Battery is the USS *Hobson* Memorial, remembering the sacrifice of the men of that vessel when it sank after a collision with the carrier USS *Wasp* in 1952. Numerous other martial memorials include a capstan from the USS *Maine,* part of an early PR effort in which pieces of the destroyed battleship were sent all over the United States to drum up support for the Spanish-American War. A less grim feature is the delightful "Little Dancer" fountain, just tall enough for small children to drink from (and pigeons as well, unfortunately).

Look for the three-story private residence where East Battery curves northward. You won't be taking any tours of it, but you should be aware that it's the **DeSaussure House** (1 E. Battery St.), best known in Charleston history for hosting rowdy, celebratory crowds on the roof and the piazzas to watch the 34-hour shelling of Fort Sumter in 1861.

Edmonston-Alston House

The most noteworthy single attraction on the Battery is undoubtedly the 1825 Edmonston-Alston House (21 E. Battery St., 843/722-7171, www.middletonplace.org, Tues.–Sat. 10 A.M.–4:30 P.M., Sun. 1–4:30 P.M., Mon. 1:30–4:30 P.M., $10 adults, $8 students), the only Battery home open to the public for tours. This is one of the most unique and well-preserved such historic homes in the United States, thanks to the ongoing efforts of the Alston family, who acquired the house from shipping merchant Charles Edmonston for $15,500 after the Panic of 1837, and still live on the third floor (tours only go to the first two stories).

Over 90 percent of the home's furnishing are original items from the Alston era, a percentage that's almost unheard of in the world of house museums. (Currently the House is owned and administered by the Middleton Place Foundation, best known for its stewardship of Middleton Place along the Ashley River.) You can still see the original paper bag used to store the houses deeds and mortgages. There's also a copy of the Ordinance of Secession and some interesting memorabilia from the golden days of Race Week, that time in February when all of Charleston society came out to bet on horses, carouse, and show off their finery.

The Edmonston-Alston House has withstood storm, fire, earthquake, and Yankee shelling, due in no small part to its sturdy construction; its masonry walls are two-bricks thick and it features both interior and exterior shutters. Originally built in the Federal style, second owner Charles Alston added several Greek Revival elements, notably the parapet, balcony, and piazza, where General Beauregard watched the attack on Fort Sumter.

Rainbow Row

From 79–107 East Bay between Tradd and Elliot Streets is one of the most photographed sights in the United States: colorful Rainbow Row. The reason for its name will become obvious when you see the array of pastel-colored mansions, all facing out over the Cooper River. The bright, historically accurate colors—nine of them, to be exact—are one of the many vestiges you'll see around town of Charleston's Caribbean heritage, a legacy of the English settlers from the colony of Barbados who were among the city's first citizens.

The homes are unusually old for this fire-, hurricane-, and earthquake-ravaged city, with most dating from 1730–1750. As you admire the Row from across East Battery Street, keep in mind you're actually walking on what used to be water. These houses were originally right on the Cooper River, their lower stories serving as storefronts on the wharf. The street was created later on top of landfill, or "made land" as it's called locally.

Besides its grace and beauty, Rainbow Row is of vital importance to American historic preservation. These were the first Charleston homes to be renovated and brought back from their early-20th-century seediness. The restoration projects on Rainbow Row directly inspired the creation of the Charleston Preservation Society, the first such group in the United States.

Continue walking up the High Battery past Rainbow Row and find Water Street. This aptly named little avenue was in fact a creek in the early days, acting as the southern border of the original walled city. The large brick building on the seaward side housing the Historic Charleston Foundation sits on the site of the old Granville bastion, a key defensive point in the wall.

Nathaniel Russell House

Considered one of the Charleston's grandest homes despite the fact that it was built by an outsider from Rhode Island, the Nathaniel Russell House (51 Meeting St., 843/724-8481, www.historiccharleston.org, Mon.–Sat. 10 A.M.–5 P.M., Sun. 2–5 P.M., last tour begins 4:45 P.M., $10) is now a National Historic Landmark and one of America's best examples of neoclassicism. Built in 1808 for the then-princely sum of $80,000 by Nathaniel Russell, a.k.a., "King of the Yankees," the home is currently furnished as accurately as possible to represent not only the lifestyle of the Russell family, but the 18 African American servants who shared the premises. The house eventually was bought by the Allson family, who amid the poverty of Civil War and Reconstruction decided in 1870 to sell it to the Sisters of Charity of Our Lady of Mercy as a school for young Catholic women.

Restorationists have identified 22 layers of paint within the home, which barely survived a tornado in 1811, got away with only minimal damage in the 1886 earthquake, but was damaged extensively by Hurricane Hugo in 1989 (and since repaired). As with fine antebellum homes throughout coastal South Carolina and Georgia, the use of faux finishing is prevalent throughout, mimicking surfaces from marble to wood to lapis lazuli. Visitors are often most impressed by the Nathaniel Russell House's magnificent "flying" spiral staircase, a work of such sublime carpentry and engineering that it needs no external support, twisting upwards of its own volition.

When you visit, keep in mind that you're in the epicenter of not only Charleston's historic preservation movement, but perhaps the nation's as well. In 1955, the Nathaniel Russell House was the first major project of the Historic Charleston Foundation, which raised $65,000 to purchase it. Two years later, admission fees from the house would support Historic Charleston's groundbreaking revolving fund for preservation, the prototype for many successful programs throughout historic areas of the United States. For an extra $6, you can gain admission to the Aiken-Rhett House farther uptown, also administered by the Historic Charleston Foundation.

Calhoun Mansion

The single largest of Charleston's surviving grand homes, the 1876 Calhoun Mansion (16 Meeting St., 843/722-8205, www.calhoun mansion.net, tours daily 11 A.M.–4:30 P.M., $15) boasts 35 opulent rooms (with 23 fireplaces!) in a striking Italianate design taking up a whopping 24,000 square feet. The grounds feature some charming garden spaces. Though the interiors at this privately run house are packed with antiques and furnishings, be aware that not all of them are accurate or period.

Miles Brewton House

A block away from the Nathaniel Russell House but much less viewed by tourists, the nearly perfect, circa-1769 Miles Brewton House (27 King St.), now a private residence, is maybe the best example of Georgian-Palladian architecture in the world. The almost medieval wrought-iron fencing, or *cheveaux de frise,* was added in 1822 after rumors of a slave uprising spread through town. This imposing double house was the site of not one but two headquarters of occupying armies, British General Clinton in the Revolution and the federal

The Miles Brewton House hosted two occupation headquarters.

© JIM MOREKIS

garrison after the end of the Civil War. The great Susan Pringle Frost, principal founder of the Charleston Preservation Society and a Brewton descendant, grew up here.

Heyward-Washington House

The Heyward-Washington House (87 Church St., 843/722-0354, www.charlestonmuseum .org, Mon.–Sat. 10 A.M.–5 P.M., Sun. 1–5 P.M., $10 adults, $5 children, combo tickets to Charleston Museum and Manigault House available) takes the regional practice of naming a historic home for the two most significant names in its pedigree to its logical extreme.

Built in 1772 by the father of Declaration of Independence signer Thomas Heyward Jr., the house also hosted George Washington himself during the president's visit to Charleston in 1791. It's now owned and operated by the Charleston Museum.

The main attraction at the Heyward-Washington House is its masterful woodwork, exemplified by the cabinetry of legendary Charleston carpenter Thomas Elfe. You'll see his work all over the house from the mantles to a Chippendale chair. Look for his signature of a figure eight with four diamonds.

Cabbage Row

You know these addresses from 89–91 Church Street better as "Catfish Row" of Gershwin's opera *Porgy and Bess* (itself based on the book *Porgy* by the great Charleston author Dubose Heyward, who lived at 76 Church St.). Today this complex—which once housed 10 families—next to the Heyward-Washington House hosts a number of shops and galleries mostly catering to tourists, but the row still has the humble appeal of the tenement housing it once was, primarily for freed African Americans after the Civil War. The house nearby at 94 Church Street was where John C. Calhoun and others drew up the infamous Nullification Acts leading to the South's secession.

St. Michael's Episcopal Church

The oldest church in South Carolina, St. Michael's Episcopal Church (71 Broad St.,

© JIM MOREKIS

the iconic steeple of St. Michael's Episcopal Church

843/723-0603, Sunday Mass 8 A.M. and 10:30 A.M., tours available after services) is actually the second sanctuary on this spot. The first church here was made out of black cypress, and called St. Philip's or "the English Church," which was later rebuilt on Church Street.

Though the designer is not known, we do know that work on this sanctuary in the style of Sir Christopher Wren began in 1752 as a response to the overflowing congregation at the rebuilt St. Philips, and didn't finish until 1761. Other than a small addition on the southeast corner in 1883 the St. Michael's you see today

is virtually unchanged, including the massive pulpit, outsized in the style of the time.

Worship services here over the years hosted such luminaries as Marquis de Lafayette, George Washington, and Robert E. Lee, the latter two of whom are known to have sat in the "governor's pew." Two signers of the U.S. Constitution, John Rutledge and Charles Cotesworth Pinckney, are buried in the sanctuary.

The 186-foot steeple, painted black during the Revolution in a futile effort to disguise it from British guns, actually sank eight inches after the earthquake of 1886. Inside the tower,

THE GREAT CHARLESTON EARTHQUAKE

The Charleston peninsula is bordered by three faults, almost like a picture frame: The Woodstock Fault above North Charleston, the Charleston Fault running along the east bank of the Cooper River, and the Ashley Fault to the west of the Ashley River. On August 31, 1886, one of them buckled, bringing one of the most damaging earthquakes ever to hit the United States.

The earthquake of 1886 was actually signaled by several shocks earlier that week. Residents of the nearby town of Summerville, South Carolina, 20 miles up the Ashley River, felt a small earthquake after midnight on Friday, August 27. Most slept through it. But soon after dawn a larger shock came, complete with a loud bang, causing many to run outside their houses. That Saturday afternoon another tremor hit Summerville, breaking windows and throwing a bed against a wall in one home. Still, Charlestonians remained unconcerned.

Then that Tuesday at 9:50 P.M. came the big one. With an epicenter somewhere near the Middleton Place plantation, the Charleston earthquake is estimated to have measured about 7 on the Richter scale. Tremors were felt across half the country, with the ground shaking in Chicago and a church damaged in Indianapolis.

A dam 120 miles away in Aiken, South Carolina, immediately gave way, washing a train right off the tracks. Cracks opened up parallel to the

Ashley River, with part of the riverbank falling into the water. Thousands of chimneys all over the state either fell or were rendered useless.

A Charleston minister at his summer home in Asheville, North Carolina, described a noise like the sound of wheels driving straight up the mountain, followed by the sound of many railroad cars going by. A moment later, one corner of his house lifted off the ground and slammed back down again.

The quake brought a series of "sand blows," a particularly disturbing phenomenon whereby craters open up and spew sand and water up into the air like a small volcano. In Charleston's case, some of the craters were 20 feet wide, shooting debris another 20 feet into the air.

The whole event lasted less than a minute.

In crowded Charleston, the damage was horrific: over 2,000 buildings destroyed, a quarter of the city's value gone, 27 killed immediately with almost 100 more to die from injuries and disease. Because of the large numbers of newly homeless, tent cities sprang up in every available park and greenspace. The American Red Cross's first field mission soon brought some relief, but the scarcity of food, and especially fresh water, made life difficult for everyone.

Almost every surviving building had experienced structural damage, in some cases severe, so a way had to be found to stabilize them. This led to the widespread use of the "earthquake bolt" now seen throughout older the famous "bells of St. Michael's" have an interesting story to tell, having made seven transatlantic voyages for a variety of reasons. They were forged in London's Whitechapel Foundry and sent over in 1764, only to be brought back as a war prize during the Revolution, after which they were returned to the church. Damaged during the Civil War, they were sent back to the foundry of their birth to be recast and returned to Charleston. In 1989 they were damaged by Hurricane Hugo, sent back to Whitechapel yet again, and returned to St. Michael's in 1993. Throughout the lifespan of the bells, the clock tower has continued to tell time, though the minute hand wasn't added until 1849.

St. Michael's offers informal, free guided tours to visitors after Sunday worship services; contact the greeter for more information.

Four Corners of Law

No guidebook is complete without a mention of this famous intersection of Broad and Meeting Streets, so named for its confluence of federal law (the Post Office building), state law (the state courthouse), municipal law (City Hall), and God's law (St. Michael's Episcopal

© JIM MOREKIS

earthquake bolts installed after the 1886 quake

Charleston homes. Essentially acting as very long screws with a washer on each end, the idea of the earthquake rod is simple: Poke a long iron rod through two walls that need stabilizing, and cap the ends. Charleston being Charleston, of course, the end caps were often decorated with a pattern or symbol.

The seismic activity of Charleston's earthquake was so intense that more than 300 aftershocks occurred in the 35 years after the event. In fact, geologists think that most seismic events measured in the region today – largely unnoticeable to those without the right instruments – are probably also aftershocks.

© JIM MOREKIS

the Old Exchange/Provost Dungeon

Church). That's all well and good, but no matter what the tour guides may tell you, the phrase "Four Corners of Law" was actually popularized by *Ripley's Believe It or Not!*

Still, there's no doubt that this intersection has been key to Charleston from the beginning. Meeting Street was laid out around 1672 and takes its name from the White Meeting House of the early Dissenters, i.e., non-Anglicans. Broad Street was also referred to as Cooper Street in the early days. Right in the middle of the street once stood the very first statue in America, a figure of William Pitt erected in 1766. You can see it today in the Charleston Museum.

WATERFRONT

Charleston's waterfront is a place where tourism, history, and industry coexist in an almost seamless fashion. Yet another of the successful—if at one time controversial—developments spearheaded by Mayor Joe Riley, the centerpiece of the harbor area as far as tourists are concerned is **Waterfront Park** down toward the High Battery. Farther up the Cooper River is

Aquarium Wharf, where you'll find the South Carolina Aquarium, the American Military Museum, the Fort Sumter Visitor Education Exhibit, and the dock where you take the various harbor ferries, whether to Fort Sumter or just a calming ride on the Cooper River.

Old Exchange/Provost Dungeon

Far from glamorous—and even bordering on the tacky—nonetheless the Old Exchange/Provost Dungeon (122 E. Bay St., 843/727-2165, www.oldexchange.com, daily 9 a.m.–5 p.m., $7 adults, $3.50 children and students) at the intersection of East Bay and Meeting Streets is brimming with history. It's known as one of the three most historically significant colonial buildings in the United States (Philadelphia's Independence Hall and Boston's Faneuil Hall being the other two). This is actually the old Royal Exchange and Custom House, with the cellar serving as a British prison, all built over a portion of the old 1698 fortification wall, some of which you can see today.

Three of Charleston's four signers of the

© JIM MOREKIS

Take a swing on the Cooper River at Waterfront Park.

Declaration of Independence did time downstairs for sedition against the crown. Later, happier times were experienced upstairs in the Exchange, as it was here where the state selected its delegates to the Continental Congress and ratified the U.S. Constitution and where George Washington took a spin on the dance floor. Nearly a victim of early 20th-century shortsightedness—it was almost demolished for a gas station in 1913—the building now fittingly belongs to the Daughters of the American Revolution.

Fans of kitsch will get a hoot out of the Animatronic, "Hall of the Presidents"–style figures. Kids might especially get a scary kick out of the basement dungeon, where the infamous pirate Stede Bonnet was imprisoned in 1718 before being hanged with his crew on the Battery.

Waterfront Park

Dubbing it "this generation's gift to the future," Mayor Joe Riley made the building of this eight-acre project another part of his ambitious and largely successful downtown renovation. Situated on Concord Street roughly between Exchange Street and Vendue Range, Waterfront Park (843/724-7327, daily dawn–dusk) was, like many waterfront locales in Charleston, built on what used to be marsh and water. This particularly massive chunk of "made land" juts about a football field's length farther out than the old waterline.

Visitors and locals alike enjoy the relaxing vista of Charleston Harbor, often from the many swinging benches arranged in an unusual front-to-back, single-file pattern all down the pier. Out on the end you can find viewing binoculars to see the various sights out on the Cooper River, chief among them the USS *Yorktown* at Patriot's Point and the big bridge to Mount Pleasant. Children will enjoy the "Vendue" fountain at the Park's entrance off of Vendue Range, while a bit farther south is the large and quite artful Pineapple Fountain with its surrounding wading pool. Contemporary art lovers of all ages will appreciate the unique **Waterfront Park City Gallery** (34 Prioleau St., Mon.–Fri. noon–5 P.M., free).

South Carolina Aquarium

Honestly, if you've been to any of the more expansive aquariums in Atlanta, Baltimore, or Monterey, you might be disappointed at the breadth of offerings at the South Carolina Aquarium (100 Aquarium Wharf, 843/720-1990, www.scaquarium.org, Mon.–Sat. 9 A.M.–5 P.M., Sun. noon–5 P.M., last ticket 4 P.M., $16 adults, $8 students, combo tickets with Fort Sumter tour available). But nonetheless, it's clean and well done and is a great place for the whole family to have some fun while educating themselves on the rich aquatic life—not only off the coast but throughout this small but ecologically diverse state.

When you enter you're greeted with the 15,000-gallon Carolina Seas tank, with placid nurse sharks and vicious-looking moray eels. Other exhibits highlight the five key South Carolina ecosystems: beach, salt marsh, coastal plain, piedmont, and mountain forest. Another neat display is the Touch Tank, a hands-on collection of invertebrates found along the coast, such as sea urchins and horseshoe crabs. The *pièce de résistance,* however, is certainly the three-story Great Ocean Tank with literally hundreds of deeper-water marine creatures, including sharks, pufferfish, and sea turtles.

Speaking of sea turtles: A key part of the Aquarium's research and outreach efforts is the Turtle Hospital, which attempts to rehabilitate and save sick and injured specimens. The hospital has so far saved 20 sea turtles, the first one being a 270-pound female affectionately known as "Edisto Mama."

Keep in mind that on weekdays during the school year the place is often chockablock with local schoolchildren on field trips. During the summer, closing time is extended an hour until 6 P.M., with the last ticket sold at 5 P.M. Note: In your research you might run across some information about an IMAX movie theater near the Aquarium. No matter what you read or hear elsewhere, this IMAX location is now closed.

American Military Museum

Slightly out of place thematically with the Aquarium, the American Military Museum (360 Concord St., 843/577-7000, www.americanmilitarymuseum.org, Mon.–Sat. 10 A.M.–6 P.M., Sun. 1–5 P.M., $6 adults, $3 students) is one of those under-the-radar types

---

C2B: YOU AND ME

Got a sailboat 30 feet long or longer? Wanna race 777 miles to Bermuda? Then batten down the hatches and enter in the annual **Charleston to Bermuda Race** (www.charlestontobermuda.com), or C2B. It's a real bluewater adventure in which sailors from around the world vie to be the first to sail from the Charleston harbor to St. David's Head on Bermuda.

While currently the *Gryphon Solo* holds the world 24-hour speed record for a 50-foot yacht, an honor secured in the C2B, many sail simply for the challenge and for the fun of it. Entries typically range from the minimum length on up to 100 feet; indeed, the winner of the inaugural event was the 30-foot *Hot Glue Gun.* The race typically takes 3–6 days to complete, with the unofficial course record so far clocking in at 73 hours.

As this is Charleston and therefore a party is never far away, part of the fun is the social whirl before the boats depart. Representatives of the Bermuda tourism board meet and mingle with crews and Charleston society in a fete usually held at the Hibernian Hall on Meeting Street. (The 2007 gala featured both South Carolina Governor Mark Sanford and Bermuda Premier Ewart Brown.) Bermuda returns the favor at the other end, hosting the finishing crews in a similar round of parties at race's end and giving out awards in a ceremony at the Bermuda Yacht Club.

With origins in a whimsical race thought up in 1997 by two local sailors, David Browder and Rick Hennigar, the C2B Race is currently owned and operated by the South Carolina Maritime Foundation. You can follow the course and speed of each entrant in real time at the online Race Tracker at www.charlestontobermuda.com.

of small, quaint museums that can be unexpectedly enriching. Certainly its location near the embarkation point for the Fort Sumter ferry hasn't hurt its profile. It's heavy on uniforms, with a wide range all the way from the Revolution to the modern day (my favorite is the 1907 naval uniform from the cruiser USS *Charleston*, part of Teddy Roosevelt's Great White Fleet). There's also a great collection of rare military miniatures.

🚩 Fort Sumter

This is it: the place that brought about the beginning of the Civil War, a Troy for modern times. Though many historians insist the war would have happened regardless of President Lincoln's decision to keep Fort Sumter (843/883-3123, www.nps.gov/fosu) in federal hands, nonetheless the stated *causus belli* was Major Robert Anderson's refusal to surrender the fort when requested to do so in the early morning hours of April 12, 1861.

A few hours later came the first shot of the war, fired from Fort Johnson by Confederate Captain George James. That 10-inch mortar shell, a signal for the general bombardment to begin, exploded above Fort Sumter, and nothing in Charleston, or the South, or America, would ever be the same again.

Notorious secessionist Edmund Ruffin gets credit for firing the first shot in anger, only moments after James's signal shell, from a battery at Cummings Point. Ruffin's 64-pound projectile scored a direct hit, smashing into the fort's southwest corner. The first return shot fired from Fort Sumter was fired by none other than Captain Abner Doubleday, the father of baseball. The first death of the Civil War also happened at Fort Sumter, not from the Confederate bombardment but on the day after. U.S. Army Private Daniel Hough died when the cannon he was loading, to be fired as part of a 100-gun surrender salute to the Stars and Stripes, exploded prematurely.

Today the battered but still-standing Fort Sumter remains astride the entrance to Charleston Harbor on the manmade, 70,000-ton sandbar begun in the early 1830s as the fort's home. Sumter was part of the so-called Third System of fortifications ordered after the War of 1812. Interestingly, the fort was still not quite finished when the Confederate guns opened up on it 50 years later, and never enjoyed its intended full complement of 135 big guns.

As you might expect, you can only visit by boat, specifically the approved concessionaire **Fort Sumter Tours** (843/881-7337, www.fort sumtertours.com, $14 adults, $8 ages 6–11, $12.50 seniors). Once at the fort, there's no charge for admission. Ferries leave from Liberty Square at Aquarium Wharf on the peninsula three times a day during the high season; call or check the website for times. Make sure to arrive about a half-hour before the ferry departs. You can also get to Fort Sumter by ferry from Patriot's Point at Mount Pleasant through the same company.

Budget at least 2.5 hours for the whole trip, including an hour at Fort Sumter. Once there, you can be enlightened by the regular ranger's talks on the fort's history and construction (generally at 11:00 A.M. and 2:30 P.M.), take in the interpretive exhibits throughout the site, and enjoy the view of the spires of the Holy City from afar.

For many, though, the highlight is the boat trip itself, with beautiful views of Charleston Harbor and the islands of the Cooper River estuary. If you want to skip Sumter, you can still take an enjoyable 90-minute ferry ride around the harbor and past the fort on the affiliated **Spiritline Cruises** (800/789-3678, www.spiritline cruises.com, $14 adults, $8 ages 6–11).

Some visitors are disappointed to find many of the gun embrasures bricked over. This was done during the Spanish-American War, when the old fort was turned into an earthwork and the newer Battery Huger (pronounced "Huge-E") was built on top of it.

FRENCH QUARTER

Unlike the New Orleans version, Charleston's French Quarter is strictly Protestant in origin and flavor. Though not actually given the name until a preservation effort hit it in the 1970s, historically this area was indeed the main place of commerce for the city's population of French Huguenots, primarily a merchant class who fled religious persecution in their native country.

Today the five-block area—roughly bounded by East Bay, Market Street, Meeting Street, and Broad Street—contains some of Charleston's most historic buildings, its most evocative old churches and graveyards, its most charming, narrow streets, and its most tasteful art galleries.

◖ St. Philip's Episcopal Church

With a pedigree dating back to the colony's fledgling years, St. Philip's Episcopal Church (142 Church St., 843/722-7734, www .stphilipschurchsc.org, sanctuary open weekdays 10 A.M.–noon and 2–4 P.M., Sunday Mass 8:15 A.M.) is the oldest Anglican congregation south of Virginia. That pedigree gets a little complicated and downright tragic at times, but any connoisseur of Charleston history needs to be clear on the fine points, so here goes:

The first St. Philip's was built in 1680 at the corner of Meeting Street and Broad Street,

© JIM MOREKIS

St. Philip's Episcopal Church

the present site of St. Michael's. That first St. Philip's was badly damaged by a hurricane in 1710, and the city fathers approved the building of a new sanctuary dedicated to the saint on Church Street. However, that building was nearly destroyed by yet another hurricane during construction. Sporadic fighting with local Native Americans further delayed rebuilding in 1721. Alas, that St. Philip's burned to the ground in 1835—a distressingly common fate for so many old buildings in this area. Construction immediately began on a replacement, and it's that building you see today. Heavily damaged by Hurricane Hugo in 1989, a $4.5-million renovation kept the church usable.

So to recap: St. Philip's was originally on the site of the present St. Michael's. And while St. Philip's is the oldest congregation in South Carolina, St. Michael's has the oldest actual church building in the state. Are we clear?

South Carolina's great statesman John C. Calhoun—who ironically despised Charlestonians for what he saw as their loose morals—was originally buried across Church Street in the former "stranger's churchyard," or West Cemetery, after his death in 1850. (Charles Pinckney and Edward Rutledge are two other notable South Carolinians buried there.) But near the end of the Civil War, Calhoun's body was moved to an unmarked grave closer to the sanctuary in an attempt to hide its location from Union troops, who it was feared would go out of their way to wreak vengeance on the tomb of one of slavery's staunchest advocates and the man who invented the doctrine of nullification. In 1880, with Reconstruction in full swing, the state legislature directed and funded the building of the current large memorial in the West Cemetery.

French Huguenot Church

One of the oldest congregations in town, the French Huguenot Church (44 Queen St., 843/722-4385, www.frenchhuguenotchurch .org, Sunday liturgy 10:30 A.M.) also has the distinction of being the only remaining independent Huguenot Church in the country. Founded around 1681 by French Calvinists,

FRENCH HUGUENOTS

A visitor can't spend a few hours in Charleston without coming across the many French-sounding names so prevalent in the region. Some are common surnames, such as Ravenel, Manigault, Gaillard, Laurens, or Huger (pronounced "Huge-E"). Some are street or place names, such as Mazyck or Legare (pronounced "Legree").

Unlike the predominantly French Catholic presence in Louisiana and coastal Alabama, the Gallic influence in Charleston was strictly of the Calvinist Protestant variety. Known as Huguenots, these French immigrants – refugees of an increasingly intolerant Catholic regime in their mother country – were numerous enough in the settlement by the 1690s that they were granted full citizenship and property rights if they swore allegiance to the British crown.

The Huguenot's quick rise in Charleston was due to two factors. Unlike other colonies, like Massachusetts and Pennsylvania, Carolina never put much of a premium on religious conformity, a trait that exists to this day despite the area's overall conservatism. And unlike many who fled European monarchies to come to the New World, the French Huguenots were far from poverty-stricken. Most had to buy their own journeys across the Atlantic, and most arrived already well educated and skilled in one or more useful trades.

In Charleston's early days, they were mostly wheat and barley farmers or tarburners. In later times their pragmatism and work ethic would lead them to higher positions in local society, such as lawyers, judges, and politicians. One of the wealthiest Charlestonians of all, the merchant Gabriel Manigault, was by some accounts the richest person in America during the early 1700s.

During that century a number of charitable aid organizations sprang up to serve various local groups, mostly along ethno-religious lines. The most wealthy and influential of them all was the South Carolina Society, founded in 1737 and first called "The Two Bit

© JIM MOREKIS

French Huguenot Church

Club" because of the original weekly dues. The Society still meets today at its building at 72 Meeting Street, designed in 1804 by none other than Manigault's grandson, also named Gabriel, who was Charleston's most celebrated amateur architect.

Another aid organization, the **Huguenot Society of Carolina** (138 Logan St., 843/723-3235, www.huguenotsociety.org, Mon.-Fri. 9 A.M.-2 P.M.), was established in 1885. Their library is a great research tool for anyone interested in French Protestant history and genealogy.

To this day, the spiritual home of Charleston's Huguenots is the same one as always: the French Huguenot Church on Church Street, one of the earliest congregations in the city. Though many of the old ways have gone, the church still holds one liturgy a year (in April) in the original French.

Dock Street Theatre, the first playhouse in the nation

the church had about 450 congregants by 1700. While refugees, they weren't destitute, as they had to pay for their passage to America.

As is the case with so many historic churches in the area, the building you see isn't the original sanctuary. The first church was built on this site in 1687, and became known as the "Church of Tides" because at that time the Cooper River lapped at its property line. This sanctuary was deliberately destroyed as a firebreak during the great conflagration of 1796. The church was replaced in 1800, but that building was in turn demolished in favor of the picturesque, stucco-coated Gothic Revival sanctuary you see today, which was completed in 1845 and subsequently survived Union shelling and heavy damage from the 1886 earthquake.

Does the church look kind of Dutch to you? There's a good reason for that. In their diaspora from their home country, French Huguenots spent a lot of time in Holland and became influenced by the tidy sensibilities of the Dutch people.

The history of the beautiful circa-1845

organ is interesting as well. A rare "tracker" organ, so named for its ultra-fast linkage between the keys the pipe valves, it was built by famed organ builder Henry Erben. After the fall of Charleston in 1865, Union troops had begun dismantling the instrument for shipment to New York when the church organist, T. P. O'Neale, successfully pleaded with them to let it stay.

Sunday services are conducted in English now, but a single annual service in French is still celebrated in April. The unique Huguenot Cross of Languedoc, which you'll occasionally see ornamenting the church, is essentially a Maltese Cross, its eight points representing the eight Beatitudes. Between the four arms of the cross are four fleurs-de-lis, the age-old French symbol of purity.

Dock Street Theatre

Unfortunately for visitors, the Dock Street Theatre (135 Church St., 843/720-3968) right down the street from the Huguenot Church will be closed for extensive (and long overdue)

© JIM MOREKIS

renovations to its infrastructure through at least spring 2010. However, any thespian or true lover of the stage must pay homage to this incarnation of the very first theater ever built in the Western Hemisphere.

So why is the Dock Street Theatre on Church Street? And where is Dock Street, anyway? In a distressingly familiar Charleston story, the original 1736 Dock Street Theatre on what's now Queen Street burned down. A second theater opened on the same site in 1754. That building was in turn demolished for a grander edifice in 1773, which, you guessed it, also burned down.

The current building dates from 1809, when the Planter's Hotel was built near the site of the original Dock Street Theatre. To mark the theater's centennial, the hotel added a stage facility in 1835, and it's that building you see today. For the theater's second centennial, the Works Progress Administration completely refurbished Dock Street back into a working theater in time to distract Charlestonians from the pains of the Great Depression. In addition to a very active and well-regarded annual season from the resident Charleston Stage Company, the 464-seat venue has hosted umpteen events of the Spoleto Festival over the past three decades, which will now be relocated until renovations are complete.

Old Powder Magazine

The Old Powder Magazine (79 Cumberland St., 843/722-9350, www.powdermag.org, Thurs.–Sun. 10 A.M.–4 P.M., $2 adults, $1 children) may be small, but the building is quite historically significant. The 1713 edifice is the oldest public building in South Carolina and also the only one that remains of the early days of the Lords Proprietors. As the name indicates, this was where the city's gunpowder was stored during the Revolution. The magazine is designed to implode rather than explode in the event of a direct hit.

This is another labor of love of the Historic Charleston Foundation, which has leased the building—which from a distance looks curiously like an ancient Byzantine church—from

The Colonial Dames since 1993. It was opened to the public as an attraction in 1997. Now directly across the street from a huge parking garage, the site has continued funding issues, so occasionally the hours for tours can be erratic. Inside you'll see displays, a section of the original brick, and an exposed earthquake rod. Right next door is the privately owned, circa-1709 Trott's Cottage, the first brick dwelling in Charleston.

Old Slave Mart Museum

Slave auctions became a big business in the South after 1808, when the United States banned further importation of slaves, thus increasing both price and demand. The auctions, with the slaves forced to stand on display on long tables, generally took place in public buildings where everyone could watch the wrenching spectacle of families being torn apart and lives ruined.

But in the 1850s, public auctions were banned in Charleston when city leaders discovered that visitors from European nations—all of which had banned slavery outright years before—were horrified and offended at the practice. So the slave trade was moved indoors to "marts" near the Cooper River waterfront where the sales could be conducted out of the public eye.

The last remaining such structure is the Old Slave Mart Museum (6 Chalmers St., 843/958-6467, www.charlestoncity.info, Mon.–Sat. 9 A.M.–5 P.M., $7 adults, $5 children, free for children five and under). Built in 1859, and originally known as Ryan's Mart after the builder, it was only in service a short time before the outbreak of the Civil War. The last auction was held in November 1863.

After the war, the Slave Mart became a tenement building, and then in 1938 an African American history museum. The city of Charleston acquired the building in the 1980s and reopened it as a museum in late 2007. There are two main areas: the orientation area, where visitors learn about the transatlantic slave trade and the architectural history of the building itself; and the main exhibit area, where visitors can see documents, tools, and displays re-creating what happened inside during this sordid chapter in local history and celebrating the resilience of the area's African American community.

NORTH OF BROAD

This tourist-heavy part of town is sometimes also called the Market area because of its proximity to the Old City Market. We'll start east at the border of the French Quarter on Meeting Street and work our way west and north toward Francis Marion Square.

Circular Congregational Church

The historic Circular Congregational Church (150 Meeting St., 843/577-6400, www .circularchurch.org, Sunday service 11 A.M., 10:15 A.M. summers) has one of the most interesting pedigrees of any house of worship in Charleston, which is saying a lot. Originally held on the site of the "White Meeting House," for which Meeting Street is named, services were held here beginning in 1681 for a polyglot mix of Congregationalists, Presbyterians, and Huguenots. For that reason it was often called the Church of Dissenters ("Dissenters" being the common term at the time for anyone not an Anglican).

As with many structures in town, the 1886 earthquake necessitated a rebuilding, and the current edifice actually dates from 1891. Ironically, in this municipality called "the Holy City" for its many high spires, the Circular Church has no steeple, and instead stays low to the ground in an almost medieval fashion. Look for the adjacent meeting house, which gave the street its name; a green-friendly addition houses the congregation's Christian outreach and has geothermal heating and cooling and boasts Charleston's only vegetative roof.

Gibbes Museum of Art

Directly across the street from the Circular Church, the Gibbes Museum of Art (135 Meeting St., 843/722-2706, www.gibbes museum.org, Tues.–Sat. 10 A.M.–5 P.M., Sun. 1–5 P.M., $9 adults, $7 students, $5 children

Gibbes Museum of Art

© JIM MOREKIS

6–12) is one of those rare Southern museums that manages a perfect blend of the modern and the traditional, the local and the international.

Beginning life in 1905 as the Gibbes Art Gallery—the final wish of James Shoolbred Gibbes, who willed $100,000 for its construction—the complex has grown through the years in both size and influence. The key addition to the original beaux arts building came in 1978 with the addition of the modern wing in the rear, which effectively doubled the museum's display space. Shortly thereafter the permanent collection and temporary exhibit space was also expanded. Serendipitously, these renovations enabled the Gibbes to become the key visual arts venue for the Spoleto Festival, begun about the same time.

The influential Gibbes Art School in the early 20th century formed a close association with the Woodstock School in New York, bringing important ties and prestige to the fledgling institution. Georgia O'Keefe, who taught college for a time in Columbia, South Carolina, brought an exhibit here in 1955. The first solo show by an African American artist here came in 1974 with an exhibit of the work of William H. Johnson.

Don't miss the gorgeous little garden and its centerpiece, the 1972 fountain and sculpture of Persephone by Marshall Fredericks. It's a perfect oasis to rest your feet before continuing on your personal art-appreciation discovery.

Unitarian Church

In a town filled with cool old church cemeteries, possibly the coolest belongs to the Unitarian Church (4 Archdale St., 843/723-4617, www.charlestonuu.org, Sunday service 11 A.M., free tours Fri.–Sat. 10 A.M.–1 P.M.) As a nod to the beauty and power of nature, vegetation and shrubbery in the cemetery have been allowed to take their natural course (walkways excepted). Virginia creeper wraps around 200-year-old-grave markers, honeybees feed on wildflowers, and tree roots threaten to engulf entire headstones. It's one of my favorite places in Charleston.

The church itself—the second-oldest such edifice in Charleston and the oldest Unitarian sanctuary in the South—is pretty cool, too. Begun in 1776 because of overcrowding at the Circular Congregational Church, the brand-new building saw rough usage by British troops during the Revolution. In 1787 the church was repaired and formally dedicated, though it was not officially chartered as a Unitarian church until 1839.

An extensive modernization happened in 1852, during which the current English Perpendicular Gothic Revival walls were installed, along with the beautiful stained-glass windows. The church was spared in the horrible fire of 1861, which destroyed the old Circular Church itself but stopped right at the Unitarian Church's property line. Sadly, it was not so lucky during the 1886 earthquake, which toppled the original tower. The version you see today is a subsequent and less grand design.

Directly next door is **St. John's Lutheran Church** (5 Clifford St., 843/723-2426, www.stjohnscharleston.org, Sunday worship 8:30

and 11 A.M.), which had its origin in 1742 when Dr. Henry Melchior Muhlenberg stopped in town for a couple of days on his way to minister to the burgeoning Salzburger colony in Ebenezer, Georgia. He would later be known as the father of the Lutheran Church in America. To see the sanctuary at times other than Sunday mornings, go by the office next door 9 A.M.–2 P.M. Mon.–Fri. and they'll let you take a walk through the interior.

◖ Old City Market

Part kitschy tourist trap, part glimpse into the old South, part community gathering place, Old City Market (Meeting and Market Streets, 843/973-7236, daily 6 A.M.–11:30 P.M.) remains Charleston's most reliable, if perhaps least flashy, attraction. It is certainly the practical center of the city's tourist trade, not least because so many tours originate nearby.

Originally built on Daniel's Creek—claimed from the marsh in the early 1800s after the city's first marketplace at Broad and Meeting Streets burned in 1796—one of City Market's early features was a colony of vultures who hung around for scraps of meat from the many butcher stalls. Sensing that the carrion eaters would keep the area cleaner than any human could, city officials not only allowed the buzzards to hang around, they were protected by law, becoming known as "Charleston eagles" in tongue-in-cheek local jargon.

Unlike Savannah's City Market (since demolished), Charleston's City Market never hosted a single slave auction—though it shared in common with Savannah's facility a preponderance of African American vendors. Indeed, when the Pinckney family donated this land to the city for a "Publick Market," one stipulation was that no slaves were *ever* to be sold here—or else the property would immediately revert to the family's descendants. And judging by the prevalence of the Pinckney name in these parts to this day, there has never been a shortage of potential claimants should that stipulation have been violated.

No matter what anyone tells you, the old train tracks around this area weren't for trolleys. During

World War II, a railroad ran from port facilities up the peninsula down here to warehouses.

Confederate Museum

Located on the second floor of City Market's main, iconic building, Market Hall on Meeting Street, the small but spirited Confederate Museum (188 Meeting St., 843/723-1541, Tues.–Sat. 11 A.M.–3:30 P.M., $5 adults, $3 children, cash only) hosts an interesting collection of Civil War memorabilia, with an emphasis on the military side, and is also the local headquarters of the United Daughters of the Confederacy. Perhaps its best contribution, however, is its research library.

Kahal Kadosh Beth Elohim Reform Temple

The birthplace of Reform Judaism in the United States and the oldest continuously active synagogue in the nation is Kahal Kadosh Beth Elohim Reform Temple (90 Hasell St., 843/723-1090, www.kkbe.org, Saturday service 11 A.M., tours Mon., Tues., Fri. 10 A.M.–noon, Wed.–Thurs. 10 A.M.–noon and 1:30–3:30 P.M., Sun. 12:30–3:45 P.M.) The congregation—Kahal Kadosh means "holy community" in Hebrew—was founded in 1749, with the current temple dating from 1840 and built in the Greek Revival style so popular at the time.

The church's Reform roots came about indirectly because of the great fire of 1838. In rebuilding, some congregants wanted to introduce musical instruments into the temple—previously a no-no—in the form of an organ. The Orthodox contingent lost the debate, and so the new building became the first home of Reform Judaism in the country, a fitting testament to Charleston's longstanding ecumenical spirit of religious tolerance and inclusiveness. Technically speaking, because the Holocaust destroyed all Reform temples in Europe, this is actually the oldest existing Reform synagogue in the world.

UPPER KING AREA

For many visitors, the area around King Street north of Calhoun Street is the most happening area of Charleston, and not only because its proximity to the Charleston Visitors Center makes it the first part of town many see up close. On some days—Saturdays when the Farmers Market is open, for instance—this bustling, active area of town seems a galaxy away from the quiet grace of the older South of Broad area.

Its closeness to the beautiful College of Charleston campus means there's never a shortage of young people around to patronize the area's restaurants and bars and to add a youthful feel to the whole place. And its closeness to the city's main shopping district, King Street, means there's never a shortage of happy shoppers toting bags of new merchandise.

Marion Square

While the Citadel moved lock, stock, and barrel almost a century ago, the college's old home, the South Carolina State Arsenal, still overlooks Francis Marion Square—a reminder of the former glory days when this was the institute's parade ground, the "Citadel Green" (the old Citadel is now a hotel). Interestingly, Marion Square (between King and Meeting Streets at Calhoun Street, 843/965-4104) can still be used as a parade ground, under agreement with the Washington Light Infantry and the Sumter Guard, which lease the square to the city. Seemingly refusing to give up on tradition—or perhaps just attracted by the many female College of Charleston students—uniformed cadets from the Citadel are still chockablock in Marion Square on any given weekend, a bit of local flavor that reminds you that you're definitely in Charleston.

Six-and-a-half acre Marion Square is named for the "Swamp Fox" himself, Revolutionary War hero and father of modern guerrilla warfare Francis Marion, for whom the hotel at the square's southwest corner is also named. The newest feature of Marion Square is the Holocaust Memorial on Calhoun Street. However, the dominant monument is the towering memorial to John C. Calhoun. Its 1858 cornerstone includes one of the more interesting time capsules you'll encounter: $100 in Continental money, a

© JIM MOREKIS

Marion Square

lock of John Calhoun's hair, and a cannonball from the Fort Moultrie battle.

Marion Square hosts many events, including the Farmers Market every Saturday from mid-April to late December, the Food and Wine Festival, and of course many Spoleto events.

College of Charleston

The oldest college in South Carolina and the first municipal college in America, the College of Charleston (66 George St., 843/805-5507, www.cofc.edu) boasts a fair share of history in addition to the way its 12,000-plus students bring a modern, youthful touch to so much of the city's public activities. While its services are no longer free, despite its historic moniker the College is now a full-blown, state-supported university in its own right.

Though the College has its share of new, modernistic buildings, a leisurely stroll around the campus will uncover some true gems of history. The oldest building on this gorgeous campus, the Bishop Robert Smith House, dates from the year of the College's founding, 1770,

and is now the president's house. Find it on Glebe Street between Wentworth and George.

The large Greek Revival building dominating the College's old quad off George and St. Philip's Streets is the magnificent Randolph Hall (1828), the oldest functioning college classroom building in the country and now hosting the president's office. The huge circular feature directly in front of it is "The Cistern," a historic reservoir that's a popular place for students to sit in the grass and enjoy the sun filtering through the surrounding live oaks. Movies that have shot scenes on campus include *Cold Mountain, The Patriot,* and *The Notebook.*

The College's main claims to academic fame are its outstanding Art History and Marine Biology departments, its performing arts program, and the groundbreaking **Avery Research Center for African American History and Culture** (843/953-7609, www.cofc.edu/avery, Mon.–Fri. 10 A.M.–5 P.M., Sat. noon–5 P.M.), which also features rotating exhibits from its permanent archive collection.

Charleston Museum

During its long history it has moved literally all over town and is currently housed in a noticeably modern building, but make no mistake: The Charleston Museum (360 Meeting St., 843/722-2996, www.charlestonmuseum.org, Mon.–Sat. 9 A.M.–5 P.M., Sun. 1–5 P.M., $10 adults, $5 children, combo tickets to Heyward-Washington and/or Manigault Houses available) is the nation's oldest museum, founded in 1773. It still strives to stay as fresh and relevant as any new museum, with a rotating schedule of special exhibits in addition to its very eclectic permanent collection.

For a long time this was the only place to get a glimpse of the CSS *Hunley,* albeit just a fanciful replica of it situated in front of the main entrance. (Now you can see the real thing at its conservation site in North Charleston, and it's even smaller than the replica would indicate.)

Most of the Charleston Museum's collection focuses on aspects of everyday life of Charlestonians from the aristocracy to the slaves, like utensils, clothing, and furniture. There are quirks as well, such as the Egyptian mummy and the fine lady's fan made out of turkey feathers. A particular and possibly surprising specialty includes work and research by noted regional naturalists like John James Audubon, André Michaux, and Mark Catesby. There are also numerous exhibits chronicling the local history of Native Americans and African Americans. There's something for children too, in the hands-on, interactive "Kidstory."

The location is particularly convenient, being close not only to the excellent Charleston Visitors Center and its equally excellent parking garage, but to the Joseph Manigault House (which the Museum runs), the Children's Museum of the Lowcountry, and the Gibbes Museum of Art.

Joseph Manigault House

Owned and operated by the nearby Charleston Museum, the Joseph Manigault House (350 Meeting St., 843/723-2926, www.charleston museum.org, Mon.–Sat. 10 A.M.–5 P.M., last tour 4:30 P.M., Sun., 1–5 P.M., last tour 4:30 P.M., $10 adults, $5 children, combo tickets to Charleston Museum and/or Heyward-Washington House available) is sometimes called the "Huguenot House." Its splendor is a good reminder of the fact that the French Protestants were far from poverty-stricken, unlike so many groups who came to America fleeing persecution.

This circa-1803 National Historic Landmark was designed by wealthy merchant and investor Gabriel Manigault for his brother, Joseph, a rice planter of local repute and fortune. (Gabriel, quite the crackerjack dilettante architect, also designed Charleston City Hall.) The three-story brick townhouse is a great example of Adams, or Federal, architecture. The furnishings are top-notch examples of 19th-century handiwork, and the rooms have been restored as accurately as possible, down to historically correct paint colors. Various outbuildings, including a privy and slaves' quarters, are clustered around the picturesque little Gate Temple to the rear of the main house in the large enclosed garden.

Each December, the Manigault House offers visitors a special treat, as the Garden Club of Charleston decorates it in period seasonal fashion, using only flowers that would have been used in the 19th century.

(Aiken-Rhett House

A comparatively recent acquisition of the Historic Charleston Foundation, the Aiken-Rhett House (48 Elizabeth St., 843/723-1159, www.historiccharleston.org, Mon.–Sat. 10 A.M.–5 P.M., Sun 2–5 P.M., last tour 4:30 P.M.) shows another side of that organization's mission. Whereas the Historic Charleston–run Nathaniel Russell House seeks to recreate and interpret a specific point in time, work at the Aiken-Rhett House, acquired in 1995, emphasizes stabilization, conservation, and research. Other than a limewash in 2006-work done under the auspices of a Save America's Treasures grant—comparatively little interpretive restoration is going on here.

And also unlike the Russell House, this is less of an ostentatious merchant's mansion than a working urban complex, a double house with a stable, a privy, and a particularly well-preserved slave quarters. Built in 1818 and expanded by South Carolina Governor William Aiken Jr., after whom we know the house today, parts of the house remained sealed from 1918 until 1975 when his family relinquished the property to the Charleston Museum, providing historians with a unique opportunity to study original documents from that period.

It was here that General Beauregard moved his headquarters during the Civil War to be out of range of the Union siege guns wreaking havoc in the lower part of the peninsula. You'd be forgiven for thinking the damaged state of some of the original wallpaper is due to the ravages of war, but it's actually water damage from Hurricane Hugo. Archaeology continues at the site, specifically in the area of the old capped well, which is giving researchers some insight into 19th-century construction methods in this high water table area.

Simply put, while there are plenty of much more vivaciously restored homes in Charleston, the Aiken-Rhett House provides the single most realistic and educational glimpse into antebellum life in the Holy City.

Children's Museum of the Lowcountry

Yet another example of Charleston's continued savvy regarding the tourist industry is the Children's Museum of the Lowcountry (25 Ann St., 843/853-8962, www.explorecml.org, Tues.–Sat. 10 A.M.–5 P.M., Sun. 1–5 P.M., $7). Recognizing that historic homes and Civil War memorabilia aren't enough to keep a family with young children in town for very long, the city established this museum in 2005 specifically to give families with kids aged 3 months to 12 years a reason to spend more time (and money) downtown.

A wide variety of hands-on activities—such as a 30-foot shrimp boat replica and a medieval castle—stretches the definition of "museum" to its limit. In truth, this is just as much an indoor playground as a museum, but there's no need to quibble. The Children's Museum has been getting rave reviews since it opened, and visiting parents and their children seem very happy with the city's wise investment.

Philip Simmons Garden

Charleston's most beloved artisan is ironworker Philip Simmons. Born on nearby Daniel Island in 1919, Simmons went through apprenticeship to become one of the most creative and sought-after decorative ironworkers in America. In 1982, the National Endowment for the Arts awarded him its National Heritage Fellowship. His work is on display at the National Museum of American History, the Smithsonian Institution, and the Museum of International Folk Art in Santa Fe, among many other places.

In 1989, the congregation at Simmons's **St. John's Reformed Episcopal Church** (91 Anson St., 843/722-4241, www.stjohnsre.org) voted to make the church garden a commemoration of life and work of the artisan, now 95. Completed in two phases, the Bell Garden and the Heart Garden, the project is a delightful blend of Simmons' signature graceful, sinuous style and fragrant flowers. Access is tricky; get there by way of tiny Menotti Street tucked beside the building.

Old Bethel United Methodist Church

The history of the Old Bethel United Methodist Church (222 Calhoun St., 843/722-3470), the third-oldest church building in Charleston, is a little confusing. Completed in 1807, the church once stood across Calhoun Street, until a schism formed in the black community over whether they should be limited to sitting in the galleries (in those days in the South, blacks and whites attended church together far more frequently than during the Jim Crow era). The entire black congregation wanted out, so in 1852 it was moved aside for the construction of a new church for whites, and then entirely across the street in 1880. Look across the street and sure enough you'll see the circa-1853 **Bethel Methodist Church** (57 Pitt St., 843/723-4587, Sunday worship 9 A.M. and 11:15 A.M.).

HAMPTON PARK AREA

Expansive, green Hampton Park is a favorite recreation spot for Charlestonians. The surrounding area near the east bank of the Ashley River has some of the earliest suburbs of Charleston, now in various states of restoration and hosting a diverse range of residents. Hampton Park is bordered by streets all around, which can be fairly heavily trafficked because this is the only way to get to the Citadel. But the park streets are closed to traffic Saturday mornings in the spring 8 A.M.–noon so neighborhood people, especially those with young children, can enjoy themselves without worrying about the traffic. This is also where the Charleston Police stable their Horse Patrol steeds.

The Citadel

Though for many its spiritual and historic center will always be at the old state Arsenal in Marion Square, The Citadel (171 Moultrie St., 843/953-3294, www.citadel.edu, daily 8 A.M.–6 P.M.) has been at this 300-acre site

WOMEN AND THE CITADEL: THE ONGOING STRUGGLE

Though a lot has certainly changed at The Citadel over a decade after courts mandated that it open its doors to female cadets, many of the same issues and obstacles remain at Charleston's formerly male-only military academy.

The first attempt to crack the gender barrier, by Shannon Faulker in 1994, failed miserably when she dropped out after less than a week, to much open celebration on campus. During her efforts, she endured not only the usual physical stress any Citadel cadet must face, but was also the subject of assorted cruelties, like bumper stickers all over town saying things like "Save the Males," one of the more printable slogans.

The star-crossed nature of Faulkner's effort was emphasized by the fact that her entrance came about because of a misunderstanding. School officials saw her first and middle names – Shannon Richey – and assumed she was a man!

The next episode came in 1996, when four female cadets were admitted, with two transferring out and filing suit against the school for sexual harassment. One of the two who remained, Nancy Mace, went on to become the first woman to graduate from The Citadel. While that accomplishment in 1999 was tempered somewhat by the fact that Mace's father was General James Emory Mace, Commandant of Cadets at the school at the time, it nonetheless marked a watershed moment in Citadel history.

In 2002, seven African American women cadets graduated from The Citadel, 32 years after Charles Foster first broke the racial barrier there in 1970 as the first African American graduate.

While the atmosphere has certainly gotten a lot more progressive at this conservative bastion – a "citadel" in more ways than one – not all is rosy. A 2006 survey found that 68 percent of women students (and 17 percent of male students) said they were victims of sexual harassment on campus. About one in five women reported a sexual assault on campus.

General John Rosa, president of The Citadel and former president of the U.S. Air Force Academy, said that though those numbers are not far off national numbers, they were "not good enough for us."

Currently over 100 of The Citadel's cadets are female – or about six percent of the student body, as opposed to about 16 percent at the service academies. And freshmen women cadets routinely have not only higher SAT scores than male cadets, but higher grade point averages as well.

Interestingly, Lu Parker, crowned Miss USA in 1994, got her master's degree in education from The Citadel. But she wasn't a cadet – all grad courses at The Citadel are night classes. And they don't even make you wear a uniform or do push-ups.

Nov.–Feb. daily 8:30 A.M.–4 P.M., Mar.–Oct. daily 8:30 A.M.–5 P.M., $14 adults, $8 ages 12–18, $6 ages 6–11, $8 for grounds only) is remarkable not only for its pedigree but for the way in which it's been preserved. This stately redbrick Georgian-Palladian building, the oldest plantation home in America open to the public, has been *literally* historically preserved—as in no electricity, heat, or running water.

Since its construction in 1738 by John Drayton, son of Magnolia Plantation founder Thomas, Drayton Hall has amazingly survived almost completely intact through the ups and downs of Lowcountry history. Drayton died while fleeing the British army in 1779; subsequently his house served as the headquarters of British General Clinton and later General Cornwallis. By 1782, however, American General "Mad Anthony" Wayne had claimed the house as his own headquarters in the name of the new country.

During the Civil War, Drayton Hall escaped the depredations of the conquering Union Army, one of only three plantation homes to survive. Three schools of thought have emerged to explain why it was spared the fate of so many other Lowcountry plantation homes: 1) A slave told the troops it was owned by "a Union Man," Drayton cousin Percival who served alongside Admiral David Farragut of "damn the torpedoes" fame; 2) General William Sherman was in love with one of the Drayton women; and 3) one of the Draytons, a doctor, craftily posted yellow smallpox warning flags at the outskirts of the property. Of the three, the last is considered the most likely, though we'll never know for sure.

Visitors expecting the more typical approach to house museums—i.e., subjective renovation with period furnishings that may or may not have any connection at all with the actual house—might be disappointed. But for others the experience at Drayton Hall is quietly exhilarating, almost in a Zen-like way. Planes are even routed around the house so that no rattles will endanger its structural integrity. There's no furniture here to speak of, only the bare rooms, decorated only with the original paint,

no matter how little remains. It can be jarring at first, but after you get into it you might wonder why anyone does things any differently.

Another way the experience is different is in the almost military professionalism of the National Trust for Historic Preservation, which has owned and administered Drayton Hall since 1974. The guides are professionals and hold degrees in the field, and a tour of the house—offered punctually at the top of the hour, except for the last of the day which starts on the half-hour—takes every bit of 50 minutes, about twice as long as most house tours. A separate 45-minute program is "Connections: From Africa to America," which chronicles the diaspora of the slaves who originally worked this plantation, from their capture to their eventual freedom. "Connections" is given at 11:15 A.M., 1:15 P.M., and 3:15 P.M.

The site comprises not only the main house but two self-guided walking trails, one along the peaceful Ashley River and another along the marsh. Note also the foundations of the two "flankers," or guest wings, at each side of the main house. They survived the Yankees only for one to fall victim to the 1886 earthquake and the other to the 1893 hurricane. Also on-site is an African American cemetery with at least 33 known graves. It's kept deliberately untended and unlandscaped to honor the final wish of Richmond Bowens (1908–1998), the seventh-generation descendant of some of Drayton Hall's original slaves.

Magnolia Plantation and Gardens

Another, completely different legacy of the Drayton family is Magnolia Plantation and Gardens (3550 Ashley Rd., 843/571-1266, www.magnoliaplantation.com, Mar.–Oct. daily 8 A.M.–dusk, call for winter hours, $15 adults, $10 children, $14 seniors). It boasts not only the first garden in the United States, dating back to the 1680s, but also the first public gardens, dating to 1872.

However, Magnolia's history spans back two full centuries before that, when Thomas Drayton Jr.—scion of Norman aristocracy, son of a wealthy Barbadian planter—came

the Maze at Magnolia Plantation and Gardens

here from the Caribbean to build his own fortune. He immediately married the daughter of Stephen Fox, who began this plantation in 1676. Throughout wars, fevers, depressions, earthquakes, and hurricanes, Magnolia has stayed in the possession of an unbroken line of Drayton descendants to this very day.

As a privately run attraction, Magnolia has little of the academic veneer of other historic plantations in the area, most of which have long passed out of private hands. There's a slightly kitschy feel here, the opposite of the quiet dignity of Drayton Hall. And unlike Middleton Place a few miles down the road, the gardens here are anything but manicured, with a wild, almost playful feel. All that being said, Magnolia can claim fame to being one of the earliest bona fide tourist attractions in the United States and the beginning of Charleston's now-booming tourist industry.

It happened after the Civil War, when John Grimke Drayton, reduced to near-poverty, sold off most of his property, including the original Magnolia Plantation, just to stay afloat. (In a common practice at the time, as a condition of inheriting the plantation Mr. Grimke, who married into the family, was required to legally change his name to Drayton.) The original plantation home was burned during the war—either by Union troops or freed slaves—so Drayton barged a colonial-era summer house in Summerville, South Carolina, down the Ashley River to this site, and built the modern Magnolia Plantation around it specifically as an attraction.

Before long, tourists regularly came here by crowded boat from Charleston (a wreck of one such ferry is still on-site). Magnolia's reputation became so exalted that at one point Baedecker's listed it as one of the three main attractions in America, alongside the Grand Canyon and Niagara Falls.

The family took things to the next level in the 1970s, when the family nursery business was no longer commercially viable. John Drayton Hastie bought out his brother and set about marketing Magnolia Plantation and Gardens as a modern tourist destination, adding more varieties of flowers so that something would always be blooming nearly year-round. While spring remains the best time to come—and also the most crowded—a huge variety of camellias blooms in the early winter, a time marked by a yearly "Winter Camellia Festival" on-site.

Today that vision is fully a reality, and Magnolia is a place to bring the whole family, picnic under the massive old live oaks, and wander the lush, almost overgrown grounds. Children will enjoy finding their way through "The Maze" of manicured camellia and holly bushes, complete with a viewing stand to look within the giant puzzle.

Plant lovers will enjoy the themed gardens such as the "Biblical Garden," the "Barbados Tropical Garden," and the "Audubon Swamp Garden," complete with alligators and named after John James Audubon, who visited here in 1851. Hundreds of varieties of camellias, clearly labeled, line the narrow walkways. House tours, the 45-minute Nature Train tour, the 45-minute Nature Boat tour, and a visit to the Audubon Swamp Garden run about $7 extra per person for each offering.

Of particular interest is the poignant old Drayton Tomb, along the Ashley River, which housed many members of the family until being heavily damaged in the 1886 earthquake. Look closely at the nose of one of the cherubs on the tomb; it was shot off by a vengeful Union soldier. Nearby you'll find a nice walking and biking trail along the Ashley among the old rice paddies.

◖ Middleton Place

Not only the first formal, landscaped garden in America but still one of the most magnificent in the world, Middleton Place (4300 Ashley River Rd., 843/556-6020, www.middleton place.org, daily 9 A.M.–5 P.M., $25 adults, $5 ages 7–15, guided house tour additional $10) is a sublime, unforgettable combination of history and sheer natural beauty. Nestled along a quiet bend in the Ashley River, the grounds contain a historic restored home, working stables, and 60 acres of breathtaking gardens,

all manicured to perfection. A stunning piece of totally modern architecture, the Inn at Middleton Place, completes the package in a surprisingly harmonic fashion.

First granted in 1675 a scant five years after the first English settlement here, Middleton Place is perhaps the culmination of the Lowcountry rice plantation aesthetic. That sensibility is most immediately seen in the graceful Butterfly Lakes at the foot of the green, landscaped terrace leading up to the Middleton Place House itself, the only surviving remnant of the vengeful Union occupation. The two wing-shaped lakes, 10 years in the construction, seem to echo the low rice paddies that once dotted this entire landscape.

In 1741 the plantation became the family seat of the Middletons, one of the most notable surnames in U.S. history. The first head of the household was Henry Middleton, president of the First Continental Congress, who began work on the meticulously planned and maintained gardens. The plantation passed to his son Arthur, a signer of the Declaration of Independence; then on to Arthur's son Henry, governor of South Carolina; and then down to Henry's son, Williams Middleton, signer of the Ordinance of Secession.

It was then that things turned sour, both for the family and for the grounds themselves. As the Civil War wound down, on February 22, 1865, the 56th New York Volunteers burned and looted the main house and destroyed the gardens, leaving only the circa-1755 guest wing, which today is the Middleton Place House Museum. The great earthquake of 1886 added insult to injury by wrecking the Butterfly Lakes.

It wasn't until 1916 that any renovation work began at all, when heir J. J. Pringle Smith took on the project as his own. No one can say he wasn't successful. At the garden's bicentennial in 1941, the Garden Club of America awarded its prestigious Bulkley Medal to Middleton Place. In 1971 Middleton Place was named a National Historic Landmark, and 20 years later the International Committee on Monuments and Sites named Middleton

Place one of six U.S. gardens of international importance.

In 1974, Smith's heirs established the non-profit Middleton Place Foundation, which now owns and operates the entire site. As development has increased along the Ashley River, several developers and at least one nearby private landowner have donated easements to protect the irreplaceable view from the site.

All that's left of the great house are the broken remains of the foundation, still majestic even in ruin. But today visitors can tour the excellently restored **Middleton Place House Museum** (4300 Ashley River Rd., 843/556-6020, www.middletonplace.org, daily 9 A.M.–5 P.M., last tour 4:30 P.M., guided tour $10) and see furniture, silverware, china, and books belonging to the Middletons, as well as family portraits by Thomas Sully and Benjamin West. A short walk takes you to the Plantation Stableyards, where costumed craftspeople still work using historically authentic tools and methods, surrounded by a happy family of domestic animals.

The newest addition to the Stableyards is a pair of magnificent young male water buffalo. Henry Middleton originally brought a pair in to work the rice fields—the first in North America—but today they're just there to relax and add atmosphere. They bear the Turkish names of Adem (the brown one) and Berk (the white one), or "Earth" and "Solid." Meet the fellas daily 9 A.M.–5 P.M.

However, if you're like most folks you'll best enjoy simply wandering and marveling at the gardens. "Meandering" is not the right word to describe them, since they're very systematically laid out. "Intricate" is the word I prefer, and that seems to sum up the attention to detail that characterizes all the garden's various portions, each with a distinct personality and landscape design template of its own. A major floral focal point of the gardens is its vast repertoire of camellia, with hundreds of varieties present including the 1786 *Reine des Fleurs,* one of the first types planted in America. While the museum closes at 5 P.M., if you're already on the grounds you can enjoy the gardens until dusk.

To get a real feel for how things used to be here, for an extra $15 per person you can take a 45-minute carriage ride through the bamboo forest to an abandoned rice field. Rides start around 10 A.M. and run every hour or so, weather permitting. And one of the most unforgettable experiences of your life may be found at the traditional grand finale of the Spoleto Festival, an orchestral performance held under the stars outside at Middleton Place, concluding with fireworks over the Ashley.

The 53-room **Inn at Middleton Place** (see *Accommodations*), besides being a wholly gratifying lodging experience, is also a quite self-conscious and largely successful experiment. Its bold, Wright-influenced modern design, comprising four units joined by walkways, is modern but both inside and outside manages to blend quite well with the surrounding fields, trees, and riverbanks. The Inn also offers kayak tours and instruction—a particularly nice way to enjoy the grounds from the waters of the Ashley—and features its own organic garden and labyrinth, intriguing modern counterpoints to the formal gardens of the plantation itself.

They still grow the exquisite Carolina Gold rice in a field at Middleton Place, harvested in the old style each September. You can sample some of it in many dishes at the **Middleton Place Restaurant** (see *Food*). Hint: You can tour the gardens for free if you arrive for a dinner reservation at 5:30 P.M. or later.

NORTH CHARLESTON

For years synonymous with crime, blight, and sprawl, North Charleston—actually a separate municipality—was for the longest time considered a necessary evil by most Charlestonians, who generally ventured there only to shop at a huge mall or see a big show at its massive concert venue, the Coliseum. But as the cost of real estate continues to rise on the peninsula in Charleston proper, more and more artists and young professionals are choosing to live here.

Make no mistake, North Charleston still has its share of crime and depressing squalor, but some of the most exciting things going on

© WWW.CHARLESTONCVB.COM

the bandshell at the Riverfront Park at the old Charleston Navy Yard

in the Charleston metro area are taking place right here. While many insisted that the closing of the U.S. Navy Yard here in the 1990s would be the economic death of the whole city, the free market stepped in and is transforming the former military facility into a hip, mixed-use shopping and residential area. This is also where you go if you want to see the raised submarine CSS *Hunley,* now in a research area on the grounds of the old Navy Yard.

In short, North Charleston offers a lot for the more adventurous traveler and will no doubt only become more and more important to the local tourist industry as the years go by. And as they're very fond of pointing out up here, there aren't any parking meters.

Magnolia Cemetery

Though not technically in North Charleston, historic Magnolia Cemetery (70 Cunnington Ave., 843/722-8638, Sept.–May daily 8 A.M.–5 P.M., June–Aug. daily 8 A.M.–6 P.M.) is on the way, in the area well north of the general downtown tourist district called "The

Neck." This historic burial ground, while not the equal of Savannah's Bonaventure, is still a stirring site for its natural beauty and ornate memorials as well as for its historic aspects. Here are buried the crewmen who died aboard the CSS *Hunley,* re-interred after their retrieval from Charleston Harbor. In all, over 2,000 Civil War dead are buried here, including five Confederate generals and 84 rebels who fell at Gettysburg and were moved here.

Charleston Navy Yard

A vast post-industrial wasteland to some and a fascinating outdoor museum to others, the Charleston Navy Yard is in the baby steps of rehabilitation from one of the Cold War era's major military centers to the largest single urban redevelopment project in the United States. The Navy's gone now, forced off the site during a phase of base realignment in the mid-1990s. But a 340-acre section, the **Navy Yard at Noisette** (1360 Truxtun Ave., 843/302-2100, www.navyyardsc.com, daily 24 hours), now hosts an intriguing mix of homes, green-friendly design firms, small nonprofits, and commercial maritime companies that was named America's sixth-greenest neighborhood by *Natural Home* magazine in 2008. It's even played host to some scenes of the Lifetime TV series *Army Wives*.

Enter on Spruill Avenue and shortly you'll find yourself on wide streets lined with huge, boarded-up warehouse facilities, old machine shops, and dormant power stations. A notable project is the restoration of **10 Storehouse Row** (2120 Noisette Blvd., 843/302-2100, Mon.–Fri. 9 A.M.–5 P.M.), which now hosts the American College of Building Arts, design firms, galleries, and a small café.

At the north end of the redevelopment lies the brand-new **Riverfront Park** (843/745-1087, daily dawn–dusk) in the old Chicora Gardens military residential area. The Park comprises a nifty little fishing pier going out into the scenic Cooper River, an excellent naval-themed bandshell, and many sleekly designed, modernist sculptures paying tribute to the sailors and ships that made history here.

From Charleston you get to the Navy Yard by taking I-26 north to exit 216-B (you can reach the I-26 junction by just going north on Meeting Street). After exiting take a left onto Spruill Avenue and a right onto McMillan, which takes you straight in.

◖ CSS *Hunley*

For the longest time the only glimpse of the ill-fated Confederate submarine was a not-quite-accurate replica outside the Charleston Museum. But after maritime novelist and adventurer Clive Cussler and his team finally found the *Hunley* in 1995 off Sullivan's Island, the tantalizing dream became a reality: We'd finally find out what it looked like, and perhaps even be lucky enough to bring it to the surface.

That moment came on August 8, 2000, when a team comprising the nonprofit **Friends of the Hunley** (Warren Lasch Conservation Center, 1250 Supply St., Building 255, 866/866-9938, www.hunley.org, Sat. 10 A.M.–5 P.M., Sun. noon–5 P.M., $12, free for children under five), the federal government and private partners

successfully implemented a plan to safely raise the vessel. It was recently moved to its new home in the old Navy Yard, named after Warren Lasch, chairman of the Friends of the Hunley.

You can now you can view the sub in a 90,000-gallon conservation tank on the grounds of the old Navy Yard, see the life-size model from the TNT movie *The Hunley,* and look at artifacts such as the "lucky" gold piece of the commander. You can even see facial reconstructions of some of the eight sailors who died onboard the sub that fateful February day in 1864, when it mysteriously sank right after successfully destroying the USS *Housatonic* with the torpedo attached to its bow.

So that research and conservation can be performed all during the week, tours to see the sub only happen on Saturdays and Sundays, so it's wise to reserve tickets ahead of time. The sub itself is completely submerged in an electrolyte formula to better preserve it, and photography is strictly forbidden. (The remains of the crew lie in Magnolia Cemetery, where they were buried in 2004 with full military honors.)

To get to the Warren Lasch Center from Charleston, take I-516 north to exit 216-B. Take a left onto Spruill Avenue and a right onto McMillan. Once in the Navy Yard, take a right on Hobson, and after about a mile take a left onto Supply Street. The Lasch Center is the low white building on your left.

Park Circle

The focus of restoration in North Charleston is the old Park Circle neighborhood (intersection of Rhett and Montague Avenues, www.parkcircle.net). The adjacent **Olde North Charleston** development has a number of quality shops, bars, and restaurants.

North Charleston and American LaFrance Fire Museum and Educational Center

It's got a mouthful of a name, but the new North Charleston Fire Museum and Educational Center (4975 Centre Point Dr., 843/740-5550, www.legacyofheroes.org, Mon.–Sat. 10 A.M.–5 P.M., last ticket 4 P.M.,

$6 adults, free for children 13 and under) right next to the huge Tanger Outlet Mall does what it does with a lot of chutzpah—which is fitting considering that it pays tribute to firefighters and the tools of their dangerous trade.

The museum, which opened in 2007 and shares a huge 25,000-square-foot space with the North Charleston Convention and Visitors Bureau, is primarily dedicated to maintaining and increasing its collection of antique American LaFrance firefighting vehicles and equipment. The 18 fire engines here date from 1857 to 1969. The museum's exhibits have taken on greater poignancy in the wake of

RAISING THE *HUNLEY*

The amazing, unlikely raising of the Confederate submarine CSS *Hunley* from the muck of Charleston harbor sounds like the plot of an adventure novel – which makes sense considering that the major player is an adventure novelist.

For 15 years, the undersea diver and bestselling author Clive Cussler looked for the final resting place of the *Hunley*. The sub was mysteriously lost at sea after sinking the USS *Housatonic* on February 17, 1864, with the high-explosive "torpedo" mounted on a long spar on its bow. It marked the first time a sub ever sank a ship in battle.

For over a century before Cussler, treasure-seekers had searched for the sub, with P. T. Barnum even offering $100,000 to the first person to find it. But on May 3, 1995, a magnetometer operated by Cussler and his group, the National Underwater Marine Agency, discovered the *Hunley*'s final resting place – in 30 feet of water and under three feet of sediment about four miles off Sullivan's Island at the mouth of the harbor.

Using a specially designed truss to lift the entire sub, a 19-person dive crew and a team of archaeologists began a process that would result in raising the vessel on August 8, 2000. But before the sub could be brought up, however, a dilemma had to be solved: For 136 years the saltwater of the Atlantic had permeated its metallic skin. Exposure to air would rapidly disintegrate the entire thing.

So the conservation team, with input from the U.S. Navy, came up with a plan to keep the vessel submerged in a special solution indefinitely at the specially constructed **Warren Lasch Conservation Center** (1250 Supply St., Building 255, 866/866-9938, www.hunley .org, Sat. 10 A.M.-5 P.M., Sun. noon-5 P.M., $12, free for children under five) in the old Navy Yard while research and conservation was performed on it piece-by-piece.

And that's how you see the *Hunley* today, submerged in its special conservation tank, still largely covered in sediment. Upon seeing the almost unbelievably tiny, cramped vessel – much smaller than most experts imagined it would be – visitors are often visibly moved at the bravery and sacrifice of the nine-man Confederate crew, who no doubt would have known that the *Hunley*'s two previous crews had drowned at sea in training accidents.

Theirs was, in effect, a suicide mission. That the crew surely realized this only makes the modern visitor's experience even more poignant and meaningful.

The Warren Lasch Center, operated under the auspices of Clemson University, is only open to the public on weekends. Archaeology continues apace during the week – inch by painstaking inch, muck and tiny artifacts removed millimeter by millimeter. The process is so thorough that archaeologists have even identified an individual eyelash from one of the crew.

Other interesting artifacts include a three-fold wallet with a leather strap, owner unknown; seven canteens; and a wooden cask in one of the ballast tanks, maybe used to hold water or liquor or even used as a chamber pot.

The very first order of business once the sub was brought up, however, was properly burying those brave sailors. In 2004, Charleston came to a stop as a ceremonial funeral procession took the remains of the nine to historic Magnolia Cemetery, where they were buried with full military honors.

the tragic loss of nine Charleston firefighters killed trying to extinguish a warehouse blaze on Highway 17 in summer 2007—second only to the 9/11 attacks as the largest loss of life for a U.S. firefighting department.

EAST COOPER

The main destination in this area on the east bank of the Cooper River across Charleston Harbor is the island of Mount Pleasant, primarily known as a peaceful, fairly affluent suburb of Charleston—a role it's played for about 300 years now. Though few old-timers (called "hungry necks" in local lingo) remain, Mount Pleasant does have several key attractions well worth visiting—the old words of former Charleston Mayor John Grace notwithstanding: "Mount Pleasant is neither a mount, nor is it pleasant." Through Mount Pleasant is also the only land route to access Sullivan's Island, Isle of Palms, and historic Fort Moultrie.

Shem Creek, which bisects Mount Pleasant, was once the center of the local shrimping industry, and while there aren't near as many shrimp boats as there once were, you can still see them docked or on their way to and from a trawling run. (Needless to say, there are a lot of great seafood restaurants around here as well.)

The most common route here for visitors is by way of Highway 17 over the massive Arthur Ravenel Jr. Bridge, with most sites requiring a turn either north or south on I-526.

Patriots Point Naval and Maritime Museum

Directly across Charleston Harbor from the old city lies the Patriots Point Naval and Maritime Museum complex (40 Patriots Point Rd., 843/884-2727, www.patriotspoint.org, daily 9 A.M.–6:30 P.M. except Christmas Day, $15 adults, $8 ages 6–11, free for active duty military), one of the first chapters in Charleston's great tourism renaissance. The project began in 1975 with what is still its main attraction, the World War II aircraft carrier USS *Yorktown*, named in honor of the carrier lost at the Battle of Midway. Much of "The Fighting Lady" is open to the public, and kids and nautical buffs

will thrill to walk the decks and explore the many stations below deck on this massive 900-foot vessel, a veritable floating city.

You can even have a full meal in the C.P.O. Mess Hall just like the crew once did (except you'll have to pay $6.99 a person). And if you really want to get up close and personal, try the Navy Flight Simulator for a small added fee.

Speaking of planes, aviation buffs will be overjoyed to see that the *Yorktown* flight deck (the top of the ship) and the hangar deck (right below) are packed with authentic warplanes, not only from World War II but from subsequent conflicts the ship participated in. You'll see an F6F Hellcat, an FG-1D Corsair, and an SBD Dauntless such as those that fought the Japanese, on up to an F4F Phantom and an F14 Tomcat from the jet era.

Patriots Point's newest exhibit is also on the *Yorktown*: the **Medal of Honor Memorial Museum,** which opened in 2007 by hosting a live broadcast of the *NBC Nightly News* with Brian Williams. Included in the cost of admission, the Medal of Honor Museum is an interactive experience documenting the exploits of the medal's honorees from the Civil War through today. It's broken up into four segments: the Wall of Honor, the Combat Tunnel, "Freedom Isn't Free," and the Hall of Heroes.

Other ships moored beside the *Yorktown* and open for tours are the Coast Guard cutter USCG *Ingham,* the submarine USS *Clamagore,* and the amazing destroyer USS *Laffey,* which survived being hit by three Japanese bombs and five kamikaze attacks—all within an hour. The Vietnam era is represented by a replica of an entire Naval Support Base Camp, featuring a river patrol boat and several helicopters.

A big plus is the free 90-minute guided tour. If you really want to make a big family history day out of it, you can also hop on the ferry from Patriots Point to Fort Sumter and back.

Old Village

It won't blow you away if you've seen Charleston, Savannah, or Beaufort, but Mount Pleasant's old town has its share of fine colonial and antebellum homes and historic churches. Indeed, Mount Pleasant's history is almost as old as Charleston's. First settled for farming in 1680, it soon acquired cachet as a great place for planters to spend the hot summers away from the mosquitoes inland at the rice paddies.

The main drag is Pitt Street, where you can shop and meander among plenty of shops and restaurants (try an ice cream soda at the historic Pitt Street Pharmacy). The huge meeting hall on the waterfront, Alhambra Hall, was the old ferry terminal.

Boone Hall Plantation

Visitors who've also been to Savannah's Wormsloe Plantation will immediately see the similarity in the majestic, live oak–lined entrance avenue to Boone Hall Plantation (1235 Long Point Rd., 843/884-4371, www .boonehallplantation.com, $17.50 adults, $7.50 children). But this site is about half a century older than Wormsloe, dating back to a grant to Major John Boone in the 1680s (the oaks of the entranceway were planted in 1743).

Unusually in this area, which made its fortune mostly on rice, Boone Hall's main claim to fame was as a cotton plantation as well as a noted brick-making plant. Boone Hall takes the phrase "living history" to its extreme, as it's not only an active agricultural facility but lets visitors go on "u-pick" walks through its fields, which boast succulent strawberries, peaches, tomatoes, and even pumpkins in October—as well as free hayrides.

Currently owned by the McRae family, which first opened it to the public in 1959, Boone Hall is called "the most photographed plantation in America." And photogenic it certainly is, with natural beauty to spare in its scenic location on the Wando River and its adorable Butterfly Garden. But as you're clicking away with your camera, do keep in mind that the plantation's "big house" is not original; it's a 1935 reconstruction.

While Boone Hall's most genuine historic buildings include the big Cotton Gin House (1853) and the 1750 Smokehouse, to me the most poignant and educational structures by far are the nine humble brick slave cabins from the 1790s. The cabins are the center of Boone Hall's educational programs, including an exploration of Gullah culture at the outdoor "Gullah Theatre" on the unfortunately named Slave Street. Summers see some serious Civil War reenacting going on.

In all, three different tours are available, a 30-minute house tour, a tour of Slave Street, and a garden tour. Boone Hall's seasonal hours are a little tricky: From Labor Day through March 31, Boone Hall is open Monday–Saturday 9 A.M.–5 P.M. and Sunday 1–4 P.M.; from April through Labor Day, it's open Monday–Saturday 8:30 A.M.–6:30 P.M. and Sunday 1–5 P.M.

Charles Pinckney National Historic Site

Though "Constitution Charlie's" old Snee Farm is down to only 28 acres from its original magnificent 700, the Charles Pinckney National Historic Site (1240 Long Point Rd., 843/881-5516, www.nps.gov/chpi, daily 9 A.M.–5 P.M., free) that encompasses it is still a charming repository of local history, though actually very little remains of Pinckney's time here.

Sometimes called "the forgotten Founder," Charles Pinckney was not only a hero of the American Revolution and a notable early abolitionist, but one of the main authors of the U.S. Constitution. His great aunt Eliza Lucas Pinckney was the first woman agriculturalist in America, responsible for opening up the indigo trade. Her son Charles Cotesworth Pinckney was one of the signers of the Constitution.

The highlight at this National Parks Service–administered site is the half-mile, self-guided walk around the site, some of it on boardwalks over the marsh. You'll see archaeological excavations and exhibits on Snee Farm's role in the agricultural life of the Lowcountry. The current main house, doubling as the visitors center, dates from 1828, 11 years after Pinckney sold Snee Farm to pay off debts. It replaced Pinckney's original home, where President George Washington slept and had breakfast under a nearby oak tree in 1791 while touring the south.

No matter what anyone tells you, no one is buried underneath the tombstone in the grove of oak trees bearing the name of Constitution Charlie's father, Colonel Charles Pinckney. The marker incorrectly states the elder Pinckney's age, so it was put here only as a monument. A memorial to the colonel is in the churchyard of the 1840s-era Christ Church about a mile down Long Point Road.

Isle of Palms

This primarily residential area of about 5,000 people received the state's first "Blue Wave" designation from the Clean Beaches Council for its very well-managed and preserved beaches. The main attraction for visitors here is **Isle of Palms County Park** (14th Ave., 843/886-3863, www.ccprc.com, daily 9 A.M.–7 P.M. May–Labor Day, daily 10 A.M.–6 P.M. Mar.–Apr. and Sept.–Oct., daily 10 A.M.–5 P.M. Nov.–Feb., $5 per vehicle, pedestrians/cyclists free), with its sweeping oceanfront beach, complete with umbrella rental, a volleyball court, a playground, and a full complement of lifeguards. Get here by taking the Isle of Palms Connector/S.C. Highway 517 from Mount Pleasant, going through the light at Palm Boulevard and taking the next left at the gate.

The island's other claim to fame is the **Wild Dunes Resort** (5757 Palm Blvd., 888/778-1876, www.wilddunes.com), with its two Fazio golf courses and 17 clay tennis courts.

Breach Inlet, between Isle of Palms and Sullivan's Island, is where the Confederate sub *Hunley* sortied to do battle with the USS *Housatonic*. During Hurricane Hugo the entire island was submerged.

Sullivan's Island

While Fort Sumter gets the vast bulk of the press, the older **Fort Moultrie** (1214 Middle St., 843/883-3123, www.nps.gov/fosu, daily 9 A.M.–5 P.M., $3 adults, $5 per family, free for children under 16) on Sullivan's Island actually has a much more sweeping history. Furthering the irony, Major Robert Anderson's detachment at Fort Sumter at the opening of the Civil War was actually the Fort Moultrie garrison, reassigned to Sumter because Moultrie was thought too vulnerable from the landward side.

Indeed, Moultrie's first incarnation, a perimeter of felled palm trees, didn't even have a name when it was unsuccessfully attacked by the British in the summer of 1776, the first victory by the colonists in the Revolution. The Redcoat cannonballs bounced off those soft, flexible trunks, and thus was born South Carolina's nickname, "The Palmetto State." The hero of the battle, Sergeant William Jasper, would gain immortality for putting the blue and white regimental banner—forerunner to the modern blue and white state flag—on a makeshift staff after the first one was shot away. (Jasper makes an appearance in Savannah history as well, leading a charge in the ill-fated attempt to retake the city from the British, during which he was mortally wounded.)

Subsequently named for the commander at the time, William Moultrie, the fort was nonetheless captured by the British at a later engagement. That first fort fell into decay and a new one was built over it in 1798, which was soon destroyed by a hurricane.

In 1809 a brick fort was built here; it soon gained notoriety as the place where the great chief Osceola was detained soon after his capture, posing for the famous portrait by George Catlin. His captors got more than they bargained for when they jokingly asked the old guerrilla soldier for a rendition of the Seminole battle cry. According to accounts, Osceola's realistic performance scared some bystanders half to death. The chief died here in 1838 and his modest gravesite is still on-site, in front of the fort.

Other famous people to have trod on Sullivan's Island include Edgar Allen Poe, who was inspired by Sullivan's lonely, evocative environment to write *The Gold Bug* and other works. (There's a Gold Bug Avenue and a Poe Avenue here today, and the local library is named after him as well.) A young Lieutenant William T. Sherman was also stationed here during his Charleston stint in the 1830s.

Moultrie's main Civil War role was as a target for Union shot during the long siege of Charleston. It was pounded so hard and for so long that its walls fell below a nearby sand hill and were finally unable to be hit anymore. A full military upgrade happened in the late 1800s, extending over most of Sullivan's Island (some private owners have even bought some of the old batteries and converted them into homes). It's the series of later forts that you'll visit on your trip to the Moultrie site, which is technically part of the Fort Sumter National Monument, and administered by the National Park Service.

Most of the outdoor tours are self-guided, but ranger programs typically happen Memorial Day through Labor Day daily at 11 A.M. and 2:30 P.M. There's also a bookstore and visitors center on-site that offers a 20-minute video on the hour and half-hour 9 A.M.–4:30 P.M.

In the wake of Hurricane Hugo's devastation, a lot of Charleston-area homeowners found a silver lining and rebuilt in a big way. Sullivan's Island is perhaps the preeminent example of this phenomenon, with some of the Charleston area's most opulent homes, almost all of them newly constructed.

You can only get to Sullivan's Island from the island of Mount Pleasant. From U.S. 17 follow the signs for S.C. Highway 703 and Sullivan's Island. Cross the Ben Sawyer Bridge and then turn right onto Middle Street; continue for about a mile and a half. Keep in mind there's no way to get to Fort Sumter from Fort Moultrie; the closest ferry to Sumter leaves from Patriots Point on Mount Pleasant.

FOLLY BEACH

Though a large percentage of the town of Folly Beach was destroyed in Hurricane Hugo—as well as nearly all of its actual beach—enough of its funky, cozy charm is left to make it worth visiting. Called "The Edge of America" during its heyday from the 1930s through the

© JIM MOREKIS

the Folly Beach Pier

'50s as a swinging resort getaway, Folly Beach is now a laid-back, provincial, and thoroughly enjoyable little getaway on this barrier island far from the crowds of greater Charleston. Though as with all areas of Charleston, the cost of living here is rapidly increasing, with many old-timers and colorful characters having long ago been priced out of the market, Folly Beach still reminds locals of a time that once was, a time of soda fountains, poodle skirts, stylish one-piece bathing suits, and growling hot rods.

Folly's main claim to larger historic fame is that it played host to George Gershwin, who stayed at a cottage on West Arctic Avenue to write the score to *Porgy and Bess,* set in downtown Charleston across the harbor. (Ironically, Gershwin's opera couldn't be performed in its original setting until 1970 because of segregationist Jim Crow laws.) Original *Porgy* author Dubose Heyward stayed around the corner at a summer cottage on West Ashley Avenue that he dubbed "Follywood."

Called Folly Road until it gets to the beach,

the aptly named Center Street is the main drag here, dividing the beach into east and west. It's capped at the ocean by the **Folly Beach Fishing Pier** (101 E. Arctic Ave., 843/588-3474, Apr.–Oct. daily 6 A.M.–11 P.M., Nov. and Mar. daily 7 A.M.–7 P.M., winter daily 8 A.M.–5 P.M., $5 parking, $8 fishing fee), which replaced the grand old wooden pier-and-pavilion structure, which tragically burned down, in 1960. Back in the day, restaurants, bars, and amusement areas with rides lined the way up to the old pavilion. As the premier musical venue in the region, the pavilion hosted legends like Tommy and Jimmy Dorsey, Benny Goodman, and Count Basie. The new fishing pier, while not nearly as grand as the old one, was recently renovated and is very much worth visiting, jutting over 1,000 feet into the Atlantic with a large, diamond-shaped pavilion at the end.

Out on the "front beach," daytime activities included regular boxing matches and extralegal drag races. Because of the fluctuating nature of the sand here, the narrow ramps from the board-walk to the beach sometimes require a big jump at the bottom. (They were long ago replaced by more practical means of access, but Folly Beach remains subject to frequent erosion.)

In the old days, the "Washout" section on the far west end was where you went to go crab-bing or fly-fishing or maybe even steal a kiss from your sweetie. Today though, the Washout is known as the prime surfing area in the Carolinas, with a dedicated group of diehards.

Another key attraction is **Folly Beach County Park** (1100 West Ashley Ave., 843/588-2426, May–Labor Day daily 9 A.M.–7 P.M., Mar., Apr., Sept., and Oct. daily 10 A.M.–6 P.M., Jan., Feb., Nov., and Dec. daily 10 A.M.–5 P.M., www.ccprc.com, $7 per vehi-cle, free for pedestrians/cyclists) at the far west end of the island. Swim, tan, and relax, maybe under a rented beach umbrella.

To get to Folly Beach from Charleston, go west on Calhoun Street and take the James Island Connector. Take a left on Folly Road/ S.C. Highway 171, which becomes Center Street on into Folly Beach.

At the far east end of Folly Island, about 300 yards offshore, you'll see the **Morris Island Lighthouse,** an 1876 beacon that was once surrounded by lush, green landscape, now completely surrounded by water as the land has eroded around it. Now privately owned, there's an extensive effort to save and preserve the light-house (www.savethelight.org). There's also an effort to keep high-dollar condo development off of beautiful, bird-friendly Morris Island it-self (www.morrisisland.org). To get there while there's still something left to enjoy, take East Ashley Street until it dead-ends. Park in the lot and take a quarter-mile walk to the beach.

SIGHTSEEING TOURS

Because of the city's small, fairly centralized layout, the best way to experience Charleston is on foot—either yours or via feet of the equine nature. Thankfully, there's a wide va-riety of walking and carriage tours for you to choose from.

The sheer number and breadth of tour op-tions in Charleston is beyond the scope of this section. For a full selection of available tours, visit the **Charleston Visitor Reception and Transportation Center** (375 Meeting St., 800/774-0006, www.charlestoncvb.com, Mon.–Fri. 8:30 A.M.–5 P.M.), where they have entire walls of brochures for all the latest tours, with local tourism experts on-site. Here are some notable highlights:

Walking Tours

If you find yourself walking around down-town soon after dark, you'll almost invariably come across a walking tour in progress (and often, several tours), with a small cluster of people gathered around a tour guide who ex-plains the various stops. There are too many walking tours to list them all, but here are the best:

For more than 10 years, **Ed Grimball's Walking Tours** (306 Yates Ave., 843/762-0056, www.edgrimballtours.com, $16 adults, $8 children) has run two-hour tours on Friday and Saturday mornings, courtesy of the knowledgeable and still-sprightly Ed himself, a native Charlestonian. All of Ed's walks start from the big Pineapple Fountain in Waterfront Park and reservations are an absolute must.

Original Charleston Walks (45 Broad St., 800/729-3420, www.charlestonwalks .com, 8:30 A.M.–9:30 P.M., $18.50 adults, $10.50 children) has received much national TV exposure. **Charleston Strolls Walk with History** (843/766-2080, www .charlestonstrolls.com, $18 adults, $10 children) is another popular tour good for a historical overview and tidbits. They have three embarkation points: Charleston Place, the Mills House, and the Days Inn. **Architectural Walking Tours** (173 Meeting St., 800/931-7761, www.architecturalwalking toursofcharleston.com, $20) offers an 18th-century tour at 10 A.M. and a 19th-century tour at 2 P.M., except Tuesdays and Sundays, which are geared more to historic preservation.

As in Savannah, ghost tours are very popular in Charleston. **Bulldog Tours** (40 N. Market St., 843/722-8687, www.bulldog tours.com) has exclusive access to the Old City Jail, and runs several other well-received ghost tours, such as a Ghost & Dungeon Tour, a Ghost & Graveyard Tour, and the adults-only Dark Side of Charleston. **Tour Charleston** (184 E. Bay St., 843/723-1670, www .tourcharleston.com, $18) offers two paranormal tours, Ghosts of Charleston I, which leaves at 5 P.M., 7:30 P.M., and 9:30 P.M. from Waterfront Park, and Ghosts of Charleston II, which leaves at 7 P.M. and 9 P.M. from Marion Square.

Pirate tours are the happening new thing, with the simply named **Pirate Tour** (843/814-6124, www.charlestonjourneys .com, Mon.–Sat. 4 P.M., $16 adults, $12 children) departing from St. Michael's, and the more kid-themed **Pirate Treasure Hunt**

DOIN' THE CHARLESTON

It's been called the biggest song and dance craze of the 20th century. Though it first entered the American public consciousness via New York City, in a 1923 Harlem musical called *Runnin' Wild*, the roots of the dance soon to be known as the Charleston were indeed in the Holy City.

Though no one is quite sure of the day and date, local lore assures us that members of Charleston's legendary Jenkins Orphanage Band were the first to start dancing that crazy "Geechie step," a development that soon became part of the band's act.

The Jenkins Orphanage was started in 1891 by the African American Baptist minister Reverend D. J. Jenkins, and originally housed in the Old Marine Hospital at 20 Franklin Street (which you can see today, though it's not open to the public). To raise money, Reverend Jenkins acquired donated instruments and started a band comprising talented orphans from the house.

The orphans traveled as far away as London, where they were a hit with the locals but not with the constabulary, who unceremoniously fined them for stopping traffic. A Charleston attorney who happened to be in London at the time, Augustine Smyth, paid their way back home, becoming a lifelong supporter of the Orphanage in the process.

From then on, playing in donated old Citadel uniforms, the Jenkins Orphanage Band frequently took its act on the road. They played at the St. Louis and Buffalo expositions, and even at President Taft's inauguration.

They also frequently played in New York, and it was there that African American pianist and composer James P. Johnson heard the Charlestonians play and dance to their Gullah rhythms, considered exotic at the time.

Johnson would incorporate what he heard into the tune "Charleston," one of many songs in the revue *Runnin' Wild*. The catchy song and its accompanying loose-limbed dance seemed tailor-made for the Roaring Twenties and its liberated, hedonistic spirit.

Before long the Charleston had swept the nation, becoming a staple of jazz clubs and speakeasies across America, and indeed, the world.

(843/817-6362, www.charlestonsidewalks .com, tours daily during summer, call for hours, $12 children, $8 adults) leaving from Waterfront Park.

Carriage Tours

The city strictly regulates the treatment of carriage horses and their upkeep, so there's not a heck of a lot of difference in service or price among the various tour companies. Typically rides take 1–1.5 hours. In summer months, night rides are often more comfortable due to cooler evening temperatures (and more romantic). They sometimes book up early, so call ahead.

The oldest service in town is **Palmetto Carriage Works** (40 N. Market St., 843/723-8145, www.carriagetour.com), which offers free parking at its "red barn" base near City Market. Another popular tour is **Old South Carriage Company** (14 Anson St., 843/723-9712, www.oldsouthcarriage.com, $20 adults, $12 children) with its Confederate-clad drivers. **Carolina Polo & Carriage Company** (16 Hayne St., 843/577-6767, www.cpcc.com, $20 adults, $12 children) leaves from several spots, including the Doubletree Hotel, the Noisy Oyster, and at their Hayne Street stables.

Motorized Tours

Leaving from Charleston Visitor Reception and Transportation Center at 375 Meeting Street, **Adventure Sightseeing** (843/762-0088, www .touringcharleston.com) offers several comfortable rides of 1.5–2 hours, including the only motorized tour to the Citadel area. You can make a day of it with **Charleston's Finest Historic Tours** (843/577-3311, www.historictoursofcharleston.com), which has a basic two-hour city tour each day at 10:30 A.M. plus offers some much longer tours to outlying plantations. They also offer free downtown pickup from most lodgings. The old faithful **Gray Line of Charleston** (843/722-4444, www.graylineofcharleston .com) departs from the Visitors Center every half-hour 9:30 A.M.–3 P.M. (hotel pickup by reservation).

African American History Tours

Charleston is extremely rich in African American history, and a couple of operators specializing in this area are worth mentioning: Al Miller's **Sites & Insights Tours** (843/762-0051, www.sitesandinsightstours .com) has several packages, including a Black History and Porgy & Bess Tour as well as a good combo city and island tour, all departing from the Visitors Center. Alphonso Brown's **Gullah Tours** (843/763-7551, www.gullah tours.com), featuring stories told in the Gullah dialect, leave from Gallery Chuma at 43 John Street near the Visitors Center at various times Monday–Saturday.

Water Tours

The best all-around tour of Charleston Harbor is the 90-minute ride offered by **Spiritline Cruises** (800/789-3678, www .spiritlinecruises.com, $14 adults, $8 ages 6–11), which leaves from either Aquarium Wharf or Patriots Point. Allow about a half-hour for ticketing and boarding. They also have a three-hour dinner cruise in the evening leaving from Patriots Point (about $50 per person). For their cruise to Fort Sumter, see *Sights.*

Sandlapper Water Tours (843/849-8687, www.sandlappertours.com) offers evening and dolphin cruises on a 45-foot catamaran.

Ecotours

This fairly new addition to Charleston's tourist scene is actually very well represented. The best operators include: **Barrier Island Eco Tours** (50 41st Ave., 843/886-5000, www .nature-tours.com), taking you up to the Cape Romaine Refuge out of Isle of Palms; **Coastal Expeditions** (843/884-7684, www .coastalexpeditions.com), offering several different-length sea kayak adventures; and **PaddleFish Kayaking** (843/330-9777, www .paddlefishkayaking.com), offering several kinds of kayaking tours (no experience necessary) from downtown, Kiawah Island, and Seabrook Island.

Entertainment and Events

Charleston practically invented the idea of diversion and culture in America, so it's no surprise that there's plenty to do here, from museums to festivals to a brisk nightlife scene.

NIGHTLIFE

One of the unique things about Charleston is the inclusiveness of its active nightlife scene. Unlike the strict locals-vs.-tourist divide you find so often in other destination cities, in Charleston it's nothing for a couple of tourists to find themselves at a table next to four or five college students enjoying themselves in that particularly Charlestonian fashion, i.e., loudly and with lots of good food and strong drink nearby.

Indeed, the Holy City is downright ecumenical in its partying. The smokiest dives also have some of the best brunches. The toniest restaurants also have some of the most hopping bar scenes. Tourist hot spots written up in all the guidebooks also have their share of local regulars.

But through it all, one constant remains: Charleston's finely honed ability to seek out and enjoy the good life. It's a trait that comes naturally and traditionally, going back to the days of the earliest Charleston drinking and gambling clubs, like the Fancy Society, the Meddlers Laughing Club, and the Fort Jolly Volunteers.

Bars close in Charleston at 2 A.M. The old days of the "mini-bottle" are gone—in which no free pour was allowed and all drinks had to be made from the little airline bottles—and it seems that local bartenders have finally figured out how to pour a decent drink after an initial breaking-in period.

At the retail level, all hard liquor sales stop at 7 P.M., with none at all on Sundays. You can buy beer and wine in grocery stores 24/7.

Upper King Street is the center of Charleston nightlife.

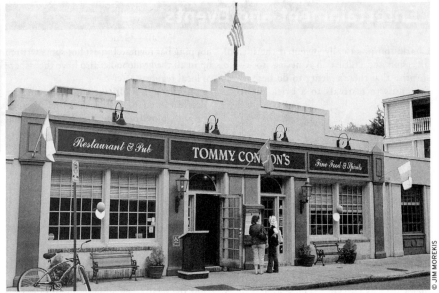

Tommy Condon's Irish Pub

Pubs and Bars

In a nod to the city's perpetual focus on well-prepared food, it's difficult to find a Charleston watering hole that *doesn't* offer really good food in addition to a well-stocked bar and boisterous camaraderie. For example, in this section you'll find not only a great bar, but one of Charleston's best restaurants, Tommy Condon's.

One of Charleston's favorite neighborhood spots is **Moe's Crosstown Tavern** (714 Rutledge Ave., 843/722-3287, daily 11 A.M.–2 A.M.) at Rutledge and Francis in the Wagener Terrace/Hampton Square area. A new second location, **Moe's Downtown Tavern** (5 Cumberland St., 843/577-8500) offers a similar vibe and menu, but the original, and best, Moe's experience is at the Crosstown.

Nipping on Moe's heels for best pub food in town is **A.C.'s Bar and Grill** (467 King St., 843/577-6742, daily 11 A.M.–2 A.M.). Though this dark, quirky watering hole might seem out of place in the increasingly tony Upper King area, that only adds to its appeal for me. A.C.'s at its best is all things to all people:

Charleston's favorite late-night bar, a great place to get a burger basket, and also one of the best (and certainly most unlikely) Sunday brunches in town, featuring their own chicken and waffles.

Frequented by locals and visitors alike in this heavily touristed area, **The Brick** (213-B E. Bay St., 843/720-7788, daily 5 P.M.–2 A.M.) gets pretty boisterous on a weekend night, serving the typical Charlestonian blend of college types and khaki-wearers. If you're hungry, be sure and check out the kitchen arm of the enterprise, the cash-only 77 Roosters, which serves cheesesteaks, burgers, and other munchies from a window in the back.

Currently one of the most popular spots on Upper King for the college crowd, **Charleston Beer Works** (468 King St., 843/577-5885, daily 5 P.M.–2 A.M.) is particularly well regarded for its beer on tap, generally thought to be one of the best selections in town—if not *the* best. The menu offers a wide range of appetizers and entrées, which while not particularly inventive, are certainly tasty.

© JIM MOREKIS

Johnson's Pub (12 Cumberland St., 843/958-0662, daily noon–2 A.M.), a quirky but popular downtown spot, offers seven varieties of burger, all incredible, plus great pizza; it's also well known for its Caesar salad. Oh, yeah, and they keep the drinks coming, too.

The Guinness flows freely at **Tommy Condon's Irish Pub** (160 Church St., 843/577-3818, www.tommycondons.com, Sun.–Thurs. 11 A.M.–2 A.M., dinner served until 10 P.M., Fri.–Sat. 11 A.M.–2 A.M., dinner served until 11 P.M.)—after the obligatory and traditional slow-pour, that is—as do the patriotic Irish songs performed live most nights. You have three sections to choose from in this large, low building right near City Market: the big outdoor deck, the cozy pub itself (my favorite), and the back dining room with classic wainscoting.

If it's a nice day out, the best place in town to relax and enjoy happy hour outside is **Vickery's Bar and Grill** (15 Beaufain St., 843/577-5300, www.vickerysbarandgrill.com, Mon.–Sat. 11:30–2 A.M., Sun. 11 A.M.–1 A.M., kitchen closes 1 A.M.), which is actually part of a small regional chain based in Atlanta. Start with the oyster bisque, and maybe try the turkey and brie sandwich or crab cakes for your entrée.

Because of its commercial nature, Broad Street can get a little sparse when the sun goes down and the officeworkers disperse back to the 'burbs. But a nice, warm little oasis can be found a few steps off Broad Street in the **Blind Tiger** (36–38 Broad St., 843/577-0088, daily 11:30–2 A.M., kitchen closes 10 P.M. Mon.– Thurs., 9 P.M. Fri.–Sun.), which takes its name from the local Prohibition-era nickname for a speakeasy. Wood panels, Guinness and Bass on tap, and some very good bar-food items (try the mussels or the Black Angus burger) make this a good stop off the beaten path if you find yourself in the area. A patio out back often features live music.

Located not too far over the Ashley River on Highway 17, Charleston institution **Gene's Haufbrau** (17 Savannah Hwy., 843/225-4363, www.geneshaufbrau.com, daily 11:30 A.M.–2 A.M.) is worth making a special trip into West Ashley. Boasting the largest beer selection in Charleston—from the Butte Creek Organic Ale from California ($3.50) to a can of PBR ($1.50)—Gene's also claims to be the oldest bar in town, established in 1952.

If you find yourself thirsty and hungry in Mount Pleasant after dark, you might want to stop in the **Reddrum Gastropub** (803 Coleman Blvd., 843/849-0313, www.reddrumpub.com, Mon. and Tues. 5:30–9 P.M., Wed.– Sat. 5:30–10 P.M.), so named because here the food is just as important as the drink. While you're likely to need reservations for the dining room, where you can enjoy Lowcountry/ Tex-Mex fusion-style cuisine with a typically Mount Pleasant–like emphasis on seafood, the bar scene is very hopping and fun—downright crowded, actually—with live music every Wednesday and Thursday night.

Though "dive" is a relative term on high-dollar Sullivan's Island, **Dunleavy's Pub** (2213-B Middle St., 843/883-9646, Sun.–Thurs. 11:30 A.M.–1 A.M., Fri.–Sat. 11:30 A.M.–2 A.M.) is the real thing. Inside is a great bar festooned with memorabilia, or you can enjoy a patio table. The other Sullivan's watering hole of note is the nearby **Poe's Tavern** (2210 Middle St., 843/883-0083, daily 11 A.M.–2 A.M., kitchen closes 10 P.M.), a nod to Edgar Allan Poe and his service on the island as a clerk in the U.S. Army. It's a lively, mostly locals scene, with a beautiful view from the outside tables. While there, you simply must have a big plate of Buddy's Nachos.

The most notable watering hole in Folly Beach is undoubtedly the **Sand Dollar Social Club** (7 Center St., 843/588-9498, Sun.–Fri. noon–1 A.M., Sat. noon–2 A.M.), the kind of cash-only, mostly local, and thoroughly enjoyable dive you often find in little beach towns. You have to pony up for a "membership" to this private club, but it's only a buck. There's a catch though: You can't get in until your 24-hour "waiting period" is over.

Live Music

Charleston's music scene is best described as hit-and-miss. There's no distinct "Charleston sound" to speak of (especially now that the heyday of Hootie and the Blowfish is long past) and there's no one place where you're assured of finding a great band any night of the week. The scene is currently in even more of a state of flux because the city's best-regarded live rock club, Cumberland's on King Street, closed in late 2007 after 15 years in business. The best place to find up-to-date music listings is the local free weekly *Charleston City Paper* (www .charlestoncitypaper.com).

These days the hippest music spot in town is way out on James Island at **The Pour House** (1977 Maybank Hwy., 843/571-4343, www .charlestonpourhouse.com, 9 P.M.–2 A.M. on nights with music scheduled, call for info), where sometimes the local characters are just as entertaining as the acts onstage.

In West Ashley, **The Map Room** (1650 Sam Rittenberg Blvd., 843/769-6336, www .themaproom.net, Mon.–Fri. 4 P.M.–2 A.M., Sat.–Sun. 6 P.M.–2 A.M.,) is bringing in some of the best local and regional acts on a consistent basis. The range of acts is really quite diverse, ranging from Athens, Georgia, alt-rock to bluegrass to the occasional Middle Eastern dance troupe. A big plus is the full menu available until 1 A.M.

The venerable **Music Farm** (32 Ann St., 843/722-8904, www.musicfarm.com) on Upper King isn't much to look at from the outside, but inside the cavernous space has played host to all sorts of bands over the past 15 years, including Talking Heads, Ween, Widespread Panic, and De La Soul. Now under new management, the beer-soaked old place won't have good old Jimbo Webb running it anymore, but it has undergone some renovations and features the same eclectic taste in booking.

For jazz, check out **Mistral** (99 S. Market St., 843/722-5708, Sun.–Thurs. 11 A.M.–11 P.M., Fri.–Sat. 11 A.M.–midnight). There's a constant stream of great performers from a variety of traditions, including Dixieland, every night of the week—not to mention some awesome food.

Another great jazz place—and, like Mistral, a very good restaurant to boot—is the relatively new **Mercato** (102 N. Market St., 843/722-

6393, www.mercatocharleston.com, bar open 4 P.M.–2 A.M., late night menu until 1 A.M.). Italian in menu and feel, the live jazz and R&B Wed.–Sat. at this establishment—owned by the same company that owns the five-star Peninsula Grill—is definitely all-American. The late kitchen hours are a great bonus.

Lounges and Tapas

Currently the undisputed queen of Upper King, the ultrachic tapas place **Raval** (453 King St., 843/853-8466, daily 5:30 P.M.–2 A.M.) always has a long line on weekend nights full of beautiful people waiting to sample the tasty bites and the vast wine selection at the oaken community tables. Try the *patatas bravas* and the Manchego cheese. For a take on Spain under the Moorish influence, go to the more exotic back bar for a trendy Euro cocktail, enjoyed in a deep comfy sofa.

Across the street from Gene's Haufbrau, the retro chic **Voodoo Lounge** (15 Magnolia Ln., 843/769-0228, Mon.–Fri. 4 P.M.–2 A.M., Sat.–Sun. 5:30 P.M.–2 A.M., kitchen open until 1 A.M.) is another very popular West Ashley hangout. It has a wide selection of trendy cocktails and some killer gourmet tacos.

The aptly named **Rooftop Bar and Restaurant** (23 Vendue Range, 843/723-0485, Tues.–Sat. 6 P.M.–2 A.M.) at the Library Restaurant in the Vendue Inn is a very popular waterfront happy hour spot from which to enjoy the sunset over the Charleston skyline. It's also a hot late-night hangout with a respectable, though far from overwhelming, menu. The crowd here is under-40, stylish, and ready to have a good time.

Located in a 200-year-old building and suitably right above a cigar store, **Club Habana** (177 Meeting St., 843/853-5900, Mon.–Sat. 5 P.M.–1 A.M., Sun. 6 P.M.–midnight) is the perfect place to sink down into a big couch, warm yourself by the fireplace, sip a martini (or port or single-malt scotch), and enjoy a good smoke in the dim light. Probably the last, best vestige of the 1990s cigar bar trend in Charleston, Club Habana remains popular. You get your cigars downstairs in Tinderbox

Internationale, which features a range of rare "Legal Cuban" smokes, i.e., rolled from pre-embargo tobacco that's been warehoused for decades in Tampa, Florida.

If martinis are your game, head to **Cintra** (16 N. Market St., 843/377-1090, Tues.–Wed. 5:30–10 P.M., Thurs.–Sat. 5:30–11 P.M.), where they boast 40 different martini recipes at last count. While you're sipping one you might decide to stay for dinner, which is also superb. Try the butternut squash ravioli or the veal Marsala.

Dance Clubs

With the closing of the popular City Bar club, Charleston's dance scene is in limbo as of this writing. But the **Trio Club** (139 Calhoun St., 843/965-5333, Thurs.–Sat. 9 P.M.–2 A.M.) right off Marion Square is still a favorite place to make the scene. There's a relaxing outdoor area with piped-in music, an intimate, sofa-filled upstairs bar for dancing and chilling, and the dark, candlelit downstairs with frequent live music.

Without a doubt Charleston's best dance club is **Club Pantheon** (see *Gay and Lesbian*).

Gay and Lesbian

Charleston is very tolerant by typical Deep South standards, and this tolerance extends to the gay and lesbian community as well. Most gay- and lesbian-oriented nightlife centers in the Upper King area.

Charleston's hottest and hippest dance spot of any type, gay or straight, is **Club Pantheon** (28 Ann St., 843/577-2582, Thurs.–Sun. 10 P.M.–2 A.M.) on Upper King on the lower level of the parking garage across from the Visitors Center (375 Meeting St.). Pantheon's not cheap—cover charges are routinely well over $10—but it's worth it for the great DJs, the dancing, and the people-watching, not to mention the drag cabaret on Friday and Sunday nights.

Just down the street from Club Pantheon—and owned by the same people—is a totally different kind of gay bar, **Dudley's** (42 Ann St., 843/577-6779, daily 4 P.M.–2 A.M.). Mellower and more appropriate for conversation or a friendly game of pool, Dudley is a nice contrast to the thumping Pantheon a few doors down.

Though **Vickery's Bar and Grill** (see *Pubs and Bars*) does not market itself as a gay and lesbian establishment, it's nonetheless become quite popular with that population—not least because of the good reputation its parent tavern in Atlanta has with that city's large and influential gay community.

THE ARTS
Theater

Unlike the more puritanical (literally) colonies farther up the American coast, Charleston was from the beginning an arts-friendly settlement. The first theatrical production in the western hemisphere happened in Charleston in January 1735, when a nomadic troupe rented a space at Church and Broad Streets to perform Thomas Otway's *The Orphan*.

The play's success led to the building of the Dock Street Theatre on now-Queen Street, which held its first production on February 12, 1736, *The Recruiting Officer*, a popular play for actresses of the time because it calls for some female characters to wear tight-fitting British army uniforms. Live theater became a staple of Charleston social life, with notable thespians performing here including both Edwin and Junius Booth, brothers of Lincoln's assassin John Wilkes, and Edgar Allan Poe's mother Eliza.

Several high-quality troupes continue to keep that proud old tradition alive, chief among them being **Charleston Stage** (843/577-7183, www.charlestonstage.com), a professional company with 20 full-time staffers founded in 1978. Also the resident company of the Dock Street Theatre, they will perform at the American Theatre (446 King St.) and the Sottile Theatre (44 George St. just off King) until Dock Street's renovations are complete. In addition to its well-received regular season of classics and modern staples, Charleston Stage has debuted more than 30 original scripts over the years, most recently *Gershwin at Folly*, recounting the composer's time at Folly Beach working on *Porgy and Bess*.

The city's most unusual players are **The**

Have Nots! (843/853-6687, www.thehavenots .com), with a total ensemble of 35 comedians who typically perform their brand of edgy improv every Friday night at Theatre 99 (280 Meeting St.). Perhaps unusually for such a dicey concept in this still-traditional arts town, The Have Nots! have managed to last 12 years, and are now partners with Piccolo Spoleto's Fringe series and a local comedy festival.

As of this writing, the players of **PURE**

STEPHEN COLBERT, NATIVE SON

A purist would insist that Charlestonians are born, not made. While it's true that Comedy Central star Stephen Colbert was actually born in Washington, D.C., he did spend most of his young life in the Charleston suburb of James Island, attending the Porter-Gaud School. And regardless of his literal birthplace, few would dispute that Colbert is the best-known Charlestonian in American pop culture today.

While it's commonly assumed that Colbert's surname is a link to Charleston's French Huguenot heritage, the truth is that it's really an Irish name. To further burst the bubble, Colbert's father, a vice president at Charleston's Medical University of South Carolina, adopted the current French pronunciation himself – historically his family pronounced the "t" at the end.

That being said, Colbert returns quite often to Charleston, as he did in a December 2007 performance at the Sottile Theater, "I am Charleston – and So Can You!," a play on the title of his most recent book. The event included a reading from the book, an interview on growing up in Charleston, and a Q&A session with the local audience. The performance benefited Charleston Stage Company, which, perhaps apocryphally, passed over Colbert for a role after an audition in 1981 for *Babes in Toyland*.

In summer 2007, Colbert cooperated with Ben & Jerry's Ice Cream to create a new flavor, "Americone Dream" (vanilla with fudge-covered waffle cone pieces and caramel swirl), proceeds from which went to the Coastal Community Foundation of South Carolina. To unveil the flavor, Colbert appeared at "The Joe" and threw out the first pitch at a Charleston River Dogs minor league game.

Soon after, Colbert told *Charleston* magazine that he and wife Evelyn "went to the Pig and bought eight pints" – a reference to the ubiquitous Southern grocery chain Piggly Wiggly, a.k.a., "the Pig."

Later that year, Colbert embarked on an ill-fated, tongue-in-cheek bid to get on the South Carolina presidential primary ballot, which never materialized. In a video message to the South Carolina Agricultural Summit in November he cried mock tears and said, "I wanted to be president of South Carolina so bad. I was going to be sworn in on a sack of pork ribs and I was going to institute the death penalty for eating Chinese shrimp."

Other famous pop culture figures born in Charleston or closely associated with the city include:

· Comedian Andy Dick

· Author Nancy Friday (grew up in Charleston, born in Pittsburgh)

· Actor Thomas Gibson ("Dharma & Greg")

· Author/lyricist Dubose Heyward

· Author Josephine Humphreys

· Actress/model Lauren Hutton

· Author Sue Monk Kidd (*The Secret Life of Bees*)

· Actress Mabel King (*The Wiz*)

· Actress Vanessa Minnillo (attended high school)

· Actor Will Patton (*Remember the Titans*)

· Author Alexandra Ripley (attended Ashley Hall)

· Singer Darius Rucker (Hootie and the Blowfish)

Theatre (843/723-4444, www.puretheatre .org) are performing in a black box space at The Cigar Factory (701 E. Bay St.). Their shows emphasize compelling, mature drama, beautifully performed. This is where to catch less-glitzy, more-gritty productions like *Rabbit Hole, American Buffalo,* and *Cold Tectonics,* a hit at Piccolo Spoleto.

The Footlight Players (843/722-4487, www.footlightplayers.net) are the oldest con- tinuously active company in town (since 1931). This community-based, amateur company performs a mix of crowd-pleasers *(The Full Monty)* and cutting-edge drama *(This War is Live)* at their space at 20 Queen Street near Waterfront Park.

On Folly Beach, the professional company **Actors Theatre of South Carolina** (843/588- 9636, www.actorstheatreofsc.org) performs a mix of Shakespeare classics along with lesser- known dramas like *Goering at Nuremberg.* Also in a state of flux venue-wise at the time of this writing, they've been performing at the new Folly Beach Fine Arts Center (55 Center St.) above the Community Center.

Music

The forerunner to the **Charleston Symphony Orchestra** (843/554-6060, www.charleston symphony.com) performed for the first time on December 28, 1936, at the Hibernian Hall on Meeting Street. During that first season the CSO accompanied the inaugural show at the renovated Dock Street Theatre, *The Recruiting Officer.* Since then, the CSO has continued to provide world-class orchestral music, gaining "Metropolitan" status in the 1970s, when they accompanied the first-ever local performance of *Porgy and Bess,* which despite its downtown setting couldn't be performed locally before then due to segregation laws.

With an annual budget over $2 million, under the baton of Maestro David Stahl, the CSO is now the largest year-round performing arts entity in South Carolina, finishing its most recent fis- cal year in the black—a notable accomplishment for anyone that follows the economics of orches- tras in midsize cities in the United States.

They perform primarily at the Gaillard Municipal Auditorium (77 Calhoun St.), but a "blue jeans" contemporary chamber music series geared toward a younger fan base, "Backstage Pass at the Sottile," is held at the Sottile Theatre (44 George St. just off King). Its "McCrady's Pops" series at the Gaillard is also a hit, featuring concerts like "Italianissimo" and—wait for it—an ABBA tribute.

Comprising mostly players with the CSO, the separate group **Chamber Music Charleston** (843/763-4941, www.chamber musiccharleston.org) is another excellent local ensemble, performing under the baton of Sandra Nikolajevs. They play a wide variety of picturesque historic venues, including the Old Exchange (120 E. Bay St.), the Calhoun Mansion (16 Meeting St.), and the Footlight Players Theatre (20 Queen St.). They can also be found at private house concerts, which tend to sell out extremely quickly.

The excellent music department at the College of Charleston sponsors the annual **Charleston Music Fest** (www.charleston musicfest.com), a series of chamber music con- certs at various venues around the beautiful campus, featuring many faculty members of the College as well as visiting guest artists.

Other College musical offerings include: The **College of Charleston Concert Choir** (www.cofc.edu/music), which performs at vari- ous venues, usually churches, around town during the fall; the **College of Charleston Opera,** which performs at least one full-length production during the school year and often performs at Piccolo Spoleto; and the popular **Yuletide Madrigal Singers,** who sing in early December at a series of concerts in historic Randolph Hall.

Dance

The premier company in town is the 20-year- old **Charleston Ballet Theatre** (477 King St., 843/723-7334, www.charlestonballet.org). Its 18 full-time dancers perform a great mix of classics, modern pieces, and, of course, a yule- tide *Nutcracker* at the Gaillard Municipal Auditorium. Most performances are at the

Sottile Theatre (44 George St., just off King), but for the past few years Charleston Ballet Theatre has offered the "King Street Series" of selected, themed pieces (e.g., *pas de deaux,* tango) geared toward a younger audience, danced at their home office on Upper King.

Cinemas

The most interesting art house and indie venue in town is currently **The Terrace** (1956 Maybank Hwy., 843/762-9494, www.terrace theater.com), and not only because they offer beer and wine, which you can enjoy at your seat. Shows before 5 P.M. are $6.50. It's west of Charleston on James Island. Get there by taking Highway 17 west out of Charleston and go south on S.C. Highway 171, then take a right on Maybank Highway (S.C. Hwy. 700).

For a generic but good multiplex experience, go over to Mount Pleasant to the **Palmetto Grande** (1319 Theater Dr., 843/216-8696). From Charleston take the Crosstown (Hwy. 17) over the Ravenel Bridge and stay on 17. Start looking for the theater when you pass the Snee Farm Country Club.

Visual Art

The premier art museum in Charleston is the **Gibbes Museum of Art** (135 Meeting St., 843/722-2706, www.gibbesmuseum.org, Tues.–Sat. 10 A.M.–5 P.M., Sun. 1–5 P.M. $9 adults, $7 students, $5 children 6–12). Recent exhibits have included cutting-edge art such as photography by Lorna Simpson, the first video installation in South Carolina, *Like Tears in Rain,* and the German Expressionism of Otto Neumann. But this is also the kind of museum where you'll see a Rembrandt, catch a Rodin exhibit, and marvel at its vast collection of painted miniatures, many by noted native son Charles Fraser.

FESTIVALS AND EVENTS

Like Savannah, its neighbor to the south, Charleston is a festival-mad city, especially in the spring and early fall. And new festivals are being added every year, further enhancing the hedonistic flavor of this city that has also

mastered the art of hospitality. Here's a look through the calendar at all the key festivals in the area:

January

Held on a Sunday in late January at historic Boone Hall Plantation on Mount Pleasant, the **Lowcountry Oyster Festival** (www.charleston lowcountry.com, 11 A.M.–5 P.M., $8, food additional) features literally truckloads of the sweet shellfish for your enjoyment. Gates open at 10:30 A.M. and there's plenty of parking. Oysters are sold by the bucket and served with crackers and cocktail sauce. Bring your own shucking knife and/or glove, or buy them on-site.

February

One of the more unique events in town is the **Southeastern Wildlife Exposition** (various venues, 843/723-1748, www.sewe.com, $12.50/day, $30/three days, free for children 12 and under). For the last quarter century, the Wildlife Expo has brought together hundreds of artists and exhibitors to showcase just about any kind of naturally themed art you can think of, in over a dozen galleries and venues all over downtown. Kids will enjoy the live animals on hand as well.

March

Generally straddling late February and the first days of March, the four-day **Charleston Food & Wine Festival** (www.charlestonfood andwine.com, various venues and admission) is a glorious celebration of one of the Holy City's premier draws: its amazing culinary community. While the emphasis is on Lowcountry gurus like Donald Barickman of Magnolia's and Robert Carter of the Peninsula Grill, guest chefs from as far away as New York, New Orleans, and Los Angeles routinely come to show off their cooking skills. Oenophiles, especially of domestic wines, will be in heaven as well. Tickets aren't cheap—an all-event pass is $650 per person—but then again, this is one of America's great food cities, so it's worth every penny.

Coming immediately before the Festival of Houses and Gardens is the **Charleston**

International Antiques Show (40 E. Bay St., 843/722-3405, www.historiccharleston.org, varied admission), held at Historic Charleston's headquarters at the Missroon House on the High Battery. It features over 30 of the nation's best-regarded dealers and offers lectures and tours.

Running mid-March through April, the perennial favorite **Festival of Houses and Gardens** (843/722-3405, www.historic charleston.org, varied admission) is sponsored by the Historic Charleston Foundation and held at the very peak of the spring blooming season for maximum effect. In all, the Festival goes into a dozen historic neighborhoods to see about 150 homes. Each day sees a different three-hour tour of a different area, at about $45 per person. This is a fantastic opportunity to peek inside some amazing old privately owned properties that are inaccessible to visitors at all other times. A highlight is a big oyster roast and picnic at Drayton Hall.

Not to be confused with the above festival, the **Garden Club of Charleston House and Garden Tours** (843/530-5164, www.thegarden clubofcharleston.com, $35) are held over a weekend in late March. Highlights include the Heyward-Washington House and the private garden of the late great Charleston horticulturalist Emily Whaley.

One of Charleston's newest and most fun events, the five-night **Charleston Fashion Week** (www.fashionweek.charlestonmag.com, varied admission) is sponsored by *Charleston Magazine* and benefits a local women's charity. Mimicking New York's Fashion Week events under tenting in Bryant Park, Charleston's version features runway action under big tents in Marion Square—and, yes, past guests have included former contestants on *Project Runway.*

April

The annual **Cooper River Bridge Run** (www .bridgerun.com) happens the first Saturday in April (unless it's Easter weekend, in which case it runs the week before) and features a 10,000-meter jaunt over the massive new Arthur Ravenel Bridge over the Cooper River,

the longest cable span in the western hemisphere. It's not for those with a fear of heights, but it's still one of Charleston's best-attended events—with well over 30,000 participants.

The whole crazy idea started when Dr. Marcus Newberry of the Medical University of South Carolina in Charleston was inspired by an office fitness trail in his native state of Ohio to do something similar in Charleston to promote fitness. Participants can walk the course if they choose, and many do.

Signaled with the traditional cannon shot, the race still begins in Mount Pleasant and ends downtown, but over the years the course has changed to accommodate growth—not only in the event itself but in the city. Auto traffic, of course, is rerouted from the night before the race. The Bridge Run remains the only elite-level track and field event in South Carolina, with runners from Kenya typically dominating year after year. Each participant in the Bridge Run now must wear a transponder chip; new "Bones in Motion" technology allows you to track a favorite runner's exact position in real-time during the race. The 2006 Run had wheelchair participants for the first time. There's now a Kid's Run in Hampton Square the Friday before, which also allows strollers.

From 1973–2000—except for 1976 when it was in Florida—the **Family Circle Cup** (161 Seven Farms Dr., Daniel Island, 843/856-7900, www.familycirclecup.com, varied admission) was held at Sea Pines Plantation on Hilton Head Island. But the popular Tier 1 Women's tennis tournament in 2001 moved to Daniel Island's brand-new Family Circle Tennis Center, specifically built for the event through a partnership of the magazine and the city of Charleston. (The Tennis Center is also open to the public and hosts many community events as well.)

Mount Pleasant is the home of Charleston's shrimping fleet, and each April sees all the boats parade by the Alhambra Hall & Park for the **Blessing of the Fleet** (843/884-8517, www.townofmountpleasant.com). Family events and lots and lots of seafood are also on tap.

May

Free admission and free parking are not the only draws at the outdoor **North Charleston Arts Festival** (5000 Coliseum Dr., www .northcharleston.org), but let's face it, that's important. Held beside North Charleston's Performing Arts Center & Convention Center, the Festival features music, dance,

A MAN, A PLAN – SPOLETO!

Sadly, Gian Carlo Menotti is no longer with us, having died in 2007 at the age of 95. But the overwhelming success of the composer's brainchild and labor of love, **Spoleto Festival USA,** lives on, enriching the cultural and social life of Charleston and serving as the city's chief calling card to the world at large.

Menotti began writing music at age seven in his native Italy. As a young man he would move to Philadelphia to study music, where he shared classes – and lifelong connections – with Leonard Bernstein and Samuel Barber.

His first full-length opera, *The Consul* would garner him the Pulitzer Prize, as would 1955's *The Saint of Bleecker Street.* But by far Menotti's best-known work is the beloved Christmas opera *Amahl and the Night Visitors,* composed especially for NBC television in 1951.

At the height of his fame in 1958, the charismatic and mercurial genius – fluent and bitingly witty in five languages – founded the "Festival of Two Worlds" in Spoleto, Italy, specifically as a forum for young American artists in Europe. But it wasn't until nearly two decades later, in 1977, that Menotti was able to make his long-imagined dream of an American counterpart a reality.

Attracted to Charleston because of its longstanding support of the arts, its undeniable good taste, and its small size – ensuring that his festival would always be the number-one activity in town while it was going on – Menotti worked closely with the man who was to become the other key part of the equation: Charleston Mayor Joe Riley, then in his first term in office. Since then, the city has built on Spoleto's success by founding its own local version, **Piccolo Spoleto** – literally, "little Spoleto" – which focuses exclusively on local and regional talent.

Things haven't always gone smoothly.

Though both festivals proved successful with audiences from their inception, internal finances have been a roller-coaster ride. Menotti and the stateside festival parted ways in 1993, when he took over the Rome Opera.

Making matters more uneasy, the Italian festival – run by Menotti's longtime partner (and later adopted son) Chip – also became estranged from what was intended to be its soul mate in South Carolina. And though Mayor Riley and Spoleto Mayor Massimo Brunini have gone public with their desire for reconciliation between the two events, as of this writing that possibility remains sketchy at best.

But perhaps this kind of creative tension is what Menotti intended all along. Indeed, each spring brings a Spoleto USA that seems to thrive on the inherent conflict between the festival's often cutting-edge offerings and the very traditional city that hosts it.

Unlike so many of the increasingly generic arts "festivals" across the nation, Spoleto still challenges its audiences, just as Menotti intended it to do. Depending on the critic and the audience member, that modern opera debut you see may be groundbreaking or gratuitous. The drama you check out may be exhilarating or tiresome. (Though pretty much everyone agrees that the annual finale, an orchestral performance with fireworks outdoors at gorgeous Middleton Place, never disappoints.)

Still, the crowds keep coming, attracted just as much for Charleston's many charms as for the art itself. Each year, a total of about half a million people attend both Spoleto and Piccolo Spoleto, bringing millions of dollars into the local economy each time.

Nearly a third of attendees are Charleston residents – the final proof that when it comes to supporting the arts, Charleston puts its money where its mouth is.

theater, multicultural performers, and storytellers. There are a lot of kid's events as well.

Held over three days at the Holy Trinity Greek Orthodox Church up towards the Neck, the **Charleston Greek Festival** (30 Race St., 843/577-2063, www.greekorthodoxchs.org, $3) offers a plethora of live entertainment, dancing, Greek wares, and of course fantastic Greek cuisine cooked by the congregation. Parking is not a problem, and there's even a shuttle to the church from the lot.

One of Charleston's newest annual events is the **Charleston International Film Festival** (various venues and prices, 843/817-1617, www .charlestonIFF.com). Despite being a relative latecomer to the film festival circuit, the event is pulled off with Charleston's usual aplomb.

The free, weekend-long, outdoor **Charleston Harbor Fest** (www.charlestonharborfest.org, free) at the Maritime Center on the waterfront is without a doubt one of the coolest events in town for the whole family. You can see and tour working tall ships, and watch master boatwrights at work building new ones. There are free sailboat rides into the harbor and the U.S. Navy provides displays. As if all that weren't enough, you get to witness the start of the 777-mile annual Charleston-to-Bermuda race.

Indisputably Charleston's single biggest and most important event, **Spoleto Festival USA** (843/579-3100, www.spoletousa.org, varied admission) has come a long way since it was a sparkle in the eye of the late Gian Carlo Menotti three decades ago. Though Spoleto long ago broke ties with its founder, his vision remains indelibly stamped on the event from start to finish. There's plenty of music, to be sure, in genres from orchestral to opera to jazz to avant-garde, but you'll find something in every other performing art here, from dance to drama to spoken word, in traditions from Western to African to Southeast Asian. For 17 days from Memorial Day weekend through early June, Charleston hops and hums nearly 24 hours a day to the energy of this vibrant, cutting-edge, yet accessible artistic celebration, which dominates everything and every

conversation for those three weeks. Events happen in historic venues and churches all over downtown and as far afield as Middleton Place, which hosts the grand finale under the stars. (Sadly, one of the most popular venues, the historic Dock Street Theatre, is closed for renovations through at least 2010.)

The 2008 event featured Anthony Davis's opera *Amistad,* the American premiere of *Monkey: Journey to the West* by Chinese director Chen Shi-Zheng, Laurie Anderson's new work *Homeland,* and a whole slew of ballet world premieres. If you want to come to Charleston during Spoleto—and everyone should at least once—book your accommodations and your tickets far in advance. Tickets usually go on sale in early January for that summer's festival.

As if all the hubbub around Spoleto didn't give you enough to do, there's also **Piccolo Spoleto** (843/724-7305, www.piccolospoleto .com, various venues and admission), literally "little Spoleto," running concurrently. The intent of Piccolo Spoleto—begun just a couple of years after the larger festival came to town and run by the city's Office of Cultural Affairs—is to give local and regional performers a time to shine, sharing some of that larger spotlight on the national and international performers at the main event. Past events have included *Amahl and the Night Visitors;* a combined jazz concert by musicians from Charleston and New Orleans; performances by Chamber Music Charleston; and "A Big Fat Middle Eastern Wedding." Of particular interest to visiting families will be Piccolo's children's events, a good counter to some of the decidedly more adult fare at Spoleto USA.

June

Technically part of Piccolo Spoleto but gathering its own following, the **Sweetgrass Cultural Arts Festival** (www.sweetgrass festival.org) is held the first week in June over in Mount Pleasant at the Laing Middle School (2213 Hwy. 17 N.). The event celebrates the traditional sweetgrass basketmaking skills of African Americans in the historical Christ Church Parish area of Mount Pleasant. If you want to buy some sweetgrass baskets made by the world's foremost experts in the field, this would be the time.

July

Each year, over 30,000 people come to see the **Patriots Point Fourth of July Blast** (866/831-1720), featuring a hefty barrage of fireworks shot off the deck of the USS *Yorktown* moored on the Cooper River in the Patriots Point complex. Food, live entertainment, and kids' activities are also featured.

September

One of Charleston's newer festivals, **Chazzfest** (161 Seven Farms Dr., www.chazzfest.com, reserved seating $75–100, general admission $35–50) has previously taken place on Saturday in the new Family Circle Tennis Center on Daniel Island, though as of this writing it is likely to change venues for future festivals. In any case, expect a laid-back day of national and regionally well-known musical artists on several stages. Of course lots of food and drink is available at concession stands. The 2007 edition featured performances by Branford Marsalis, Son Volt, and Toots & the Maytals. To get to Daniel Island from Charleston, take I-26 north and then I-526 east. Take Exit 24 to Daniel Island and then take a left on Seven Farms Drive.

From late September into the first week of October, the city-sponsored **MOJA Arts Festival** (843/724-7305, www.mojafestival .com, varied venues and admission), highlights the cultural contributions of African Americans and people from the Caribbean with dance, visual art, poetry, cuisine, crafts, and music in genres from gospel to jazz to reggae to classical. In existence since 1984, MOJA's name comes from the Swahili word for "one," and its incredibly diverse range of offerings in so many media have made it one of the Southeast's premier events. Highlights include a Reggae Block Party and the always-fun Caribbean Parade. Some events are ticketed, while others, such as the kids' activities and many of the dance and film events, are free.

For five weeks from the last week of September into October, the Preservation Society of Charleston hosts the much-anticipated **Fall Tours of Homes & Gardens** (843/722-4630, www.preservationsociety.org, $45). The tour takes you into over a dozen local residences and is the nearly 90-year-old organization's biggest fundraiser. Tickets typically go on sale the previous June, and they tend to sell out very quickly.

October

Another great food event in this great food city, the **Taste of Charleston** (1235 Long Point Rd., 843/577-4030, www.charlestonrestaurant association.com, 11 A.M.–5 P.M., $12) is held at Boone Hall Plantation in Mount Pleasant and sponsored by the Greater Charleston Restaurant Association. Over 50 area chefs and restaurants come together so you can sample their wares, including a wine and food pairing, with proceeds going to charity.

November

Plantation Days at Middleton Place (4300 Ashley River Rd., 843/556-6020, www .middletonplace.org, daily 9 A.M.–5 P.M., last tour 4:30 P.M., guided tour $10) happen each Saturday in November, giving visitors a chance to wander the grounds and see artisans at work practicing the authentic crafts as they would have been done in antebellum days on the grounds, with a special emphasis on the contributions of African Americans. A special treat comes on Thanksgiving, when a full meal is offered at the Middleton Place restaurant (843/556-6020, www.middletonplace.org) on the grounds (reservations highly recommended).

Though the **Battle of Secessionville** actually took place in June 1862, interestingly November is the time the battle is reenacted at Boone Plantation (1235 Long Point Rd., 843/884-4371, www.boonehallplantation .com, $17.50 adults, $7.50 children) on Mount Pleasant. Call for specific dates and times.

December

A yuletide in the Holy City is an experience

you'll never forget, as the **Christmas in Charleston** (843/724-3705, www.charleston city.info) events clustered around the first week of the month prove. For some reason—whether it's the old architecture, the friendly people, the churches, the carriages, or all of the above—Charleston feels right at home during Christmas. The festivities begin with Mayor Joe Riley lighting the city's 60-foot Tree

of Lights in Marion Square, followed by a parade of brightly lit boats from Mount Pleasant all the way around Charleston up the Ashley River. The key event is the Sunday Christmas Parade through downtown featuring bands, floats, and performers in the holiday spirit. The Saturday Farmer's Market in the square continues through the middle of the month with a focus on holiday items.

Shopping

For a relatively small city, Charleston has an impressive amount of big-name, big-city stores to go along with its charming, one-of-a-kind locally owned shops. I've never known anyone to leave Charleston without bundles of good stuff.

KING STREET

Without a doubt, King Street is by far the main shopping thoroughfare in the area—actually in the entire region. It's unique not only for the fact that so many national name stores are lined up so close to each other, but because there are so many great restaurants of so many different types scattered in and amongst all the retail outlets, ideally positioned for when you need to take a break to rest and refuel.

Though I don't necessarily recommend doing so—Charleston has so much more to offer—a visitor could easily spend an entire weekend doing nothing but shopping, eating, and carousing up and down King Street from early morning to the wee hours of the following morning.

King Street has three distinct areas with three distinct types of merchandise: Lower King is primarily top-of-the-line antique stores (most are closed Sundays, so plan your trip accordingly); Middle King is where you'll find upscale name-brand outlets from traditional (Saks Fifth Avenue) to hip (American Apparel), as well as some excellent shoe stores; and Upper King north of Calhoun is where you'll find funky housewares shops, generally locally owned.

Antiques

On the 100 block of Lower King, **George C. Williams American Antiques** (155 King St., 843/377-0290, Mon.–Fri. 10 A.M.–5:30 P.M., Sat. 10 A.M.–5 P.M.) has some fine local and regional pieces. A relatively new addition to Lower King's cluster of antique shops, **Alexandra AD** (156 King St., 843/722-4897, Mon.–Sat. 10 A.M.–5 P.M.) features great chandeliers, lamps, and fabrics.

As the name implies, **English Patina** (179 King St., 843/853-0380, Mon.–Sat. 10 A.M.–5 P.M.) specializes in European furniture, brought to its big James Island warehouse three times a year in shipping containers. Since 1929, **George C. Birlant & Co.** (191 King St., 843/722-3842, Mon.–Sat. 9 A.M.–5:30 P.M.) has been importing 18th- and 19th-century furniture, silver, china, and crystal, and also deals in the famous "Charleston Battery Bench."

On the 200 block, **A'riga IV** (204 King St., 843/577-3075, Mon.–Sat. 10:30 A.M.–4:30 P.M.) deals in a quirky mix of 19th-century decorative arts, including rare apothecary items. **Carlton Daily Antiques** (208 King St., 843/853-2299, Mon.–Sat. 10 A.M.–5:30 P.M.) intrigues with its unusual focus on deco and modernist pieces and furnishings.

Art Galleries

Ever since native son Joseph Allen Smith began one of America's first art collections in Charleston in the late 1700s, the Holy City has been fertile ground for visual artists.

For most visitors, the center of visual arts activity is in the French Quarter between South Market and Tradd Streets. Thirty galleries reside there within short walking distance, including: **Charleston Renaissance Gallery** (103 Church St., 843/723-0025, www.fineart south.com, Mon.–Sat. 10 A.M.–5 P.M.) specializing in 19th- and 20th-century oils and sculpture featuring artists from the American South, including some splendid pieces from the Charleston Renaissance; the city-funded **City Gallery at Waterfront** (34 Prioleau St., 843/958-6484, Tues.–Fri. 11 A.M.–6 P.M., Sat.–Sun. noon–5 P.M.); the **Pink House Gallery** (17 Chalmers St., 843/723-3608, http://pinkhousegallery.tripod.com, Mon.–Sat. 10 A.M.–5 P.M.), in the oldest tavern building in the South, circa 1694; **Helena Fox Fine Art** (12 Queen St., 843/723-0073, www.fraserfoxfineart.com, Mon.–Sat. 10 A.M.–5 P.M.), dealing in 20th-century representational art; and the **Anne Worsham Richardson Birds Eye View Gallery** (119-A Church St., 843/723-1276, Mon.–Sat. 10 A.M.–5 P.M.), home of South Carolina's official painter of the state flower and state bird.

The best way to experience the area is to go on one of the popular **French Quarter ArtWalks** (843/724-3424, www.frenchquarter arts.com), held the first Friday of March, May, October, and December 5–8 P.M. and featuring lots of wine, food, and, of course, art. You can download a map at the website.

One of the most important single venues, the nonprofit **Redux Contemporary Art Center** (136 St. Philip St., 843/722-0697, www.redux studios.org, Wed.–Sat. noon–5 P.M.) features modernistic work in a variety of media, from illustration to video installation to blueprints to performance art to graffiti. Outreach is hugely important to this venture, including lecture series, classes, workshops, and internships.

For a more modern take from local artists, check out the **Sylvan Gallery** (171 King St., 843/722-2172, www.thesylvangallery.com, Mon.–Fri. 9 A.M.–5 P.M., Sat. 10 A.M.–5 P.M., Sun. 11 A.M.–4 P.M.), which specializes in 20th- and 21st-century art and sculpture.

Right up the street and incorporating works from the estate of Charleston legend Elizabeth O'Neill Verner is **Ann Long Fine Art** (177 King St., 843/577-0447, www.annlongfineart .com, Mon.–Sat. 11 A.M.–5 P.M.), which seeks to combine the painterly aesthetic of the Old World with the edgy vision of the New. Its Old Master–inspired Florentine gallery is nicely juxtaposed with a modern gallery, featuring works from the estate of German Expressionist Otto Neumann, among other modernists. You'll find the African American–themed portraiture of Mario Robinson here as well.

Farther up King and specializing in original Audubon prints and antique botanical prints is **The Audubon Gallery** (190 King St., 843/853-1100, www.audubonart.com, Mon.–Sat. 10 A.M.–5 P.M.), the sister store of the Joel Oppenheimer Gallery in Chicago.

In the Upper King area is **Gallery Chuma** (43 John St., 843/722-7568, www.gallery chuma.com, Mon.–Sat. 10 A.M.–6 P.M.), which specialized in the art of the Gullah people of the South Carolina coast. They do lots of cultural and educational events about Gullah culture as well as displaying art on the subject.

By far Charleston's favorite art supply store is **Artist & Craftsman Supply** (434 King St., 843/579-0077, www.artistcraftsman.com, Mon.–Sat. 10 A.M.–7 P.M., Sun. noon–5 P.M.), part of a well-regarded Maine-based chain. They cater to the pro as well as the dabbler, and have a fun children's art section as well.

Books and Music

It's easy to overlook at the far southern end of retail development on King, but the excellent **Preservation Society of Charleston Book and Gift Shop** (147 King St., 843/722-4630, Mon.–Sat. 10 A.M.–5 P.M.) is perhaps the single best place in town to pick up books on Charleston lore and history as well as locally themed gift items.

The charming **Pauline Books and Media** (243 King St., 843/577-0175, Mon.–Sat. 10 A.M.–6 P.M.) is run by the Daughters of St. Paul and has Christian books, Bibles, rosaries, and images from a Roman Catholic perspective.

Housed in an extremely long and narrow storefront on Upper King, Jonathan Sanchez's funky and friendly **Blue Bicycle Books** (420 King St., 843/722-2666, www.bluebicycle books.com, Mon.–Sat. 10 A.M.–6 P.M., Sun. 1–6 P.M.) deals primarily in used books and has a particularly nice stock of local and regional books, art books, and fiction.

The local bastion of indie music and the best place to find that rare vinyl is **52.5 Records** (561 King St., 843/722-3525, Mon.–Thurs. 11 A.M.–7 P.M., Fri.–Sat. 11 A.M.–9 P.M., Sun. 1–6 P.M.).

Clothes

Cynics may scoff at the proliferation of high-end national retail chains on Middle King, but rarely will a shopper find so many so conveniently located, and in such a pleasant environment. The biggies are: **Saks Fifth Avenue** (211 King St., 843/853-9888, Mon.–Wed. 10 A.M.–6 P.M., Thurs.–Sat. 10 A.M.–7 P.M., Sun. noon–5 P.M.); **Banana Republic** (247 King St., 843/722-6681, Mon.–Fri. 10 A.M.–7 P.M., Sat. 10 A.M.–8 P.M., Sun. noon–6 P.M.); **J. Crew** (264 King St., 843/534-1640, Mon.–Thurs. 10 A.M.–6 P.M., Fri.–Sat. 10 A.M.–8 P.M., Sun. noon–6 P.M.); and **American Apparel** (348 King St., 843/853-7220, Mon.–Sat. 10 A.M.–8 P.M., Sun. noon–7 P.M.).

As for locally owned clothing shops, try **Lula Kate** (231 King St. 843/723-5885, Mon.–Sat. 10 A.M.–6 P.M., Sun. noon–5 P.M.), which specializes in professional, business attire, or the innovative **Worthwhile** (268 King St., 843/723-4418, Mon.–Sat. 10 A.M.–6 P.M., Sun. noon–5 P.M.), which has lots of organic fashion.

On the next block, some way-cool indie stores include the upscale **Copper Penny** (311 King St. 843/723-2999, Mon.–Sat. 10 A.M.–7 P.M., Sun. noon–6 P.M.) and the all-around excellent **Luna** (334 King St., 843/853-5862, Mon.–Sat. 10:30 A.M.–7 P.M., Sun. noon–5 P.M.). After living for a time in L.A., native Charlestonian Guilds Bennett brought back a fun and flirty West Coast vibe to her boutique **Miostile** (346 King St.,

843/722-7073, Mon.–Sat. 10 A.M.–7 P.M., Sun. noon–5 P.M.), which offers designer items in a beautifully restored setting.

Also in this area is one of the city's most unique locally owned shops: the nationally famous **Mary Norton** (318 King St., 843/724-1081, www.marynorton.com, Mon.–Sat. 10 A.M.–6 P.M.), formerly Moo Roo, where native Charlestonian Mary Norton creates and sells her one-of-a-kind designer handbags.

Big companies' losses are your gain at **Oops!** (326 King St., 843/722-7768, Mon.–Fri. 10 A.M.–6 P.M., Sat. 10 A.M.–7 P.M., Sun. noon–6 P.M.), which buys factory mistakes and discontinued lines from major brands at a discount, passing along the savings to you. The range here tends towards colorful and preppy.

The fun and unique "lifestyle boutique" **b'zar** (541 King St., 843/579-2889, www .shopbzar.com, Mon.–Sat. 11 A.M.–6 P.M., Sun. noon–5 P.M.) on Upper King has cutting-edge women's and men's clothes, as well as accessories, great candles, books, and music.

If hats are your thing, make sure you visit **Magar Hatworks** (by appointment only, 843/345-4483, leighmagar@aol.com, www .magarhatworks.com), where Leigh Magar makes and sells her whimsical, all-natural hats, some of which she designs for Barneys New York.

Notable locally owned clothing stores on King Street include the classy **Berlins Men's and Women's** (114–120 King St., 843/722-1665, Mon.–Sat. 9:30 A.M.–6 P.M.), dating from 1883, and **Jos. A. Bank** (328 King St., 843/723-9770, Mon.–Sat. 9 A.M.–8 P.M., Sun. noon–6 P.M.), a mecca for reasonably priced preppy menswear.

Health and Beauty

The Euro-style window display of **Stella Nova** (292 King St., 843/722-9797, Mon.–Sat. 10 A.M.–7 P.M., Sun. 1–5 P.M.) beckons at the corner of King and Society. Inside this locally owned cosmetics store and studio, you'll find a wide selection of high-end makeup and beauty products. There's also a Stella Nova day spa location at 78 Society Street (843/723-0909, Mon.–Sat. 9 A.M.–6 P.M., Sun. noon–5 P.M.).

Inside the Francis Marion Hotel near Marion Square is **Spa Adagio** (387 King St., 843/577-2444, Mon.–Sat. 10 A.M.–7 P.M., Sun. appointment only), offering massage, waxing, and skin and nail care. On Upper King you'll find **Allure Salon** (415 King St., 843/722-8689, Tues. & Thurs. 10 A.M.–7 P.M., Wed. and Fri. 9 A.M.–5 P.M., Sat. 10 A.M.–3 P.M.) for stylish haircuts.

Home, Garden, and Sporting Goods

With retail locations in Charleston and Savannah and a new cutting-edge, green-friendly warehouse in North Charleston, **Half Moon Outfitters** (280 King St., 843/853-0990, www.halfmoonoutfitters.com, Mon.–Sat. 10 A.M.–7 P.M., Sun. noon–6 P.M.) is something of a local legend. Here you can find not only top-of-the-line camping and outdoor gear and good tips on local recreation, but some really stylish, outdoorsy apparel as well.

Probably Charleston's best-regarded home goods store is the nationally recognized **ESD, Elizabeth Stuart Design** (314 King St., 843/577-6272, www.esdcharleston.com, Mon.–Sat. 10 A.M.–6 P.M.), with a wide range of antique and new furnishings, art, lighting, jewelry and more.

Several great home and garden stores are worth mentioning on Upper King: **Global Awakening Market** (499 King St., 843/577-8579, www.globalawakeningmarket.com, Mon.–Sat. 11 A.M.–6 P.M.), which deals exclusively in fair trade clothing, crafts, and furnishing from all over the world; **Charleston Gardens** (650 King St., 843/723-0252, www.charlestongardens.com, Mon.–Sat. 9 A.M.–5 P.M.) for furniture and accessories; and **Haute Design Studio** (489 King St., 843/577-9886, Mon.–Fri. 9 A.M.–5:30 P.M.) for upper-end furnishings with an edgy feel.

Jewelry

Joint Venture Estate Jewelers (185 King St., 843/722-6730, www.jventure.com, Mon.–Sat. 10 A.M.–5:30 P.M.) specializes in antique, vintage, and modern estate jewelry as well as pre-owned watches, including Rolex, Patek Philippe, and Cartier. Since 1919, **Croghan's Jewel Box** (308 King St., 843/723-3594, Mon.–Fri. 9:30 A.M.–5:30 P.M., Sat. 10 A.M.–5 P.M.) has offered amazing locally crafted diamonds, silver, and designer pieces to generations of Charlestonians. An expansion in the late 1990s tripled the size of the historic location. **Art Jewelry by Mikhail Smolkin** (312 King St., 843/722-3634, Mon.–Sat. 10 A.M.–5 P.M.) features one-of-a-kind pieces by this St. Petersburg, Russia, native.

Shoes

Rangoni of Florence (270 King St., 843/577-9554, Mon.–Sat. 9:30 A.M.–6 P.M., Sun. 12:30–5:30 P.M.) imports the best women's shoes from Italy, with a few men's designs as well. **Copper Penny Shooz** (317 King St., 843/723-3838, Mon.–Sat. 10 A.M.–7 P.M., Sun. noon–6 P.M.) combines hip and up-scale fashion. Funky and fun **Phillips Shoes** (320 King St., 843/965-5270, Mon.–Sat. 10 A.M.–6 P.M.) deals in Dansko for men, women, and kids (don't miss the awesome painting above the register of Elvis fitting a customer). **Mephisto** (322 King St., 843/722-4666, www.mepcomfort.com, Mon.–Sat. 10 A.M.–6 P.M.) deals in that incredibly comfortable, durable brand.

The most famous locally owed place for footwear is **Bob Ellis Shoe Store** (332 King St., 843/722-2515, Mon.–Sat. 9 A.M.–6 P.M.), which has served Charleston's elite with high-end shoes since 1950. Hip and popular **Pete Banis Shoes** (375 King St., 843/577-0950, Mon.–Sat. 10 A.M.–6 P.M., Sun. noon–5 P.M.) still does layaway. **Farushga** (377A King St., 843/722-3131, Mon.–Sat. 10:30 A.M.–6:30 P.M., Sun. 11:30 A.M.–5:30 P.M.) has provocative European styles for men and women.

CHARLESTON PLACE

Charleston Place (130 Market St., 843/722-4900, www.charlestonplaceshops.com, Mon.–Wed. 10 A.M.–6 P.M., Thurs.–Sat. 10 A.M.–8 P.M., Sun. noon–5 P.M.), a combined

The Trunk Show on Meeting Street

retail/hotel development begun to much controversy in the late 1970s, was the first big downtown redevelopment project of Mayor Riley's tenure. While naysayers said people would never come downtown to shop for boutique items, Riley proved them wrong, and 30 years later The Shops at Charleston Place and the Riviera (the entire complex has itself been renovated through the years) remains a big shopping draw for locals and tourists alike.

Highlights inside the large, stylish space include Crabtree & Evelyn, Gucci, Talbot's Laura Ashley, VSOE Boutique, Everything But Water, and Godiva.

NORTH OF BROAD

In addition to the myriad of tourist-oriented shops in the Old City Market itself, there are a few gems in the surrounding area that also appeal to locals.

A laid-back flea market vibe dominates at **Old City Market** (Meeting and Market Streets, 843/973-7236, daily 6 A.M.–11:30 P.M.), with the front, westward Market Hall featuring

meandering halls lined with smallish, tourist-oriented shops and the subsequent, less-grand buildings purely for touristy flea market stalls. Pricier establishments, such as the famous Peninsula Grill, line the perimeter. Tip: If you must have one of the handcrafted sweet-grass baskets, try out your haggling skills—the prices have wiggle room built in.

Women come from throughout the region to shop at the incredible consignment store **The Trunk Show** (281 Meeting St., 843/722-0442, Mon.–Sat. 10 A.M.–6 P.M.). You can find one-of-a-kind vintage and designer wear and accessories at hard-to-believe prices.

Indigo (4 Vendue Range, 800/549-2513, Sun.–Thurs. 10 A.M.–6 P.M., Fri.–Sat. 10 A.M.–7 P.M.), a favorite home accessories store, has plenty of one-of-a-kind pieces, many of them by regional artists and rustic in flavor, almost like outsider art.

Affiliated with the hip local restaurant chain Maverick Kitchens, **Charleston Cooks!** (194 East Bay St., 843/722-1212, www.charleston cooks.com, Mon.–Sat. 10 A.M.–9 P.M., Sun.

MAYOR JOE'S LEGACY

Few cities anywhere have been as greatly influenced by one mayor as Charleston has by Joseph P. "Joe" Riley, re-elected in November 2007 to his ninth four-year term. Now mayor for over 30 years, "Mayor Joe," as he's called, is not only responsible for instigating the vast majority of redevelopment in the city, he continues to set the bar for its award-winning tourist industry – always a key component in his long-term plans.

Riley won his first mayoral race at the age of 32. He was the second Irish American mayor of the city, the first being the great John Grace, who was first elected in 1911 and eventually defeated by the allegedly anti-Catholic Thomas P. Stoney.

Legend has it that soon after winning his first mayoral election in 1975, Riley was handed an old envelope written decades before by the Bishop of Charleston, addressed to "The Next Irish Mayor." Inside was a note with a simple message: "Get the Stoneys."

Though young, the well-regarded lawyer, Citadel grad, and former member of the state legislature had a clear vision for his administration: It would bring unprecedented numbers of women and minorities into city government, rejuvenate then-seedy King Street, and enlarge the city's tax base by annexing surrounding areas (during Riley's tenure the city has grown from 16.7 square miles to over 100).

But in order to make any of that happen, one thing had to happen first: Charleston's epidemic street crime had to be brought under control. Enter a vital and perhaps underrated partner in Riley's effort to remake Charleston: Chief of Police Reuben Greenberg. From 1982–2005, Greenberg – who intrigued locals and the national media not only for his dominant personality but because he was that comparative rarity, an African American Jew – turned old ideas of law enforcement in Charleston upside down through his introduction of "community policing." Charleston cops would have to have a college degree. Graffiti would not be toler-

ated. And for the first time in recent memory, they would have to walk beats instead of stay in their cars. With Greenberg's help, Riley was able to keep together the unusual coalition of predominantly white business and corporate interests and African American voters that brought him into office in the first place.

It hasn't all been rosy. Riley was put on the spot in 2007 after the tragic deaths of the "Charleston 9" firefighters, an episode which seemed to expose serious policy and equipment flaws in the city's fire department. And he's often been accused of being too easily infatuated with high-dollar development projects instead of paying attention to the needs of regular Charlestonians.

But while every four years there's talk around town that somebody might finally be able to beat Mayor Joe, every four years the naysayers are disappointed as he's re-elected again.

Here's only a partial list of the major projects and events Mayor Joe has made happen in Charleston that visitors are likely to enjoy:

- Charleston Maritime Center

- Charleston Place

- Children's Museum of the Lowcountry

- Hampton Park rehabilitation

- King Street/Market Street retail district

- Mayor Joseph P. Riley Ballpark (named after the mayor at the insistence of city council over his objections)

- MOJA Arts Festival

- Piccolo Spoleto

- The South Carolina Aquarium

- Spoleto USA

- Waterfront Park

- West Ashley Bikeway & Greenway

11 A.M.–6 P.M.) has gourmet items and kitchen ware, and even offers cooking classes.

OFF THE PENINSULA

Though the best shopping is in Charleston proper, there are some noteworthy independent stores in the surrounding areas. The biggest music store in the region is **The Guitar Center** (7620 Rivers Ave., 843/572-9063, Mon.–Fri. 11 A.M.–7 P.M., Sat. 10 A.M.–7 P.M., Sun. noon–6 P.M.) in North Charleston across from the (also huge) Northwood Mall. With just about everything a musician might want or need, it's part of a chain that's been around since the late 1950s, but the Charleston location is relatively new.

Though the peninsula is known for its antiques, **Linda Page's Thieves Mart** (1460 Ben Sawyer Blvd., 843/884-9672, Mon.–Fri., 9 A.M.–5:30 P.M., Sat. 9 A.M.–5 P.M.) in Mount Pleasant isn't a slouch, especially for items from the first half of the 20th century. Near the Old Village, the Thieves Mart has just about every kind of item or knick-knack, depending on what Linda's been able to bring in.

SHOPPING CENTERS

The newest and most pleasant mall in the area is the retro-themed, pedestrian-friendly **Mount Pleasant Towne Center** (1600 Palmetto Grande Dr., 843/216-9900, www.mtpleasant townecentre.com, Mon.–Sat. 10 A.M.–9 P.M., Sun. noon–6 P.M.), which opened in 1999 to serve the growing population of East Cooper residents tired of having to cross a bridge to get to a big mall. In addition to national chains you'll find a few cool local stores in here, like Stella Nova spa and day salon, Shooz by Copper Penny, and the men's store Jos. A. Banks.

You'll find the big **Northwoods Mall** (2150 Northwoods Blvd., North Charleston, 843/797-3060, www.shopnorthwoodsmall.com, Mon.–Sat. 10 A.M.–9 P.M., Sun. noon–6 P.M.) up in North Charleston. Anchor stores include Dillard's, Belk, Sears, and J.C. Penney.

North Charleston also hosts the **Tanger Outlet** (4840 Tanger Outlet Blvd., 843/529-3095, www.tangeroutlet.com, Mon.–Sat. 10 A.M.–9 P.M., Sun. 11 A.M.–6 P.M.). Get factory-priced bargains from stores such as Adidas, Banana Republic, Brooks Brothers, Corningware, Old Navy, Timberland, and more.

Citadel Mall (2070 Sam Rittenberg Blvd., 843/766-8511, www.shopcitadel-mall.com, Mon.–Sat. 10 A.M.–9 P.M., Sun. noon–6 P.M.) is in West Ashley (and not at all close to the real Citadel). Anchors here are Dillards, Parisian, Target, Belk, and Sears.

Sports and Recreation

Because of the generally gorgeous weather in the Charleston area, helped immensely by the steady, soft sea breeze, outdoor activities are always popular and available. Though it's not much of a spectator sports town, there are plenty of things to do on your own, such as golf, tennis, walking, hiking, boating, and fishing.

ON THE WATER
Beaches

Folly Beach is the area's most famous beach. In addition to the charming town of Folly Beach itself, there's the Charleston County–run **Folly Beach County Park** (1100 West Ashley Ave.,

843/588-2426, www.ccprc.com, daily 10 A.M.–dark, open 9 A.M. March and April, $7 per vehicle, free for pedestrians and cyclists) at the far west end of Folly Island. It has a picnic area, restrooms, outdoor showers, and beach chair and umbrella rentals. Get there by taking S.C. Highway 171/Folly Road until it turns into Center Street, and then take a right on West Ashley.

On Isle of Palms you'll find **Isle of Palms County Park** (14th Ave., 843/886-3863, www.ccprc.com, daily 10 A.M.–dark, open 9 A.M. summer, $5 per vehicle, free for pedestrians and cyclists), which has restrooms, showers, a picnic area, a beach volleyball area, and beach chair and umbrella rentals. Get there by taking the Isle of Palms Connector/Highway 517 to the island, go through the light at Palm Boulevard and take the next left at the park gate. Or you can park on the street and access the beach yourself.

On the west end of Kiawah Island to the south of Charleston is **Kiawah Island Beachwalker Park** (843/768-2395, www.ccprc.com, Mar.–Apr. weekends only 10 A.M.–6 P.M., summer 9 A.M.–7 P.M., Sept. 10 A.M.–6 P.M., Oct. weekends only 10 A.M.–6 P.M., closed Nov.–Feb., $7 per vehicle, free for pedestrians and cyclists), the only public facility on this mostly private resort island. It has restrooms, showers, a picnic area with grills, and beach chair and umbrella rentals. Get there from downtown by taking Lockwood Avenue onto the Highway 30 Connector bridge over the Ashley River. Turn right onto Folly Road, then a left onto Maybank Highway. After about 20 minutes you'll take a left onto Bohicket Road, which leads you to Kiawah in 14 miles. Turn left from Bohicket onto the Kiawah Island Parkway. Just before the security gate, turn right on Beachwalker Drive and follow the signs to the park.

For a totally go-it-alone type of beach day, go to the three-mile beach on the Atlantic Ocean at Sullivan's Island. There are no facilities, no lifeguards, strong offshore currents, and no parking lots on this residential island (park on the side of the street). There's also a lot of dog-walking on this beach since no leash is required November–February. Get there from downtown by crossing the Ravenel Bridge over the Cooper River and bearing right onto Coleman Boulevard, which turns into Ben Sawyer Boulevard. Take the Ben Sawyer Bridge onto Sullivan's Island. Beach access is marked.

Kayaking

There are many gorgeous, fun, and safe paddles in the Charleston area. While all are a drive out of the peninsula, they are worth the trip. One of the best experiences is north of Charleston at **Cape Romaine National Wildlife Refuge** (5801 Hwy. 17 N., 843/928-3264, www.fws

.gov/caperomain, open sunrise–sunset year-round). Essentially comprising four barrier islands, the 66,000-acre refuge provides a lot of great paddling opportunities, chief among them **Bull Island** (no overnight camping). A fairly lengthy trek from where you put in lies famous Boneyard Beach, where hundreds of downed trees lie on the sand, bleached by sun and salt.

Slightly to the south within the refuge, **Capers Island Heritage Preserve** (843/953-9300, www.dnr.sc.gov, daily dawn–dusk, free) is a popular camping locale (get permits in advance by calling the South Carolina Department of Natural Resources).

The best local outfit for guided kayak tours is **Coastal Expeditions** (654 Serotina Ct., 843/881-4582, www.coastalexpeditions.com), which also runs the only approved ferry service to the Refuge. They'll rent a kayak for roughly $50 a day. Coastal Expeditions also sells an outstanding kayaking/boating/fishing map of the area for about $12. Another good tour operator is **Nature Adventures Outfitters** (1900 Iron Swamp Rd., 800/673-0679) out of Awendaw Island.

Closer to town, many kayakers put in at the **Shem Creek Marina** (526 Mill St., 843/884-3211, www.shemcreekmarina.com) or the public **Shem Creek Landing** in Mount Pleasant. From there it's a safe, easy paddle—sometimes with appearances by dolphins or manatee—to the Intracoastal Waterway. Some kayakers like to go from Shem Creek straight out into Charleston Harbor to **Crab Bank Heritage Preserve,** a prime birding island. Another good place to put in is at **Isle of Palms Marina** (50 41st Ave., 843/886-0209) on Morgan Creek behind the Wild Dunes Resort, emptying into the Intracoastal Waterway.

Local company **Half Moon Outfitters** (280 King St., 843/853-0990; 425 Coleman Blvd., 843/881-9472, www.halfmoonoutfitters.com, Mon.–Sat. 10 A.M.–7 P.M., Sun. noon–6 P.M.) sponsors an annual six-mile Giant Kayak Race at Isle of Palms Marina in late October, benefiting the Coastal Conservation League.

Behind Folly Beach is an extensive network of waterways, including lots of areas that are great for camping and fishing. The Folly

River Landing is just over the bridge to the island. On Folly a good tour operator and rental house is **OceanAir Sea Kayak** (520 Folly Rd., 800/698-8718, www.seakayaksc.com).

Fishing and Boating

For casual fishing off a pier, try the **Folly Beach Fishing Pier** (101 E. Arctic Ave., 843/588-3474, $5 parking, $8 fishing fee, rod rentals available) on Folly Beach or the **North Charleston Riverfront Park** (843/745-1087, www.northcharleston.org, daily dawn–dusk) along the Cooper River on the grounds of the old Navy Yard. Get onto the Navy Yard grounds by taking I-26 north to exit 216-B. Take a left onto Spruill Avenue and a right onto McMillan Avenue.

Key local marinas include **Shem Creek Marina** (526 Mill St., 843/884-3211, www.shemcreekmarina.com), **Charleston Harbor Marina** (24 Patriots Point Rd., 843/284-7062, www.charlestonharbormarina.com), **Charleston City Marina** (17 Lockwood Dr., 843/722-4968), **Charleston Maritime Center** (10 Wharfside St., 843/853-3625, www.cmcevents.com), and the **Cooper River Marina** (1010 Juneau Ave., 843/554-0790, www.ccprc.com).

Good fishing charter outfits include **Barrier Island Eco Tours** (50 41st Ave., 843/886-5000, www.nature-tours.com, about $80) out of Isle of Palms; **Bohicket Boat Adventure & Tour Co.** (2789 Cherry Point Rd., 843/559-3525, www.bohicketboat.com) out of the Edisto River; and **Reel Fish Finder Charters** (315 Yellow Jasmine Ct., Moncks Corner, 843/697-2081). Captain James picks clients up at many different marinas in the area.

For a list of all public landings in Charleston County, go to www. ccprc.com.

Diving

Diving in the area can be quite challenging because of the fast currents, and visibility can be low. But as you'd expect in this historic area, there are plenty of wrecks, fossils, and artifacts. In fact, there's an entire Cooper River Underwater Heritage Trail with the key sites marked for divers.

Offshore diving centers on the network of offshore artificial reefs (go to www.dnr .sc.gov for a list and locations), particularly the "Charleston 60" sunken barge and the new and very popular "Train Wreck," comprising 50 deliberately sunk New York City subway cars. The longtime popular dive spot known as the "Anchor Wreck" was recently identified as the Norwegian steamer *Leif Erikkson,* which sank in 1905 after a collision with another vessel. In addition to being fun dive sites, these artificial reefs have proven to be important feeding and spawning grounds for marine life.

Probably Charleston's best-regarded outfitter and charter operator is **Charleston Scuba** (335 Savannah Hwy., 843/763-3483, www .charlestonscuba.com) in West Ashley. You also might want to check out **Cooper River Scuba** (843/572-0459, www.cooperriverdiving.com) and **Atlantic Coast Dive Center** (843/884-1500, www.atlanticcoastdivecenter.com).

Surfing and Boarding

The surfing at the famous **Washout** area on the eastside of Folly Beach isn't what it used to be due to storm activity and beach erosion. But the diehards still gather at this area when the swell hits—generally about 3–5 feet (occasionally with dolphins!). Check out the conditions yourself from the three views of the Folly Surfcam (www.follysurfcam.com).

The best local surf shop is undoubtedly the historic **McKevlin's Surf Shop** (8 Center St., 843/588-2247, www.mckevlins.com) on Folly Beach, one of the first surf shops on the entire East Coast, dating to 1965 (check out an employee's "No Pop-Outs" blog at http://mckevlins .blogspot.com). Other shops include **Barrier Island Surf Shop** (2013 Folly Rd., 843/795-4545) on Folly Beach and **The Point Break** (369 King St., 843/722-4161) on the peninsula.

For lessons, **Folly Beach Shaka Surf School** (843/607-9911, www.shakasurfschool .com) offers private and group sessions at Folly; you might also try **Sol Surfers Surf Camp** (843/881-6700, www.solsurfers.net).

Kiteboarders might want to contact **Air** (843/388-9300, www.catchsomeair.us), which offers several levels of lessons, as well as **Whitecap Windsurfing** (706/833-9463, www.whitecapwindsurfing.com).

Water Parks

During the summer months, Charleston County operates three water parks, though none are on the peninsula: **Splash Island Waterpark** (444 Needlerush Pkwy., 843/884-0832) in Mount Pleasant; **Whirlin' Waters Adventure Waterpark** (University Blvd., 843/572-7275) in North Charleston; and **Splash Zone Waterpark at James Island County Park** (871 Riverland Dr., 843/795-7275) on James Island west of town. Admission runs about $10 per person. Go to www.ccprc.com for more information.

ON LAND
Golf

America's first golf course was constructed in Charleston in 1786. The term "green fee" is alleged to have evolved from the maintenance fees charged to members of the South Carolina Golf Club and Harleston Green in what's now downtown Charleston. So as you'd expect, there's some great golfing in the area, generally in the outlying islands. Here are some of the highlights (green fees are averages and are subject to season and time):

The folks at the nonprofit **Charleston Golf, Inc.** (423 King St., 843/958-3629, www.charlestongolfguide.com) are your best one-stop resource for tee times and packages.

The main public course is the 18-hole **Charleston Municipal Golf Course** (2110 Maybank Hwy., 843/795-6517, www.charleston city.info, green fees about $40). To get there from the peninsula, take U.S. 17 south over the Ashley River, take S.C. 171/Folly Road south, and then take a right onto Maybank Highway.

Probably the most renowned area facilities are at the acclaimed **Kiawah Island Golf Resort** (12 Kiawah Beach Dr., 800/654-2924, www.kiawahgolf.com) about 20 miles from Charleston. The Resort has five courses in all, the best known of which is the **Kiawah Island Ocean Course,** site of the famous "War by the Shore" 1991 Ryder Cup. This 2.5-mile course, which is walking-only until noon each day, hosted the Senior PGA Championship in 2007 and will host the 2012 PGA Championship. The Resort offers a golf academy and private lessons galore. These are public courses, but be aware that tee times are limited for golfers who aren't guests at the Resort.

Two excellent resort-style public courses are at **Wild Dunes Resort Golf** (5757 Palm Blvd., 888/845-8932, www.wilddunes.com, $165 green fees) on Isle of Palms.

The 18-hole **Patriots Point Links** (1 Patriots Point Rd., 843/881-0042, www.patriotspointlinks.com, green fees about $100) on the Charleston Harbor right over the Ravenel Bridge in Mount Pleasant is one of the most convenient courses in the area and it boasts some phenomenal views.

Also on Mount Pleasant is perhaps the best course in the area for the money, the award-winning **Rivertowne Golf Course** (1700 Rivertown Country Club Dr., 843/856-9808, www.rivertownecountryclub.com, $150 green fees) at the Rivertowne Country Club. This relatively new course, opened in 2002, was designed by Arnold Palmer.

Tennis

Tennis fans are in for a treat at the brand-new **Family Circle Tennis Center** (161 Seven Farms Dr., 800/677-2293, www.familycirclecup.com, Mon.–Thurs. 8 A.M.–8 P.M., Fri. 8 A.M.–7 P.M., Sat. 8 A.M.–5 P.M., Sun. 9 A.M.–5 P.M., $15/hr.) on Daniel Island. This multimillion-dollar facility is owned by the city of Charleston, and was built in 2001 specifically to host the annual Family Circle Cup women's competition, which was previously held in Hilton Head for many years. But it's also open to the public year-round (except when the Cup is on) with 17 courts.

The best resort tennis activity is at the **Kiawah Island Golf Resort** (12 Kiawah Beach Dr., 800/654-2924, www.kiawahgolf.com), with a total of 28 courts.

There are four free, public, city-funded facilities on the peninsula: **Moultrie Playground** (Broad St. and Ashley Ave.,

843/769-8258, www.charlestoncity.info, six lighted hard courts), **Jack Adams Tennis Center** (290 Congress St., six lighted hard courts), **Hazel Parker Playground** (70 East Bay St. on the Cooper River, one hard court), and **Corrine Jones Playground** (Marlowe and Peachtree Streets, two hard courts).

Over in West Ashley, the city also runs the public **Charleston Tennis Center** (19 Farmfield Rd., 843/769-8258, www.charleston city.info, 15 lighted courts).

Hiking and Biking

If you're like me, you'll walk your legs off just making your way around the sights on the peninsula. Early risers will especially enjoy the incredible beauty of a dawn breaking over the Cooper River as they walk or jog along the Battery or a little farther north at Waterfront Park.

Charleston-area beaches are perfect for a leisurely bike ride on the sand. Sullivan's Island is a particular favorite, and it's worth the drive just to enjoy a sunset after pedaling nearly the whole length of the island. Indeed, you might be surprised at how long you can ride in one direction on these beaches.

Those desiring a more demanding use of their legs can walk or ride their bike in the dedicated pedestrian/bike lane on the massive **Arthur Ravenel Jr. Bridge** over the Cooper River, the longest cable-stayed bridge in the western hemisphere. The extra lanes are a huge advantage over the old span on the same site, and a real example for other cities to follow in practical, sustainable transportation solutions. There's free parking on the Mount Pleasant side on the road to Patriots Point. Keep in mind there's a long walk or ride to the bridge from the lot. **Bike the Bridge Rentals** (360 Concord St., 843/853-2453, www.bikethe bridgerentals.com) offers self-guided tours over the Ravenel Bridge and back on a Raleigh Comfort bike, and also rents road bikes for lengthier excursions.

In West Ashley, there's a good urban walking/biking trail, the **West Ashley Greenway,** built on a former rail bed. The 10-mile trail runs parallel to U.S. 17 and passes parks,

schools, and the Clemson Experimental Farm, ending near John Island. To get to the trailhead from downtown, drive west on U.S. 17. About a half-mile after you cross the bridge, turn left onto Folly Road (S.C. Highway 171). At the second light, turn right into South Windermere Shopping Center; the trail's behind the center on the right.

The most ambitious trail in South Carolina is the **Palmetto Trail** (www.palmetto conservation.org), begun in 1997 and covering 425 miles from the Atlantic to the Appalachians—including a section across the state house lawn in Columbia! The coastal terminus near Charleston, the seven-mile Awendaw Passage through the Francis Marion National Forest, begins at the trailhead at the Buck Hall Recreational Area (843/887-3257, $5 vehicle fee), which has parking and bathroom facilities. Get there by taking U.S. 17 north about 20 miles out of Charleston and through the Francis Marion National Forest and then Awendaw. Take a right onto Buck Hall Landing Road.

Another good nature hike outside town is on the eight miles of scenic and educational trails at **Caw Caw Interpretive Center** (5200 Savannah Hwy., 843/889-8898, www.ccprc.com, Wed.–Fri. 9 A.M.–3 P.M., Sat.–Sun. 9 A.M.–5 P.M., $1) in nearby Ravenel on an old rice plantation.

One of the best outfitters in town is **Half Moon Outfitters** (280 King St., 843/853-0990, www.halfmoonoutfitters.com, Mon.–Sat. 10 A.M.–7 P.M., Sun. noon–6 P.M.). They have a Mount Pleasant location (425 Coleman Blvd., 843/881-9472) as well (and it has better parking).

Bird-Watching

Cape Romaine National Wildlife Refuge (5801 Hwy. 17 N., 843/928-3264, www .fws.gov/caperomain, sunrise–sunset year-round) is a birder's paradise, especially **Bull Island,** which is accessible only by boat. You can kayak there yourself or take the only approved ferry service from **Coastal Expeditions** (654 Serotina Ct., 843/881-4582, www.coastalexpeditions.com). **Barrier Island Eco Tours** (50 41st Ave., 843/886-5000, www.nature-tours.com) on Isle of Palms also runs trips to the area.

Right in Charleston Harbor is the amazing **Crab Bank Heritage Preserve,** where thousands of migratory birds can be seen depending on the season. You can either kayak there yourself or take a charter with **Nature Adventures Outfitters** (1900 Iron Swamp Rd., 800/673-0679) out of Awendaw Island.

On James Island southwest of Charleston is **Legare Farms** (2620 Hanscombe Point Rd., 843/559-0763, www.legarefarms.com), which holds migratory bird walks each Saturday in autumn at 8:30 A.M. ($6 adults, $3 children).

Well northwest of Charleston is **Francis Beidler Forest** (336 Sanctuary Rd., Harleyville, S.C., 843/462-2150, www.sc.audubon.org, Tues.–Fri. 9 A.M.–5 P.M., $7 adults, $3.50 children 6–18, free for children under five), a largely pristine habitat jointly owned by the Nature Conservancy and the Audubon Society. See the rare and beautiful Northern Parula, the Yellow-Throated Wrbler, and many other species drawn to old-growth stands such as the cypress and tupelo forests here.

Ice Skating

Ice skating in South Carolina? Yep, 100,000 square feet of it, year-round at the two NHL-size rinks of the **Carolina Ice Palace** (7665 Northwoods Blvd., 843/572-2717, www.carolina icepalace.com, $7 adults, $6 children) in North Charleston. This is also the practice facility for the local hockey team, the Stingrays, as well as where the Citadel hockey team plays.

SPECTATOR SPORTS
Charleston River Dogs

A New York Yankees farm team playing in the South Atlantic League, the Charleston River Dogs (360 Fishburne St., www.riverdogs.com, $5 general admission) play April–August at Joseph P. Riley, Jr., Park, a.k.a., "The Joe." The park is great, and there are a lot of fun promotions to keep things interesting should the play on the field be less than stimulating (as minor league ball often can be). Because of the intimate, retro design of the park, there are no bad

seats, so you might as well save a few bucks and go for the general admission ticket.

From downtown, get to The Joe by taking Broad Street west until it turns into Lockwood Drive. Follow that north until you get to Brittlebank Park and The Joe, next to the Citadel. Expect to pay $3–5 for parking.

Family Circle Cup

Moved to Daniel Island in 2001 from its long-time home in Hilton Head, the prestigious Family Circle Cup women's tennis tournament is held each April at the Family Circle Tennis Center (161 Seven Farms Dr., Daniel Island, 843/856-7900, www.familycirclecup.com, varied admission). Almost 100,000 people attend the multiweek event. Individual session tickets go on sale the preceding January.

Charleston Battery

The professional, A-League soccer team Charleston Battery (1990 Daniel Island Dr., 843/971-4625, www.charlestonbattery .com, about $10) play April–July at Blackbaud Stadium on Daniel Island north of Charleston. To get there from downtown, take I-26 north and then I-526 to Mount Pleasant. Take Exit 23A, Clements Ferry Road, and then a left on St. Thomas Island Drive. Blackbaud Stadium is about a mile on the left.

South Carolina Stingrays

The ECHL professional hockey team the South Carolina Stingrays (843/744-2248, www.sting rayshockey.com, $15) get a good crowd out to their rink at the North Charleston Coliseum, playing October–April.

Citadel Bulldogs

The Citadel (171 Moultrie St., 843/953-3294, www.citadelsports.com) plays Southern Conference football home games at Johnson-Hagood Stadium next to the campus on the Ashley River near Hampton Park. The basketball team plays home games at McAlister Field House on campus. The school's hockey team skates home games at the Carolina Ice Palace (see *Ice Skating*).

Accommodations

As one of America's key national and international destination cities, Charleston has a very well-developed infrastructure for housing visitors—a task made much easier by the city's longstanding tradition of and pride in hospitality. Because the bar is set so high, few visitors experience a truly bad stay in town. Hotels and bed-and-breakfasts are generally well maintained and have a high level of service, ranging from good to excellent. There's a 12.5 percent tax on hotel rooms in Charleston.

SOUTH OF BROAD
Over $300

On the south side of Broad Street is a great old Charleston lodging and one of the city's best bargains, **《 Governor's House Inn** (117 Broad St., 843/720-2070, www.governors house.com, $285–585). This circa-1760 building, a National Historic Landmark, is associated with Edward Rutledge, signer of the Declaration of Independence. Though most of its 11 rooms—all with four-poster beds, period furnishings, and high ceilings—go for around $300, some of the smaller rooms here can be had for closer to $200 in the off-season. The Governer's House is highly recommended not only for its good value and location, but also for its service and romantic feel.

The nine rooms of the **《 Two Meeting Street Inn** (2 Meeting St., 843/723-7322, www.twomeetingstreet.com, $220–435) way down by the Battery are individually appointed, with themes like "The Music Room" and the "The Spell Room." The decor in this 1892 Queen Anne bed-and-breakfast is very traditional, with lots of floral patterns and hunt club–style pieces and artwork; it's considered by many to be the most romantic lodging in town, and you won't soon forget the experience of sitting on the veranda enjoying the sights, sounds, and breezes of the Battery South of Broad. The Spell family has run the house as an inn since the 1940s, and their care and attention to detail are obvious to all guests, many

of whom come back again and again. Three of the rooms, the Canton, Granite, and Roberts, can be had for not much over $200.

WATERFRONT
$150-300

About as close to the Cooper River as a hotel gets, the **Harbourview Inn** (2 Vendue Range, 843/853-8439, www.harbourviewcharleston .com, $259) comprises a "historic wing" and a larger, newer, but still tastefully done main building. For the best of those eponymous harbor views, try to get a room on the third floor or you might have some obstructions. It's the little touches that keep guests happy here, with wine, cheese, coffee, tea, and cookies galore, and an emphasis on smiling, personalized service. The rooms are quite spacious, with big bathrooms and 14-foot ceilings. You can take your complimentary breakfast—good but not great—in your room or eat it on the nice rooftop terrace. The valet parking might sound steep at $15 a night, but this is downtown Charleston, after all.

Over $300

The rooms are the focus at the nearby **Vendue Inn** (19 Vendue Range, 843/577-7970, www .vendueinn.com, $359). With a range of decor from Colonial to French Provincial, all rooms are sumptuously appointed in that "boutique" style, with lots of warm, rich fabrics, unique pieces, and high-end bath amenities. The Inn gets a lot of traffic in the evenings because of the popular Library restaurant and its hopping Rooftop Bar, which has amazing views of the city and the river.

FRENCH QUARTER
Over $300

Suitably enough, the best place in this part of town is the **《 French Quarter Inn** (166 Church St., 843/722-1900, www.fqicharleston .com, $359). And the decor in the 50 surprisingly spacious rooms is suitably high-period French, with low-style, non-canopied beds and

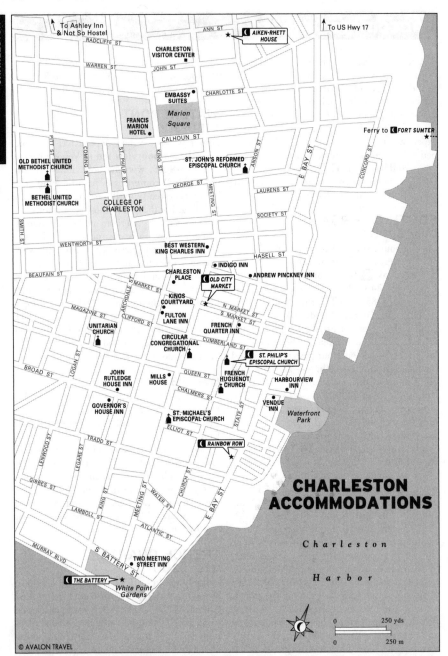

To Ashley Inn & Not So Hostel
To US Hwy 17

RADCLIFFE ST
ANN ST
★ ☾ AIKEN-RHETT HOUSE

CHARLESTON VISITOR CENTER
WARREN ST
JOHN ST

CHARLOTTE ST

EMBASSY SUITES

FRANCIS MARION HOTEL
Marion Square
CALHOUN ST

Ferry to ☾ FORT SUMTER ★

PITT ST
COMING ST
ST. PHILIP ST
KING ST
ST. JOHN'S REFORMED EPISCOPAL CHURCH ✝
ANSON ST
E BAY ST
CONCORD ST

OLD BETHEL UNITED METHODIST CHURCH ✝
GEORGE ST
MEETING ST
LAURENS ST

BETHEL UNITED METHODIST CHURCH ✝
COLLEGE OF CHARLESTON
SOCIETY ST

SMITH ST
WENTWORTH ST
BEST WESTERN KING CHARLES INN
HASELL ST

BEAUFAIN ST
● INDIGO INN
● ANDREW PINCKNEY INN

MAGAZINE ST
ARCHDALE ST
MARKET ST
CLIFFORD ST
CHARLESTON PLACE
☾ OLD CITY MARKET ★
N MARKET ST
S MARKET ST

UNITARIAN CHURCH ✝
KINGS COURTYARD
● FULTON LANE INN
FRENCH QUARTER INN ●
CUMBERLAND ST

CIRCULAR CONGREGATIONAL CHURCH ✝
ST. PHILIP'S EPISCOPAL CHURCH ✝

BROAD ST
LOGAN ST
JOHN RUTLEDGE HOUSE INN
MILLS HOUSE ●
QUEEN ST
FRENCH HUGUENOT CHURCH ✝
HARBOURVIEW INN

CHALMERS ST
VENDUE INN
Waterfront Park

GOVERNOR'S HOUSE INN
ST. MICHAEL'S EPISCOPAL CHURCH ✝
STATE ST

ELLIOT ST
☾ RAINBOW ROW ★

LENWOOD ST
LEGARE ST
TRADD ST

GIBBES ST
KING ST
MEETING ST
WATER ST
CHURCH ST
E BAY ST

CHARLESTON ACCOMMODATIONS

LAMBOLL ST
ATLANTIC ST
Charleston

MURRAY BLVD
S BATTERY ST
TWO MEETING STREET INN ●
Harbor

☾ THE BATTERY ★
White Point Gardens

0   250 yds
0   250 m

© AVALON TRAVEL

crisp, fresh linens. Many rooms feature fireplaces, whirlpool baths, and private balconies. One of Charleston's hottest restaurants, Tristan, is on ground floor. You're treated to champagne on your arrival, and goodies are available all day, with wine and cheese served every night at 5 P.M. As you'd expect at a place with the word "French" in its name, the continental silver service breakfast is particularly good.

NORTH OF BROAD
$150-300

It calls itself a boutique hotel, perhaps because each room is totally different and sumptuously appointed. But the charming **(Andrew Pinckney Inn** (199 Church St., 843/937-8800, www.andrewpinckneyinn.com, $170–260) is very nearly in a class by itself in Charleston not only for its great rates, but for its casual, West Indies–style decor, charming courtyard, gorgeous three-story atrium, and rooftop terrace on which you can enjoy your complimentary (and delicious) breakfast. With 37 rooms and four suites, it's larger than it looks, but the friendly staff—including a concierge—does a good job of making everyone feel special. For the money and the amenities, it's possibly the single best lodging package in town.

Aside from its surprisingly low rates, a central location near the Market and a beautiful interior courtyard are the main selling points of the **Indigo Inn** (1 Maiden Lane, 843/577-5900, www.indigoinn.com, $150–189) Despite its fairly large size—40 rooms—this is a cozy, romantic place that doesn't take itself too seriously, with a very friendly staff who enjoy telling you cool things to do around town.

Free parking, a great location, friendly staff, and reasonable prices are the highlights of the **Best Western King Charles Inn** (237 Meeting St., 843/723-7451, www.kingcharles inn.com, $200–250). It's not necessarily where you would want to spend your honeymoon, but it's plenty nice enough and frequent visitors to town swear by it. The rooms have armoires and poster beds, and some suites have fireplaces.

If you plan on some serious shopping, you might want to stay right on the city's main shopping thoroughfare at the **Kings Courtyard Inn** (198 King St., 866/720-2949, www.kingscourtyardinn.com, $245–285). This 1853 Greek Revival building houses a lot more rooms—more than 40—than meets the eye, and can get a little crowded at times. Still, its charming courtyard and awesome location on King Street are big bonuses, as is the convenient but cramped parking lot right next door (about $12 a day, a bargain for this part of town), with free in/out privileges.

Affiliated with the Kings Courtyard—and right next door, in fact—is the smaller, cozier **Fulton Lane Inn** (202 King St., 866/720-2940, www.fultonlaneinn.com, $245), with its lobby entrance on tiny Fulton Lane between the two inns. Small, simple guest rooms—some with fireplaces—have comfortable beds and spacious bathrooms. This is the kind of place for active people who plan to spend most of their days out and about, but want a cozy place to come back to at night. You mark down your continental breakfast order at night, leave it on your doorknob, and it shows up at the *exact* time you requested the next morning. Then when you're ready to shop and walk, just go down the stairs and take the exit right out onto busy King Street. Also nice is $12-a-day parking with free in/out privileges.

Over $300

Considered Charleston's premier hotel, **(Charleston Place** (205 Meeting St., 843/722-4900, www.charlestonplace.com, $419–529) maintains a surprisingly high level of service and decor considering its massive, 440-room size. Now owned by the London-based Orient-Express Hotels, Charleston Place is routinely rated as one of the best hotels in North America by *Condé Nast Traveler* and other publications. The rooms aren't especially large but they are well appointed, featuring Italian marble baths, high-speed Internet, and voice messaging—and, of course, there's a pool available. A series of suite offerings—Junior, Junior Executive, Parlor, and the 800-square-foot Senior—feature enlarged living areas and multiple TVs and phones. A Manager's Suite on

© JIM MOREKIS

the Mills House Hotel

the Private Club level up top comprises 1,200 square feet of total luxury that will set you back at least $1,600 a night. But it's the additional offerings that make Charleston Place closer to a lifestyle decision than a lodging decision. The on-site spa (843/937-8522) offers all kinds of massages, including couples and "mommy to be" sessions. Diners and tipplers have three fine options to choose from: the famous **Charleston Grill** (843/577-4522, dinner nightly beginning at 6 P.M.) for fine dining; the breakfast, lunch, and brunch hot spot **Palmetto Cafe** (843/722-4900, breakfast daily 6:30 A.M.–11 A.M., lunch daily 11:30 A.M.–3 P.M.); and the **Thoroughbred Club** (daily 11 A.M.–midnight) for cocktails and afternoon tea.

On the north side of Broad Street, the magnificent (**John Rutledge House Inn** (116 Broad St., 843/723-7999, www.johnrutledge houseinn.com, $300–405) is very close to the old South of Broad neighborhood not only in geography, but in feel. Known as "America's most historic inn," the Rutledge House boasts a fine old pedigree indeed: Built for Constitution signer John Rutledge in 1763, it's one of only 15 homes belonging to the original signers to survive. George Washington breakfasted here with Mrs. Rutledge in 1791. The interior is stunning: Italian marble fireplaces, original plaster moldings, and masterful ironwork abound in the public spaces. The inn's 19 rooms are divided among the original mansion and two carriage houses. All have antique furnishings and canopy beds, and some suites have fireplaces and whirlpool baths. A friendly and knowledgeable concierge will give you all kinds of tips and make reservations for you.

Though this is a new building owned by Holiday Inn, the **Mills House Hotel** (115 Meeting St., 843/577-2400, www.ichotels group.com, $309–359) boasts an important pedigree and still tries hard to maintain the old tradition of impeccable Southern service at this historic location. An extensive round of renovations completed in 2007 has been well received, though it also means prices have gone up (even parking is up to $19 a day now). Centrally located and within walking distance of almost all key historic sites, the original Mills House was built in 1853 and immediately became one of the South's premier hotels, hosting luminaries like Robert E. Lee and President Theodore Roosevelt.

UPPER KING AREA
Under $150

Stretching the bounds of the "Upper King" definition, we come to the ◖ **Ashley Inn** (201 Ashley Ave., 843/723-1848, www.charleston -sc-inns.com, $139) well northwest of Marion Square, almost in the Citadel area. Though it's too far to walk from here to most any historic attraction in Charleston, the Ashley Inn does provide free bikes to its guests, as well as free off-street parking, a particularly nice touch. It also deserves a special mention not only because of the romantic, well-appointed nature of its six guest rooms, suite, and carriage house, but for its outstanding breakfasts. You get to pick a main dish, such as Carolina sausage pie, stuffed waffles, or cheese blintzes.

$150-300

In a renovated 1924 building overlooking beautiful Marion Square, the **Francis Marion Hotel** (387 King St., 843/722-0600, www .francismarioncharleston.com, $189–329) offers quality accommodation in the hippest, most bustling area of the peninsula—though be aware that it's quite a walk down to the Battery from here. The rooms are plush and big, though the bathrooms, for some reason, are downright cramped. The hotel parking garage is $12 a day, with valet parking until about 8 P.M. A Starbucks in the lobby pleases many a guest on their way out or in. Most rooms hover around $300, but some are a real steal.

Over $300

What to do with a historic military school that looks like a castle? Renovate it into a hotel, of course. That's just what the **Embassy Suites Charleston** (337 Meeting St., 843/723-6900, www.embassysuites1.hilton.com, $329–369) did with the old Citadel building, a circa-1840 National Historic Landmark overlooking

Marion Square. Needless to say, the architecture is amazing, but Embassy actually did a good job with the public spaces inside as well. The rooms themselves are not always ideal, mostly due to the physical limitations of the building itself. There's a complimentary full breakfast. One catch: Parking pushes $20 a day. While the location is fun and bustling, it's a hefty walk to historic areas farther south on the peninsula.

HAMPTON PARK AREA
Under $150

Charleston's least-expensive lodging is also by far its most unique, the ◖ **Not So Hostel** (156 Spring St., 843/722-8383, www.notsohostel.com, $21 dorm, $60 private). The already-reasonable prices also include a great make-your-own breakfast, off-street parking, bikes, high-speed Internet access in the common room, and even an airport/train/bus shuttle. The inn actually comprises three 1840s Charleston single houses, all with the obligatory piazzas to catch the breeze. (However, unlike some hostels, there's air-conditioning in all the rooms.)

Because the free bike usage makes up for its off-the-beaten-path location, a stay ay the Not So Hostel is a fantastic way to enjoy the Holy City on a budget, while having a great time with some cool people to boot.

WEST ASHLEY
$150-300

Looking like Frank Lloyd Wright parachuted into a 300-year-old plantation and got to work, the ◖ **The Inn at Middleton Place** (4290 Ashley River Rd., 843/556-0500, www .theinnatmiddletonplace.com, $220) is one of Charleston's most unique lodgings—and not only because it's on the grounds of the historic and beautiful Middleton Place Plantation. The four connected buildings comprising over 50 guest rooms are modern, yet deliberately blend in with the forested, neutral-colored surroundings. The very spacious rooms have that same woody minimalism, with excellent fireplaces, spacious Euro-style baths, and huge, floor-to-ceiling windows overlooking the grounds and the river. Guests also have full access to the rest of the gorgeous Middleton grounds. The only downside is that you're a lengthy drive from the peninsula and all its attractions, restaurants, and nightlife. While those who need constant stimulation will be disappointed in the deep quietude here, nature-lovers and those in search of peace and quiet will find this almost paradise. And don't worry about food—the excellent Middleton Place Restaurant is open for lunch and dinner.

CAMPING

Charleston County runs a family-friendly, fairly boisterous campground at **James Island**

County Park (871 Riverland Dr., 843/795-7275, www.ccprc.com, $31 tent site, $37 pull-thru site). A neat feature here is the $5 per person round-trip shuttle to the Visitors Center downtown, Folly Beach Pier, and Folly Beach County Park. The Park also has 10 furnished cottages for rental, sleeping up to eight people (843/795-4386, $138 a day). Reservations are recommended.

For more commercial camping in Mount Pleasant, try the **KOA of Mt. Pleasant** (3157 Hwy. 17 N., 843/849-5177, www.koa.com, $30+ tent sites, $50+ pull-thrus).

Food

If you count the premier food cities in the United States on one hand, Charleston has to be one of the fingers. Its long history of good taste and livability has combined with an affluent and sophisticated population to attract some of the brightest chefs and restaurateurs in the country today.

Kitchens here eschew fickle trends and innovation for innovation's sake, instead emphasizing quality, professionalism, and most of all, freshness of ingredients. In a sort of Southern Zen, the typical Charleston chef seems to take pride in making a melt-in-your-mouth masterpiece out of the culinary commonplace—in not fixing what ain't broke, as they say down here. (I've heard Charleston's cuisine described as "competent classics," which also isn't far off the mark.)

Unlike Savannah, its more drink-oriented neighbor to the south, even Charleston's bars have great food. So don't assume you have to make reservations at a formal restaurant to fully enjoy the cuisine here. Truth is, it's all around you. Though an entire volume could easily be written about Charleston restaurants, here's a baseline foundation of recommended places to begin your epicurean journey through town.

SOUTH OF BROAD
Classic Southern
The only restaurant in the quiet old South

of Broad area is also one of Charleston's best and oldest: **Carolina's** (10 Exchange St., 843/724-3800, Sun.–Thurs. 5–10 P.M., Fri.–Sat. 5–11 P.M., $18–30). There's a new chef in town, Jeremiah Bacon, a Charleston native who spent the last seven years honing his craft in New York City. His Lowcountry take on European classics includes grilled salmon with potato gnocchi, tagliatelle with Lowcountry prosciutto, and pan-roasted diver scallops, with as many fresh ingredients as possible from the nearby Kensington Plantation. A tried-and-true favorite that predates Bacon's tenure, however, is Perdita's fruit de mer—a recipe that goes back to the restaurant's predecessor, Perdita's, in the 1950s, commonly regarded as Charleston's first fine-dining restaurant. If you can get the whole table to agree, try the $49-per-person Perdita's four-course tasting menu (wine flights extra). A recent renovation of this Revolutionary War–ra building—once the legendary Sailor's Tavern—hasn't negatively affected the romantic ambience of the three themed areas: Perdita's Room (the oldest dining area), the Sidewalk Room, and the Bar Room. Free valet parking is a big plus.

WATERFRONT
New Southern
No restaurant in Charleston inspires such

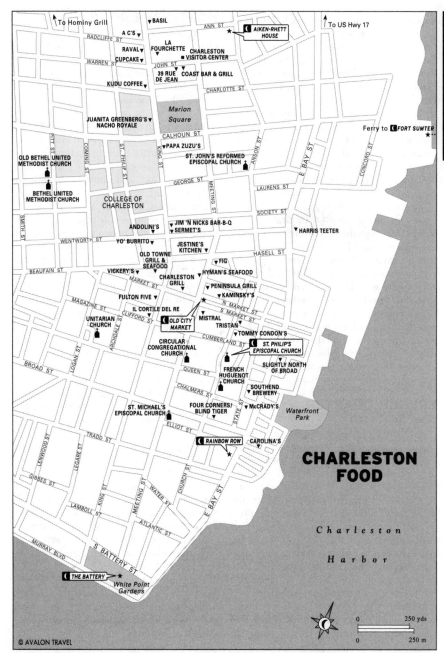

CHARLESTON FOOD

To Hominy Grill

BASIL
ANN ST
AIKEN-RHETT HOUSE
A C'S
RADCLIFFE ST
RAVAL
LA FOURCHETTE
CHARLESTON VISITOR CENTER
CUPCAKE
WARREN S
JOHN ST
39 RUE DE JEAN
COAST BAR & GRILL
KUDU COFFEE
CHARLOTTE ST
To US Hwy 17

Marion Square

JUANITA GREENBERG'S NACHO ROYALE
CALHOUN ST
Ferry to FORT SUMTER

PITT ST
COMING ST
ST. PHILIP ST
KING ST
PAPA ZUZU'S
ST. JOHN'S REFORMED EPISCOPAL CHURCH
ANSON ST
E BAY ST
CONCORD ST

OLD BETHEL UNITED METHODIST CHURCH
GEORGE ST
MEETING ST
LAURENS ST

BETHEL UNITED METHODIST CHURCH
COLLEGE OF CHARLESTON
SOCIETY ST

SMITH ST
ANDOLINI'S
JIM 'N NICKS BAR-B-Q
SERMET'S
HARRIS TEETER

WENTWORTH ST
YO' BURRITO
JESTINE'S KITCHEN
HASELL ST

OLD TOWNE GRILL & SEAFOOD
FIG

BEAUFAIN ST
VICKERY'S
CHARLESTON GRILL
HYMAN'S SEAFOOD

MARKET ST
PENINSULA GRILL

FULTON FIVE
KAMINSKY'S

MAGAZINE ST
IL CORTILE DEL RE
N MARKET ST
S MARKET ST

CLIFFORD ST
OLD CITY MARKET
MISTRAL
TRISTAN

UNITARIAN CHURCH
ARCHDALE ST
CUMBERLAND ST
TOMMY CONDON'S

BROAD ST
LOGAN ST
CIRCULAR CONGREGATIONAL CHURCH
ST. PHILIP'S EPISCOPAL CHURCH

QUEEN ST
FRENCH HUGUENOT CHURCH
SLIGHTLY NORTH OF BROAD

CHALMERS ST
SOUTHEND BREWERY

ST. MICHAEL'S EPISCOPAL CHURCH
FOUR CORNERS/ BLIND TIGER
STATE ST
McCRADY'S
Waterfront Park

TRADD ST
ELLIOT ST

LENWOOD ST
LEGARE ST
RAINBOW ROW
CAROLINA'S

GIBBES ST
KING ST
MEETING ST
WATER ST
CHURCH ST
E BAY ST

LAMBOLL ST
ATLANTIC ST

Charleston Harbor

MURRAY BLVD
S BATTERY ST

THE BATTERY
White Point Gardens

0   250 yds
0   250 m

© AVALON TRAVEL

impassioned, vocal advocates as ◖ **McCrady's** (2 Unity Alley, 843/577-0025, www.mccradys restaurant.com, Sun.–Thurs. 5:30–10 P.M., Fri.–Sat. 5:30–11 P.M., $25–34). Housed in Charleston's oldest tavern building (circa 1788), McCrady's is also known as Charleston's best-kept secret, since despite its high quality it's managed to avoid the siege of tourists common at many local fine-dining spots. But their loss can be your gain, as you enjoy the prodigious talents of young chef Sean Brock, whose *sous vide,* or vacuum cooking, is spoken of in hushed tones by his clientele. The restaurant's relatively low profile undoubtedly has to do with Brock's daring choices, all based on his unending quest for fresh and adventurous local ingredients. This is not the place to gorge on usual Lowcountry fare. Portions here are small and dynamic, and range from a yam soup with marshmallow and roasted chestnuts to seared foie gras with maple syrup to seared Hawaiian tuna in a saffron-vegetable juice emulsion. The menu changes seasonally according to the local market and the chef's whim. Many diners find the seven-course, $70 Chef's Tasting a near-religious experience. For an extra $60, master sommelier Clint Sloan provides paired wine selections.

FRENCH QUARTER
New Southern

One of the hottest new downtown spots for those with a more adventurous palate, **Tristan** (55 Market St., 843/534-2155, www.tristan dining.com, Mon.–Thurs. 11:30 A.M.–10 P.M., Fri.–Sat. 11:30 A.M.–11 P.M., Sun. 11 A.M.– 10 P.M., $18–32) inside the French Quarter Inn draws raves for the globally influenced cuisine of Chef Ciaran Duffy, who's equally at home with seafood, game, and multicultural barbecue. (His dramatic flair extends to the restaurant's website, which features a chef's-eye view webcam, worn on his head as he cooks.) At last count, the copious wine list boasted over 400 labels. The real scene here is for Sunday brunch, a hedonistic, à la carte affair with crab cake benedicts, corned beef hash, frittatas, omelets, and Bloody Marys galore.

NORTH OF BROAD
New Southern

Don't be put off by the initials of ◖ **Slightly North of Broad** (192 East Bay St., 843/723-3424, www.mavericksouthernkitchens.com, lunch Mon.–Fri. 11:30 A.M.–3 P.M., dinner daily 5:30–11 P.M., $15–35). Its acronym is an ironic play on the common, often-pejorative reference to the insular "South of Broad" neighborhood. This hot spot, routinely voted best restaurant in town in such contests, is anything but snobby. Hopping with happy foodies for lunch and dinner, the fun is enhanced by the long, open kitchen with its own counter area. Chef Frank Lee's dynamic but comforting menu here is practically a bible of the new wave of Lowcountry cuisine, with dishes like beef tenderloin, jumbo lump crab cakes, grilled BBQ tuna—and of course the sinful Wednesday night dinner special: deviled crab-stuffed flounder. An interesting twist at SNOB is the selection of "medium plates," i.e., dishes a little more generous than an app but with the same adventurous spirit. Examples include the sesame-encrusted tuna medallions, a charcuterie plate for the paté-lovers, and the to-die-for shrimp and grits. Lunch reservations only accepted for parties of five or more; reservations for dinner are highly recommended.

Just across the street from Hyman's Seafood is that establishment's diametrical opposite, the intimate bistro and stylish bar ◖ **FIG** (232 Meeting St., 843/805-5900, www.eatatfig .com, Mon.–Thurs. 6–11 P.M., Fri.–Sat. 6 P.M.– midnight, $20–25)—but the two do share one key thing: a passion for fresh, simple ingredients. While Hyman's packs in the tourists, who in turn pack in giant plates of seafood, FIG—short for "Food Is Good"—attracts young professional scenesters, as well as the diehard foodies. Chef Mike Lata was nominated in 2007 for James Beard's Best Chef of the Southeast. FIG is one of Charleston's great champions of the Sustainable Seafood Initiative, and the kitchen staff strives to work as closely as possible with local farmers and anglers in determining its seasonal menu.

Inside the plush Charleston Place Hotel

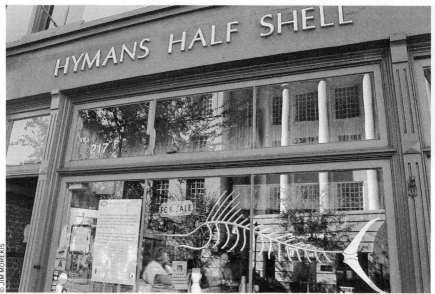

© JIM MOREKIS

Hymans Half Shell oyster bar

you'll find ⟨ **Charleston Grill** (224 King St., 843/577-4522, www.charlestongrill.com, dinner nightly beginning at 6 P.M., $27–50), one of the city's favorite (and priciest) fine-dining spots for locals and tourists alike. Chef Bob Waggoner, who in 1988 became the first American to own his own restaurant in France (Le Monte Cristo), divides his menu into four categories: Pure, Lush, Southern, and Cosmopolitan. He specializes in French-influenced Lowcountry cuisine like a nicoise vegetable tart, but there are a lot of great fusion dishes as well, such as the tuna and hamachi sashimi topped with pomegranate molasses and lemongrass oil. Reservations are a must.

The hard-to-define **Mistral** (99 S. Market St., 843/722-5708, Sun.–Thurs. 11 A.M.–11 P.M., Fri.–Sat. 11 A.M.–midnight, $10–25) is part seafood restaurant, part sexy French bistro, part Lowcountry living. With live, serious jazz blowing it hot Monday–Saturday nights and some of the best mussels and shrimp in the area served up fresh, all you really need to do is enjoy. If you're not a shellfish fan, try the sweetbreads or

their excellent veal. This is a great place to relax and enjoy an evening of great music and great food in a dimly lit, unhurried environment.

Seafood

Routinely voted the best seafood restaurant in the South, ⟨ **Hymans Seafood** (215 Meeting St., 843/723-6000, www.hymanseafood .com, Mon.–Thurs. 11 A.M.–9 P.M., Fri.–Sun. 11 A.M.–11 P.M., $14–25), actually comprises two affiliated establishments: Hymans Seafood (with its boisterous oyster bar, Hymans Half Shell), and Aaron's Deli, which has an awesome club sandwich and genuine key lime pie. The dividing line between the two is ambiguous at best, and both live up to the hype—and the routine hour-plus wait for a table—with a stubborn adherence to good old-fashioned quality control rare in this corporate age (rest assured that some member of the same family that began Hymans in 1890 will be on the premises any time it's open for business, without exception). To keep things manageable, Hymans offers the same menu and prices for both lunch and dinner. After asking for some complimentary fresh boiled peanuts in lieu of bread, start with the Carolina Delight, a delicious app (also available as an entrée) involving a lightly fried cake of grits topped with your choice of delectable seafood, or maybe a half-dozen oysters from the Half Shell oyster bar. In any case, definitely try the she-crab soup, some of the best you'll find anywhere. As for entrées, the ubiquitous Lowcountry crispy scored flounder is always a good bet, as is any fish special; but the real action at Hymans comes from anything that has a shell. The lump crab cakes, in particular, are a melt-in-your-mouth wonder. Or you can simply pay five bucks extra and have your fish stuffed with lump crab meat, though admittedly it's just not the same. A full bar is available, as well as a decent wine list, reasonably priced. Alas, this establishment, extremely popular with locals and tourists as well as the occasional movie star (Anthony Hopkins, Barbra Streisand, Mel Gibson), rock band (AC/DC, Metallica), and astronaut (Neil Armstrong) doesn't take reservations, so budget your time accordingly. Lunch crowds are generally lighter, though that's a relative term.

Perhaps only in Charleston would the best-known Irish pub also be one of its best-known seafood restaurants. But then again, **(Tommy Condon's Irish Pub** (160 Church St., 843/577-3818, www.tommycondons.com, dinner Sun.–Thurs. until 10 P.M., Fri. and Sat. until 11 P.M., bar daily until 2 A.M.) is unusual in a lot of ways: Irish in a town that tends to celebrate all things English and French, and fairly expensive in a town where pub food is surprisingly reasonable for the high quality. The food is some of the best in town, pub or non-pub, with the best picks being the unreal shepherd's pie and a great shrimp and grits. Other specialties include crab cakes with roasted red pepper dijon cream sauce, and a seafood platter featuring delectable deep-fried shrimp, scallops, oysters, and fish. If you're feeling particularly adventurous and/or have had a few Guinnesses, try the Irish nachos, featuring the usual ingredients but on fried potatoes instead of tortilla chips.

Mediterranean

One of the most romantic restaurants in Charleston—which is saying a lot—**(II Cortile del Re** (193A King St., 843/853-1888, Mon.–Sat. 5–10:30 P.M., $18–30) stands out amidst the antique stores on Lower King. Thankfully the Italian owners don't overdo the old country sentimentality, either in atmosphere or in menu. Sure, the tablecloths are white and the interior is warm, dark, and decorated with opera prints. But the piped-in music is long on cool jazz and short on over-the-top tenors, and the skinny wine bar in the front room is a favorite destination all its own. Portions here manage to be simultaneously large and light, as in the overtopped mussel plate in a delightfully thin and spicy tomato sauce, or the big spinach salad with goat cheese croutons sprinkled with a subtle vinaigrette. The entrées emphasize the Tuscan countryside, focusing both on slow-roasted meats and sublime takes on traditional pasta dishes, all somehow managing the same blend of heartiness and melt-in-your mouth lightness. My favorite is the simply perfect roasted lamb in a dark juniper and rosemary sauce, served on a bed of what are likely the best mashed potatoes in the world. Save room for the gelato dessert, served swimming in a pool of dark espresso.

Literally right around the corner from Il Cortele del Re is the other in Charleston's one-two Italian punch, **Fulton Five** (5 Fulton St., 843/853-5555, Mon.–Sat. from 5:30 P.M., $15–32). The cuisine of Northern Italy comes alive in this bustling, dimly lit room, from the *bresaola* salad of spinach and thin dried beef to the caper-encrusted tuna on a bed of sweet pea risotto. It's not cheap and the portions aren't necessarily the largest, but with these tasty, non-tomato-based dishes and this romantic, gusto-filled atmosphere, you'll be satiated with life itself.

You'll find the best gyros this side of the Mediterranean at **(Papa Zuzu's** (370 King St., 843/534-1666, daily 11 A.M.–9 P.M., $6–10), a long, narrow, funky eatery for which the phrase "hole in the wall" seems to have been invented. It's perfectly situated to feed the hungry shoppers passing by on King Street. Look for the fresh tomatoes in the window, ripening in the sun. The cuts of lamb—generously but artfully sliced—are perfectly cooked and complimented by a tangy but light tzaziki sauce. The service is mellow and friendly, and they'll either call your name to come get your order or just bring it out to you if it's not too busy. If you're not a gyro fan, the Greek pizza's awesome, too. There's also a nice range of alternative beverages and juices for the health-conscious.

Commonly known as the oldest family-run restaurant in Charleston, **Old Towne Grill and Seafood** (229 King St., 843/723-8170, www .oldtownerestaurant.com, Sun.–Thurs. 11 A.M.– 10 P.M., Fri.–Sat. 11 A.M.–11 P.M., $10–20), right next to the Riviera Theatre, brings a little taste of Greece to King Street. It's the usual moussaka, avgolemono, and roasted chicken type of place in the usual taverna atmosphere, but in this city of foodies who sometimes take themselves a little too seriously, it's a nice place to take a break from the scene, bring the family, and indulge in the Western world's original comfort cuisine.

One of Charleston's original hip people-watching spots, and still a personal favorite, is **Sermet's Corner** (276 King St., 843/853-7775, lunch daily 11 A.M.–3 P.M., dinner Sun.–Thurs. 4–10 P.M., Fri.–Sat. 4–11 P.M., $9–16), on a bustling intersection of King and Wentworth. Charismatic chef and owner Sermet Aslan—who also painted most of the artwork on the walls of this charming, high-ceilinged space—dishes up large, inexpensive portions of Mediterranean-style goodies like panini, pastas, pestos, calamari, and inventive meat dishes.

The best pizza in Charleston can be found at the multiple locations of the local chain **Andolini's** (82 Wentworth St., 843/722-7437, daily 11 A.M.–11 P.M., $2–10). As if the great taste, long hours, and fun decor weren't enough, it's also cheap. One of the best deals in town at this quirky, college-friendly institution is the lunch special: six bucks even for a huge one-topping slice of their signature New York–style pies, a salad, and a soda. Or for the same money you can have two cheese slices and a Bud. Their best special, however, might be a massive 19-inch with one topping and a pitcher of beer for

$20. In any event, know that all the sauce and dough is made and hand-tossed daily. There's a less funky but just as tasty incarnation in Mount Pleasant (414 W. Coleman Blvd., 843/849-7437) and a fun retro-style location in West Ashley (1117 Savannah Hwy., 843/225-4743), in addition to branches way out on James Island (967 Folly Rd., 843/576-7437) and up in North Charleston (6610 Rivers Ave., 843/266-7437).

Classic Southern

Walk through the gaslit courtyard of the Planter's Inn at Market and Meeting Streets into the stately yet surprisingly intimate dining room of the [**Peninsula Grill** (112 N. Market St., 843/723-0700, www.peninsulagrill.com, nightly from 5:30 P.M., $28–35) and begin an epicurean journey you'll not soon forget. Known far and wide for impeccable service as well as the mastery of Chef Robert Carter, Peninsula Grill is perhaps Charleston's quintessential purveyor of high-style Lowcountry cuisine and the odds-on favorite as best restaurant in town. From the lobster skillet cake and crab cake appetizer to the bourbon-grilled jumbo shrimp to the benne-crusted rack of lamb to sides like wild mushroom grits and hoppin' John, the menu reads like a "greatest hits" of regional cooking. You'll almost certainly want to start with the sampler trio of soups and finish with Carter's legendary coconut cake, a family recipe (only huge, whole cakes are served, so you'll definitely be leaving with some). Whatever you choose in between those bookends is almost guaranteed to be excellent. To accompany your inevitably near-perfect meal, choose from 20 wines by the glass or from over 300 bottles. Four stars from the Mobil Travel Club, four diamonds from AAA, and countless other accolades have come this restaurant's way in its relatively brief (by Charleston standards) decade of existence. Needless to say, reservations are highly recommended.

The long lines at Wentworth and Meeting Streets across from the fire station are waiting to follow Rachael Ray's lead and get into **Jestine's Kitchen** (251 Meeting St., 843/722-7224, Tues.–Thurs. 11 A.M.–9:30 P.M., Fri.–Sat.

11 A.M.–10 P.M. $8–15) and enjoy a simple, Southern take on such meat-and-three comfort food classics as meatloaf, pecan-fried fish, and fried green tomatoes. Instead of bread, you're greeted with a plate of cucumber pickles. Most of the recipes are handed down from the restaurant's namesake, Jestine Matthews, the African American woman who raised owner Dana Berlin. Mrs. Matthews passed away in 1997 at the age of 112, her longevity perhaps a testament to the healthy qualities of traditional Southern country cooking. Save room for her signature Coca-Cola cake.

Asian

For whatever reason, the Asian influence is not prevalent in Charleston cuisine. But **Wasabi** (61 State St., 843/577-5222, Mon.–Thurs. 11 A.M.–9:30 P.M., Fri.–Sat. 11 A.M.–11 P.M., Sun. noon–9 P.M., $10–15) has made quite a name for itself as the place for sushi downtown, though its hibachi work is impressive as well if you're more in the mood for the classic Japanese steakhouse experience. The bar gets hopping after dinner.

Mexican

If you suddenly find yourself craving Mexican while shopping on King Street, duck about a block down Wentworth to find the cavernous, delightful **Yo' Burrito** (86 Wentworth St., 843/853-3287, www.yoburrito.com, Sun.–Thurs. 11 A.M.–10 P.M., Fri.–Sat. 11 A.M.–11 P.M., $5–8), a local legend in its own right. Order from a variety of overstuffed specialty burritos, tasty quesadillas, and stacked nachos at the counter and take a seat at one of the large, communal-style tables, perhaps enjoying a freshly squeezed lemonade while you wait. But the real kicker is the condiment bar of homemade salsas, including a smoky chipotle number that is the closest thing to real red salsa I've had this side of New Mexico. But I suggest trying them all. In typical Charleston tradition, there's a great little bar area in back of this large space, where $5 mason jar margaritas and other drink specials make happy hour (Mon.–Fri. 4–7 P.M.) very happy indeed.

Barbecue

Jim 'n' Nick's (288 King St., 843/577-0406, www.jimnnicks.com, Sun.–Thurs. 10:30 A.M.–9 P.M., Fri.–Sat. 10:30 A.M.–10 P.M., $10–30) is a college scene masquerading as a roadside joint, but don't let that dissuade you from enjoying the 'Bama style tomato and vinegar barbecue—not to mention the fresh collards and homemade cheese biscuits.

UPPER KING
French

A taste of the 1930s Left Bank on Upper King, the intimate little bistro **(La Fourchette** (432 King St., 843/722-6261, Mon.–Sat. from 6 P.M., $15–20) is regarded as the best French restaurant in town and, *naturalment,* one of the most romantic as well. You'll be pleasantly surprised at the reasonable prices as well. Cassoulet, the French national dish, is front and center among Chef Perig Goulet's concoctions, arriving in its own casserole dish on a trivet. Whatever you do, make sure you start with the *pommes frites* double-fried in duck fat. Your arteries may not thank you, but your taste buds will. Finish with perhaps the best cup of coffee in Charleston, served in a French press (of course).

Seafood

Many say that the cashew-encrusted seared rare tuna on a bed of crabmeat and buckwheat noodles at **(COAST Bar and Grill** (39-D John St., 843/722-8838, www.coastbarandgrill.com, open nightly from 5:30 P.M., $18–30) is the single best dish in Charleston. I wouldn't necessarily go that far, but it's certainly up there. To be honest, the buttery, smoky, bacon-wrapped scallop appetizer is just as good. A new darling of local scenesters, COAST makes the most of its loud, hip former warehouse setting. Beautifully textured Lowcountry-themed paintings and kitschy faux-Polynesian items ring the walls, as the clanging silverware competes with the boisterous conversation. It may sound stressful, but the effect is actually quite warmly energizing. While the fun-loving decor in the dining room will suck you in, what keeps you happy is what goes on in

© JIM MOREKIS

Juanita Greenberg's Nacho Royale

the kitchen—specifically on its one-of-a-kind hickory-and-oak grill, which cooks up some of the freshest seafood in town. The raw bar is also satisfying, with a particularly nice take on and selection of ceviche. COAST is perhaps the strongest local advocate of the Sustainable Seafood Initiative, whereby restaurants work directly with local fishermen to make the most out of the area's stock while making sure it thrives for future generations. This forward focus extends to the wine list, which features plenty of organic selections. Right next to and affiliated with the more Old World seafood stylings of Rue de Jean, COAST is one of the most happening places in the bustling Upper King scene. Getting there's a little tricky: Find Rue de Jean on John Street and then duck about 100 feet down the alley beside it.

Asian
There's usually a long wait to get a table at the great Thai place **Basil** (460 King St., 843/724-3490, www.basilthairestaurant.com, lunch Mon.–Thurs. 11:30 A.M.–2:30 P.M., dinner Mon.–Thurs. 5 P.M. 10:30 P.M., Fri.–Sat. 5–11 P.M., Sun. 5–10 P.M., $15–23) on Upper King, since they don't take reservations. But Basil also has one of the hippest, most happening bar scenes in the area as well, so you won't necessarily mind. (Tip: Basil calls your cell phone when your table is ready, so a lot of people go across the street to Chai's to have a drink while they wait.) Basil is a long, loud room, with big open windows to people-watch. But most of the action takes place inside, as revelers down cosmos and diners enjoy fresh, succulent takes on Thai classics like cashew chicken and pad thai, all cooked by Asian chefs under the direction of owner Henry Eang. The signature dish at Basil, as you might imagine, is the basil duck.

Mexican
The best quesadilla I've ever had was at **◖ Juanita Greenberg's Nacho Royale** (439 King St., 843/723-NACHO, www.juanita greenbergs.com, daily 11 A.M.–11 P.M., $6–8)— perfectly packed with Jack cheese but not overly so, full of spicy sausage, and finished with a

delightful *pico de gallo*. This modest Mexican joint on Upper King—owned by Edie and Michael Rabin, the same folks that run the local Andolini's chain—caters primarily to a college crowd, as you can tell from the reasonable prices, the large patio out back, the extensive tequila list, and the bar that stays open 'til 2 A.M. on weekends. But don't let that give you pause. The service is quick and friendly, the margarita pitchers rock, and the food—from quesadillas to burritos to the eponymous nachos—constitutes one of the tastiest bargains in town.

HAMPTON PARK AREA
Classic Southern

With a motto like "Grits are good for you," you know what you're in store for at **Hominy Grill** (207 Rutledge Ave., 912/937-0930, breakfast Mon.–Fri. 7:30 A.M.–11:30 A.M., lunch and dinner 11:30 A.M.–8:30 P.M., brunch Sat.–Sun. 9 A.M.–3 P.M., $10–20), set in a renovated barbershop at Rutledge and Cannon over near the Medical University of South Carolina. Open for breakfast, lunch, and dinner but primarily revered for its Sunday brunch, Chef Robert Stehling has fun, almost mischievously so, breathing new life into American and Southern classics. Because this is almost a locals-only place, you can really impress your friends back home by saying you had the rare pleasure of the Hominy's sautéed shad roe with bacon and mushrooms—when the shad are running, that is.

Casual Dining

Moe's Crosstown Tavern (714 Rutledge Ave., 843/722-3287, Mon.–Sat., 11 A.M.–midnight, bar until 2 A.M., $10–15) is not only one of the classic Southern dives, but they've got one of the best kitchens on this side of town, known for handcut fries, great wings, and, most of all, excellent burgers. On Tuesdays, the burgers are half-price at happy hour—one of Charleston's best deals.

WEST ASHLEY
Classic Southern

Tucked away on the grounds of the Middleton Place Plantation is the romantic and charming **Middleton Place Restaurant** (843/556-

6020, www.middletonplace.org, lunch daily 11 A.M.–3 P.M., dinner Tues.–Thurs. 6–8 P.M., Fri.–Sat. 6–9 P.M., Sun. 6–8 P.M., $15–25). Theirs is a respectful take on traditional plantation fare like hoppin' John, gumbo, she-crab soup, and collards. The special annual Thanksgiving buffet is a real treat. Reservations are required for dinner. A nice plus is being able to wander the gorgeous landscaped gardens before dusk if you arrive at 5:30 P.M. or later with a dinner reservation.

Casual Dining

The kitchen at **Gene's Haufbrau** (17 Savannah Hwy., 843/225-4363, www.geneshaufbrau .com, daily 11:30 A.M.–1 A.M.) complements its fairly typical bar-food menu with some good wraps. Start with the "Drunken Trio" (beer-battered cheesesticks, mushrooms, and onion rings) and follow with a portobello wrap or a good old-fashioned crawfish po' boy. One of the best meals for the money in town is Gene's rotating, $6.95 blue plate special, offered Monday–Friday 11:30 A.M.–4:30 P.M. The late-night kitchen hours, 'til 1 A.M., are a big plus.

Barbecue

To get the best barbecue in Charleston, you've got to go over the bridge a little ways into West Ashley. But for connoisseurs, **❮ Bessinger's** (1602 Savannah Hwy., 843/556-1354, www .bessingersbbq.com, prices and hours vary) is certainly worth the trip for its mustard-based wizardry—best exemplified by the legendary "Big Joe" sandwich, named for old family patriarch Joseph "Big Joe" Bessinger, founder of the legendary "Eat at Joe's" on the road to Orangeburg. It's eight ounces of hand-pulled pork and a one-way passport to nirvana. Smaller tummies might opt for the Little Joe, a five-ounce version of same. You can always leave with a bottle or two of the "family secret" Gold Recipe sauce. There are two scenes at Bessinger's, the sit-down Southern buffet (open Thurs. 5–8 P.M., Fri.–Sat. 5–9 P.M., and Sun. noon–8 P.M., $11.50 adults, $5.95 children)— Friday is fried catfish night—and the Sandwich

Shop (Mon.–Sat. 10:30 A.M.–9:30 P.M., $6.35 for a "Big Joe" basket) for quick takeout. In old-school tradition, Bessinger's is a dry joint that doesn't sell alcohol.

Many local cognoscenti insist that another West Ashley joint, the new **Fiery Ron's Home Team** (1205 Ashley River Rd., 843/225-7427, www.hometeambbq.com, Mon.–Sat. 11 A.M.–9 P.M., Sun. 11:30 A.M.–9 P.M., $7–22) is even better than Bessinger's, though purists might object to the fact that Ron cooks without a sauce, instead letting you pick one: vinegar, mustard, or tomato-based. (Some fans insist you need no sauce at all on Ron's barbecue.) The Home Team offers sandwiches, but the best course of action is any of the platters, with a choice of two of Ron's already legendary sides, including perfect collards, awesome mashed potatoes, and tasty mac-and-cheese. As if that weren't enough, the owners' close ties to the regional jam-band community means there's great live blues and indie rock after 10 P.M. most nights (Thursday is bluegrass night) to spice up the bar action, which goes until 2 A.M.

Mediterranean

Anything on this Northern Italian–themed menu is good, but the risotto—legacy of original chef John Marshall—is the specialty dish at **Al Di La** (25 Magnolia Rd., 843/571-2321, Tues.–Sat. 6–10 P.M.), West Ashley's most popular fine dining spot and perhaps Charleston's best trattoria. Reservations are recommended.

For pizza, chain **Andolini's** (1117 Savannah Hwy., 843/225-4743) has a location in West Ashley.

MOUNT PLEASANT

Most restaurant action in Mount Pleasant centers on the picturesque, historic, and still fairly rustic shrimping village of Shem Creek, which is dotted on both banks with bars and restaurants, most dealing in fresh local seafood.

Seafood

One of the best regarded is **Water's Edge** (1407 Shrimp Boat Lane, 843/884-4074, daily 11 A.M.–11 P.M., $20–30), which consistently takes home a Wine Spectator Award of Excellence for its great selection of vintages. Native Charlestonian Jimmy Purcell concentrates on fresh seafood with a slightly more upscale flair than many Shem Creek places. Offerings include a pepper-seared tuna appetizer and seafood paella with lobster, fish, scallops, clams, mussels, and shrimp over saffron rice in a traditional tomato broth. But steak lovers are in luck here as well—the prime rib is a specialty, as is the big Kansas City strip.

Right down the road from Water's Edge is another popular spot, especially for a younger crowd: **Vickery's Shem Creek Bar and Grill** (1313 Shrimp Boat Lane, 843/884-4440, daily 11:30 A.M.–1 A.M., $11–16). With a similar menu to its partner location on the peninsula, this Vickery's has the pleasant added bonus of a beautiful view overlooking the Creek. You'll get more of the Vickery's Cuban flair here, with a great black bean soup and an awesome Cuban sandwich.

Vegetarian

For a vegetarian-friendly change of pace from seafood, go to the excellent (and reasonably priced) **Mustard Seed** (1026 Chuck Dawley Blvd., 843/849-0050, Mon.–Sat. 11 A.M.–2:30 P.M., Mon.–Sat. 5–9:30 P.M., $14–18). The pad thai is probably the best thing on New York–trained Chef Sal Parco's creative and dynamic menu, but you might also get a kick out of the sweet potato ravioli.

For a *real* change of pace, try **The Sprout Cafe** (629 Johnnie Dodds Blvd., 843/849-8554, www.thehealthysprout.com, Mon.–Fri. 6 A.M.–8 P.M., Sat. 9 A.M.–3 P.M., Sun. 11 A.M.–3 P.M., $3–10), whose motto is "no meat, no heat." Dealing totally in raw foods, the obvious emphasis here is on health and freshness of ingredients. You might be surprised at the inventiveness of their breakfast-through-dinner, seasonal menu—memorably described as "grab and go" by the staff—which might include a tasty crepe topped with a pear-and-nut puree and topped with maple syrup, or a raw squash and zucchini "pasta" dish topped with walnut "meatballs." The desserts may be the biggest surprise, like the lemon brulee and the chocolate mousse, a skillful blend of raw cocoa, almond milk, and agave. There's also an abundance of herbal and organic teas and beverages. This is a great place not only for vegans, but for those with severe food allergies as well.

FOLLY BEACH
Breakfast and Brunch
The closest thing to a taste of old Folly is the **Lost Dog Café** (106 W. Huron St., 843/588-9669, daily 6:30 A.M.–3 P.M., $5–7), so named for its bulletin board stacked with alerts about lost pets, pets for adoption, and newborns for sale or giveaway. They open early, the better to offer a tasty, healthy breakfast to the surfing crowd. It's a great place to pick up a quick, inexpensive, and tasty meal while you're near the beach.

Seafood
Fans of the legendary ◖ **Bowen's Island Restaurant** (1870 Bowens Island Rd., 843/795-2757, Tues.–Sat. 5–10 P.M., $5–15, cash only) on James Island off the main road to Folly nearly went into mourning when a major fire burned it to the ground in late 2006. But you can't keep a good oysterman down; owner Robert Barber rebuilt and regulars insist that this institution, which began in the 1940s as a fishing camp, is as old-school as ever.

A universe removed from the Lexus-and-navy-blue-jacket scene downtown, Bowen's Island isn't the place for the hung-up, the uptight, or the well dressed. This is the place to go when you want shovels of oysters—literally thrown onto your table, freshly steamed and delicious and all-you-can-eat. The fried shrimp, flounder, and hush puppies are incredible, too. The bizarre setting—a nondescript building, little to no signage, set near a junkyard of sorts—only adds to the authenticity of the whole experience. To get there from the peninsula, take Calhoun Street west onto the James Island Connector/S.C. Highway 30. Take Exit 3 onto S.C. Highway 171 South roughly five miles and look for Bowens Island Road on your right. The restaurant will be on your left in a short while.

Mexican
Owned by the same folks that run chic Raval on the peninsula, the new **Taco Boy** (15 Center St., 843/588-9701, Sun.–Thurs. 11 A.M.–10 P.M., Fri.–Sat. 11 A.M.–11 P.M., $5–15) is a fun place to get a fish taco, have a margarita, and take a walk on the nearby beach afterward. Though no one is under any illusions that this is an authentic Mexican restaurant, the fresh guacamole is particularly rave-worthy, and there's a good selection of tequilas and beers *hecho en Mexico,* with the bar staying open until 2 A.M. on weekends.

NORTH CHARLESTON
Quick Bites
If you have a hankering for pizza in North Charleston, don't miss **EVO Pizzeria** (1075 E. Montague Ave., 843/225-1796, www.evopizza.com, lunch Tues.–Fri. 11 A.M.–2:30 P.M., dinner 5–10 P.M., Sat. 6–10 P.M., $10–15) in the Olde North Charleston area at Park Circle. They specialize in a small but rich menu of unusual gourmet pizza toppings, like pistachio pesto.

Nearby is North Charleston's best coffeehouse, **Park Circle Coffee** (1078 E. Montague Ave., www.parkcirclecoffee.com, Mon.–Fri. 7 A.M.–4 P.M., Sat. 8 A.M.–2 P.M., Sun. 9 A.M.–2 P.M.), which specializes in organic Counter Culture coffee and also has some good lunch wraps for under $10.

Vegans might also want to make a special trip up I-26 to find **Soul Vegetarian** (3225-A Rivers Ave., 843/744-1155, $5–10), the only all-vegan place in the state. Owned and operated by members of the African Hebrew Israelites of Jerusalem, they make their own soy "dairy" products. You'll find barbecue tofu, vegan lasagna, and even faux milkshakes. Hours are flexible, so call ahead.

COFFEE, TEA, AND SWEETS
By common consensus, the best java joint in Charleston is John Saunders' ◖ **Kudu Coffee** (4 Vanderhorst Ave., 843/853-7186, Mon.–Sat. 6:30 A.M.–7 P.M., Sun. 9 A.M.–6 P.M.) in the Upper King area. (A kudu is an African

antelope). John's Africa theme extends to his beans, which all have an African pedigree. Poetry readings and occasional live music add to the mix. A lot of green-friendly, left-of-center community activism goes on here as well; a recent discussion group was titled "How to Survive the Bible Belt but Still Find God." The adjacent African art store shop, Kudu Kitu, is owned by the coffeehouse.

If you find yourself needing a quick pick-me-up while shopping on King Street, avoid the lines at the two Starbucks on the avenue and instead turn east on Market and duck inside **City Lights Coffeehouse** (141 Market St., 843/853-7067, Mon.–Thurs. 7 A.M.–9 P.M., Fri.–Sat. 7 A.M.–10 P.M., Sun. 8 A.M.–6 P.M.). The sweet goodies are delectable in this cozy little Euro style place, and the Counter Culture organic coffee is to die for. If you're really lucky they'll have some of their Ethiopian Sidamo brewed.

Though technically a retail location of a national chain rather than a traditional tea room per se, the truth is that you can get an outstanding fresh cup of herbal tea or maté at **Teavana** (340 King St., 843/723-0600, www.teavana .com, Mon.–Thurs. 10 A.M.–6 P.M., Fri.–Sat. 10 A.M.–9 P.M., Sun. noon–6 P.M.) and even take the time to enjoy it in the little courtyard out back. Stored in big cans along the back wall, all the tea here is loose, fresh, and of extremely high quality. The friendly and quite knowledgeable staff will let you do sniff tests until you find the aroma that appeals to you most.

A unique Charleston phenomenon on Upper King by Marion Square is the aptly named ◖ **Cupcake** (433 King St., 843/853-8181, www.freshcupcakes.com, Mon.–Sat. 10 A.M.–7 P.M.). Their eponymous specialty compels Charlestonians to form lines onto the sidewalk, waiting to enjoy one or more of the 30 flavors of little cakes. My favorite is the coffee, which is simply their famous vanilla cake with a coffee cream cheese frosting, topped with a single espresso bean.

Routinely voted as having the best desserts in the city, **Kaminsky's** (78 N. Market St., 843/853-8270, daily noon–2 A.M.) cakes alone

are worth the trip to the City Market area. The fresh fruit torte, the red velvet, and the "Mountain of Chocolate" are the three bestsellers. There's a Mount Pleasant location, too (1028 Johnnie Dodds Blvd., 843/971-7437).

Some key **Starbucks** locations in Charleston are 239 King Street, 387 King Street, 168 Calhoun Street, and 475 East Bay Street.

MARKETS AND GROCERIES

A fun and favorite local fixture from April through mid-December, the **Charleston Farmers Market** (843/724-7309, www .charlestoncity.info) rings beautiful Marion Square with stalls of local produce, street eats, local arts and crafts, and kids activities 8 A.M.–2 P.M. each Saturday.

Running April through October, East Cooper has its own version in the **Mount Pleasant Farmers Market,** (843/884-8517, http://townofmountpleasant.com) each Tuesday from 3 P.M. until dark at the Moultrie Middle School on Coleman Boulevard.

For organic groceries and/or a quick, healthy bite while you're in Mount Pleasant, check out **Whole Foods** (923 Houston Northcutt Blvd., 843/971-7240, daily 8 A.M.–9 P.M.).

The biggest and best supermarket near the downtown tourist area is the regional chain **Harris Teeter** (290 E. Bay St., 843/722-6821, 24 hours daily). As you might expect from the location, they have a very good wine selection here. There are other Harris Teeter stores in Mount Pleasant (920 Houston Northcutt Blvd. and 620 Long Point Rd., 843/881-4448) and Folly Beach (675 Folly Rd., 843/406-8977).

For a charming grocery shopping experience, try **King Street Grocery** (435 King St., 843/958-8004, daily 8 A.M.–midnight) on Upper King. If you're down closer to the Battery, go to the delightful and historic **Burbage's Self-Serv** (157 Broad St., 843/723-4054, 8 A.M.–6 P.M. Sun.–Fri., 8 A.M.–2 P.M. Sat.), serving the South of Broad neighborhood and nearby points since 1874.

Need groceries at 4 A.M. on Folly Beach? Go to **Bert's Market** (202 E. Ashley Ave., 843/588-9449), which is open 24 hours.

Information and Services

VISITORS CENTERS

I highly recommend a stop at the **Charleston Visitor Reception and Transportation Center** (375 Meeting St., 800/774-0006, Mon.–Fri. 8:30 A.M.–5 P.M., www.charleston cvb.com). Housed in a modern building with an inviting, open design, the Visitors Center has several high-tech, interactive exhibits, including an amazing model of the city under glass. Wall after wall of well-stocked, well-organized brochures will keep you informed on everything a tourist would ever want to know or see about the city. A particularly welcoming touch is the inclusion of the work of local artists all around the Center.

I particularly recommend using the attached parking garage not only for your stop at the Visitors Center but also anytime you want to see the many sights this part of town has to offer, such as the Charleston Museum, the Manigault and Aiken-Rhett Houses, and the Children's Museum.

But most of all, the big selling point at the Visitors Center is the friendliness of the smiling and courteous staff, who welcome you in true Charleston fashion and are there to book rooms and tours, find tickets for shows and attractions, and to fill you in on every aspect of what to expect and look for while you're in the area.

If for no other reason, you should go to the Visitors Center to take advantage of the great deal offered by the **Charleston Heritage Passport** (www.heritagefederation.org), which gives you 40 percent off admission to all of Charleston's key historic homes, the Charleston Museum, and the two awesome plantation sites on the Ashley River: Drayton Hall and Middleton Place. You can get the Heritage Passport *only* at the Visitors Center on Meeting Street.

Other area visitors centers include the **Mt. Pleasant-Isle of Palms Visitor Center** (Johnnie Dodds Blvd., 843/853-8000, daily 9 A.M.–5 P.M.), and the new **North Charleston Visitor Center** (4975-B Centre Pointe Dr., 843/853-8000, Mon.–Sat. 10 A.M.–5 P.M.).

HOSPITALS

If there's a silver lining in getting sick or injured in Charleston, it's that there are plenty of high-quality medical facilities available. The premier institution is the **Medical University of South Carolina** (171 Ashley Ave., 843/792-2300, www.muschealth.com) in the northwest part of the peninsula.

Two notable facilities are near each other downtown: **Roper Hospital** (316 Calhoun St., 843/402-2273, www.roperhospital.com) and **Charleston Memorial Hospital** (326 Calhoun St., 843/792-2300).

In Mount Pleasant there's **East Cooper Regional Medical Center** (1200 Johnnie Dodds Blvd., www.eastcoopermedctr.com). In West Ashley there's **Bon Secours St. Francis Hospital** (2095 Henry Tecklenburg Ave., 843/402-2273, www.ropersaintfrancis.com).

POLICE

For non-emergencies in Charleston, West Ashley, and James Island, contact the **Charleston Police Department** (www .charlestoncity.info) at 843/577-7434. In Mount Pleasant, call 843/884-4176.

North Charleston (www.northcharleston .org) is a separate municipality with its own police department; for non-emergencies, call 843/308-4718.

Of course, for emergencies always call **911.**

MEDIA

The daily newspaper of record is the *Post and Courier* (www.charleston.net). Its entertainment insert, *Preview,* comes out on Thursdays.

The free alt-weekly is the decade-old *Charleston City Paper* (www.charlestoncity paper.com), which comes out on Wednesdays and is the best place to find local music and arts listings.

A particularly well done and lively metro glossy is *Charleston Magazine* (www.charleston mag.com), which comes out once a month.

LIBRARIES

The main branch of the **Charleston County Public Library** (68 Calhoun St., 843/805-6801, www.ccpl.org, Mon.–Thurs. 9 A.M.–9 P.M., Fri.–Sat. 9 A.M.–6 P.M., Sun. 2–5 P.M.) has been on its current site since 1998. Named for Sullivan's Island's most famous visitor, the **Edgar Allan Poe** (1921 I'On Ave., 843/883-3914, www.ccpl.org, Mon. and Fri. 2–6 P.M., Tues., Thurs., and Sat. 10 A.M.–2 P.M.) has been housed in Battery Gadsden, a former Spanish-American War gun emplacement, since 1977.

The College of Charleston's main library is the **Marlene and Nathan Addlestone Library** (205 Calhoun St., 843/953-5530, www.cofc .edu), home to special collections, the Center for Student Learning, the main computer lab, the media collection, and even a café. The college's **Avery Research Center for African American History and Culture** (125 Bull St., 843/953-7609, www.cofc. edu/avery, Mon.–Fri. 10 A.M.–5 P.M., Sat. noon–5 P.M.) houses documents relating to the history and culture of African Americans in the Lowcountry.

For other historical research on the area, check out the collections of the **South Carolina Historical Society** (100 Meeting St., 843/723-3225, www.southcarolinahistoricalsociety.org, Mon.–Fri. 9 A.M.–4 P.M., Sat. 9 A.M.–2 P.M.). There's a $5 research fee for non-members.

GAY AND LESBIAN RESOURCES

Contrary to many media portrayals of the region, Charleston is quite open to gays and lesbians, who play a major role in arts, culture, and business. As with any other place in the South, however, it's generally expected that people— straights as well—will keep personal preferences and politics to themselves in public settings.

A key local advocacy group is the **Alliance for Full Acceptance** (29 Leinbach Dr., Ste. D-3, 843/883-0343, www.affa-sc.org).

The **Lowcountry Gay and Lesbian Alliance** (843/720-8088) holds a potluck the last Sunday of each month.

For the most up-to-date happenings, try the Gay Charleston blog (http:///gaycharleston. ccpblogs.com) of the *Charleston City Paper.*

Getting There and Around

AIR

Way up in North Charleston is **Charleston International Airport** (5500 International Blvd., 843/767-1100, airport code CHS, www .chs-airport.com), served by AirTran (www.air tran.com), American Airlines (www.aa.com), Continental Airlines (www.continental.com), Delta (www.delta.com), Northwest Airlines (www.nwa.com), United Airlines (www.ual .com), and US Airways (www.usairways.com).

As in most cities, taxi service from the airport is regulated. The fare from the airport is $2.15 per mile, with $12 fee for each passenger over two (no additional charge up to two people). For example, this translates to about $27 for two people from the airport to Charleston Place downtown. For the airport vicinity there's a fixed rate of $9 per person.

CAR

There are two main routes in to Charleston, I-26 from the west/northwest (which dead-ends downtown) and U.S. 17 from the west (called Savannah Highway when it gets close to Charleston proper), which continues on over the Ravenel Bridge into Mount Pleasant and beyond.

There's a fairly new perimeter highway, I-526 (Mark Clark Expressway), which loops around the city from West Ashley to North Charleston to Daniel Island and into Mount Pleasant. It's accessible both from I-26 and U.S. 17.

Keep in mind that I-95, while certainly a gateway to the region, is actually a good ways out of Charleston, about 30 miles west of the city.

BUS

Public transportation by **Charleston Area Regional Transit Authority** (843/724-7420, www.ridecarta.com), or CARTA, is a fairly convenient and inexpensive way to enjoy Charleston without the more structured nature of an organized tour. There are a wide variety of routes all over the area, but most visitors will limit their acquaintance to the tidy, trolley-like DASH (Downtown Area Shuttle) buses run by CARTA throughout the peninsula, primarily for tourists. Each ride is $1.25 per person (seniors are $0.60). The best deal is the $4 one-day pass, which you get at the Charleston Visitor Center (375 Meeting St.). Keep in mind that DASH only stops at designated places.

DASH has three routes: the 210, which runs a northerly circuit from the Aquarium to the College of Charleston; the 211, running up and down the parallel Meeting and King Streets from Marion Square down to the Battery; and the 212 Market/Waterfront shuttle from the Aquarium area down to Waterfront Park.

RENTAL CAR

Charleston International Airport has rental kiosks for Avis (843/767-7031), Budget (843/767-7051), Dollar (843/767-1130), Enterprise (843/767-1109), Hertz (843/767-4550), National (843/767-3078), and Thrifty (843/647-4389).

There are a couple of rental locations downtown: Budget (390 Meeting St., 843/577-5195) and Enterprise (398 Meeting St., 843/723-6215). Hertz has a location in West Ashley (3025 Ashley Town Center Dr., 843/573-2147), as does Enterprise (2004 Savannah Hwy., 843/556-7889).

TAXI

The South is generally not big on taxis, and Charleston is no exception. The best bet is simply to call, rather than try to flag one down. Charleston's most fun service is **Charleston Black Cabs** (843/216-2627, www.charleston blackcabcompany.com), using Americanized versions of the classic British taxi (at over $50,000 a pop, they're not a cheap investment). A one-way ride anywhere on the peninsula below the bridges is a flat $10 per person, and rates go up from there. They're very popular, so call as far ahead as you can or try to get one at their stand at Charleston Place.

Two other good services are **Safety Cab** (843/722-4066) and **Yellow Cab** (843/577-6565).

You can also try a human-powered taxi service from **Charleston Rickshaw** (843/723-5685). A cheerful (and energetic) young cyclist will pull you and a friend to most points on the lower peninsula for about $10–15. Call 'em or find one by City Market. They work late on Friday and Saturday nights, too.

PARKING

As you will quickly see, parking is at a premium in downtown Charleston. An exception seems to be the large number of free spaces all along the Battery, but unless you're an exceptionally strong walker, that's too far south to use as a reliable base from which to explore the whole peninsula.

Most metered parking downtown is on and around Calhoun Street, Meeting Street, King Street, Market Street, and East Bay Street. That may not sound like a lot, but it constitutes the bulk of the area that most tourists visit. Most meters have three-hour limits but you'll come across some as short as 30 minutes. Technically you're not supposed to "feed the meter" in Charleston, as city personnel put little chalk marks on your tires to make sure people aren't overstaying their welcome. Metered parking is free 6 P.M.–6 A.M. and all day on Sunday. On Saturdays, expect to pay.

The city has several conveniently located and comparatively inexpensive parking garages. I strongly suggest that you make use of them. They're located at: The Aquarium, Camden and Exchange Streets, Charleston

Place, Concord and Cumberland Streets, East Bay and Prioleau Streets, Marion Square, Gaillard Auditorium, Liberty and St. Philip Streets, Majestic Square, the Charleston Visitor Reception and Transportation Center, and Wentworth Street.

There are several private parking garages as well, primarily clustered in the City Market area. They're convenient, but many of them have parking spaces that are simply too small for some cars.

The city's website (www.charlestoncity.info) has a pretty good interactive map of parking possibilities on the peninsula.

Greater Charleston

Though one could easily spend a lifetime enjoying the history and attractions of Charleston itself, there are several wholly unique experiences to be had in the less-developed areas surrounding the city. Whether farther inland or on the water, life in this outer region largely centers on the quiet enjoyment of nature, its bounty, and its beauty. While food and accommodations tend to be much more scattered in quality and quantity the farther outside Charleston you go, do consider visiting these areas to get a full flavor of the region.

EDISTO ISLAND

One of the last great unspoiled, down-home places in the Lowcountry—for now—Edisto Island has been highly regarded as a getaway spot since the Edisto tribe first starting coming here for shellfish. (Proof of their patronage is in the huge shell midden, or debris pile, near the beach.) In fact, locals here swear that the island was settled by English-speaking colonists even before Charleston was settled in 1670.

In any case, we do know that the Spanish established a short-lived mission on St. Pierre's Creek. Then in 1674, the island was purchased from the Edistos for a few trinkets by the perhaps appropriately named Earl of Shaftesbury. For most of its modern history, cotton plantations were Edisto Island's main claim to fame, though after the Civil War fishing became the primary occupation. Because of several hurricanes in the mid-20th century, little remains of previous eras. Probably the best-known Edisto native is James Jamerson, a well-regarded session bassist with Motown Records's Funk Brothers, playing on Marvin Gaye's "I Heard it Through the Grapevine."

Now this barrier island, for the moment unthreatened by the encroachment of planned communities and private resorts so endemic to the Carolina coast, is a nice getaway for area residents in addition to just plain being a great—if a little isolated—place to live for its 800 or so full-time residents. The beaches are beautiful, the shells are plentiful, the walks are romantic, the people are friendly, and the food is good but casual. The residents operate on "Edisto Time," with a *mañana* philosophy (i.e., it'll get done when it gets done) that results in a mellow pace of life out in these parts.

Orientation

There's basically one main land route here, south on S.C. Highway 174 off U.S. 17. Most activity on the island centers on the township of Edisto Beach, which voted to align itself with Colleton County for its lower taxes (the rest of Edisto Island is part of Charleston County). Flanked by the North Edisto River and the South Edisto River, Edisto Beach has two ends, joined by Palmetto Boulevard running the seaward length of the island's Atlantic face. Docksite Road is a key avenue around the curved western end of the island, known since the plantation days as the Neck. The Plantation Course at Edisto takes up most of the southwest part of the island.

◖ Edisto Beach State Park

Edisto Beach State Park (8377 State Cabin Rd., 843/869-2156, www.southcarolinaparks.com,

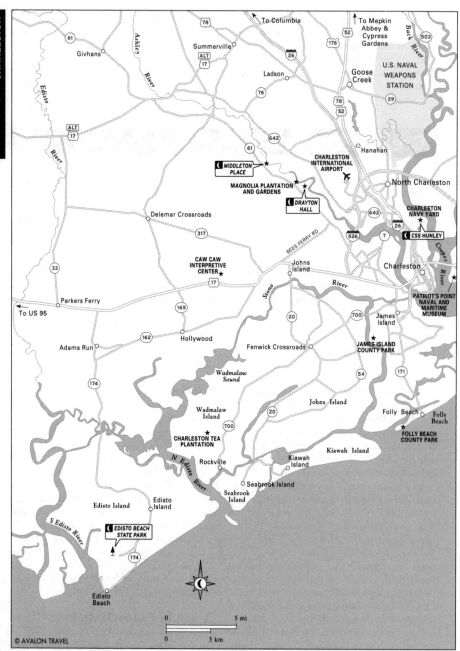

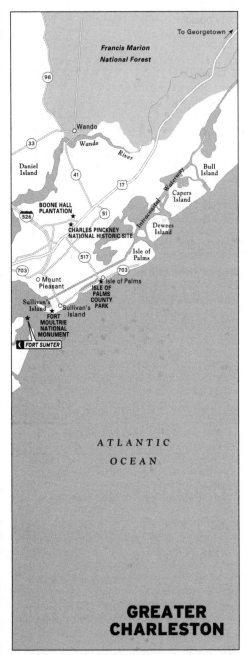

**GREATER
CHARLESTON**

daily 8 A.M.–6 P.M. Nov.–mid-Mar.,
6 A.M.–10 P.M. mid-Mar.–Oct., $4 adult, $1.50
children, free for children five and under) is
one of the most beautiful, romantic beaches
in the Carolinas, its tall palmettos having escaped much of Hurricane Hugo's wrath. It's
one of the world's foremost destinations for
shell collectors; largely because of fresh loads
of silt from the adjacent ACE Basin, there are
always new shells, many of them fossils, washing ashore.

The park stretches almost three miles and
features the state's longest system of fully accessible hiking and biking trails, including
one leading to the 4,000-year-old shell midden. There's also an educational center with
exhibits about the nature and history of both
the park as well as the surrounding ACE Basin.
Like many state recreational facilities in the
South, Edisto Beach State Park was developed
by the Civilian Conservation Corps (CCC),
one of President Franklin D. Roosevelt's New
Deal programs during the Great Depression,
which had the doubly beneficial effect of
employing large numbers of people while establishing much of the conservation infrastructure
we enjoy today. You'll still find many 1930s-era
buildings throughout the park.

Sights

The charming **Edisto Museum** (8123 Chisolm
Plantation Rd., 843/869-1954, www.edisto
museum.org, Tues.–Sat. 1–4 P.M., adults $3,
free for children under 10), a project of the
Edisto Island Historic Preservation Society, is
in the midst of plans for a major expansion that
will incorporate a nearby slave cabin. In addition to well-done little exhibits on area culture
and history, there's a cute gift shop as well, all
for a very good cause.

Opened in 1999 by local snake-hunters
the Clamp brothers, the **Edisto Island
Serpentarium** (1374 Hwy. 174, 843/869-
1171, www.edistoserpentarium.com, Thurs.–
Sat. 10 A.M.–5 P.M., $10.95 adults, $8.95
children 6–12, $4.95 children 4–5, children
under 3 free) is educational and fun, taking
you up-close and personal with a variety of

reptilian creatures native to the area. Inside, venomous and non-venomous snakes and frogs slide, slither, and hop in hand-painted cages with indigenous vegetation, while the larger specimens (including 19 gators in two ponds, as well as Bubba and Shelly, two big alligator snapping turtles) are outside behind a low enclosure for easy viewing. The serpentarium is on the main route into Edisto before you get to the beach area.

Shopping

For various ocean gear, try the **Edisto Surf Shop** (145 Jungle Rd., 843/869-9283, daily 9 A.M.–5 P.M.). For a new or used beach read, go right next door to the **Cozy Corner** (145 Jungle Rd., 843/869-1221), which also serves a mean espresso. You can find whimsical Lowcountry-themed art for enjoyment or purchase at **Fish or Cut Bait Gallery** (142 Jungle Rd., 843/869-2511, Tues.–Sat. 10 A.M.–5 P.M., www.fishorcutbaitgallery.com).

If you're camping and need some groceries, there's always the **Piggly Wiggly** grocery store, a.k.a., "The Pig" (104 Jungle Rd., 843/869-0055, Sun.–Thurs. 7 A.M.–9 P.M., Fri.–Sat. 7 A.M.–10 P.M.). For fresh seafood, try **Flowers Seafood Company** (1914 Hwy. 174, 843/869-0033, Mon.–Sat. 9 A.M.–7 P.M., Sun. 9 A.M.–5 P.M.).

Sports and Recreation

As the largest river of the ACE (Ashepoo, Combahee, Edisto) Basin complex, the Edisto River figures large in the lifestyle of Edisto Island's residents and visitors. A good public landing is at Steamboat Creek off S.C. Highway 174 on the way down to the island. Take Steamboat Landing Road (S.C. Hwy. 968) off 174 near the James Edwards School. Live Oak Landing is farther up Big Bay Creek near the Interpretive Center at the State Park. The **Edisto Marina** (3702 Docksite Rd., 843/869-3504) is on the far west side of the island.

Captain Ron Elliott of **Edisto Island Tours** (843/869-1937) offers various eco-tours and fishing trips, as well as canoe and kayak rentals.

Ugly Ducklin' (843/869-1580) offers creek and inshore fishing charters.

You can get gear as well as book boat and kayak tours of the area at **Edisto Watersports & Tackle** (3731 Docksite Rd., 843/869-0663, www.edistowatersports.com).

Riding a bike on Edisto Beach and all around the island is a great, relaxing way to get some exercise and see the sights. The best place to rent a bike—or a kayak or canoe, for that matter—is **Island Bikes and Outfitters** (140 Jungle Rd., 843/869-4444, Mon.–Sat. 9–4 P.M.). Bike rentals there run about $16 a day; single kayaks are about $60 a day.

There's one golf course on the island, the 18-hole **Plantation Course at Edisto** (21 Fairway Dr., 843/869-1111, $60 green fees), finished in 2006.

Accommodations

One of the great things about Edisto Island is the dearth of chain lodging. The recommended option is staying at the Edisto Beach State Park itself, either at a campsite by the ocean on the Atlantic side or in a marsh-front cabin on the northern edge (843/869-2156, www.south carolinaparks.com, $75–100 cabins, $25 tent sites). During high season (Apr.–Nov.), there's a minimum week-long stay in the cabins; during the off-season, the minimum stay is two days. You can book cabins up to 11 months in advance, and I highly recommend doing so as they go very quickly.

You can also rent a privately owned house along the beach; call **Edisto Sales and Rentals Realty** (1405 Palmetto Blvd., 800/868-5398, www.edistorealty.com) for more information.

Food

One of the most popular joints on the island is **Whaley's** (2801 Myrtle St., 843/869-2161, lunch Tues.–Sat. 11:30 A.M.–2 P.M., dinner Tues.–Sat. 5–9 P.M., bar daily 5 P.M.–2 A.M., $5–15), a down-home place in an old gas station a few blocks off the beach. This is a good place for casual seafood like boiled shrimp, washed down with a lot of beer. The bar is open seven days a week.

If working-class barbecue is more your speed, try **Po-Pigs BBQ** (2410 Hwy. 174, 843/869-9003, Thurs.–Sat. 11:30 A.M.–9 P.M., $4–10) on the way into town. This is the real thing, the full pig cooked in all its many ways: white meat, dark meat, cracklin's, and hash.

The rowdy but friendly **Dock Side Lounge** (3730 Docksite Rd., 843/869-3018, Mon.–Sat. 4 P.M.–2 A.M., kitchen closes 9 P.M.) is a good place to get a casual bite since two longtime popular eating spots, the Old Post Office and the Sunset Grille, closed down. Though their stated credo is "Get naked—everyone else does," you will actually need to stay dressed.

The only thing approximating fast food on Edisto Island is the takeout-only **McConkey's Jungle Shack** (108 Jungle Rd., 843/869-0097, Mon.–Fri. 11 A.M.–8 P.M., Sat.–Sun. 8 A.M.–8 P.M., $4–10) on the eastern end of the beach, known for its shrimp-and-chips basket and great burgers.

NORTH OF CHARLESTON
Mepkin Abbey
The little Berkeley County berg of Moncks Corner is actually named for a person, not a vocation. But nonetheless that's where you'll find a fully active, practicing Trappist monastery, Mepkin Abbey (1098 Mepkin Abbey Rd., Moncks Corner, 843/761-8509, www.mepkinabbey.org, Tues.–Fri. 9 A.M.–4:30 P.M., Sat. 9 A.M.–4 P.M., Sun. 1–4 P.M., free), notable for the fact that it's not only open to visitors, but welcomes them.

The beautiful Abbey and grounds on the Cooper River is on what was once the plantation of the great Carolina statesman Henry Laurens (whose ashes are buried here), and later the home of famous publisher Henry Luce and his wife Clare Boothe Luce. The focal point of natural beauty is the Luce-commissioned **Mepkin Abbey Botanical Garden** (closed Mon.), a 3,200-acre tract with a camellia garden designed by noted landscape architect Loutrel Briggs, a native New Yorker who made Charleston his adopted home.

When they're not in prayer, the monks generally observe silence. In accordance with the emphasis the order puts on the spiritual value of manual labor, farming is the main physical occupation, with the monks' efforts producing eggs, honey, preserves, soap, and even compost from the gardens, all of which you can purchase in the Abbey gift shop in the reception center, which will always be your first stop. Tours of the Abbey itself are usually given at 11:30 A.M. and 3 P.M. most days.

The majority of visitors to the Abbey are casual day visitors, eager to enjoy the relaxing quiet, the kiss of the river's breeze, and the humming of the honeybees. But for those wanting a contemplative, quiet retreat of a distinctly Christian nature, the Abbey lets you stay up to six nights in one of their guesthouses (married couples can also take advantage of this).

As you'd imagine, the accommodations are Spartan—a bed, desk, and reading chair, with a private bathroom. Linens, towels, and soap are provided, but other than access to the library there's no other modern stimulation. Retreatants eat together with the monks at the same time, enjoying the same strict vegetarian diet and the same strict mealtime silence (though at lunch a single monk reads aloud from a book). Monks will assist retreat guests in the protocols of the Abbey's prayer schedule.

Cypress Gardens
Nature lovers can also enjoy Cypress Gardens (3030 Cypress Gardens Rd., Moncks Corner, 843/553-0515, www.cypressgardens.info, daily 9 A.M.–5 P.M., last admission 4 P.M., $10 adults, $5 children 6–12), which carries with it a lot of the same quiet, meditative nature of the Abbey, though it's entirely secular. One of the first nature preserves in the Lowcountry, Cypress Garden is the life's work of Benjamin R. Kittredge and his son Benjamin, Jr. Together they brought back the former glory of the old Dean Hall plantation, which the elder Kittredge, a New Yorker who married into a wealthy Charleston family, had bought in 1909.

Only instead of rice, the main crop was to be flowers. *Millions* of flowers, from azaleas to daffodils to camellias to wisteria to dogwoods to roses to lotus and then some. The

THE MONKS OF MONCKS CORNER

© WWW.CHARLESTONCVB.COM

Mepkin Abbey

Near Moncks Corner, South Carolina, the old Mepkin Plantation is now the home of the monks of Mepkin Abbey. How and why a monastery came to be in this semi-rural corner of the Deep South is worth a closer look.

Originally the plantation of the great South Carolina statesman and Revolutionary War hero Henry Laurens, by 1936 the grounds had come into the hands of famed *Time* magazine publisher Henry Luce. In 1949, Henry and his wife Clare Boothe – a renowned congresswoman and playwright herself – donated a large portion of Mepkin to the Roman Catholic Church to be used as a monastery. In response, 29 monks from the Abbey of Gethsemane in Kentucky answered the call and moved to the Lowcountry to begin Mepkin Abbey. (Though it does contain actual monks, the little town of Moncks Corner north of Charleston was actually named for Thomas Monk, a merchant in the area.)

Mepkin Abbey's monks are of the Order of Cistercians of the Strict Observance, more commonly known simply as Trappists. With the credo "pray and work," the Trappists believe manual labor provides worshippers with the best opportunity to share and experience creation and restoration. They also view manual labor as following in the footsteps of the "Poor Christ" – since their work enriches and provides for the surrounding community, especially the disadvantaged.

Much of the monks' labor centers on various farm activities. Until recently the harvesting of chicken eggs – almost 10 million annually – was the main source of revenue to maintain the Abbey. In the wake of a controversy surrounding those eggs – which began when a member of the animal rights group PETA masqueraded as a retreat guest and secretly filmed the Abbey's chicken coops – the Abbey has decided to phase out egg production and sale and turn to other products to raise money.

As part of their vows, Mepkin Abbey's monks remain silent during the early and late parts of the day. Their daily schedule is very strict, as follows:

- 3 A.M.: Rise

- 3:20 A.M.: Vigils followed by half an hour of meditation, then a reading or private prayer

- 5:30 A.M.: Lauds followed by breakfast

- 7:30 A.M.: Eucharist followed by 15 minutes thanksgiving and Terce

- 8:30-11:30 A.M.: Silence ends and morning work period begins

- Noon: Midday prayer followed by dinner

- 1-1:40 P.M.: "Siesta" (optional)

- 1:45-3:30 P.M.: Afternoon work period

- 5 P.M.: Supper

- 6 P.M.: Vespers

- 7:35 P.M.: Compline

- Silence begins as monks retire for the day.

old paddy system was made navigable for small boats—today they're glass-bottomed—to meander among the tall cypress trees. The city of Charleston acquired the tract from the family, and later Berkeley County would come into possession of it.

The current 170-acre park was heavily damaged during Hurricane Hugo in 1989, but has made quite a comeback, and its inspiring and calming natural beauty remains true to the vision of the Kittredges. The founders would certainly approve of a particularly modern addition, the "Butterfly House," a 2,500-square-foot building packed full of butterflies, caterpillars, turtles, and birds. Just go in quietly, remain as quiet as you can, and the butterflies will find you, an unforgettable experience for child and adult alike.

You can also walk two nature trails and enjoy the flora and fauna of this area untouched by modern development. There's a new "Crocodile Isle" exhibit with several rare species of the reptile. A freshwater Aquarium has 30 species of fish as well and about 20 species of reptiles

and amphibians. Out on the water, you can enjoy one of those glass-bottomed boat rides on the blackwater or—and this is what I recommend—paddle yourself in a canoe (included in the admission price) amongst the gorgeous cypress trees.

Cape Romaine National Wildlife Refuge

Cape Romaine National Wildlife Refuge (5801 U.S. Hwy. 17 N., 843/928-3264, www.fws.gov/caperomain, open sunrise–sunset year-round) just north of Charleston off U.S. 17 comprises 66,000 acres, most of them water. A popular kayaking and ecotourism destination on the refuge is **Bull Island,** which has two nature trails (no bikes), restrooms, a shelter, and a picnic area (no overnight camping allowed).

Pretty much the only land-based activity at Cape Romaine is the **Sewee Visitor Center** (5821 U.S. Hwy. 17 N., Awendaw, 843/928-3368, www.fws.gov/seweecenter, Tues.–Sat. 9 A.M.–5 P.M.), a partnership of various governmental and conservation groups that also

© WWW.CHARLESTONCVB.COM

Cypress Gardens

serves as the gateway for visitors into the southern portion of the huge Francis Marion National Forest. Facilities include a big nature exhibit hall, a map room with a 3-D model of the forest and refuge, and a one-mile nature trail. It's on that trail that you'll find Sewee's signature: the red wolves housed at the facility. Their residence here is the legacy of a historic program begun on nearby Bulls Island in the 1970s to bring the rare canines back from the verge of extinction. Watch them eat on Fridays at 4 P.M.

Francis Beidler Forest

Though a full hour's drive northwest of Charleston, this National Natural Landmark is worth mentioning. The Francis Beidler Forest (336 Sanctuary Rd., Harleyville, S.C., 843/462-2150, www.sc.audubon.org, Tues.–Fri. 9 A.M.–5 P.M., $7 adults, $3.50 children 6–18, free for children under five) is jointly owned by the Nature Conservancy and the Audubon Society to conserve this rare and special 15,000-acre habitat in the blackwater Four Holes Swamp. An 1,800-acre section of the forest contains the largest and most ancient old-growth stands of bald cypress and tupelo trees in the world, with some trees well over 1,000 years old. Explore this section on a two-mile boardwalk.

To get there from Charleston, take I-26 west out of town to Exit 187. Make a left onto S.C. Highway 27 south to U.S. 78, where you'll turn right. Veer right on Highway 178 and then take a right on Francis Beidler Forest Road. To get to the visitors center, veer right onto Mims Road after a few miles.

Accommodations

Moncks Corner isn't exactly awash in world-class lodging, but you might try the **Holiday Inn Express** (505 Rembert C. Dennis Blvd., Moncks Corner, 843/761-7509, $100–140).

In the Cape Romaine National Wildlife Refuge, wilderness camping is permissible at **Capers Island Heritage Preserve** (843/953-9300, www.dnr.sc.gov, daily, free)

with advance permission from the South Carolina Department of Natural Resources.

If you find yourself in dire need of a place to stay in Harleyville after visiting the Francis Beidler Forest, I recommend taking the short drive to nearby St. George and trying the pet-friendly **Quality Inn** (6014 W. Jim Bilton Blvd., Saint George, 843/563-4581, www.qualityinn.com, $60) or the **Best Value Inn** (125 Motel Dr., St. George, 843/563-2360, www.bestvalueinn.com, $50).

Food

If you get hungry while you're up in Moncks Corner, your best bet is to go for seafood at **Gilligan's at the Dock** (582 Dock Rd., Moncks Corner, 843/761-2244, Sun.–Thurs. 11 A.M.–9 P.M., Fri.–Sat. 11 A.M.–10 P.M., $12–20). They have awesome fried catfish and a nice view of the Cooper River.

Up near Awendaw and Cape Romaine, near the entrance to the Francis Marion National Forest, get some of the best she-crab soup in the region at **See Wee Restaurant** (4808 Hwy. 17, Awendaw, 843/928-3609, Mon.–Sat. 11 A.M.–9 P.M., Sun. 11 A.M.–3 P.M., $5–15), run by the mother-and-son team of Mary Rancourt and Kurt Penninger, who use old family recipes.

WEST OF CHARLESTON
Caw Caw Interpretive Center

Just west of town on Highway 17, you'll find the unique Caw Caw Interpretive Center (5200 Savannah Hwy., Ravenel, 843/889-8898, www.ccprc.com, Wed.–Fri. 9 A.M.–3 P.M., Sat.–Sun. 9 A.M.–5 P.M., $1), a treasure trove for history buffs and naturalists wanting to learn more about the old rice culture of the South. With a particular emphasis on the expertise of the those who worked on the rice plantations using techniques they brought with them from Africa, the county-run facility comprises 650 acres of land (on an actual former rice plantation built on former cypress swamp), eight miles of interpretive trails, an educational center with exhibits, and a wildlife sanctuary with seven different habitats. Walking on the trails, some of them boardwalks, you can still see the old dikes, canals, and sluice gates that were key to the whole operation. Most Wednesday and Saturday mornings, guided bird walks are held at 8:30 A.M. ($5 per person). Keep in mind that bikes and dogs aren't allowed on the grounds.

Johns Island

Now a rapidly growing suburb of Charleston, the outlying community of Johns Island is where you'll find **Angel Oak Park** (3688 Angel Oak Rd., Mon.–Sat. 9 A.M.–5 P.M., Sun. 1–5 P.M.) home of a massive live oak, 65 feet in circumference, that's well over 1,000 years old and commonly considered the oldest tree east of the Mississippi River. The tree and the park are owned by the city of Charleston, and the grounds are often used for weddings and special events. Get here from Charleston by taking U.S. 17 over the Ashley River, then S.C. Highway 171 to Maybank Highway. Take a left onto Bohicket Road near the Piggly Wiggly, and then look for signs on your right. Here is also where you'll find **Legare Farms** (2620 Hanscombe Point Rd., 843/559-0763, www.legarefarms.com), open to the public for various activities, like its annual pumpkin patch in October and bird walks each Saturday in autumn at 8:30 A.M. ($6 adults, $3 children).

Charleston Tea Plantation

Currently owned by the R.C. Bigelow Tea corporation, the Charleston Tea Plantation (6617 Maybank Hwy., 843/559-0383, www.bigelow tea.com, Wed.–Sat. 10 A.M.–4 P.M., free) is no cute living history exhibit: It's a big, working tea plantation, with acre after acre of *Camilla sinensis* being worked by modern farm machinery. Visitors get to see a sample of how the tea is made, "from the field to the cup," as they put it here, first by a trolley tour of the "Back 40" and then at a viewing gallery of the processing machines at work. And of course there's a gift shop where you can sample and buy all types of teas and tea-related products.

Unlike many agricultural sites in the area, the 127-acre Charleston Tea Plantation was never actually a plantation. It was first planted at the relatively late date of 1960, when the Lipton tea company moved some plants from Summerville, South Carolina, to its research facility on Wadmalaw Island. Lipton decided the climate and high labor costs of the American South weren't conducive to making money, so they sold the land to two employees, Mack Fleming and Bill Hall, in 1987. The two held onto the plantation until 2003, when R.C. Bigelow won it at auction for $1.28 million. Growing season is from April through October. The tea bushes, direct descendants of plants brought over in the 1800s from India and China, "flush up" 2–3 inches every few weeks during growing season.

To get here from Charleston, take the Ashley River Bridge, stay left to Folly Road (S.C. Highway 171), turn right onto Maybank Highway for 18 miles, and look for the sign on your left.

Kiawah Island

Only one facility for the general public exists on beautiful Kiawah Island, the **Kiawah Island Beachwalker Park** (843/768-2395, www.ccprc.com, Mar., Apr., and Oct. weekends only 10 A.M.–6 P.M., summer 9 A.M.–7 P.M., Sept. 10 A.M.–6 P.M., closed Nov.–Feb., $7 per vehicle, free for pedestrians/cyclists). Get there from downtown by taking Lockwood Avenue onto the Highway 30 Connector bridge over the Ashley River. Turn right onto Folly Road, then a left onto Maybank Highway. After about 20 minutes you'll take a left onto Bohicket Road, which leads you to Kiawah in 14 miles. Turn left from Bohicket onto the Kiawah Island Parkway. Just before the security gate, turn right on Beachwalker Drive and follow the signs to the park.

The island's other main attraction—and quite private—is the **Kiawah Island Golf Resort** (12 Kiawah Beach Dr., 800/654-2924, www.kiawahgolf.com), which is a key location for PGA tournaments. Several smaller private, family-friendly resorts exist on Kiawah, with fully furnished homes and villas and every amenity you could ask for and then some, giving you full access to the island's 10 miles of beautiful beach. Go to www.explorekiawah.com for a full range of options or call 800/877-0837.

Through the efforts of the **Kiawah Island Conservancy** (23 Beachwalker Dr., 843/768-2029, www.kiawahconservancy.org), over 300 acres of the island have been kept as undeveloped nature preserve. The island's famous bobcat population has made quite a comeback, with somewhere between 24 and 36 animals currently active. The bobcats are vital to the island ecosystem, since as top predator they help cull what would otherwise become untenably large populations of deer and rabbit. As a side note, while you're enjoying the beautiful scenery of the islands on the Carolina coast, it's always important to remember that most, including Kiawah, were logged and/or farmed extensively in the past. While they're certainly gorgeous now, it would be incorrect to call them "pristine."

Seabrook Island

Like its neighbor Kiawah, Seabrook Island is also a private resort-dominated island.

In addition to offering miles of beautiful beaches, on its 2,200 acres are a wide variety of golfing, tennis, equestrian, and swimming facilities, as well as extensive dining and shopping options. There are also a lot of kids' activities as well. For information on lodging options and packages, go to www.seabrook.com or call 866/249-9934.

Food

If you find your tummy growling in the suburb of Johns Island southwest of Charleston, try **Fat Hen** (3140 Maybank Hwy., Johns Island, 843/559-9090, Tues.–Sat. 11:30 A.M.–3 P.M. and 5:30–10 P.M., Sun. 10 A.M.–3 P.M., $15–20), a self-styled "country French bistro" begun by a couple of old Charleston restaurant hands. The fried oysters are a particular specialty. There's also a bar menu for late-night hours (10 P.M.–2 A.M.).

On nearby James Island, vegetarians will enjoy **Daily Dose** (1622 Highland Ave., James Island, 843/225-3367, Tues.–Fri. 11 A.M.–9 P.M., $5–10), which specializes in healthy, organic wraps. But you don't have to be overly healthy—they've got a good beer selection, too.

BEAUFORT AND THE LOWCOUNTRY

For many people around the world, the Lowcountry is the first image that comes to mind when they think of the American South. For the people that live here the Lowcountry is altogether unique, but it does embody many of the region's most noteworthy qualities: an emphasis on manners, a respect for and a reliance upon nature, a constant look back into the past, and a slow and leisurely pace (embodied in the joking but largely accurate nickname "Slowcountry").

History hangs in the humid air where first the Spanish came to interrupt the native tribes' ancient reverie, then the French, followed by the English. Though time, erosion, and development have erased most traces of these multicultural occupants, you can almost hear their ghosts in the rustle of the branches in a sudden sea breeze, or in the piercing call of a heron over the marsh.

Artists and arts lovers the world over are drawn here to paint, photograph, or otherwise be inspired by some of the most gorgeous wetlands in the United States, so vast that human habitation appears fleeting and intermittent. Sprawling between Beaufort and Charleston is the huge ACE (Ashley, Combahee, Edisto) Basin, an extraordinarily beautiful and important estuary and a national model for good conservation practices.

In all, the single most defining characteristic of the Lowcountry is its liquid nature—not only literally, in the hundreds of creeks and waterway that dominate every vista and the preponderance of delicious seafood cooked in all manner of ways, but figuratively, too, in the

© JIM MOREKIS

BEAUFORT

HIGHLIGHTS

◖ **Henry C. Chambers Waterfront Park:** Walk the dog or while away the time on a porch swing at this clean and inviting gathering place on the serene Beaufort River (page 133).

◖ **St. Helena's Episcopal Church:** To walk through this Beaufort sanctuary and its walled graveyard is to walk through Lowcountry history (page 136).

◖ **Penn Center:** Not only the center of modern Gullah culture and education, but a key site in civil rights history as well (page 148).

◖ **Hunting Island:** This is one of the most peaceful natural getaways on the East Coast, but it's only minutes away from the more civilized temptations of Beaufort (page 154).

◖ **ACE Basin National Wildlife Refuge:** You can take a lifetime to learn your way around this massive, marshy estuary – or just a few hours soaking in its lush beauty (page 155).

◖ **Pinckney Island National Wildlife Refuge:** This excellently maintained sanctuary is a major birding location and a great little getaway from nearby Hilton Head (page 160).

◖ **Old Bluffton:** Gossipy and gorgeous by turns, this charming village on the May River centers on a thriving artist colony (page 172).

LOOK FOR ◖ TO FIND RECOMMENDED SIGHTS, ACTIVITIES, DINING, AND LODGING.

slow but deep quality of life here. Once outside what passes for urban areas here, you'll find yourself taking a look back through the decades to a time of roadside produce stands, shadetree mechanics, and men gathered along tidal creeks fishing and crabbing—not for sport but for the family dinner.

Indeed, not so very long ago, before the influx of resort development, retirement subdivisions, and tourism, much of the Lowcountry was like a flatter, more humid Appalachia—poverty-stricken and sometimes desperately underserved. While the archetypal South has been marketed in any number of ways to the

rest of the world, here you get a sense that this is the real thing—timeless, endlessly alluring, but somehow very familiar.

South of Beaufort is the historically significant Port Royal area and the East Coast Marine Recruit Depot of Parris Island. East of Beaufort is the center of Gullah culture, St. Helena Island, and the scenic and unspoiled gem of Hunting Island. To the south is the also scenic but entirely developed golf and tennis mecca, Hilton Head Island, and Hilton Head's close neighbor but diametrical opposite in every other way, Daufuskie Island, another important Gullah center. Nestled in between is

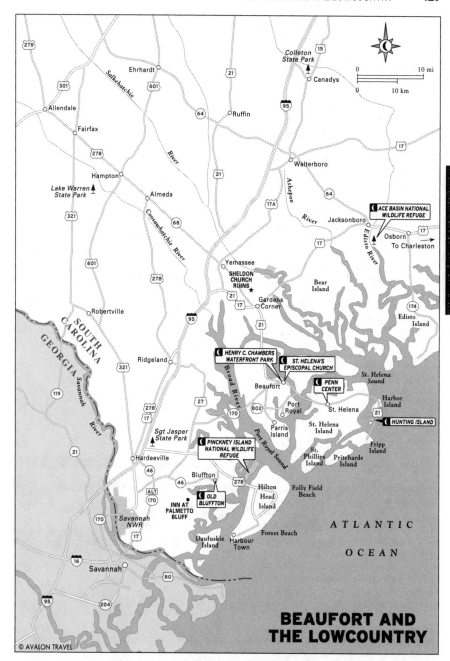

BEAUFORT

BEAUFORT AND THE LOWCOUNTRY

© AVALON TRAVEL

the charming, close-knit, and gossipy little village of Bluffton on the gossamer May River.

PLANNING YOUR TIME

The small-scale accessibility and comparative lack of traffic in most of the Lowcountry is one of its more charming aspects. Don't let that fool you into thinking you can knock everything out in a day, though. That would defeat the purpose, which is not only to see the sights of this historically and naturally rich region, but to fully enjoy its laidback, slow, and leisurely pace.

The most common-sense game plan is to use the centrally located Beaufort as a home base. Not only is it easy to get from there to anywhere else in the area, but there's also a preponderance of affordable and charming lodging.

Keep a full day of leisure to walk all over Beaufort. There's no need to hurry; just do what the locals do and take everything in its own time. Another full day should go to St. Helena's Penn Center and on to Hunting Island. If you're in the mood for a road trip, dedicate another full day to tour the surrounding area to the north and northeast, perhaps a jaunt to the ACE Basin National Wildlife Refuge, stopping at the Old Sheldon Church Ruins in the late afternoon on your way back to Beaufort. If you have extra time, split it between Port Royal and a tour of the historic and military sites of interest on Parris Island.

While the New York accents fly fast and furious on Hilton Head Island, that's no reason for you to rush. Certainly a casual visitor can do Hilton Head in a day, but that would be a shame, because its more natural attractions beg for a more considered sort of enjoyment. Plan on at least a half-day just to enjoy the fine, broad beaches alone. I recommend another half-day to tour the island itself, maybe including a stop in Sea Pines for late lunch or dinner. While most of the marketing materials make scant mention of it, nature-lovers mustn't miss the Pinckney Island National Refuge, gorgeous enough to be a must-see but small enough and convenient enough to fully enjoy in a few hours.

There's a lot to choose from in terms of stores and wares, so make sure you allot some extra time to enjoy what the island has to offer shopping-wise. And then double it to be on the safe side.

Water is an integral part of Lowcountry life.

Beaufort

Sandwiched exactly halfway between the prouder, louder cities of Charleston and Savannah, Beaufort is in many ways a more authentic slice of life from the past than either of those two. Long a staple of movie crews seeking to portray some archetypal aspect of the old South *(Prince of Tides, The Great Santini, Forrest Gump)* or just to film beautiful scenery for its own sake *(Jungle Book, Last Dance)*, Beaufort—pronounced "Byoofert," by the way, not "Bo-fort"—features some of the most glorious and well-preserved examples of Southern architecture, most all of them in idyllic, family-friendly neighborhoods.

The pace in Beaufort is languid, slower even than the waving Spanish moss in the hundreds of massive old live oak trees. The line between business and pleasure is a blurry one here. As you can tell from the signs you see on storefront doors saying things like "Back in an hour or so," time is an entirely negotiable commodity. The locals here exemplify the old Lowcountry ideals of hospitality, grace, and ready but dry humor.

The architecture combines the relaxed Caribbean flavor of Charleston with the Anglophilic dignity of Savannah. In fact, plenty of people prefer the well-kept, highly individualistic old homes of Beaufort, seemingly tailor-made for the exact spot on which they sit, to the historic districts of either Charleston or Savannah in terms of sheer architectural delight.

While you'll no doubt run into plenty of charming and gracious locals during your time here, you might be surprised at the amount of transplanted Northerners. That's due not only to the high volume of retirees who've moved to the area, but the active presence of three major U.S. Navy facilities, the Marine Corps Air Station Beaufort, the Marine Corps Recruit Depot on nearby Parris Island, and the Beaufort Naval Hospital. Many's the time a former sailor or Marine has decided to put down roots in the area after being stationed here, the most famous

example being author Pat Conroy's father, a.k.a. "The Great Santini."

HISTORY

Though little known to most Americans, the Port Royal Sound area around Beaufort is not only one of the largest natural harbors on the East Coast, it's one of the nation's most historic places. It's a fact made all the more maddening in how little of that history remains.

This was the site of the second landing by the Spanish on the North American continent, the expedition of Captain Pedro de Salazar in 1514. (Ponce de Leon's more famous landing at St. Augustine was but a year earlier.) A Spanish slaver named Francisco Cordillo made a brief stop in 1521, long enough to name the area Santa Elena—one of the oldest European place names in America.

Port Royal Sound didn't get its modern name until the first serious attempt at a permanent settlement, Jean Ribaut's exploration in 1562. Though ultimately disastrous, Ribault's historic expedition was the first French settlement in America. Ribaut returned to France for reinforcements to find his country in an all-out religious civil war. He sought safety in England only to be clapped in the Tower of London. Meanwhile his soldiers at Charlesfort became restive and essentially revolted against their absentee commander, with most moving to a subsequent French settlement, Fort Caroline, near present-day Jacksonville, Florida. In a twist straight out of Hollywood, in 1565 Fort Caroline bought food and a ship to return to France from a passing vessel, which turned out to be commanded by the infamous English privateer John Hawkins. While the French waited for a favorable wind for the trip home, who should arrive but none other than Jean Ribault himself, fresh out of prison and at the head of 600 French soldiers and settlers sent to rescue his colony!

In yet another unlikely development, the Spanish fleet of Pedro Menéndez de Avilés

BEAUFORT

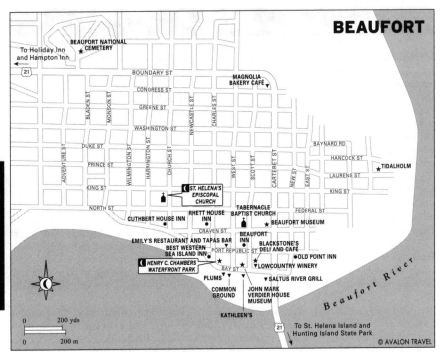

BEAUFORT

To Holiday Inn and Hampton Inn · 21

BEAUFORT NATIONAL CEMETERY

BOUNDARY ST
CONGRESS ST
GREENE ST
WASHINGTON ST

MAGNOLIA BAKERY CAFÉ

BLADEN ST
MONSON ST
NEWCASTLE ST
CHARLES ST

DUKE ST
PRINCE ST
KING ST
NORTH ST

ADVENTURE ST
WILMINGTON ST
HARRINGTON ST
CHURCH ST
WEST ST
SCOT ST
CARTERET ST
NEW ST
EAST ST

BAYNARD RD
HANCOCK ST
LAURENS ST
KING ST

TIDALHOLM

ST. HELENA'S EPISCOPAL CHURCH

TABERNACLE BAPTIST CHURCH

FEDERAL ST

RHETT HOUSE INN
CUTHBERT HOUSE INN
CRAVEN ST

BEAUFORT MUSEUM

BEAUFORT INN
BLACKSTONE'S DELI AND CAFÉ

EMILY'S RESTAURANT AND TAPAS BAR
BEST WESTERN SEA ISLAND INN
PORT REPUBLIC ST
OLD POINT INN

HENRY C. CHAMBERS WATERFRONT PARK
BAY ST
LOWCOUNTRY WINERY

PLUMS
SALTUS RIVER GRILL

COMMON GROUND
JOHN MARK VERDIER HOUSE MUSEUM

KATHLEEN'S

Beaufort River

21 To St. Helena Island and Hunting Island State Park

0   200 yds
0   200 m

© AVALON TRAVEL

soon appeared, intent on driving the French out for good. Ribault went on the offensive, intending to mount a preemptive attack on the Spanish base at St. Augustine. However, a storm wrecked the French ships and Ribault was washed ashore near St. Augustine and killed by waiting Spanish troops.

As if the whole story couldn't get any stranger, back at Charlesfort things had become so desperate for the 27 original colonists who stayed behind that they decided to build a ship to sail back home to France—technically the first ship built in America for a transatlantic crossing. The vessel made it across the Atlantic, but not without price; running out of food, the French soldiers began eating shoe leather before moving on, so the accounts say, to eating each other. Twenty survivors were rescued in the English Channel.

After the French faded from the scene, Spaniards from Florida came to garrison Santa Elena. But steady Indian attacks and Francis Drake's attack on St. Augustine forced the Spanish to abandon the area entirely in 1587. Within the next generation British indigo planters had established a firm presence in the Port Royal area, chief among them John "Tuscarora Jack" Barnwell of Port Royal Island and Thomas Nairn of St. Helena. These men would go on to found the town of Beaufort, named for Henry Somerset, Duke of Beaufort, and chartered in 1711 as part of the original Carolina colony.

In 1776, Beaufort planter Thomas Heyward Jr. signed the Declaration of Independence. After independence was gained, Lowcountry planters turned to cotton as the main cash crop, since England had been their prime customer for indigo. The gambit paid off, and Beaufort soon became one of the wealthiest and highest-regarded towns in the new nation.

The so-called "Golden Age" of Sea Island

cotton saw storm clouds gather on the horizon as the Lowcountry became the hotbed of secession, with the very first Ordinance of Secession being drawn up in Beaufort's Milton Maxey House. Only seven months after secessionists fired on Fort Sumter in nearby Charleston in 1861, a huge Union fleet sailed into Port Royal and occupied Hilton Head, Beaufort, and the rest of the Lowcountry for the duration of the war. While this ensured that many of the classic plantation homes would survive, it also meant economic distress for local residents who chose to stay rather than flee.

Gradually evolving their own distinct dialect and culture, much of it solidly linked to their West African roots, the Lowcountry island's African American population became known as the Gullah. Evolving from an effort by abolitionist missionaries early in the Civil War, in 1864 the Penn School was formed on St. Helena Island specifically to teach the children of the Gullah communities. Now known as the Penn Center, the facility has been a beacon for the study of this aspect of African American culture ever since.

The 20th century ushered in a time of increased dependence on military spending, with the opening of a training facility on Parris Island in the 1880s (the Marines didn't begin training recruits there until 1915). The Lowcountry got a further boost from wartime spending in the '40s. Parris Island, already thriving as a Marine hub, was joined by the Marine Corps Naval Air Station in nearby Beaufort in 1942. In 1949, the Naval Hospital opened. Today, the tourism industry has joined the military as a major economic driver in the Lowcountry. Hollywood discovered its charms as well, in a series of critical and box-office hits like *The Big Chill, The Prince of Tides,* and *Forrest Gump.*

ORIENTATION

Don't be discouraged by the big-box sprawl that assaults you on the approaches to Beaufort on Boundary Street, lined with the usual discount megastores, fast food outlets, and budget motels. This is a popular area for relocation as well as for tourists, and when you add to the mix the presence of several bustling military facilities you have a recipe for occasional gridlock and general architectural ugliness.

But after you make the big ninety-degree bend where Boundary turns into Carteret Street—known locally as the "Bellamy Curve"—it's like entering a whole new world of slow-paced, Spanish moss–lined avenues, friendly people, gentle breezes, and inviting storefronts. This is the Beaufort Historic District, often called simply the "Old Point" or even more simply, "the Point." Whatever you call it, it's surely one of the most beguiling little towns you'll ever visit.

While you can make your way to downtown by taking Carteret all the way to Bay Street—don't continue over the big bridge unless you want to go straight to Lady's Island and St. Helena Island—I suggest availing yourself of one of the "Downtown Access" signs before you get that far. Because Carteret Street is the only way to that bridge, it can get backed up at rush hour. By taking a quick right and then a left all the way to Bay Street, you can you can come into town from the other, quieter end, with your first glimpse of downtown proper being its timelessly beguiling views of the Beaufort River.

Once there, try to park your car slightly outside the town center and simply walk everywhere you want to go, or conversely you can park in the long-term metered spaces at the marina. Unlike Charleston or Savannah, any visitor in reasonably good shape can walk the entire length and breadth of Beaufort's 300-acre downtown with little trouble. In fact, that's by far the best way to experience it.

SIGHTS
◖ Henry C. Chambers Waterfront Park

Before you get busy shopping and dining and admiring Beaufort's fine old homes, go straight to the town's pride and joy since 1980, the Henry C. Chambers Waterfront Park (843/525-7054, www.cityofbeaufort .org, daily 24 hours), stretching for hundreds

PAT CONROY'S LOWCOUNTRY

I was always your best subject, son. Your career took a nose dive after The Great Santini *came out.*

– Colonel Donald Conroy to his son Pat

Though born in Georgia, no other single person is associated with the South Carolina Lowcountry as much as author Pat Conroy. After moving around as a child of a military family, he began high school in Beaufort. His painful teen years there formed the basis of his first novel, a brutal portrait of his domineering Marine pilot father, Colonel Donald Conroy, a.k.a., Colonel Bull Meecham of *The Great Santini* (1976). Many scenes from the 1979 film adaptation were filmed at the famous "Tidalholm," or Edgar Fripp House, at 1 Laurens Street in Beaufort. (The house was also front and center in *The Big Chill*.)

Conroy's pattern of thinly veiled autobiography actually began with his first book, the self-published *The Boo*, a tribute to a teacher at The Citadel in Charleston while Conroy was still a student there. His second work, *The Water is Wide* (1972), is a chronicle of his experiences teaching in a one-room African American school on Daufuskie Island. Though ostensibly a straightforward, first-person journalistic effort, Conroy changed the location to the fictional Yamacraw Island, supposedly to protect its fragile culture from curious outsiders. (The 1974 film adaptation starring Jon Voight was titled *Conrack* after the way his students mispronounced his name.)

You can visit that same two-room school today on Daufuskie. Known as the Mary Field School, the building is now a local community center. (Conroy wrote the forward to the excellent cookbook *Gullah Home Cooking the Daufuskie Way: Smokin' Joe Butter Beans, Ol' 'Fuskie Fried Crab Rice, Sticky-Bush Blackberry Dumpling, and Other Sea Island Favorites*, by Daufuskie native and current Savannah resident Sallie Ann Robinson.)

Conroy would go on in 1980 to publish *The Lords of Discipline*, a reading of his real-life experience with the often-savage environment faced by cadets at The Citadel – though Conroy would change the name, calling it the Carolina Military Institute. Still, when it came time to make a film adaptation in 1983, The Citadel refused to allow it to be shot there. So the "Carolina Military Institute" was filmed in England instead!

For many of his fans, Conroy's *The Prince of Tides* is his ultimate homage to the Lowcountry. Surely, the 1991 film version starring Barbra Streisand and Nick Nolte – shot on location and awash in gorgeous shots of the Beaufort River marsh – did much to implant an idyllic image of the area to audiences around the world. According to local legend, Streisand originally didn't intend to make the film in Beaufort, but a behind-the-scenes lobbying effort allegedly coordinated by Conroy himself and including a stay at the Rhett House Inn, convinced her.

The Bay Street Inn at 601 Bay Street in Beaufort was seen in the film, as was the football field at the old Beaufort High School. The beach scenes were shot on nearby Fripp Island. Interestingly, some scenes set in a Manhattan apartment were actually shot within the old Beaufort Arsenal on 713 Craven Street, now a museum. Similarly, the Beaufort Naval Hospital doubled as New York's Bellevue.

Despite the many personal tribulations he faced in the area, Conroy has never given up on the Lowcountry and still makes his home there with his family in Fripp Island, South Carolina. As for the "Great Santini" himself, you can visit the final resting place of Colonel Conroy in the Beaufort National Cemetery – Section 62, Grave 182.

© JIM MOREKIS

Henry C. Chambers Waterfront Park

of feet directly on the Beaufort River. A taste-fully designed and user-friendly mix of walk-ways, bandstands, and patios, Waterfront Park is a favorite gathering place for locals and visi-tors alike, beckoning one and all with its open greenspace and wonderful marsh-front views. My favorite part is the long row of swinging benches on which to peacefully sit and while away the time looking out over the marsh.

Many of the popular restaurants on Bay Street have back entrances and outdoor seating facing Waterfront Park, but you may opt for a casual picnic. Kids will especially enjoy the park not only because there's so much room to run around, but for the charming playground at the east end near the bridge, complete with a jungle gym in the form of a Victorian home. The clean, well-appointed public restrooms are particularly welcome feature here.

John Mark Verdier House Museum

A smallish but stately Federalist building on the busiest downtown corner, the Verdier House Museum (801 Bay St., 843/379-6335, Mon.–Sat. 11 A.M.–4 P.M., $6 adults, $4 students) is the only historic Beaufort home open to regu-lar tours. Built in 1805 for the wealthy planter John Mark Verdier, its main claim to fame was acting as the Union headquarters during the long occupation of Beaufort during the Civil War. However, perhaps its most intriguing link to history—a link it shares with Savannah's Owens-Thomas House—is its connection to the Revolutionary War hero the Marquis de Lafayette, who stayed at the Verdier House on the Beaufort leg of his 1825 U.S. tour. Despite the late hour of his arrival, a crowd gathered at the corner of Bay and Scott Streets, and Lafayette finally had to come to the entrance-way to satisfy their desire for a speech. When the Verdier House was faced with demolition in the 1940s, the Historic Beaufort Foundation purchased the house and renovated it to its cur-rent state, reflective of the early 1800s.

Beaufort Museum

Housed in the imposing yellow-gray tabby

BEAUFORT

© JIM MOREKIS

the historic St. Helena's Episcopal Church cemetery

facade of the historic 1852 Beaufort Arsenal, the Beaufort Museum (713 Craven St., 843/379-3331, www.historicbeaufort.org, Mon.–Sat. 11 A.M.–4 P.M., $3) capably tells the story of Beaufort from its early plantation days through its key role in the secession movement to the modern era. I suggest purchasing the discounted combo ticket to the Beaufort Museum and the Verdier House Museum ($8 adults, $4 students).

(St. Helena's Episcopal Church

Nestled within the confines of a low brick wall surrounding this historic church and cemetery, St. Helena's Episcopal Church (505 Church St., 843/522-1712, Tues.–Fri. 10 A.M.–4 P.M., Sat. 10 A.M.–1 P.M.) has witnessed some of Beaufort's most compelling tales. Built in 1724, this was the parish church of Thomas Heyward, one of South Carolina's signers of the Declaration of Independence. John "Tuscarora Jack" Barnwell, early Indian fighter and one of Beaufort's founders, is buried on the grounds.

The balcony upstairs in the sanctuary was

intended for black parishioners; as was typical throughout the region before the Civil War, both races attended the same church services. After the entire congregation fled with the Union occupation, Federal troops decked over the second floor and used St. Helena's as a hospital—with surgeons using tombstones as operating tables. The wooden altar was carved by the crew of the USS *New Hampshire* while the warship was docked in the harbor during Reconstruction.

While the cemetery and sanctuary interior are likely to be your focus, be sure to take a close look at the church exterior—many of the bricks are actually ship's ballastones. Also be aware that you're not looking at the church's original footprint; the building has been expanded several times since its construction (a hurricane in 1896 destroyed the entire east end). A nearly $3 million restoration, mostly for structural repairs, was completed in 2000.

Tabernacle Baptist Church

Built in 1845, this handsome sanctuary at 911

Craven Street (843/524-0376) had a congregation of over 3,000 before the Civil War, most of them slaves—though the vast majority of slaves generally worshipped separately on plantation ground. During the war, freed slaves purchased the church for their own use. A congregant was the war hero Robert Smalls, who is buried in the church cemetery and has a nice memorial dedicated to him there, proudly facing the street.

Beaufort National Cemetery

It's not as poignantly ornate as Savannah's big Victorian cemeteries, but Beaufort National Cemetery (1601 Boundary St., daily 8 A.M.–sunset) is worth a stop as you enter or leave Beaufort for its history. Begun by order of Abraham Lincoln in 1863, this is one of the few cemeteries containing the graves of both Union and Confederate troops, mostly the former. National Cemetery is where 19 soldiers of the all-black Massachusetts 54th and 55th Infantry were re-interred with full military honors after being found on Folly Island near Charleston. Sergeant Joseph Simmons, "Buffalo Soldier" and veteran of both World Wars, is buried here, as is none other than the "Great Santini" himself, novelist Pat Conroy's father Donald.

Organized Tours

Colorful character Jon Sharp runs the very popular **Jon Sharp's Walking History Tour** (843/575-5775, www.jonswalkinghistory.com, Tues.–Sat. 11 A.M., Sun. 1 P.M., $20), taking a break during the summer months. The two-hour jaunt begins and ends at the Downtown Marina and takes you all through the downtown area.

The Spirit of Old Beaufort (103 West St. Extension, 843/525-0459, www.thespiritof oldbeaufort.com, 10:30 A.M., Mon.–Sat. 2 P.M., 7 P.M., $13 adults, $8 children) runs a series of good, year-round walking tours, roughly two hours long, with guides usually in period dress. If you don't want to walk, you can hire one of their guides and take them in your own vehicle for a $50 minimum.

As you might expect, few things could be more Lowcountry than an easy-going carriage ride through the historic neighborhoods. **Southurn Rose Buggy Tours** (843/524-2900, www.southurnrose.com, $18 adults, $7 children)—yes, that's how they spell it—offers 50-minute narrated carriage rides of the entire Old Point, including movie locations, embarking and disembarking near the Downtown Marina. Another similarly-priced carriage operator is **Carolina Buggy Tours** (901 Port Republic St., 843/525-1300).

An important specialty bus tour in the area is **Gullah-N-Geechie Man Tours** (843/838-7516, www.gullahngeechietours.net, $20 adults, $18 children), focusing on the rich Gullah history and culture of the St. Helena's Island area, including the historic Penn Center. Call for pickup information.

ENTERTAINMENT AND EVENTS
Nightlife

Those looking for a rowdy time will be happier seeking it in the notorious party towns of Charleston or Savannah. However, a few notable places in downtown Beaufort do double duty as dining havens and neighborhood watering holes. Sadly, the well-regarded restaurant within the Beaufort Inn on Port Republic Street closed for good in 2007. But several establishments tucked together on Bay Street, all with café seating out back facing the waterfront, can also show you a good time.

A charming little bar is **Hemingway's Bistro** (920 Bay St., 843/521-4480, daily 11 A.M.–2 A.M.), which is a great place to relax over a cocktail. There's live music on the weekend.

The convivial **Kathleen's Grill** (822 Bay St., 843/524-2500, daily 11 A.M.–2 A.M.) features live music by a variety of regional artists. Weekend tunes crank up about 10 P.M.

Plum's (904½ Bay St., 843/525-1946, daily 5 P.M.–2 A.M.) offers not only a tasty menu but some fun at 10 P.M. when the kitchen closes down and the focus turns to its great beer selection. Close by is **Luther's Rare & Well Done** (910 Bay St., 843/521-1888, 5 P.M.–midnight), which offers a late-night appetizer menu to go with its rock-oriented live music on weekends.

BEAUFORT

A WALKING TOUR OF BEAUFORT HOMES

© JIM MOREKIS

Lewis Reeve Sams House in Beaufort

One of the unique aspects of the Lowcountry and Georgia coast is the large amount of historical homes in totally private hands. When a homeowner purchases one of these fine old homes, they generally know what's in store: a historical marker of some sort will be nearby, organized tours will periodically swing by their home, and production companies will sometimes approach them about using the home as a film set. It's a trade-off most homeowners are only too glad to accept.

Here's a walking tour of some of Beaufort's fine historic homes in private hands. You won't be taking any tours of the interior, but these homes are part of the legacy of the area and are locally valued as such. Be sure to respect the privacy of the inhabitants by keeping the noise level down and not trespassing on private property to take photos.

- **Thomas Fuller House:** Begin at 1211 Bay St., at the corner of Harrington and Bay, and view this 1796 home, one of the oldest in existence in Beaufort and even more unique in that much of the building material is tabby (hence the home's other name, the Tabby Manse).

- **Milton Maxcy House:** Walk east on Bay Street one block and take a left on Church Street; walk up to the corner of Church and Craven Streets. Otherwise known as the Secession House (113 Craven St.), this 1813 home was built on a tabby foundation dating from 1743. In 1860, when it was the residence of attorney Edmund Rhett, the very first Ordinance of Secession was signed here and the rest, as they say, was history.

- **Lewis Reeve Sams House:** Pick up the walking tour on the other side of the historic district, at the foot of the bridge. This gorgeous house at 602 Bay Street, at the corner of Bay and New Streets with its double-decker veranda dates from 1852 and served as a Union hospital during the Civil War.

- **Berners Barnwell Sams House:** Continue up New Street until you get to 310 New Street, where you'll find this 1818 home, which served as the African American hospital during the Union occupation. Harriet Tubman of Underground Railroad fame worked here for a time as a nurse.

- **Joseph Johnson House:** Continue up New Street and take a right on Craven Street. Cross East Street and stop at 411 Craven Street to find this 1850 home, nicknamed The Castle, with the massive live oak in the front yard. Legend has it that when the Yankees occupied Hilton Head, Mr. Johnson buried his valuables under an outhouse. After the war he returned to find his home for sale due to unpaid back taxes. He dug up his valuables, paid the taxes, and resumed living in the home. You might recognize the home from the film *Forces of Nature*.

- **Marshlands:** Backtrack to East Street and walk north to Federal Street. Take a right and go to the end to find 501 Pinckney Street. Built by James R. Verdier, Marshlands is a National Historic Landmark, used as hospital during the Civil War, as many Beaufort homes were. It was the setting of Francis Griswold's 1931 novel *A Sea Island Lady*.

- **The Oaks:** Walk up to King Street, take a right and go to the corner of King and Short Streets. The Oaks at 100 Laurens Street at this intersection was owned by the Hamilton family, who lost a son who served with General Wade Hampton's cavalry in the Civil War. After the conflict, the family couldn't afford the back taxes, and neighbors paid the debts and returned the deed to the Hamiltons.

- **Edgar Fripp House:** Walk east on Laurens toward the water to find this handsome Lowcountry mansion, sometimes called Tidalholm, at 1 Laurens Street. Built in 1856 by the wealthy planter for whom nearby Fripp Island is named, this house was a key setting in *The Big Chill* and *The Great Santini*.

- **Francis Hext House:** Go back to Short Street, walk north to Hancock Street and take a left. This palatial estate, known as Riverview, at 207 Hancock Street is one of the oldest structures in Beaufort, built in 1720.

- **Robert Smalls House:** Continue west on Hancock Street, take a short left on East Street, and a quick right on Prince Street. This 1834 home at 511 Prince Street was the birthplace of Robert Smalls, a former slave and Beaufort native who stole the Confederate ship *Planter* from Charleston Harbor while serving as its helmsman and delivered it to Union troops in Hilton Head. Smalls and a few compatriots commandeered the ship while the officers were at a party at Fort Sumter, taking it right past Confederate pickets. Smalls used the bounty he received for the act of bravery to buy his boyhood home for his own. After the war, Smalls was a longtime U.S. congressman.

Performing Arts

Beaufort's fine arts scene is small but professional in outlook. Most performances are based in the nice new Performing Arts Center on the oak-lined campus of the University of South Carolina Beaufort (801 Carteret St., 843/521-4100).

A prime mover of the local performing arts scene is **Beaufort Performing Arts, Inc.** (www.uscb.edu), formed by a mayoral task force in 2003 specifically to encourage arts and cultural development within the area. The most recent season, with performances at USCB's Performing Arts Center, included performances by famed Celtic fiddler Natalie MacMaster, the Claremont Trio, and the Bee Gees. Prices typically range $12–40. Of particular note is a series of children's shows, such as a recent one based on the popular Junie B. Jones books.

Perhaps surprisingly for such a small place, Beaufort boasts its own full orchestra, the **Beaufort Orchestra** (1106 Carteret Street, 843/986-5400, www.beaufortorchestra.org), which plays in the Performing Arts Center. A recent season included Paganini's Violin Concerto in D, Tchaikovsky's "Pathetique" Symphony No. 6, and "Beaufort Goes to Broadway."

The closest place for quality live theatre is Hilton Head; however, just across the bridge from Beaufort on Lady's Island is the **Sea Island Dinner Theatre** in the little Sea Island Conference Center (178 Sam's Point Rd., 843/522-3924, www.seaislandconference center.com).

Film

One of only two fully functional drive-ins in the state, the **Highway 21 Drive In** (55 Parker Dr., 843/846-4500, www.hwy21drivein.com) has two screens, great sound, and awesome concessions including Angus beef hamburgers. All you need to provide is the car and the company.

Festivals and Events

Surprisingly for a town so prominent in so many films, Beaufort didn't have its own film festival until 2007. The **Beaufort Film Festival** (843/986-5400, www.beaufortfilmfestival .com) is held in late winter. It's small in scale—the inaugural festival was only two days, at a now-defunct theater—but boasts a diverse range of high-quality, cutting edge entries, including shorts and animation.

Technically the film festival is part of a larger event, **Kaleidoscope: Film, Food, and Fine Arts** (843/986-5400, www.beaufortkaleido scope.com), a celebration of Lowcountry culture in various venues around town. Highlights include an "arts walk" (basically a town-wide art gallery open house), an "Iron Chef Beaufort" chef competition, and Friday night wine dinners wherein some leading Southern chefs take over the kitchen at a number of local restaurants.

Foodies will also enjoy **A Taste of Beaufort** (www.downtownbeaufort.com), usually held the first Saturday in May, which features the offerings of two dozen or so local restaurants with live music, all along historic Bay Street.

Now over 20 years old, the **Gullah Festival of South Carolina** celebrates Gullah history and culture on Memorial Day weekend at various locations throughout town, mostly focusing on the Waterfront Park.

By far the biggest single event on the local festival calendar is the over 50-year-old **Beaufort Water Festival** (www.bftwater festival.com), held over two weeks in June or July each year, centering on the Waterfront Park area. One of the most eclectic and idiosyncratic events of its kind in a region already known for quirky, hyperlocal festivals, the Beaufort Water Festival features events as diverse as a raft race, badminton, bocce, billiards, croquet, and golf tournaments, a children's toad fishing tournament, a ski show, a bed race, a street dance, and all sorts of live music and local art exhibits.

The signature events are two galas, the Commodore's Ball and the Regatta Ball, and the Saturday morning two-hour Grand Parade, historically organized by the local Lions Club. A delightfully regional touch completes the festival, with a blessing and parade of the shrimp fleet on the closing Sunday.

Fall in the Lowcountry means shrimping season, and early October brings the **Beaufort**

Shrimp Festival (www.beaufortsc.org). Highlights include an evening concert with specially lighted shrimpboats docked along the river, a 5K run over the Woods Memorial Bridge, and a more laid-back 5K walk through the historic district. Various cooking competitions are held, obviously centering around the versatile crustaceans that are the raison d'être of the shrimp fleet.

October also brings a relatively new event, the **Chalk on the Walk** (www.beaufortcounty arts.com). Based on European street festivals—and similar to Savannah's Sidewalk Arts Festival—Chalk on the Walk features a delightful blend of street painting and performing, live music, and an art market.

St. Helena Island hosts the three-day **Penn Center Heritage Days** (www.penncenter.com) each November, without a doubt the Beaufort area's second-biggest celebration after the Water Festival. Focusing on Gullah culture, history, and delicious food, Heritage Days does a great job of combining fun with education. The event culminates in a colorful Saturday morning parade, featuring lots of traditional Gullah garb, from St. Helena Elementary School to the Penn Center Historic District.

SHOPPING

The Beaufort area's shopping allure comes from the rich variety of independently owned shops, most of which keep a pretty high standard and don't deal too much in touristy schlock. As you might expect, the main drag in town, Bay Street, is also the shopping hub. Note that in Beaufort's shops as well as most everything else in town, hours of operation are loose guidelines and not rigidly observed.

My favorite shop in Beaufort is **The Bay Street Trading Company** (808 Bay St., 843/524-2000, www.baystreettrading .com, Mon.–Fri. 10 A.M.–5:30 P.M., Sat. 10 A.M.–5 P.M., Sun. noon–5 P.M.), sometimes known simply as "The Book Shop," which has a very friendly staff and the best single collection of Lowcountry-themed books I've ever seen in one place. Across the street, the fairly recently renovated, so-bright-red-you-can't-

miss-it Old Bay Marketplace houses a few very cute shops, most notably the **McIntosh Book Shoppe** (917 Bay St., 843/524-1119, Mon.–Sat. noon–5 P.M., Sun. 1–5 P.M.). Also in the Marketplace is the stylish **Lulu Burgess** (917 Bay St., 843/524-5858, Mon.–Sat. 10 A.M.–6 P.M., Sun. noon–5 P.M.), an eclectic store that brings a rich, quirky sense of humor to its otherwise tasteful assortment of gift items for the whole family.

A unique gift item, as well as something you can heartily enjoy on your own travels, can be found at **Lowcountry Winery** (705 Bay St., 843/379-3010, Mon.–Sat. 10 A.M.–5 P.M.). Not only can you purchase bottles of their various red and white offerings, they host tastings daily in their tasting room (because of state law they must charge a fee for the tasting, but it's only a buck per person).

One of the more unusual shops in town is **Cravings by the Bay** (928 Bay St., 843/522-3000, Mon.–Sat. 10 A.M.–5 P.M., Sun. noon–4 P.M.), primarily known for its collection of gift baskets incorporating regional gourmet goodies like She-Crab Soup, Praline Mustard Glaze, and Benne Wafers, any of which you can purchase separately, of course.

Art Galleries

As you'd expect in such a visually stirring locale, there's a plethora of great art galleries in the Beaufort/St. Helena's area. While most are clustered on Bay Street, there are gems scattered all over. Almost all are worth a look, but here are a few highlights:

My favorite gallery in town is the simply named **The Gallery** (802 Bay St., 843/470-9994, www.thegallery-beaufort.com, Mon.–Sat. 11 A.M.–5 P.M.). Deanna Bowdish brings in the most cutting-edge regional contemporary artists in a large, friendly, loft-like space.

The **Beaufort Art Association Gallery** (1001 Bay St., 843/379-2222, www.beaufort artassociation.com, Mon.–Sat. 10 A.M.–5 P.M.) hosts rotating exhibits by member artists in the stately and historic Elliott House.

Lovers of the Lowcountry will enjoy the aesthetic at the two-floor **Rhett Gallery** (901

Bay St., 843/524-3339, www.rhettgallery.com, Mon.–Sat. 9 A.M.–5:30 P.M., Sun. variable hours). Owner Nancy Rhett submitted one of the designs for the state's Friends of Hunting Island license plate. Close by in the Old Bay Marketplace is **Art and Soul** (917 Bay St., 843/379-9710, Mon.–Sat. 10 A.M.–5:30 P.M.), featuring over 50 regional artists.

A complete art experience blending the traditional with the cutting-edge is at the **I. Pinckney Simons Art Gallery** (711 Bay St., 843/379-4774, www.ipinckneysimons gallery.com, Tues.–Fri. 11 A.M.–5 P.M., Sat. 11 A.M.–3 P.M.), which is pronounced "Simmons" despite the spelling. There you will find not only painting, but compelling photography, sculpture and jewelry as well, all by local and regional artists of renown.

There aren't many local artists featured at **Four Winds Gallery** (709 Bay St., 843/379-5660, www.fourwindstraders.com, Mon.–Wed. and Sat. 10:30 A.M.–5:30 P.M., Thurs. 10:30 A.M.–7 P.M., Sun. 11 A.M.–4 P.M.), but it's a great place to find religious folk art from around the world, from wooden African tribal votives to Orthodox icons from Greece.

A few blocks from Bay Street is a fun local favorite, the **Longo Gallery** (103 Charles St., 843/522-8933, Mon.–Sat. 11 A.M.–5 P.M.). Friendly owners Suzanne and Eric Longo provide a whimsical assortment of less traditional art than you might find in the more touristy waterfront area. Take Charles Street as it works its way toward the waterfront, and the gallery is right behind a storefront on the corner of Charles and Bay Streets.

You'll find perhaps the area's best-known gallery over the bridge on St. Helena's Island. Known regionally as one of the best places to find Gullah folk art, **Red Piano Too** (870 Sea Island Parkway, 843/838-2241, www.redpiano too.com, Mon.–Sat. 10 A.M.–5 P.M.) is on the corner before you turn onto the road to the historic Penn Center. Over 150 artists from a diverse range of traditions and styles are represented in this charming little 1940 building with the red tin awning, historically significant in its own right because it once hosted a produce cooperative that was the first store in the area to pay African Americans with cash rather than barter for goods.

SPORTS AND RECREATION

Beaufort County comprises over 60 islands, so it's no surprise that nearly all recreation in the area revolves around the water, which dominates so many aspects of life in the Lowcountry. The closer to the ocean you get, the more it's a salt marsh environment. But as you explore more inland, in the sprawling ACE Basin, you'll encounter primarily blackwater.

Kayaking

The Lowcountry is tailor-made for kayaking. A no-brainer for Beaufort is to put in at the public ramp at the **Downtown Marina** (1006 Bay St., 843/524-4422) and paddle along the peaceful Intracoastal Waterway, either north up the Beaufort River or south into the Sound. A 10-minute drive away from Beaufort in little Port Royal is **The Sands** public boat ramp into Battery Creek. You can also put in at the ramp at the **Ladys Island Marina** (73 Sea Island Pkwy., 843/522-0430) just across the bridge from Beaufort. A great compendium of Beaufort-area landings is at www.beaufortusa .com/marinas.htm.

The catch here, as with all the Lowcountry, is to know your way around if you choose to leave the main shoreline. It's easy to get lost because of the sheer number of creeks, and they all seem to look the same once you get into them a good ways. If you don't feel comfortable with your navigation skills, it's a good idea to contact Kim and David at **Beaufort Kayak Tours** (843/525-0810, www.beaufortkayaktours.com), who rent kayaks and can guide you on a number of excellent tours of all three key areas. They charge about $40 for adults, $30 for children for a two-hour trip. A tour with Beaufort Kayak Tours is also the best (and nearly the only) way to access the historically significant ruins of the early British tabby Fort Frederick, now located on the grounds of the Beaufort Naval Hospital and inaccessible by car.

North and northeast of Beaufort lies the big

ACE Basin region, with about two dozen public ramps indicated by brown signs. Comprising hundreds of miles of creeks and tributaries in addition to its three eponymous rivers, the ACE Basin also features a fun paddling bonus: canals from the old rice plantations. A good service for rental and knowledgeable guided tours of the Basin is **Outpost Moe's** (843/844-2514, www .geocities.com/outpostmoe), where the basic 2.5-hour tour costs $40 per person, and an all-day extravaganza through the Basin is $80. Moe's provides lunch for most of its tours.

Another premier local outfitter for ACE Basin tours is **Carolina Heritage Outfitters** (Hwy. 15, Canadys, S.C., 843/563-5051, www .canoesc.com), who focus on the Edisto River trail. In addition to guided tours and rentals, you can camp overnight in their cute treehouses along the kayak routes ($125). They load you up with your gear, drive you 22 miles up river, then you paddle downriver to the treehouse for the evening. The next day you paddle yourself the rest of the way downriver back to home base.

To have a more dry experience of the ACE Basin from the deck of a larger vessel, try **ACE Basin Tours** (One Coosaw River Dr., 843/521-3099, www.acebasintours.com, Mar.–Nov. Wed. and Sat. 10 A.M., $35 adults, $15 children), which will take you on a three-hour tour in the 40-passenger *Dixie Lady*. To get to their dock, take Carteret Street over the bridge to St. Helena Island and then take a left on SC 802 east (Sam's Point Rd.). Continue until you cross Lucy Point Creek, and the ACE Basin Tours marina is on your immediate left after you cross the bridge.

If you prefer self-guided paddling, keep in mind that you can spend a lifetime learning your way around the ACE Basin. But the state of South Carolina has conveniently gathered some of the best self-guided kayak trips at www.acebasin.net/canoe.html.

Fishing and Boating

Key public marinas in the area are the Downtown Marina in Beaufort, the **Lady's Island Marina** (73 Sea Island Pkwy., 843/522-0430), and the **Port Royal Landing Marina**

(843/525-6664). Hunting Island has a popular thousand-foot fishing pier at the south end. A good local fishing charter service is Captain Josh Utsey's **Lowcountry Guide Service** (843/812-4919, www.beaufortscfishing.com). Captain Ed Hardee (843/441-6880) offers good inshore charters.

The huge ACE Basin is a very popular fishing, crabbing, and shrimping area. It has about two dozen public boat ramps, with colorful names like Cuckold's Creek and Steamboat Landing. There's a useful map of them all at www.acebasin.net, or look for the brown signs along the highway.

Hiking and Biking

Despite the Lowcountry's, well, lowness, fun biking opportunities abound. It might not get your heart rate up like a ride in the Rockies, but the area lends itself to laid-back two-wheeled enjoyment. Many local B&Bs provide bikes free for guests, and you can rent your own just across the river from Beaufort in Lady's Island at **Lowcountry Bikes** (102 Sea Island Pkwy., 843/524-9585, Sun.–Tues. and Thurs.–Fri. 10 A.M.–6 P.M., Wed. 10 A.M.–1 P.M., Sun. 10 A.M.–3 P.M., about $5/hr). They can also hook you up with some good routes around the area.

Bicycling around Beaufort is a sheer delight, for its relative paucity of traffic as well as its picturesque beauty. Port Royal is close enough that you can easily make a circuit to that evenless trafficked little town. To get to Port Royal from Beaufort, take Bay Street west to Ribault Road (U.S. 21) and veer left onto Paris Avenue into downtown Port Royal, where the biking is easy, breezy, and fun.

For a visually delightful ride, the bridge over the Beaufort River also features a pedestrian/bike lane with some awesome views of the town and the marsh. You can either turn back at the base of the bridge and go back into Beaufort or push on to Lady's Island and St. Helena Island, though the traffic on U.S. 21 can get daunting.

An interesting, if long (about 20 miles round-trip) bike route on St. Helena Island begins at St. Helena Elementary School on U.S.

21. From there you take Land's End Road past the Penn Center, all the way to—you guessed it—land's end, whereupon you circle back on Seaside Road. Cut back to Land's End Road and the school via Club Bridge Road.

Some good, if marshy, hiking is at the large **Bear Island Wildlife Management Area** (843/844-8957, www.dnr.sc.gov, Feb.–Oct. Mon.–Sat. dawn–dusk). To get there, take U.S. 21 north out of Beaufort to U.S. 17 north. Take a right on Bennett's Point Road and continue south about 13 miles. The entrance is about a mile on your left after crossing the Ashepoo River.

Bird-Watching

Because of its abundance of both saltwater and freshwater environments and its relatively low human density, the Lowcountry offers a sometime-stunning glimpse into the diversity and majesty of the Southeast's bird population, both regional and migratory.

Serious birders swear by **Hunting Island State Park** (2555 Sea Island Pkwy., 866/345-7275, www.huntingisland.com, daily 6 A.M.–6 P.M., until 9 P.M. DST, $4 adults, $1.50 children), which thanks to its undeveloped state and its spot on key migratory routes makes it a great place to see brown pelicans, loons, herons, falcons, plovers, and egrets of all types. Park naturalists conduct frequent guided walks.

The tall observation tower at Port Royal's The Sands, where Battery Creek joins the Beaufort River, is a convenient vantage point from which to see any number of local bird species. The big, wild **ACE Basin** (8675 Willtown Rd., 843/889-3084, www.fws.gov/acebasin, grounds year-round daylight–dark, office Mon.–Fri. 7:30 A.M.–4 P.M.) hosts at least 19 species of waterfowl and 13 species of wading birds. At the northeast corner of the ACE Basin is the **Bear Island Wildlife Management Area** (843/844-8957, www.dnr.sc.gov, Feb.–Oct. Mon.–Sat. dawn–dusk), considered one of the best birding spots in South Carolina. To get there, take U.S. 21 north out of Beaufort to U.S. 17 north. Take a right on Bennett's Point

Road and continue south about 13 miles. The entrance is about a mile on your left after crossing the Ashepoo River.

Golf

The best-regarded public course in the area, and indeed one of the best military courses in the world, is **Legends at Parris Island** (Building 299, Parris Island, 843/228-2240, www.mccssc.com, $30 green fees). You need to call in advance for a tee time before you can come on Parris Island to golf.

Another popular public course is **South Carolina National Golf Club** (8 Waveland Ave., Cat Island, 843/524-0300, www.scnational.com, $70 green fees). Get to secluded Cat Island by taking the Sea Island Parkway onto Lady's Island and taking it south as it turns into Lady's Island Drive. Take Island Causeway and continue.

ACCOMMODATIONS

Beaufort's historic district is blessed with an abundance of high-quality accommodations that blend in well with their surroundings. There are plenty of budget-minded chain places, some of them very acceptable, in the sprawl of Boundary Street outside of downtown, but here are some suggestions within bicycle distance of the Point. That's not a hypothetical, as most inns offer free bicycles to use as you please during your stay.

Under $150

The aptly named **⟪ Old Point Inn** (212 New St., 843/524-3177, www.oldpointinn.com, $115–175) is not only a great value, but it's also the only historic inn in Beaufort with full views of the river and marsh. Tucked between the historic Lewis Reeve Sams House and the circa-1717 Thomas Hepworth House, the oldest building in town, the Old Point Inn combines Southern style with a delightful lack of pretension. There's a hammock on the upstairs veranda and a small garden patio. Owners Paul and Julie Michau have furnished each themed suite with their own eclectic collection of international furniture and objets d'art.

The **Best Western Sea Island Inn** (1015 Bay St., 843/522-2090, www.bestwestern .com, $135–170) is a great value for those for whom the B&B experience is not paramount. Anchoring the southern end of the historic district in a low, tasteful brick building, the Best Western offers decent service, basic amenities, and surprisingly attractive rates for the location on Beaufort's busiest street.

$150-300

Any list of upscale Beaufort lodging must highlight the **(Beaufort Inn** (809 Port Republic St., 843/379-4667, www.beaufort inn.com, $152–425), consistently voted one of the best B&Bs in the nation. It's sort of a hybrid, in that it comprises not only the 1897 historic central home but a cluster of freestanding historical cottages, each with a charming little porch and rocking chairs. With everything connected by gardens and pathways, you could almost call it a campus. Still, for its sprawling nature-44 rooms in total—the Beaufort Inn experience is intimate, with attentive service and top-flight amenities such as wet bars, large baths, and sumptuous king beds. Within or without the main building, each suite has a character all its own, whether it's the 1,500-square-foot Loft Apartment (complete with guest bedroom and full kitchen) or one of the cozier (and more affordable) Choice Rooms with a queen-size bed.

The 18-room, circa 1820 **Rhett House Inn** (1009 Craven St., 843/524-9030, www .rhetthouseinn.com, $175–320) is known as the local vacation getaway for the stars. Such arts and entertainment luminaries as Robert Redford, Julia Roberts, Ben Affleck, Barbara Streisand, Dennis Quaid, and Demi Moore have all stayed here at one time or another. Owner Steve Harrison is also a local realtor and no doubt has helped many a guest relocate to town after they've fallen in love with it while staying at his inn. As if Beaufort's great restaurants weren't caloric enough, you can put on a few pounds just staying at the Rhett House. Of course you get the requisite full Southern breakfast, but you'll also be treated to afternoon tea and pastries, more munchies at cocktail hour, and homemade late-night desserts.

There's nothing like enjoying the view of the Beaufort River from the expansive porches of the **(Cuthbert House Inn** (1203 Bay St., 843/521-1315, www.cuthberthouseinn.com, $205–250), possibly the most romantic place to stay in Beaufort. This grand old circa-1790 Federal mansion was once the home of the wealthy Cuthbert family of rice and indigo planters and is now on the National Register of Historic Places. General Sherman himself spent a night here in 1865. Some of the king rooms have fireplaces and clawfoot tubs. Of course you get a full Southern breakfast, in addition to sunset hors d'oeuvres on the veranda.

Situated in a restored 1890 farmhouse smack in the heart of Port Royal's little downtown, the **Beaulieu Guest House at Port Royal** (1103 Paris Ave., Port Royal, 843/770-0303, www .beaulieuhouse.com, $155–225) has three suites to choose from. They claim to have the oldest live oaks in Port Royal on the grounds, which are right next to the historic Union Church.

Camping
Hunting Island State Park (2555 Sea Island Pkwy., 866/345-7275, www.huntingisland .com, daily 6 A.M.–6 P.M., until 9 P.M. DST, $4 adults, $1.50 children, $25 campsites, $87–172 cabins) has 200 campsites on the north end of the island, with individual water and electric hookups. Most are available by reservation only, but 20 are available on a first-come, first-served basis. On the south end the park has 15 two- or three-bedroom cabins for rent, fully heated and air-conditioned and equipped with TVs and kitchens. The cabins sometimes fill up a full year in advance, so book as early as you can. There's a one-week minimum stay during the high season (Mar.–Nov.) and a two-night minimum at other times. Also be aware that checkout time, which is strictly enforced, at the cabins is a chipper 10 A.M.

Another neat place to camp is **Tuck in De Wood** (22 Tuc In De Wood Lane, St. Helena, 843/838-2267, $25 for tent and RV sites), a

74-site campground just past the Penn Center on St. Helena Island.

FOOD
Breakfast and Brunch
One of the best breakfasts I've had anywhere in the world was a humble two-egg plate for five bucks at Beaufort's most popular morning hangout, **(Blackstone's Café** (205 Scott St., 843/524-4330, Mon.–Sat. 7:30 A.M.–2:30 P.M., Sun. 7:30 am.–2 P.M., under $10), complete with unbelievably tasty hash browns, a comparative rarity in this part of the country where grits rule as the breakfast starch of choice. Many come from miles around just for Blackstone's large-portion shrimp-and-grits entrée and "shrimpburger" specials. Tucked on a side street just off busy Bay Street, Blackstone's roomy but inviting interior—festooned with various college, nautical, and military motifs and a checkerboard floor—has more than enough room for you to spread out and relax before continuing on with your travels (there's even free Wi-Fi). The friendly,

Blackstone's Café in Beaufort

chipper waitstaff are on a firm first-name basis with the many regulars, but don't worry—in true Lowcountry fashion, they'll treat you like a regular, too.

Casual Dining
Comfort food mecca **Kathleen's Grill** (822 Bay St., 843/524-2500, daily 11 A.M.–10 P.M., open for breakfast on weekends 7–11 A.M., $7–20) is a longtime favorite of locals and tourists alike. Like most places on Bay Street, indoor dining as well as outdoor dining overlooking the water is available. Start with fried green tomatoes or peel-and-eat shrimp, then move on to one of the house specialties, a grouper or oyster sandwich piled high. Pricier seafood and steak entrées are also available, including a great soft-shell crab plate. Kathleen's is also a nightlife hub, with live music almost every night of the week starting up around 8 P.M. or so, later on Friday and Saturday nights.

Another longtime lunch favorite is **(Magnolia Bakery Café** (703 Congress St., 843/524-1961, Mon.–Sat. 9 A.M.–5 P.M.). It's a little ways north of the usual tourist area, but well worth going out of your way for (Beaufort's pretty small, after all). Lump crab cakes are a particular specialty item, but you can't go wrong with any of the lunch sandwiches. They even offer a serviceable crepe. Veggie diners are particularly well taken care of with a large selection of black bean burger plates. As the name indicates, the range of desserts here is tantalizing, to say the least, with the added bonus of a serious espresso bar.

Luther's Rare & Well Done (910 Bay St., 843/521-1888, daily 10 A.M.–midnight) on the waterfront is the kind of meat-lover's place where even the French onion soup has a morsel of rib eye in it. While the patented succulent, rubbed steaks are a no-brainer here, the hand-crafted specialty pizzas are also quite popular. Housed in a historic pharmacy building, Luther's is also a great place for late eats after many other places in this quiet town have rolled up the sidewalk. A limited menu of appetizers and bar food is available after 10 P.M.

LOWCOUNTRY BOIL

What we now know as "Lowcountry Boil" was originally called Frogmore Stew – not because of any amphibian presence, but for the tiny township on St. Helena Island, South Carolina, where the first pot was made, supposedly by Mr. Richard Gay of the Gay Fish Company. Old-timers still call it Frogmore Stew, however.

As with any vernacular dish, dozens of local and family variants abound. The key ingredient that makes Lowcountry Boil what it is – a well-blended mélange with a character all its own rather than just a bunch of stuff thrown together in a pot of boiling water – is some type of crab boil seasoning. You'll find Zatarain's suggested on a lot of websites, but in my experience Old Bay is far more common in the eponymous Lowcountry where the dish originated.

In any case, here's a simple six-serving Lowcountry Boil recipe to get you started. The only downside to is that it's pretty much impossible to make it for just a few people. The dish is intended for large gatherings, whether a football tailgating party on a Saturday or a family afternoon after church on Sunday. Note the typical ratio of one ear of corn per person and half a pound each of meat and shrimp.

- 6 ears fresh corn on the cob, cut into three-inch sections
- 3 pounds smoked pork sausage, cut into three-inch sections
- 3 pounds fresh shrimp, shells on
- 5 pounds new potatoes
- 6 ounces Old Bay Seasoning

In two gallons of boiling water, put in the sausage and potato pieces with half of the Old Bay. When the potatoes are about half-way done – approximately 15 minutes – put in the corn and boil for about half that time, seven minutes. Add the shrimp and boil for three minutes, until they just turn pink. *Do not overcook the shrimp.* Take the pot off the heat and drain; serve immediately. If you cook the shrimp just right, the oil from the sausage will cause those shells to slip right off.

This is but one of countless recipes. Some cooks add some lemon juice and beer in the water as it's coming to a boil; others add onion, garlic, and/or green peppers.

Fine Dining

The hottest table in town these days is without a doubt at the (**Saltus River Grill** (802 Bay St., 843/379-3474, Sun.–Thurs. 5–9 P.M., Fri.–Sat. 5–10 P.M., $10–39). Executive Chef Jim Spratling has made this fairly new restaurant, housed in a historic tabby building on the waterfront, famous throughout the state for its unbelievable raw bar menu featuring oysters from Nova Scotia to the Chesapeake Bay to Oregon and British Columbia. Sushi lovers can also get a fix here as well, whether it's a basic California roll or great sashimi. Other specialties include she-crab bisque, lump crab cakes, flounder fillet, and of course the ubiquitous shrimp-and-grits. The Saltus River Grill is definitely more upscale in feel and in price than most Lowcountry places, with a very see-and-be-seen type of attitude and a hopping bar. Reservations recommended.

Sharing an owner with the Saltus River Grill is **Plum's** (904½ Bay St., 843/525-1946, daily lunch 11 A.M.–4 P.M., daily dinner 5–10 P.M., $15–25). The short and focused menu keys on daringly prepared entrées highlighting local ingredients, such as the shrimp penne al'amatriciana and fresh black mussel pasta. Because of the outstanding microbrew selection, Plum's is a big nightlife hangout as well; be aware that after 10 P.M., when food service ends but the bar remains open until 2 P.M., it's no longer smoke-free, though there's a friendly porch from which you can get some fresh air and feed the resident cat.

An up-and-comer downtown is **Breakwater Restaurant and Bar** (205 West St., 843/379-0052, www.breakwater-restaurant.com, dinner

Thurs.–Sat. 6–9:30 P.M., bar until 2 A.M., $10–20). The concise menu makes up in good taste what it lacks in comprehensiveness, with an emphasis on seafood, of course, with some especially enticing marine-oriented tapas like diver scallops in a vanilla cognac sauce. Yum!

Right around the corner from Breakwater is **Emily's** (906 Port Republic St., 843/522-1866, dinner Mon.–Sat. 4–10 P.M., bar until 2 A.M., $10–20), a very popular fine dining spot that specializes in a more traditional brand of rich, tasty tapas (available 4–5 P.M.) and is known for its active bar scene.

Coffeehouses

The charming and popular **[Common Ground** (102 West St., 843/524-2326, daily 7:30 A.M.–10 P.M.) coffeehouse on the waterfront park is not only a great place for a light sandwich or sweet treat, the java is a cut above most such places, featuring a wide selection of excellent fair trade "Dancing Goat" brews.

INFORMATION AND SERVICES

The U.S. Postal Service has a **post office** in downtown Beaufort at 501 Charles Street (843/525-9085).

An alternative weekly focusing mostly on the arts is **Lowcountry Weekly** (www .lcweekly.com).

GETTING THERE AND AROUND

While the Marines can fly their F-18s directly into Beaufort Naval Air Station, you won't have that luxury. The closest major airport to Beaufort is the **Savannah/Hilton Head International Airport** (400 Airways Ave., 912/964-0514, airport code SAV, www.savannahairport.com) off I-95 outside Savannah. If you're not going into Savannah for any reason, from the airport the easiest route to the Beaufort area is to take Exit 8 off I-95, and from there take U.S. 278 east to S.C. 170.

Conversely, you could fly into the **Charleston International Airport** (5500 International Blvd., airport code CHS, www .chs-airport.com), but because that facility is on the far north side of Charleston it actually might take you longer to get to Beaufort. From the Charleston Airport the best route south to Beaufort is U.S. 17 south, exiting at U.S. 21 at Gardens Corner and then into Beaufort.

If you're coming into the region by car, I-95 will be your likely primary route, with your main point of entry being Exit 8 off I-95 connecting to U.S. 278.

OUTSIDE BEAUFORT

The areas outside tourist-traveled Beaufort can take you even further back into sepia-toned Americana, into a time of sharecropper homesteads, sturdy oystermen, and an altogether variable and subjective sense of time.

[Penn Center

By leaving town and going over the long, low Richard V. Woods Memorial Bridge over the Beaufort River on the Sea Island Parkway (which eventually turns into U.S. 21), you'll pass through little Lady's Island and eventually reach St. Helena Island. Known to old-timers as Frogmore, the area took back its old, Spanish-derived place name in the 1980s. Today St. Helena Island is most famous for the Penn Center (16 Martin Luther King Jr. Dr., 843/838-2474, www.penn center.com, Mon.–Sat. 11 A.M.–4 P.M., $4 adults, $2 seniors and children), without a doubt the absolute spiritual home of Gullah culture and history.

When you visit here among the preserved live oaks and humble but well-preserved buildings, you'll instantly see why Dr. Martin Luther King Jr. chose this as one of his major retreat and planning sites during the civil rights era. The dream began as early as 1862, when a group of abolitionist Quakers from Philadelphia came down during the Union occupation with the specific goal of teaching recently freed slave children. With a student body of about 50, they were soon joined by African American educator

© JIM MOREKIS

the Penn Center's Butler Building

Charlotte Forten. After Reconstruction, the Penn School continued its mission by offering teaching and agricultural/industrial trade curricula.

The migration of blacks out of the South during World War II took a toll on the school, however, which became a community improvement center after classes ceased in 1948. In the late 1960s, the Southern Christian Leadership Conference used the school as a retreat and planning site, with both the Peace Corps and the Conscientious Objector Programs training here.

In addition to its role as an education and research hub for the study of Gullah culture, the Penn Center continues to serve in an important civil rights role in providing legal counsel to African American homeowners on St. Helena. Because clear title is extremely difficult to acquire in the area due to the fact that so much of the land has stayed in the families of former slaves, developers are constantly making shady offers so that ancestral land can be opened up to upscale development.

The beautiful 50-acre campus of the Penn Center is part of the Penn School Historic District, a National Historic Landmark comprising 19 buildings, most of key historical significance, including Darrah Hall, the oldest building on the campus; the old "Brick Church" right across MLK Jr. Drive; and Gantt Cottage, where Dr. King himself stayed periodically in the 1963–1967 period. Another building, the Retreat House, was intended for Dr. King to continue his yearly strategy meetings, but he was assassinated before being able to stay there. The museum and bookshop are housed in the Cope Building, now called the York W. Bailey Museum, situated right along MLK Jr. Drive. A self-guided nature trail takes you all around the campus. The key public event each year happens each November with the Penn Center Heritage Days, when the entire St. Helena community comes together to celebrate and enjoy entertainment such as the world-famous, locally based Hallelujah Singers.

Continue a few hundred yards down MLK

Jr. Drive past the Penn Center and look for the ancient tabby ruins on the left side of the road. This is the **Chapel of Ease,** the remnant of a 1740 church destroyed by forest fire in the late 1800s.

To get to the Penn Center from Beaufort, proceed over the bridge until you get to St. Helena Island. Take a right when on MLK Jr. Drive when you see the Red Piano Too Art Gallery. The Penn Center is a few hundred yards on your right.

Old Sheldon Church Ruins

A short ways to the north of Beaufort are the poignantly desolate ruins of the once-magnificent Old Sheldon Church (Old Sheldon Church Rd. off U.S. 17 just past Gardens Corner, daily dawn–dusk). Set a couple of miles off the highway on a narrow road, the serene, oak-lined grounds containing this massive, empty edifice give little hint of the violence so intrinsic to its history. One of the first Greek Revival structures in

THE LOST ART OF TABBY

St. Helena Island's Chapel of Ease is a great example of tabby construction.

Let's clear up a couple of misconceptions about tabby, that unique construction technique combining oyster shells, lime, water, and sand found all along the South Carolina and Georgia coast.

First, it did not originate with Native Americans. The confusion is due to the fact that the native population left behind many shell middens, or enormous trash heaps, of oyster shells. These middens indeed provided the bulk of the shells for tabby buildings to come, though Native Americans themselves had little else to do with it.

Secondly, though the Spanish were responsible for the first use of tabby in the Americas, contrary to lore almost all remaining tabby ruins in the area date from later English settlement. The British first fell in love with tabby after the siege of Spanish – held St. Augustine, Florida. General James Oglethorpe, who especially admired the British tabby forts in Port Royal, South the United States, the house of worship held its first service in 1757 as Prince William's Parish Church. The sanctuary was first burned by the British in 1779, mainly because of reports that the Patriots were using it to store gunpowder captured from a British ship. After being rebuilt in 1826, the sanctuary survived until General Sherman's arrival in 1865, whereupon Union troops razed it once more. Nothing remains now but these towering walls and columns, made of red

brick instead of the tabby often seen in similar ruins on the coast. It's now owned by the nearby St. Helena's Episcopal Church in Beaufort, which holds outdoor services here the second Sunday after Easter. In all, an almost painfully compelling bit of history set amid stunning natural beauty, and well worth the short drive.

Oyotunji Village

By continuing north of the Sheldon Church a

Carolina, became an eager advocate for the art in Georgia – so much so that it became known as "Oglethorpe tabby" or "Georgia tabby." A "tabby revival" of sorts, centering in Georgia, took place in the early 1800s, but petered out as the great prehistoric middens began to be depleted.

Scholars remain divided as to whether tabby was invented by West Africans, or its use spread to Africa from Spain and Portugal, circuitously coming to America through the knowledge of imported slaves. The origin of the word itself is also unclear, as similar words exist in Spanish, Portuguese, Gullah, and Arabic to describe various types of wall.

We do know for sure how tabby is made: The primary technique was to burn alternating layers of oyster shells and logs in a deep hole in the ground, thus creating lime. The lime was then mixed with oyster shells, sand, and water and poured into molds to dry and then be used as building blocks, much like large bricks.

Tabby is remarkably strong and resilient, able to easily survive the hurricanes that often batter the area. Its one flaw, however, is a tendency to disintegrate when in contact with living vegetation. That's one reason you'll often find tabby ruins in a clearing (another reason being it's easier to see enemies approach that way).

Here are the best examples of true tabby you can see today:

· Maybe the most imposing living example

of tabby construction is at **Fort Frederica** on St. Simons Island, Georgia. The tough little fort, built in 1736, is still commanding its military presence. There are also tabby ruins of the barracks nearby.

· Several younger tabby buildings still exist in downtown Beaufort: the **Barnwell-Gough House** (705 Washington St.); the magnificent Thomas Fuller House, or **"Tabby Manse"** (1211 Bay St.); and the **Saltus House** on the 800 block of Bay, perhaps the tallest surviving tabby structure.

· **Wormsloe Plantation** near Savannah has the remains of Noble Jones's fortification of the Skidaway Narrows.

· The remarkably intact walls of the **Horton-DuBignon House** on Jekyll Island, Georgia, date from 1738, and the house was occupied into the 1850s.

· The **Chapel of Ease** off Land's End Road on St. Helena Island, South Carolia, dates from the 1740s. If someone tells you Sherman burned it down, don't believe them; the culprit was a forest fire in 1886.

· Surrounding the **Haig Point Lighthouse** on Daufuskie Island, South Carolina, are the original foundations of the old Haig Point Mansion, considered the largest tabby structure ever built, razed by Union troops in 1861. Some ruins of tabby slave quarters are also nearby.

Old Sheldon Church ruins

short ways, the more adventurous can find the most quirky of all Lowcountry attractions, the Oyotunji Village (56 Bryant Lane, 843/846-8900, hours vary). Built in 1970 by self-proclaimed "King" Ofuntola Oseijeman Adelabu Adefunmi I, a former used car dealer with an interesting past, Oyotunji claims to be North America's only authentic African village, with 5–10 families residing on its 30 acres. It also claims to be a separate kingdom and not a part of the United States—though I'm sure the State Department begs to differ. With a mission to preserve the religious and cultural aspects of Yoruba Orisa culture of West Africa, each spring the village hosts an annual Warrior's Festival, celebrating traditional male rites of passage. Truth is, there's not much to see here but a few poorly built "monuments." But connoisseurs of roadside Americana will no doubt be pleased.

Yemassee

Going still further north on U.S. 17 you'll come to the small town of Yemassee. Its main claim to fame is nearby **Auldbrass,** designed by Frank Lloyd Wright in 1939. The home is privately owned by Hollywood producer Joel Silver, but rare, much-sought-after tours happen every other year in November through the auspices of the Beaufort County Open Land Trust. To find out about the next tour and to get on the list, email your mailing address to bcolt2@islc.net or call 843/521-2175 to receive ticket information the summer prior.

Port Royal

This sleepy little town of about 4,000 nestled between Beaufort and Parris Island touts itself as a leader in "small town New Urbanism." This is certainly true, with its manicured emphasis on livability, retro-themed shopping areas, and relaxing walking trails. However, Port Royal is still pretty sleepy—but not without very real charms, not the least of which is the fact that everything in town is within easy walking distance of everything else.

The highlight of the year is the annual Soft Shell Crab Festival, held each April to mark

© JIM MOREKIS

Port Royal is a charming fishing town.

the short-lived harvesting season for that favorite crustacean. Indeed, the rhythms of the
sea mean everything to Port Royal, as indicated
by the recent hubbub over a proposal to close
the town's Port Authority dock. Though the
controversy happened at the height of the season, anxious shrimp-boat captains refused to
leave the dock for fear that demolition might
begin in the middle of the night while they
were offshore.

While much of the tiny historic district has a
scrubbed, tidy feel, the main historic structure
is the charming little **Union Church** (11th St.,
843/524-4333, Mon.–Fri. 10 A.M.–4 P.M.), one
of the oldest buildings in town, with guided
docent tours.

Don't miss the new boardwalk and observation tower at **The Sands** municipal beach and
boat ramp. The 50-foot-tall structure provides
a commanding view of the gorgeous Battery
Creek. To get to The Sands, go to 7th Street
and then turn onto Sands Beach Road.

Another environmentally oriented point of
pride is the new **Lowcountry Estuarium** (1402

Paris Ave., 843/524-6600, www.lowcountry
estuarium.org, Fri. and Sat. 10 A.M.–5 P.M.,
feedings at 11:30 A.M. and 3 P.M., $4 adults,
$2 children). The point of the facility is to give
hands-on opportunities to learn more about
the flora and fauna of the various ecosystems of
the Lowcountry, such as salt marshes, beaches,
and estuaries.

Parris Island

Though more commonly known as the home
of the legendary **Marine Corps Recruit Depot
Parris Island** (283 Blvd. de France, 843/228-
3650, www.mcrdpi.usmc.mil, free), the island
is also of extreme historic significance as the
site of some of the oldest European presence
in America. The U.S. Marine Corps began its
association with Parris Island in 1891, though
the island's naval roots actually go back to its
use as a coaling station during the long Union
occupation. By the outbreak of World War
I, a full-blown military town had sprung up,
now with its own presence on the National
Register of Historic Places. In November 1915.

Parris Island officially went in business as a recruit depot, and today it's where all female Marine recruits and all male recruits east of the Mississippi River go through the infamous, grueling 13-week boot camp.

Currently about 19,000 recruits are processed each year—2,000 of them women—with almost every Friday during the year marking the graduation of a company of newly minted Marines. That's why you might notice an influx of visitors to the area each Thursday, a.k.a. "Family Day," with the requisite amount of celebration on Fridays after that morning's ceremony. This begins a 10-day leave period, after which the recruits go to Camp Lejeune, North Carolina. Unlike many military facilities in the post-9/11 era, Parris Island still hosts plenty of visitors, about 120,000 a year. While the vast majority come by invitation only to witness one of the weekly graduations, a few important facilities exist of interest to the history buff. But word to the wise: Thursdays and Fridays can get crowded.

The **Parris Island Museum** (Bldg. 111, 111 Panama St., 843/228-2951, daily 8:30 A.M.–4:30 P.M.) near the entrance not only lovingly details the entire U.S. military experience in the area, but also features many surprisingly good exhibits on the area's earliest colonial history. The Spanish built Santa Elena directly on top of the original French settlement, Charlesfort. They then built two other settlements, San Felipe and San Marcos. All are now on the circa-1950s depot golf course and available to the public for self-guided tours. Archaeological exploration has continued since 1979, with intensive research on the long-lost Santa Elena/Charlesfort site (http://santaelena.us), now a National Historic Landmark, beginning in the late 1990s. Many artifacts are viewable at the nearby clubhouse/interpretive center, open daily 7 A.M.–5 P.M.

The **Douglas Visitor Center** (Bldg. 283, Blvd. de France, 843/228-3650, Mon. 7:30 A.M.–noon, Tues. and Wed. 7:30 A.M.–4:30 P.M., Thurs. 6:30 A.M.–7 P.M., Fri. 7:30 A.M.–3 P.M.) is a great place to find maps and touring information. All visitors to the

Parris Island Recruit Depot must get a pass at the gate. You must have a valid driver's license, registration, and proof of insurance. Rental car drivers must show a copy of the rental agreement. Do *not* use your cell phone while driving. While Parris Island kindly welcomes visitors, be aware that all traffic rules within the camp are strictly enforced, and your vehicle is subject to inspection at any time.

C Hunting Island

Rumored to be a hideaway for Blackbeard himself, the aptly named Hunting Island was indeed for many years a notable hunting preserve, and its incredible abundance of wildlife holds true to this day. The island is one of the East Coast's best birding spots, and you can also spot dolphins, loggerheads, alligators, and deer. However, thanks to preservation efforts by President Franklin Roosevelt and the Civilian Conservation Corps, the island is no longer for hunting but for sheer enjoyment. And enjoy it people do, to the tune of a million visitors a year.

A true family-family friendly outdoor adventure spot, **Hunting Island State Park** (2555 Sea Island Pkwy., 866/345-7275, www.huntingisland.com, daily 6 A.M.–6 P.M., until 9 P.M. DST, $4 adults, $1.50 children) has something for everyone—kids, parents, and newlyweds. Yet it still retains a certain sense of lush wildness—so much so that it doubled as Vietnam in *Forrest Gump*. At the north end past the campground is the island's main landmark, the historic Hunting Island Light, which dates from 1875. Though the lighthouse ceased operations in 1933, a rotating light—not strong enough to serve an actual navigational aid—is turned on at night. While the 167-step trek to the top ($2 donation per person) is quite strenuous, the view from the little observation area at the top of the lighthouse is stunning, a complete panorama of Hunting Island and much of the Lowcountry coast.

At the south end of the island is a marsh walk, nature trail, and a fishing pier complete with a cute little nature center. Hunting Island's three miles of beautiful beaches also serve as a major center of loggerhead turtle nesting and hatching, a process that begins around June as the mothers lay their eggs and culminates in late summer and early fall, when the hatchlings make their daring dash to the sea. At all phases the turtles are strictly protected, and while there are organized events to witness the hatching of the eggs, it is strictly forbidden to touch or otherwise disturb the turtles or their nests. Contact the park ranger for more detailed information.

Getting to Hunting Island couldn't be easier—just take the Sea Island Parkway (U.S. 21) about 20 minutes beyond Beaufort and you'll run right into it.

Fripp Island

If you keep driving past Hunting Island you'll reach Fripp Island, one of South Carolina's totally private, developed barrier islands. Unlike its more egalitarian neighbor, Fripp only welcomes visitors who are guests of the **Fripp Island Golf and Beach Resort** (800/845-4100, www.frippislandresort.com), which offers a range of lodging from oceanfront homes to villas to golf cottages. Family-friendly recreation abounds, not only in 36 holes of high-caliber golf, but in over three miles of uncrowded beach. A major allure is Camp Fripp, providing activities for kids.

◀ ACE Basin National Wildlife Refuge

Occupying pretty much the entire area between Beaufort and Charleston, the ACE Basin—the acronym signifies its role as the collective estuary of the Ashepoo, Combahee, and Edisto Rivers—is one of the most enriching natural experiences America has to offer. The Basin's three core rivers, the Edisto being the largest, are the framework for a matrix of waterways criss-crossing its approximately 350,000 acres of salt marsh. It's this intimate relationship with the tides that makes the area so enjoyable, and also what attracted so many rice plantations throughout its history (canals and dikes from the old rice paddies are still visible throughout). Other uses have included

tobacco, corn, and lumbering. While the ACE Basin can in no way be called "pristine," it's a testament to the power of nature that after 6,000 years of human presence and often intense cultivation the Basin manages to retains much of its untamed feel.

The ACE Basin is so big that it is actually broken up into several parts for management purposes under the umbrella of the ACE Basin Project (www.acebasin.net), a task force begun in 1988 by the state of South Carolina, the U.S. Fish and Wildlife Service, and various private firms and conservation groups. The Project is now considered a model for responsible watershed preservation techniques in a time of often rampant coastal development. A host of species, both common and endangered, thrive in the area, including wood storks, alligators, sturgeon, loggerheads, teals, and bald eagles.

About 12,000 acres of the ACE Basin Project comprise the Ernest F. Hollings ACE Basin National Wildlife Refuge (8675 Willtown Rd., 843/889-3084, www.fws.gov/acebasin, grounds open year-round daylight–dark, office open weekdays 7:30 A.M.–4 P.M.), run by the U.S. Fish and Wildlife Service. The historic 1828 Grove Plantation House is in this portion of the Basin and in fact houses the refuge's headquarters. It's an interesting attraction in and of itself and is sometimes featured on local tours of homes. To get to the refuge's main entrance, take U.S. 17 to SC 174, and turn right onto Willtown Road. The entrance road is two miles from there.

About 135,000 acres of the Basin falls under the protection of the South Carolina Department of Natural Resources as part of the **National Estuarine Research Reserve System** (www.nerrs.noaa.gov/acebasin). The South Carolina DNR also runs two Wildlife Management Areas, **Donnelly WMA** (843/844-8957, www.dnr.sc.gov, Mon.–Sat. 8 A.M.–5 P.M. year-round) and **Bear Island WMA** (843/844-8957, www.dnr.sc.gov, Feb. 1–Oct. 14 Mon.–Sat., dawn–dusk), both of which provide rich opportunities for birding and wildlife observation.

Over 128,000 acres of the ACE Basin Project are permanently protected through conservation easements, management agreements, and fee title purchases. While traditional uses such as farming, fishing, and hunting do indeed continue in the ACE Basin, the area is off-limits to the gated communities, which are sprouting like mildew all along the Carolina coast. Because it is so well defended, the ACE Basin also functions like a huge outdoor laboratory for the coastal scientific community, with constant research going on in botany, zoology, microbiology, and marine science.

Food

If you find yourself in charming little Port Royal, try the waterfront seafood haven **11th Street Dockside** (1699 11th St., Port Royal, 843/524-7433, daily 4:30–10 P.M., $17–27). The Dockside Dinner is a great sampler plate with lobster tail, scallops, crab legs, and shrimp, and the views of the waterfront and the adjoining shrimp-boat docks are relaxing and beautiful.

For more upscale dining in Port Royal, try **《 Bateaux** (610 Paris Ave., Port Royal, 843/379-0777, www.bateauxrestaurant.net, Mon.–Sat. 5–9 P.M., $20–30). On Lady's Island for many years, Bateaux has moved a few miles away to a new Port Royal location in the historic Customs House downtown. It's highly regarded for its adventurous small-plate items such as foie gras and scallops, and its daring Lowcountry seafood creations such as the Bateaux seafood stew. Reservations recommended.

A Lady's Island hot spot is the very casual **Steamer Oyster and Steak House** (168 Sea Island Pkwy., 843/522-0210, daily 11 A.M.– 9:30 P.M., $15–20). The big hit here is the Frogmore stew, a.k.a. Lowcountry Boil.

For vegan/vegetarian soups, salads, and sandwiches on Lady's Island, jump across the Beaufort River Bridge a short ways and try **It's Only Natural** (45 Factory Creek Court, 843/986-9595, Mon.–Fri. 8 A.M.–6 P.M., Sat. 9 A.M.–4:30 P.M., $5). It's visible right off the main road, the Sea Island Parkway (U.S. 21). They also offer a range of health food items and produce.

Right before you take a right to get to the Penn Center on St. Helena Island is **Gullah Grub** (877 Sea Island Pkwy., 843/838-3841, Mon.–Thurs. 11:30 A.M.–7 P.M., under $20), an unpretentious, one-room lunch spot focusing on down-home Southern specialties with a Lowcountry touch, such as hushpuppies, collard greens, and shrimp-'n'-shark.

Information and Services

The nice, new, Chamber of Commerce–run **Beaufort Visitors Information Center** (1106 Carteret St., 843/986-5400, daily 9 A.M.– 5:30 P.M., www.beaufortsc.org) is easy to find as you enter the historic district.

The daily newspaper of record in Beaufort is the *Beaufort Gazette* (www.beaufort gazette.com).

Hilton Head Island

Literally the prototype of the modern planned resort community, Hilton Head Island is also a case study in how quickly and utterly a landscape can change when enough money is introduced. Once consisting almost entirely of African Americans with deep historic roots in the area, in the mid-1950s Hilton Head began its transformation into an almost all-white, upscale golf, tennis, and shopping mecca populated largely by northern transplants and retirees. As you can imagine, the flavor here is now quite different from surrounding areas of the Lowcountry, to say the least, with an emphasis on material excellence, top prices, get-it-done-yesterday punctuality, and the attendant aggressive traffic.

Giving credit where it's due, however, Hilton Head knows what its target audience is and delivers the goods in a thoroughly professional manner. While it's easy to dismiss it as a sort of Disney World for the elite—a disjointed collection of gated communities comprising 70 percent of its area—the truth is that millions of visitors—not

BEAUFORT

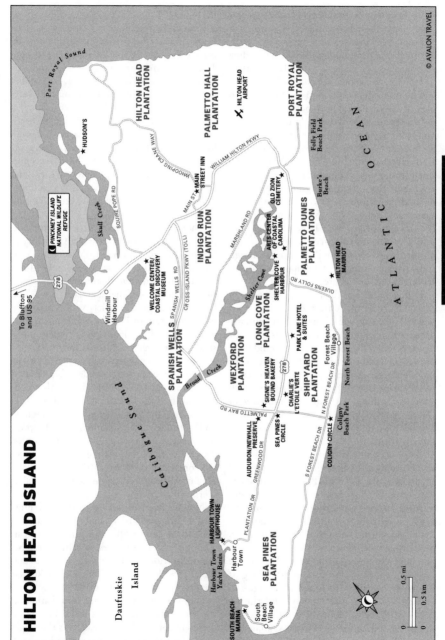

all of them elite by any stretch—not only enjoy what Hilton Head has to offer, they swear by it, returning year after year. The attraction is quality, whether in the stunning beaches, outstanding cultural offerings, plush accommodations, attentive service, or copious merchandise.

The intentional elimination of risk is also part of the island's appeal, both to the senior demographic as well as the family segment. You won't see any litter during your stay, and you're very unlikely to experience any crime. Certainly that's to Hilton Head's credit and no small reason for its continued success.

One of the great unsung positive aspects of modern Hilton Head is its dedication to sustainable living. With the support of voters, the town routinely buys large tracts of land to preserve as open space. Seemingly every hundred yards or so you'll come across a sign indicating how many acres have been preserved in the immediate area.

Hilton Head was the first municipality in the country to mandate the burying of all power lines, and one of the first to regularly use covenants and deed restrictions. All new development must conform to rigid guidelines on setbacks and tree canopy. It has one of the most comprehensive signage ordinances in the country as well, which means no garish commercial displays will disrupt your views of the night sky. If those are "elite" values, then certainly we might do well in making them more mainstream.

Just outside Hilton Head are two of the Lowcountry's true gems, Bluffton and Daufuskie Island. While Bluffton's outskirts have been taken over by the same gated community sprawl spreading throughout the coast, at its core is a delightfully charming little community on the quiet May River, now called Old Bluffton, where you'd swear you just entered a time warp. Daufuskie Island, though home to a top-flight golf resort, still maintains much of its age-old isolated, timeless personality, and the island—still accessible by boat only—is still one of the spiritual centers of the Gullah culture and lifestyle.

HISTORY

The second-largest barrier island on the East Coast, Hilton Head Island was inhabited by Native Americans at least 10,000 years ago. The first European to sight the island was Spain's Francisco Cordillo in 1521, but it didn't enter mainstream consciousness until the 1663 sighting by Sir William Hilton, who thoughtfully named the island—with its notable headland or "Head"—after himself. Hilton, who like many of Charleston's original settlers was from the British colony of Barbados, was purposely trying to drum up interest in the island as a commercial venture, famously describing his new namesake as having "sweet water" and "clear sweet air."

Though Hilton Head wasn't the first foothold of English colonization in Carolina, as Hilton wanted it to be, it did acquire commercial status first as the home of several rice and indigo plantations. Later it gained fame as the first location of the legendary "Sea Island Cotton," a long-grain variety which, following its introduction in 1790 by William Elliott II of the Myrtle Bank Plantation, would soon be the dominant version of the cash crop.

Hilton Head planters were outspoken in the cause of American independence. The chief pattern in the Lowcountry during that conflict involved the British raiding Hilton Head and surrounding areas from their stronghold on Daufuskie, burning plantations and capturing slaves to be resold in Caribbean colonies. As a reminder of the savage guerrilla nature of the conflict in the South, British hit-and-run raids on Hilton Head continued for weeks after Cornwallis surrendered.

Nearby Bluffton was settled by planters from Hilton Head Island and the surrounding area in the early 1800s as a summer retreat. Though Charleston likes to claim the label today, Bluffton was actually the genuine "cradle of secession." Indeed, locals still joke that the town motto is "Divided We Stand."

Fort Walker, a Confederate installation on the site of the modern Port Royal Plantation development on Hilton Head, was the target of the largest fleet ever assembled in North

America at the time, when a massive Union force sailed into Port Royal Sound in October 1861. A month later, the Fort—and effectively the entire area—had fallen, though by that time most white residents had long since fled. During the Civil War, Bluffton was also evacuated and, like Hilton Head, escaped serious action. However, in June 1863, Union troops destroyed most of the town of Bluffton except for about a dozen homes and two churches.

Though it seems unlikely given the island's modern demographics, Hilton Head was almost entirely African American through much of the 20th century. Given its role as a plantation site, the population was always mostly African American, becoming even more so when Union troops occupied the island at the outbreak of the Civil War. Freed and escaped slaves flocked to the island, and most of the dwindling number of African Americans on the island today are descendants of this original Gullah population.

For the first half of the 20th century, logging was Hilton Head's main commercial pursuit. Things didn't take their modern shape until the 1950s, when the Fraser family bought 19,000 of the island's 25,000 acres with the intent to continue forestry on them. But in 1956—not at all coincidentally the same year the first bridge to the island was built—Charles Fraser convinced his father to sell him the southern tip of Hilton Head Island. Fraser's brainchild and decades-long labor of love—some said his obsession—Sea Pines Plantation was the prototype of the golf-oriented resort community so common today on both U.S. coasts.

Though Fraser himself was killed in a boating accident in 2002, he survived to see Sea Pines encompass much of Hilton Head's economic activity, including Harbour Town, and to see the Town of Hilton Head incorporated in 1983. Fraser is buried under the famous Liberty Oak in Harbour Town, which he personally made sure wasn't harmed during the development of the area.

ORIENTATION

Hilton Head Islanders have long referred to their island as the "shoe" (and speak of driving to the toe, going to the heel, etc.). If you take a look at a map, you'll see why. Hilton Head bears an uncanny resemblance to a running shoe in action pointed toward the southeast, with the aptly named Broad Creek forming a near facsimile of the Nike "swoosh" symbol.

Running the length and circumference of the shoe is the undisputed main drag, U.S. 278 Business (William Hilton Parkway), which crosses onto Hilton Head right at the "tongue" of the shoe, a relatively undeveloped area where there are still a few old African American communities. The new Cross Island Parkway toll route (U.S. 278), beginning up toward the ankle as you first get on the island, is a quicker, much more convenient route straight to the toe near Sea Pines.

While it is technically the business spur, when locals say "278" they're talking about the William Hilton Parkway, which takes you the entire sole of the shoe, including the beaches and on down to the toe, where you'll find a confusing, crazy British-style roundabout called Sea Pines Circle. It's also the site of the Harbour Town Marina and the island's oldest planned development, Sea Pines Plantation.

There's no "town center" per se, but activity here tends to revolve around just a few places: the Shelter Cove mall and residential development near the entrance to the island; Coligny Plaza, an older, more casual shopping center near the main beach entrance; Sea Pines Circle, a center of nightlife; and two spots within Sea Pines itself, Harbour Town and South Beach—the former a blend of upscale and family attractions, and the latter catering a bit more to the beach crowd.

While precious little history is left on Hilton Head, place names reverberate with the names of key figures long-gone: Cordillo Parkway, named for the first Spaniard to come to the area; Coligny Plaza, named for the admiral who sent the first French expedition to the area; and Ribault Road, named for the leader of that expedition. In any case, while making your way around the island always keep in mind that the bulk of it consists of private developments, and local law enforcement frowns

BEAUFORT

on people who aimlessly wander among the condos and villas.

SIGHTS

Contrary to what many think, there are actually quite a few things to do on Hilton Head that don't involve swinging a club at a little white ball or shopping for designer labels, but instead celebrate the area's rich history and natural setting. Below is a list of those attractions, arranged in geographical order from where you first access the island.

◖ Pinckney Island National Wildlife Refuge

Though actually consisting of many islands and hammocks, Pinckney Island NWR (912/652-4415, daily dawn–dusk, free) is the only part of this small but very well-managed 4,000-acre refuge that's open to the public. Almost 70 percent of the former rice plantation is salt marsh and tidal creeks, making it a perfect microcosm for the Lowcountry as a whole. Native Americans liked the area as well, with an approximately 10,000-year presence, with over 100 archaeological sites being identified to date. Like many coastal refuges, it was a private game preserve for much of the 20th century. Some of the state's richest birding opportunities abound here, with observers able to spot gorgeous white ibis, rare wood storks, herons, egrets, eagles, and ospreys with little trouble from its miles of trails.

Getting there is easy: On U.S. 278 east to Hilton Head, the refuge entrance is right between the two bridges onto the island. There are no restrooms or water.

Coastal Discovery Museum

Surprisingly in an area as awash in money as Hilton Head, the island abounds with small, underfunded, but worthwhile endeavors such as the Coastal Discovery Museum (100 William Hilton Pkwy., 843/689-6767, www .coastaldiscovery.org, Mon.–Sat. 9 A.M.–5 P.M., Sun. 10 A.M.–2 P.M., free) just as you get onto Hilton Head. The exhibits here are small-scale but heartfelt, like the excellent little dioramas

of traditional island life. The Museum hosts a variety of specialty guided tours, such as a Native Americans on the Sea Islands tour, a Pinckney Island walking tour, and a Sea Pines Plantation Overview. The cost for most of the tours is $12 adults, $7 children.

The Museum is a partner with the state in a sea turtle protection program, which you can learn more about once there. Standing exhibits include a historical timeline of Hilton Head, a Butterfly Garden, and the Sea Island Biodiversity Room, intended for use with local schoolchildren (the Museum helps develop science curricula for local schools) but fully available to the public. The Museum also plays an important role locally as the steward of the 68-acre **Honey Horn** greenspace at the intersection of the Cross Island Parkway and U.S. 278. Purchased by the town in the late 1990s, the plan is for the Honey Horn parcel, which contains several historic structures, to be a cultural attraction preserving the heritage of the island. Currently many annual events are hosted there, including wine tastings and the annual Chili Cookoff.

Green's Shell Enclosure

Less-known than the larger Native American shell ring farther south at Sea Pines, the Green's Shell Enclosure (803/734-3886, daily dawn–dusk) is certainly easier to find and you don't have to pay five bucks to enter the area, as with Sea Pines. This three-acre Heritage Preserve dates back to at least the 1300s. The heart of the site comprises a low embankment, part of the original fortified village. To get here, take a left at the intersection of U.S. 278 and Squire Pope Road. Turn left into Greens Park, pass the office on the left, and the entrance to the shell enclosure is on the left. Park and walk the rest of the way. No camping.

Zion Chapel of Ease Cemetery

More like one of the gloriously desolate scenes common to the rest of the Lowcountry, this little cemetery in full view of the William Hilton Parkway at Folly Field Road is all that remains of one of the "Chapels of Ease," a string of chapels set up in the 1700s. The cemetery (daily dawn–dusk, free) is said to be haunted by the ghost of William Baynard, whose final resting place is in a mausoleum on-site (the remains of his ancestral home are farther south at Sea Pines Plantation).

Audubon-Newhall Preserve

Plant lovers shouldn't miss this small but very well-maintained 50-acre wooded tract in the south-central part of the island on Palmetto Bay Road between the Cross Island Parkway and Sea Pines circle. Almost all plant life, even that in the water, is helpfully marked and identified, but if all you want to do is just enjoy, that's fine too, because the preserve has two miles of nature trails. Unusually, there's a well-preserved bog environment (*pocosin* to the indigenous tribes here). The preserve is open dawn to dusk year-round and it's free and open to the public—but you can't camp here, though it sure is inviting. For more information, call the Hilton Head Audubon Society at 843/842-9246.

Harbour Town

Okay, it's not that historic and not all that natural, but Harbour Town is still pretty cool. Everybody loves the huge, colorful **Harbour Town Lighthouse** (149 Lighthouse Rd.), which has never really helped a ship navigate its way to the island. The 90-foot structure was built in 1970 purely to give the tourists a little atmosphere, and that it does, as kids especially love climbing the stairs to the top (at $2 per person, that is) and looking out over the island's expanse. This being Hilton Head, of course, there's a gift shop at the top, too. The other attraction here is the boisterous café and shopping scene around the marina and the nearby park area. The public can access Sea Pines Plantation, which contains Harbour Town, but it'll cost you a $5 "road use fee." It's worth it especially if you also pay a visit to the following Sea Pines attractions.

Stoney-Baynard Ruins

These tabby ruins on Plantation Drive in Sea Pines are what remains of the circa-1790

central building of the old Braddock's Point Plantation, first owned by patriot and raconteur Captain "Saucy Jack" Stoney and then the Baynard family. Active during the island's heyday as a cotton center, the plantation was destroyed after the Civil War. Two other foundations are nearby, one for slave quarters and one whose use is still unknown. It's open dawn–dusk and it's free, but there is that $5 fee to enter Sea Pines.

Sea Pines Forest Preserve

The Sea Pines Forest Preserve (175 Greenwood Dr., 843/363-4530, free) is set amid the famous Sea Pines Plantation golf resort development at the extreme southern end of the island, the first such development of its kind anywhere. You don't need a bag of golf clubs to enjoy this 600-acre preserve, built on the site of an old rice plantation (dikes and logging trails are still visible as you tread the elevated boardwalks over the marsh). Here you can ride a horse, ride your bike, fish, or just take a walk on the eight miles of trails (open dawn–dusk) and enjoy the natural beauty around you.

Hilton Head may not by synonymous with archaeology in your mind, but the Sea Pines Forest Preserve boasts a Native American shell ring, one of only about 20 such sites on the East Coast. A combination ceremonial area and communal common space, the shell ring today is actually a series of low rings made of discarded oyster shells covered with earth. Scientists date the ring itself to about 1450 B.C., though human habitation on the island goes as far back as 8000 B.C.

Tours

Almost all guided tours on Hilton Head focus on the water. **Harbour Town Cruises** (843/363-9023, www.vagabondcruise.com) offers several sightseeing tours, as well as excursions to Daufuskie and Savannah. They also offer a tour on a former America's Cup racing yacht.

"Dolphin tours" are extremely popular on Hilton Head and there is no shortage of proprietors. **Dolphin Watch Nature**

Cruises (843/785-4558, $25 adults, $10 children) departs from Shelter Cove, as does **Lowcountry Nature Tours** (843/683-0187, $40 adult, $35 children, two and under free). **The Gypsy** (843/363-2900, $12 adults, $6 children) sails out of South Beach Marina on the Oceanside, taking you all around peaceful Calibogue Sound.

Two dolphin tours are based on Broad Creek, the large body of water which almost bisects the island through the middle. "Captain Jim" runs **Island Explorer Tours** (843/785-2100, $40 per person for two-hour tour) from a dock behind the old Oyster Factory on Marshland Road. Not to be outdone, "Captain Dave" leads tours at **Dolphin Discoveries** (843/681-1911 $40 adults, $30 children 12 and under for two-hour tour), leaving out of Simmons Landing next to the Broad Creek Marina on Marshland Road.

Outside Hilton Head (843/686-6996, www.outsidehiltonhead.com) runs a variety of eco/dolphin waterborne tours as well as a guided day-trip excursion to Daufuskie complete with golf cart rental. **Calibogue Cruises** (843/342-8687, thehiltonhead-daufuskie connection.com) provides a similar service.

For an in-depth look at Hilton Head's rich Gullah history, you might want to call **Gullah Heritage Trail Tours** (843/681-7066, www .gullahheritage.com, $22 adults, $11 children), which departs from the Coastal Discovery Museum Wednesday–Saturday 10 A.M. and 2 P.M., Sunday 2 P.M.

ENTERTAINMENT AND EVENTS
Nightlife

The crowd is definitely on the older side, but without a doubt the most high-quality live entertainment on the island is at **The Jazz Corner** (1000 William Hilton Pkwy., 843/842-8620, www.thejazzcorner.com, dinner daily 6–9 P.M., late-night menu after 9 P.M.), which brings in the best names in the country—and outstanding regulars like Bob Masteller and Howard Paul—to perform in this space in the somewhat unlikely setting of a boutique mall,

the Village at Wexford. The dinners are great, but the attraction here is definitely the music. Reservations recommended. Live music starts around 7 P.M.

Hip professionals are the target clientele at the dance club **Stages** (33 Office Park Rd., 843/686-3545), which operated for years under the name Monkey Business. Like many nightlife spots on the island, it's within a shopping center—this one a part of the notorious "Barmuda Triangle," so named for the preponderance of bars within walking distance of Sea Pines Circle.

The longtime heart of the Barmuda Triangle is the **Tiki Hut** (1 S. Forest Beach Dr., 843/785-5126, Sun.–Thurs. 11 A.M.–8 P.M., Fri.–Sat. 11 A.M.–10 P.M., bar until 2 A.M.), actually part of the Holiday Inn Oceanfront Hotel at the entrance to Sea Pines. This popular watering hole is the only beachfront bar on the island, which technically makes it the only place you can legally drink alcohol on a Hilton Head beach.

Another Barmuda Triangle staple is **Casey's Sports Bar and Grille** (37 New Orleans Rd., 843/785-2255, daily 11 A.M.–2 A.M.), which despite its moniker and its 40 TVs is not just for sports fans—there's also a lively karaoke scene.

Inside Sea Pines is the **Quarterdeck Lounge and Patio** (843/842-1999, www.seapines.com, Sun.–Thurs. 5:30–10 P.M., Fri.–Sat. 5:30 P.M.–midnight) at the base of the Harbour Town Lighthouse. This is where the party's at after a long day on the fairways during the Verizon Heritage golf tournament.

Within Sea Pines is also where you'll find **The Salty Dog Cafe** (232 S. Sea Pines Dr., 843/671-2233, www.saltydog.com, lunch daily 11 A.M.–3 P.M., dinner daily 5–10 P.M., bar daily until 2 A.M.), one of the South Beach area's most popular institutions (some might even call it a tourist trap) and something akin to an island empire, with popular T-shirts, a gift shop, books, and an ice cream shop, all overlooking the marina. It's a fun place at night, with live entertainment and a fun-loving, reasonably diverse crowd.

Margaritas are great here, but skip the food; if you're hungry, try the affiliated Wreck of the Salty Dog nearby.

Performing Arts

Because so many of its residents migrated here from art-savvy metropolitan areas in the northeast, Hilton Head maintains a very high standard of top-quality entertainment. Much of the activity centers on the multimillion-dollar **Arts Center of Coastal Carolina** (14 Shelter Cove Ln., 843/842-2787, www.artshhi.com), which hosts touring shows, resident companies, musical concerts, dance performances, and visual arts exhibits.

Now over a quarter-century old and under the masterful direction of maestro Mary Woodmansee Green, the **Hilton Head Symphony Orchestra** (843/842-2055, www.hhso.org) performs a year-round season of masterworks and pops programs, generally at the First Presbyterian Church (540 William Hilton Pkwy.). They also take their show on the road with several concerts in Bluffton, and even perform several "Symphony Under the Stars" programs at Shelter Cove.

Chamber Music Hilton Head (www.cmhh.org) performs throughout the year with selections ranging from Brahms to Smetana at All Saints Episcopal Church (3001 Meeting St.).

The **South Carolina Repertory Company** (136B Beach City Rd., Studio B, 843/342-2057, www.hiltonheadtheatre.com) performs an eclectic, challenging season, from musicals (*Tomfoolery*) to cutting-edge drama (*The Drawer Boy*) to the outright avant-garde (*Some Things you Need to Know Before the World Ends [A Final Evening with the Illuminati]*).

Film

There's an art house on Hilton Head, the charming little **Coligny Theatre** (843/686-3500, www.colignytheatre.com) in the Coligny Plaza shopping center before you get to Sea Pines. For years this was the only movie theatre for miles around, but it reincarnated as a primarily indie film venue in 2002. Look for the entertaining murals by local artist Ralph Sutton.

The main multiplex on Hilton Head is **Northridge Cinema 10** (Hwy. 278 and Mathews Dr., 843/342-3800, www.southeastcinemas.com) in the Northridge Plaza shopping center. Off the island is the way-cool new **Sea Turtle Cinemas** (106 Buckwalter Pkwy., 843/706-2888, www.seaturtlecinemas.com) in the Berkeley Place shopping center. To get there take the William Hilton Parkway/U.S. 278 west off Hilton Head about 10 miles. Turn left at Buckwalter Parkway. Sea Turtle Cinemas is a half-mile on the right.

Festivals and Events

Late February and early March brings the Hilton Head **WineFest** (www.hiltonheadhospitality.org), which culminates in what they call "The East Coast's Largest Outdoor Public Tasting and Auction" in Shelter Cove Community Park. Some events charge admission.

A small but delightful event is the **Hilton Head Quilt Festival** (www.palmettoquiltguild.org), sponsored each March by the Palmetto Quilt Guild and held at the St. Andrew by the Sea Methodist Church. A nominal fee gets you in to see a display of over 100 handcrafted quilts.

Hilton Head's premier event is the **Verizon Heritage Classic Golf Tournament** (843/671-2248, www.verizonheritage.com), held each April at the Harbour Town Golf Links on Sea Pines Plantation. Formerly known as the MCI Heritage Classic, the event is South Carolina's only PGA Tour event and brings thousands of visitors to town yearly.

September brings one of Hilton Head's most beloved events, the **Food Fest** (www.hiltonheadhospitality.org). Activity centers on the Shelter Cove shopping district, and features diverse culinary entertainment such as a Drink Making Contest, a Tailgate Gourmet Challenge, and a Hospitable Waiters Race. Some events charge admission.

A fairly new event happens each October in Bluffton, the **Arts & Seafood Festival** (www.blufftonartsandseafoodfestival.com). The emphasis is on locally harvested shrimp and oysters. A 5K run is featured on Saturday morning, with Sunday bringing a traditional Blessing of the Fleet ceremony on the river.

A fun and fondly anticipated yearly event is the **Kiwanis Club Chili Cookoff** (www.hilton headkiwanis.org), held each October at Honey Horn on the island's south end. A low admission price gets you all the chili you can eat plus free antacids. All funds go to charity, and all excess chili goes to a local food bank.

Every November brings Hilton Head's second-largest event, the world-famous **Hilton Head Concours d'Elegance & Motoring Festival** (www.hhiconcours.com), a multiday event bringing together vintage car clubs from throughout the nation, culminating in a prestigious "Best of Show" competition.

SHOPPING

As you'd expect, Hilton Head is a shopper's delight, with an emphasis on upscale stores and prices to match. Keep in mind that hours may be shortened in the off-season (Nov.–Mar.). Here's a rundown of the main island shopping areas in the order you'll encounter them as you enter the island:

Shelter Cove

Associated with the attached residential community, this shopping area on Broad Creek right off the William Hilton Parkway actually comprises three entities, the larger **Mall at Shelter Cove,** the smaller **Plaza at Shelter Cove,** and the dockside **Shelter Cove Harbour.**

The Mall opens at 10 A.M. Monday–Saturday and noon on Sunday and features the usual national stores you'd expect, but with a few typically Hilton Head upgrades like **Off 5th/ Saks Fifth Avenue Outlet** (843/341-2088) and **Williams-Sonoma** (843/785-2408). Other neat stores in the Mall are **DeGullah Creations** (843/686-5210), specializing in authentic Gullah wares, and **Blue Parrot** (800/252-6653), with gift lines such as Wee Forest Folk and Swarovski Crystal.

The most interesting store at the Plaza is no doubt the flagship location of **Outside Hilton Head** (843/686-6996, www.outsidehilton head.com, Mon.–Sat. 10 A.M.–5:30 P.M., Sun. 11 A.M.–5:30 P.M.), a complete outdoor outfitter with a thoroughly knowledgeable staff (they have a smaller satellite store in Sea Pines). Whatever outdoor gear you need and whatever tour you want to take, they can most likely hook you up.

Shelter Cove Harbour hosts a few cute shops hewing to its overall nautical/vacation theme, such as the clothing stores **Camp Hilton Head** (843/842-3666, Mon.–Sat. 10 A.M.–9 P.M., Sun. noon–5 P.M.) and the marine supplier **Ship's Store** (843/842-7001, Mon.–Sat. 7:30 A.M.–5 P.M., Sun. 7:30 A.M.–4 P.M.).

Village at Wexford

This well-shaded shopping center on William Hilton Parkway hosts the Lily Pulitzer signature women's store **S.M. Bradford Co.** (843/686-6161, Mon.–Sat. 10 A.M.–6 P.M.) and the aromatic **Scents of Hilton Head** (843/842-7866, Mon.–Fri. 10 A.M.–6 P.M., Sat. 10 A.M.–5 P.M.).

Coligny Circle

This is the closest Hilton Head comes to funkier beach towns like Tybee Island or Folly Beach, though it's doesn't really come that close. You'll find some delightful and somewhat quirky stores here, many keeping long hours in the summer, like the self-explanatory **Coligny Kite & Flag Co.** (843/785-5483, Mon.–Sat. 10 A.M.–9 P.M., Sun. 11 A.M.–6 P.M.), the hippie-fashion **Loose Lucy's** (843/785-8093, Mon.–Sat. 10 A.M.–6 P.M., Sun. 11 A.M.–5 P.M.), and the Caribbean-flavored **Jamaican Me Crazy** (843/785-9006, daily 10 A.M.–10 P.M.). Kids will love both **The Shell Shop** (843/785-4900, Mon.–Sat. 10 A.M.–9 P.M., Sun. noon–9 P.M.) and **Black Stone Minerals** (843/785-7090, Mon.–Sat. 10 A.M.–10 P.M., Sun. 11 A.M.–8 P.M.).

Harbour Town

The Shoppes at Harbour Town are a collection of 20 mostly boutique stores along Lighthouse Road. Probably the most interesting is **Match**

(843/671-4653, www.matchgoods.com, daily 10 A.M.–9 P.M.), an upscale vintage store that acquires antiques, designer items, and home goods through a corporate partnership for resale, also boasting its own walk-in humidor. Other highlights include the clothier **Knickers Men's Store** (843/671-2291, daily 10 A.M.–9 P.M.), and the **Top of the Lighthouse Shoppe** (149 Lighthouse Rd., 843/671-2810, www.harbourtownlighthouse.com, daily 10 A.M.–9 P.M.), where many a climbing tourist has been coaxed to part with some of their disposable income.

South Beach Marina

On South Sea Pines Drive at the Marina you'll find several worthwhile shops, including an "outpost" location of the great local outfitter **Outside Hilton Head** (800/686-6996, www.outsidehiltonhead.com) as well as a good ship's store and all-around grocery dealer **South Beach General Store** (843/671-6784, daily 8 A.M.–10 P.M.). And of course right on the water there's the ever-popular **Salty Dog Café** (843/671-2233, www.saltydog.com, lunch daily 11 A.M.–3 P.M., dinner daily 5–10 P.M.), whose ubiquitous T-shirts seem to adorn every other person on the island.

Thrift Shops

Don't scoff. Every thrift store connoisseur knows the best place to shop second-hand is in an affluent area like Hilton Head, where the locals try hard to stay in style and their castoffs are first-class. Key stops here are **The Bargain Box** (546 William Hilton Pkwy., 843/681-4305, Mon., Wed., and Fri. 1–4 P.M., Sat. 9:15 A.M.–12:15 P.M.) and **St. Francis Thrift Store** (2 Southwood Dr., 843/689-6563, Wed.–Sat. 10 A.M.–3 P.M.) right off the William Hilton Parkway.

Art Galleries

As with all the Lowcountry, visual artists are inexorably drawn to this area. Despite the wealth apparent in some quarters here, there's no freestanding art museum in the area, that role being filled by dozens of independent galleries.

My favorite gallery in the Hilton Head area would perhaps be more at home in Bluffton. The folk-art oriented **America. Oh Yes!** (1540 Fording Island Rd., 15 Bridge Center, 843/757-0088, Mon.–Sat. 11 A.M.–4 P.M.) has as its motto "art for people who don't care what their neighbors think." Fittingly for a gallery devoted to outsider art, America. Oh Yes! is actually just outside Hilton Head before you cross the bridge to the island.

For a more formal approach, go to **Morris & Whiteside Galleries & Sculpture Garden** (807 William Hilton Pkwy., 843/842-4433, www.morris-whiteside.com, daily 10 A.M.–5 P.M.), which features a variety of paintings and sculpture, heavy on landscapes but also showing some fine figurative work.

Not to be confused with the Red Piano Too on St. Helena Island, the **Red Piano Art Gallery** (220 Cordillo Pkwy., 843/785-2318, www.redpianoartgallery.com, daily 10 A.M.–5 P.M.) isn't devoted to Gullah art, but rather concentrates on natural landscapes with an often-whimsical touch.

The nonprofit **Art League of Hilton Head** (Pineland Station, Suite 207, Mon.–Sat. 10 A.M.–6 P.M.) displays work by member artists in all media.

SPORTS AND RECREATION
Beaches

First, the good news: Hilton Head Island has 12 miles of some of the most beautiful, safe beaches you'll find anywhere. The bad news is that there are only a few ways to gain access, generally at locations referred to as "beach parks." Don't just drive into a residential neighborhood and think you'll be able to park and find your way to the beach; for better or worse, Hilton Head is not set up for that kind of casual access.

Driessen Beach Park has 207 long-term parking spaces, costing $0.25 for 30 minutes. There's free parking but fewer spaces at the Coligny Beach Park entrance and at Fish Haul Creek Park. Also, there are 22 metered spaces at Alder Lane Beach Access, 51 at Folly Field Beach Park, and 13 at Burkes Beach

BEAUFORT

Hilton Head has 12 miles of beautiful, wide beaches.

Road. Most other beach parks are for permit parking only. Clean, well-maintained public restrooms are available at all the beach parks. You can find beach information at 843/342-4580 and www.hiltonheadislandsc.gov. Beach Park hours vary: Coligny Beach Park is open daily 24 hours. All other beach parks are open March–September 6 A.M.–8 P.M. and October–February 6 A.M.–5 P.M.

Unlike Savannah's Tybee Island and Charleston's Folly Beach, alcohol is strictly prohibited on Hilton Head's beaches. This may cut down on your vacation fun, but the plus side is the ban makes the beaches very friendly for families. There are lifeguards on all the beaches during the summer, but be aware that the worst undertow is on the northern stretches. Also please remember to leave the sand dollars where they are; their population is dwindling due to souvenir hunting.

Kayaking

Kayakers will enjoy Hilton Head Island, which offers several gorgeous routes, including Calibogue Sound to the south and west and Port Royal Sound to the north. You can also make your way up the May River to Bluffton. For particularly good views of life on the salt marsh, try Broad Creek, which nearly bisects Hilton Head Island, and Skull Creek, which separates Hilton Head from the natural beauty of Pinckney Island. Broad Creek Marina is a good place to put in. (For more area landings, see *Fishing and Boating*.)

If you want a guided tour, there are plenty of great kayak tour outfits to choose from in the area. Chief among them is certainly **Outside Hilton Head** (32 Shelter Cove Ln., 800/686-6996, www.outsidehiltonhead.com). They offer a wide range of guided trips, including "The Outback," in which you're first boated to a private island and then take on a tour of tidal creeks, and five- or seven-hour "Ultimate Lowcountry Day" trips to Daufuskie, Bluffton, or Bull Creek.

Other good places to book a tour or just rent a kayak are **Water-Dog Outfitters** (Broad Creek Marina, 843/686-3554) and

Kayak Hilton Head (Broad Creek Marina, 843/684-1910). **Cool Breeze Kayaking** (Broad Creek Landing, 843/683-4040) offers two-hour dolphin kayak tours.

Kayaking on the May River in nearby Bluffton is quite enriching, not only for the serene beauty but for the well-preserved nature of the river, which makes it very wildlife-friendly. The best places to put in are the Wharf Street Landing at the Bluffton Oyster Company at 63 Wharf Street and the Alljoy Landing down Alljoy Road a little ways out of Old Bluffton.

Fishing and Boating

As you'd expect, anglers and boaters love the Hilton Head/Bluffton area, which offers all kinds of saltwater, freshwater, and fly-fishing opportunities. Captain Brian Vaughn runs **Off the Hook Charters** (843/298-4376, www .offthehookcharters.com), which offers fully licensed trips at $400 for a half-day. **Carolina Sportfishing** offers deep-sea action on the 58-foot Viking yacht *Judith E* at about $200 per hour. Captain Dave Fleming of **Mighty Mako Sport Fishing Charters** (843/785-6028, www.mightymako.com) can take you saltwater fishing, both backwater and near-shore, on the 25-foot *Mighty Mako* for about $400 for a half-day.

Public landings in the Hilton Head area include the Marshland Road Boat Landing and the Broad Creek Boat Ramp under the Charles Fraser Bridge. Bluffton landings include the Bluffton Public Dock on Calhoun Street, the Alljoy Landing on Alljoy Road, and the Bluffton Oyster Factor on Wharf Street.

Hiking and Biking

Though the very flat terrain is not challenging, Hilton Head provides some scenic and relaxing biking opportunities. Thanks to wise planning and foresight, the island has an extensive 40-mile-plus network of biking trails that does a great job of keeping bikers out of traffic. A big plus is the long bike path paralleling the William Hilton Parkway, enabling cyclists to use that key artery without braving its traffic.

There is even an underground bike path beneath the Parkway to facilitate crossing that busy road. In addition, there are also routes along Pope Avenue and North and South Forest Beach Drive.

While several bike routes go into and through various private developments like Sea Pines and Palmetto Dunes, be aware that access technically is limited to residents and you may be challenged and asked where you're residing. Also, please pay attention to the miniature stop signs on the bike paths, ignorance of which can lead to some nasty scrapes or worse.

But the best bike path on Hilton Head is the simplest of all, where no one will ask you where you're staying that night: the beach. For a few hours before and after low tide the beach effectively becomes a 12-mile bike path around most of the island, and a pleasant morning or afternoon ride may well prove to be the highlight of your trip to the island.

There's a plethora of bike rental facilities on Hilton Head with competitive rates. Be sure and ask if they offer free pick-up and delivery. Try **Coconut Bike Rentals** (81 Pope Ave., 843/686-5055, daily 8 A.M.–5 P.M.) or **Hilton Head Bicycle Company** (112 Arrow Rd., 843/686-6888, Mon.–Sat. 9 A.M.–5 P.M., Sun. noon–5 P.M.).

Hikers will particularly enjoy Pinckney Island National Wildlife Refuge, which takes you through several key Lowcountry ecosystems, from maritime forest to salt marsh. Other peaceful, if non-challenging, trails are at the Audubon-Newhall Preserve on Hilton Head Island.

Bird-Watching

Without doubt the premier birding locale in the area is the fabulous **Pinckney Island National Wildlife Refuge** (U.S. 278 East just before Hilton Head, 912/652-4415, www.fws .gov). You can see bald eagles, ibis, wood storks, painted buntings, and many more species. Birding is best in spring and fall. The refuge has several freshwater ponds that serve as wading bird rookeries. During migratory season, so many beautiful birds abound here making such a ruckus that you'll think you wandered onto an Animal Planet shoot.

Golf

Hilton Head is one of the world's great golf centers, with no less than 23 courses, and one could easily write a book about nothing but that. This, however, is not that book. Perhaps contrary to what you might think, most courses on the island are public and some are downright affordable. (All courses are 18 holes unless otherwise described; green fees are averages and vary with season and tee time.)

The best-regarded course, with prices to match, is **Harbour Town Golf Links** (Sea Pines Plantation, 843/363-4485, www .seapines.com, $239 green fees). It's on the island's south end at Sea Pines and is the home of the annual Verizon Heritage Classic, far and away the island's number-one tourist draw.

There are two Arthur Hills–designed courses on the island, **Arthur Hills** at Palmetto Dunes Resort (843/785-1140, www.palmetto dunes.com, $125 green fees) and **Arthur Hills at Palmetto Hall** (Palmetto Hall Plantation, 843/689-4100, www.palmettohallgolf.com, $130 green fees), both of which now offer the use of Segway vehicles on the fairways.

The reasonably priced **Barony Course** at Port Royal Plantation (843/686-8801, www .portroyalgolfclub.com, $98 green fees) also boasts some of the toughest greens on the island. Another challenging and affordable course is the **George Fazio** at Palmetto Dunes Resort (843/785-1130, www.palmettodunes .com, $105 green fees).

Hilton Head National Golf Club (60 Hilton Head National Dr., 843/842-5900, www.golf hiltonheadnational.com), which is actually on the mainland just before you cross the bridge to Hilton Head, not only boasts a total of 27 challenging holes, but is consistently rated among the best golf locales in the world for both condition and service. *Golf Week* has named it one of America's best golf courses. All three courses here are public and green fees at each are below $100.

The closest public courses to Bluffton are

the Arnold Palmer–designed **Crescent Pointe Golf Club** (1 Crescent Pointe Dr., 888/292-7778, www.crescentpointegolf.com, green fees $90) and the nine-hole **Old Carolina Golf Club** (89 Old Carolina Rd., 888/785-7274, www .oldcarolinagolf.com, green fees $26), certainly one of the best golf deals in the region.

It's a good idea to book tee times through the **Golf Island Call Center** (888/465-3475, www.golfisland.com), which can also hook you up with good packages.

Tennis

One of the top tennis destinations in the country, Hilton Head has over 20 tennis clubs, some of which offer court time to the public (walk-on rates vary; call for information). They are: **Palmetto Dunes Tennis Center** (Palmetto Dunes Resort, 843/785-1152, www.palmettodunes.com, $30/hr.), **Port Royal Racquet Club** (Port Royal Plantation, 843/686-8803, www.portroyalgolfclub.com, $25/hr.), **Sea Pines Racquet Club** (Sea Pines Plantation, 843/363-4495, www.seapines .com, $25/hr.), **South Beach Racquet Club** (Sea Pines Plantation, 843/671-2215, www .seapines.com, $25/hr.), and **Shipyard Racquet Club** (Shipyard Plantation, 843/686-8804, $25/hr.).

Free, first-come-first-serve play is available at the following public courts maintained by the Island Recreation Association (www.island reccenter.org): **Chaplin Community Park** (Singleton Beach Rd., four courts, lighted), **Cordillo Courts** (Cordillo Pkwy., four courts, lighted), **Fairfield Square** (Adrianna Ln., two courts), **Hilton Head High School** (School Rd., six courts), and **Hilton Head Middle School** (Wilborn Rd., four courts).

ACCOMMODATIONS
Under $150

It won't blow you away, but you can't beat the price at **Park Lane Hotel and Suites** (12 Park Ln., 843/686-5700, www.hiltonheadparklane hotel.com, $120). This is your basic suite-type hotel (formerly a Residence Inn) with the basic free continental breakfast, but the allure here is the price, hard to find anywhere these days at a resort location, especially one as toney as Hilton Head. For a non-refundable $50 fee, you can bring your pet. The one drawback, probably reflected in the price, is that the beach is a couple of miles away. The hotel does offer a free shuttle, however, so it would be wise to take advantage of that and avoid the usual beach parking hassles.

$150-300

By Hilton Head standards, the (**Main Street Inn** (2200 Main St., 800/471-3001, www .mainstreetinn.com, $229) can be considered a bargain stay, and with high quality to boot. With its Old World touches, sumptuous appointments, charming atmosphere, and attentive service, this 33-room inn on the grounds of Hilton Head Plantation seems like it would be more at home in Charleston than Hilton Head. They serve a great full breakfast—not continental—daily 7:30–10:30 A.M. As a bonus, most of the less-expensive rooms have a great view of the formal garden, another part of that old Lowcountry appeal that's hard to come by on the island. If you want to upgrade, there are larger rooms with a fireplace and a smallish private courtyard for not much more. Overall, it's one of Hilton Head's best values.

Another good place for the price is the **South Beach Marina Inn** (232 S. Sea Pines Dr., 843/671-6498, www.sbinn.com, $186) in Sea Pines. Located near the famous Salty Dog Café and outfitted in a similar nautical theme, the inn not only has some pretty large rooms for the price, it offers a great view of the marina and has a very friendly feel, great for families with kids and romantic couples alike (especially with a beach on calm Calibogue Sound only a couple minutes' walk away). As with all Sea Pines accommodations, staying on the plantation means you don't have to wait in line with other visitors to pay the $5 a day "road fee." Sea Pines also offers a free trolley to get around the plantation.

One of Hilton Head's favorite hotels for true beach-lovers is the **Holiday Inn Oceanfront** (1 South Forest Beach Dr., 843/785-5126, www.hihiltonhead.com, $200), home of the famed Tiki Hut bar on the beach. Staff turnover is less frequent here than at other local accommodations, and while it's no Ritz-Carlton and occasionally shows signs of wear, it's a good value on a bustling area of the island. Parking has always been a problem here, but at least there's a free valet service.

One of the better resort-type places for those who prefer the putter and the racquet to the Frisbee and the surfboard is the (**Inn at Harbour Town** (7 Lighthouse Ln., 843/363-8100, www.seapines.com, $199) in Sea Pines. The big draw here is the impeccable service, delivered by a staff of "butlers" in kilts, comprising mostly Europeans who take the venerable trade quite seriously. While it's not on the beach, you can take advantage of the free Sea Pines Trolley every 20 minutes.

Over $300

Located smack-dab on the beach in Palmetto Dunes, the **Hilton Head Marriott Beach and Golf Resort** (One Hotel Circle, 843/686-8400, www.hiltonheadmarriott.com, $310–350) is somewhat corporate in flavor, with the generally more attentive service you'd expect in that genre. Beach access is the strong point here, but you can always just hang out by the pool if you'd prefer.

For longer-term stays and a more condo-style vacation in the fun and convenient Forest Beach area, rent a villa from a private owner at **North Shore Place** (N. Forest Beach Dr., 843/785-7616, www.hhidirect.com, prices vary). Moments away from the beach, your villa will also have a well-equipped kitchen and a covered veranda. A plus is you can use the oceanfront pool facilities at nearby **Sea Crest Villas** (1 N. Forest Beach Dr., 843/842-6212, prices vary), which also is a great place to stay for a condo-style stay.

FOOD

You'll have no problem finding very good restaurants in and around Hilton Head and Bluffton. Because of the fairly cosmopolitan nature of the population, with so many transplants from the northeastern United States and Europe, you might be surprised by the quality. Because of another demographic quirk of the area, its large percentage of senior citizens, you can also find some great deals by looking for some of the common "early bird" dinner specials, usually starting around 5 P.M.

Breakfast and Brunch

There are a couple of great diner-style places on the island. Though known more for its hamburgers and Philly cheesesteaks, locals swear that **(Harold's Diner** (641 William Hilton Pkwy., 843/842-9292, Mon.–Sat. 7 A.M.–3 P.M., $4–6) has the best pancakes in the Lowcountry, as well as the most hilariously sarcastic service. Unpretentious and authentic in a place where those two adjectives are rarely used, Harold's is one of a few must-visit restaurants on Hilton Head. As one patron has said, "The lack of atmosphere *is* the atmosphere."

You'll find another great locally owned breakfast spot at **Skillets** (1 N. Forest Beach Dr., 843/785-3131, www.skilletscafe.com, breakfast daily 7 A.M.–5 P.M., dinner daily 5–10 P.M., $5–23) in Coligny Plaza in the Forest Beach area. Their eponymous stock in trade is a layered breakfast dish of sautéed ingredients served in a porcelain skillet, like the "Kitchen Sink" (pancakes ringed with potatoes, sausage, and bacon, topped with two poached eggs). Breakfast is served 7 A.M.–5 P.M., but lunches are good too, including, believe it or not, an excellent meatloaf. Dinner is surprisingly upscale; try any of the excellent seafood dishes, like the blackened shrimp and scallops with tasso ham and blue cheese.

A very good all-day breakfast place with a twist is **Signe's Heaven Bound Bakery & Café** (93 Arrow Rd., 843/785-9118, www.signesbakery.com, Mon.–Fri. 8 A.M.–4 P.M., Sat. 9 A.M.–2 P.M., $5–10). The breakfast comprises tasty dishes like frittatas and breakfast polenta, while the twist is the extensive artisan bakery. You'll be surprised at the quality of the food for the low prices.

Casual Dining

In the case of this next restaurant, "casual" definitely refers to the atmosphere, not the prices. It's not cheap, but fresh seafood lovers will enjoy one of Hilton Head's staples, the huge **(Hudson's on the Docks** (1 Hudson Rd., 843/681-2772, www.hudsonsonthedocks.com, daily lunch 11 A.M.–4 P.M., opens for dinner at 5 P.M., $14–23) on Skull Creek just off Squire Pope Road on the less-developed north side. Much of the catch—though not all of it by any means—comes directly off the boats you'll see dockside. Built on the old family oyster factory, Hudson's is now owned by transplants from, of all places, Long Island, New York. Still, its record of satisfied customers, heavy on the families, remains intact. Try the stuffed shrimp, filled with delicious crabmeat, or just go for a combination platter. Leave room for one of the homemade desserts by Ms. Bessie, a 30-year Hudson's veteran employee.

Like many other affluent areas in the United States, Hilton Head is almost entirely dependent on Mexican-American skilled labor, so it's no surprise that there are a couple of excellent and authentic Mexican restaurants on the island. Just off the William Hilton Parkway near the island's entrance, **(Mi Tierra** (160 Fairfield Square, 843/342-3409, lunch daily 11 A.M.–4 P.M., dinner weekdays 4–9 P.M., weekends until 10 P.M., $3–15) has a clientele about half-Gringo and half-Hispanic. (They also run a taco stand, **Baja Tacos,** right outside.) The tacos at both places are the real thing, nothing like what you'd find in a Taco Bell, as is the homemade and perfect guacamole. You'll find lots of traditional seafood dishes here, like ceviche, octopus, shrimp, and oysters. Mondays often have a real Mariachi band. There's a Bluffton location, too (101 Mellichamp Center, Bluffton, 843/757-7200, lunch daily 11 A.M.–4 P.M., dinner Mon.–Fri. 4–9 P.M. Sat.–Sun. 4–10 P.M.).

On the other end of the island, **Fiesta Fresh** (51 New Orleans Rd., 843/785-4788, Mon.–Sat. 9 A.M.–9 P.M., Sun. 9 A.M.–8 P.M.) is a little harder to find but well worth the trip. More of a counter-style place, Fiesta Fresh's specialty is the guacamole burrito, every bit as delicious as it sounds. Check out the incredible homemade condiment bar with several homemade salsas and fresh chopped cilantro. To get there, hit the Sea Pines traffic circle and come out going south on Pope Avenue. Take a left on College Center Drive, and a left on New Orleans Road.

Fine Dining
Not to be confused with Charley's Crab House next door to Hudson's, seafood lovers will also enjoy the experience down near Sea Pines at **C Charlie's L'Etoile Verte** (8 New Orleans Rd., 843/785-9277, www.charliesofhiltonhead .com, lunch Tues.–Sat. 11:30 A.M.–2 P.M., dinner Mon.–Sat. 6–9:30 P.M., $25–40), which is considered by many connoisseurs to be Hilton Head's single best restaurant. The emphasis here is on "French country kitchen" cuisine— think Provence, not Paris. In keeping, each day's menu is concocted from scratch and handwritten. Listen to these recent entrées and feel your mouth water: flounder saute Meuniere, grilled wild coho salmon with a basil pesto, and breast of duck in a raspberry demi-glace. Get the picture? Of course you'll want to start with the escargot and leeks vol-au-vent, the house paté, or even some pan-roasted Bluffton oysters. As you'd expect the wine selection is absolutely celestial. Reservations essential.

Perhaps the most unique restaurant on Hilton Head is **C Red Fish** (8 Archer Rd., 843/686-3388, www.redfishofhiltonhead.com, lunch Mon.–Sat. 11:30 A.M.–2 P.M., dinner nightly beginning with early-bird specials at 5 P.M., $20–37). Strongly Caribbean in decor as well as menu, with romanticism and panache to match, this is a great place for couples. The creative but accessible menu by Executive Chef Sean Walsh incorporates unique spices, fruits, and vegetables for a fresh, zesty palate. The recommended course of action is to pick your own wine from the truly vast, thousand-bottle-plus, award-winning selection from the attached wine shop and cellar to go with your dinner (there's a small corkage fee). You can't go wrong with any entrée here, but highlights include the grilled grouper with a mango avocado salsa, the horseradish-encrusted salmon, and the Dominican braised pork cooked in coconut milk, with cilantro, chilies, fried bananas, jasmine rice, and Cuban black beans. Reservations essential.

For upscale Italian, try **Bistro Mezzaluna** (55 New Orleans Rd., 843/842-5011, daily 5–9:30 P.M.). Known far and wide for its osso bcco as well as its impeccable service, there's also a great little bar for cocktails before or after dinner.

Staying with that Southern European vibe, you might also like **Vassili's Mediterranean Tavern** (11 Lagoon Rd., 843/842-4033, lunch daily 11 A.M.–3 P.M., dinner daily 5–10 P.M., www.vassilisofhiltonhead.com, $15–40), owned by the locally revered restaurateurs of the Maniotis family. At this friendly place near Coligny Plaza you'll find all the high points of a typical Greek menu, including calamari, spanakopita, and of course a Greek salad, but there are some great non-Greek items on the menu as well, including crab-stuffed grouper and a fine chicken piccata.

INFORMATION AND SERVICES
The best place to get information on Hilton Head, book a room, or secure a tee time is just as you come onto the island at the **Hilton Head Island Chamber of Commerce Welcome Center** (100 William Hilton Pkwy., 843/785-3673, www.hiltonheadisland.org, daily 9 A.M.–6 P.M.). It's in the same building as the Coastal Discovery Museum.

You'll find Bluffton's visitors center in the **Heyward House Historic Center** (70 Boundary St., 843/757-6293, www.heyward house.org).

Hilton Head's paper of record is the *Island Packet* (www.islandpacket.com). A good Bluffton publication is *Bluffton Today* (www .blufftontoday.com).

The easy-to-find **Hilton Head post office** is at 13 William Hilton Parkway (843/893-3490). Bluffton has a post office at 32 Bruin Road (843/757-3588).

GETTING THERE AND AROUND

A few years back, the Savannah International Airport added Hilton Head to its name specifically to identify itself with that lucrative market. It's been a success, and that facility remains the closest airport to Hilton Head Island and Bluffton. From the airport go north on I-95 into South Carolina, and take Exit 8 onto U.S. 278 east.

If you're entering the area by car, the best route is also Exit 8 off of I-95 onto U.S. 278, which takes you by Bluffton and right into Hilton Head. Near Bluffton, U.S. 278 is called Fording Island Road, and on Hilton Head proper it becomes the William Hilton Parkway business route. Technically, 278 turns into the new Cross Island Parkway, but when most locals say "278" they're almost always referring to the William Hilton Parkway.

Other than taxi services, there is no public transportation to speak of in the Lowcountry, unless you want to count the free shuttle around Sea Pines Plantation. Taxi services include **Yellow Cab** (843/686-6666), **Island Taxi** (843/683-6363), and **Ferguson Transportation** (843/842-8088).

BLUFFTON

Similar to Beaufort, except even quieter and smaller, Bluffton is an idyllic village on the banks of the wide, hypnotically serene, and well-preserved May River. Despite its friendly, open ways today, Bluffton was the original hotbed of secession, with Charleston diarist Mary Chestnut famously referring to the town as "the center spot of the fire eaters."

◖ Old Bluffton

While its outskirts (so-called "Greater Bluffton") are now a haven for new planned communities hoping to mimic some aspect of Bluffton's historic patina, the town center itself remains an authentic and charmingly retro look at old South Carolina. Retro cuts both ways, however, and Bluffton has been a notorious speed trap for generations. Always obey the speed limit.

When General Sherman came through, he repaid the favor of those original Bluffton secessionists, which is why only nine homes in Bluffton are of antebellum vintage; the rest his troops torched. One of the survivors is the **Heyward House Historic Center** (70 Boundary St., 843/757-6293, www.heywardhouse.org, Mon.–Fri. 10 A.M.–3 P.M., Sat. 11 A.M.–2 P.M., $5 adults, $2 students), which is not only open to tours but serves as Bluffton's visitors center. Built in 1840 as a summer home for the owner of Moreland Plantation, John Cole, the house was later owned by George Cuthbert Heyward, grandson of Declaration of Independence signer Thomas Heyward. (Remarkably, it stayed in the family until the 1990s.) Of note are the intact slave quarters on the grounds.

The center of tourist activity focuses on the **Old Bluffton Historic District,** several blocks of 1800s buildings clustered between the parallel Boundary and Calhoun Streets (old-timers sometimes call this the "original square mile"). Many of the buildings are private residences, but most have been converted into art studios and antiques stores. The wares feature a whimsical, folk art quality very much in tune with Bluffton's whole Southern Shangri-la feel. While the artists and shopkeepers are serious about their work, they make a point to warmly invite everyone in, even when they're busy at work on the latest project.

Whatever you do, don't fail to go all the way to the end of Calhoun Street as it dead-ends on a high bluff on the May River at the Bluffton Public Dock. Overlooking this peaceful marsh-front vista is the sublimely photogenic **Church of the Cross** (110 Calhoun St., 843/757-2661, www.thechurchofthecross.net, tours Mon.–Sat. 10 A.M.–2 P.M.). Though the current sanctuary was built in 1854 and is one of only two local churches not burned in the Civil War, the parish itself began in 1767, with the first services on this spot held in the late 1830s. Standing here on this bluff, with the steady south breeze blowing the bugs away and relieving the Lowcountry heat, you'll see why affluent South Carolinians began building summer homes here in the 1800s.

You might want to get a gander at the state's

Bluffton features many interesting art galleries.

last remaining working oyster house, the **Bluffton Oyster Company** (63 Wharf St., 843/757-4010, Mon.–Sat. 9 A.M.–5:30 P.M.), while you still can. The adjoining five acres were recently purchased by the Beaufort County Open Land Trust with the intention of the area evolving into a community greenspace celebrating a key aspect of local heritage, the celebrated May River oyster. Meanwhile Larry and Tina Toomer continue to oversee the oyster harvesting-and-shucking family enterprise with roots back to the early 1900s.

While the oysters are growing scarce on the May River, get a close-up look at an interesting state-funded seafood farm on the Colleton River estuary, the **Waddell Mariculture Center** (Sawmill Creek Rd., 843/837-3795). Free tours are available n Monday, Tuesday, Wednesday, and Friday mornings. Shrimp, fish, and shellfish are some of the "product" raised and harvested there. Get to Waddell by taking U.S. 278 east out of Bluffton and take a left on Sawmill Creek Road.

Shopping

Bluffton's eccentric little art studios, most

clustered in a two-block stretch on Calhoun Street, are by far its main shopping draw. Named for the Lowcountry phenomenon you find in the marsh at low tide amongst the fiddler crabs, Bluffton's **Pluff Mudd Art** (27 Calhoun St., 843/757-5551, Mon.–Sat. 10 A.M.–5:30 P.M.) is a cooperative of 16 great young painters and photographers from throughout the area.

The **Guild of Bluffton Artists** (20 Calhoun St., 843/757-5590, Mon.–Sat., 10 A.M.–4:30 P.M.) features work from many local artists, as does the outstanding **Society of Bluffton Artists** (48 Boundary St., 843/757-6586).

For cool custom handcrafted pottery, try **Preston Pottery and Gallery** (10 Church St., 843/757-3084). Another great Bluffton place is the hard-to-define **eggs'n'tricities** (71 Calhoun St., 843/757-3446). The name pretty much says it all for this fun and eclectic vintage/junk/jewelry/folk art store.

While the most unique gift items in Bluffton are in its many local art galleries and studios, there are a couple of charming, non-art related shops that are very much worth checking out—and conveniently, they're right next to each other! The aptly named **The Store** (56 Calhoun St., 843/757-3855, Mon.–Sat. 10 A.M.–5 P.M.) is located, sure enough, in the historic 1904 Peeples Store building. Babby Guscio's place not only offers a lot of neat knick-knacks and gifts in addition to tasty comestibles, it's also a great place to meet locals and strike up a conversation. But no high heels, please! Literally right next door in an adjoining space is the tiny but thoroughly delightful **Scuppernongs** (56-A Calhoun St., 843/757-8463, Mon.–Sat. 11 A.M.–7 P.M.) wine shop.

If you want to score some fresh local seafood for your own culinary adventure, the no-brainer choice is the **Bluffton Oyster Company** (63 Wharf St., 843/757-4010), the state's only active oyster facility. They also have shrimp, crab, clams, and fish, nearly all of it from the nearly pristine May River on whose banks it sits.

For a much more commercially intense experience, head just outside of town on U.S. 278 on the way to Hilton Head to find the dual **Tanger Outlet Centers** (1414 Fording Island Rd., 843/837-4339, Mon.–Sat. 10 A.M.–9 P.M., Sun. 11 A.M.–6 P.M.), an outlet-shopper's paradise with virtually every major brand represented, from Nine West to Ralph Lauren to Abercrombie & Fitch and dozens more, including new additions Skechers and the Limited Too. A serious shopper can easily spend most of a day here between its two sprawling malls, Tanger I and Tanger II, so be forewarned!

Sports and Recreation

The premier kayaking outfitter in Bluffton is no doubt **Native Guide Kayak Tours** (8 2nd St., 843/757-5411), which features tours of the May and New Rivers led by native Ben Turner.

You can find a great 12-mile tour of Old Town Bluffton at www.greaterbluffton pathways.org. It starts at the Piggly Wiggly grocery store in town, goes south on Thomas Heyward Street, east on Bridge Street, north on Calhoun Street, south on Bluffton Road, and east on Alljoy Road. The route includes spurs to the Church of the Cross, Myrtle Island, the marsh on the May River, and Pine Island.

Accommodations

UNDER $150

A quality bargain stay right between Bluffton and Hilton Head is the **Holiday Inn Express Bluffton** (35 Bluffton Rd., 843/757-2002, www.ichotelsgroup.com, $120), on U.S. 278 as you make the run onto Hilton Head proper. It's not close to the beach or to Old Town Bluffton, so you'll definitely be using your car, but its central location will appeal to those who want to keep their options open.

OVER $300

For an ultra-upscale spa/golf resort environment near Bluffton, the clear pick is the **(Inn at Palmetto Bluff** (476 Mt. Pelia Rd., 843/706-6500, www.palmettobluffresort.com, $650–900) just across the May River. This Auberge property was picked in 2006 as the number-two U.S. resort by *Condé Nast Traveler* magazine. Despite its glitzy pedigree and extremely upper-end prices, it's more Tara than Trump Tower. The main building is modeled after a Lowcountry plantation home, and the idyllic views of the May River are blissful. Lodging is dispersed among a series of cottages and "village home" rentals. Needless to say, virtually your every need is provided for here, though the nearest off-site restaurant of any quality is quite a drive away. That will likely make little difference to you, however since there are three top-flight dining options on the grounds: the fine dining **River House Restaurant** (843/706-6542, breakfast daily 7–11 A.M., lunch or "porch" menu daily 11 A.M.–10 P.M., dinner daily 6–10 P.M., mains $30–40); the **May River Grill** (Tues.–Sat. 11 A.M.–4 P.M., mains $9–13) at the golf clubhouse; and the casual **Buffalo's** (843/706-6630, Sun.–Tues. 11:30 A.M.–5 P.M., Wed.–Sat. 11:30 A.M.–9 P.M., mains $10–15).

Food

BREAKFAST AND BRUNCH

No discussion of Bluffton cuisine is complete without the famous **(Squat 'n' Gobble** (1231 May River Rd., 843/757-4242, Mon.–Fri. 7 A.M.–9 P.M., Sat.–Sun. 7 A.M.–3 P.M.), a wholly local phenomenon—and not to be

the famous Squat 'n' Gobble in Bluffton

© JIM MOREKIS

confused with a similarly named chain of eateries in California. Long a site of gossiping and politicking as well as, um, squatting and gobbling, this humble diner on the May River Road in town is an indelible part of the local consciousness. Believe it or not, despite the totally unpretentious greasy-spoon ambience—or because of it—the food's actually quite good. They specialize in the usual "American" menu of eggs, bacon, hamburgers, hot dogs, and fries. There's a tie for best thing on the menu—I can't decide whether the Greek pizza is better or the barbecue, so I'll go with both.

Another imaginatively named breakfast/brunch spot is the **Sippin' Cow Cafe** (1230 May River Rd., 843/757-5051, Tues.–Sat. 7 A.M.–3 P.M.) just across the street from the Squat 'n' Gobble. One of their specialties is a great breakfast burrito.

CASUAL DINING
Another beloved Bluffton institution (and believe me, Blufftonians love their institutions) is **Pepper's Porch** (1255 May River Rd., 843/757-2295, Tues.–Sun. 11:30 A.M.–9 P.M., $12–20). Housed in an old barn for drying a

local herb called deer tongue, this is the kind of distinctly Southern place where they bring out a basket of little corn muffins instead of bread. Entrées include a great stuffed grouper and delicious, fresh-fried shrimp. Don't miss the fried strawberry dessert, which tastes a million times better than it sounds. Weekends see live music and karaoke in the aptly named Back Bar, a favorite local hangout.

Prime rib is the house specialty at **Myrtle's Bar & Grill** (32 Bruin Rd., 843/757-6300, Tues.–Fri. lunch 11:30 A.M.–2:30 P.M., Tues.–Sat. dinner 5–9:30 P.M., Sunday brunch 10 A.M.–2 P.M.), generally served on Tuesday nights. They also do a mean flounder. Housed in the old post office, Myrtle's is a favorite local hangout and has recently begun hosting an interactive murder-mystery dinner theatre show.

FINE DINING
Most dining in Bluffton is pretty casual, but you'll get the white tablecloth treatment at **Claude & Uli's Signature Bistro** (1533 Fording Island Rd., 843/837-3336, lunch Mon.–Fri. 11:30 A.M.–2:30 P.M., open for dinner Mon.–Sat. at 5 P.M., $18–25) just outside of town in

WHO ARE THE GULLAH?

A language, a culture, and a people with a shared history, Gullah is more than that – it's also a state of mind.

Simply put, the Gullah are African Americans of the Sea Islands of South Carolina and Georgia. (In Georgia, the term "Geechee," from the nearby Ogeechee River, is more or less interchangeable.) Protected from outside influence by the isolation of this coastal region, the Gullahs' culture is considered the closest living cousin to the West African traditions of their ancestors, imported as slaves from the mid-1600s to the mid-1800s into Charleston and Savannah. While you often hear that "Gullah" is a corruption of "Angola," some linguists think it simply means "people" in a West African language.

In any case, the Gullah speak what's known as a "creole" language, i.e., one derived from several sources. Gullah combines elements of Elizabethan English, Jamaican patois, and several West African dialects; for example "goober" (peanut) comes from the Congo *n'guba*.

Though several white writers in the 1900s published collections of Gullah folk tales in the original language, the first linguist to seriously study Gullah was Lorenzo Dow Turner. His groundbreaking *Africanisms in the Gullah Dialect* (1949) explicitly traced elements of the language to Sierra Leone in West Africa and traced more than 300 Gullah words directly to Africa. Prior to Turner's seminal book, Gullah was simply considered broken English.

Another creole element is a word with multiple uses, for example Gullah's "shum," could mean "see them," "see him," "see her," or "see it," in either past or present tense, depending on the context. Gullah is spoken very rapidly, which of course only adds to its impenetrability to the outsider. Gullah also relies on colorful turns of phrase. If you hear "'E tru mout'" (literally "He true mouth"), that means

the speaker is referring to someone who doesn't lie. "Ie een crack muh teet" (literally "I didn't even crack my teeth") means "I kept quiet." A forgetful Gullah speaker might say, "Mah head leab me," or "My head left me."

Gullah music, as practiced by the world-famous Hallelujah Singers of St. Helena Island, also uses many distinctly African techniques, such as call and response (the folk hymn "Michael Row the Boat Ashore" is a good example). Many traditional folkways are still observed to this day, such as the practice of passing a young child over the casket or gravesite of a relative to keep the dead person from coming back and haunting the child.

The most famous Americans with Gullah/Geechee roots are Supreme Court Justice Clarence Thomas (Pin Point, Ga., near Savannah), boxer Joe Frazier (Beaufort, S.C.), NFL great Jim Brown (St. Simons Island, Ga.), and hip-hop star Jazzy Jay (Beaufort).

Upscale development continues to claim more and more traditional Gullah areas of the Sea Islands, generally by pricing them out through rapidly increasing property values. Today, the major pockets of living Gullah culture in South Carolina are in Beaufort, St. Helena Island, Daufuskie Island, and a northern section of Hilton Head Island. In Georgia you'll find Geechee communities in Sapelo Island, St. Simon's Island, and Harris Neck in McIntosh County.

The old ways are not as prevalent as they were, but two key educational and outreach institutions are keeping alive the spirit of Gullah: the **Penn Center** (16 Martin Luther King Dr., 843/838-2474, www.penncenter.com, $4 adults, $2 seniors and children, Mon.-Sat. 11 A.M.-4 P.M.) on St. Helena Island, South Carolina, and the **Avery Research Center** (66 George St., 843/953-7609, www.cofc.edu/avery, Mon.-Fri. 10 A.M.-5 P.M., Sat. noon-5 P.M.) at the College of Charleston.

Moss Village. Chef Claude has brought his extensive European training and background (including Maxim's in Paris) to this romantic little spot. Claude does a great veal cordon bleu as well as a number of fine seafood entrées, such as an almond-crusted tilapia and an excellent seafood pasta. Don't miss their specialty soufflé for dessert, which you should order with dinner as it takes almost a half-hour to bake.

DAUFUSKIE ISLAND

Sitting right between Savannah and Hilton Head Island and accessible only by water, Daufuskie Island has about 500 full-time residents, most of whom ride around on golf carts or bikes (there's only one paved road, Haig Point Road, and cars are a rare sight). Once the home of rice and indigo plantations and rich oyster beds—the latter destroyed by pollution—the two upscale residential resort communities on the island, begun in the 1980s, give a clue as to where its future lies. Fortunately, a 300-acre portion of the so-far undeveloped Webb Tract was recently put under a conservation easement.

The area of prime interest to tourists is the unincorporated western portion, or "Historic District," the old stomping grounds of Pat Conroy during his stint as a teacher of resident African American children. His old two-room schoolhouse of *The Water is Wide* fame, the **Mary Field School,** is still there, as id the adjacent 140-year-old **Union Baptist Church,** but Daufuskie students now have a surprisingly modern new facility (middle school students are still ferried to mainland schools every day).

Farther north on Haig Point Road is the new **Billie Burn Museum,** housed in the old Mt. Carmel Church and named after the island's resident historian. On the southern end you'll find the **Bloody Point Lighthouse,** named for the vicious battle fought nearby during the Yamasee War of 1815 (the light was actually

moved a half-mile inland in the early 1900s). Other areas of interest throughout the island include Native American sites, tabby ruins, the old Baptist Church, and a couple of cemeteries.

Otherwise there's really not much to do on Daufuskie. It's a place where you go to see a slice of Sea Island and Gullah history and relax, relax, relax. One place to do just that in high style is the **Daufuskie Island Resort and Breathe Spa** (800/648-6778, www.daufuskie islandresort.com), a top-flight facility affiliated with the island's resort, with all the ultra-pampering amenities you'd expect, including 45 therapeutic treatments for men and women. They take you there from their "embarkation center" on Squire Pope Road on Hilton Head Island or Savannah's River Street.

For the freshest island seafood, check out the **Old Daufuskie Crab Company** (Freeport Marina, 843/785-6652, daily 11:30 A.M.–9 P.M., $7–22). There are also several places to get a bite, from casual to classy, within the Daufuskie Island Resort.

Two good public ferries to and from Daufuskie from Hilton Head are **Calibogue Cruises** (843/342-8687) and **Daufuskie Island Resort Ferry** (421 Squire Pope Rd., 843/341-4870, www.daufuskieislandresort .com), the latter also operating a public ferry that leaves Savannah from River Street Market (425 E. River St.). Both ferries bring you in on the Cooper River side of the island. From there you can take shuttles or rent golf carts or bikes.

Many tour operators offer guided package excursions to Daufuskie. If you want to spend a night or two there, go upscale at the **Daufuskie Island Resort** (843/842-2000, www.daufuskieislandresort.com, $189 for two queens, $339 and up for suites and villas, winter rates surprisingly cheap). Or rent a humble cabin at **Freeport Marina** (843/785-8242, rates vary).

SAVANNAH

Rarely has a city owed so much to the vision of one person than Savannah owes to General James Edward Oglethorpe. Given the mission by King George II of England to set up a buffer to protect Charleston's rice plantations from Spanish incursion, this committed reformer had a far more sweeping vision in mind.

After befriending a local Creek tribe, Oglethorpe laid out his settlement in a deceptively simple plan that is studied today the world over as a model of nearly perfect urban design. Many of his other progressive ideas—such as prohibiting slavery and hard liquor, to name two—soon went by the wayside, but the legacy of his original city plan lives on to this day.

Savannah would comprise a series of rectangular "wards," each built around a central square. Growth was simple and orderly, with wards simply added to the grid as needed. The center of each square was designed for militia to take up a defensive position. But the structures around the squares were built facing *within,* thereby engendering a feeling of community and solidarity during peacetime.

As Savannah grew, each square took on its own characteristics depending on who lived on the square and how they made their livelihood. It's this individuality that instilled Savannah's innate love of the eccentric, so well-documented in John Berendt's *Midnight in the Garden of Good and Evil.*

The squares of Savannah's downtown—since 1965 part of the National Landmark Historic District—are also responsible for the city's walkability, another defining characteristic. You can't call Savannah a true pedestrian

© JIM MOREKIS

HIGHLIGHTS

☾ River Street: Despite River Street's occasional tourist tackiness, there's still nothing like strolling the cobblestones amid the old cotton warehouses, enjoying the cool breeze off the river, and watching the huge ships roll in and out on their way to and from the bustling port (page 185).

☾ First African Baptist Church: The oldest black congregation in America still meets in this historic sanctuary, a key stop on the Underground Railroad (page 191).

☾ Owens-Thomas House: Possibly America's best example of Regency architecture and definitely an example of state-of-the-art historic preservation in action. For now and all time, Savannah's single greatest historical home (page 200).

☾ Telfair Museum of Art: Old-school meets new-school in this museum complex comprising the traditional collection of the Telfair Academy of Arts and Sciences and the ultramodern Jepson Center for the Arts, both within a stone's throw of each other on charming Telfair Square (page 201).

☾ Cathedral of St. John the Baptist: This soaring Gothic Revival edifice is complemented by its ornate interior and its matchless location on verdant Lafayette Square, stomp-ing ground of the young Flannery O'Connor (page 204).

☾ Monterey Square: Perhaps Savannah's quintessential square, with some of the best examples of local architecture – including the Mercer-Williams House and Temple Mickve Israel – and absolutely world-class ironwork all around its periphery (page 206).

☾ Forsyth Park: A verdant expanse ringed with old live oaks, with memorials chocka-block. The true center of downtown life, it's Savannah's backyard, hosting public events year-round (page 212).

☾ Bonaventure Cemetery: Simply unforgettable, this historic burial ground is the final resting place for some of Savannah's favorite citizens, including the great Johnny Mercer, and makes great use of its setting on the banks of the Wilmington River (page 214).

☾ Fort Pulaski National Monument: This well-run site, built with the help of a young Robert E. Lee, is not only quite historically significant, its beautiful, spacious setting and associated nature walks make it a great place for the entire family (page 220).

☾ Tybee Lighthouse: One of America's best-preserved historic beacons, offering a stunning view of Tybee Island (page 221).

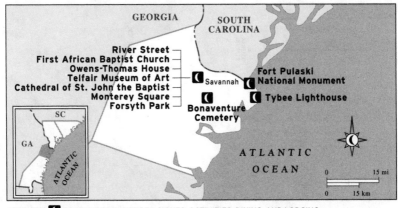

LOOK FOR ☾ TO FIND RECOMMENDED SIGHTS, ACTIVITIES, DINING, AND LODGING.

SAVANNAH

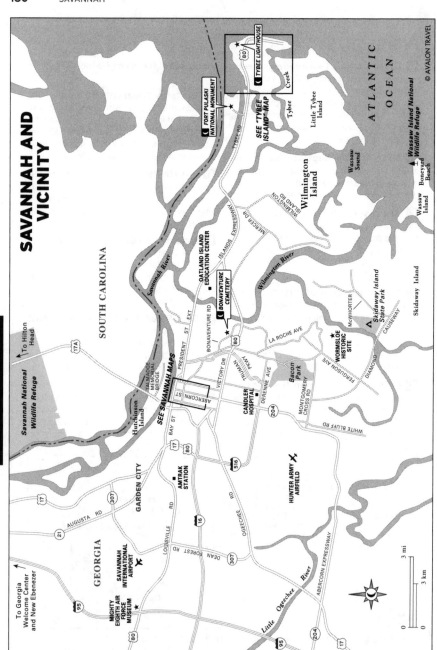

SAVANNAH AND VICINITY

© AVALON TRAVEL

ATLANTIC OCEAN

SOUTH CAROLINA

GEORGIA

Savannah River

To Hilton Head

17A

Savannah National Wildlife Refuge

Hutchinson Island

TALMADGE MEMORIAL BRIDGE

SEE SAVANNAH MAPS

ABERCORN ST

PRESIDENT ST EXT

BONAVENTURE RD

★ BONAVENTURE CEMETERY

OATLAND ISLAND EDUCATION CENTER

ISLANDS EXPRESSWAY

MERCER DR

WILMINGTON ISLAND RD

Wilmington Island

Wilmington River

FORT PULASKI NATIONAL MONUMENT

TYBEE RD

SEE "TYBEE ISLAND" MAP

★ ★ TYBEE LIGHTHOUSE

80

Tybee Creek

Tybee Island

Little Tybee Island

Wassaw Sound

Wassaw Island

Wassaw Island National Wildlife Refuge

Boneyard Beach

80

VICTORY DR

BAY ST

17

80

PAYNE

TRUMAN

DERENNE AVE

LA ROCHE AVE

CANDLER HOSPITAL

516

WORMSLOE HISTORIC SITE ★

FERGUSON AVE

McWHORTER

Skidaway Island State Park

Skidaway Island

SKIDAWAY RD CAUSEWAY

DIAMOND

Bacon Park

MONTGOMERY CROSS RD

204

WHITE BLUFF RD

GARDEN CITY

AMTRAK STATION

HUNTER ARMY AIRFIELD ✈

17

307

16

OGEECHEE RD

LOUISVILLE RD

DEAN FOREST RD

AUGUSTA RD

21

307

204

ABERCORN EXPRESSWAY

Little Ogeechee River

95

17

SAVANNAH INTERNATIONAL AIRPORT ✈

MIGHTY EIGHTH AIR FORCE MUSEUM ★

80

95

To Georgia Welcome Center and New Ebenezer

0   3 mi

0   3 km

city, since like Charleston its downtown area suffers from too many cars and too few parking spaces. But it is just as true that a visitor needs no car at all to fully enjoy all the sights and hospitality Savannah has to offer.

Savannah's squares act as a governor on speed, literally and figuratively. Just as cars entering a square must yield to traffic already within, pedestrians are obliged to slow down and interact with the environment around them, both built and natural. You become participant and audience simultaneously, a feat made easier by the local penchant for easy conversation.

Visitors from more inhibited parts of the country are sometimes taken aback by how easy Savannahians are to approach, how quick they are to smile and laugh, and how eagerly and casually they seek out conversation. You might enter a small boutique to do some shopping and quickly find yourself in a meandering yet very entertaining exchange of gossip with the shopkeeper. Indeed, gossiping is the pastime of choice for most Savannahians, performed not so much with rancor or pettiness but with flair, in a spirit of gregarious one-upmanship.

While Savannah is beginning to suffer from the same influx of cookie-cutter development the rest of the country is dealing with, it's seemingly one of the last places left where eccentricity is celebrated and even encouraged. This outspoken, often stubborn determination to make one's own way in the world is personified by the old Georgia joke about Savannah being the capital of "the state of Chatham," a reference to the county in which it resides. In typical contrarian fashion, Savannahians take this moniker, ostensibly a pejorative, as a compliment instead.

Savannah is also known for being able to show you a good time. It's not only about the massive, world-famous St. Patrick's Day celebration each year—though certainly that's something everyone should experience at least once in their lives. The truth is that Savannahians, like New Orleanians, will use any excuse for a party, and any excuse to drink in the full flavor of natural beauty here—whether in the heady glory of a spring day with all the flowers blooming, or the sweet release of the long-awaited autumn, brisk and bracing but not so crisp that you can't wear shorts.

And, like Charleston, this is a city moving forward. While Savannah has the same racial tension and socioeconomic disparity typical of many Southern cities, and, though it may not be the next Charleston, it is coming into its own: a small-scale yet cosmopolitan city with a fun-loving mix of history and modernity.

While Charleston's outlying areas tend to compliment the history and outlook of the Holy City itself, Savannah's outskirts are more self-contained. Despite the fact that Tybee Island is largely dependent on Savannah's economy, it has willfully kept its own fun and funky persona. More rural areas outside town, such as New Ebenezer and Midway, are reflective of a wholly different side of the state—a Georgia of country churches and tight-knit descendants of original plantation owners.

PLANNING YOUR TIME

More than just a day and much more than just a parade, St. Patrick's Day in Savannah—an event generally expanded by the city to include several days before and after it—is also a time of immense crowds, with the city's usual population of about 150,000 more than tripling with the influx of partying visitors. Be aware that lodging on and around March 17 fills up well in advance. Unless you know someone that lives here or you're really into crashing on people's floors, it's best not to just spontaneously show up in Savannah on St. Patrick's weekend.

Like Charleston, you don't necessarily need access to a car to have a great time and see most sights worth enjoying. A strong walker can easily traverse the length and breadth of downtown in a day, though less energetic travelers should consider a central location and/or use of the free downtown shuttle.

To fully enjoy Savannah, however, you'll need access to a vehicle so that you can go east to Tybee Island and south to various historical sights with spottier public transportation. You

OGLETHORPE: VISIONARY ARISTOCRAT

statue of General James Oglethorpe in Chippewa Square

One of the greatest products of the Enlightenment, James Edward Oglethorpe was a study in contrasts, embodying all the vitality, contradiction, and ambiguity of that turbulent age.

A stern moralist yet an avowed liberal, an aristocrat with a populist streak, an abolitionist and an anti-Catholic, a man of war who sought peace – the founder of Georgia would put his own inimitable stamp on the new nation to follow, a legacy personified to this day in the city he designed.

After making a name for himself fighting the Turks, the young London native and Oxford graduate would return home only to serve a two-year prison sentence for killing a man in a brawl. The experience was a formative one for Oglethorpe, scion of a large and upwardly mobile family now forced to see how England's underbelly really lived.

Upon his release from prison, the 25-year-old Oglethorpe ran for the "family" House of Commons seat once occupied by his fathers and two brothers, and won. He immediately made a name for himself an aggressive campaigner for human rights and an outspoken opponent of slavery.

Another jail-related epiphany came when Oglethorpe, then on the Prison Discipline Committee of Parliament, saw a dear friend die of smallpox in debtors' prison. More than ever, Oglethorpe was determined to right what he saw as a colossal wrong in the draconian English justice system.

His crusade took the form of establishing a sanctuary for debtors in North America. To that end, he and his friend Lord Perceval established the Trustees, a 21-member group who lobbied King George for permission to establish such a colony. The grant from the king – who was more interested in containing the Spanish to the south than in any humanitarian concerns – would include all land between the Altamaha and Savannah Rivers and from the headwaters of these rivers to the "south seas."

Though ironically no debtors were among Savannah's original colonists, the new settlement was indeed a reflection of its founder's core values, banning rum as a bad influence (though beer and wine were allowed), prohibiting slavery, and eschewing lawyers on the theory that a gentleman should always able to defend himself.

Nearing 40 and distracted by an increasingly nasty guerrilla war with the Spanish – Savannah's proximity to whom was the reason no Catholics were originally allowed – Oglethorpe's ambitious agenda gradually eroded in the face of opposition from the settlers, who craved not only the more hedonistic lifestyle of their neighbors to the north in Charles Town but the economic advantage that city enjoyed in the use of slave labor.

In nearly the same hour as his greatest military victory, crushing the Spanish at the Battle of Bloody Marsh on St. Simon Island, Oglethorpe also suffered an ignominious defeat: being replaced as head of the 13th colony which he had founded.

He went back to England, never to see the New World again. But his heart was always with the colonists. After successfully fending off a political attack and an unsuccessful attempt at a court-martial, Oglethorpe married and eventually commenced a healthy retirement. He supported independence for the American colonies, making a point to enthusiastically receive the new ambassador from the United States, one John Adams.

At age 88, the old general died on June 30, 1785. Fittingly for this life-long philanthropist and humanitarian, his childhood home in Godalming, Surrey, is now a nursing home.

© JIM MOREKIS

will appreciate downtown all the more when you can get away and smell the salt air.

And also like Charleston, it's hard to imagine fully enjoying Savannah in a single day. Plan on two nights at an absolute minimum—not only to enjoy all the sights, but to fully soak in the local color and attitude.

ORIENTATION

It's tempting for newcomers to assume that Savannah jumps across the river into South Carolina, as do other riverine cities from Kansas City to Paris. But this is not the case, as Savannah emanates strictly southward from the river and never crosses the state line. (Don't be confused by the spit of land you see across the main channel of the Savannah River, the one bearing the squat new Trade and Convention Center and the towering Westin Savannah Harbour hotel. That's not South Carolina, it's Hutchinson Island, Georgia, annexed by the city of Savannah for development. South Carolina begins farther north, after you cross the river's Back Channel.)

The downtown area is bounded on the east by East Broad Street and on the west by Martin Luther King Jr. Boulevard (formerly West Broad St.). For quick access to the south, take the one-way streets Price (on the east side of downtown) or Whitaker (on the west side of downtown). Conversely, if you want to make a quick trip north into downtown, three one-way streets taking you there are East Broad, Lincoln, and Drayton. Technically, Gwinnett Street is the southern boundary of the National Historic Landmark District, though in practice locals typically extend the boundary several blocks southward.

When you're driving downtown and come to a square, the law says traffic within the square *always* has the right of way. In other words, if you haven't yet entered the square, you must yield to any vehicles already in the square.

Many of the following neighborhood designations, like City Market and the Waterfront, are well within the National Landmark Historic District, but locals tend to think of them as separate entities, and we'll follow their lead.

While largely in private hands, the Victorian District—with historical certification and protection of its own—contains some wonderful architecture that unfortunately is often overshadowed by the more ornate buildings in the Historic District proper.

The Eastside includes many areas that are technically islands, but their boundaries are so blurred by infill of the marsh and by well-constructed roads that you'll hardly sense a difference from the mainland.

To most locals, "Southside" refers to the generic strip mall sprawl below Derenne Avenue, but for our purposes here the term also includes some outlying islands. I include them in the southern part of town because of the general direction and length of travel.

HISTORY

To understand the inferiority complex that Savannah feels to this day with regards to Charleston, you have to remember that literally from day one, Savannah was intended to play second fiddle to its older, richer neighbor to the north. By the early 1700s, the land south of Charles Town was a staging area for attacks by the Spanish and Native Americans. So in 1732, King George II granted a charter to the Trustees of Georgia, a proprietary venture that was the brainchild of a 36-year-old general and member of Parliament, General James Edward Oglethorpe.

On February 12, 1733, the ship *Anne* landed with 114 passengers along the bluff on the south bank of the Savannah River. Oglethorpe bonded with Tomochichi, the local Creek Indian chief, and the colony prospered. (Contrary to what locals might tell you, Savannah did not get its name because it resembles a grassy savanna. The city is christened for the Savannah River, which itself is named for a wandering, warlike offshoot of the Shawnee tribe that dominated the waterway in the late 1600s.)

Ever the idealist, Oglethorpe had a plan for the new "classless society" in Savannah that prohibited slavery, rum, and—wait for it—lawyers! But as the settlers enviously eyed the economic dominance of Charleston's slave-based rice economy, the Trustees bowed to public pressure and relaxed restrictions on slavery and rum. By 1753, the crown reclaimed the charter, making Georgia America's 13th colony.

Though part of the new United States in 1776, Savannah was captured by British forces in 1778, who successfully held the city against a combined assault a year later. After the Revolution, Savannah became the first capital of Georgia, a role that lasted until 1786.

Despite hurricanes and yellow fever epidemics, Savannah's heyday was the antebellum period from 1800 to 1860, when for a time it outstripped Charleston as a center of commerce. By 1860, Savannah's population doubled after an influx of European immigrants, chief among them Irish workers coming to lay track on the new Central of Georgia line.

Blockaded for most of the Civil War, Savannah didn't see much action other than the fall of Fort Pulaski, which had worldwide ramifications. In April 1862, a Union land/sea force successfully laid siege to Fort Pulaski using rifled artillery, a revolutionary new technology that instantly rendered the world's masonry forts obsolete.

War came to Savannah's doorstep when General William T. Sherman's March to the Sea concluded with his capture of the town in December 1864. Sherman sent a now-legendary telegram to President Lincoln granting him the city as a Christmas present with these words: "I beg to present you as a Christmas gift, the City of Savannah with 150 heavy guns and plenty of ammunition and also about 25,000 bales of cotton."

After a lengthy Reconstruction period, Savannah began reaching out to the outside world. From 1908–1911, it was a national center of road racing. In the Roaring Twenties, native son Johnny Mercer rose to prominence and the great Flannery O'Connor was born in downtown Savannah.

World War II provided an economic lift to Savannah, but the city was still known as the "pretty woman with a dirty face," as Britain's Lady Astor famously described it in 1946.

Almost in answer to Astor's quip, city leaders in the '50s began a misguided program to retrofit the city's infrastructure for the automobile era. This frenzy of demolition cost such irreplaceable civic treasures as Union Station, the City Auditorium, and the old Desoto Hotel. Savannah's preservation movement had its seed in the fight by seven Savannah women to save the Davenport House and other buildings from similar fates. Preservation took a huge step forward in 1966, when the historic district was named a National Historic Landmark.

Savannah played a pioneering, though largely unsung, role in the civil rights movement. Ralph Mark Gilbert, pastor of the historic First African Baptist Church, launched one of the first black voter registration drives in the South, which led the way for the historic integration of the police department in 1947. Gilbert's efforts were kept alive in the '50s and '60s by the forceful and beloved W. W. Law, head of the local chapter of the NAACP for many years.

Savannah's longstanding diversity was further proved in 1970, when Greek American John P. Rousakis began his 21-year stint as mayor. During Rousakis' tenure, the first African American city alderman was elected, the movie industry discovered the area, and Atlanta was awarded the 1996 Summer Olympics, which brought several venues to Savannah. Once-decrepit River Street and Broughton Street were revived. The opening of the Savannah College of Art and Design (SCAD) in 1979 ushered another important chapter in Savannah's renaissance.

After the publication of John Berendt's *Midnight in the Garden of Good and Evil* in 1994, nothing would ever be the same in Savannah. Old-money families cringed as idiosyncrasies and hypocrisies were laid bare in "The Book." Local merchants and politicians, however, delighted in the influx of tourists.

Savannah's first African American mayor, Floyd Adams Jr., was elected in 1995. Immediately succeeding him was current mayor Otis Johnson, the first black Savannahian to graduate from the University of Georgia.

Sights

It's best to introduce yourself to the sights of Savannah by traveling from the river southward. It's no small task to navigate the nation's largest contiguous Historic District, but when in doubt it's best to follow James Oglethorpe's original plan of using the five "monumental" squares on Bull Street (Johnson, Wright, Chippewa, Madison, and Monterey) as focal points.

WATERFRONT

It's only natural to start one's adventures in Savannah where Oglethorpe's adventures themselves began: on the waterfront, now dominated by scenic and historic River Street. Once the bustling center of Savannah's thriving cotton and naval stores export industry, the waterfront is also generally thought of as including Factor's Walk and Bay Street.

◖ River Street

It's much tamer than it was 30 years ago—when muscle cars cruised its cobblestones and a volatile mix of local teenagers, sailors on shore leave, and soldiers on liberty made things less-than-family-friendly after dark—but River Street still has more than enough edginess to keep things interesting. Families are now safe and welcome here, but energetic pub crawling remains a favorite pastime for locals and visitors alike. And of course the collected history in this block stretch of waterfront, representative of the era of King Cotton, will interest those of a more introspective bent as well.

If you have a car, park it somewhere else and walk. The cobblestones—actually old ballast stones from some of the innumerable ships that docked here over the years—are tough on the suspension, and much of River Street is dedicated to pedestrian traffic anyway. If you do find yourself driving here, keep in mind that the north–south "ramps" leading up and off River Street are all extensions of major downtown

a tugboat on the Savannah River

© JIM MOREKIS

SAVANNAH

SAVANNAH

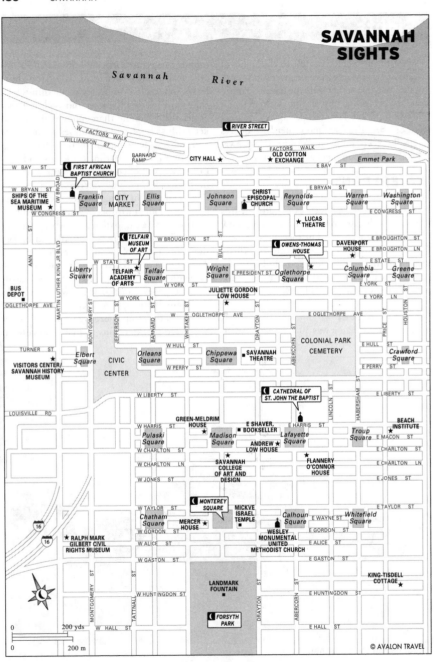

SAVANNAH SIGHTS

Savannah River

☾ RIVER STREET

W. FACTORS WALK
WILLIAMSON ST
BARNARD RAMP
E FACTORS WALK
CITY HALL ★
OLD COTTON ★ EXCHANGE
Emmet Park

W BAY ST
☾ FIRST AFRICAN BAPTIST CHURCH
E BAY ST

W BRYAN ST
SHIPS OF THE SEA MARITIME MUSEUM ★
E BRYAN ST

Franklin Square
CITY MARKET
Ellis Square
Johnson Square
CHRIST EPISCOPAL CHURCH
Reynolds Square
Warren Square
Washington Square

W CONGRESS ST
E CONGRESS ST

LUCAS ★ THEATRE

☾ TELFAIR MUSEUM OF ART
W BROUGHTON ST
E BROUGHTON ST

☾ OWENS-THOMAS HOUSE
DAVENPORT HOUSE ★
E BROUGHTON LN

W STATE ST
E STATE ST

Liberty Square
TELFAIR ACADEMY OF ARTS
Telfair Square
Wright Square
E PRESIDENT ST
Oglethorpe Square
Columbia Square
Greene Square

BUS DEPOT
E YORK ST

OGLETHORPE AVE
W YORK ST
JULIETTE GORDON LOW HOUSE ★
E YORK LN

W YORK LN
W OGLETHORPE AVE
E OGLETHORPE AVE

TURNER ST
Crawford Square

Elbert Square
CIVIC CENTER
Orleans Square
W HULL ST
Chippewa Square
SAVANNAH THEATRE ■
COLONIAL PARK CEMETERY

VISITORS CENTER/ SAVANNAH HISTORY MUSEUM ★
W PERRY ST
E PERRY ST

LOUISVILLE RD
W LIBERTY ST
E LIBERTY ST

☾ CATHEDRAL OF ST. JOHN THE BAPTIST
BEACH INSTITUTE ★

GREEN-MELDRIM HOUSE ★
W HARRIS ST
E SHAVER, BOOKSELLER ■
E HARRIS ST
Troup Square ★
E MACON ST

Pulaski Square
Madison Square
Lafayette Square

W CHARLTON ST
ANDREW ★ LOW HOUSE
E CHARLTON ST

W CHARLTON LN
SAVANNAH COLLEGE OF ART AND DESIGN ★
FLANNERY O'CONNOR HOUSE ★
E CHARLTON LN

W JONES ST
E JONES ST

W TAYLOR ST
E TAYLOR ST

☾ MONTEREY SQUARE
Chatham Square
MERCER ★ HOUSE
MICKVE ISRAEL TEMPLE ■
Calhoun Square
E WAYNE ST
Whitefield Square

W GORDON ST
WESLEY MONUMENTAL UNITED METHODIST CHURCH ♦
E GORDON ST

RALPH MARK ★ GILBERT CIVIL RIGHTS MUSEUM
W ALICE ST
E ALICE ST

W GASTON ST
E GASTON ST

LANDMARK FOUNTAIN ■
KING-TISDELL COTTAGE ★

W HUNTINGDON ST
E HUNTINGDON ST

☾ FORSYTH PARK

W HALL ST
E HALL ST

MARTIN LUTHER KING JR BLVD
ANN ST
MONTGOMERY ST
JEFFERSON ST
BARNARD ST
WHITAKER ST
BULL ST
DRAYTON ST
ABERCORN ST
LINCOLN ST
HABERSHAM ST
PRICE ST
HOUSTON ST
TATTNALL ST

16
16
OGLETHORPE AVE

0   200 yds
0   200 m

© AVALON TRAVEL

streets, so you can easily drive or walk up them and find yourself in the middle of bustling Bay Street and on to points beyond.

THE WAVING GIRL

Begin your walking tour of River Street on the east end, at the statue of Florence Martus, a.k.a. *The Waving Girl,* set in the emerald green expanse of little Morrell Park. Beginning at the age of 19, Martus—who actually lived several miles downriver on Elba Island—took to greeting every passing ship with a wave of a handkerchief by day and a lantern at night, without fail for the next 40 years. Ship captains would often return the greeting with a salute of their own on the ship's whistle, and word spread all over the world of the beguiling woman who waited on the balcony of that lonely house.

Was she looking for a sign of a long lost love who went to sea and never returned? Was she trying to get a handsome sea captain to sweep her off her feet and take her off that little island? No one knows for sure, but the truth is probably more prosaic. Martus was a life-long spinster who lived with her brother the lighthouse keeper, and was by most accounts an eccentric, if delightful, person—which of course makes her an ideal Savannah character. After her brother died, Martus moved into a house on the Wilmington River, whiling away the hours by—you guessed it—waving at passing cars.

Martus became such an enduring symbol of the personality and spirit of Savannah that a U.S. Liberty ship was named for her in 1943. She died a few months after the ship's christening at the age of 75.

ROUSAKIS PLAZA

Continue walking west to Rousakis Plaza (River Street behind City Hall), a focal point for local festivals. It's a great place to sit, feed the pigeons, and watch the huge container ships go back and forth from the Georgia Ports Authority's sprawling complex farther upriver (you can see the huge Panamax cranes in the distance).

The **African American Monument** at the edge of Rousakis Plaza was erected in 2002

The Waving Girl, in Morrell Park

© JIM MOREKIS

SAVANNAH

to controversy for its stark tableau of a dazed-looking African American family with broken shackles around their feet. Adding to the controversy was the graphic content of the inscription at the base of the 12-foot statue, written especially for the monument by famed poet Maya Angelou. It reads: "We were stolen, sold and bought together from the African continent. We got on the slave ships together. We lay back to belly in the holds of the slave ships in each other's excrement and urine together, sometimes died together, and our lifeless bodies thrown overboard together. Today, we are standing up together, with faith and even some joy."

At this point you can't miss the huge, vaguely cubist Hyatt Regency Savannah, another controversial local landmark. The modern architecture of the Hyatt caused quite a stir when it was first built in 1981, not only because it's so contrary to the area's historic architecture but because its superstructure effectively cuts off one end of River Street from the other.

"Underneath" the Hyatt—actually still River Street—you'll find elevators to the hotel lobby, the best way to get up off the waterfront if you're not up for a walk up the cobblestones. Immediately outside the west side of the Hyatt up towards Bay Street is another exit/entry point, a steep and solid set of antebellum stairs, which, despite its decidedly pre–Americans with Disabilities Act aspect, is nonetheless one of the quicker ways to leave River Street for those with strong legs and good knees.

FACTOR'S WALK

One level up from River Street, Factor's Walk has nothing to do with math, though a lot of money has been counted here. In arcane usage, a "factor" was a broker, i.e., a middleman for the sale of cotton, Savannah's chief export during most of the 1800s. Factors mostly worked in Factor's Row, the traditional phrase for the actual buildings on River Street, most all of which were used in various import/export activities before their current transformation into a mélange of shops, hotels, restaurants, and taverns.

Factor's Walk is divided into Lower Factor's Walk, comprising the alleys and back entrances behind Factor's Row, and Upper Factor's Walk, the system of crosswalks at the upper levels of Factor's Row that lead you directly to Bay Street.

BAY STREET

Because so few downtown streets can accommodate 18-wheelers, Bay Street unfortunately has become the default route for much industrial traffic in the area on its way to and from the industrial west side of town.

In front of the Hyatt Regency is a concrete bench, marking the exact spot on which Oglethorpe pitched his first tent. But dominating Bay Street is **City Hall** (2 E. Bay St.) next door, with its gold-leaf dome. The 1907 building was designed by acclaimed architect Hyman Witcover and erected on the site of Savannah's first town hall.

The large gray Greek Revival building directly across from City Hall is the **U.S. Custom House** (1 E. Bay St.), not "Customs" regardless of what the tour guides may say. Built on

the spot of Georgia's first public building in 1852, the Custom House was also Georgia's first federal building and was the first local commission for renowned New York architect John Norris, who would go on to design 22 other buildings in Savannah. Within its walls was held the trial of the captain and crew of the notorious slave ship *Wanderer,* which illegally plied its trade after a national ban on the importation of slaves. Local newspaper publisher and educator John H. DeVeaux worked here after his appointment as the first African American U.S. Collector of Customs.

Directly adjacent to City Hall on the east is a small canopy sheltering two cannon, which together comprise the oldest monument in Savannah. These are the **Chatham Artillery Guns,** presented to the local militia group of the same name by President George Washington during his one and only visit to town in 1791. Today, locals use the phrase "Chatham Artillery" differently, to refer to a particularly potent local punch recipe that mixes several hard liquors.

Look directly behind the cannon and you'll see the ornate **Savannah Cotton Exchange** (100 E. Bay St.), built in 1886 to facilitate the city's huge cotton export business. Once nicknamed "King Cotton's Palace" but now a Masonic lodge, this delightful building by William Gibbons Preston is one of Savannah's many great examples of the Romanesque style. You'll become well acquainted with Preston's handiwork during your stay in Savannah—the Boston architect built many of Savannah's finest buildings. Note the fanciful lion figure in front—sometimes mistakenly referred to as a gryphon—representing Mark the Evangelist.

CITY MARKET

In local parlance, the phrase "City Market" generally refers not only to the refurbished warehouses comprising this tourist-friendly area of shops and restaurants in the Historic District's western portion, but its bookend squares as well—both of which had close scrapes with the bulldozer and wrecking ball before their current renaissance.

THE TWO PAULAS

It's odd that in a conservative Southern city like Savannah, its two biggest empire-builders are women – both of whom overcame contentious divorces to get where they are today. Odder still is the fact that they both share the same first name.

In any case, the empires that Paula Deen and Paula Wallace have built are two of the major reasons people visit Savannah today. Deen's empire centers on The Lady & Sons restaurant in City Market and her high profile on the Food Network. Wallace's empire centers on the Savannah College of Art and Design, the largest art school in the nation (and growing).

Their names are similar, but that's about their only similarity. These two powerhouse women and their stories of how they rose to the top could not be more different in every other way.

Deen, an Albany, Georgia, native, came to Savannah after divorcing her first husband in 1989, arriving with only $200 and her two teenage sons (now Food Network stars in their own right). Always ready with a self-deprecating quip, Deen still refers to herself as a former "bag lady" – the name of her first catering company – who still has a yen for shopping at Wal-Mart.

Severely agoraphobic (fearing crowds), Deen gradually increased her public presence first with a job cooking at a local hotel and then with her own restaurant, Lady & Sons, which was initially on West Congress Street. Her gregarious aw-shucks style caught the attention of producer Gordon Elliott, formerly with the seminal tabloid show *A Current Affair*.

His first cooking show pilot with Deen fizzled in 1999. But soon after the 9/11 attacks, Elliott spotted an opportunity to market a good old-fashioned comfort food show, *Paula's Home Cooking* to the trendy foodies at the Food Network. The result was, as they say, ratings gold. Initially taped at Elliott's New York home, taping has now moved to Savannah.

Sometimes known by local wags as "the white Oprah," Deen has expanded her presence into publishing, with a series of cookbooks, a glossy magazine, and a memoir. She had a brief but entertaining role as – you guessed it, a chef – in the 2005 film *Elizabethtown*. She's currently married to tugboat captain Michael Groover.

Petite, soft-spoken, and often surrounded by a coterie of devoted assistants, Paula Wallace is Deen's polar opposite in temperament. She arrived in Savannah in 1979 with her then-husband Richard Rowan to establish an art school. The two twenty-somethings, young children in tow, came armed with the guts to take a chance on depressed downtown real estate, the willingness to roll up their sleeves, and her parent's deep pockets.

The power couple soon became the toast of the town. Then came a bitter divorce. After the smoke cleared, Paula was the clear and undisputed *presidente* of SCAD.

It's hard to overstate the college's impact on Savannah. It's renovated over 50 historic properties and is estimated to own at least $200 million in assets, returning about $95 million a year into the local economy and employing approximately 1,400 people.

Now happily remarried, Wallace continues to expand SCAD's presence, with satellite campuses in Atlanta and Lacoste, France. In addition to her presidential duties, she authors children's and interior design books and manages the college's permanent art collection.

Ellis Square

Just across Bay Street on the western edge of the Historic District, Ellis Square has a history as Savannah's main open-air marketplace that goes back to 1755, when there was actually a single City Market building in the square itself. Three market buildings would come and go until the building of the fourth City Market in 1872, an ornate Romanesque affair with a 50-foot roofline.

In the 1954, the city, under the thrall of autoworship that was sweeping the country, decided a parking garage in the square was more important than fresh food or a sense of community. So the magnificent City Market building—and Ellis Square—simply ceased to exist.

However, several large warehouses surrounding City Market survived. They carried with them the seed of real renewal, which grew with the nascent preservation movement in the '50s and '60s. Now a year-round hub of tourism, City Market's eclectic scene encompasses working art studios, hip bars, cute cafés, live music in the east end of the courtyard, cutting edge art galleries, gift shops, and some great restaurants. This is also where you pick up one of the horse-drawn carriage tours, which embark from Jefferson Street running down the middle of City Market.

The eyesore that was the Ellis Square parking garage is now gone, and an ambitious attempt is underway to rebuild the square on top of a huge underground parking garage. It will cost taxpayers millions of dollars before all is said and done, but as any Savannahian will tell you, the return of one of their precious squares is priceless.

Franklin Square

Just west of City Market is Franklin Square, once known simply as "Water Tank Square" because that's where the city reservoir was. Don't be alarmed by the numbers of men hanging around in the square. Scruffy heirs to an old Savannah tradition, most of them are day laborers for hire.

Until recently, Franklin Square was, like Ellis

THE REBIRTH OF ELLIS SQUARE

One of the great tragedies of Savannah's 1950s love affair with "urban renewal" was the paving over of Ellis Square, site of the original City Market, replaced by a squat, drab parking garage.

Savannah is finally making amends for its bad karma by bringing Ellis Square back from the grave. In the massive $22 million "Ellis Square Project" – also called "The Big Dig" in a nod to a similarly ambitious project in Boston – city taxpayers are funding a complete facelift that will boast a new, fairly modern landscape design.

After a few initial rough spots – in which the walls of the dig began leaning inward, cracking the foundations of some nearby buildings – the project has progressed, with an estimated completion about the time you're reading this book. One major unanswered question is just how much groundwater will have to be continuously pumped out of the hole, both during and after construction.

While not everyone in town is enamored of the proposed design – many local landscape architects see its self-conscious modernity as a slap in the face to Oglethorpe's original design – there's no doubt that Savannah welcomes the return of one of its most beloved squares.

There's also no doubt that the city welcomes the 1,000 or so new parking spaces that will be available in a massive parking garage *under* the new Ellis Square.

Ellis Square is not the only one to have been partially or completely destroyed, however. A small plot of worn grass on the west side of the Savannah Civic Center is all that remains of Elbert Square, eviscerated by the construction of the block-long building.

And, ironically, Liberty Square was annihilated to make room for a place where some people lose their liberty – the new Chatham County Courthouse and Jail.

Square, a victim of "progress," this time in the form of a highway going right through the middle of it. But as part of the city's general effort to reclaim its history, Franklin Square was returned to its integral state in the mid-1980s.

(FIRST AFRICAN BAPTIST CHURCH

Without a doubt the premier historic attraction on Franklin Square—and indeed one of the most significant historic sites in Savannah—is the First African Baptist Church (23 Montgomery St., 912/233-2244, www.oldestblackchurch.org, tours Mon.–Fri. 10 A.M.–4 P.M.). It's the oldest black congregation in North America, dating from 1777. The church would also host the first African American Sunday school in North America, begun in 1826.

The church's founding pastor, George Liele, was the first black Baptist in Georgia. Here Liele, perhaps the first black missionary in America, would baptize his eventual successor, Andrew Bryan, a slave who opted to stay in Savannah and preach the Gospel instead of leaving with many other blacks after the British vacated the city. Third pastor Andrew Marshall was an ardent supporter of American independence and purchased his freedom shortly after the end of the Revolution. He actually served as George Washington's personal servant during his visit here. This founding trio is immortalized in stained-glass windows in the sanctuary.

The present building dates from 1859, and was built almost entirely by members of the congregation themselves, most of whom were enslaved at the time. It houses the oldest church organ in Georgia. Unusually for African American buildings of the period, it was built of brick, and indeed would be known as "The Brick Church" for many years.

A key staging area for the fabled Underground Railroad, First African still bears the scars of that turbulent time. When you're in the sanctuary, look for small holes in the floorboard. These were used as breathing holes for escaped slaves hiding in a cramped crawlspace. Some original pews remain in the balcony, with a few bearing African tribal signatures etched in the wood.

When Reverend Ralph Mark Gilbert occupied the pulpit during early 1950s, First African Baptist was the nerve center of the early civil rights movement in Savannah. A civil rights museum a few blocks away on MLK Jr. Boulevard is named for this influential pastor.

HISTORIC DISTRICT
Johnson Square

Due east of City Market, Oglethorpe's very first square is named for Robert Johnson, governor of South Carolina at the time of Georgia's founding. This is where Savannah's town crier did his thing back in the day; in modern times as well, political candidates usually choose Johnson Square to make major speeches and announcements.

It was here where Savannah's Liberty Pole was erected in 1774 to celebrate a new nation. And it was here where a gathering in 1861 celebrated Georgia's secession, ironically with a huge banner draped over the Greene Monument bearing the words "Don't Tread on Me"—a slogan used in the founding of the very union they sought to dissolve.

The roomy, shady square, ringed with major bank branches and insurance firms, is dominated by the **Nathanael Greene Monument** in honor of George Washington's second-in-command, who was granted nearby Mulberry Grove plantation for his efforts. Marquis de Lafayette dedicated the towering obelisk during his one and only visit to Savannah in 1825. At the time it did not honor any one person. Its dedication to Greene came in 1886, followed by the re-interment of Greene's remains directly underneath the monument in 1901. (In typically maddening Savannah fashion, there is a separate square named for Greene, which has no monument to him at all.)

A much smaller but more charming and personable little monument in Johnson Square, though, is the **William Bull Sundial** at the south side. Bull Street was named for this South Carolinian who accompanied Oglethorpe on his first journey to the new colony, helping him choose and survey the site—hence a sundial is an appropriate remembrance.

CHRIST EPISCOPAL CHURCH

The southeast corner of Johnson Square is dominated by Christ Episcopal Church (18 Abercorn St., 912/232-4131, www .christchurchsavannah.org), a.k.a. Christ Church, a historic house of worship also known as the "Mother Church of Georgia" because its congregation traces its roots to that first Anglican service in Savannah, held the

same day Oglethorpe landed. While this spot on Johnson Square was reserved for the congregation from the very beginning, this is actually the third building on the site, dating from 1838. Much of the interior is more recent than that, however, since a fire gutted the interior in 1895. In the northeast bell tower is a bell forged in 1919 by Revere and Sons of Boston.

For a special treat, walk right in to Christ Church's Compline service, held every Sunday evening at 9 P.M., and enjoy a selection of calming liturgical music sung by

© JIM MOREKIS

monument to John Wesley in Reynolds Square

JOHN WESLEY AND THE SEEDS OF METHODISM

In December 1735, General Oglethorpe returned to the new colony after taking Tomochichi and a few other Yamacraw for an eventful tour of England. Among others, on his return he brought with him two brothers, the ambitious John Wesley and his musical brother Charles.

John Wesley had already made a name for himself in Anglican circles for founding the "Holy Club" at Oxford University. The club gained the then-pejorative name "Methodists" because of their piety and overly regular ways, though the Wesleys still at that point considered themselves devout Anglicans.

The brothers had just lost their father and were at a turning point in life, so they came to Savannah with the mission to help Christianize the local Native Americans. The 1979 sculpture of John Wesley in Reynolds Square, in fact, portrays him evangelizing outdoors to native peoples.

John Wesley felt called to the Christian faith at a remarkably early age. When he was five, his home in England caught fire, his room in the attic and thus unreachable. But he managed to lean out of the window until someone was able to save him. From that time on he believed he'd been saved for a special task.

During his year and a half tenure in Savannah, Wesley founded what's commonly known as the first Sunday school in America while rector of Christ Church, a congregation known as "the mother church of Georgia," which continues to this day in a sanctuary on Johnson Square.

Wesley's pioneering, almost radical spirit immediately began testing the patience of his High Anglican parishioners, including his attempt to revise the Book of Common Prayer

Christ Church's excellent Compline Choir. Colloquially known as "saying good night to God," the Compline service is free and open to those of all faiths.

Reynolds Square

Walk directly east of Johnson Square to find yourself at Reynolds Square, named for John Reynolds, the first (and exceedingly unpopular) royal governor of Georgia. First called "Lower New Square," Reynolds originally served as site of the "filature," or cocoon storage warehouse, during the fledgling colony's ill-fated flirtation with the silk industry (a federal building now occupies that site).

As with Johnson Square, the monument in Reynolds Square has nothing to do with its namesake, but is instead a likeness of John Wesley dedicated in 1969 near the spot believed to have been his home. On the northeast corner of the square is the parish house of Christ Church, Wesley's congregation during his stay in Savannah.

A Reynolds Square landmark, the **Olde Pink**

SAVANNAH

and his habit of drawing lots whenever he needed to make an important decision. Ever the innovator, Wesley taught himself Spanish in order to better communicate with Savannah's large population of Sephardic Jews. One of the earliest British abolitionists, Wesley constantly preached against the evils of slavery.

All this change proved too much of a good thing for many Savannahians, and eventually two women began spreading gossip about the rector. For awhile Oglethorpe himself was convinced, and punished Wesley by making him a literal pariah, forced to sleep on the ground.

However, Wesley eventually returned to the general's favor, even becoming a sort of proxy for Oglethorpe whenever the founder was away. Unfortunately, this put him at odds with a young up-and-comer in the colony, Thomas Causton, who had designs on running the colony himself.

The final blow to Wesley's American ministry came in typical Savannah fashion, through a failed love affair – with, of all people, Thomas Causton's niece, Sophia Hopkey. (Wesley and Hopkey became romantically involved, suitably enough, while he was giving her French lessons.)

In a pang of conscience, Wesley abruptly stopped speaking to Hopkey, and she quickly married someone else. However, a jealous and vindictive Wesley then refused to allow Hopkey to take Communion, whereupon her new husband – backed behind the scene by Causton – sued the minister for defamation, asking for the then-astronomical sum of 1,000 pounds sterling.

The case against him never went to trial and a challenge to a duel by Causton didn't pan out, either. But the damage to Wesley's credibility and reputation was done. He packed his bags and left Georgia, never to return, lamenting, "I came to convert the Indians, but, oh, who will convert me?"

The Wesleys were long gone from Savannah by the time the first true Methodist church opened here, appropriately named Wesley Monumental United Methodist. Because this "beautiful and commodious edifice" was built by funds gathered from Methodists all over the world, it's considered to belong to all who practice that faith.

One aspect of his Georgia experience seemed to have a deep and lasting positive impact on Wesley, however. On his initial trip over the Atlantic, a storm destroyed one of the ship's masts. A group of devout Moravian settlers on the ship impressed Wesley when instead of panicking, they began calmly singing hymns. Wesley would go on to say the Moravians "were the only genuine Christians" he had ever met.

So it was no surprise that upon his return to England, Wesley immediately sought out the company of Moravian congregation to fine-tune his upgrading of Anglican doctrine, which would eventually become the first evangelical movement in the United Kingdom – known then as now as Methodism.

House (23 Abercorn St.), is not only one of Savannah's most romantic restaurants but quite a historic site as well. It's the oldest Savannah mansion from the 18th century still extant, as well as the first place in Savannah where the Declaration of Independence was read aloud. Pink inside as well as out, the Georgian mansion was built in 1771 for rice planter James Habersham Jr., one of America's richest men at the time and member of the notorious "Liberty Boys" who plotted revolution against the Crown. The building's pink exterior was a matter of serendipity, resulting from its core red brick seeping through the formerly white stucco outer covering.

At the southwest corner of Reynolds Square is the understated **Oliver Sturgis House** (27 Abercorn St.), former home of the partner with William Scarbrough in the launching of the S.S. *Savannah*. This is one of the few Savannah buildings to feature the stabilizing earthquake rods which are much more common in Charleston. Don't miss the dolphin downpour spouts at ground level.

LUCAS THEATRE FOR THE ARTS

The other major Savannah landmark occupying Reynolds Square is the Lucas Theatre for the Arts (32 Abercorn St., 912/525-5040, www.lucastheatre.com). Built in 1921 as part of Arthur Lucas' regional chain of movie houses, the Lucas also featured a stage for road shows. Ornate and stately but with cozy warmth to spare, the venue was a hit with Savannahians for four decades, until the advent of TV and residential flight from downtown led to financial disaster. In 1976, the Lucas closed after a screening of *The Exorcist*. Several attempts to revive the venue followed, including a comedy club in the '80s, but to no avail.

When the building faced demolition in 1986, a group of citizens created a nonprofit specifically to raise money to save it. Despite numerous starts, stops, and bureaucratic and personal obstacles, that 14-year campaign finally paid off in a grand reopening in December 2000, an event helped immeasurably by timely donations from *Midnight* star Kevin Spacey and the cast and crew of the locally shot *Forrest Gump*.

the historic Lucas Theatre for the Arts

Administered by a fairly unique public/private partnership between local taxpayers and the Savannah College of Art and Design, the Lucas now hosts world-class entertainment and civic events year-round. The theater's schedule stays pretty busy, so it should be easy to check out a show while you're in town. Once inside, be sure to check out the extensive gold-leaf work throughout the interior, all painstakingly done by hand.

Columbia Square

Named for the mythical patroness of America, this square features at its center not an expected portrait of that female warrior figure, but the original fountain from Noble Jones's Wormsloe Plantation, placed there in 1970.

ISAIAH DAVENPORT HOUSE MUSEUM

Columbia Square is primarily known as the home of the Isaiah Davenport House Museum (324 E. State St., 912/236-8097, www.davenporthousemuseum.org, Mon.–Sat. 10 A.M.–4 P.M., Sun. 1–4 P.M., $8 adults, $5 children). The house museum is a delightful stop in and of itself because of its elegant simplicity, sweeping double staircase, and near-perfect representation of the Federalist style. But the Davenport House occupies an exalted place in Savannah history as well, because it was the fight to save it that began the preservation movement in Savannah.

In 1955 the Davenport House, then a tenement, was to be demolished to make way for a parking lot. But Emma Adler and six other feisty Savannah women, angered by the recent paving over of City Market, refused to go down quietly. Together they formed the Historic Savannah Foundation in order to raise the $22,500 needed to purchase the Davenport House. By 1963, the Davenport House—built in 1820 for his own family by master builder Isaiah Davenport—was open to the public as a museum. Another major restoration from 2000–2003 brought the home back to its original early 1800s state as you enjoy it today.

Across the corner from the Davenport House is the Classical Revival masterpiece **Kehoe**

House (123 Habersham St.), designed for local ironworks owner William Kehoe in 1892 by DeWitt Bruyn. Sadly, the proof of Kehoe's self-described "weakness for cupolas" is no longer extant, the cupola having rotted away. But that's where Kehoe would often go to get some peace and quiet from his many children. Once a funeral home and then an inn owned briefly for a time by football legend Joe Namath, the Kehoe House is now one of Savannah's premier bed-and-breakfasts. It's unique not only in its exuberantly Victorian architecture, but in its twin fireplaces and ubiquitous rococo ironwork, courtesy naturally of the irrepressible Kehoe himself.

WARREN AND WASHINGTON SQUARES

Warren Square and its neighbor Washington Square formed the first extension of Oglethorpe's original four, and still boast some of the oldest houses in the historic district. Both squares are lovely little garden spots, ideal for a picnic in the shade. Two houses near Washington Square were restored by the late Jim Williams of *Midnight* fame: The **Hampton Lillibridge House** (507 E. Saint Julian St.), which once hosted an Episcopal exorcism, and the **Charles Oddingsells House** (510 E. Saint Julian St.). Now a hotel, the **Mulberry Inn** on Washington Square was once a cotton warehouse and subsequently a Coca-Cola bottling plant.

GREENE SQUARE

Named for Revolutionary War hero Nathanael Greene but bearing no monument to him whatsoever, this square is of particular importance to local African American history. At the corner of Houston (pronounced "House-ton") and East State Streets is the 1810 **Cunningham House,** built for Henry Cunningham, former slave and founding pastor of the **Second African Baptist Church** (124 Houston St., 912/233-6163) on the west side of the square, in which General Sherman made his famous promise of "40 acres and a mule." In 1818, the residence at 542 East State Street was constructed for free blacks Charlotte and William

SAVANNAH

THE IRISH IN SAVANNAH

© JIM MOREKIS

the Celtic cross in Emmet Park

It seems Savannah's close connection to St. Patrick's Day was ordained from the beginning. The very first baby born here, Georgia Close, came into the world on March 17, 1733.

Two hundred and fifty years later Savannah holds what's commonly considered the second-largest St. Patrick's Day celebration in the world, second only to New York City's. Three presidents have visited during the shindig – William Howard Taft in 1912, Harry Truman in 1962, and Jimmy Carter in 1978.

With its fine spring weather and walkability – not to mention its liberal "to-go cup" rules allowing you to carry your own adult beverage with you on the street – Savannah seems tailor-made for such a boisterous outdoor celebration. But most of all, what makes it a perfect fit is the city's large Irish-American population and their collective legacy.

The earliest Irish in Georgia were descendants of the Calvinist Scots who "planted" Ireland's northern province of Ulster in the 1600s. Often called "crackers" – perhaps from the Gaelic *craic*, "enjoyable conversation" – these early Irish made their living trading, trapping, or soldiering, and generally entered Georgia from upstate South Carolina. One such "cracker" and one of Savannah's earliest Irish heroes was Sergeant William Jasper, mortally wounded leading the charge to retake the city from the British in 1779.

The main chapter in local Irish history, however, really began in the 1830s with the arrival of the first wave of Irish to help build the Central of Georgia Railroad's first leg to Macon, Georgia, completed in 1843. The story goes that Irish were employed to build the railroad because, un-

like slaves, their bodies had no commercial value and could be worked to exhaustion with impunity. A second wave of Irish immigration followed two decades later when the Potato Famine in the old country forced many to seek new shores.

Though the Irish initially received a similar reception to the one they experienced in Manhattan – prejudice, police scrutiny, "No Irish need apply" signs in shop windows – their willingness to work long hours for low pay soon made them irreplaceable in Savannah's economy. And also as in New York, in short order Irish became major players in politics and business.

In the early days, Irish neighborhoods were clustered around East Broad Street in the Fort Wayne (or "Old Fort") area, and on the west side of town near West Broad Street (now MLK Jr. Boulevard). It's no coincidence that those areas also had large African American populations. Because of their shared link as victims of poverty and prejudice, in the early days Savannah Irish tended to live near black neighborhoods, often socializing with them after-hours – much to the chagrin of Savannah's elite.

Ironically given St. Patrick's Day's current close association with the Catholic faith, the first parade in Savannah was organized by Irish *Protestants*. In 1813, 13 members of the local Hibernian Society – America's oldest Irish society – took part in a private procession to Independent Presbyterian Church. The first public procession was in 1824, when the Hibernians invited all local Irishmen to parade through the streets. The first recognizably modern parade, with bands and a "grand marshal," happened in 1870.

Today's parade is a far cry from those early beginnings. Organized by a "committee" of about 700 local Irishmen – with but a tiny sprinkling of lasses – the three-hour procession includes marchers from all the local Irish organizations, from Hibernians to Clan na Erin to Sinn Fein (no relation to the political party in Ireland). Rain or shine, the assembled clans march – amble is perhaps a more accurate word – wearing their kelly green blazers, brandishing their walking canes and to-go cups, some pushing future committee members in strollers, fair skin gradually getting redder in the Georgia sun.

Wall. The property at 513 East York Street was built for the estate of Catherine DeVeaux, part of a prominent African American family.

Old Fort

One of the lesser-known aspects of Savannah history is this well-trod neighborhood at the east end of Bay Street, once the site of groundbreaking experiments and piratical intrigue, then a diverse melting pot of Savannah citizenry.

TRUSTEES GARDEN

At the east end of Bay Street where it meets East Broad Street rises a large bluff behind a masonry retaining wall—at 40 feet off the river, still the highest point in Chatham County. This is Trustees Garden, the nation's first experimental garden. Modeled on the Chelsea Botanical Garden in London, it was intended to be the epicenter of Savannah's silk industry. Alas, the colonists had little knowledge of native soils or climate—they thought the winters would be milder—and the experiment was not as successful as hoped.

Soon Trustees Garden became the site of Fort Wayne, a defensive installation overlooking the river named after General "Mad Anthony" Wayne of Revolutionary War fame, who retired to a plantation near Savannah. The Fort Wayne area—still called the "Old Fort" neighborhood by old-timers—fell from grace and became associated with the "lowest elements" of Savannah society, which in the 19th and early 20th centuries were Irish and African Americans.

It also became known for its illegal activity and as the haunt of sea salts such as the ones who frequented what is now the famed and delightfully schlocky Pirates' House restaurant. That particular building began life in 1753 as a seamen's inn, and later became chronicled by Robert Louis Stevenson in *Treasure Island* as a rogue's gallery of pirates and assorted nautical ne'er-do-wells. Find the old "Herb House," the older-looking clapboard structure next to the Pirates' House entrance, on East Broad Street. You're looking at what's considered the single oldest building in Georgia and one of the oldest in the United States. Constructed in 1734, it was originally the home of Trustees Garden's chief gardener.

To the rear of Trustees Garden is the 1881 Hillyer building, now the **Charles H. Morris Center,** a mixed-use performing arts and meeting space.

EMMET PARK

Just north of Reynolds Square on the north side of Bay Street you'll come to Emmet Park, first a Native American burial ground and then known as "the Strand" or "Irish Green" because of its proximity to the Irish slums of the Old Fort area. In 1902, the park was named for Robert Emmet, an Irish patriot of the early 1800s who was executed by the British for treason. Within it is the eight-foot **Celtic cross,** erected in 1983 and carved of Irish limestone. The Celtic cross is the center of a key ceremony for local Irish Catholics during the week prior to St. Patrick's Day.

Close by is one of Savannah's more recent monuments, the **Vietnam War Memorial** at East Bay Street and Rossiter Lane. The reflecting pool is in the shape of Vietnam itself, and the names of all 106 Savannahians killed in the conflict are carved into an adjacent marble tablet. Walk a little farther east and you'll find my favorite little chapter of Bay Street history, the **Beacon Range Light.** Tucked into a shady corner, few tourists bother to check out this masterfully crafted 1858 navigation aid, intended to warn approaching ships of the old wrecks sunk in the river as a defense during the Revolutionary War.

Broughton Street

Downtown's main shopping district for most of the 20th century, Broughton Street once dazzled shoppers with decorated gaslights, ornate window displays, and fine examples of terrazzo, a form of mosaic that still adorns many shop entrances. Post-war suburbs and "white flight" brought neglect to the area by the 1960s, and many thought Broughton was gone for good. But with the downtown renaissance brought about largely by the Savannah College of Art and Design, Broughton was able not only to get back on its feet but begin to thrive as a commercial and recreational nerve center once again.

Around the corner from the Lucas Theatre on Reynolds Square is the *art moderne* **Trustees Theatre** (216 E. Broughton St., 912/525-5051, www.scad.edu), a SCAD-run operation that seats 1,200 and hosts concerts, film screenings, and the school's much-anticipated spring fashion show. It began life in the post-war boom of 1946 as the Weis Theatre, another one of those ornate Southern movie houses that took full commercial advantage of being the only buildings at the time to have air conditioning. But by the end of the '70s it followed the fate of Broughton Street, laying dormant and neglected until its purchase and renovation by SCAD in 1989. This block of Broughton in front of Trustees Theatre is usually blocked off to mark the gala opening of the Savannah Film Festival each fall. Searchlights criss-cross the sky, limos idle in wait, and Hollywood guests strike poses for the photographers.

Across the street is SCAD's **Jen Library** (201 E. Broughton St.), a state-of-the-art facility set in the circa-1890 Levy and Maas Brothers department stores. The Chinese characters on the modest marquee, which simply say "Jen Library," are a nod to SCAD benefactors Jim and Lancy Jen, administrators of the Pei Ling Chan Charitable Trust established by Lancy's Chinese father.

An important piece of Broughton Street history happened at its intersection with Whitaker Street. Tondee's Tavern was where the infamous "Liberty Boys" met over ale and planned Savannah's role in the upcoming American Revolution. Only a plaque marks the site's contribution to Savannah's colonial history.

Wright Square

By now you know the drill. The big monument in Wright Square, Oglethorpe's second square, has nothing to do with James Wright, royal governor of Georgia right before the Revolution, for whom it's named. Instead the monument honors William Gordon, former mayor and founder of the Central of Georgia Railroad, which upon completion of the Savannah–Macon run was the longest railroad in the world. Gordon is in fact the only native Savannahian to be honored in a city square.

But more importantly, Wright Square is the final resting place for the great Yamacraw chief Tomochichi, buried in 1737 in an elaborate state funeral at James Oglethorpe's insistence. A huge boulder of Stone Mountain granite honoring the chief was placed in a corner of the square in 1899 under the auspices of William Gordon's daughter-in-law. However, Tomochichi is not buried under the boulder, but rather somewhere underneath the Gordon monument. So why not rename it Tomochichi Square? Old ways die hard down here, my friend.

On the west side of the square is the **Federal Courthouse and Post Office,** built in 1898 out of Georgia marble. The building's stately facade makes an appearance in several films, including the original *Cape Fear* and *Midnight in the Garden of Good and Evil.*

Across the square stands another Preston design, the **Old Chatham County Courthouse,** no longer an active judicial facility but still known as "the old courthouse." Note the yellow brick construction, quite rare for this area.

Next to the old courthouse is the historic **Evangelical Lutheran Church of the Ascension** (120 Bull St., 912/232-4151, www .elcota.org), built in the 1870s for a congregation that traced its roots to some of the first Austrian Salzburgers to come to Savannah in 1734. While most moved to adjacent Effingham County, many stayed and thrived in town, where they were universally well regarded for their work ethic and honest dealings.

JULIETTE GORDON LOW BIRTHPLACE
Around the corner from Wright Square at Oglethorpe and Bull is the Juliette Gordon Low Birthplace (10 E. Oglethorpe Ave., 912/233-4501, www.girlscouts.org, year-round Mon.–Tues. and Thurs.–Sat. 11 A.M.–4 P.M., Sun. 11 A.M.–4 P.M., Wed. Mar.–Oct.

SCOUT'S HONOR: JULIETTE GORDON LOW

Known simply as "Daisy" to family and friends, Juliette Magill Kinzie Gordon was perhaps born to be a pioneer. Her father's family took part in the original settlement of Georgia, and her mother's kin were among the founders of Chicago.

Though mostly known as the founder of the Girl Scouts of America, Daisy was also an artist, adventurer, and healer. Born and raised in the house on Oglethorpe Avenue in Savannah known to Girl Scouts across the nation as simply "The Birthplace," she was an animal lover with an early penchant for theater, drawing, and poetry.

After school she traveled, returning home to marry a wealthy cotton heir named William Mackay Low, son of the builder of Savannah's exquisite Andrew Low House, in which Daisy was to spend most of her adult life. A harbinger of her troubled marriage happened on her wedding day, on the steps of Christ Church downtown. A grain of rice, thrown for good luck, struck her eardrum and led to a painful infection and the loss of hearing in that ear. Things went downhill from there, as she and her ne'er-do-well husband spent most of their unhappy time together in England, where he enjoyed hunting.

Daisy returned to Savannah with the outbreak of the Spanish-American War in 1898. Though virtually unknown and unstudied by most Americans today, that conflict represented a transformative period in Savannah history. Because of the city's proximity to Cuba, one of the main theaters of the war, it became staging area for U.S. Army troops from all over the country.

For Savannah, taking such an active role in the conflict was an opportunity to make amends for the alienation and strife of the Civil War and effectively rejoin the union again. For the first time since Sherman's March to the Sea, Savannahians actively and proudly displayed the Stars and Stripes in an honest show of patriotism, of which Daisy was a part, tending to wounded soldiers returning from Cuba.

After the war Daisy, returned to England to spend the last fractious days of her marriage, which existed in name only until her husband's death in 1905. She then did a lot of restless traveling, until in 1911 while in England

the gravesite of Juliette Gordon Low in Laurel Grove cemetery

she met another man who would change her life: Robert Baden-Powell, founder of the Boy Scout and Girl Guides in Britain. Struck by the simplicity and usefulness of his project, she carried the seeds of a similar idea back with her to the United States.

"I've got something for the girls of Savannah, and all of America, and all the world, and we're going to start it tonight!" were her famous words in a phone call to a cousin after meeting Baden-Powell. So on March 12, 1912, Daisy gathered 18 girls in the garden floor of the Andrew Low House to register the first troop of American Girl Guides, to be renamed the Girl Scouts of America a year later.

From that humble beginning in Savannah, the Girl Scouts now have nearly four million members. Since its inception, over 50 million girls have taken part in the organization. Through her outreach efforts during World War I, she also helped begin the World Association of Girl Guides and Girl Scouts.

Juliette "Daisy" Gordon Low died of breast cancer in her bed upstairs in the Andrew Low House on January 17, 1927. She was buried in Laurel Grove Cemetery on the city's west side. Girl Scout troops from all over America visit her birthplace, the Andrew Low House, and her gravesite to this day, often leaving flowers and small personal objects near her tombstone as tokens of respect and gratitude.

SAVANNAH

10 A.M.–4 P.M., $8 adults, $7 children), declared the city's very first National Historic Landmark in 1965. The founder of the Girl Scouts of America lived here from her birth in 1860 until she left for school. The house was built in 1821 for Mayor James Moore Wayne, a future Supreme Court Justice, but the current furnishings, many original, are intended to reflect the home during the 1880s.

Also called the Girl Scout National Center, the Low birthplace is probably Savannah's most festive historic site because of the heavy traffic of Girl Scout troops from across the United States. They flock here year-round to take part in programs and learn more about their organization's founder, whose family sold the house to the Girl Scouts in 1953.

You don't have to be affiliated with the Girl Scouts to tour the home. Tours are given every 15 minutes, and tickets are available at the Oglethorpe Avenue entrance. Be aware the site is closed most holidays, sometimes for extended periods; be sure to check the website for details.

Oglethorpe Square

Don't look for a monument to Georgia's founder in the square named for him. That would be way too easy, so of course his monument is in Chippewa Square. Originally called "Upper New Square," Oglethorpe Square was created in 1742.

◖ OWENS-THOMAS HOUSE

The square's main claim to fame, the Owens-Thomas House (124 Abercorn St., 912/233-9743, www.telfair.org, Mon. noon–5 P.M., Tues.–Sat. 10 A.M.–5 P.M., Sun. 1–5 P.M., $10 adults, $4 children), lies on the northeast corner. Widely known as the finest example of Regency architecture in the United States, the Owens-Thomas House was designed by brilliant young English architect William Jay. One of the first professionally trained architects in America, Jay was only 24 when he designed the home for cotton merchant or "factor" Richard Richardson, who lost the house in the depression of 1820 (all that remains of his tenure at the house are three marble-top tables).

Owens-Thomas House

© WWW.SAVANNAHVISIT.COM

The house's current name is derived from Savannah Mayor George Welshman Owens, who bought the house in 1830. It remained in his family until 1951, when his granddaughter Margaret Thomas bequeathed it to the Telfair Academy of Arts and Sciences, which currently operates the site.

Several things about the Owens-Thomas House stand out. First, it's constructed mostly of tabby, a mixture of lime, oyster shells, and sand. Its exterior is English stucco while the front garden balustrade is a type of artificial stone called coade stone. Perhaps most interestingly, a complex plumbing system features rain-fed cisterns, flushing toilets, sinks, bathtubs, and a shower. While inside, notice the unusual curved walls, with doors bowed to match. While many Owens family furnishings are part of the collection, much of it is representative American and European work from 1750 to 1830. On the south facade is a beautiful cast-iron veranda from which Revolutionary War hero Marquis de Lafayette addressed a crowd of star-struck Savannahians during his visit in 1825.

The 1990s marked the most intensive phase of restoration for the home, which began with a careful renovation of the carriage house and the associated slave quarters—discovered in a surprisingly intact state, including the original "haint blue" paint. The carriage house, where all tours begin, is now the home's gift shop.

Look across the square from the Owen-Thomas House. That's the former site of the Unitarian church where James L. Pierpont first performed "Jingle Bells." The entire building was moved to Troup Square to the south, in 1997 the local Unitarian congregation acquired the building and is now holding services in it once again.

Telfair Square

One of the few Savannah squares to show consistency in nomenclature, Telfair Square was indeed named for Mary Telfair, last heir of a family that was one of the most important in early Savannah history. A noted patron of the arts, Mary bequeathed the family mansion to the Georgia Historical Society upon her death in 1875 to serve as a museum. Originally called St. James Square after a similar square in London, Telfair is the last of Oglethorpe's original four squares.

◖ TELFAIR MUSEUM OF ART

Also consistent with its name, Telfair Square indeed hosts two of the three buildings operated by the Telfair Museum of Art (912/790-8800, www.telfair.org), an umbrella organization that relies on a combination of private and public funding and drives much of the arts agenda in Savannah.

The original part of the complex and the oldest art museum in the South, the **Telfair Academy of Arts and Sciences** (121 Barnard St.) was built in 1821 by the great William Jay for Alexander Telfair, scion of that famous Georgia family. The five statues in front are of Phidias, Raphael, Rubens, Michelangelo, and Rembrandt. Inside, the sculpture gallery and rotunda were added in 1885, the year before the building's official opening as a museum.

As well as displaying Sylvia Judson Shaw's now-famous "Bird Girl" sculpture originally in Bonaventure Cemetery (actually the third of four casts by the sculptor), the Telfair Academy features an outstanding collection of primarily 18th- and 20th-century works, most notably the largest public collection of visual art by Kahlil Gibran. Major paintings include work by Childe Hassam, Frederick Frieseke, Gari Melchers, and, of course, the massive *Black Prince of Crécy* by Julian Story.

The latest and proudest addition to the Telfair brand is the striking, 64,000-square-foot **Jepson Center for the Arts** (207 W. York St.), whose ultramodern exterior sits catty-corner from the old Telfair. Promoting a massive, daringly designed new facility devoted to nothing but modern art was a hard sell in this traditional town, especially when renowned architect Moshe Safdie, who also designed the Salt Lake City Public Library and Peabody Essex Museum, insisted on building a glassed-in flyover across a lane between two buildings. But no one regrets it now, as Safdie's

SAVANNAH

vision has exceeded even his supporters' high expectations. After a few delays in construction, Jepson opened its doors to the public in March 2006 and has since wowed locals and visitors alike with its cutting-edge assortment of late 20th- and 21st-century modern art, including digital installation pieces.

Its exterior covered in Portuguese stone, the Jepson is anchored around a high entrance atrium often used for wine and cheese receptions. A grand marble staircase sweeps you to the upper two floors. The second floor contains the Artzeum, a popular kids section offering a variety of hands-on activities for the art lover. The Nieses Auditorium is a screening room with a small performance stage.

Both museums are open Monday noon–5 P.M., Tuesday–Saturday 10 A.M.–5 P.M., and Sunday 1–5 P.M. Admission to each one singly is $10 adults and $4 children, but I recommend the Telfair's three-site combination ticket, which at the bargain price of $15 allows you to visit both art museums as well as the must-see Owens-Thomas House.

TRINITY UNITED METHODIST CHURCH

Directly between the Telfair and the Jepson stands Trinity United Methodist Church (225 W. President St., 912/233-4766, www.trinity church1848.org, Sunday services 8:45 A.M. and 11 A.M., sanctuary open to public daily 9 A.M.–5 P.M.), Savannah's first Methodist church. Built in 1848 on the site of the Telfair's family garden, its masonry walls are of famous "Savannah Gray" bricks—a lighter, more porous, and elegant variety—under stucco. Virgin long-leaf pines were used for most of the interior, fully restored in 1969. A fire in 1991 brought enough smoke and water damage to close the sanctuary for two years; the congregation met instead at a local mortuary! Back and better than ever, Trinity UMC had a nearly million-dollar exterior facelift in 2000. Call ahead for a tour.

Unfortunately, Telfair Square's charm is dampened by two glum federal buildings, one at the east side occupied by the IRS and one on the southeast corner, facing Oglethorpe Avenue. The latter edifice houses the U.S. Army Corps of Engineers, and its remarkably bland design prompted a horrified Savannah Mayor John Rousakis to famously quip that it looked like "bathroom tiles."

Chippewa Square

Named for a battle in the War of 1812, Chippewa Square has a large monument not to the battle, natch, but to James Oglethorpe, clad in full soldier's regalia. Notice the general is still facing south, toward the Spanish!

Yes, the bench on the square's north side is in the same location as the one Tom Hanks occupied in *Forrest Gump*, but it's not the same bench that hosted the two-time Oscar winner's backside—that one was donated by Paramount Pictures to be displayed in the Savannah History Museum on MLK Jr. Boulevard.

From Chippewa Square look south for the huge rectangular steel-and-glass structure dominating the skyline along Liberty Street. That's the infamous **Drayton Tower,** an outstanding, nearly pure example of the Internationalist architecture style nonetheless loathed by traditionalists since its construction in 1955. Until recently it served hundreds of students and seniors as one of downtown's few areas of low-cost housing. They've all since been kicked out, as now the building is subdivided into high-end condos with retail on the ground floor.

HISTORIC SAVANNAH THEATRE

At the northeast corner is the Historic Savannah Theatre (222 Bull St., 912/233-7764, www. savannahtheatre.com), which claims to be the oldest continuously operating theatre in America. Designed by William Jay, it opened in 1818 with a production of *The Soldier's Daughter.* In the glory days of gaslight theatre in the 1800s, some of the nation's best actors, including Edwin Booth, brother to Lincoln's assassin, regularly trod the boards of its stage. Other notable visitors were Sarah Bernhardt, W. C. Fields, and Oscar Wilde. Due to a fire in 1948, little remains of Jay's original design except a small section of exterior wall. It's currently home to a semi-professional revue company specializing in oldies shows.

INDEPENDENT PRESBYTERIAN CHURCH

Built in 1818, possibly by William Jay—scholars are unsure of the scope of his involvement—Independent Presbyterian Church (207 Bull St., 912/236-3346, www.ipc sav.org, Sunday service 11 A.M., Wednesday service noon) is called the "mother of Georgia Presbyterianism." A fire destroyed most of Independent Presbyterian's original structure in 1889, but the subsequent rebuilding was a very faithful rendering of the original design, based on London's St. Martin in the Field. The marble baptism font survived the fire and is still used today. Note also the huge mahogany pulpit, another original feature. The church's steeple made a cameo appearance in *Forrest Gump* as a white feather floated by.

Lowell Mason, composer of the hymn "Nearer My God to Thee," was organist at Independent Presbyterian. In 1885 President Woodrow Wilson married local parishioner Ellen Louise Axson in the manse to the rear of the church. Presiding was her grandfather, minister at the time. During the Great Awakening in 1896, almost 3,000 people jammed the sanctuary to hear famous evangelist D. L. Moody preach. Call ahead for a tour.

FIRST BAPTIST CHURCH

The nearby First Baptist Church (223 Bull St., 912/234-2671, www.heideldesign.com, Sunday service 11 A.M.) claims to be the oldest original church building in Savannah, with a cornerstone dating from 1830. Services were held here throughout the Civil War, with Union troops attending during the occupation. The church was renovated by renowned local architect Henrik Wallin in 1922. Call ahead for a tour.

COLONIAL CEMETERY

Just north of Chippewa Square is Oglethorpe Avenue, originally called South Broad and the southern boundary of the original colony. At Oglethorpe and Abercorn Streets is Colonial Cemetery, first active in 1750. You'd be forgiven for assuming it's the "D.A.R." cemetery; the Daughters of the American Revolution contributed the ornate iron entranceway in 1913, thoughtfully dedicating it to themselves instead of the cemetery itself.

Unlike the picturesque beauty of Bonaventure and Laurel Grove cemeteries, Colonial Cemetery has a morbid feel. The fact that burials stopped here in 1853 plays into that desolation, but maybe another reason is because it's the final resting ground of many of Savannah's yellow fever victims.

Famous people buried here include Button Gwinnett, one of Georgia's three signers of the Declaration of Independence. The man who reluctantly killed Gwinnett in a duel, General Lachlan McIntosh, is also buried there. The original burial vault of Nathanael Greene is in the cemetery, though the Revolutionary War hero's remains were moved to Johnson Square over a century ago. Vandalism through the years, including by Union troops, has taken its toll on the old gravestones. Many remain lined up along the east wall of the cemetery, with no one alive being able to remember where they originally stood.

Madison Square

Though named for the nation's fourth president, Madison Square memorializes a local hero who gave his life for his city during the American Revolution. Irish immigrant Sergeant William Jasper, hero of the Battle of Fort Moultrie in Charleston three years earlier, was killed leading the American charge at Spring Hill during the Siege of Savannah, when an allied army failed to retake the city from the British. Though the monument in the square honors Jasper, he isn't buried there. His body was interred in a mass grave near the battlefield along with other colonists and soldier-immigrants killed in the horrifically one-sided battle.

Though suitably warlike, the two small cannon in the square have nothing to do with the Siege of Savannah. They commemorate the first two highways in Georgia, today known as Augusta Road and Ogeechee Road.

GREEN-MELDRIM HOUSE

Given the house's beauty and history, visitors will be forgiven for not immediately realizing that the Green-Meldrim House (1 W. Macon St., 912/232-1251, tours every half-hour Tues.– Fri. 10 A.M.–3:30 P.M., Sat. 10 A.M.–12:30 P.M., $7 adults, $3 children) is also the rectory of the adjacent St. John's Episcopal Church, which acquired it in 1892. Though known primarily for serving as General. William T. Sherman's headquarters during his occupation of Savannah, visitors find the Green-Meldrim House a remarkably calming, serene location in and of itself, quite apart from its role as the place where Sherman issued his famous "40 Acres and a Mule" Field Order Number 15.

A remarkably tasteful example of Gothic Revival architecture, this 1850 design by John Norris features a beautiful external gallery of filigree ironwork. The interior is decorated with a keen and rare eye for elegant minimalism in this sometimes-rococo-minded town.

Nearby, the old **Scottish Rite Temple** at Charlton and Bull Streets was designed by Hyman Witcover, who also designed City Hall at Bay and Bull. A popular drugstore with a soda fountain for many years, it currently houses the Gryphon Tea Room, run by the Savannah College of Art and Design.

Directly across from that is SCAD's first building, **Poetter Hall,** known to old-timers as the Savannah Volunteer Guards Armory. With its imposing but somewhat whimsical facade right out of a Harry Potter movie, this brick and terra-cotta gem of a Romanesque Revival building was built in 1893 by William Gibbons Preston. It housed National Guard units (as well as a high school) until World War II, when the USO occupied the building during its tenant unit's service in Europe.

At the north side of Madison Square is the **Hilton Savannah DeSoto.** Imagine occupying that same space the most glorious, opulent, regal building you can think of, a paradise of brick, mortar, and buff-colored terra-cotta. That would have been the old DeSoto Hotel, which from its opening in 1890 was known as one of the world's most beautiful hotels and the

clear masterpiece in Boston architect William Gibbons Preston's already-impressive Savannah portfolio. Alas, it didn't have air conditioning, so the Hilton chain demolished it in 1968 for the current nondescript box.

Lafayette Square

Truly one of Savannah's favorite squares, especially on St. Patrick's Day, verdant Lafayette Square boasts a number of important sights and attractions.

◖ CATHEDRAL OF ST. JOHN THE BAPTIST

Spiritual home to Savannah's Irish community and the oldest Catholic church in Georgia, the Cathedral of St. John the Baptist (222. E. Harris St., 912/233-4709, www.savannah cathedral.org, daily 9 A.M.–5 P.M. with a break for Mass noon–12:30 P.M., Sunday services 8 A.M., 10 A.M., 11:30 A.M., Latin Mass 1 P.M.) was initially known as Our Lady of Perpetual Help. It's the place to be for Mass at 8 A.M. the morning of March 17, as the clans gather in their green jackets and white dresses to take a sip of communion wine before moving on to harder stuff.

Despite its overt Celtic character today, the parish was originally founded by Haitian émigrés who arrived after an uprising in their native country in the late 1700s. They were joined by other Gallic Catholics when some nobles fled from the French Revolution. The first sanctuary on the site was built in 1873, after the diocese traded a lot at Taylor and Lincoln Streets to the Sisters of Mercy in exchange for the cathedral's site on Abercorn. In a distressingly common event in Savannah, fire swept the edifice in 1898, leaving only two spires and the external walls. In an amazing story of determination and skill, the cathedral was completely rebuilt within a year and a half.

In the years since, many renovations have been undertaken, including an interior renovation following the Vatican Council II to incorporate some of its sweeping reforms, for example, a new altar allowing the celebrant to face the congregation. The most recent renovation, from 1998–2000, involved the intricate removal, cleaning, and re-leading of more than 50 of the cathedral's stained-glass windows, a roof replacement, and an interior makeover.

When inside, look for the new 9,000-pound altar and the 8,000-pound baptismal font, both made of Italian marble. The stained-glass window of the Virgin Mary is the largest of the three windows that survived the great fire of 1898. In 2003, an armed man entered the Cathedral and set the pulpit and bishop's chair on fire, resulting in nearly $400,000 of damage. The pulpit you see now is an exact replica, crafted by local woodworker Guenther Wood, with the Four Evangelists specially carved in Italy. The arsonist was arrested by a SWAT team, later saying he did it as a statement against organized religion.

ANDREW LOW HOUSE MUSEUM

Another major landmark on Lafayette Square is the Andrew Low House Museum (329 Abercorn St., 912/233-6854, www.andrew lowhouse.com, Mon.–Wed. and Fri.–Sat. 10 A.M.–4:30 P.M., Sun. noon–4:30 P.M., last tour at 4 P.M. $8 adults, $4.50 children), in which the founder of the Girl Scouts of America, Juliette "Daisy" Gordon Low, spent her short, unhappy marriage to William "Billow" Low, heir to the Low cotton fortune. Despite their happy-go-lucky nicknames, the union of Daisy and Billow was a notably unhappy one. Still, divorce was out of the question, so the couple lived separate lives until William's death in 1905. The one good thing that came out of the marriage was the germ for the idea for the Girl Scouts, which Juliette got from England's "Girl Guides" while living with her husband there, Savannah being the couple's winter residence.

Designed by the great New York architect John Norris, the Low House is a magnificent example of the Italianate style. Check out the cast-iron balconies on the long porch, a fairly rare feature in historic Savannah homes. Antiques junkies will go nuts over the furnishings, especially the massive secretary in

the parlor, one of only four such in existence (a sibling is in the Metropolitan Museum of Art). Poet William Makepeace Thackeray ate in the dining room, now sporting full French porcelain service, and slept in an upstairs room (he also wrote at the desk by the bed). Also on the second floor you'll see the room where Robert E. Lee stayed during his visit, and the bed where Juliette Gordon Low died.

FLANNERY O'CONNOR CHILDHOOD HOME

On the other corner of Lafayette Square stands the rather Spartan facade of the Flannery O'Connor Childhood Home (207 E. Charlton St., 912/233-6014, www.flannery oconnorhome.org, Sat.–Sun. 1–4 P.M., $5). The Savannah-born novelist lived in this three-story townhome from her birth in 1925 until 1938 and attended church at the Cathedral across the square. Once a fairly nondescript attraction for so favorite a native daughter, a just-concluded round of renovations has returned the main two floors to the state Flannery would have known, including an extensive library. A nonprofit association sponsors O'Connor-related readings and signings. While the current backyard garden is circa-1993, it is the place where five-year-old Flannery is said to have taught a chicken to walk backwards, foreshadowing the eccentric, gothic flavor of her writing.

Across from the O'Connor house is the **Hamilton-Turner Inn** (330 Abercorn St., 912/233-1833, www.hamilton-turnerinn.com). Now a privately owned bed-and-breakfast, this 1873 Second Empire mansion is best known for the showmanship of its over-the-top Victorian appointments and its role in "The Book" as the home of Joe Odom's girlfriend "Mandy Nichols" (real name Nancy Hillis). In 1883 it was reportedly the first house in Savannah to have electricity.

Troup Square

This low-key square boasts the most modern-looking monument downtown, the **Armillary Sphere.** Essentially an elaborate sundial, the sphere is a series of astrologically themed rings with an arrow that marks the time by shadow. It's supported by six tortoises.

Troup Square is also the home of the historic **Unitarian Universalist Church of Savannah** (313 E. Harris St., 912/234-0980, www.jinglebellschurch.org, Sunday service 11 A.M.). This original home of Savannah's Unitarians, who sold the church when the Civil War came, was recently re-acquired by the congregation. It is where James L. Pierpont first performed his immortal tune "Jingle Bells." However, when he did so the church was actually on Oglethorpe Square. The entire building was moved to Troup Square in the mid-1800s.

Just east of Troup Square, near the intersection of Harris and Price Streets, is the **Beach Institute** (502 E. Harris St., 912/234-8000, www.kingtisdell.org, Tues.–Sun. noon–5 P.M., $4). Built as a school by the Freedmen's Bureau soon after the Civil War, it was named after its prime benefactor, Alfred Beach, editor of *Scientific American,* and served as an African American school through 1919. Restored by SCAD and given back to the city to serve as a museum, the Beach Institute houses the permanent Ulysses Davis collection and a rotating calendar of art with a connection to black history.

JONES STREET

There aren't a lot of individual attractions on Jones Street, the east–west avenue between Taylor and Charlton Streets just north of Monterey Square. Rather, it's the small-scale, throwback feel of the place and its tasteful, dignified homes, including the former home of Joe Odom at 16 East Jones Street, that are the attraction.

The **Eliza Thompson House** (5 W. Jones St.), now a bed-and-breakfast, was in fact the first home on Jones Street. Cotton factor Joseph Thompson built the house for his wife Eliza in 1847. The carriage house is not original to the structure, having been built almost from scratch in 1980.

◀ Monterey Square

For many, this is the ultimate Savannah square.

Originally named "Monterrey Square" to commemorate the local Irish Jasper Greens' participation in a victorious Mexican-American War battle in 1846, the spelling morphed into its current version somewhere along the way. But Monterey Square remains one of the most visually beautiful and quietly serene spots in all of Savannah—despite the stream of tourist trolleys trundling around its periphery.

At the center of the square is a monument not to the victory for which it's named but to Count Casimir Pulaski, killed while attempting to retake the city from the British, and whose remains supposedly lie under the 55-foot monument. As early as 1912, people began noticing the disintegration of the monument due to substandard marble used in some key parts, but it wasn't until the 1990s that a full restoration attempt was accomplished. (The restoration company discovered that one of the monument's 34 sections had been accidentally installed upside-down. So in the true spirit of preservation, they dutifully put the section back—upside down!) The "Goddess of Liberty" atop the monument, however, is not original; you can see her in the Savannah History Museum.

MERCER-WILLIAMS HOUSE MUSEUM

Many tourists come to see the Mercer-Williams House Museum (429 Bull St., 912/236-6352, www.mercerhouse.com, Mon.–Sat. 10:30 A.M.–3:40 P.M., Sun. 12:30–4 P.M., $12.50 adults, $8 students). While locals will never begrudge the business Savannah's enjoyed since "The Book," it's a shame that this grand John Norris building is now primarily known as a crime scene involving antiques dealer Jim Williams and his lover. Therefore it might come as no real surprise that if you take a tour of the home, you might hear less about "The Book" than you may have expected. Now proudly owned by Jim Williams' sister Dorothy Kingery, an established academic in her own right, the Mercer-Williams House deliberately concentrates on the early history of the home and her brother's prodigious talent as a collector and conservator of fine art and antiques.

THE STORY OF "JINGLE BELLS"

Long after the Civil War ended, a North/South feud of a more harmless kind still simmers, as Boston and Savannah vie over bragging rights as to where the classic Christmas song "Jingle Bells" was written.

The song's composer, James L. Pierpont, led a life at times as seemingly carefree as his song itself. Born in Boston the son of an outspokenly abolitionist Unitarian minister, Pierpont's wanderlust manifested early, when he ventured from his new wife and young children to follow the Gold Rush to San Francisco, coming back East after one of that city's periodic enormous fires.

When his brother John was named minister of the new Unitarian congregation in Savannah in 1853 – a novelty down South at the time – Pierpont followed him, becoming music director and organist, again leaving behind his wife and children in Boston. During this time Pierpont became a prolific composer of secular, good-time tunes, including polkas, ballads, and minstrel songs.

Pierpont's first wife, by then mostly a memory, died of tuberculosis in 1856. By August 1857, he had remarried the daughter of the mayor of Savannah. That same month, a Boston-based publisher, Oliver Ditson and Co., first published his song "One Horse Open Sleigh." Two years later it was re-released under the current title, "Jingle Bells." However, at neither time was the song a popular hit.

In 1859, with slavery beginning to tear the country apart and the storm clouds of civil war gathering, the Unitarian Church in Savannah closed due to its abolitionist stance, then untenable anywhere in the Deep South. By the outbreak of war, Pierpont's brother John had gone back up North. James Pierpont, however, opted to stay in Savannah with his second wife Eliza Jane, even going so far as to sign up with the Isle of Hope Volunteers

of the First Georgia Cavalry (he served as a company clerk). During this Yankee's sojourn in the Confederate Army he wrote several forgettable patriotic tunes for the nascent nation, including "Our Battle Flag," "Strike for the South," and "We Conquer or Die."

After the war Pierpont taught music in sleepy Valdosta, Georgia, and then plied his trade in nearby Quitman. It took action by his son Juriah in 1880 to renew the copyright to what would become one of the most famous songs of all time. Pierpont died in 1883 in Winter Haven, Florida, and by his own request was buried in Savannah's Laurel Grove Cemetery near his beloved father-in-law, former Mayor Thomas Purse.

The provenance of his now-famous song is more in doubt. In Massachusetts, they swear Pierpont wrote the song while at the home of one Mrs. Otis Waterman. Down in Georgia, local scholars assure us a homesick Pierpont wrote the tune during a typical balmy Savannah winter at a house at Oglethorpe and Whitaker streets, long since demolished.

The Savannah contingent's ace in the hole is the fact that "Jingle Bells" was first performed in public at a Thanksgiving program at the local Unitarian Universalist Church in 1857. And despite persistent claims in Massachusetts that he wrote the song in that state in 1850, Southern scholars point out that Pierpont was actually in California in 1850.

So in this case at least, it appears the South can claim victory over the Yankees.

In one of those delightful happenstances of serendipity, Pierpont's old church – moved to Troup Square from its original site on Oglethorpe Square – went on the market in the 1990s and the local Unitarian Universalist congregation was able to raise enough money to buy it. They held their first service in their "new" home in 1997 and remain there to this day.

(That being said, Dr. Kingery's mama didn't raise no fool, as we say down here. The house was known to generations of Savannahians as simply the Mercer House until *Midnight* took off, at which time the eponymous nod to the late, great Mr. Williams was added.)

Built for General Hugh W. Mercer, Johnny Mercer's great-grandfather, in 1860, the war interrupted construction. General Mercer—descendant of the Revolutionary War general and George Washington's close friend Hugh Mercer—survived the war, in which he was charged with the defense of Savannah. But he soon fell into hard times and was forced to sell the house to John Wilder, who moved in after completion in 1868. (Just so you know, and despite what any tour guide might tell you, the great Johnny Mercer himself never lived in the house. Technically, no member of his family ever did.)

Tours of the home's main four rooms begin in the carriage house to the rear of the mansion. They're worth it for art aficionados even though the upstairs, Dr. Kingery's residence, is off-limits. Be forewarned that if you're coming just to see things about the book or movie, you might be disappointed.

TEMPLE MICKVE ISRAEL

Directly across Monterey Square from the Mercer House is Temple Mickve Israel (20 E. Gordon St., 912/233-1547, www.mickveisrael .org), a notable structure for many reasons: It's Georgia's first synagogue; it's the only Gothic

FACT VS. FICTION: *MIDNIGHT IN THE GARDEN OF GOOD AND EVIL*

There's no doubt about it: John Berendt's *Midnight in the Garden of Good and Evil* is a masterfully crafted true crime classic. And you can't argue with success: It was on the *New York Times* bestseller list for over four years, and is a major reason for Savannah's tourism boom of the 1990s, which continues today.

However, as Berendt himself admits in his author's note, many events and characters are embellished, a few names are changed, and some conversations are made up out of whole cloth. Berendt didn't arrive in town until a year after the murder that is the core of the book's narrative, thus rendering impossible his "conversation" with the murder victim, Danny Hansford.

Midnight's sometimes-tenuous relationship with reality is clear and has been remarked upon elsewhere, but there are other, more subtle anomalies as well that are worth mentioning.

For example, in the introduction Mary Hardy tells the author that Savannah has a bad taste in its mouth about New York writers. Actually, before the Civil War Savannah and New York City had a remarkably close association. Savannah's leading citizens self-consciously aped New York fashion, and many of them kept leading Manhattan architect John Norris quite busy designing their homes (the exquisite Andrew Low house is but one of the 23 buildings Norris designed in Savannah). Many a young socialite, including famous native Juliette Gordon Low, was sent off to finishing school in New York.

By the 1850s Savannah's infatuation with all things New York was so pronounced that one Charleston writer opined that "northern influence is very potent in Savannah; the Yankees exert themselves to the utmost to carry the elections their way."

Also, much is made in "The Book" of Savannah's isolated geography and how it supposedly turned the city's citizens into "hothouse plants" incapable of existing elsewhere. But as Berendt himself writes, Savannah is the westernmost point of the Eastern seaboard, minutes away from I-95. That proximity to the interior is one reason why Savannah's port is so successful and so many rail lines and industrial warehouses are active in the area to this synagogue in the country; and it's the third-oldest Jewish congregation in North America (following New York and Newport, R.I.). Notable congregants have included Dr. Samuel Nunes Ribiero, who helped stop an epidemic in 1733 his descendant Raphael Moses, considered the father of the peach industry in the Peach State; and current Mickve Israel Rabbi Arnold Mark Belzer, one of Savannah's most beloved community leaders. A specialist in the study of small, often-persecuted Jewish communities around the world, Belzer met Pope John Paul II in 2005 as a part of that Pontiff's historic rapprochement between the Catholic Church and Judaism.

Mickve Israel offers 30–45 minute tours of the sanctuary and museum, which are open daily 10 A.M.–1 P.M. and 2–4 P.M. It's closed weekends and on Jewish holidays.

Calhoun Square

The last of the 24 squares in Savannah's original grid, Calhoun Square is also the only square with all its original buildings intact—a rarity indeed in a city ravaged by fire so many times in its history.

Dominating the south side of the square is Savannah's first public elementary school and spiritual home of Savannah's community of educators, the **Massie Heritage Center** (207 E. Gordon St., 912/201-5070, www.massieschool .com, Mon.–Fri. 9 A.M.–4 P.M., self-guided tour $3, guided tour $5). In 1841, Peter Massie, a Scots planter with a populist streak, endowed

day. Charleston, by contrast, is about an hour away from I-95.

Most importantly, however, the single most jarring aspect of this book that purports to be about the "real" Savannah is this: Almost none of the lead characters is actually from Savannah.

Jim Williams, Joe Odom, Lady Chablis, Emma Kelly, "Mandy Nichols" (real name Nancy Hillis) – all were from other places.

For a riveting fiction experience that gives a telling – and just as entertaining – glimpse into the life of real Savannahians, you have to go back 70 years to the 1939 potboiler classic *The Damned Don't Cry*, by Harry Hervey. The Joe Odom of his day, Hervey was a profligate spender who loved parties. The Texas native, who lived in Savannah and is buried in Bonaventure Cemetery, wrote his tabloid-trashy novels purely to make enough money to continue his hedonistic way of life, penning them in a room in the ornate and now-sadly demolished Desoto Hotel.

That frenzied do-or-die sense informs *The Damned Don't Cry* (not to be confused with the 1950 Joan Crawford movie of the same name) with a surprisingly modern tone as it tells its tale of the hapless Zelda O'Brien, a poor Irish resident of the old Fort Wayne neighborhood who dreams of a better way of life in one of Savannah's uppercrust mansions, now identified as likely being the McAlpin House at 230 Barnard Street. (Interestingly, Zelda's own address is listed as 18 E. Broad St., which never actually existed.)

In an outrageously politically incorrect storyline by today's standards – and perhaps 1939's as well – *The Damned Don't Cry's* storyline makes *Midnight* look tame. Zelda's life becomes a soap opera as her mother has affairs, her brother is jailed, her family goes broke, and she bears a soldier's love child. Unlike the recent arrivals documented in Berendt's book, all the quirky characters and scenes in *The Damned Don't Cry* are Savannah through and through, from the grizzled neighborhood characters to Zelda's own eccentric family to her visit with her father to Fort Pulaski, then desolate and overgrown with vegetation and swamp creatures.

Long out of print, Hervey's offbeat masterpiece` was republished in 2003 by the Georgia-based Cherokee Publishing. Interestingly, the new editions are based on direct scans from the original, including the delightfully kitschy cover design.

the school to give poor children as good an education as the children of rich families, like Massie's own, received.

Another of Savannah's masterpieces by John Norris—whose impressive oeuvre includes the Low House, the Mercer House, and the Green-Meldrim House—the central portion of the trifold building was completed in 1856 and is a great example of Greek Revival architecture (the two large wings on each side were added later by different architects).

After the Civil War, the "Massie school," as it's locally known, was designated as the area's African American public school. Classes ceased in 1974 and it now operates as a living history museum, centering on the period-appointed one-room "heritage classroom." If you're in town during the school year you may find yourself amidst a throng of local schoolchildren on field trips.

Catty-corner to the Massie School is the **Wesley Monumental United Methodist Church** (429 Abercorn St., 912/232-0191, www.wesleymonumental.org, Sunday services 8:45 A.M. and 11 A.M., sanctuary open to public daily 9 A.M.–5 P.M.). This home of Savannah's first Methodist parish was named not only for movement founder John Wesley but for his musical younger brother Charles. Built in 1875 on the model of Queen's Kirk in Amsterdam and the fourth incarnation of the parish home, this is another great example of Savannah's Gothic churches.

In addition to regular services, the church often hosts musical performances of both secular and liturgical music. Its acoustically wonderful sanctuary features a magnificent Noack Organ, which would no doubt please the picky ears of Charles Wesley himself, author of the lyrics to "Hark! The Herald Angels Sing." When inside, check out the stained-glass "Wesley Window," with busts of the church's dual namesakes and a globe adorned with John's famous phrase, "The world is my parish."

Martin Luther King Jr. Boulevard

Originally known as West Broad Street (you'll still hear old-timers refer to it that way), Martin Luther King Jr. Boulevard is the spiritual home of Savannah's African American community, though it has gone through several transformations. In the early 1800s, West Broad was a fashionable address, but during the middle of that century its north end got a bad reputation for crime and blight, as thousands of Irish immigrants packed in right beside the area's poor black population.

West Broad's glory days as a center of black culture happened in the first half of the 20th century, beginning and ending with the late, great Union Station terminal. Built in 1902, the terminal was the main gateway to the city and ushered in a heyday on West Broad that saw thriving black movie theaters like the Star. Here were packed venues on the "chitlin circuit" such as The Dunbar, hosting such legends as Little Richard. Black-owned small businesses like Thrifty Supply Center and Laura's Tailors provided goods and services during this time of segregation. Doctors, dentists, and lawyers flourished. The great number of African American–owned banks on the street gave it the name "the Wall Street of black America."

The end came with the razing of the gorgeous Union Station in 1963 to make way for an on-ramp to I-16. The poorly planned project cut the historic boulevard in two, with several entire neighborhoods being destroyed to make way for it. While the hideous on-ramp remains, every now and then talk surfaces of moving it in an attempt to recreate the magic of old West Broad.

Renamed for the civil rights leader in 1990, MLK Jr. Boulevard currently is undergoing another renaissance. A city-sponsored facelift of the median and a low-interest facade loan program, begun in 1996, have beautified some formerly run-down areas near the Historic District, while an increase in businesses servicing the SCAD student population brings a vibrant, edgy hustle to the area on into the night. During his visit to town for the 2007 Savannah Music Festival, jazz great Wynton Marsalis dedicated a plaque to Louis Armstrong's mentor King Oliver in front of the building at 514 MLK Jr. Boulevard where Oliver spent his last days.

RALPH MARK GILBERT CIVIL RIGHTS MUSEUM

One of the former black-owned bank buildings on MLK Jr. Boulevard is now home to the Ralph Mark Gilbert Civil Rights Museum (460 MLK Jr. Blvd., 912/231-8900, www.sip.armstrong.edu, Mon.–Sat. 9 A.M.–5 P.M., $4 adults, $2 children). Named for the pastor of the First African Baptist Church and a key early civil rights organizer, the building was also the local NAACP headquarters for a time.

Three floors of exhibits here include photos and interactive exhibits, the highlight for historians being a fiber optic map of nearly 100 significant civil rights sites. The first floor features a re-creation of the Azalea Room of the local Levy's department store, an early boycott diner where blacks were not allowed to eat, though they could buy goods from the store. The second floor is more for hands-on education, with classrooms, a computer room, and a video/reading room. A film chronicles mass-meetings, voter registration drives, boycotts, sit-ins, kneel-ins (integration of churches), and wade-ins (integration of beaches).

SHIPS OF THE SEA MARITIME MUSEUM

One of Savannah's more unique museums is the quirky Ships of the Sea Maritime Museum (41 MLK Jr. Blvd., 912/232-1511, http://ships ofthesea.org, Tues.–Sun. 10 A.M.–5 P.M., $7 adults, $5 students). The stunning Greek Revival building in which it resides is known as the Scarbrough House because it was initially built in 1819 by the great William Jay for local shipping merchant William Scarbrough, owner of the SS *Savannah*, the first steamship to cross the Atlantic. After the Scarbroughs sold the property it became the West Broad School for African Americans from Reconstruction through integration.

One of the Historic Savannah Foundation's key restoration projects in the 1970s, the museum recently got another major facelift in 1998, including a roof based on the original Jay design and a delightful enlargement of the mansion's garden out back. Inside, children, maritime buffs, and crafts connoisseurs can find intricate and detailed scale models of various historic vessels, such as Oglethorpe's *Anne*, the SS *Savannah*, and the NS *Savannah*, the world's first nuclear-powered surface vessel. There's even a model of the *Titanic*.

BATTLEFIELD PARK

Under this fairly new name, three very important sites are clustered together on MLK Jr. Boulevard under the auspices of the Coastal Heritage Society: the Savannah History Museum, the Roundhouse Museum, and the Siege of Savannah battlefield.

The **Savannah History Museum** (303 MLK Jr. Blvd., 912/651-6825, www.chsgeorgia.org, Mon.–Fri. 8:30 A.M.–5 P.M., Sat.–Sun. 9 A.M.–5 P.M., $4.25 adults, $3.75 students), first stop for many a visitor to town because it's in the same restored Central of Georgia passenger shed as the Visitors Center, contains many interesting exhibits on local history, concentrating mostly on colonial times. Towards the rear of the museum is a room for rotating exhibits, as well as one of Johnny Mercer's two Oscars and of course the historic "*Forrest Gump* bench" that Tom Hanks sat on during his scenes in Chippewa Square.

The **Roundhouse Railroad Museum** (601 W. Harris St., 912/651-6823, www.chsgeorgia.org, daily 9 A.M.–5 P.M., $4.25 adults, $3.75 students) is an ongoing homage to the deep and strangely underreported influence of the railroad industry on Savannah. Constructed in 1830 for the brand-new Central of Georgia line, the Roundhouse's design was cutting-edge for the time, the first facility to put all the railroad's key facilities in one place. Spared by Sherman, the site saw its real heyday after the Civil War. But as technology changed, so did the Roundhouse, which gradually fell further into neglect until the 1960s, when preservation-minded buffs banded together to raise enough money to save it.

There's a large (and growing) collection of various period locomotives and rail cars. Some of Savannah's greatest artisans have contributed their preservation skills over the years to bring back much of the facility's muscular splendor. For a complete experience, take your time walking through the various building, noting not only the displays but the impressive workmanship. The real highlight of the Roundhouse is the thing in the middle that gave it its name, a huge central turntable for positioning rolling stock for repair and maintenance. Frequent demonstrations occur with an actual steam locomotive firing up and taking a turn on the turntable.

Right off MLK Jr. Boulevard is the brand-new **Battle Memorial Park,** a.k.a. the Spring Hill Redoubt, a reconstruction of the British fortifications at the Siege of Savannah with an interpretive site. Note the redoubt is not at the actual location of the original fort; that lies underneath the nearby Sons of the Revolution marker. Eight hundred granite markers will signify the battle's casualties, most of whom were buried in mass graves soon afterward. To Savannah's everlasting shame, most of the remains of these brave men were simply bulldozed up and discarded without ceremony during later construction projects.

VICTORIAN DISTRICT

Boasting 50 blocks of gorgeous Victorian and Queen Anne frame houses built between 1870 and 1910, Savannah's Victorian District, which technically begins at Gwinnett Street, is bisected by the city's premier design landmark of the era, one-of-a-kind Forsyth Park.

◖ Forsyth Park

A favorite with locals and tourists alike, the vast, lush expanse of Forsyth Park is a center of local life, abuzz with activity and events year-round. The park owes its existence to William B. Hodgson, who donated its core 10 acres to the city for use as a park. Deeply influenced by the then-trendy design of municipal greenspace areas in France, the landscape design of Forsyth Park by William Bischoff dates to 1851. Named for Georgia Governor John Forsyth, the park comprises 30 acres and its perimeter is about a mile. Here's a walking tour, beginning at the north end:

As you approach the park down Bull Street,

don't miss the ornate ironwork on the west side of the street marking the **Armstrong House,** designed by Henrik Wallin. Featured in the 1962 film *Cape Fear* as well as 1997's *Midnight in the Garden of Good and Evil,* this Italianate mansion was once home to Armstrong Junior College before its move to the south side. When he's not practicing law in this building, Sonny Seiler, one of the characters in The Book, still raises the University of Georgia's signature bulldog mascots. Directly across Bull Street is another site of *Midnight* fame, the Oglethorpe Club, one of the many brick and terra-cotta designs by local architect Alfred Eichberg.

It's easy to miss, but as you enter the park's north side, you encounter the **Marine Memorial,** erected in 1947 to honor the 24 Chatham County Marines killed in World War II. Subsequently the names of Marines killed in Korea and Vietnam were added.

Look west at the corner of Whitaker and Gaston Streets. That's **Hodgson Hall,** home of the Georgia Historical Society. This 1876 building was commissioned by Margaret Telfair to honor her late husband William Hodgson, chief benefactor of the park the house overlooks. The Georgia Historical Society (912/651-2125, www.georgiahistory.com) administers a treasure of books, documents, maps, photos, and prints that has been a boon to writers and researchers since it was chartered by the state legislature in 1839.

Looking east at the corner of Drayton and Gaston Streets, you'll see the old **Poor House and Hospital,** in use until 1854 when it was converted to serve as the headquarters for the Medical College of Georgia. During the Civil War, Genereal Sherman used the hospital to treat Federal soldiers. From 1930–1980 the building was the site of Candler Hospital.

Behind Candler Hospital's cast-iron fence you can soak in the venerable beauty of Savannah's most famous tree, the 300-year-old **Candler Oak.** During Sherman's occupation, wounded Confederate prisoners were treated within a barricade around the oak. The tree is on the National Register of Historic Trees and was the maiden preservation project of the Savannah Tree Foundation, which secured America's first-ever conservation easement on a single tree.

Walking south into the park proper you can't miss the world-famous **Forsyth Fountain,** an iconic Savannah sight if there ever was one. Cast in iron on a French model, the fountain was dedicated in 1858. Its water is typically dyed green a few days before St. Patrick's Day. Interestingly, two other versions of this fountain exist—one in Poughkeepsie, New York, and the other in, of all places, the central plaza in Cuzco, Peru. Various acts of vandalism and natural disaster took its toll on the fountain until a major restoration in 1988 brought it to its present level of beauty.

Continuing south you'll encounter two low buildings in the center of the park. The one on the east side is the so-called "Dummy Fort," circa 1909, formerly a training ground for local militia. To the west is the charming **Fragrant Garden for the Blind.** One of those precious little Savannah gems that is too often overlooked in favor of other attractions, the Fragrant Garden was sponsored by the local Garden Club and based on others of its type throughout the United States.

The tall monument dominating Forsyth Park's central mall area is the **Confederate Memorial,** which recently received a major facelift. Dedicated in 1875, it wasn't finished in its final form until several years later. A New York sculptor carved the Confederate soldier atop the monument. A copy of it is in Poughkeepsie, New York, as a memorial to Federal dead—with the "C.S.A." on the soldier's rucksack changed to "U.S.A." The Bartow and McLaws monuments surrounding the Confederate Memorial were originally in Chippewa Square.

We'll close the walking tour with my favorite Forsyth Park landmark, at the extreme southern end. It's the Memorial to Georgia Veterans of the Spanish-American War, more commonly known as **"The Hiker"** because of the subject's almost casual demeanor and confident stride. Savannah was a major staging area for that conflict, and many troops were bivouacked in the park. Sculpted in 1902 by Alice Ruggles Kitson, more than 50 replicas of "The Hiker" were made and put up all over the United States; because the same bronze formula was used for all 50 of them, the statues are used by scientists today to gauge the effects of acid rain across the nation.

Carnegie Branch Library

Looking like Frank Lloyd Wright parachuted into Victorian Savannah, the Carnegie Branch Library (537 E. Henry St., 912/652-3600, Mon. 10 A.M.–8 P.M., Tues.–Thurs. 10 A.M.–6 P.M., Fri.–Sat. 2–6 P.M.) is the only example of Prairie-style architecture in town, designed by Savannah architect Julian de Bruyn Kops and built, as the name implies, with funding from tycoon/philanthropist Andrew Carnegie in 1914. But much more importantly, the Carnegie Library was for decades the only public library for African Americans in Savannah. One of its patrons was a young Clarence Thomas, who would grow up to be a Supreme Court justice.

EASTSIDE
Old Fort Jackson

The oldest standing brick fort in Georgia, Old Fort Jackson (912/232-3945, http://chsgeorgia.org, daily 9 A.M.–5 P.M., $4.25, free for children six and under), named for Georgia Governor James Jackson, is also one of eight remaining examples of the so-called Second System of American forts built prior to the War of 1812. Its main claim to fame is its supporting role in the saga of the CSS *Georgia,* a Confederate ironclad now resting under 40 feet of water directly in front of the fort.

Built with $115,000 in funds raised by the Ladies Gunboat Society, the *Georgia*—wrapped in an armor girdle of railroad ties—proved too heavy for its engine. So it was simply anchored in the channel opposite Fort Jackson as a floating battery. With General Sherman's arrival in 1864, Confederate forces evacuating to South Carolina scuttled the vessel where she lay to keep her out of Yankee hands.

Maritime archaeology on the *Georgia*

continues apace, with dive teams bringing up cannon, ammunition, and other artifacts. (Unlike Charleston's CSS *Hunley* submarine, no lives were lost in the *Georgia* incident, therefore there are no concerns about disrupting a gravesite.) Every now and then, talk surfaces of raising the ironclad—both for research and because the port views it as an impediment to dredging the channel even deeper—but most experts say it's unlikely to survive the stress.

Operated by the nonprofit Coastal Heritage Society, Fort Jackson is in an excellent state of preservation and provides loads of information for history buffs as well as for kids, who will enjoy climbing the parapets and running on the large parade ground (this area was once a rice field). Inside the fort's casemates underneath the ramparts you'll find well-organized exhibits on the fort's construction and history. Most visitors especially love the daily cannon firings during the summer. If you're really lucky, you'll be around when Fort Jackson fires a salute to passing military vessels on the river—the only historic fort in America that does so.

To get to Fort Jackson, take President Street Extension (Islands Expressway) east out of downtown. The entrance is several miles on your left.

Oatland Island Wildlife Center

The closest thing Savannah has to a zoo is the vast, multipurpose Oatland Island Wildlife Center (711 Sandtown Rd., 912/898-3980, www.oatlandisland.org, Mon.–Fri. 9 A.M.–4 P.M., Sat.–Sun. 10 A.M.–4 P.M., $5 adults, $3 children). Set on a former Centers for Disease Control site, it's undergone an extensive environmental cleanup and is now owned by the local school system, though supported purely by donation. Families by the hundreds come here for a number of special Saturdays throughout the year, including an old-fashioned cane-grinding in November, a day of sheep-shearing in April, and Savannah's only Medieval Festival, which happens in September.

The main attraction here are the critters, located at various points along a meandering two-mile nature trail through the woods and alongside the marsh. All animals at Oatland are there because they're somehow unable to return to the wild, usually because of injury (often at the hands of humans). Highlights include a tight-knit pack of Eastern wolves, a pair of bison, some really cute foxes, and an extensive raptor aviary. Kids will love the petting zoo of farm animals, some of which are free to roam the grounds at will. But the crown jewel in Oatland's menagerie is no doubt the magnificent Florida panther, a rare cousin to the American cougar.

The massive central building was designed by noted local architect Henrik Wallin as a retirement home for railroad conductors. Check out the huge set of whalebones on display inside, the remains of a 50-foot-long endangered fin whale that washed ashore on Tybee Island in 1989.

To get there from downtown, take President Street Extension (Islands Expressway) about five miles. Begin looking for the Oatland Island sign on your right. You'll go through part of a residential neighborhood until you take a bend to the right; Oatland's gate is then on the left. To get there from Bonaventure Cemetery, go straight out the gate on Bonaventure Road and take a right on Pennsylvania Avenue. As you dead-end on Islands Expressway, take a right and look for the entrance on the right.

◖ Bonaventure Cemetery

On the banks of the Wilmington River just east of town lies one of Savannah's most unique sights, Bonaventure Cemetery (330 Bonaventure Rd., 912/651-6843, daily 8 A.M.–5 P.M.). John Muir, who would go on to found the Sierra Club, wrote of Bonaventure's Spanish moss–bedecked beauty in his 1867 book *A Thousand-Mile Walk to the Gulf,* marveling at the screaming bald eagles that then frequented the area. The bald eagles are long gone, but, like Muir, Savannahians to this day reserve a special place for Bonaventure in their hearts.

While its pedigree as Savannah's premier public cemetery goes back 100 years, it was used as a burial ground as early as 1794, when Governor Tattnall buried a relative there. In the years since, this achingly poignant vista of live oaks and azaleas has been the final resting place of such local and national luminaries as Johnny Mercer, Conrad Aiken, Wormsloe founder Noble Jones, and, of course, the Trosdal plot, former home of the famous "Bird Girl" statue (the original is now in the Telfair Academy of Arts and Sciences). Fittingly, the late, great Jack Leigh, who took the "Bird Girl" photo for the cover of *Midnight in the Garden of Good and Evil,* is interred here as well.

Go to Section K and see the Greek cemetery, a veritable stone chronicle of that local community's history from the late 1800s. Section K also holds many memorials to Spanish-American War veterans, commemorated by a special cross. Close by is the Jewish section, established by congregants of Temple Mickve Israel, with many evocative inscriptions on the tombs of the many Holocaust survivors buried here. Section A is home to a large plot for Confederate veterans of the Georgia Hussars. Veterans of both World Wars are buried in the American Legion Field. Closer to the river is an interesting plot set aside for railroad conductors.

While strolling through Bonaventure, you might see some burial sites lined with reddish-brown tiles, their tops studded with half-circles. Mistakenly known as "slave tiles," these are actually a rare type of Victorian garden tile that has nothing whatsoever to do with slaves.

Several local tour companies offer options that include a visit to Bonaventure (see *Tours*). If you're doing a self-guided tour, go by the small visitors center at the entrance and pick up one of the free guides to the cemetery, lovingly assembled by members of the local volunteer Bonaventure Historical Society. By all means do the tourist thing and pay your respects at Johnny Mercer's final resting place and go visit beautiful little "Gracie" in Section E, lot 99, and leave her a little offering of a coin or even a Christmas present in December, as many visitors do. But I also suggest doing as the locals do: Bring a picnic lunch and a blanket and set yourself beside the breezy banks of the Wilmington River, taking in all the lazy beauty and evocative bygone history surrounding you.

To get there from downtown, take President Street Extension east and take a right on

the memorial to Gracie in Bonaventure Cemetery

© SONJA WALLEN

SAVANNAH

Pennsylvania Avenue, then a left on Bonaventure Road. Alternately, go east on Victory Drive (Hwy. 80) and take a left on Whatley Road in the town of Thunderbolt. Veer left onto Bonaventure Road. The cemetery is a mile ahead on the right.

Thunderbolt

Take a left out of Bonaventure Cemetery and continue on Bonaventure Road to find yourself in the little fishing village of Thunderbolt, almost as old as Savannah itself. According to Oglethorpe, the town was named after "a rock which was here shattered by a thunderbolt, causing a spring to gush from the ground, which continued ever afterward to emit the odor of brimstone."

Just off Victory Drive is the **Thunderbolt Museum** (at the corner of Victory Dr. and Mechanics Ave., open Wed. 10 A.M.–2 P.M. and second and third Sun. 3–5 P.M., free) housed in the humble former town hall. Cross Victory onto River Road and notice how the road is built around the live oak tree in the middle of it. Though most of the nice views of the river have been obscured by high-rise condos, there's a cute public fishing pier.

Continue on River Road to and you'll soon be at the entrance to **Savannah State University** (3219 College St., 912/356-2186, www.savstate .edu). This historically black university began life in 1890 as the Georgia State Industrial College for Colored Youth. Famous graduates include current Savannah Mayor Otis Johnson and NFL great Shannon Sharpe. The main landmark is the newly restored Hill Hall, a 1901 building featured in the film *The General's Daughter*.

Daffin Park

A century spent in Forsyth Park's more genteel shadow doesn't diminish the importance of Daffin Park (1500 E. Victory Dr.) as Savannah's second major greenspace. Designed by John Nolen in 1907 and named for a former local parks commissioner, Daffin not only hosts a large variety of local athletes on its various fields and courts, it's home to Historic Grayson Stadium on the park's east end. Recently given a serious facelift, Grayson Stadium hosts the single-A exploits of the Savannah Sand Gnats. One of the great old ballparks of America, this venue dates from 1941 and has hosted greats such as Babe Ruth, Jackie Robinson, and Mickey Mantle.

Most picturesque for the visitor, however, is the massive fountain set in the middle of the expansive central pond on the park's west side. Originally built in the shape of the continental United States, the pond was the backdrop for a presidential visit by Franklin D. Roosevelt in 1933, which included a speech to an African American crowd. On the far west end of Daffin Park along Waters Avenue is a marker commemorating the site of the Grandstand for the Great Savannah Races of 1911.

WESTSIDE
Laurel Grove Cemetery

Its natural vista isn't as alluring as Bonaventure's, but Laurel Grove Cemetery boasts its own exquisitely carved memorials and a distinctly Victorian type of surreal beauty that not even Bonaventure can match. In keeping with the racial apartheid of Savannah's early days, there are actually two cemeteries: **Laurel Grove North** (802 W. Anderson St., daily 8 A.M.–5 P.M.) for whites, and **Laurel Grove South** (2101 Kollock St., daily 8 A.M.–5 P.M.) for blacks. Both are well worth visiting.

By far the most high-profile site in the North Cemetery is that of Juliette Gordon Low, founder of the U.S. Girl Scouts. Other historically significant sites there include the graves of 8th Air Force founder Frank O. Hunter, Central of Georgia founder William Gordon and "Jingle Bells" composer James Pierpont.

But it's the graves of the anonymous and near-anonymous that are the most poignant sights here. The various sections for infants known as "Babylands" cannot fail to move. "Mr. Bones," a former Savannah Police dog, is the only animal buried at Laurel Grove. There's an entire site reserved for victims of the great yellow fever epidemic. And don't blink or you'll miss the small rock pile, or cairn, near Governor James Jackson's tomb, the origin and purpose of which remains a mystery.

Make sure to view the otherworldly display of Victorian statuary, originally from the grand Greenwich Plantation near Bonavenure Cemetery. As with Bonaventure, throughout Laurel Grove you'll find examples of so-called "slave tiles," actually Victorian garden tiles, lining gravesites.

Laurel Grove South features the graves of Savannah's early black Baptist ministers, such as Andrew Bryan and Andrew Cox Marshall. Some of the most touching sites are those of African Americans who obtained their freedom and built prosperous lives for themselves and their families. The vast majority of local firefighters in the 1800s were African Americans, and their simple graves are among the most touching, such as the headstone for one known simply as "August," who died fighting a fire.

To get to Laurel Grove North, take MLK Jr. Boulevard to Anderson Street and turn west. To get to Laurel Grove South, take Victory Drive (Hwy. 80) west to Ogeechee Road. Take a right onto Ogeechee then a right onto West 36th Street. Continue on to Kollock Street.

Mighty Eighth Air Force Museum

Military and aviation buffs absolutely mustn't miss the large new Mighty Eighth Air Force Museum (175 Bourne Ave., 912/748-8888, www.mightyeighth.org, daily 9 A.M.–5 P.M., $10 adults, $6 children) in Pooler, Georgia, right off I-95. The 8th Air Force was born at Hunter Field, Savannah as the 8th Bomber Command in 1942, becoming the 8th Air Force in 1944 (it's now based in Louisiana). About 350,000 Americans served in the unit during the war, under such legendary generals as Ira Eaker and Jimmy Doolittle.

A moving testament to the men and machines who conducted those strategic bombing campaigns over Europe in World War II—losing over 26,000 men—the museum also features later 8th Air Force history such as the Korean War, the Linebacker II bombing campaigns over North Vietnam, and the Persian Gulf. Inside you'll find not only airplanes like the P-51 Mustang and the German ME-109, there's also a well-done interactive B-17 waist gunner exhibit. Outside are several more aircraft, including a MIG-17, an F4 Phantom, and a B-47 Stratojet bomber just like the one that dropped the fabled "Tybee Bomb" in 1958. A nearby "Chapel of the Fallen Eagles" is a fully functioning sanctuary to honor the more than 26,000 members of the Mighty Eighth to die during World War II.

To get to the Mighty Eighth Museum from downtown, take I-16 west until it intersects I-95. Take I-95 north and take Exit 102. Follow the signs.

Savannah-Ogeechee River Canal

A relic of the pre-railroad days, the Savannah-Ogeechee River Canal (681 Ft. Argyle Rd., 912/748-8068, www.savannahogeecheecanal.com, daily 9 A.M.–5 P.M., $2 adults, $1 students) is a 17-mile barge route joining the two rivers. Finished in 1830, it saw three decades of prosperous trade in cotton, rice, bricks, guano, naval stores, and agriculture before the coming of the railroads finished it off.

You can walk some of its length today near the Ogeechee River terminus, admiring the impressive engineering of its multiple locks to stabilize the water level in the canal. Back in the day, the canal would continue through four lift locks as it traversed 16 miles, before reaching the Savannah River. Naturalists will also enjoy the built-in nature trail that walking along the canal provides. Be sure to check out the unique sand hills nearby, a vestige of a bygone geological era when this area was an offshore sandbar. Kids will enjoy the impromptu menagerie of gopher turtles near the site's entrance.

To get there, get on I-95 south and take Exit 94. The canal is a little over two miles west.

SOUTHSIDE
Wormsloe State Historic Site

The one-of-a-kind Wormsloe State Historic Site (7601 Skidaway Rd., 912/353-3023, www.gastateparks.org/info/wormsloe, Tues.–Sat. 9 A.M.–5 P.M., Sun. 2–5:30 P.M., $4 adults, $2 children) was first settled by Noble Jones, who landed with Oglethorpe on the *Anne* and fought beside him in the War of Jenkin's Ear. One of the great renaissance men of history, this soldier was also an accomplished carpenter, surveyor, forester, botanist, and physician. Wormsloe became famous for its bountiful gardens, so much so that the famed naturalist William Bartram mentioned them in his diary after a visit in 1765 with father John Bartram.

After his death, Noble Jones was originally buried in the family plot on the waterfront, but now his remains are at Bonaventure Cemetery. Jones' descendants donated 822 acres to The Nature Conservancy, which transferred the property to the state. The house, dating from 1828, and 65.5 acres are still owned by his family, and no, you can't visit them.

The stunning entrance canopy of 400 live oaks, Spanish moss dripping down the entire length, is one of those iconic images of Savannah that will stay with you the rest of your life. An interpretive museum, one-mile nature walk, and living history demonstrations make this a great site for the entire family.

Walk all the way to the Jones Narrows to see the ruins of the original 1739 fortification, one of the oldest and finest examples of tabby construction in the United States. No doubt the area's abundance of Native American shell middens, where early inhabitants discarded their oyster shells, came in handy for its construction. You can see one nearby.

To get to Wormsloe, take Victory Drive (U.S. 80) to Skidaway Road. Go south on Skidaway Road for about 10 miles and follow the signs; you'll see the grand entrance on your right.

Isle of Hope

A charming, friendly seaside community and National Historic District, Isle of Hope is one of a dwindling number of places where parents still let their kids ride around all day on bikes, calling them in at dinnertime. It doesn't boast many shops or restaurants—indeed, the marina is the only real business—but the row of waterfront cottages on Bluff Drive should not be missed. You might even recognize some of them from movies such as *Forrest Gump* and *Glory*. Built from 1880–1920, they reflect Isle of Hope's reputation as a healing area and serene Wilmington River getaway from Savannah's age-old capitalist hustle.

To get to Isle of Hope, take Victory Drive (U.S. 80) east and take a right on Skidaway Road. Continue south on Skidaway and take a left on Laroche Avenue. Continue until you hit Bluff Drive.

Bethesda Home for Boys

Another beloved local institution is Bethesda Home for Boys (9520 Ferguson Ave., 912/351-2055, www.bethesdahomeforboys.net, Mon.–Fri. 9 A.M.–5 P.M.), the first orphanage in the United States and quite possibly America's first charitable organization. Still in operation today, Bethesda began life in 1740 with a grant of 500 acres to evangelist George Whitefield, a key figure in America's "Great Awakening," for the express purpose of an orphanage. Now known as The Bethesda School for Boys, the institution has helped over 10,000 children since its inception.

This original building burned down in 1773, with its replacement being partially demolished

in the 20th century. However, the west wing, dating from 1883, remains standing and now serves as a museum. Walk out to the marsh and take a long look—that's the historic Moon River, long known simply as the Back River until it was renamed to honor Savannah songwriter Johnny Mercer and his signature tune of the same name.

Across Moon River is **Pin Point, Georgia,** a tiny, predominantly African American township better known as the boyhood home of Supreme Court Justice Clarence Thomas. Pin Point traces its roots to a community of former slaves on Ossabaw Island. Displaced by a hurricane, they settled at this idyllic site, itself a former plantation. Many new residents made their living shucking oysters at the Varn Oyster Company, the central shed of which still remains. Pin Point is small—about 500 people—and very tightly knit. The area is best experienced by taking a local tour focused on African American history (see *Tours*).

Skidaway Island

Though locals primarily know Skidaway Island as the site of The Landings, the first gated community in Savannah, for your purposes Skidaway Island is notable for two beautiful and educational nature-oriented sites.

The first, the **University of Georgia Marine Educational Center and Aquarium** (30 Ocean Science Circle, 912/598-3474, www .uga.edu/aquarium, Mon.–Fri. 9 A.M.–4 P.M., Sat. noon–5 P.M., $2 adults, $1 children) shares a gorgeous 700-acre campus on the scenic Skidaway River with the research-oriented **Skidaway Institute of Oceanography,** also UGA-affiliated. It hosts scientists and grad students from around the nation, often on trips on is research vessel, the RV *Sea Dawg*. The main on-site attraction of the Marine Center is the small but well-done aquarium featuring 14 tanks with 200 live animals. Don't expect Sea World here; remember you're essentially on a college campus and the emphasis here is on education, not flash.

The second site of interest to visitors is **Skidaway Island State Park** (52 Diamond

Causeway, 912/598-2300, www.gastateparks .org/info/skidaway, daily 7 A.M.–10 P.M., $2 parking fee). Yeah, you can camp there, but the awesome nature trails leading out to the marsh—featuring an ancient Native American shell midden and an old whiskey still—are worth a trip just on their own, especially when combined with the Marine Education Center Aquarium. To get there, take Victory Drive (Hwy. 80) until you get to Waters Avenue and continue south as it turns into Whitefield

Avenue and then the Diamond Causeway. The park is on your left after the drawbridge. An alternate route from downtown is to take the Truman Parkway all the way to its dead end at Whitefield Avenue; take a left and continue as it turns into Diamond Causeway into Skidway.

TYBEE ISLAND

Its name means "salt" in the old Euchee tongue, indicative of the island's chief export in those days. And Tybee Island—"Tybee" to locals—is

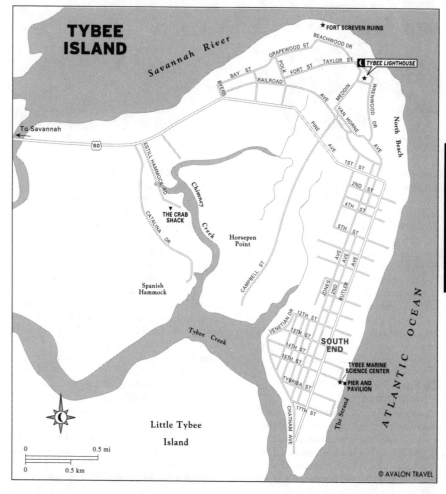

the Tybee Island Marine Science Center

© JIM MOREKIS

indeed one of the essential seasonings of life in Savannah. First incorporated as Ocean City and then Savannah Beach, the island has since reclaimed its original name.

While 18 miles from Savannah, in truth Tybee is part and parcel of the city's social and cultural fabric. Many of the island's 3,000 full-time residents, known for their boozy bonhomie and quirky personal style, commute to work in the city. And those living "in town" often reciprocate by visiting Tybee to dine in its few but excellent restaurants, drink in its casual and crazy watering holes, and frolic on its wide, beautiful beaches lined with rare sea oats waving in the Atlantic breeze.

◖ Fort Pulaski National Monument

There's one must-see before you get to Tybee Island proper. On Cockspur Island, you'll find Fort Pulaski National Monument (Hwy. 80 E., 912/786-5787, www.nps.gov, fort daily 8:30 A.M.–5:15 P.M., visitors center daily 9 A.M.–5 P.M., $2 per person 17 and up). Not

only a delight for any history buff, the fort's also a fantastic place to take the kids. They can climb on the parapets, earthworks, and cannon, and burn off calories on the great nature trail nearby. Along the way they'll no doubt learn a few things as well.

Synchronicity and irony practically scream from every brick. Perhaps prophetically named for Count Casimir Pulaski, who died leading an ill-fated charge on the British in 1779, Fort Pulaski is also symbolic of a catastrophic defeat, this one in 1862 when Union forces using new rifled cannon reduced much of it to rubble in 30 hours. Robert E. Lee—yes, *that* Robert E. Lee—helped build the fort while a lieutenant with the U.S. Army Corps of Engineers. And the Union general who reduced the fort, Quincy A. Gillmore, was in the Corps of Engineers himself, helping to oversee the fort's construction.

Very well managed by the National Park Service, Fort Pulaski is old enough to convey a real sense of history, but young and strong enough to withstand hands-on attention from visitors. By all means visit the visitors center a few hundred yards from the fort itself, but the palpable pleasure starts when you cross the drawbridge over the moat and see a cannon pointed at you from a narrow gunport.

Enter the inside of the fort itself and take in just how big it is—Union occupiers regularly played baseball on the huge, grassy parade ground. Take a walk around the perimeter, underneath the ramparts. This is where the soldiers lived and worked, and you'll see re-creations of officer's quarters, meeting areas, sick rooms, and prisoners' bunks among the cannon, where Confederate prisoners-of-war were held after the fort's surrender. Cannon firings happen most Saturdays.

And now for the pièce de résistance: Take the steep corkscrew staircase up to the ramparts themselves and take in the jaw-droppingly beautiful view of the lush marsh around the fort, the Savannah River and Tybee Island spreading out in the distance. Stop and sit near one of the several remaining cannon and contemplate what went on here a century and a half ago. (Warning: There's no railing of any kind on the inboard side of the ramparts. Keep the kids well back from the edge, because it's a lethal fall to the fort interior.)

Afterwards take a stroll all the way around the walls and see for yourself the power of those Yankee guns. Though much of the devastation was soon repaired, some sections of the wall remain in their damaged state. You can even pick out a few cannonballs still stuck in the masonry like blueberries in a pie.

Save some time and energy for the extensive palmetto-lined nature trail through the sandy upland of Cockspur Island on which the fort is located. There are informative markers, a picnic area, and, as a bonus, there's a coastal defense facility from the Spanish-American War, Battery Hambright.

Cockspur Beacon

Continue east on Highway 80, passing over Lazaretto Creek, named for the quarantine or "lazaretto" built in the late 1700s to make sure newcomers, mostly slaves, were free of disease. As you cross, look to your left over the river's wide south channel. On a tiny oyster shell islet find the little Cockspur Beacon lighthouse, in use from 1848–1909, when major shipping was routed through the deeper north channel of the river. The site is now preserved by the National Park Service, and is accessible only by boat.

◖ Tybee Lighthouse

Reaching Tybee proper on Highway 80, you'll soon arrive at the intersection with North Campbell Avenue. This is the entrance to the less-populated, more historically significant north end of the island, once almost entirely taken up by Fort Screven, a coastal defense fortification of the early 1900s. Take a left onto North Campbell Avenue then left again on Van Horn. Once on Van Horn, take an immediate right onto Meddin Drive. Continue until you see a lighthouse on your left and a parking lot on the right.

Rebuilt several times in its history, the Tybee Lighthouse (30 Meddin Ave., 912/786-5801, www.tybeelighthouse.org, Wed.–Mon. 9 A.M.–5 P.M., $6 adults, $5 children) traces its construction to the first year of the colony, based on a design by the multitalented Noble Jones. At its completion in 1736, it was the tallest structure in America. One of a handful of working 18th-century lighthouses today, the facility has been restored to its 1916–1964 incarnation, featuring a nine-foot-tall first order Fresnel lens installed in 1867.

The entrance fee gives you admission to the lighthouse, the lighthouse museum, and the nearby Tybee Island Museum. All the outbuildings on the lighthouse grounds are original, including the residence of current lighthouse keeper and Tybee Island Historical Society Director Cullen Chambers, which is also the oldest building on the island. If you've got the legs and the lungs, definitely take all 178 steps up to the top of the lighthouse for a stunning view of Tybee, the Atlantic, and Hilton Head Island.

All around this area of the north end, you'll see low-lying concrete bunkers. Though many are in private hands, these are remains of Fort

Screven's coastal defense batteries. Battery Garland is open to tours, and also houses the aforementioned **Tybee Island Museum** (30 Meddin Ave., 912/786-5801), a charming, almost whimsical little collection of exhibits from various eras of local history.

Take Van Horne around the delightful Jaycee Park to the row of ornate mansions with expansive porches facing the Atlantic.

This is Officer's Row, former home of Fort Screven's commanding officers and now a mix of private residences, vacation rentals, and B&Bs.

South End

Now scoot out Van Horne to Butler Avenue and take a left on a path that looks as if it will take you right into the Atlantic Ocean. Follow

THE TYBEE BOMB

On a dark February night in 1958 at the height of the Cold War, a USAF B-47 Stratojet bomber based at Homestead, Florida, made a simulated nuclear bombing run somewhere over southeast Georgia. A Charleston-based F-86 fighter on a mock intercept came too close, clipping the big bomber's wing.

Before bringing down the wounded B-47 at Savannah's Hunter Airfield – then a Strategic Air Command base – Commander Howard Richardson decided he first had to jettison his lethal cargo: a 7,000-pound Mark 15 hydrogen bomb, serial number 47782.

We know for sure that he jettisoned it over water. Richardson, who won the Distinguished Flying Cross for his efforts that night, said so himself. What no one knows is exactly where.

And thus began the legend of "the Tybee bomb." Go in any Tybee watering hole and ask 10 people where they think it is and you'll get 10 different answers. Some say it's in the north side of Wassaw Sound, some the south. Some say it's in the shallows, some in deepwater.

Many local shrimpers, crabbers, and fishermen have claimed at various times to have ripped their nets on the bomb. Or on something...

Speculation ran wild, with some locals fearing nuclear explosion, radioactive contamination, or even that a team of scuba-diving terrorists would secretly retrieve the ancient weapon.

Former Army colonel and present-day raconteur and soldier-of-fortune Derek Duke took it as his personal mission to find the bomb. He says the Air Force could easily find it, but won't do so either because they don't want to go to the expense of finding it or they don't want to

admit they lost a thermonuclear weapon for half a century. Duke claims to have found a radiation-emitting object off Little Tybee Island during a search in 2004.

Commander Richardson, now retired and living in Jackson, Mississippi, says the point is moot because the bomb wasn't armed when he jettisoned it. Environmentalists say that doesn't matter, because the enriched uranium the Air Force admits was in the bomb is toxic whether or not there's the risk of a nuclear detonation. Tybee fishermen say the fact that the bomb also had 400 pounds of high explosive "nuclear trigger" is reason enough to get it out of these waterways, which hosted the 1996 Olympic yachting competition.

And what of the owners of the Tybee Bomb, the Air Force? In 2000, they sent a team to Savannah to find the bomb, concluding it was buried somewhere off the coast in 5-15 feet of mud. In 2005, in another attempt to find the weapon – and also to shut down the rampant conspiracy theories, most of them propagated by Duke – they sent down another team of experts to look one last time.

Their verdict: The bomb's still lost.

That won't stop local speculation about its whereabouts, however. Who can resist a real-life cloak-and-dagger story? Certainly very few people around here.

Postscript: No one was injured that night in 1958, except for some frostbite the F-86 pilot suffered as a result of ejecting from his damaged plane. In an interesting bit of synchronicity, the fighter pilot, Clarence Wilson, and the B-47 commander Howard Richardson grew up miles away from each other in Winston County, Mississippi.

this road as it veers right along the coast and you're on Tybee's main drag, the beach fully public and accessible from any of the streets to your left.

Go all the way down to **Tybrisa** (formerly 16th St.) to get a flavor of old Tybee. Here's where you'll find the tacky old five-and-dimes like T. S. Chu's, still a staple of local life, and little diners, ice cream spots, and taverns. The new pride of the island is the large, long pier structure called the **Tybrisa Pavilion II,** built in 1996 in an attempt to recreate the lost glory of the Tybrisa Pavilion, social and spiritual center of the island's gregarious resort days. Built in 1891 by the Central of Georgia railroad, the grand old Tybrisa hosted name entertainers and big bands on its expansive dance floor. Sadly, fire destroyed it in 1967, an enormous blow to area morale.

Literally at the foot of the Pavilion you'll find the **Tybee Island Marine Science Center** (1510 Strand, 912/786-5917, www .tybeemsc.org, Wed.–Mon. 9 A.M.–5 P.M., Tues. noon–5 P.M., $4 adults, $3 children), an outstanding resource with nine aquariums and a touch tank featuring native species. Here is the nerve center for the Tybee Island Sea Turtle Project, an ongoing effort to document and preserve the local comings-and-goings of the island's most beloved inhabitant and unofficial mascot, the endangered sea turtle. A very kid-friendly facility despite the seriousness of its mission, the Center holds summer Sea Camps for area children, and indeed one of its goals is to bring a hands-on aspect to educating the public about the area's rich variety of ocean, dune, and marsh life—only steps away.

TOURS

Savannah's tourist boom has resulted in a similar explosion of well over 50 separate tour services, ranging from simple guided trolley journeys to horse-drawn carriage rides to specialty tours to eco-tourism adventures. There's even an iPod walking tour. Here's a listing of the key categories with the most notable offerings in each (and don't forget to tip your guide if you were satisfied with the tour):

Trolley Tours

The vehicle of choice for the bulk of the tourist masses visiting Savannah, trolley tours allow you to sit back and enjoy the views in a reasonably comfortable. As in other cities, the guides provide commentary while attempting, with various degrees of success, to navigate the cramped downtown traffic environment. Though the city of Savannah forces tourist guides to learn a 90-page manual on local history and general knowledge and pass a tough test on the material, I've overheard enough egregious errors of fact emanating from the PA systems of passing trolleys to know that not all guides are staying true to the manual. Some, in fact, seem to spend much of their time straying noticeably from it. In any event, locals are happy that a portion of each trolley ticket goes to fund historic preservation.

The main trolley companies in town are **Old Savannah Tours** (912/234-8128, www.old savannahtours.com, basic on-off tour $20 adults, $9 children), **Old Town Trolleys** (800/213-2474, www.trolleytours.com, basic on-off tour $23 adults, $10 children), **Oglethorpe Trolley Tours** (912/233-8380, www.oglethorpetours.com, basic on-off tour $20 adults, $10 children), and **Gray Line Tours** (912/234-8687, www.graylineof savannah.com, basic on-off tour $10). All embark from the Savannah Visitors Center on Martin Luther King Jr. Boulevard about every 20–30 minutes on the same schedule, 9 A.M.–4:30 P.M. Frankly there's not much difference between them, as they all offer a very similar range of services for similar prices, with most offering pickup at your downtown hotel. While the common "on-off privileges" allow trolley riders to disembark for awhile and pick up another of the same company's trolleys at marked stops, be aware there's no guarantee the next trolley will have enough room to take you onboard. Or the one after that.

Specialty Tours

Besides the standard narrated Historic District tours, all the above companies also offer a

SAVANNAH

number of spin-off tours. Samples include the Pirate's House Dinner & Ghost Tour, Belles of Savannah, the Evening Haunted Trolley, and multiple Paula Deen tours.

The copious ghost tours, offered by all the companies, can be fun for the casual visitor. But students of the paranormal are likely to be disappointed by the cartoonish, Halloween aspect of some of them, with guides reading from hokey scripts and cursory stops where an actor will pop up out of the shadows and say "Boo!"

A standout in the ghost field is the **Hearse Ghost Tours** (912/695-1578, www.hearse ghosttours.com), a unique company that also operates tours in New Orleans and St. Augustine, Florida. Up to eight guests at a time ride around in the open top of a converted hearse, painted all black of course, and get a 90-minute, suitably over-the-top narration from the driver/guide. Still pretty cheesy, but a hip kind of cheesy.

For those who take their paranormal activity *very* seriously, there's Shannon Scott's **Sixth Sense Savannah Ghost Tour** (866/666-3323, www.sixthsensesavannah .com, $18, $30 midnight tour), an uncensored, straightforward look at Savannah's poltergeist population.

Longtime tour guide and raconteur Greg Proffit and his staff offer fun walking "pub crawls," **Savannah Tours by Foot** (912/238-3843, www.savannahtours.com), wherein the point is to meet your guide at some local tavern, ramble around, learn a little bit, and imbibe a lot, though not necessarily in that order. The adult tour is the "Creepy Crawl" ($15) whereas the kid-and-Girl Scout-appropriate tour is the "Creepy Stroll" ($10). You may not want to believe everything you hear, but you're sure to have a lot of fun. The tours book up early, so make arrangements in advance.

A good selection of more narrowly focused specialty walking tours is offered by **See Savannah Walking Tours** (912/234-3571, www.seesavannah.com). All tours depart from 135 Bull Street, and among the offerings are a "Savannah Saunter" ($20 adults, $5 children

6–14) and the "Homemade Thunder" Civil War tour ($16 adults, $5 children 6–14).

Ron Higgins leads both a **Savannah Movie Tour** (912/234-3440, savannahmovietours.net, $25 adults, $15 children), taking you to various film locations in town, and a newer **Savannah Foody Tour** (912/234-3440, savannahmovie tours.net, $45) featuring 6–9 local eateries.

Storyteller and author Ted Eldridge leads **A Walk Through Savannah Tours** (912/921-4455, www.awalkthroughsavannah.brave host.com) and offers all kinds of specialty walking tours, such as a garden tour, a ghost tour, a historic churches tour, and of course a *Midnight* tour.

Truly independent travelers might want to use Phil Sellers' **Citytrex** (912/228-5608, www.citytrex.com, $10 average download), which as of this writing is Savannah's only podcast-based self-guided walking tour. Just go to the website and download a tour from the wide array offered directly to your iPod or cellphone. Some downloads offer enhanced content such as photos.

The unique **Negro Heritage Trail Tour** (912/234-8000, www.kingtisdell.org, $19 adults, $10 children) takes you on a 90-minute air-conditioned bus tour of over 30 of Savannah's key African American history sites. Pick up the Negro Heritage Tour at the Visitors Center downtown (301 MLK Jr. Blvd.) at 10 A.M. and noon Tuesday–Saturday.

Carriage Tours

Ah, yes—what could be more romantic and more traditional than enjoying downtown Savannah the way it was originally intended to be traveled, by horse-drawn carriage? Indeed, this is one of the most fun ways to see the city, for couples as well as for those with horse-enamored children. Yes, the horses sometimes look tired, but the tour operators generally take great care to keep the horses hydrated and out of the worst of the heat.

There are three main purveyors of equine tourism in town: **Carriage Tours of Savannah** (912/236-6756, www.carriagetoursofsavannah .com, pick up in City Market), **Historic**

Savannah Carriage Tours (888/837-1011, www
.savannahcarriage.com, pick up at the
Hampton Inn), and **Plantation Carriage
Company** (912/201-0001, pick up in City
Market). As with the trolleys, the length of
the basic tour and the price is about the same
for all—45–60 minutes, about $20 for adults
and $10 for children. All offer specialty tours
as well, from ghost tours to evening romantic
rides with champagne. Some will pick you up
at your hotel.

Water Tours

The heavy industrial buildup on the Savannah
River means that the main river tours for tourists, all departing from the docks in front of the
Hyatt Regency hotel, tend to be quite disappointing in their constant, unrelenting views
of cranes, docks, storage tanks, and smoke-
stacks. Still, for those into that kind of thing,
narrated trips up and down the river on the
Georgia Queen and the *Savannah River Queen*
are offered by **Savannah Riverboat Cruises**
(912/232-6404, www.savannahriverboat.com,
$17.95 adults, $9.95 children 4–12).

If you've just *got* to get out on the river
for a short time, by far the best bargain is to
take one of the two little **Savannah Belles**
(daily 7:30 A.M.–10:30 P.M., free) water ferries,
which shuttle passengers from River Street to
Hutchinson Island and back every 15–20 minutes. Pick up either the *Juliette Gordon Low* or
the *Susie King Taylor* on River Street in front
of City Hall or at the Waving Girl landing a
few blocks east.

Ecotours

By far the most complete and passionate eco-
tourism operator in the Savannah area is the
35-year-old nonprofit **Wilderness Southeast**
(912/897-5108, www.wilderness-southeast.org,
$10–35). Run more like the educational outfit
that it is rather than a typical tour company,

the emphasis on any of Wilderness Southeast's
tours is on the wonder and science of nature,
leaving the more Disneyfied, show-biz aspects
of local tourism to others. Guided trips include
paddles to historic Mulberry Grove, birding
trips, and beach explorations. Regularly scheduled "Walks on the Wild Side" run the gamut
from "Alligators to Anhingas" to the "Urban
Forest" to "Explore the Night Sky" to the
"Blackwater River Float." Custom tours are
also available.

On Highway 80 just as you get on
Tybee Island is another quality tour service, **Sea Kayak Georgia** (1102 Hwy. 80,
888/529-2542, www.seakayakgeorgia.com).
Run by locals Marsha Henson and Ronnie
Kemp, both certified kayak and canoe in-
structors, Sea Kayak offers many different
types of kayak tours of the coast, and can
even customize one to your tastes. Instruction
classes are also offered.

Tucked away on Lazaretto Creek before you
get to Tybee is **Capt. Mike's Dolphin Tours**
(1 U.S. Hwy 80, 912/786-5848, www.tybee
dolphins.com) offering a "Dolphin Cruise"
($15 adults, $8 children) and a "Sunset Cruise"
($18 adults, $11 children) on an open-decked,
tented Coast Guard–approved vessel. Yes, you
more than likely will see dolphins—they're
chockablock in the area's tidal creeks, especially at feeding time. Captain Mike also
offers half- and full-day onshore and offshore
fishing charters.

Priding himself on giving more than "just
another dolphin tour," Michael Neal at **Bull
River Cruises** (8005 Old Tybee Rd., 800/311-
4779, www.bullriver.com) gives great tours of
local waters in the 49-foot *Island Explorer*.
These are largely chartered group tours, so
I suggest calling ahead to see if you can be
included on an existing charter. Bull River
Cruises is in the Bull River Marina on U.S. 80
before it crosses Bull River.

SAVANNAH

Entertainment and Events

If you like to have a good time, you're in the right place. Savannah is known for its heavy yearly schedule of festivals, many of them outdoors, as well as its copious variety of watering holes hosting a diverse range of local residents and adventurous tourists.

NIGHTLIFE

Let's face it: Savannah is a hard-drinking town, and not just on St. Patrick's Day. Visitors expecting a Bible Belt atmosphere are sometimes surprised—often, it must be said, pleasantly so—at Savannah's high tolerance for intoxication and its associated behavior patterns. (Not long ago, a city councilman decided he'd had a few too many and simply got a ride home from an on-duty cop.) The ability to legally walk downtown streets with beer, wine, or a cocktail also contributes to the overall joie de vivre.

A party here is never far away, any night of the week, so it makes sense to begin this section with a close, loving look at the bars, pubs, and taverns that are the heart of Savannah's social scene and really make it tick. Bars close in Savannah at 3 A.M., a full hour later than in Charleston.

One catch though: Due to Georgia's notorious Bible Belt blue laws, establishments that serve alcohol that do not derive at least 50 percent of their revenue from food may not open on Sundays. Supermarkets and convenience stores cannot sell alcoholic beverages of any kind on Sundays, and liquor stores are closed all day.

Bars and Pubs

Savannah's best dive—and I mean that in the nicest way—is without a doubt **Pinkie Masters** (318 Drayton St., 912/238-0447, Mon.–Fri. 4 P.M.–3 A.M., Sat. 5 P.M.–3 A.M.). Small, dark, crowded, and dusty, but oh-so alive, Pinkie's, named for a legendary local political kingmaker, is a favorite not only with students, artists, and professors, but also with lawyers, journalists, and grizzled war vets. Traditionally the watering hole for local political types, the walls are plastered over with signed photos of a diverse range of politicos and entertainers from the 1970s through today, from all sides of the spectrum. This is where Jimmy Carter, ironically a teetotaler, stood on the bar and announced his candidacy for Georgia governor. The selection may be basic (Pabst Blue Ribbon is the drink of choice) but the company far from it. The service is friendly but casual; bartenders often finish their shift and simply take their place on a barstool with the customers.

Think of **Hang Fire** (27 Whitaker St., 912/443-9956, Mon.–Sat. 5 P.M.–3 A.M.) as Pinkie's, the new generation. Though only a couple of years old, this Whitaker Street haunt, occupying the site of downtown's last strip bar, is already one of the most popular bars in town, and like Pinkie's caters to a wide range of people who seem to get along in more or less perfect harmony. Trivia nights on Tuesdays are a hoot.

Long known as Savannah's premier place for young hotties to meet other young hotties, the **Bar-Bar** (219 W. Julian St. in City Market, 912/231-1910, www.thebarbar.com, Mon.–Sat. 7 P.M.–3 A.M.) is a little hard to find, being a basement-level establishment. (Stand in front of the Wild Wing Caf– on the east end of City Market, then walk west until you see the steps down to the Bar-Bar entrance.) A sprawling underground den underneath an old warehouse, the low-ceilinged but spacious Bar-Bar boasts a great little dance floor, pool tables, and plenty of places to sit and relax in privacy. And oh, yeah, plenty of hotties.

Also a decent restaurant, the bar at **1790** (307 E. President St., 912/236-7122, lunch Mon.–Fri. 11:30 A.M.–2 P.M., dinner daily 6–10 P.M., bar Mon.–Fri. 11 A.M.–3 A.M., Sat.–Sun. 6–3 A.M.) has long been a gathering place for some of Savannah's most well-connected businesspeople to let their hair down and gossip about each other 'til last call. But you don't have to be in the old-school clique to

SAVANNAH

© JIM MOREKIS

Kevin Barry's Irish Pub on West River Street

enjoy 1790's very Southern form of garrulous trash-talking; it's a welcoming place, with its big, rectangular bar adding to the clubby atmosphere. And you can order from the restaurant menu until 10 P.M.

The main landmark on the west end of River Street is the famous (or infamous, depending on which side of "The Troubles" you're on) **Kevin Barry's Irish Pub** (117 W. River St., 912/233-9626, www.kevinbarrys.com, daily 11 A.M.–3 A.M.), one of Savannah's most beloved establishments. K.B.'s keeps alive the spirit of Irish independence, so don't be alarmed when you see a tribute on the wall to some martyr or other, killed fighting the English. It's open seven days a week, with evenings seeing performances by a number of Irish troubadours, all veterans of the East Coast trad circuit. An eclectic mix of tourists, local Irish, military, and sailors keeps this place always interesting and alive. While no one in their right mind goes to an Irish pub for the food, Kevin Barry's offers a good, solid range of typical fare, including a serviceable corned beef and cabbage.

Don't get too excited about the "rooftop dining" advertised at **Churchill's Pub & Restaurant** (13–17 W. Bay St., 912/232-8501, www.thebritishpub.com, opens Mon.–Fri. 5 P.M., Sat. 10 A.M., kitchen closes 10 P.M. Sun.–Thurs., 11 P.M. Fri.–Sat.), unless you enjoy looking at the sides of other buildings. The real attractions at Churchill's are threefold: the great selection of beer; the great company; and perhaps most of all, the fish and chips, which are hands-down the best in town. Don't forget to be liberal with the malt vinegar; it's key.

The "other" English pub in town, **Six Pence Pub** (245 Bull St., 912/233-3151, daily 11:30 A.M.–midnight) is centrally located off Chippewa Square downtown, and is an especially good place to stop in for a pint on a rainy day. On nice days, the sidewalk tables go quickly, so grab one if it's open. Look for the big red London telephone booth out front.

The only brewpub in Savannah, **Moon River Brewing Company** (21 W. Bay St.,

912/447-0943, www.moonriverbrewing .com, Mon.–Thurs. 11 A.M.–11 P.M., Fri.–Sat. 11 A.M.–midnight, Sun. 11 A.M.–10 P.M.) directly across from the Hyatt Regency, offers half a dozen handcrafted beers—from a pale ale to a stout to all points between. The quality of the batches can vary widely, but you can always order a sampler round to get a feel for what you'd like to have more of. I like the Claire de Lune, a Cologne-style light ale. The kitchen offers a range of items (including soups, salads, seafood, and steaks), but you might want to stick with the beer.

Live Music and Karaoke

Despite its high-volume offerings, the hardcore/heavy metal club **The Jinx** (127 W. Congress St., 912/236-2281, www.thejinx.net, Mon.–Sat. 4 P.M.–3 A.M.) is a friendly watering hole and probably the closest thing Savannah has to a full-on Athens, Georgia, music club. Shows start *very* late here, never before 11 P.M. and often later than that. If you're here for the show, bring earplugs.

In the basement of the well-known Olde Pink House restaurant, **Planter's Tavern** (23 Abercorn St., 912/232-4286, Sun.–Thurs. 5–10:30 P.M., Fri.–Sat. 5–11 P.M.) is worth a trip all by itself. Appointed in classic English hunt club decor, the highlight of Planter's Tavern are the regular performances by pianist/singer Gail Thurmond, who knows a wide range of jazz and pop standards, including lots and lots of Johnny Mercer. You can also order dinner from the Pink House menu down here. I like to plop down on the sofa right in front of the fireplace next to Gail's piano; it drowns out the clinking silverware. Planter's Tavern is open daily, but Gail takes Mondays off.

Having nothing whatsoever to do with the 1982 film of the same name, **Savannah Smiles Dueling Pianos** (314-B Williamson St., 912/527-6453, Wed.–Sun. 7 P.M.–3 A.M.) is hard to define, but I'll give it a shot: Imagine a piano bar, only with two pianos, within a sports bar the size of an airplane hangar. For all that, it's actually a very fun place, with a friendly staff and a good mix of locals and tourists. Send in your suggested song titles on a cocktail napkin to the eponymous dueling pianists. You get here by walking west on Factors Walk.

Savannah's undisputed karaoke champion is **McDonough's** (21 E. McDonough St., 912/233-6136, www.mcdonoughsof savannah.com, Mon.–Sat. 8 P.M.–3 A.M., Sun. 8 P.M.–2 A.M.), an advantage compounded by the fact that a lot more goes on here than karaoke. The kitchen at McDonough's is quite capable, and many locals swear you can get the best burger in town here. Despite the sports bar atmosphere, the emphasis here is on the karaoke, which ramps up every night at 9:30 P.M., and a very competent group of regulars never fails to entertain. The crowd here is surprisingly diverse, racially and socioeconomically mixed, featuring lawyers and students, rural folks and Rangers in equal numbers.

Gay and Lesbian

Any examination of gay and lesbian nightlife in Savannah must of course begin with **Club One Jefferson** (1 Jefferson St., 912/232-0200, www.clubone-online.com) of *Midnight* fame, with its famous drag shows, including the notorious Lady Chablis, upstairs in the cabaret, and its rockin' 1,000 -square-foot dance floor downstairs. Cabaret showtimes are Thurs.–Sat. 10:30 P.M. and 12:30 A.M., Sunday 10:30 P.M. and Monday 11:30 P.M. Call for Chablis's showtimes. As with all local gay nightclubs, straights are more than welcome here.

A friendly, kitschy little tavern at the far west end of River Street near the Jefferson Street ramp, **Chuck's Bar** (301 W. River St., 912/232-1005, www.myspace.com/chucks _bar, Mon.–Wed. 8 P.M.–3 A.M., Thurs.–Sat. 7 P.M.–3 A.M.) is a great place to relax and see some interesting local characters. Karaoke at Chuck's is especially a hoot, and they keep the Christmas lights up all year.

Though technically it doesn't market itself as a gay and lesbian venue, **Venus de Milo** (38 MLK Jr. Blvd., 912/447-0901, Mon.–Sat. 4:30 P.M.–3 A.M.) is historically a favorite gathering place for the community. It's also by far the best wine bar in Savannah, with an excellent selection of all varietals.

Blaine's Back Door (13 E. Perry Lane, 912/233-6765, www.blainesbar.com, Mon.–Sat. 2 P.M.–3 A.M.) is the closest thing in Savannah to the classic East Village or West Coast gay bar, with lots of pictures of muscular men in various degrees of undress on the wall and a small but active dance floor.

THE ARTS
Theater

After going through a spell of the doldrums, live theatre is back in Savannah—and it may be better than ever. An abundance of artists and students makes the city a natural for theater, and you might be surprised at the caliber of the talent.

The most consistently high-quality productions are by the City of Savannah's **Cultural Arts Theatre** (9 W. Henry St., 912/651-6782, www.savannahga.gov), a taxpayer-supported company that puts on a surprisingly eclectic range of shows, from chestnuts like *The Sound of Music* to more modern productions like *Bat Boy: The Musical*. Most productions are in the Black Box space on Henry Street, but large musicals are generally staged at the Lucas Theatre.

The semi-pro troupe at the **Historic Savannah Theatre** (222 Bull St., 912/233-7764, www.savannahtheatre.com) performs a busy, rotating schedule of oldies revues (typical title: *Return to the '50s*), which make up for their lack of originality with the tightness and energy of their talented young cast of regulars.

The upstart **Cardinal Rep** (703D Louisville Rd., 912/232-6080, www.savannahactorstheatre.org) operates in a restored train depot just west of the Historic District. Concentrating on cutting-edge drama and sketch comedy, Cardinal Rep relies on a cadre of SCAD students and directors.

Occupying the same former Belk building in east Savannah, Savannah Childrens Theatre and Savannah Community Theatre put on solid, year-round seasons of high-quality productions, mostly musicals.

Savannah Childrens Theatre (2160 E. Victory Dr., 912/238-9015, www.savannah childrenstheatre.org) has an entrance in front of the building, facing Victory Drive, while **Savannah Community Theatre** (2160 E. Victory Dr., 912/898-9021, www.savannah communitytheatre.com) is reached by simply driving around to the building's rear.

For a fun evening of boozy, interactive theatre, go down to the River Street docks on a Thursday night for **Murder Afloat** (boards next to the Hyatt Regency, cruise starts at 9:30 P.M., 912/232-6404, www.murderafloat.com, $26.95 adults, $18.95 children under 12). The mysterious fun happens during a 90-minute cruise on the Savannah River aboard on of two riverboats, during which you can talk to the actors and try to figure out "whodunit." Food is included and there's a cash bar onboard.

There are few things to recommend Savannah's south side to the visitor, but one of them is the **Armstrong Atlantic State University Masquers** (11935 Abercorn St., 912/927-5381, www.finearts.armstrong.edu), the second-oldest college theater group in the country (only Harvard's Hasty Pudding Theatricals is older). Now nearing their 75th anniversary, the Masquers boast a newly restored performance space at the Jenkins Theatre, and might surprise you with the high quality of their performances—despite being a student program. Parking is never a problem.

Music and Dance

The Savannah Symphony is no more, victim of the same economic and demographic challenges facing orchestras in small-to-mid-sized cities all over the United States. But carrying on their proud tradition—and using many of the same musicians—is the **Savannah Orchestra** (800/514-3849, www.savannahsinfonietta.org) a professional troupe that performs concertos and sonatas at various venues around town and is always worth checking out. Recent performances have included Mendelssohn's Violin Concerto in E Minor, Bach's Brandenburg Concerto No. 5, and Brahms' Serenade No. 1.

A prime dance company in town is

Savannah Danse Theatre (912/897-2100, www.savannahdansetheatre.org), known chiefly for its complete *Nutcracker* performance each December at the Lucas Theatre, with live accompaniment by a full symphony orchestra hired especially for the occasion—quite a rarity in a city this size.

Another local ballet troupe is **Ballet Savannah** (912/352-7487, www.balletsavannah.com), with various performances during the year.

Dancing primarily in the modern/African style, **Sankofa Dance Theatre** (912/661-1286, www.sankofadancetheatre.com) is the closest thing to cutting-edge dance in town.

Spoken Word

Perhaps the single most vibrant cultural scene in Savannah is that of spoken word poetry. Practiced at open mics at coffeehouses all over town, these passionate, untutored

---

FROM *GATOR* TO *GUMP*: CINEMA IN SAVANNAH

OK, so *Gator* wasn't actually the first high-profile movie filmed primarily in Savannah. That honor would have to go to 1962's *Cape Fear*, starring Gregory Peck and Robert Mitchum (who years before filming was arrested and briefly jailed for public indecency while wandering in a drunken state through Savannah).

But 1975's *Gator*, directed by and starring Burt Reynolds, definitely put the city on the Hollywood map in practical terms, due in no small part to the then-mega star power of Reynolds himself, whose personal filmmaking mission was, in his words, to "say some nice things about the South."

Old-timers still tell stories of hanging around the pool with Burt and the crew at the old Oglethorpe Hotel on Wilmington Island, once owned by the Teamsters and rumored to be the final resting place of Jimmy Hoffa (it's now the Wilmington Plantation condos). Current Chatham County Commission Chairman Pete Liakakis, a black belt in karate and the fittest septuagenarian you'll ever meet, served as Burt's bodyguard during the shoot.

In short order, parts of the landmark 1970s TV miniseries *Roots* were filmed in and around Savannah, as were part of the follow-up *Roots: The Next Generation*.

Film aficionados fondly remember the sadly forgotten 1980 TV movie *The Ordeal of Dr. Mudd,* starring Dennis Weaver. There are other reasons to remember the film other than the infamous story from "The Book" where Jim Williams unfurls a swastika banner to ruin a shot on Monterey Square. The film also ex-

pertly uses interiors of Fort Pulaski to tell this largely sympathetic account of the historical Dr. Samuel Mudd, accused of aiding Abraham Lincoln's assassin John Wilkes Booth. In a chilling bit of synchronicity, Booth's brother Edwin, the most famous actor in America during the 1800s, played in Savannah often.

A key chapter in local filmography came with the filming of 1989's *Glory* in coastal Georgia, despite the fact that the real-life events it depicted actually happened near Charleston. River Street was the set for the parade scenes, and as Colonel Shaw, Matthew Broderick delivered his stirring address to the troops one block west of Mrs. Wilkes Boarding House on Jones Street. The railroad roundhouse off MLK Jr. Boulevard stood in for a Massachusetts training ground, but local preservationists were aghast when they discovered that some black paint the film crew had applied to the historic facility wouldn't come off. There were calls for Savannah never again to host another film crew, but luckily cooler heads prevailed.

Perhaps Savannah's most important brush with Hollywood came with the filming of 1994's *Forrest Gump* in and around Savannah. Let's face it: The list of hits filmed in Savannah is a short one, let alone critical and box office successes the likes of *Gump*. Look for the long-running series of shots of Tom Hanks sitting on a bench in Chippewa Square – and note how the traffic runs the wrong direction around the square! The famous bench itself now resides in the Savannah History Museum on MLK Jr. Boulevard. The steeple you see in the shot of performances can blow you away with their often brutal honesty and charismatic delivery. The main spoken word collective in town is **AWOL (All Walks of Life)** (912/341-8306, awolinc.org). They not only spearhead performance of the art form at various venues around town, but work in local schools to build self-esteem; in the words of one of their participants, "not every kid can be an athlete."

Film

First, the bad news: Savannah's a horrible town for mainstream film. The moviehouses themselves are pretty underwhelming, both in service and projection equipment. Many high-profile films simply never get around to showing here, while the worst pap tends to stay for weeks and weeks.

The closest multiplex to downtown is the **Victory Square Stadium 9** (1901 E. Victory

the floating white feather is of nearby Independent Presbyterian Church.

Ben Affleck and Sandra Bullock filmed many scenes of 1999's *Forces of Nature* on Tybee Island and in Savannah (yours truly's house is in the final scene for about two seconds). Both actors would become infatuated with coastal Georgia from their experiences on the film, with Bullock buying property on Tybee and Affleck buying a pricey compound on the newly developed Hampton Island farther down the coast.

Longtime Hollywood producer and Savannah native Stratton Leopold, who also owns Leopold's Ice Cream on Broughton Street, helped Savannah land 1999's *The General's Daughter* starring John Travolta (look for the grand exterior of the main building at Oatland Island and shots of The Crab Shack seafood restaurant on Tybee, actually an old fishing camp).

Trotting out a serviceable Southern accent for a Brit, Kenneth Branagh came to town to play a disgruntled Savannah lawyer in Robert Altman's *Gingerbread Man*. Despite the late Altman's reputation as an actor's director, he's one of the few directors to grasp the extent of the Georgia coast's natural beauty; the views of the Tybee marsh are some of the best landscape shots of the area you'll ever see.

Though I'm sure quite a few downtown art students had no idea what the fuss was about, Robert Redford still turned female heads of a certain age when he came to town to direct 2000's *The Legend of Bagger Vance*, with Will Smith as the eponymous caddie. In the film, watch for the facsimile of a

Depression-era storefront specially built around City Market.

Cate Blanchett and Katie Holmes starred in 2000's *The Gift*, one of the few movies to take full advantage of the poignant and stunning natural beauty of Bonaventure Cemetery.

Ironically, considering the impact of "The Book" on Savannah, Clint Eastwood's *Midnight in the Garden of Good and Evil* (1997) is arguably the all-time worst movie ever filmed here. Though now lionized as one of Hollywood's great directors, Eastwood's famously laissez faire attitude toward filmmaking – reportedly there were no rehearsals before cameras rolled – did not serve the story or the setting well, perhaps because Savannah's already a pretty darn laissez faire kind of place to begin with. Still, it's fun to watch *Midnight* and count the local celebrities with parts who are in the actual book, from gossipy hairdresser Jerry Spence to a line-fumbling Lady Chablis to Jim Williams' real-life lawyer, Sonny Seiler, who plays the judge who tried the case.

Lately the pickings have been pretty thin, and Savannahians are grumbling that the golden age of Savannah films is over. Chief among the complaints is that until recently, Georgia had refused to keep pace with other states in tax incentives to attract the film industry.

Case in point: Alyssa Milano was set to play a Savannah lawyer in a locally shot TV pilot. When filmmakers realized how much money they could save by crossing the river into South Carolina, they rewrote the entire script and moved the shoot.

And that's how Alyssa Milano became a Charleston lawyer.

Dr., 912/355-5000, www.trademarkcinemas
.com), which also hosts the screenings of **The
Reel Savannah Group** (www.reelsavannah
.org, reelsavanah@hotmail.com), a nonprofit
that brings in foreign independent releases one
Sunday a month.

The **Sentient Bean Coffeehouse** (13 E.
Park Ave., 912/232-4447, www.sentientbean
.com) hosts counterculture and political docu-
mentaries and kitsch classics at least two nights
a week.

Visual Arts

It's true: There are more art galleries per cap-
ita in Savannah than in New York City—one
gallery for every 2,191 residents, to be exact.

The no-brainer package experience for the
visitor is the combo of the **Telfair Academy
of Arts and Sciences** (121 Barnard St.,
912/790-8800, www.telfair.org) and the
Jepson Center (207 W. York St., 912/790-
8800, www.telfair.org). These two affiliated
arms of the Telfair Museum of Art run the
gamut, from the Academy's impressive collection of Kahlil Gibran drawings to the 2008
installation by local favorite Marcus Kenney
at the Jepson, comprising dozens of tiny heads
arranged on the entrance stairs in the building's atrium.

Naturally, SCAD galleries (912/525-5225,
www.scad.edu) are in great abundance all over
town, displaying the handiwork of students,
faculty, and alumni. The ones with the most
consistently impressive exhibits are the **Pei
Ling Chan Gallery** (324 MLK Jr. Blvd.), **Red
Gallery** (201 E. Broughton St.) and **Pinnacle
Gallery** (320 E. Liberty St.). The college also
runs its own museum, the **SCAD Museum of
Art** (227 MLK Jr. Blvd., 912/525-7191, www
.scad.edu), home of the Evans Collection of
African American art and the Newton Center
for British American Studies.

FESTIVALS AND EVENTS

Savannah's calendar fairly bursts with festivals, many outdoors. Dates shift from year to
year, so it's best to consult the listed websites
for details.

January

Floats and bands take part in the **Martin Luther
King Jr. Day Parade** downtown to commemo-
rate the civil rights leader and Georgia native.
The bulk of the route consists of historic MLK
Jr. Boulevard, formerly West Broad Street.

February

Savannah loves its history, and makes sure everyone else does too with its two-week-long
Georgia Days (www.georgiahistory.com) celebration in February, sponsored by the Georgia
Historical Society to mark the founding of the
city by James Oglethorpe in 1733. The most
camera-friendly event of the celebration is the
delightful parade downtown by thousands of
area elementary schoolchildren, clad in their
choice of either a colonist outfit or Native
American garb. But there's plenty to do for the
visiting history buff, including a series of free
lectures by noted scholars, a "Colonial Faire and
Muster" at historic Wormsloe Plantation, and a
"Super Museum Sunday," in which most of the
area's museums are open to the public for free.

Definitely *not* to be confused with St.
Patrick's Day, the **Savannah Irish Festival**
(912/232-3448, www.savannahirish.org) fo-
cuses on Celtic music. A regular performer and
Savannah's most popular "Irishman at large"
is folk singer Harry O'Donoghue, a native of
Ireland who regularly plays at Kevin Barry's
Irish Pub on River Street and hosts his own
Celtic music show, "The Green Island," on local
public radio 91.1 FM Saturday evenings.

Hosted by the historically African American
Savannah State University at various venues
around town, the month-long **Black Heritage
Festival** (912/691-6847) is tied into Black
History Month and boasts name entertainers like
the Alvin Ailey Dance Theatre (performing free!).
This event also usually features plenty of historical lectures devoted to the very interesting and
rich history of African Americans in Savannah.

March

One of the most anticipated events for house-
proud Savannahians, the **Tour of Homes and
Gardens** (912/234-8054, www.savannah

tourofhomes.org) offers guests the opportunity to visit six beautiful sites off the usual tourist-trod path. This is a great way to expand your understanding of local architecture and hospitality beyond the usual house museums.

More than just a day, the citywide **St. Patrick's Day** (www.savannahsaintpatricks day.com) celebration generally lasts at least half a week and temporarily triples the population. The nearly three-hour parade—second-biggest in the United States—always begins at 10 A.M. on St. Patrick's Day (unless that falls on a Sunday, in which case it's generally on the previous Saturday) and includes an interesting mix of marching bands, wacky floats, and sauntering local Irishmen in kelly green jackets.

The appeal of the event comes not only from the festive atmosphere and generally beautiful spring weather, but from Savannah's unique law allowing partiers to walk the streets with a plastic cup filled with the adult beverage of their choice. Because of this, however, there is inevitably going to be over-imbibing, which Savannahians generally think of as "local character." While you may disagree, there's no escaping the event if it's going on while you're here. Your best course of action is to simply put on a "Kiss Me I'm Irish" button, sample a beverage yourself, and live and let live if possible.

While the parade itself is very family-friendly, afterwards hardcore partiers generally head en masse to River Street, which is blocked off for the occasion and definitely *not* where you want to take small children. Five bucks will buy those 21 and over a bracelet allowing them to drink alcohol. For information on this aspect of the celebration, go to www .riverstreetsavannah.com. If you want to hear traditional Celtic music on St. Patrick's Day in Savannah, River Street isn't the place to go, with the single exception of Kevin Barry's on the west end. Outdoor entertainment on River Street during the celebration is generally a lame assortment of cover bands. For authentic Irish music on St. Paddy's Day, wander around the pubs in the City Market area, where the *real* trad musicians perform.

Savannah's answer to Charleston's Spoleto,

the three-week **Savannah Music Festival** (912/234-3378, www.savannahmusicfestival .org) is held at various historic venues around town and begins right after St. Patrick's Day. Past festivals have featured Wynton Marsalis, the Beaux Arts Trio, and Diane Reeves. The jazz portion is locked down tight, thanks to the efforts of festival director Rob Gibson, a Georgia native who cut his teeth as the founding director of Jazz at Lincoln Center. You can often see Gibson racing from venue to venue by bicycle in order to be able to personally introduce each act. The classical side is equally impressive, helmed by one of the world's great young violinists, Daniel Hope, acting as associate director. Other genres are featured in abundance as well, from gospel to bluegrass to zydeco to world music to the always-popular American Traditions vocal competition.

The most economical way to enjoy the Music Festival is to purchase tickets online before December of the previous year at a 10 percent discount. However, if you just want to take in a few events, individual tickets are available at a tiered pricing system that allows everyone to enjoy this popular event. You can buy tickets to individual events in town at the walk-up box office beside the Trustees Theatre on Broughton Street. Don't miss the intimate chamber music concerts held inside the historic rotunda of the Telfair Museum of Art. Indeed, aficionados often find that the smaller-scale concerts are generally the most memorable experiences of the entire festival.

April

Short for "North of Gaston Street," the **NOGS Tour of Hidden Gardens** (912/961-4805, www .gcofsavnogstour.org, $30) is available two days in April and focuses on Savannah's amazing selection of private gardens selected for excellence of design, historical interest, and beauty.

Everyone loves the annual free **Sidewalk Arts Festival** (912/525-5865, www.scad.edu) presented by the Savannah College of Art and Design in Forsyth Park. Contestants claim a rectangular section of sidewalk on which to display their chalk art talent. But you don't have to compete to have fun; there's a non-contest section with chalk provided. Live entertainment and food round out this delightful outdoor spring event.

May

The SCAD-sponsored **Sand Arts Festival** (www.scad.edu) on Tybee Island's North Beach centers on a competition of sand castle design, sand sculpture, sand relief, and wind sculpture. You might be amazed at the level of artistry lavished on the sometimes-wondrous creations, only for them to wash away with the tide.

The annual celebration of Scottish and Celtic heritage known as the **Savannah Scottish Games** is generally held at the historic Bethesda Home For Boys. Expect food, dancing, music, and, of course, the requisite lifting and throwing of heavy objects by stocky gentlemen in kilts.

If you don't want to get wet, don't show up at the **Tybee Beach Bum Parade,** an uproarious Memorial Day event with a distinctly boozy overtone. This unique 20-year-old event—so typical of eccentric Tybee Island—features homemade floats filled with partiers who squirt the assembled crowds with various water pistols. The crowds, of course, pack their own heat and squirt right back.

June

Though performers at the downtown **Savannah Asian Festival** range from Japanese taiko drummers to Korean tae kwon do teams to hula dancers, the real attraction is the food, provided by a wide and diverse range of local ethnic restaurants. Another lure of this early summer festival is that it's held in the air-conditioned confines of the Savannah Civic Center downtown.

July

Two key events happen around **Fourth of July,** primarily the large fireworks show on River Street, always on July 4, and also an impressive fireworks display from the Tybee Pier and Pavilion, which sometimes is on a different night. A nice bonus of the Tybee event is that sometimes you can look out over the Atlantic

and see a similar fireworks display held on nearby Hilton Head Island, South Carolina, a few minutes away by boat (but nearly an hour by car).

September

The second-largest gay and lesbian event in Georgia (only Atlanta's version is larger), the **Savannah Pride Festival** (www.savannah pride.org, various venues, free) happens every September. Crowds get pretty big for this festive, fun event, which usually features lots of dance acts and political booths.

Though the quality of the acts has been overshadowed lately by the Savannah Music Festival in the spring, the **Savannah Jazz Festival** (www.savannahjazzfestival.org) has two key things going for it: It's free, and it's outside (weather permitting) in the glorious green expanse of Forsyth Park. Generally spread out over several nights, the volunteer-run festival draws a good crowd regardless of the lineup, and concessions are available.

October

The Savannah Symphony Orchestra is defunct, but area classical musicians unite to play a free evening at **Picnic in the Park** (www.savannah ga.gov), a concert in Forsyth Park that draws thousands of noshers. This is one of Savannah's favorite events. And did I mention it's free? Arrive early to check out the ostentatious, whimsical picnic displays, which compete for prizes. Then set out your blanket, pop open a bottle of wine, and enjoy the sweet sounds of some of the region's best professional musicians.

That combined aroma of beer, sauerkraut, and sausage that you smell coming from the waterfront is the annual **Oktoberfest on the River** (www.riverstreetsavannah.com), which has evolved to be Savannah's second-largest celebration (behind only St. Patrick's Day). Live entertainment of varying quality is featured, though of course the attraction is the aforementioned beer and German food. A highlight is the Saturday morning "Weiner Dog races" involving, you guessed it, competing dachshunds.

If pickin' and grinnin' is your thing, don't miss the low-key but always entertaining **Savannah**

Folk Music Festival (www.savannahfolk.org). The main event of the weekend is held on a Sunday night in the historic Grayson Stadium in Daffin Park, but a popular Old-Time Country Dance is usually held the Saturday prior. Members of the Savannah Folk Music Society will help you learn how to do the dance, so don't be shy!

Sponsored by St. Paul's Greek Orthodox Church, the popular **Savannah Greek Festival** (www.stpaul.ga.goarch.org) features food, music, and Greek souvenirs. The weekend event is held across the street from the church at the parish center—in the gym, to be exact, right on the basketball court. Despite the pedestrian location, the food is authentic and delicious, and the atmosphere convivial and friendly.

Despite its generic-sounding name, the **Fall Festival** (www.bamboo.caes.uga.edu) is actually quite interesting, given its location in the unique Bamboo Farm and Coastal Garden. A joint project of the University of Georgia and Chatham County, the Bamboo Farm features a wide array of native species, all lovingly tended. The festival features tours, displays, arts and crafts, food, and lots of kid's activities. The event is free, but you'll pay $1 to park. To get there, take Exit 94 off of I-95 and take U.S. 204 east towards Savannah. Turn right on East Gateway Boulevard, then left on Canebrake Road. Enter at the Canebrake gate.

Hosted by the Savannah College of Art and Design, the week-long **Savannah Film Festival** (www.scad.edu) beginning in late October is rapidly growing not only in size but in prestige. Lots of older, more established Hollywood names appear as honored guests for the evening events, while buzz-worthy, up-and-coming actors, directors, producers, writers, and animators give excellent workshops during the day. Many of these usually-jaded show-biz types really let their hair down for this festival, because, as you'll see, Savannah is the real star.

The best way to enjoy this excellent event is to buy a pass, which enables you to walk from event to event. Most importantly, the passes gain you admission to what many locals consider the best part of the festival: the after-parties, where you'll often find yourself rubbing up against some famous star or director while in line for a drink. But whatever you do, don't ask for an autograph. The thing at these parties is to be cool—and if you can't *be* cool, at least act that way!

One of Savannah's most unique events is October's **"Shalom Y'all" Jewish Food Festival** (912/233-1547, www.mickveisrael.org), held in Forsyth Park and sponsored by the historic Temple Mickve Israel. Latkes, matzo, and other nibbles are all featured along with entertainment.

November

Generally kicking off the month is the popular **Telfair Art Fair** (www.telfair.org), a multiday annual art show and sale under a huge tent in Telfair Square between the two museums there, the Telfair Academy and the Jepson Center. Browse or buy, either way it's a culturally enlightening good time.

The name says it all. The **Savannah Seafood Festival** (www.riverstreetsavannah.com) on River Street offers mouthwatering fare from a variety of local vendors plus live entertainment.

Two of the South's favorite pastimes come together at the aptly named **Blues & BBQ Festival** (www.roundhousebluesandbbq.com), held at the historic Roundhouse and featuring some of the biggest names in blues and the best purveyors of barbecue in the region. Something about all that railroad paraphernalia just makes the tunes and the food that much more enticing and real.

December

Arts and crafts and holiday entertainment highlight the **Christmas on the River and Lighted Parade** (www.riverstreetsavannah .com) that happens on River Street.

Another beloved local tour, the annual **Holiday Tour of Homes** (912/236-8362, www.dnaholidaytour.net) sponsored by the Downtown Neighborhood Association is a great way to get up close with a half-dozen or so of some of Savannah's best private homes, all dolled up in their finest for the holidays. There's an afternoon tour and a candlelight tour by trolley.

SAVANNAH

Shopping

Downtown Savannah's main shopping district is Broughton Street, which is included here along with several other key shopping areas of note.

BROUGHTON STREET

The historic center of downtown shopping has recently seen an influx of large chain stores, like Banana Republic, The Gap, and American Apparel, to name but a few. You can find those on your own, but here's a rundown of some other, perhaps less obvious, shopping choices.

Art Supply

A great art town needs a great art supply store, and in Savannah that would be **Primary Art Supply** (14 E. Broughton St., 912/233-7624, http://primaryartsupply.com, Mon.–Fri. 8 A.M.–8 P.M., Sat.–Sun. 10 A.M.–6 P.M.), which has two full floors of equipment and tools for the serious artist—priced to be affordable for students.

Clothes and Fashion

The newest, biggest splash on Broughton has no doubt been the opening of the überhip **Marc Jacobs** (322 W. Broughton St., 912/234-2800, www.marcjacobs.com, Mon.–Sat. 11 A.M.–7 P.M.), which focuses on the more affordable Marc by Marc Jacobs line of men's and women's clothing and accessories. Be sure to check out the wild window displays, the talk of the town.

The clothing store for Savannah's hippest, up-and-coming women, **Bleu Belle** (205 W. Broughton St., 912/443-0011, www.bleu belle.com, Mon.–Sat. 10 A.M.–6 P.M., Sun. noon–5 P.M.) stays on top of the trends with a wide selection, from casual chic to drop-dead evening wear.

Gaucho is another popular choice for women, with an emphasis on accessories, jewelry, and shoes. There are two locations: 18 East Broughton Street (912/234-7414, Mon.–Sat.

10 A.M.–6 P.M.) and the original location at 250 Bull Street (912/232-7414, Mon.–Sat. 10 A.M.–6 P.M., Sun. 1–5 P.M.).

Popular Georgia/South Carolina chain **Loose Lucy's** (212 W. Broughton St., 912/201-2131, www.looselucys.com, Mon.–Fri. 10 A.M.–7 P.M., Sat. 10 A.M.–9 P.M., Sun. 11 A.M.–6 P.M.) features cool clothes and shoes heavy on 1960s psychedelic chic, including lots of tie-dye and batik.

Home Goods

While Savannah is an Anglophile's dream, Francophiles will enjoy **The Paris Market & Brocante** (36 W. Broughton St., 912/232-1500, www.theparismarket.com, Mon.–Sat. 10 A.M.–6 P.M., Sun. 11 A.M.–4 P.M.) on a beautifully restored corner of Broughton Street. Home and garden goods, bed and bath accoutrements, and a great selection of antique and vintage items combine for a rather opulent shopping experience. In addition to the decadent Old World fun of wandering through the expert displays of gorgeous Continental-inspired merchandise, you can actually find some decent bargains here.

Those looking for great home decorating ideas with inspiration from both global and Southern aesthetics should check out **24e Furnishings at Broughton** (24 E. Broughton St., 912/233-2274, www.twentyfoure.com, Mon.–Thurs. 10 A.M.–6 P.M., Fri.–Sat. 10 A.M.–7 P.M., Sun. noon–5 P.M.), located in an excellent restored 1921 storefront.

Outdoor Outfitters

Outdoor lovers should make themselves acquainted with **Half Moon Outfitters** (15 E. Broughton St., 912/201-9313, www.half moonoutfitters.com, Mon.–Sat. 10 A.M.–7 P.M., Sun. noon–6 P.M.), a full-service camping, hiking, skiing, and kayaking store. Half Moon is part of a regional chain that also has two locations in Charleston.

WATERFRONT

Amid the T-shirt shops, candy stores, and tchotchke places, Savannah's waterfront area does have a few worthy shopping options.

Antiques

Probably the coolest antique shop in town is **Jere's Antiques** (9 N. Jefferson St., 912/236-2815, www.jeresantiques.com, Mon.–Sat. 9:30 A.M.–5 P.M.). It's in a huge historic warehouse on Factors Walk, and has a concentration on fine European pieces.

Art

The fun River Street co-op **Gallery 209** (209 E. River St., 912/236-4583, www.gallery209 .com, daily 10:30 A.M.–9 P.M.) showcases more than 30 of Savannah's best-known artists and craftspeople.

Clothes and Fashion

The river's most popular clothing store by far is the boutique **Jezebel Limited** (25 E. River St., 912/236-4333, Mon.–Sun. 10 A.M.–6 P.M.), which packs a lot of cute, wearable high fashion into a small place.

Clothe your inner biker at **Harley-Davidson** (503 E. River St., 912/231-8000, Mon.–Sat. 10 A.M.–6 P.M., Sun. noon–6 P.M.).

CITY MARKET

A borderline tourist trap, City Market strongly tends towards more touristy, less unique items. Here are a few exceptions:

An absolutely one-of-a-kind shopping experience is in City Market at **Universe Trading Company** (27 Montgomery St., 912/233-1585, Tues.–Sat. 10 A.M.–5 P.M.) on the southwest corner of Franklin Square. This mind-blowing collection of kitsch—including, at last check, an actual cigar store Indian—is the real thing: a great old-fashioned junk shop, in the best sense of the term.

The whimsical **A. T. Hun Gallery** (302 W. St. Julian St., 912/233-2060, www.athun .com, Mon.–Thurs. 10 A.M.–6 P.M., Fri.–Sat. 10 A.M.–10 P.M., Sun. 11 A.M.–5 P.M.) is one of the first true art galleries in town and features a variety of adventurous art from local and regional favorites.

Another City Market favorite is **Chroma Gallery** (31 Barnard St., 912/232-2787, www.chromaartgallery.com, daily 10 A.M.–5:30 P.M.), run by two of Savannah's most beloved artists, Lori Keith Robinson and Jan Clayton Pagratis.

Check out some whimsical watches at **Time After Time** (305 W. Bryan St., 912/233-0568, daily 10 A.M.–6 P.M.).

If you're dying for a good smoke, try **Savannah Cigars** (308 W. Congress St., 912/233-2643, Mon.–Thurs. 11 A.M.–6 P.M., Fri.–Sat. 11 A.M.–11 P.M., Sun. noon–6 P.M.).

DOWNTOWN DESIGN DISTRICT

This relatively new shopping district, comprising storefronts in renovated historic buildings, runs for three blocks on Whitaker Street downtown beginning at Charlton Lane and ending at the Mercer-Williams House.

Antiques and Home Goods

An eclectic, European-style home goods store popular with locals and tourists alike is **One Fish Two Fish** (401 Whitaker St., 912/484-4600. Mon.–Sat. 10 A.M.–5 P.M., Sun. noon–5 P.M.). Owner Jennifer Beaufait Grayson, a St. Simons Island native, came to town a decade ago to set up shop in this delightfully restored old dairy building on the corner of Whitaker and Jones and has been getting rave reviews since.

Southern Charm Antiques (412-C Whitaker St., 912/233-9797, Mon.–Sat. 10 A.M.–5 P.M., Sun. noon–5 P.M.) takes a fresh look at old traditions, while **12 West Jones** (12 W. Jones St., 912/231-0622) has lots of antiques and decorative items.

Art Galleries

The **Whitney Gallery** (415 Whitaker St., 912/495-0024, Tues.–Sat. 10 A.M.–5 P.M.) features fresh contemporary art with a respect for tradition.

The **Julian Christian Gallery** (114

W. Taylor St., 912/234-1960, Mon.–Fri. 11 A.M.–5 P.M.) focuses on interiors and painted furniture.

VICTORIAN DISTRICT
Antiques
The huge **J. D. Weed** (102 W. Victory Dr., 912/234-8540, www.jdweedco.com, Mon.–Fri. 8:30 A.M.–5 P.M., Sat. 8:30 A.M.–noon), established in 1816, has a host of high-end, one-of-a-kind pieces.

Right around the corner, **Pinch of the Past** (2603 Whitaker St., 912/232-5563, www.pinchofthepast.com, Tues.–Sat. 9:30 A.M.–5:30 P.M.) concentrates on hard-to-find antique furnishings for renovation projects.

Art Galleries
South of downtown off Whitaker Street is the Starland Design District—actually an artists' colony of sorts on the grounds of the old Starland Dairy building. Here you'll find several experimental, avant-garde galleries, chief among them the **DesotORow Gallery** (2427 Desoto Ave. between Whitaker and Bull Sts., 912/236-4421, www.desotorow.com) and the **Starland Café** (11 E. 41st St., 912/443-9355, Mon.–Fri. 11 A.M.–3 P.M.), which also serves lunch during the week.

BOOKS
The fact that **E. Shaver Bookseller** (326 Bull St., 912/234-7257, Mon.–Sat. 9 A.M.–6 P.M.) is one of the few locally owned independent bookstores left in town should not diminish the fact that it is also the best bookstore in town. Esther Shaver and her friendly, well-read staff can help you around the rambling old interior of their ground-level store and its generous stock of regionally themed books. Don't miss the rare map room, with some gems from the 17th and 18th centuries.

Specializing in "gently used" books in good condition, **The Book Lady** (6 E. Liberty St., 912/233-3628, Mon.–Sat. 10 A.M.–5:30 P.M.) on Wright Square is a great place to pass some time while you're waiting on the heat to ebb. Many rare first editions are available.

© JIM MOREKIS

E. Shaver Bookseller on Madison Square, a Savannah institution

The beautiful Monterey Square location and a mention in *Midnight in the Garden of Good and Evil* combine to make **V&J Duncan** (12 E. Taylor St., 912/232-0338, www.vjduncan.com, Mon.–Sat. 10:30 A.M.–4:30 P.M.) a Savannah "must-shop." Owner John Duncan and his wife Virginia ("Ginger" to friends) have collected an impressive array of prints, books, and maps over the past quarter-century, and are themselves a treasure trove of information.

OTHER UNIQUE STORES

Not only a valuable outlet for SCAD students and faculty to sell their artistic wares, **shopSCAD** (340 Bull St., 912/525-5180, www.shopscadonline.com, Mon.–Wed. 9 A.M.–5:30 P.M., Thurs.–Fri. 9 A.M.–8 P.M., Sat. 10 A.M.–8 P.M., Sun. noon–5 P.M.) is also one of Savannah's most unique boutiques. You never really know what you'll find, but whatever it is, it will be one-of-a-kind. The jewelry in particular is always cutting-edge in design and high-quality in craftsmanship. The designer T-shirts are a hoot, too.

A delightful little slice of Europe on Abercorn, **Fabrika** (140 Abercorn St., 912/236-1122, www.fabrikasavannah.com, Mon.–Sat. 10 A.M.–6 P.M., Sun. noon–4 P.M.) seems more like a store in Holland or France than one in Savannah. Tiny and personable, the store is jammed with high-quality, buzz-worthy bolts of fabric, oodles of beads, and lots of sewing paraphernalia. They even offer custom sewing and sewing lessons.

MALLS

The mall closest to downtown—though it's not that close at about 10 miles south of downtown—is **Oglethorpe Mall** (7804 Abercorn St., 912/354-7038, www.oglethorpemall.com, Mon.–Sat. 10 A.M.–9 P.M., Sun. noon–6 P.M.), which despite being totally renovated and upgraded is still referred to by old-timers as "the old mall." Its anchor stores are Sears, Belk, J. C. Penney, and Macy's.

Much farther out on the south side is the **Savannah Mall** (14045 Abercorn St., 912/927-7467, www.savannahmall.com, Mon.–Sat. 10 A.M.–9 P.M., Sun. noon–6 P.M.). Its anchor stores are Dillard's, Target, and Bass Pro Shops Outdoor World.

GROCERIES AND MARKETS

Savannah's first and still premiere health food market, **Brighter Day Natural Foods** (1102 Bull St., 912/236-4703, www.brighterdayfoods.com, Mon.–Sat. 10 A.M.–7 P.M., Sun. 12:30–5:30 P.M.) has been the labor of love of Janie and Peter Brodhead for 30 years, all of them in the same location at the southern tip of Forsyth Park. Boasting organic groceries, regional produce, a sandwich and smoothie bar in the back, and an extensive vitamin, supplement, and herb section, Brighter Day is an oasis in Savannah's sea of chain supermarkets.

The **Starland Farmers Market** (Apr.–Oct. Sat. 9 A.M.–noon, www.starlandfarmersmarket.com) is a bit off the beaten tourist path in the Starland Design District at Whitaker Street just before it dead-ends into Victory Drive; but it's reputation is growing as a good place to stock up on local produce like onions, blueberries, collards, watermelon, potatoes, and yellow squash, and to meet an interesting and diverse crowd. Get there early, though, because the good stuff gets snapped up.

A throwback to the South's old ways and a pleasant spot to pick up some fresh area produce downtown is **Polk's Fresh Market** (530 E. Liberty St., 912/238-3032, Mon.–Sat. 8 A.M.–6 P.M.).

A local tradition for 20 years, **Keller's Flea Market** (5901 Ogeechee Rd., Exit 94 off I-95, 912/927-4848, Sat.–Sun. 8 A.M.–6 P.M., www.ilovefleas.com) packs in about 10,000 shoppers over the course of a typical weekend, who find a range of bargains in antiques, home goods, produce, and general kitsch. Free admission, concessions on-site.

A short ways into southside Savannah is a **Fresh Market** (5525 Abercorn St., 912/354-6075, Mon.–Sat. 9 A.M.–9 P.M., Sun. 11 A.M.–8 P.M.). Currently there's only one true supermarket in downtown Savannah, **Kroger** (311 E. Gwinnett St., 912/231-2260, daily 24 hours).

SAVANNAH

Sports and Recreation

Savannah more than makes up for its sad organized sports scene with copious outdoor options that take full advantage of its temperate climate and the natural beauty of its marshy environment next to the Atlantic Ocean.

ON THE WATER
Kayaking and Canoeing

Probably the single best single kayak/canoe adventure in Savannah is the run across the Back River from Tybee to **Little Tybee Island,** an undeveloped State Heritage Site that despite its name is actually twice as big as Tybee, albeit mostly marsh. Many kayakers opt to camp on the island. You can even follow the shoreline out into the Atlantic, but be aware that wave action can get intense offshore.

Begin the paddle at the public boat ramp on the Back River. To get there, take Butler all the way to 18th Street and take a right, then another quick right onto Chatham Avenue. The parking lot for the landing is a short way up Chatham on your left. (Warning: Do not attempt to swim to Little Tybee no matter how strong a swimmer you think you are—the currents are exceptionally vicious. Also, do not be tempted to walk far out onto the Back River beach at low tide. The tide comes in very quickly and often strands people on the sandbar.)

By paddling west up the Back River and turning right into the first tidal creek, you find yourself taking a relaxing jaunt down Chimney Creek. You can even put in at The Crab Shack and enjoy a seafood meal before going back to the boat ramp.

One of the great overall natural experiences in the area is the massive **Savannah National Wildlife Refuge** (912/652-4415, www.fws.gov/savannah, no fee). This 30,000-acre reserve—half in Georgia, half in South Carolina—is on the Atlantic Flyway, so you'll be able to see birdlife in abundance, in addition to alligators and manatee. Earthen dikes criss-crossing the refuge are vestigial remnants of rice paddies from plantation days.

You can kayak on your own, but many opt to take guided tours offered by **Wilderness Southeast** (912/897-5108), **Sea Kayak Georgia** (888/529-2542), and **Swamp Girls Kayak Tours** (843/784-2249). To get there, take U.S. Highway 17 north over the big Talmadge Bridge, over the Savannah River into South Carolina. Turn left on South Carolina Highway 170 South and look for the entrance to Laurel Hill Wildlife Drive on the left.

Another pleasant kayaking route is the **Skidaway Narrows.** Begin this paddle at the public boat ramp, which you find by taking Waters Avenue all the way until it turns to Whitefield Avenue and then Diamond Causeway. Continue all the way over the Moon River to a drawbridge; park at the foot of the bridge. Once in the water, paddle northeast. Look for the osprey nests on top of the navigational markers in the Narrows as you approach Skidaway Island State Park. Continuing on you'll find scenic Isle of Hope high on a bluff to your left, with nearly guaranteed dolphin sightings around marker 62.

Farther out of town but worth the trip for any kayaker is the beautiful blackwater **Ebenezer Creek,** near the tiny township of New Ebenezer in Effingham County. Cypress trees lining this nationally designated Wild and Scenic River hang overhead and wildlife abounds in this peaceful paddle. Look for old wooden sluice gates, vestiges of the area's rice plantation past. To get there, take Exit 109 off I-95. Go north on Highway 21 to Rincon, Georgia, then east on Highway 275 (Ebenezer Rd.). Put in at the Ebenezer Landing ($5).

The one-stop shop for local kayaking information, tours, and equipment is **Sea Kayak Georgia** (1102 Hwy. 80, 888/529-2542, www.seakayakgeorgia.com), run by Tybee Islanders Marsha Henson and Ronnie Kemp.

Another popular tour operator is **Savannah Canoe & Kayak** (2169 Tennessee Ave., 912/341-9502, www.savannahcanoeandkayak.com).

Fishing

Savannah is a saltwater angler's paradise, rich in trout, flounder, and king and Spanish mackerel. Offshore there's a fair amount of deep-sea action, including large grouper, white and blue marlin, wahoo, snapper, sea bass, and big amberjack near some of the many offshore wrecks.

Perhaps the best-known local angler is Captain Judy Helmey, a.k.a. "Miss Judy." In addition to her frequent and entertaining newspaper columns, she runs a variety of well-regarded charters out of **Miss Judy Charters** (912/897-2478, www.missjudycharters.com). Four-hour trips start at $500. To get there, go west on U.S. 80, take a right onto Bryan Woods Road, a left onto Johnny Mercer Boulevard, a right onto Wilmington Island Way, and a right down the dirt lane at her sign.

Another highly regarded local fishing charter is the Tybee-based **Amick's Deep Sea Fishing** (912/897-6759, www.amicksdeepsea fishing.com). Captain Steve Amick and crew run offshore charters starting at $110 per person daily. Go east on U.S. 80 and turn right just past the Lazaretto Creek Bridge; boats are behind Café Loco.

Another charter service is offered at **Lazaretto Creek Marina** (1 U.S. 80, 912/786-5848, www.tybeedolphins.com). Half- and full-day inshore and offshore fishing charters are available, starting at $250 for four hours. Go east on Hwy. 80 and turn right just past the Lazaretto Creek Bridge. Turn right at the dead end.

Shallow-water fly fishers might want to contact **Savannah Fly Fishing Charters** (56 Sassafras Trail, 912/308-3700, www.savannah fly.com). Captain Scott Wagner takes half- and full-day charters both day and night from Savannah all the way down to St. Simons Island. Half-day rate starts at $300. Book early.

Diving

Diving is a challenge off the Georgia coast because of the silty nature of the water and its mercurial currents. Though not particularly friendly to the novice, plenty of great offshore opportunities abound around the many artificial reefs created by the Georgia Department of Natural Resources. An excellent guidebook in PDF form with full GPS data is available at http://crd.dnr.state.ga.us/assets/documents/ReefBooklet.pdf.

Certainly no underwater adventure in the area would be complete without a dive at **Gray's Reef National Marine Sanctuary** (912/598-2345, www.graysreef.noaa.gov). Administered by the National Oceanic and Atmospheric Administration, this fully protected marine sanctuary 17 miles offshore is in deep enough water to provide divers good visibility of its live-bottom habitat. Not a classic living coral reef, but rather one built by sedimentary deposits, Gray's Reef's provides a look at a truly unique ecosystem.

Some key dive charter operators that can take you to Gray's Reef are Captain Walter Rhame's **Mako Dive Charter** (600 Priest Landing Dr., 912/604-6256) which leaves from the Landings Harbor Marina; **Georgia Offshore** (1191 Lake Dr., Midway, 912/658-3884); and **Fantasia Scuba** (3 E. Montgomery Cross Rd., 912/921-8933). The best all-around dive shop in town is **Diving Locker and Ski Chalet** (74 W. Montgomery Cross Rd., 912/927-6603, www.divinglockerskichalet.com) on the south side.

Surfing and Boarding

Other than some action around the pier, the surfing is poor on Tybee Island, with its broad shelf, tepid wave action, and lethal rip currents. But board surfers and kiteboarders have a lot of fun on the south end of Tybee beginning at about 17th Street. The craziest surf is past the rock jetty, but be advised that the rip currents are especially treacherous there.

The best—and pretty much only—surf shop in town is **High Tides Surf Shop** (405 Hwy. 80, 912/786-6556, www.hightidesurfshop .com). You can get a good local surf report and forecasts at their website.

ON THE LAND
Golf

There are several strong public courses in Savannah that are also great bargains. Chief among these has to be the **Henderson Golf Club** (1 Al Henderson Blvd., 912/920-4653, www.hendersongolfclub.com), an excellent municipal course with reasonable green fees of $39 during the week and $48 on the weekend, both of which include a half-cart.

Another local favorite and unbeatable bargain is the circa-1926 **Bacon Park Golf Course** (Shorty Cooper Dr., 912/354-2625, www.baconparkgolf.com), comprising three nine-hole courses with a choice of three 18-hole combinations and some very small, fast greens. Green fees hover around $30.

A relatively new course but not one you'd call a bargain is the **Club at Savannah Harbor** (2 Resort Dr., 912/201-2007, www.theclubat savannahharbor.com) across the Savannah River on Hutchinson Island, adjacent to the Westin Savannah Harbor Resort. Home to the Liberty Mutual Legends of Golf Tournament each spring, the Club's tee times are 7:30 A.M.–3 P.M., with half-light play 2–5 P.M. Green fees are $135, or $70 for twilight fees.

The **Wilmington Island Club** (501 Wilmington Island Rd., 912/897-1612) has arguably the quickest greens in town and is

---

SHOELESS JOE AND SAVANNAH BASEBALL

Long before gaining notoriety for his role on the infamous Chicago "Black Sox" that threw the 1919 World Series, baseball legend Shoeless Joe Jackson was a stalwart on the South Atlantic or "Sally" League circuit. Playing for the Savannah Indians in 1909, Joe played ball predominantly at Bolton Street Park off what's now Henry Street. That year Jackson hit .358, a Sally League performance bested only twice that century.

The South Carolina native must have remembered his days in Savannah fondly, for after his major league career ended ignominiously Joe returned to town, began a thriving dry cleaning business and lived with his wife first at 143 Abercorn Street and then on East 39th Street. No doubt tired of the jokes up north about his Southern accent and his alleged illiteracy – the degree of which is a matter of some dispute among baseball scholars – Joe said he simply felt more at home here.

Another early great who played in Savannah was Georgia native Ty Cobb, who visited in 1905 with an Augusta team. He's remembered, typically enough, for getting into a fistfight with a teammate who voiced his displeasure at Cobb eating popcorn in the outfield and muffing an easy catch.

Savannah got a proper ballpark in 1926, named Municipal Stadium. After a hurricane destroyed it in 1940, rebuilding began but abruptly stopped when Pearl Harbor was attacked the

next year and all the laborers rushed off to enlist. So abruptly did they drop their tools, in fact, that to this day behind third base you can still clearly see the jagged line indicating where construction halted. The stadium was renamed Grayson Stadium in honor of Spanish-American War hero William Grayson, who spearheaded the venue's eventual renovation.

The great Babe Ruth played in the stadium once in 1935 in his final year as a major leaguer, as his Boston Braves beat the South Georgia Teachers College (now Georgia Southern University) 15-1 in an exhibition game. Ruth, of course, hit a home run.

There's a common thread between Jackson and Babe Ruth, who wasn't known as a hitter until after he'd already established himself as a standout pitcher. Shoeless Joe – perhaps the game's most consummate hitter until Ted Williams' arrival on the scene 30 years later – tried to change Ruth's stance in the batter's box to improve his hitting. The rest, as they say, is history.

"I was able to help Ruth a little before he began to hit," Jackson told the *Savannah Morning News* in 1932. "When I first knew him, he was a spraddle-legged hitter, and I taught him to change to pivot hitting. He's the only fellow I ever tried to convert who jumped on to the idea in a minute."

Mickey Mantle and the defending world champion New York Yankees played the unarguably the most beautiful local course, set close by the Wilmington River amid lots of mature pines and live oaks. Green fees are $69.

Tennis

The closest public courts to the downtown area are at the south end of **Forsyth Park** (912/351-3850), which features four, free lighted courts. As you might expect, they get serious use. Farther south in **Daffin Park** (1001 E. Victory Dr., 912/351-3850), there are nine courts ($3), three of which are available for night play. On the south side, **Bacon Park** (6262 Skidaway Rd., 912/351-3850) has 14 lighted courts ($3).

If you get the tennis jones on Tybee, there are two free courts at **Tybee Island Memorial Park** (912/786-4573, www.cityoftybee.org) at Butler Avenue and Fourth Street.

Hiking

Though hiking in Savannah and the Lowcountry is largely a 2-D experience given the flatness of the terrain, there are plenty of good nature trails from which to observe the area's rich flora and fauna up close. My favorite

---

Cincinnati Reds in a 1959 exhibition game in Savannah. The switch-hitting slugger hit two of his trademark mammoth home run shots during the game — both left-handed and each over 500 feet, according to witnesses.

Atlanta Braves great Hank Aaron, then a skinny second baseman with a Jacksonville club, played in Grayson's first game with both black and white players in 1953. Frank Robinson played one of the first games of his storied career here with the Columbia Reds. He showed up late to the game and still hit two home runs. Jackie Robinson stole home base in an exhibition game.

But in a way, all these names pale in comparison to one Savannah player whose influence can be felt to this day, not only in sports but in the business world at large.

Curt Flood gave the world free agency.

Flood, who played for the Savannah Redlegs in 1957, refused to report to the Phillies after the Cardinals traded him in 1969. Flood sued Major League Baseball the next year, saying the so-called "reserve clause" allowing the trade violated antitrust laws. While Flood would lose the lawsuit in the U.S. Supreme Court in 1971, the narrowly worded decision left the way open for collective bargaining and today's massive free agent salaries.

The Savannah minor league team has taken on various incarnations over the years. The 1962 Savannah White Sox was the most suc-cessful, contributing an amazing 14 players to the majors. But the taste of success was short-lived. That was the year local civil rights great W. W. Law, then a postman, called for African Americans to boycott Grayson Stadium to protest its segregated seating policy. (The concession stand off the third base line is a reminder of that shameful era. It was once the "colored" restroom.)

Rather than risk violence at the stadium, the White Sox disbanded. Grayson was dormant until the Savannah Braves, a double-A team, began a very successful run in 1971 (including a 12-game winning season by pitcher and controversial *Ball Four* writer Jim Bouton), followed in 1984 by the Savannah Cardinals.

The current single-A team, the Savannah Sand Gnats, had their name chosen by a poll of daily newspaper readers. While their level of play rarely conjures mental images of Shoeless Joe or the Babe, Grayson Stadium itself has just been given an impressive new facelift courtesy of the city, with a new scoreboard and upgraded seating. By far the Sand Gnats' most famous face so far has been Cy Young Award–winning pitcher Eric Gagne, who pitched his very first professional game with the local club.

The old left field bleachers, only remaining part of the original Municipal Stadium, were recently torn down after the lawyers decided they were too rickety. They've been replaced by a grass hillock.

trails are at **Skidaway Island State Park** (52 Diamond Causeway, 912/598-2300, www .gastateparks.org, daily 7 A.M.–10 P.M., $2 per vehicle daily parking fee). The three-mile Big Ferry Trail is the best overall experience, taking you out to a wooden viewing tower from which you can see the vast expanse of the Skidaway Narrows. A detour takes you past a Native American shell midden, Confederate earthworks, and even a rusty old still—a nod to Skidaway Island's former notoriety as a bootlegger's sanctuary. The shorter but still fun Sandpiper Trail is wheelchair-accessible.

An interesting, if hardly challenging, trail is the **McQueen Island Trail,** more commonly known as "Rails to Trails." This paved, palm-lined walking trail along the Savannah River was built on the old bed of the Savannah-to-Tybee railroad, which operated during Tybee's heyday as a major East Coast vacation spot in 1930s and '40s. To get there, cross the long, low Bull River Bridge and take an *immediate* left into the small parking area, being very mindful of fast-moving inbound traffic on U.S. 80.

Biking

Most biking activity centers on Tybee Island, with the **McQueen Island Trail** (see *Hiking*) being a popular and simple ride. Many locals like to load up their bikes and go to **Fort Pulaski** (912/786-5787, www.nps .gov, open every day except Christmas, fort hours 8:30 A.M.–5:15 P.M., visitors center 9 A.M.–5 P.M., $2 per person 17 and up). From the grounds you can ride all over scenic and historic Cockspur Island.

It's not a strenuous ride, but pedaling around the idyllic little neighborhoods of **Isle of Hope** is relaxing fun.

Bird-Watching

Birding in the Savannah area is excellent at two spots on the **Colonial Coast Birding Trail** (http://georgiawildlife.dnr.state.ga.us). Chief among them is **Skidaway Island State Park** (52 Diamond Causeway, 912/598-2300, www.gastateparks.org, daily 7 A.M.–10 P.M., $2 per vehicle daily parking fee). Spring and fall bring a lot of the usual warbler action, while spring and summer feature nesting osprey and painted bunting, always a delight.

The other trail spot is Tybee Island's **North Beach** area ($5 per day parking fee, meters available). You'll see a wide variety of shorebirds and gulls, as well as piping plover, northern gannets, and purple sandpiper (winter).

Wading birds in particular are in wide abundance at the **Savannah National Wildlife Refuge** (see *Kayaking and Canoeing*). The views are excellent all along the Lauren Hill wildlife drive, which takes you through the heart of the old rice paddies that criss-crossed the entire area.

SPECTATOR SPORTS

Topping the list of local spectator sports—indeed, it's basically the entire list—is the **Savannah Sand Gnats** (1401 E. Victory Dr., 912/351-9150, www.sandgnats.com) baseball franchise, currently a single-A affiliate of the New York Mets. The attraction here is not the level of play but the venue itself, Grayson Stadium in Daffin Park in the city's midtown area, a historic venue that's hosted such greats as Babe Ruth, Jackie Robinson, and Mickey Mantle over the years. The Gnats' season runs April–September.

There's not a bad seat in the house, so your best bet by far is to just buy a $6 general admission ticket. The games never sell out, so there's no need to stress. Entertainment runs the usual gamut of minor league shenanigans, including frequent fireworks displays after the games.

Accommodations

First the bad news about hotels in Savannah: They can be horribly overpriced considering the poor service and limited amenities. There are several high-profile, high-dollar hotels downtown associated with big-name chains that seem to get in all the guidebooks. However, I cannot in good conscience list some of them here because the chance of a disappointing experience is too high to qualify them for a clear recommendation.

On the bright side, however, Savannah's many historic bed-and-breakfasts are competitive with the hotels on price, and far outperform them on service and ambience. If you don't need a swimming pool and don't mind climbing some stairs every now and then, a B&B is usually your best bet. And of course the breakfasts are great, too!

A precious few full-service hotels exist downtown that truly live up to that description, and they are listed below, along with the best of the B&Bs. There's a standard tax of 13 percent.

CITY MARKET
$150-300

Considering its price, location, and relatively good level of service, one of the best deals in town for the value-minded is the **Quality Inn Heart of Savannah** (300 W. Bay St., 912/236-6321, www.qualityinn historicsavannah.com, $160). I'm not saying it's romantic, and I'm not saying it's plush; it's neither of those, and in fact, this is more motel than hotel. However, with its location just off City Market and a range of affordable, somewhat-decently maintained rooms, this is worth looking into.

A Days Inn property, the **Inn at Ellis Square** (201 W. Bay St., 912/236-4440, www .innatellissquare.com, $189) is smack dab between City Market and Bay Street: in other words, the heart of the tourist action. Set in the renovated 1851 Guckenheimer

Building, the Inn is one of the better-appointed chain hotels in town.

WATERFRONT
$150-300

Probably the best experience for the money as far as downtown chain hotels go, the **Hampton Inn Historic District** (201 E. Bay St., 912/231-9700, www.hamptoninn .com, $250) isn't for those who love peace and quiet. Set on the busy corner of Bay and Abercorn Streets, the noise and crowd level here is high (in fact the corner is a key pickup spot for trolley and carriage tours). However, if you're the type who wants to be in the thick of things, this is your place—with the added benefit of having a significantly better level of service than most chain spots, including the high-rise Desoto, its decrepit sibling Hilton location downtown. The breakfast here is quite good.

A cut above the Holiday Inn chain, to which it's affiliated, the **Mulberry Inn** (601 E. Bay St., 912/238-1200, www.holiday inn.com, $189) is a longtime favorite with travelers to Savannah. The one flaw is its location on loud, busy Bay Street. However, with a charming central courtyard and with peaceful little Washington Square right on the other side of the building, it's hard to complain too much. Don't miss the genuine English teatime, complete with jazz piano accompaniment, observed in the lobby each afternoon at 4 P.M. (as if there's another English teatime). Another nifty touch is a dedicated parking garage—an amenity only someone who's spent half an hour looking for a parking space in downtown Savannah will truly appreciate. Parking is free for Holiday Inn "priority members," (you can sign up for membership at check-in). The building formerly housed a Coca-Cola bottling plant; look for the historical photos all around the building.

SAVANNAH

SAVANNAH

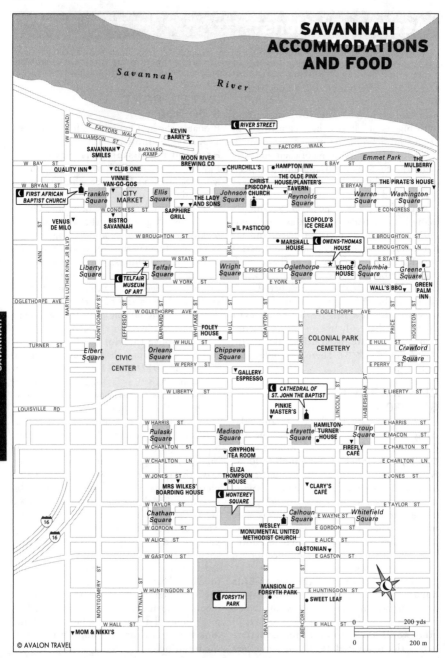

SAVANNAH ACCOMMODATIONS AND FOOD

Savannah River

KEVIN BARRY'S

RIVER STREET

W FACTORS WALK

WILLIAMSON ST

W BROAD

BARNARD RAMP

E FACTORS WALK

SAVANNAH SMILES

MOON RIVER BREWING CO

CHURCHILL'S

HAMPTON INN

E BAY ST

Emmet Park

THE MULBERRY

W BAY ST

QUALITY INN

CLUB ONE

THE OLDE PINK HOUSE/PLANTER'S TAVERN

THE PIRATE'S HOUSE

VINNIE VAN-GO-GOS

CHRIST EPISCOPAL CHURCH

E BRYAN ST

W BRYAN ST

FIRST AFRICAN BAPTIST CHURCH

Franklin Square

CITY MARKET

Ellis Square

Johnson Square

Reynolds Square

Warren Square

Washington Square

E CONGRESS ST

THE LADY AND SONS

W CONGRESS ST

ANN ST

VENUS DE MILO

BISTRO SAVANNAH

SAPPHIRE GRILL

IL PASTICCIO

LEOPOLD'S ICE CREAM

E BROUGHTON ST

W BROUGHTON ST

MARSHALL HOUSE

OWENS-THOMAS HOUSE

E BROUGHTON LN

MARTIN LUTHER KING JR BLVD

W STATE ST

BULL

E STATE ST

Liberty Square

TELFAIR MUSEUM OF ART

Telfair Square

Wright Square

E PRESIDENT ST

Oglethorpe Square

KEHOE HOUSE

Columbia Square

Greene Square

W YORK ST

E YORK ST

WALL'S BBQ

GREEN PALM INN

OGLETHORPE AVE

W OGLETHORPE AVE

WHITAKER

E OGLETHORPE AVE

PRICE ST

HOUSTON ST

TURNER ST

Elbert Square

CIVIC CENTER

MONTGOMERY ST

JEFFERSON ST

BARNARD ST

Orleans Square

FOLEY HOUSE

W HULL ST

Chippewa Square

BULL

DRAYTON

COLONIAL PARK CEMETERY

E HULL ST

Crawford Square

W PERRY ST

E PERRY ST

GALLERY ESPRESSO

W LIBERTY ST

CATHEDRAL OF ST. JOHN THE BAPTIST

ABERCORN

LINCOLN

E LIBERTY ST

LOUISVILLE RD

PINKIE MASTER'S

W HARRIS ST

HABERSHAM ST

E HARRIS ST

Pulaski Square

Madison Square

Lafayette Square

HAMILTON-TURNER HOUSE

Troup Square

E MACON ST

W CHARLTON ST

E CHARLTON ST

GRYPHON TEA ROOM

FIREFLY CAFÉ

W CHARLTON LN

E CHARLTON LN

W JONES ST

ELIZA THOMPSON HOUSE

E JONES ST

MRS WILKES' BOARDING HOUSE

CLARY'S CAFÉ

MONTEREY SQUARE

W TAYLOR ST

E TAYLOR ST

Chatham Square

Calhoun Square

E WAYNE ST

Whitefield Square

W GORDON ST

E GORDON ST

WESLEY MONUMENTAL UNITED METHODIST CHURCH

W ALICE ST

E ALICE ST

GASTONIAN

W GASTON ST

E GASTON ST

MONTGOMERY ST

TATTNALL ST

W HUNTINGDON ST

MANSION OF FORSYTH PARK

E HUNTINGDON ST

FORSYTH PARK

SWEET LEAF

DRAYTON

ABERCORN

E HALL ST

W HALL ST

MOM & NIKKI'S

0   200 yds

0   200 m

© AVALON TRAVEL

Over $300

Yes, it's an insult to architecture and to history. That being said, one of the few name-brand hotels in Savannah worth the price and providing a consistent level of service is one of its original chain hotels, the **Hyatt Regency Savannah** (2 E. Bay St., 912/238-1234, www.savannah.hyatt.com, $379). Though it's more than three decades old, a competent if uninspiring renovation means that the Hyatt has avoided the neglect of many older chain properties downtown. While the price may seem daunting, consider the location—literally smack dab on top of River Street, mere blocks from the bulk of the important attractions downtown and some of its best restaurants. Three sides of the hotel offer views of the bustling Savannah waterfront, with its massive ships coming in from all over the world. Parking fees in the on-site garage are high ($20 daily), but hey, it's downtown Savannah, so by the end of your stay you might be thankful to pay even that much.

HISTORIC DISTRICT
$150-300

Easily the best bed-and-breakfast for the price in Savannah is (**The Green Palm Inn** (546 E. President St., 912/447-8901, www.greenpalminn.com, $179), a folksy and romantic little Victorian number with some neat gingerbread exterior stylings and four cute rooms, each named after a species of palm tree. It's situated on the very easternmost edge of the Historic District—hence it's reasonable rates—but let's face it, being right next to charming little Greene Square is far from the worst place you could be. Delightful innkeeper Diane McCray provides a very good and generous breakfast plus a pretty-much-constant dessert bar.

One of Savannah's original historic B&Bs, the (**Eliza Thompson House** (5 W. Jones St., 912/236-3620, www.elizathompson house.com, $269) is a bit out of the bustle on serene, beautiful Jones Street but still close enough to get involved whenever you feel the urge. You can enjoy the various culinary offerings—breakfast, wine and cheese, nighttime munchies—either in the parlor or on the patio overlooking the house's classic Savannah garden. One of the half-dozen lodging properties owned by the locally based HLC group, the Eliza Thompson House hews to their generally high standard of service.

Another great place in the thick of things is the **Marshall House** (123 E. Broughton St., 912/644-7896, www.marshallhouse.com, $249). Beautifully restored to its original grandeur, the Marshall is an intriguing combination of New Orleans (for its elaborate iron balcony), Manhattan (for the cozy smallness of its rooms), and Savannah (for its location dominating an eastern block of busy Broughton Street). A fine restaurant, 45 Bistro, is downstairs, and has a delightful bar. The location's main flaw, a painful lack of parking, is solved by valet service. Don't count on booking a room here during the last week of October; the Savannah Film Festival typically rents out the entire hotel for movie types.

Over $300

The circa-1896 (**Foley House Inn** (14 W. Hull St., 912/232-6622, www.foleyinn.com, $295–325) is a four-diamond B&B with rooms available at a three-diamond price. Its 19 individualized, Victorian-decor rooms, in two townhouses, range from the smaller Newport overlooking the "grotto courtyard" to the four-poster, bay-windowed Essex room, complete with fireplace and whirlpool bath. The location on Chippewa Square is pretty much perfect: well off the busy east–west thoroughfares but in the heart of Savannah's active theater district and within walking distance of anywhere. And of the service here, as at most any local B&B, will be appreciably higher than at a comparably priced hotel.

One of Savannah's favorite bed-and-breakfasts, (**The Kehoe House** (123 Habersham St., 912/232-1020, www.kehoe house.com, $329) is a great choice for its

the Kehoe House bed-and-breakfast on Columbia Square

© JIM MOREKIS

charm and attention to guests. Its historic location on quiet little Columbia Square catty-corner to the Isaiah Davenport House is within walking distance to all the downtown action, but far enough from the bustle to get some peace out on one of the rocking chairs on the veranda.

Once a bordello, the 1838 mansion that is home to the 16-room **Ballastone Inn** (14 E. Oglethorpe Ave., 912/236-1484, www.ballastone .com, $235–395) is one of Savannah's favorite inns. Highlights include an afternoon tea service and one of the better full breakfasts in town. Note that some rooms are at what Savannah calls the "garden level," i.e., sunken basement-level rooms with what amounts to a worm's-eye view.

Hardcore fans of *Midnight in the Garden of Good and Evil* might want to stay at the **Hamilton-Turner Inn** (330 Abercorn St., 888/448-8849, www.hamilton-turnerinn .com, $319–326). Though no longer owned by Nancy Hillis, a.k.a. "Mandy," this over-the-top Second Empire mansion on gorgeous Lafayette Square still carries all the mystery you'd expect, in 17 suitably ornate rooms.

VICTORIAN DISTRICT
$150-300
A short walk from Forsyth Park, the **Dresser-Palmer House** (211 E. Gaston St., 912/238-3294, www.dresserpalmerhouse .com, $189–319) features 15 rooms in two wings, but still manages to make things feel pretty cozy. Garden-level rooms go for a song (under $200).

Over $300
The 1868 **(Gastonian Inn** (220 E. Gaston St., 912/232-2869, www.gastonian.com, $245–455) got a major renovation in 2005 and remains a favorite choice for travelers to Savannah, mostly for its 17 sumptuously decorated rooms and suites (all with working fireplaces) and the always-outstanding full breakfast. They pile on the epicurean delights with teatime, evening nightcaps, and complimentary wine. This is one of the six properties

owned by the local firm HLC, which seems to have consistently higher standards than most out-of-town chains here.

How ironic that a hotel built in a former mortuary would be one of the few Savannah hotels not to have a resident ghost story. But that's the case with **Mansion on Forsyth Park** (700 Drayton St., 912/238-5158, www.mansiononforsythpark.com, $339–419), which dominates an entire block alongside Forsyth Park in the wildly high-Victorian former Fox & Weeks Mortuary building. Despite the circa-1888 vintage of the building itself, the Mansion is one of the newer hotels in town. Its sumptuous, big-bed, big-bath, big-screen-TV-equipped rooms scream "boutique hotel," as does the swank little bar and the alfresco patio area. But the Mansion has received mixed reviews for service, which, to be fair, is a common complaint throughout Savannah. Much of that early friction seems to have evaporated, and the Mansion—complete with its own art gallery, the Grand Bohemian, and fine-dining restaurant, 700 Drayton, which offers guests fun culinary classes—has had no problem entering the first tier of Savannah lodging. The Mansion's Addams Family decor of thick velvet and vaguely Dadaist artwork isn't for everyone, but still, it certainly beats seagulls and pink flamingoes.

CAMPING

The best overall campground in town is at the well-managed and never overcrowded **Skidaway Island State Park** (52 Diamond Causeway, 912/598-2300, www.gastateparks.org, $2 per vehicle daily parking fee, $24 per night tent and RV sites, $35 per night for group camping). There are 88 sites with 30-amp service. A two-night minimum stay is required on weekends and a three-night minimum for Memorial Day, Labor Day, Independence Day, and Thanksgiving. Despite these restrictions, the natural beauty of the park and its easy access to some great nature trails makes it worth the price.

There's one campground on Tybee, the **River's End Campground and RV Park** (915 Polk St., 912/786-5518, www.cityoftybee.org). Owned by the city of Tybee Island itself, River's End on the north side of the island offers 100 full-service sites plus some primitive tent sites. During Tybee's sometimes-chilly off-season, you can relax and get warm inside the common "River Room." There's also a swimming pool and laundry facilities. Basic water and electric sites are $34 per night, while 50-amp full hook-ups with water and electric are $45.

Totally wilderness camping can be done on state-owned Little Tybee, accessible across the Back River by boat only. No facilities.

The best camping and wilderness resource locally is **Half Moon Outfitters** (15 E. Broughton St., 912/201-9393, www.halfmoonoutfitters.com).

TYBEE ISLAND

Most of the hotels on Butler Avenue are what we describe in the South as "rode hard and put away wet," i.e., they see a lot of wear and tear from eager vacationers. That doesn't make them bad, just be aware. Also be aware that any place on Butler, even the substandard places, charges a premium during the high season of March–October.

Here are a few places that are clearly a cut above. All cluster at $200 or below.

On glorious Officer's Row on the North End, the sumptuous suites of the **Savannah Beach Inn** (21 Officers Row, 800/844-1398, www.savannahbeachinn.com, $200) are tastefully restored, without a hint of the usual Tybee kitsch. The breezy veranda boasts some of the island's most awesome views over the Atlantic. This is easily one of the most romantic spots in the area, with access to the dunes and total seclusion from the partying at the South End.

One of Tybee's most worthwhile lodging experiences for the money, the single-suite **Bluebird Bed and Breakfast** (1206 Venetian Dr., 912/786-0786, www.tybeebandb.com, $125) is tucked away on Horsepen Creek and the Back River, away from the general beach-town hubbub—but that's what makes it all the more romantic, in a whimsical sort of way. Its spacious and charming interior comprises a master bedroom, a large kitchen/den area, and a delightful breakfast nook overlooking the marsh. There's even a resident dock if you want to put in your kayak or canoe. You wouldn't know it from the loving and personalized care lavished on the little inn by owner Shirley Sessions, but the building itself is a former Army barracks, moved all the way from Fort Screven on Tybee's north end in the 1940s. The cottage was purchased in the '70s by one of Juliette Gordon Low's original Girl Scouts, George McDonald, who was the moving force behind changing the name back to Tybee Island from Savannah Beach, as it was then incorporated. Two-night minimum on weekends.

Available for daily or weekly rental, the delightful and well-appointed upstairs apartment of **The Octopus Lair** (12th Street, 912/660-7164, www.octopuslair.com, $125) is tucked away on the south side of the island, equidistant from both the beach and the more active areas. There's even a propane grill on the porch so you can cook out.

A popular place for singles looking for a getaway and families with kids (12 and over only, though) is the whimsical **Atlantis Inn** (20 Silver Ave., 912/786-6044, www.atlantisinntybee.com, $155–380). Twelve *very* themed rooms are offered, in over-the-top stylings such as Some Like It Hot, Poseidon's Palace, and Hog Gone Wild (a Harley theme, natch). The cutesy quotient may be off the chart, but the service is pleasant and personable, and the location—right around the corner from action-packed 16th Street a block from the beach—is hard to top.

Right around the corner from the bustling 16th Street corridor, the **Hunter House Inn** (1701 Butler Ave., 912/786-7515, $150) is still a relatively peaceful getaway. There are two ground-level suites for larger groups of people, each with a large living room with sleeper sofa in addition to a queen-size bed. Upstairs are two smaller rooms, also with queens. Whimsically appointed and more on the casual side, these are not ultra-plush accommodations, but are great for people who want a laid-back fun time at the beach.

Food

Though Charleston's cuisine scene is clearly a cut above Savannah's, the Georgia city is still a foodie's paradise, with a big-city selection of cuisine at competitive prices, concocted by a cast of executive chefs, who despite their many personal idiosyncrasies, tend to go with what works rather than experimenting for the sake of experimentation.

Here's a breakdown of the most notable offerings, by area and by type of cuisine. You'll note there's no separate "Seafood" section listed. That's because seafood is an intrinsic part of most restaurant fare in Savannah, whether through regular menu offerings or through specials.

CITY MARKET
Classic Southern

Every year, thousands of visitors come to

Savannah for the privilege of waiting for hours outside in all weather, the line stretching a full city block, for a chance to eat at **The Lady & Sons** (102 W. Congress St., 912/233-2600, www.ladyandsons.com, lunch Mon.–Sat. 11 A.M.–3 P.M., dinner Mon.–Sat. begins at 5 P.M. Sundays buffet 11 A.M.–5 P.M., $17–25) and sample some of local celebrity Paula Deen's "home" cooking—actually a fairly typical Southern buffet with some decent fried chicken, collard greens, and mac and cheese. For the privilege, you must begin waiting in line as early as 9:30 A.M. for lunch and as early as 3:30 P.M. for dinner in order to be assigned a dining time. You almost assuredly will never see Paula, who has precious little to do with the restaurant these days.

Eating at this Savannah landmark provides

a story that visitors will be able to tell friends and family for the rest of their lives, and far be it from me to look down upon them for doing so. That being said—if it were me, I'd take that four hours spent waiting in line and instead go to one of Savannah's many other excellent eating establishments, leaving lots of time left over for an afternoon beer or coffee or dessert, and leaving yet more time to see one of Savannah's many interesting and beautiful sights. A chef friend of mine puts it best: When food sits out under a heat lamp too long, it all tastes the same anyway.

New Southern

Accomplishing the difficult task of being achingly hip while also offering some of the best food in town, **(The Sapphire Grill** (110 W. Congress St., 912/443-9962, www.sapphire grill.com, Fri.–Sat. at 5:30–11:30 P.M., Sun.–Thurs. 6–10:30 P.M., $25–40) comes closer than any other Savannah restaurant to replicating a high-class, trendy Manhattan eatery—at prices to match. With its bare stone walls, lean ambience, and romantically dark interior, you'd be tempted to think it's all sizzle and no steak. But executive chef Chris Nason, former exec at Charleston's Anson Restaurant, has a way with coastal cuisine, relying on the freshest local seafood. But his classic meat dishes like lamb, filet mignon, and veal are equally skillful. Sauces are vibrant but not overpowering, the presentation artful but not distracting, the ingredients always impeccably fresh, and the vegetables out of this world. Nason's signature style is definitely Southern, but think high-Southern, not breaded and heavy. The lobster Bisque is a must-have, and the benne-encrusted local black grouper is always a good choice. As you'd expect, the wine list is impressive, but a close look shows a refined taste for some of the lesser-known labels that other local places miss. Reservations are essential, and while there's no dress code per se, you don't want to go here looking unkempt.

(Bistro Savannah (309 W. Congress St., 912/233-6266, Mon.–Thurs. 5:30–10:30 P.M., Fri.–Sat. 5:30–11 P.M., Sun. 5:30–10 P.M.,

$12–25) is one of those long-lived local establishments that seems to outlast every trend. As the name implies, the menu and atmosphere are more French than Southern, with small marble-topped tables and high ceilings that enhance the general clang and echo of silverware, dishes, and conversation. Still, it's definitely romantic in that Parisian way, and hence especially enjoyable for couples. Everything on the menu is great, with a definite lean towards fruit and chutney, but the specials tend to be the strongest offerings. Start with the appetizer of shrimp and tasso with grits. Reservations are a good idea, but not essential.

Italian

One would never call Savannah a great pizza town, but the best pizza in Savannah is without a doubt **(Vinnie VanGoGo's** (317 W. Bryan St., 912/233-6394, www.vinnie vangogos.com, Mon.–Thurs. 4–11:30 P.M., Fri. 4 P.M.–1 A.M., Sat. noon–1 A.M., Sun. noon–11:30 P.M., $3–13) at the far west end of City Market on Franklin Square. Featuring some of the best local characters both in the dining area and behind the counter, Vinnie's is a classic, can't-miss Savannah hang-out, due in no small part to its excellent beer selection and late hours on weekends. Their pizza is a thin-crust Neapolitan style—though the menu claims it to be New York style—with a delightful tangy sauce and fresh cheese. Pesto pizza (with pesto instead of sauce) is available, as is a white pizza (no sauce). Watching the pies being made is part of the whole experience. Individual slices are huge, so don't feel obliged to order a whole pie, though at these bargain prices you'll be tempted to. Personally I opt for Italian sausage and extra cheese to offset the richness of the sauce. Calzones are also massive and well stuffed. The waiting list for a table can get pretty long these days, but take heart: Vinnie's offers free delivery throughout downtown, delivered by bicycle courier. Cash only!

Many Savannahians remember a time when the charmingly old-school **Garibaldi Café** (315 W. Congress St., 912/232-7118, daily 5–10 P.M., $11–33) was the only fine dining restaurant

© JIM MOREKIS

Pirate's House in Trustees Garden

in town. And you know what? It's still great. More like a spot you'd find in Little Italy than Savannah, Garibaldi features many of the over-the-top decor touches typical of the genre, from Roman busts to massive brocade curtains and the huge chandelier in the "Grand Ballroom." But longtime master chef Gerald Green's food is still the draw, a dependable Northern Italian menu known far and wide for its well-made veal dishes, its raw bar offerings, and Garibaldi's signature dish, the very popular crispy scored flounder with apricot glaze (don't forget to flip the flounder over; there's more fish under there to enjoy). Reservations recommended.

WATERFRONT
Classic Southern

Locals rarely eat at the Savannah institution called the **Pirate's House** (20 E. Broad St., 912/233-5757, www.thepirateshouse.com, lunch daily 11 A.M.–4 P.M., dinner Sun.–Thurs. 4–9:30 P.M., Fri.–Sat. 4–10 P.M., $17–26), known primarily for its delightfully kitschy pre–Jack Sparrow pirate decor and its

dependably pedestrian food. Still, the history here is undeniable: One of America's oldest buildings, built in 1753, the Pirate's House hosted many a salty sea dog in its day as a seamen's inn—though perhaps few actual pirates. And anyplace that rates a shout-out in Robert Louis Stevenson's *Treasure Island* has to be worth a visit.

The rambling interior of the old house, each of the 15 dining rooms with its own different nautical flavor, just adds to the general air of jaunty buccaneer insouciance. "The Captain's Room" is allegedly where shipmasters would shanghai unwary men to complete their chronically short-handed crews. Supposedly a tunnel from there goes all the way to the river, the better to transport the drugged kidnapping victims. Yes, the old tunnel to River Street really does exist, and no, your waiter will not let you have a look. Instead, settle for the "Southern Buffet," each day 11 A.M.–3 P.M., featuring the Pirate House's signature honey pecan fried chicken.

A favorite breakfast and lunch place with the downtown office crowd is **B. Matthews**

Eatery (325 E. Bay St., 912/233-1319, www
.bmatthewseatery.com, daily 7:30–3:30 P.M.,
dinner Tues.–Sat. from 5:30 P.M.), which
offers a variety of sandwiches (like their signature black-eyed pea cake sandwich, some great
soups, and fresh bakery items. Lunch will run
you about $10, dinner twice that.

Very few restaurants on River Street rise
above tourist schlock, but a clear standout is ◖ **Vic's on the River** (16 E. River
St., 912/721-1000, www.vicsontheriver
.com, Sun.–Thurs. 11 A.M.–10 P.M., Fri.–Sat.
11 A.M.–11 P.M., $22–40). Hewing more
to Charleston-style fine dining than most
Savannah restaurants—with dishes like wild
Georgia shrimp, stone-ground grits, and blue
crab cakes with a three-pepper relish—Vic's
combines a romantic, old Savannah atmosphere
with an adventurous take on Lowcountry cuisine. Note the entrance to the dining room is
not on River Street, but on the Bay Street level
on Upper Factors Walk.

HISTORIC DISTRICT
Classic Southern
The meteoric rise of Paula Deen and her
Lady & Sons has only made local epicure-
ans even more exuberant in their praise for
◖ **Mrs. Wilkes' Dining Room** (107 W. Jones
St., 912/232-5997, www.mrswilkes.com,
Mon.–Fri. 11 A.M.–2 P.M., $13), Savannah's
original comfort food mecca. Though the delightful Sema Wilkes herself has passed on,
nothing has changed—not the communal
dining room, the cheerful service, the care
taken with take-out customers, and, most
of all, not the food—a succulent mélange of
the South's Greatest Hits, from the best fried
chicken in town to snap beans to black-eyed
peas to collard greens. While each day boasts
a different set menu, most all the classics are
on the table meal.

A very authentic Southern eating experience is at **Mom & Nikki's** (714 MLK Jr. Blvd.,
912/233-7636, Tues.–Sat., call for hours,
$5–10). Another success story in the burgeon-
ing renaissance of the Martin Luther King Jr.
Boulevard corridor, Mom & Nikki's is in a

former YMCA building, with cafeteria-style
decor to match. But the food! The menu ro-
tates, but you can usually find the fried chicken
and collards that are among the best in town.
And whatever you do, make sure and try the
amazing smothered shrimp over rice.

Some writers would be tempted to put
◖ **Cha Bella** (102 E. Broad St., 912/790-
7888, www.cha-bella.com, Tue.–Sun. 5:30–0,
$17–35) in the "New Southern" category, but
I prefer to think that this restaurant's forte—
savory dishes using only the freshest locally
grown organic ingredients—makes it a classic throwback to the way food was always intended to be. This new spot is getting a large
local following eager to enjoy its concise menu
from Chef Matthew Roher, featuring fresh salads like grilled eggplant and plum tomatoes
topped with local artisan goat cheese, and entrées like the Georgia white shrimp risotto. The
patio bar is a favorite hangout for downtown's
hip movers and shakers.

Barbecue
A local legend, ◖ **Wall's BBQ** (515 E. York
Lane, 912/232-9754, Thurs.–Sat., call for
hours, $6–9) is one family's labor of love, tucked
away in a back alley—they're called "lanes" in
Savannah—that you'll miss if you blink. People
love the barbecue, but the crab cakes are a
lesser-known but still world-class item.

Another great local barbecue joint tucked
away in a lane is **Angel's BBQ** (21 W.
Oglethorpe Lane, 912/495-0902, www
.angels-bbq.com, Tues. 11:30 A.M.–3 P.M.,
Wed.–Sat. 11:30 A.M.–6 P.M., $5–9). Get there
by finding Independent Presbyterian Church
at the northwest corner of Chippewa Square
and walking down the lane next to the church.
They offer a particularly Memphis-style take
on barbecue, but you might try the unique
house specialty, the barbecued bologna. Don't
miss the peanuts-and-greens on the side.

One of Savannah's great characters and ra-
conteurs, Gerald Schantz is also a great cook
and caterer, specializing in Southern comfort
foods at his own **Gerald's Diner** (corner of
Montgomery and Bolton Sts., 912/786-4227,

Leopold's Ice Cream is in the heart of Savannah's theater district.

Mon.–Fri. 11 A.M.–2 P.M., $7–12). His pulled-pork BBQ is up there with most anything else in town, and his certified wild Georgia fried shrimp, cooked to order, are to die for. It's an unpretentious diner atmosphere and Gerald is never short of entertaining stories.

Breakfast and Brunch

Downtowners swear by the low-key little **Firefly Café** (321 Habersham St., 912/234-1971, Tues.–Sun. 7:30 A.M.–9:30 P.M., $12–25) on quiet Troup Square, and not only for the excellent omelets (maybe the best in town), great sandwiches (one word: Reuben!), and fresh salads (try the spinach salad with goat cheese). It's also a neighborhood place to see old friends and catch up over coffee, with the charming interior only enhancing the general bonhomie. This is a particularly good choice for vegetarians and vegans for all meals of the day. While mostly considered a breakfast and lunch spot, dinner is great, too; you can't go wrong with any pasta dish, but be sure to check out the specials first.

Actually part of a regional chain, the spacious

and charming **J. Christopher's** (122 E. Liberty St., 912/236-7494, daily 7 A.M.–2 P.M., $6–12), set in a former auto garage right across from the Desoto Hilton. It's a big hit for Sunday brunch, and appeals to couples, college students, and families with kids alike. Service can be achingly slow at times, but it's always friendly. Build your own omelet or "skillet" (roasted potatoes with two sunny-side-up eggs on top and your choice of toppings).

Casual Dining

He helped produce *Mission Impossible III* and other Hollywood productions, but Savannah native Stratton Leopold's other claim to fame is running the old family business at **Leopold's Ice Cream** (212 E. Broughton St., 912/234-4442, www.leopoldsicecream .com, Sun.–Thurs. 11 A.M.–10 P.M., Fri.–Sat. 11 A.M.–11 P.M.). The family tradition goes back to 1919, when Leopold's father and uncles founded the first store bearing the family name at Gwinnett and Habersham Streets. Now in a new location but the same delicious family ice cream recipe, Leopold's also offers soup and sandwiches to go with its delicious sweet treats. Memorabilia from Stratton's various movies is all around the shop, which always stays open after every evening performance at the Lucas Theatre around the corner. You can occasionally find Stratton himself behind the counter doling out scoops.

Today Show watchers might recall Al Roker's visit to the **Starfish Café** (719 E. Broad St., 912/790-8512, www.thestarfishcafe.com, Mon.–Fri. 8 A.M.–2 P.M., $7–10), a unique Savannah establishment that's part restaurant, part social project. Under the careful tutelage of Chef Rachel Petraglia, disadvantaged Savannahians learn valuable job skills as cooks and food prep workers. The result might surprise you; you can actually get a very good lunch here for a bargain price, while knowing you're helping the needy make a better life for themselves. All of the lunch sandwiches are great choices, but make sure you check out the specials of the day first, which usually include an interesting seafood dish. And save room for their famous bread pudding for dessert. A joint project of the local Union Mission and Savannah Technical College and a true local success story, Starfish Café hosts some of Savannah's most important opinion leaders on a regular basis; don't be surprised to run into the mayor here.

New Southern
Once the home of General James Habersham and the first place the Declaration of Independence was read aloud in Savannah, the **◖ Olde Pink House** (23 Abercorn St., 912/232-4286, Sun.–Thurs. 5:30–10:30 P.M., Fri.–Sat. 5:30–11 P.M., $15–30) is still a hub of activity in Savannah, as tourists and locals alike frequent the classic interior of the dining room and the downstairs Planter's Tavern. Regularly voted "Most Romantic Restaurant in Savannah"—though make no mistake, they pack you in pretty tight here—the Pink House is known for its savvy (and often sassy!) service and the uniquely regional flair it adds to traditional dishes, with liberal doses of pecans,

the Olde Pink House on Reynolds Square

© JIM MOREKIS

Vidalia onions, shrimp, and crab. The she-crab soup and lamb chops in particular are crowd-pleasers, and the scored crispy flounder stacks up to similar versions of this dish at several other spots in town. Reservations are essential, but don't worry about how you're dressed.

Moroccan
Savannah's single most unique dining experience happens at **Casbah** (118 E. Broughton St., 912/234-6168, daily 5:30–10:30 P.M., $10–20). This Moroccan restaurant features nightly belly dancing shows, with the dancers doing their thing from table to table to pre-recorded (and loud) music beginning at 6:30 or 7 P.M. with continuing shows through the evening. Beware—sometimes they grab a guest for a quick "lesson"! But don't let the over-the-top floor show or the "market" of authentic but overpriced Moroccan goods take away from the incredible food. Served in communal Moroccan style—with a waiter rinsing your hands with rose water before the meal, though utensils are provided on request—these

SAVANNAH

CHATHAM ARTILLERY PUNCH

Christened in honor of Georgia's oldest military unit, you'd think Chatham Artillery Punch was named for the ridiculously big bang it packs. But the story goes that when wives of the unit's soldiers made some punch for a party, individual artillery officers began sneaking their own wildly disparate additions to the concoction, until it became the veritable encyclopedia of hard liquor that it is today.

When George Washington visited Savannah in 1792, the Chatham Artillery gave him a 26-gun salute. Washington returned the respect by giving the unit the so-called "Washington Guns," captured at Yorktown in 1781 and now on display on Bay Street.

To this day the Chatham Artillery, now a unit of the Georgia Army National Guard, drinks the punch at its annual Saint Barbara's Day, honoring the patron saint of the artillery.

Here's the classic Chatham Artillery Punch recipe, intended to lay waste to an entire company of cannoneers. Most modern recipes substitute any sweet red wine for the Catawba wine.

- 1 ½ gallons Catawba wine
- ½ gallon rum
- 1 quart gin
- 1 quart brandy
- ½ pint Benedictine
- 2 quarts Maraschino cherries

- 1 ½ quarts rye whiskey
- 1 ½ gallons strong tea
- 2 ½ pounds brown sugar
- 1 ½ quarts orange juice
- 1 ½ quarts lemon juice

Most recipes say to mix all the ingredients 36-48 hours before serving, adding a case of champagne when ready to serve. But connoisseurs say to soak the tea overnight in the water, then mix the tea with the lemon juice, then add brown sugar and the liquors. At this point you let the mix set for a week in a covered container.

Local experts insist that you should never refrigerate the mix – when ready to serve you're supposed to pour it over a cake of ice. Then you add the cherries, the pineapple, and finally the champagne.

dishes hew to the deceptively simple cuisine of North Africa, with an emphasis on expertly grilled and seasoned meats and saffron rice. The lamb kabobs are to die for—the best I've had anywhere.

Asian

Downtown's hippest sushi spot is 【 **Sushi Zen** (41 Whitaker St., 912/233-1188, www .sushi-zensga.com, Tues.–Wed. 5:30–11 P.M., Thurs.–Sat. 5:30 P.M.–4 A.M., Sun. 5–11 P.M., $8–10), and it's one of the few kitchens open until 11 P.M. on weekends. You can take a seat at the sushi bar or at the rather cramped

small tables. There's also a small mezzanine level so you can see who else is hanging out. While most come for the sushi, made by highly trained artisans under the watchful eye of the great chef Yoshi, the extensive Japanese menu includes tempura, teriyaki, and noodle dishes. Sake is warmed to perfection and served with the respect it deserves, and beer drinkers will love the selection of Asian beers.

Part of the renovation of the Martin Luther King Jr. Boulevard corridor, the relatively new 【 **Wasabi's** (113 MLK Jr. Blvd., 912/233-8899, daily 11 A.M.–10:30 P.M., $8–20) is making a name for itself for its sushi, in a town with several very good sushi restaurants already. The à la carte tempura is also especially tasty and the Sapporo on draft is a real plus. There's an early-bird sushi boat for two offered 4–6:30 P.M., $29.95.

It's not much for decor, but **Saigon** (4 W. Broughton St., 912/232-5288, lunch Mon.–Sat. 11 A.M.–3 P.M., dinner Fri. and Sat. 5–11 P.M., Sun.–Thurs. 5–10 P.M., $8–12) provides some good and reasonably priced Vietnamese fare, served quickly and efficiently. I'm all about the thin rice noodles and barbecued skewered pork, but others swear by the *pho*. Find it centrally located in a storefront in Broughton Street's crowded shopping district.

Italian

Though the dining room stays busy, the entrées at **Il Pasticcio** (2 E. Broughton St., 912/231-8888, www.ilpasticciosavannah .com, Mon.–Thurs. 5:30–10 P.M., Fri. and Sat. 5:30–11:30 P.M., Sun. 5:30–9:30 P.M., $20–36) take a back seat to its atmosphere: dark, sexy, and Euro-trendy—think Florence or Milan. I suggest taking a seat at the cozy, ornate circular bar and ordering an appetizer while you enjoy the cosmopolitan crowd of beautiful people and the spacious views of this busy corner of Broughton Street. After 10 P.M. Tuesday–Saturday, one corner becomes the "Luna Lounge," with low-key live entertainment. Dress to impress: Not only will everyone inside check you out, but everyone walking by can see in.

Mexican and Southwestern

Visitors from anywhere west of the Mississippi River will be sorely disappointed at this glaring blind spot in Savannah cuisine. However, when you need a fix, you need a fix.

A popular option for Mexican downtown is the relatively new **Carlito's Mexican Bar & Grill** (119 MLK Jr. Blvd, 912/232-2525, Mon.–Thurs. 11 A.M.–10 P.M., Fri.–Sat. 11 A.M.–10:30 P.M., Sun. noon–10 P.M., $5–15). It won't impress anyone from New Mexico or Texas, but it's the best you're going to do here. It's pretty much the classic big-room, big-booth

Mexican place, down to the stereotypical "Monster Margaritas."

Your standard Mexican-owned salsa-and-cerveza restaurant, **Juarez** (420 E. Broughton St., 912/236-0530, Mon.–Fri. 11 A.M.–9:30 P.M., Sat. noon–9:30 P.M., Sun. 4–9:30 P.M., $7–13) offers large portions of typical dishes, such as enchiladas and fajitas.

Coffee and Tea

A coffeehouse before coffeehouses were cool, Savannah's original java joint, **Gallery Espresso** (234 Bull St., 912/233-5348, www.galleryespresso.com, Mon.–Fri. 7:30 A.M.–10 P.M., Sat.–Sun. 8 A.M.–11 P.M.), currently occupies a prime corner lot on beautiful Chippewa Square. Of course there's the requisite free Wi-Fi, and while you sip and surf you can also enjoy the regular rotating modern art exhibits by well-known local artists, all curated by owner Jessica Barnhill.

Deadsville in the summer, the art student hangout **Metro Coffeehouse** (402 MLK Jr. Blvd., 912/232-9545, www.metrocoffeehouse online.com, Mon.–Fri. 8 A.M.–2 A.M., Sat. 10 A.M.–2 A.M., Sun. noon–2 A.M.) comes alive whenever SCAD's in session—which is understandable, since it's owned by a SCAD graduate film student. The coffee's great, but Metro's really more like a big, comfy living room. This coffeehouse, with its scattered sofas, free Wi-Fi, occasional very plugged-in entertainment, and very late hours caters to a slice of the kind of real Savannah life rarely mentioned in the guidebooks. Great for vegan drinks and smoothies. There are also several vegan and vegetarian sandwiches on the menu.

VICTORIAN DISTRICT
New Southern

Before there was Paula Deen, there was Elizabeth Terry, Savannah's first well-known high-profile chef and founder of this most elegant of all Savannah restaurants, **(Elizabeth on 37th** (105 E. 37th St., 912/236-5547, daily 6–10 P.M., $25 and up). Terry has since sold the place to two of her former waiters, Greg and Gary Butch, but this restaurant has for the most part continued to maintain her high standards—though, frankly, there have been a few complaints from those who think its hey-day has past. In a beautifully restored Victorian mansion just outside the historic district, with its own lovingly tended herb garden and emphasis on local suppliers, Elizabeth on 37th continues to be—a quarter-century after its founding—where many Savannahians go when the evening calls for something really memorable. Executive chef Kelly Yambor uses eclectic, seasonally shifting ingredients that blend the South with the South of France. Along with generally attentive service, it makes for a wonderfully old-school fine dining experience. Reservations recommended.

The newest darling of serious local foodies is the aptly named **Local 11 Ten** (1110 Bull St., 912/790-9000, www.local11ten.com, Tues.–Thurs. 6–10 P.M., Fri.–Sat. 6–10:30 P.M., $22–39), just off the south end of Forsyth Park. Its wide-open dining room has a great view of the streetscape, adventurous cuisine (the handiwork of Memphis-born Keith Latture), and cute bar have proven big attractions. Try the hanger steak with a side of Vidalia onion rings. Or try the rabbit. Yes, the rabbit.

Casual Dining

Though it's primarily known for its sublime sweet treats, **C Back in the Day Bakery** (2403 Bull St., 912/495-9292, www.backinthedaybakery.com, Tues.–Fri. 7:30 A.M.–4 P.M., Sat. 9 A.M.–3 P.M., $7) in the Starland Design District at the southern edge of the Victorian area also offers a small but delightfully tasty (and tasteful) range of lunch soups, salads, and sandwiches 11 A.M.–2 P.M. There's even free Wi-Fi. Lunch highlights are the baguette with camembert, roasted red peppers, and lettuce, and the caprese, the classic tomato/mozzarella/basil trifecta on a perfect ciabatta. But whatever you do, save room for dessert, which runs the full sugar spectrum from red velvet cupcakes, lemon bars, macaroons, carrot cake, Cosmopolitan Cake, Nana's Pudding, and my favorite, Omar's Mystic Espresso Cheesecake.

Coffee and Tea

The coffee at **C The Sentient Bean** (13 E. Park Ave., 912/232-4447, www.sentientbean.com, daily 7:30 A.M.–10 P.M.) is all fair-trade and organic, and the all-vegetarian fare is a major upgrade above the usual coffeehouse offering. But "The Bean" is more than a coffeehouse—it's a community. Probably the best indie film venue in town, the Bean regularly hosts screenings of various cutting-edge, left-of-center documentary and kitsch films, as well as rotating art exhibits. When there's no movie, there's usually some low-key live entertainment or spoken word open mic action going on.

EASTSIDE
New Southern

The aptly named **New South Café** (2601 Skidaway Rd., 912/233-7568, www.numediaservices.com/newsouth, Tues.–Sat. 11 A.M.–3 P.M., 5–10 P.M., $9–34) on the city's eastside is a relative newcomer, but is getting rave reviews for its bold yet unpretentious take on Southern cuisine, including specialties like hushpuppy-crusted fried catfish fingers, shrimp and grits, and the signature, award-winning crab cake burger.

SOUTHSIDE
Southwestern

Should you find yourself shopping at Oglethorpe Mall on Savannah's ugly, paved-over southside, take a quick jaunt across Abercorn to **Moe's Southwestern Grill** (7801 Abercorn St., 912/303-6688, daily 11 A.M.–10 P.M., $5–10) in the Chatham Plaza shopping center. This regional franchise offers made-to-order Southwestern fare—or a Southeastern version of it, anyway—in a whimsical, boisterous atmosphere where you'll be treated with a shouted "Welcome to Moe's!" the second you step foot inside. Any of the homemade salsas are great; just take a sampling of all three to your table. Local vegetarians and vegans love this spot, since you tell the counter staff exactly what you want in your burrito and you can always substitute tofu for any meat.

Japanese

In the cozy Habersham Village shopping center near Ardsley Park, locally owned **Hirano's** (4426 Habersham St., 912/353-8337, daily 5–9 P.M., $6–8) is a longtime favorite. The main dining room offers a truncated but quick, inexpensive, and delicious menu of teriyaki-and-rice items, with California rolls and gyoza appetizers available. The door to your left leads you to a traditional Japanese sushi bar, with low tables and the classic pencil-and-paper, fill-it-out-yourself menu.

TYBEE ISLAND
Breakfast and Brunch

Considered the best breakfast in the Savannah area for 30 years and counting, **❤ The Breakfast Club** (1500 Butler Ave., 912/786-5984, www.tybeeisland.com/dining/brclub/Default.htm, daily 6:30 A.M.–1 P.M., $4–10), with its brisk, diner atmosphere and hearty, Polish sausage–filled omelettes, is like a little bit of Chicago in the South. Lines start early for a chance to enjoy such house specialties as Helen's Solidarity, the Athena Omelette, and the Chicago Bear Burger, but don't worry—you'll inevitably strike up a conversation with someone interesting while you wait.

Caribbean

Don't be deceived by the very casual decor and attire at the **❤ North Beach Grill** (41 Meddin Dr., 912/786-9003, daily 11:30 A.M.–10 P.M., $7–17). The kitchen is run by the same two partners that run the fine-dining restaurant bearing their names, Georges' On Tybee, and as such has the same consistently high quality and reliance on fresh ingredients. Jerk chicken and pork are the order of the day here, though the seafood specials are definitely worth checking out. In any event, you must start with the plantains and salsa! No china or white glove service here—just a place to enjoy a beautiful view of the North Beach dunes, some Buffett tunes, a cold Red Stripe, and some of the best Caribbean food for miles around.

Casual Dining

Set in a large former fishing camp overlooking Chimney Creek, **❤ The Crab Shack** (40 Estill Hammock Rd., 912/786-9857, www.thecrabshack.com, Mon.–Thurs. 11:30 A.M.–10 P.M., Fri.–Sun. 11:30 A.M.–11 P.M., $6–30) is the Savannah area's favorite seafood place and also something of an attraction in itself. Owner Jack Flanagan, a modern-day pirate in the best Jimmy Buffett tradition, is an unpretentious former sea captain with a pronounced flair for living for the moment. So don't expect fine gourmet fare or quiet seaside dining here; the emphasis is on mounds of fresh, tasty seafood, heavy on the raw bar action, all in a very casual and boisterous outdoor atmosphere where enjoying yourself is the only goal. Did I mention the alligators? There are alligators in a 25,000-gallon exhibit, not to mention a colony of cats that have the run of the place (other than the gator pit, of course). Have I made myself clear that this is not the place for the chronically uptight? Getting there is a little tricky: Take U.S. 80 to Tybee, cross the bridge over Lazaretto Creek, and begin looking for Estill Hammock Road to Chimney Creek on your right. Take Estill Hammock and veer right. After that, it's hard to miss.

If you're hanging out on the south end near the Pier, you can't miss the three-story pink building with the open decks and the words "Time to Eat" in six-foot letters across the top of the facade. That's not the name of the restaurant—it's actually **Fannie's on the Beach** (1613 Strand Ave., 912/786-6109, www.fanniesonthebeach.com, Mon.–Thurs. 11 A.M.–10 P.M. Fri.–Sun. 11 A.M.–11 P.M., $8–24) a great-for-all-ages restaurant and bar with a menu that's a cut above the usual tavern fare. You can't go wrong with any of their fine, rich, cheese-heavy pizzas; my favorite is the spinach and feta with sun-dried tomatoes. Live, boozy entertainment and a fun wait and bar staff add to the overall Tybee flavor. Sunday brunches noon–3 P.M. are a local favorite.

New Southern

There are some excellent restaurants on Tybee—in truth, some of the best in the region—but keep in mind that "fine-dining" here doesn't mean you have to dress to the nines. As elsewhere on the island, a casual look is just fine.

My favorite restaurant on Tybee, the **Hunter House** (1701 Butler Ave., 912/786-7515, www.hunterhouseinn.com, Mon.–Sat. from 6 P.M., $20–30), boasts the one-of-a-kind talents of legendary local chef Espy Geissler. With equal mastery of continental cuisine and Southern classics alike—and a particularly brilliant touch with seafood—Espy never fails to amaze with his perfectly textured sauces, delightful presentation, and constant striving for excellence. In fact, the story goes that Espy got his job at the Hunter House, also a small inn, because owner John Hunter got tired of hearing him complain about the food. So he hired him, and the rest is culinary history. (Espy's talents go beyond the kitchen; he's an excellent painter in his own right, an artistic pursuit that clearly informs his cooking as well.) The dining room, softly lit and dominated by forest green, is elegant without being overwhelming, romantic without being cloying, keeping just enough seaside touches to remind you that you are, after all, on Tybee. The tiny but perfect bar, off in a side dining room, is often cheerfully

manned by John Hunter himself, who also makes a point of visiting each table. Start with the seafood bisque, a tomato-based delight that doesn't skimp on the crab, and the succulent fried green tomatoes, unlike any others you've had. Listen closely to the specials, but know that any seafood entrée is a good bet, especially grouper and snapper. To get here, take U.S. 80 onto Tybee until you veer right at the Atlantic Ocean. Now called Butler Avenue, this road takes you all the way past 16th Street. Look for the Hunter House on your right.

The owner of North Beach Grill, George Spriggs, also runs a fine-dining restaurant, **Georges' on Tybee** (1105 U.S. 80, 912/786-9730, Tue.–Sun. 5:30–10 P.M., Sun. brunch 11 A.M.–2 P.M., mains $10–21). While the plural in the name is because Spriggs once ran this restaurant with a partner also named George, the new incarnation focuses on a "refined Southern bistro menu," as Spriggs himself describes it. Any seafood here is recommended, but try the flounder sautéed in Pernod. Save room for dessert, a particular specialty; the banana-and-ginger spiced cheesecake is a good pick.

Information and Services

VISITORS CENTERS
The main clearinghouse for tourist information is undoubtedly the downtown **Savannah Visitors Center** (301 MLK Jr. Blvd., 912/944-0455, Mon.–Fri. 8:30 A.M.–5 P.M., Sat., Sun., and holidays 9 A.M.–5 P.M.).

Other visitors centers in the area include the **River Street Hospitality Center** (1 River St., 912/651-6662, daily 10 A.M.–10 P.M.), the **Tybee Island Visitor Center** (S. Campbell Ave. and Highway 80, 912/786-5444, daily 9 A.M.–5:30 P.M.), and the **Savannah Airport Visitor Center** (464 Airways Ave., 912/964-1109, daily 10 A.M.–6 P.M.).

The **Savannah Convention and Visitors Bureau** (101 E. Bay St.) keeps an accurate

and up-to-date list of lodgings at its website at www.savcvb.com and can be reached at 877/SAVANNAH (877/728-2662).

HOSPITALS
Savannah has two very good hospital systems. Centrally located near midtown, **Memorial Health University Hospital** (4700 Waters Ave., 912/350-8000, www.memorialhealth.com) is the region's only Level-1 Trauma Center and is one of the best in the nation. The St. Joseph's/Candler Hospital System (www.sjchs.org) has two units, **St. Joseph's Hospital** (11705 Mercy Blvd., 912/819-4100) on the extreme southside and **Candler Hospital** (5401 Paulsen St., 912/819-6000) closer to midtown.

POLICE

The city and county police forces recently merged to form the **Savannah/Chatham County Metropolitan Police Department.** For non-emergencies, call 912/651-6675. For emergencies, call 911.

MEDIA
Newspapers

The daily newspaper of record is the *Savannah Morning News* (912/525-0796, www.savannah now.com). It puts out an entertainment insert on Thursdays called "Do."

The free weekly newspaper in town is *Connect Savannah* (912/721-4350, www .connectsavannah.com), hitting stands each Wednesday. Look to it for culture and music coverage, as well as an alternative take on local politics and issues.

Two glossy magazines compete, the hipper *The South* magazine (912/236-5501, www.the southmag.com) and the more establishment *Savannah* magazine (912/652-0293, www.sa-vannahmagazine.com).

Radio and Television

The National Public Radio affiliate is the Georgia Public Broadcasting station WSVH 91.1 FM. Savannah State University offers jazz, reggae, and Latin music at WHCJ 90.3 FM.

Georgia Public Broadcasting is on WVAN. The local NBC affilate is WSAV, the CBS affiliate WTOC, the ABC affiliate is WJCL, and the Fox affiliate is WTGS.

LIBRARIES

The **Live Oak Public Library** (www.liveoak pl.org) is the umbrella organization for the libraries of Chatham, Effingham, and Liberty counties. By far the largest branch is south of downtown Savannah, the **Bull Street Branch** (222 Bull St., 912/652-3600, Mon.–Thurs. 9 A.M.–9 P.M., Fri.–Sat. 9 A.M.–6 P.M., Sun. 2–6 P.M.). Farthest downtown and tucked away on Upper Factor's Walk is the charming little **Ola Wyeth Branch** (4 E. Bay St., 912/232-5488, Mon.–Fri. noon–3 P.M.). In midtown Savannah is the **Carnegie Branch** (537 E.

Henry St., 912/231-9921, Mon. 10 A.M.–8 P.M., Tues.–Thurs. 10 A.M.–6 P.M., Fri.–Sat. 2–6 P.M.). The beach has its own **Tybee Island Branch** (405 Butler Ave., 912/786-7733, open Mon., Fri.–Sat. 2–6 P.M., Tues. 10 A.M.–8 P.M., Wed. 10 A.M.–6 P.M.).

The **Georgia Historical Society** (501 Whitaker St., 912/651-2128, www.georgia history.com, Tues.–Sat. 10 A.M.–5 P.M.) has an extensive collection of clippings, photos, maps, and other archived material at its headquarters at the corner of Forsyth Park in Hodgson Hall. Their website has been extensively revamped and is now one of the Southeast's best online resources for Georgia history information.

The SCAD-run **Jen Library** (201 E. Broughton St., 912/525-4700, www.scad .edu) features 3,000 Internet connections in its cavernous 85,000-square-foot space. Its main claim to fame is the remarkable variety of art periodicals it subscribes to, nearly 1,000 at last count. Though built for the school's 7,000-plus art students, the public can enter and use it as well with photo ID (you just can't check anything out). It's open Monday–Friday 7:30 A.M.–1 A.M., Saturday 10 A.M.–1 A.M., Sunday 11 A.M.–1 A.M., with shorter hours when class is out of session.

POST OFFICES

There are two post offices of note for most visitors to Savannah. The largest with the longest hours is the **Main Branch** (2 N. Fahm St., open Mon.–Fri. 8 A.M.–5:30 P.M., Sat. 9 A.M.–1 P.M.). It's off Bay Street just past the western edge of the Historic District. A smaller but more convenient branch downtown is the **Telfair Square Station** (118 Barnard St., open Mon.–Fri. 8 A.M.–5 P.M.).

GAY AND LESBIAN RESOURCES

Visitors often find Savannah to be surprisingly cosmopolitan and diverse for a Deep South city, and nowhere is this more true than with its sizeable and influential gay and lesbian community. In line with typical Southern protocol, the community is largely apolitical and more concerned with integration than provocation. But they're still very much aware of their growing impact on the local economy and are major players in art and commerce.

The **Savannah Pride Festival** is held every September at various venues in town. Topflight, dance-oriented musical acts perform, restaurants show off their creativity, and activists staff information booths.

The chief resource for local gay and lesbian information and concerns is the First City Network, whose main website (www.first citynetwork.org) features many useful links, though many might find its MySpace page (www.myspace.com/firstcitynetwork) useful as well. Another great Internet networking resource is Gay Savannah (www.gay savannah.com).

For specifically gay-friendly accommodations, try the **Under the Rainbow Inn** (104–106 W. 38th St., 912/790-1005, www .under-the-rainbow.com, $109–155), a great B&B in the historic Thomas Square district, a former streetcar suburb of Savannah.

Getting There and Around

AIR

Savannah is served by the fairly new and efficient **Savannah/Hilton Head International Airport** (400 Airways Ave., 912/964-0514, airport code SAV, www.savannahairport.com) directly off I-95 at exit 104. The airport is about 20 minutes from downtown Savannah and an hour from Hilton Head Island. Airlines with routes into and out of SAV include AirTran (www.airtran.com), American Eagle (www .aa.com), Continental (www.continental.com), Delta (www.delta.com), Northwest Airlink (www.nwa.com), United Express (www.ual .com), and US Airways (www.usairways.com).

Taxi stands are available for transportation to Savannah at the following regulated fares and conditions: The cost is $2 for the first ⅙ of a mile and $0.30 per ⅙ mile thereafter, not to exceed $3.50 for the first mile and $1.80 per mile thereafter. Waiting charge is $21/hour. No charge for baggage. The maximum fare for destinations in the Historic District is $25.

CAR

Savannah is the eastern terminus of I-16, and that Interstate is the most common entrance to the city. However, most travelers get to I-16 via I-95, taking the exit for downtown Savannah (Historic District). Once on I-16, the most common entry points into Savannah proper are via the Gwinnett Street exit, which puts you near the southern edge of the Historic District near Forsyth Park, or, more commonly, the Montgomery Street exit farther into the heart of downtown.

Paralleling I-95 is the old coastal highway, now U.S. 17, which goes through Savannah. U.S. 80 is Victory Drive for most of its length through town; however, after you pass through Thunderbolt on your way to the islands area, including Tybee, it reverts to U.S. 80.

TRAIN

Savannah is on the north–south "Silver Service" of Amtrak (2611 Seaboard Coastline Dr., 912/234-2611, www.amtrak.com). To get to the station on the westside of town, take I-16 west and get off on I-516 north. Immediately take the Gwinnett Street/Railroad Station exit and follow the Amtrak signs.

BUS

Chatham Area Transit (www.catchacat .org), Savannah's publicly supported bus system, is quite thorough and efficient considering Savannah's relatively small size. Plenty of routes criss-cross the entire area, with one-way fares of $1 per person, exact change only, which includes one connecting route. Service runs weekdays and Saturdays 5:30 A.M.–11:30 P.M., Sundays 7 A.M.–9 P.M. Young children are free. A weekly pass is $12. Buy advance tickets at two locations: 900 East Gwinnett Street and 124 Bull Street.

Of primary interest to visitors is the completely free **CAT Shuttle,** which travels a continuous circuit route throughout the Historic District, keyed around hotels, historic sites, and the Savannah Visitors Center. The Shuttle is wheelchair-accessible and runs weekdays and Saturdays 7 A.M.–7 P.M., Sundays 9:30 A.M.–5 P.M.

RENTAL CAR

The vast bulk of rental car facilities are at the Savannah/Hilton Head International Airport, including Avis (800/831-2847), Budget (800/527-0700), Dollar (912/964-9001), Enterprise (800/736-8222), Hertz (800/654-3131), National (800/227-7368), and Thrifty (800/367-2277).

Rental locations away from the airport are Avis (7810 Abercorn St., 912/354-4718), Budget (7070 Abercorn St., 912/355-0805), Enterprise (3028 Skidaway Rd., 912/352-1424; 9505 Abercorn St., 912/925-0060; 11506-A Abercorn Expy., 912/920-1093; 7510 White Bluff Rd., 912/355-6622).

TAXI

Taxi services in Georgia tend to be less regulated than other states, but services are plentiful in Savannah and are generally reasonable. The chief local service is **Yellow Cab** (866/319-9646, www.savannahyellowcab.com). For wheelchair accessibility, request cab #14. Other services include **Adam Cab** (912/927-7466), **Magikal Taxi Service** (912/897-8294), and **Sunshine Cab** (912/272-0971).

If you like some local flavor to go with your cab ride, call **Concierge Taxi Services** (912/604-8466), the one-man show of local author Robert S. Mickles. He's very friendly and always has a great Savannah story to tell.

If you're not in a super hurry, it's always fun to take a **Savannah Pedicab** (912/232-7900, www.savannahpedicab.com) for quick trips around downtown. Your friendly driver will pedal one or two passengers anywhere within the Historic District for a reasonable price.

PARKING

Parking is at a premium in downtown Savannah. The city's Parking Services Department is extremely vigilant about parking violations, ostensibly to encourage "turnover" of the valuable spaces, but also of course to generate revenue. Traditional coin-operated metered parking is available throughout the city, ranging from 15 minutes to a precious few 10-hour meters. More and more, the city is going to self-pay kiosks where you purchase a stamped receipt to display inside your dashboard.

Bottom line: Be sure to pay for all parking weekdays 8:30 A.M.–5 P.M. No matter what the printed information on the meter tells you, there is *no* enforcement of parking meters at all on weekends or after 5 P.M. any day. That information has been on the meters for years and almost seems intended to bilk tourists. That being said, you should also know that illegally parking and parking in sweep zones will get you ticketed and/or towed any time of day.

Tybee Island is even more strict about parking regulations than Savannah. If the meter says to feed it until 8 P.M. on the weekend. then feed the meter until 8 P.M. on the weekend!

The city operates four parking garages at various costs and hours: The **Bryan Street Garage** (100 E. Bryan St.) is open 24/7 and costs $1 per hour for the first hour and $0.75 each additional hour Monday–Friday. Evenings 6 P.M.–6 A.M. are a $2 fee and anytime Saturday and Sunday is a $1 fee. The **Robinson Garage** (132 Montgomery St.) is open 24/7 and costs $1 per hour for the first hour and $0.75 each additional hour Monday–Friday. Evenings 6 P.M.–6 A.M. and weekends are free. The **State Street Garage** (100 E. State St.) is open Monday–Friday 6 A.M.–1 A.M., Saturday 5 A.M.–3 A.M., and Sunday 5 A.M.–1 A.M. and costs $1 per hour for the first hour and $0.75 each additional hour Monday–Friday. Evenings 6 P.M.–1 A.M. are free, as are Saturdays 5 A.M.–3 A.M. and Sundays 5 A.M.–1 A.M. The **Liberty Street Garage** (401 W. Liberty St.) is open Monday–Friday 6 A.M.–1 A.M., Saturday 5 A.M.–3 A.M., and Sunday 5 A.M.–1 A.M. and costs $1 per hour for the first hour and $0.75 each additional hour Monday–Friday. Evenings Monay–Friay 6 P.M.–1 A.M. are a $2 fee and Saturdays and Sundays anytime are $1.

SAVANNAH

Outside Savannah

As is the case with Charleston, Savannah's outlying areas still bear the indelible marks of the plantation era. The marsh still retains traces of the old rice paddies, and the economics of the area still retain a similar sense of strict class and racial stratification.

While history is no less prominent, it is more subtle in these largely semi-rural areas, and the tourist infrastructure is much less well-developed than Savannah proper. This area contains some of the most impoverished communities in Georgia, so keep in mind that life is harder here than in the city and the locals may have more on their minds than keeping you entertained—though certainly at no point will their Southern manners fail them.

And also keep in mind that you are traveling in one of the most unique ecosystems in the country and natural beauty is never far away.

© FRANK MCINTOSH

the historic Midway Church

MIDWAY AND LIBERTY COUNTY

Locals will tell you that Midway is named because it's equidistant from the Savannah and Altamaha Rivers on Oglethorpe's old "river road," which it certainly is. But others say the small but very historic town is actually named after the Medway River in England. In any case, we know that in seeking to pacify the local Creek tribe, the Council of Georgia in 1752 granted a group of Massachusetts Puritans then residing in Dorchester, South Carolina, a 32,000-acre land grant as incentive to move south. After moving into Georgia and establishing New Dorchester, they soon founded a nearby settlement that would later take on the modern spelling of Midway.

Midway's citizens were very aggressive early on in the cause for American independence. That's the very reason the area's three original parishes were combined and named Liberty County in 1777—the only Georgia county named for a concept rather than a person. Two of Georgia's three signers of the Declaration of Independence, Lyman Hall and Button Gwinnett, resided primarily in Midway and both attended the historic Midway Church. But a key part of Liberty County history is no more: the once-thriving seaport of Sunbury, which formerly challenged Savannah for economic supremacy in the region but is now nonexistent.

Because Midway is only an easy 45 minutes from Savannah on I-95, it makes a particularly fun and easy day trip.

Midway

Into Midway proper is the charming **Midway Museum** (Highway 17, 912/884-5837, Tues.–Sat. 10 A.M.–4 P.M., Sun. 2–4 P.M., $3 per person) and the adjacent **Midway Church,** sometimes called the "Midway meetinghouse." The museum contains a variety of artifacts, most from the 18th and 19th centuries, and an extensive genealogy collection.

The Midway Church, built in 1756, was burned during the Revolution but rebuilt in 1792. Both Button Gwinnett and Lyman Hall attended services here, and during the Civil War some of Sherman's cavalry set up camp. The church is particularly noteworthy in that throughout its history black and white parishioners worshipped together simultaneously. The nearby cemetery is the final resting place of two Revolutionary War generals; Union cavalry kept horses within its walls. The museum, church, and cemetery are easy to find: You take Exit 76 off I-95 South, and take a right on U.S. 84. Turn right on U.S. 17, and all are at the intersection of 17 and Martin Road.

Liberty County

One of the most interesting private eco-tourism and cultural sites in the region is the **Melon Bluff Nature and Heritage Preserve** (2999 Islands Hwy., 912/884-5779, www.melonbluff .com, Sept.–May, call for further details, $3 day use, $15 riding fee). The site, within the historical boundaries of the Springfield Plantation, is run by the charming and knowledgeable Devendorf family, who boast roots in the area going back to the original royal land grant.

Melon Bluff is a key part of the Colonial Birding Trail. Its 20 miles of trails, on 2,200 acres, wind through virtually every type of ecosystem in coastal Georgia, from ancient live oak stands to salt marsh to maritime forest. Visitors can bring their hiking boots, mountain bikes, or horses and explore the site on their own, or take part in guided activities such as kayak trips on the meandering, marshy Midway River. Melon Bluff has expanded its cultural tourism interpretive offerings, keying on the important recent discovery in the area of the earliest known artifact of the first European settlement in North America: a Spanish coin near the site of the fabled San Miguel de Gualdalpe colony.

The base of operations for Melon Bluff is the Nature Center three miles east of I-95 at Exit 76, on your right. Parking is available there and that's also the main trailhead.

Nearby is **Seabrook Village** (660 Trade Hill Rd., 912/884-7008, Tues.–Sat. 10 A.M.–4 P.M., $3 per person), a unique living history museum chronicling the everyday life of Liberty County's African American community, with a direct link to Sherman's famous "40 Acres and a Mule" Field Order No. 15. There are eight restored vernacular buildings on the 100-acre site, including the simple but sublime one-room Seabrook School.

Youmans Pond (daily, free) is a prime stop for migratory fowl. Its main claim to fame is being visited in 1773 by the great naturalist William Bartram on one of his treks across the Southeast. Youmans Pond has changed little since then, with its tree-studded pond and oodles of owls, ospreys, herons, egrets, wood storks, and many more. To get there, take I-95 south from Savannah to Exit 76. Go east on GA 38, which becomes a dirt road until you find the freshwater pond on the right.

Less easy to find is **LeConte-Woodmanston Botanical Garden** (912/884-6500, www.hist .armstrong.edu/publichist/LeConte/leconte -home.htm, Tues.–Sat. 9 A.M.–5 P.M., closed Dec. 18–Feb. 14, call first to verify times and road conditions, $2). Part of William Bartram's historic nature trail, this was the home of Dr. Louis LeConte, renowned 19th-century botanist, and his sons John LeConte, first president of the University of California at Berkeley, and Joseph LeConte, who with John Muir founded the Sierra Club. The highlight here is the rare tidally influenced freshwater wetland, featuring the blackwater Bulltown Swamp. This visit is best done in a four-wheel-drive vehicle. From Savannah, take I-95 south to Exit 76. Turn right on U.S. 84, then left on U.S. 17. Turn right on Barrington Ferry Road until pavement ends at Sandy Run Road. Continue until you see the historic markers. Turn left onto the dirt road then another mile.

Dorchester Academy and Museum (8787 E. Oglethorpe Hwy., 912/884-2347, www .dorchesteracademy.com, open Tues.–Fri. 11 A.M.–2 P.M., Sat. 2–4 P.M., free) was built as a boarding and day school for freed African Americans after the Civil War. Its early teachers were mostly idealistic transplants from

THE DEAD TOWN OF SUNBURY

If you spend much time in Liberty County you'll probably hear someone mention that a certain place or person is "over near Sunbury." Such is the lasting legacy of this long-gone piece of Georgia history on the Midway River that locals still refer to it in the present tense, though the town itself is no more.

Founded soon after Midway in 1758, by 1761 Sunbury rivaled Savannah as Georgia's main commercial port, with a thriving trade in lumber, rice, indigo, corn, and, unfortunately, slaves as well. At one time, one writer recalls, seven square-rigged vessels called on the port in a single day. At various times, all three of Georgia's signers of the Declaration of Independence – Button Gwinnett, Lyman Hall, and George Walton – had connections to Sunbury.

The beginning of the end came with those heady days of revolution, however, when Sun-

bury was the scene of much fighting between colonists and the British army in 1776-1779. A British siege in 1778 culminated in this immortal reply from the colonial commander, Colonel John McIntosh, to a redcoat demand for surrender: "Come and take it."

By the beginning of 1779, however, a separate British assault did indeed "take it," adding to the increasingly violent pillage of the surrounding area. Though after American independence Sunbury remained the Liberty County seat until 1797, it was never the same, beset by decay, hurricanes, and yellow fever outbreaks. (Fort Morris, however, would defend the area against the British once more time, in the War of 1812 as Fort Defiance.)

By 1848, nothing of the town remained but the old cemetery, which you can find adjacent to the Fort Morris State Historic Site.

New England. Liberty County was one of the earliest integrated school districts in Georgia, and Martin Luther King Jr. came to Dorchester in 1962 to plan the march on Birmingham. In 1997, an extensive renovation brought the facility to its current state. The museum is small but features an interesting display of memorabilia. Take Exit 76 off I-95 and go west on U.S. Highway 84, about two miles past the intersection with U.S. Highway 17.

Built to defend the once-proud port of Sunbury, **Fort Morris State Historic Site** (2559 Ft. Morris Rd., 912/884-5999, www.gastateparks.org/info/ftmorris, Tues.–Sat. 9 A.M.–5 P.M., Sun. 2–5:30 P.M., $3) was reconstructed during the War of 1812 and was an encampment during the Civil War. It was here that Colonel John McIntosh gave his famous reply to the British demand for his surrender: "Come and take it." The museum has displays of military and everyday life of the era. Reenactments and cannon firings are highlights. There's a visitors center and a nature trail. To get there, take Exit 76 off I-95

south. Go east on Islands Highway and take a left on Trade Hill Road. Turn onto Fort Morris Road; the site is two miles down.

Liberty County is also home to part of the sprawling Fort Stewart army installation, home of the U.S. Army "Rock of the Marne" 3rd Infantry Division. The only thing open to the public is the **Fort Stewart Museum** (Bldg. T904, 2022 Frank Cochran Dr., 912/767-7885, Tues.–Sat. 10 A.M.–4 P.M., free), which chronicles the division's activity in World War II, Vietnam, Korea, Desert Storm, and Iraq. All visitors must stop at the main gate and provide proof of registration, insurance, and drivers license to receive a visitor's pass. To get there, take Exit 87 off I-95 south. Take a left on Hwy. 17, then veer right onto GA 196 west. Turn right at U.S. 84. Turn right onto General Stewart Way and follow directions to the main gate.

Accommodations and Food

While industry is coming quickly to Liberty County, it's still a small, self-contained community with not much in the way of tourist amenities (many would say that is part of its charm). A great choice for a stay is the **❰ Palmyra Barn and Cottage** (5836 Islands Hwy., 912/884-5779, www.palmyraplantation.com). The B&B ($165–205) is in a 1940s converted barn, and the self-catered circa-1840 Cottage ($300) nearby is right on the river. Your hosts, Laura and Meredith Devendorf, couldn't be more charming or informed about the area, and the breakfasts are absurdly rich and filling in that hearty and deeply comforting Southern tradition.

Restaurants of note include the **Sunbury Crab Company** (541 Brigantine Dunmore Rd., 912/884-8640, lunch Sat.–Sun., dinner Wed.–Sun., $10–30), providing, you guessed it, great crab cakes in a casual atmosphere on the Medway River. Many locals eat at least once a week at **Holton's Seafood** (13711 E. Oglethorpe Hwy., 912/884-9151, daily lunch and dinner, $7–17), an unpretentious and fairly typical family-run fried seafood place just off I-95 at the Midway exit.

But real local connoisseurs swear that the historic 1930s-era truck stop known as **Ida Mae & Joe's North Midway Restaurant** (912/884-3388) is by far the best eating establishment in the area, with fried catfish and homemade pies that are worth the trip. It's west of I-95 toward Midway on East Oglethorpe Highway (U.S. 84).

Getting There and Around

When traveling in this area keep in mind that if you want to avoid I-95 you can always take the more scenic "back door" route into Liberty County out of Savannah on U.S. 17.

RICHMOND HILL AND BRYAN COUNTY

Known as the "town that Henry Ford built," Richmond Hill is a growing bedroom community of Savannah in adjacent Bryan County. Sherman's March to the Sea ended here with much destruction, so little history before that time is left. Most of what remains is due to Ford's philanthropic influence, still felt in many place names around the area,

including the main drag, GA 144, known as Ford Avenue.

After the auto magnate and his wife Clara made the area, then called Ways Station, a summer home, they were struck by the area's incredible poverty and determined to help improve living conditions, building hospitals, schools, churches, and homes. The Fords eventually acquired over 85,000 acres in Bryan County, including the former Richmond plantation. What is now known as Ford Plantation—currently a private luxury resort—was built in the 1930s and centered on the main house, once the central building of the famous Hermitage Plantation on the Savannah River, purchased and moved by Ford south to Bryan County.

Sights

The little **Richmond Hill Historical Society and Museum** (corner Ford Ave. and Timber Trail Rd., 912/756-3697, daily 10 A.M.–4 P.M., donations encouraged) is housed in a former kindergarten built by Henry Ford.

Perhaps the main attraction here, especially for Civil War buffs, is **Fort McAllister State Historic Site** (3894 Ft. McAllister Rd., 912/727-2339, www.gastateparks.org/info/ftmcallister, daily 7 A.M.–10 P.M., $4 adults, $2.50 children). Unlike the masonry forts of Savannah, Fort McAllister is an all-earthwork fortification on the Ogeechee River, the site of a short but savage assault by Sherman's troops in December 1864, in which 5,000 Union soldiers quickly overwhelmed the skeleton garrison of 230 Confederate defenders. After the war, the site fell into disrepair until Henry Ford funded and spearheaded restoration of it in the 1930s, as he did so many historic sites in Bryan County. The fort, which features many reenactments throughout the year, has a well-run new **Civil War Museum** (Mon.–Sat. 9 A.M.–5 P.M., Sun. 2–5 P.M.). An adjacent recreational site features a beautiful, oak-lined picnic ground, a nature trail, and the nearby 65-site Savage Island Campground. To get there off I-95, take Exit 90 and go 10 miles east on GA Spur 144.

Practicalities

There's no end to the chain food offerings here, but one of the better restaurants in town is **The Upper Crust** (1702 U.S. 17, 912/756-6990, Mon.–Sat. lunch and dinner, Sun. dinner only, $7–12), a casual American place with great pizza in addition to soups, salads, and hot sandwiches. Another popular place, also on Highway 17, is **Steamers Restaurant & Raw Bar** (4040 U.S. Hwy. 17, 912/756-3979, daily 5–10 P.M. $10–20), home of some good Lowcountry Boil.

To get to Richmond Hill, drive south of Savannah on I-95 and take Exit 90. Most lodgings in the area are clustered off I-95 at Exit 87 (Exit 90 also gets you to Richmond Hill). Keep in mind the two most important thoroughfares are the north–south U.S. 17 and the east–west GA 144, also known as Ford Avenue.

NEW EBENEZER

Few people visit New Ebenezer today, west of Savannah in Effingham County. Truth is, there's not much there anymore except for one old church. But oh, what a church. The **Jerusalem Evangelical Lutheran Church** (2966 Ebenezer Rd., Rincon, 912/754-3915, www.effga.com/jerusalem) hosts the oldest continuous congregation in the United States. Built out of local clay brick in 1769, its walls are 21 inches thick. Some original panes of glass remain, and its European bells are still rung before each service, which begins each Sunday at 11 A.M. Several surrounding structures are also heirs to New Ebenezer's Salzburg legacy.

Around the corner from the church is a much newer spiritually themed site, the **New Ebenezer Retreat and Conference Center** (2887 Ebenezer Rd., 912/754-9242, www.new ebenezer.org). Built in 1977, the Retreat provides acres of calm surroundings, lodging, and meals in an ecumenical Christian setting.

Scenic, blackwater **Ebenezer Creek** is best experienced by putting in at the private Ebenezer Landing ($5).

To get to New Ebenezer, take Exit 109 off I-95. Go north on GA 21 to Rincon, Georgia, then east on GA 275 (Ebenezer Road).

The above-mentioned New Ebenezer Retreat and Conference Center offers a range of very reasonably priced lodgings, most including meals, in a beautiful setting. The extremely fast-growing town of Rincon, through which you will most likely drive on your way to New Ebenezer, offers an assortment of the usual chain food and lodging establishments.

WASSAW ISLAND NATIONAL WILDLIFE REFUGE

Totally unique in that it's the only Georgia barrier island never cleared for agriculture or development, the 10,000-acre Wassaw Island National Wildlife Refuge (www.fws.gov/wassaw) is accessible only by boat. There are striking, driftwood-strewn beaches, while the interior of the island has some beautiful old-growth stands of longleaf pine and live oak.

Wassaw is a veritable paradise for nature-lovers and bird-watchers, with migratory activity in the spring and fall, waterfowl in abundance in the summer, and manatee and loggerhead turtle activity (about 10 percent of Georgia's transient loggerhead population makes use of Wassaw for nesting). There are also about 20 miles of trails and a decaying Spanish-American War–era battery, Fort Morgan, on the north end. National Wildlife Refuge Week is celebrated in October.

Because of its comparatively young status—it was formed only about 1,600 years ago—Wassaw also has some unique geographical features. You can still make out the parallel ridge features, vestiges of successive ancient shorelines. A central ridge forms the backbone of the island, reaching an amazing (for this area) elevation of 45 feet above sea level at the south end.

Native Americans first settled the island, whose name comes from an ancient word for "sassafras," which was found in abundance there. During the Civil War, both Confederate and Union troops occupied the island successively. In 1866 the wealthy New England businessman George Parsons bought the island, which stayed in that family's hands until it was sold to the Nature Conservancy in 1969 for $1 million. The Conservancy in turn sold Wassaw to the U.S. government for $1 to be managed as a wildlife refuge.

It's easiest to get to Wassaw Island from Savannah. Charters and schedule trips are available from **Captain Walt's Charters** (Thunderbolt Marina, 912/507-3811), the **Bull River Marina** (8005 E. Hwy. 80, 912/897-7300), **Delegal Marina** (912/598-0023), **Capt. Joe Dobbs** (912/598-0090), and **Isle of Hope Marina** (912/354-8187). Most docking is either at the beaches on the north and south ends or in Wassaw Creek, where the Fish and Wildlife Service dock is also located (temporary mooring only).

There's no camping allowed on Wassaw Island; it's for day use only.

OSSABAW ISLAND

Owned and operated by Georgia as a heritage and wildlife preserve, the island was a gift to

NEW EBENEZER AND THE SALZBURGERS

Perhaps the most unsung chapter in Europe's great spiritual diaspora of the 1700s, the Salzburgers of New Ebenezer – a thrifty, peaceful, and hard-working people – were Georgia's first religious refugees and perhaps the most progressive as well.

The year after Oglethorpe's arrival, a contingent of devout Lutherans from Salzburg in present-day Austria arrived after being expelled from their home country for their beliefs. Oglethorpe, mindful of Georgia's mission to provide sanctuary for persecuted Protestants and also wishing a military buffer to the west, eagerly welcomed them.

Given land about 25 miles west of Savannah, the Salzburgers named their first settlement Ebenezer ("stone of help" in Hebrew). Disease prompted them to move the site to better land nearer to the river and call it – in pragmatic Germanic style – New Ebenezer, and so it remains to this day.

Because they continued to speak German instead of English, the upriver colony maintained its isolation. Still, the Salzburgers were among Oglethorpe's most ardent and loyal supporters. Their pastor and de facto political leader Johann Martin Boltzius, seeking to build an enlightened agrarian utopia of small farmers, was an outspoken foe of slavery and the exploitative plantation system of agriculture.

His system largely worked: The fragile silk industry thrived in New Ebenezer where it had failed miserably in Savannah, and the nation's first rice mill was built here.

However, don't get the idea that the Salzburgers were all work and no play. They enjoyed their beer, so much so that Oglethorpe was forced to send regular shipments, rationalizing that "cheap beer is the only means to keep rum out."

For 10 years, Georgia hosted another progressive Lutheran sect, the Moravians, who John Wesley called the only genuine Christians he'd ever met. Despite their professed pacifism, however, they had to leave New Ebenezer because they didn't get along with the Salzburgers and their communal living arrangements led to internal discord.

The Trustees' turnover of Georgia back to the crown in 1750 signaled the final victory of pro-slavery forces – so much so that even Pastor Boltzius acquired a couple of slaves as domestic servants. New Ebenezer's influence began a decline that rapidly accelerated when British forces pillaged much of the town in the Revolution, even burning pews and Bibles.

Fifty years later nothing at all remained except the old Jerusalem Church, now the Jerusalem Evangelical Lutheran Church. Built in 1769, it still stands today and hosts regular worship services. Right around the corner is the New Ebenezer Retreat nestled along the banks of the Savannah, providing an ecumenical meeting and natural healing space for those of all faiths.

Though New Ebenezer's often called a "ghost town," this is a misnomer. Extensive archaeological work continues in the area, and the Georgia Salzburger Society works hard to maintain several historic buildings and keep the legacy alive through special events.

the state from Eleanor Torrey-West and family in 1978, who still retain some property on the island. All public use of the island is managed by the **Ossabaw Island Foundation** (www .ossabawisland.org).

The 12,000-acre island is much older than Wassaw Island to its north, and so has traces of human habitation back to 2000 B.C. The island's name comes from an old Muskogean word referring to yaupon holly, found in abundance on the island and used by Native Americans in purification rituals to induce vomiting. Wading birds and predators such as bald eagles make their homes on the island, as do feral horses and a transient population of loggerhead turtles, who lay eggs in the dunes during the summer. There are several tabby ruins on the island, along with many miles of walking trails.

Unlike the much-younger Wassaw, Ossabaw Island was not only timbered extensively but hosted several rice and cotton plantations, particularly on the north end. The first property transfer in Georgia involved Ossabaw, St. Catherine's, and Sapelo Islands, which were ceded to the Yamacraws in exchange for the English getting the coastal region. The Yamacraws then granted those islands to Mary Musgrove, who began the modern era on the island by planting and introducing livestock.

Descendants of the island's slaves moved to the Savannah area after the Civil War, founding the community of Pin Point. Similarly to Jekyll Island to the south, Ossabaw was a hunting preserve for wealthy families in the Roaring Twenties. Even today hunting is an important activity on the island, with lotteries choosing who gets a chance to pursue its overly large populations of deer and wild hog, the latter of which are descended from pigs brought by the Spanish.

Now reserved exclusively for educational and scientific purposes, the island is accessible only by boat. Georgia law provides public access to all beaches up to the high-tide mark—which simply means that the public can ride out to Ossabaw and go on the beach for day-use, but any travel to the interior is restricted and you must have permission first. Contact the Ossabaw Island Foundation at info@ ossabawisland.org for information. For day trips, call any of the numbers for tour operators listed under *Wassaw Island*.

THE GOLDEN ISLES

More than any other area in the Charleston and Savannah region, the Georgia coast retains a timeless mystique evocative of a time before the coming of Europeans, even of humankind itself. Often called the Golden Isles because of the play of the afternoon sun on the vistas of marsh grass, its other nickname, "the Debatable Land," is a nod to its centuries-long role as a constantly shifting battleground of European powers.

Though on the map it looks relatively short, Georgia's coastline comprises the longest contiguous salt marsh environment in the world—a third of America's remaining salt marsh—and is one of the planet's greatest estuaries. Abundant with wildlife, vibrant with exotic, earthy aromas, constantly refreshed by a steady, salty sea breeze, it's a place with no real match anywhere else.

Filled with rich sediments from rivers far upstream and replenished with nutrients from the twice-daily ocean tide, Georgia's marshes from the mainland to the barrier islands are an amazing engine of natural production. Producing more food energy than any estuary on the East Coast, each acre of marsh produces about 20 tons of biomass—four times more productive than an acre of corn.

Ancient Native Americans held the area in special regard, intoxicated not only by the easy sustenance it offered but its spiritual solace. Their shell middens, many still in existence, are not only a sign of a well-fed people, but one thankful for nature's bounty.

Avaricious for gold as they were, the Spanish also admired the almost monastic enchantment of Georgia's coast, choosing it as the site

HIGHLIGHTS

◖ **Historic District:** A charming, pedestrian-friendly area of restored buildings, art galleries, and shrimp boats in the heart of Brunswick (page 277).

◖ **Jekyll Island Historic District:** Relax and soak in the salty breeze at this one-time playground of the world's richest people (page 287).

◖ **The Village:** The center of social life on St. Simons Island has shops, restaurants, a pier, and a beachside playground (page 296).

◖ **Fort Frederica National Monument:** An excellently preserved tabby fortress from the first days of English settlement in Georgia (page 297).

◖ **Harris Neck National Wildlife Refuge:** This former wartime airfield is now one of the East Coast's best birding locations (page 305).

◖ **Cumberland Island National Seashore:** Wild horses – such as the ones that live here – might not be able to drag you off of this evocative, undeveloped island paradise (page 312).

◖ **Okefenokee National Wildlife Refuge:** More than just a swamp, the Okefenokee is a natural wonderland that takes you back into the mists of prehistory (page 315).

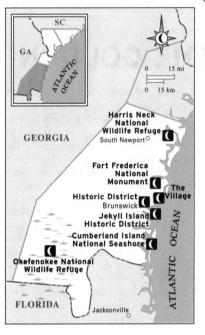

LOOK FOR ◖ TO FIND RECOMMENDED SIGHTS, ACTIVITIES, DINING, AND LODGING.

of their first colony in North America. Their subsequent chain of Roman Catholic missions are now long gone, but certainly testified to their own quest here.

While the American tycoons who used these barrier islands as personal playgrounds had an avarice of their own, we must give credit where it's due: Their self-interest kept these places largely untouched by the kind of development that has plagued many of South Carolina's barrier islands to the north.

Though isolated even today, the Golden Isles played an irreplaceable role in the defense of the young United States. It was here where massive live oaks were forested and used in the construction of the bulked-up, super-fast frigates of the fledgling U.S. Navy. The USS *Constitution* got its nickname, "Old Ironsides," from the strength of these pieces of Georgia oak, so resilient as to literally repel British cannonballs during the War of 1812.

Though the South Carolina Sea Islands are generally seen as the center of Gullah culture, the African American communities of the Golden Isles, Georgia's Sea Islands, also boast a long and fascinating history of survival, resourcefulness, and proud cultural integrity carried on to this day.

HISTORY

For over 5,000 years, the Golden Isles of what would become Georgia were an abundant

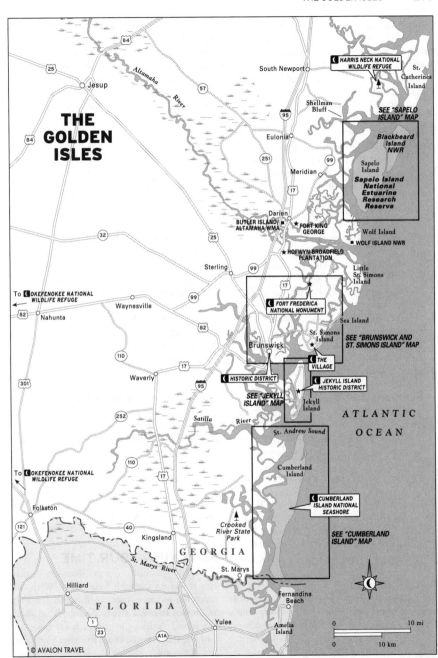

THE GOLDEN ISLES

THE GOLDEN ISLES

HARRIS NECK NATIONAL WILDLIFE REFUGE

St. Catherines Island

South Newport

Shellman Bluff

SEE "SAPELO ISLAND" MAP

Jesup

Eulonia

Blackbeard Island NWR

Meridian

Sapelo Island

Sapelo Island National Estuarine Research Reserve

Darien

BUTLER ISLAND/ ALTAMAHA WMA

FORT KING GEORGE

Wolf Island

WOLF ISLAND NWR

HOFWYN-BROADFIELD PLANTATION

Sterling

Little St. Simons Island

To OKEFENOKEE NATIONAL WILDLIFE REFUGE

Waynesville

FORT FREDERICA NATIONAL MONUMENT

Nahunta

Sea Island

St. Simons Island

SEE "BRUNSWICK AND ST. SIMONS ISLAND" MAP

Brunswick

THE VILLAGE

Waverly

HISTORIC DISTRICT

JEKYLL ISLAND HISTORIC DISTRICT

SEE "JEKYLL ISLAND" MAP

Jekyll Island

ATLANTIC OCEAN

Satilla River

St. Andrew Sound

To OKEFENOKEE NATIONAL WILDLIFE REFUGE

Cumberland Island

CUMBERLAND ISLAND NATIONAL SEASHORE

Folkston

Crooked River State Park

SEE "CUMBERLAND ISLAND" MAP

Kingsland

GEORGIA

St. Marys River

St. Marys

Hilliard

Fernandina Beach

FLORIDA

Yulee

Amelia Island

THE GOLDEN ISLES

Altamaha River

0   10 mi
0   10 km

© AVALON TRAVEL

food and game source for Native Americans. In those days long before erosion and channel dredging had taken their toll, each barrier island was an easy canoe ride away from the next one—a sort of early Intracoastal Waterway—and there was bounty for everyone.

But in 1526 all that changed when the Golden Isles became the site of the first European settlement in America, the fabled San Miguel de Guadalpe, founded nearly a century before the first English settlements in Virginia. Historians remain unsure where expedition leader Lucas de Allyon actually set up camp with his 600 colonists and slaves, but recent research breakthroughs have put it somewhere around St. Catherine's Sound.

Though San Miguel disintegrated within a couple of months, it set the stage for a lengthy Spanish presence on the Georgia coast that culminated in the mission period of 1580–1684. Working with the coastal chiefdoms of Guale and Mocama, almost all of Georgia's barrier islands and many interior spots hosted Catholic missions, each with an accompanying contingent of Spanish regulars.

The missions began retreating with the English incursion into the American Southeast in the 1600s, and the coast was largely free of European presence until an early English outpost, Fort King George near modern-day Darien, Georgia, was established decades later in 1721. Fetid, isolated, and hard to provision, the small fort was abandoned seven years later.

The next English project was Fort Frederica on St. Simons Island, commissioned by General James Edward Oglethorpe following his establishment of Savannah to the north. Oglethorpe's settlement of Brunswick and Jekyll Island came soon afterward. With the final vanquishing of the Spanish at the Battle of Bloody Marsh near Fort Frederica, the Georgia coast became an exclusively British-dominated area. It quickly emulated the profitable rice-based plantation culture of the South Carolina Lowcountry, and indeed many notable Carolina planters expanded their holdings with marshland on the Georgia coast.

Though comparatively little fighting took place this far south, the American Revolution would find an affluent class of local planters energetically engaged in the cause of independence. The area's seaports hosted a steady stream of agricultural goods and naval stores for domestic and international markets.

The southern reaches of Sherman's March to the Sea came down as far as Darien, a once-vital trading port which was burned to the ground by Union troops. With slavery gone and the plantation system in disarray, the coast's African American population was largely left to its own devices. Though the famous "40 Acres and a Mule" land and wealth redistribution plan for freed slaves was not to see fruition, the black population of Georgia's Sea Islands, like that of South Carolina's, developed an inward-looking culture that persists to this day. The generic term for this culture is Gullah, but in Georgia you'll also hear it referred to as Geechee, local dialect for the nearby Ogeechee River.

As with much of the South after the war, business carried on much as before, with the area becoming a center of lumber, the turpentine trade, and an increasing emphasis on fishing and shrimping. But by the start of the 20th century, the Golden Isles had become firmly established as a playground for the rich, who hunted and dined on the sumptuous grounds of exclusive retreats such as the Jekyll Island Club.

As elsewhere, World War II brought new economic growth in the form of military bases, even as German U-boats ranged off the coast. Today the federal presence is most notable in the massive Trident submarine base at Kings Bay toward the Florida border.

PLANNING YOUR TIME

Generally speaking, the peak season in this area is March through Labor Day. With the exception of some resort accommodations on St. Simons Island, Little St. Simons Island, and Sea Island, lodging is generally far more affordable than up the coast in either Savannah or Charleston.

Though many travelers take I-95 south from Savannah to the Golden Isles, U.S. 17 roughly parallels the interstate—in some cases so closely that cars on both roads can see each other—and is a far more scenic and enriching drive for those with a little extra time to spend. Indeed, U.S. 17 is an intrinsic part of the life and lore of the region and you are likely to spend a fair amount of time on it regardless.

Geographically, Brunswick is similar to Charleston in that it lies on a peninsula situated roughly north/south. And like Charleston, it's separated from the Atlantic by barrier islands, in Brunswick's case St. Simons Island and Jekyll Island. Once you get within city limits, however, Brunswick has more in common with Savannah due to its Oglethorpe-designed grid layout.

Brunswick itself can easily be fully experienced in a single afternoon. But really—as its nickname "Gateway to the Golden Isles" indicates—Brunswick's main role is as an economic and governmental center for Glynn County, to which Jekyll Island and St. Simons Island, the real attractions in this area, belong.

Both Jekyll Island and St. Simons Island are well worth visiting, and have their own separate pleasures—Jekyll more contemplative, St. Simons more upscale. Give a full day to Jekyll so you can take full advantage of its relaxing, open feel. A half-day can suffice for St. Simons because most of its attractions are clustered in the Village area near the pier, and there's little beach recreation to speak of.

Getting to the undeveloped barrier islands, Sapelo and Cumberland, takes planning in advance because there is no bridge to either. Both require a ferry booking and a hence more substantial commitment of time. There are no real stores and few facilities on these islands, so pack along whatever you think you'll need, whether it be food, water, medicine, suntan lotion, insect repellant, or otherwise.

Sapelo Island is limited to day use unless you have prior reservations, with the town of Darien in McIntosh County as your gateway. The same is true for Cumberland Island National Seashore, with the town of St. Marys in Camden County as your gateway.

Brunswick and Glynn County

Consider Brunswick sort of a junior Savannah, sharing with that city twice its size to the north a heavily English flavor, great manners, a city plan with squares courtesy of General James Oglethorpe, a thriving but environmentally intrusive seaport, and a busy shrimping fleet.

While Brunswick never became the dominant commercial center, à la Savannah, that it was envisioned to be, it has followed the Savannah model in modern times, both in terms of downtown revitalization and an increasing emphasis on port activity. Sadly, unlike Savannah, Brunswick has not seen fit to preserve the integrity of its six existing squares, all but one of which (Hanover Square) have been bisected by streets and/or built on.

Though the first real English-speaking settler of the area, Mark Carr, began cultivating

land near Brunswick in 1738, the city wasn't laid out until 1771, in a grid design similar to Savannah's. Originally comprising nearly 400 acres, Brunswick was named for Braunschweig, the seat of the House of Hanover in Germany and also for the Duke of Brunswick, a brother of King George III.

The Brunswick area hosted a number of profitable plantations and a burgeoning lumber industry, but a series of financial panics in the late 1830s hit particularly hard. When the Civil War started, most white citizens fled to nearby Waynesville, Georgia, and wharves and key buildings were burned to keep them out of Union hands.

Brunswick's longstanding status as "Gateway to the Golden Isles" happened in the 1880s with the increasing popularity of nearby Jekyll Island

THE GOLDEN ISLES

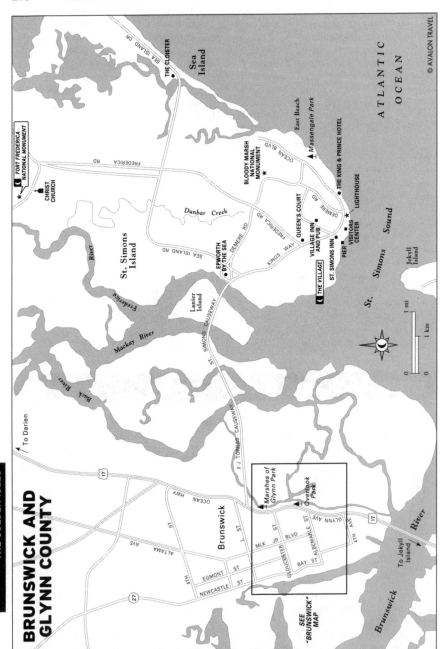

BRUNSWICK AND GLYNN COUNTY

© AVALON TRAVEL

as a millionaires' getaway. Two terrible hurricanes, one in 1893 and another in 1898, put the city underwater, but it was quickly rebuilt.

Brunswick saw a boom in population during World War II as a home of wartime industry such as the J. A. Jones Construction Company, which in a two-year span built 99 massive Liberty ships and at its peak employed 16,000 workers (they managed to build seven ships in a single month in 1944).

Since the war, the shrimping industry has played a big role in Brunswick's economy, so much so that it calls itself the "Shrimp Capital of the World." But lately the local shrimping industry is in steep decline, both from depleted coastal stocks and increased competition from Asian shrimp farms.

SIGHTS
◖ Historic District

Technically Brunswick has an "Old Town" district on the National Register of Historic Places as well as an adjacent district called "Historic Brunswick" centering on the storefronts of Newcastle Street. Since it's all pretty close together, for our purposes here we'll consider it all one nice package.

the historic Ritz Theatre in Brunswick

© JIM MOREKIS

Unlike Savannah, which renamed many of its streets in a fit of patriotism after the American Revolution, Brunswick's streets bear their original Anglophilic names, like Gloucester, Albemarle, and Norwich. You'd be forgiven for thinking that Brunswick's Union Street is a post–Civil War statement of national unity, but the name actually commemorates the union of Scotland and England in 1707!

Though its layout mimics Savannah's, Brunswick's downtown assortment of low, brick, Main Street America–style buildings actually gives it a feel more like Athens or Macon, Georgia, than Savannah. Most of the visitor-friendly activity centers on **Newcastle Street,** where you'll find the bulk of the galleries, shops, and restored buildings. Adjacent in the more historic areas are some nice residential homes.

The new pride of downtown is **Old City Hall** (1212 Newcastle St.), an amazing circa 1889

Richardsonian Romanesque edifice designed by noted regional architect Alfred Eichberg, who also planned many similarly imposing buildings in Savannah. City Hall reopened in 2004 after extensive renovations, bringing back to life its great vintage fireplaces and refitting its original gaslight fixtures.

Another active restored building is the charming **Ritz Theatre** (1530 Newcastle St., 912/262-6934, www.goldenislesarts.org), built in 1898 to house the Grand Opera House and the offices of the Brunswick and Birmingham Railroad. This ornate three-story Victorian transitioned with the times, becoming a vaudeville venue, then a movie house. Under the management of the Golden Isles Arts and Humanities Association since 1989, the Ritz now hosts performances, studios, an art gallery, and classes.

The privately owned **Mahoney-McGarvey House** (1705 Reynolds St.) is considered the

THE GOLDEN ISLES

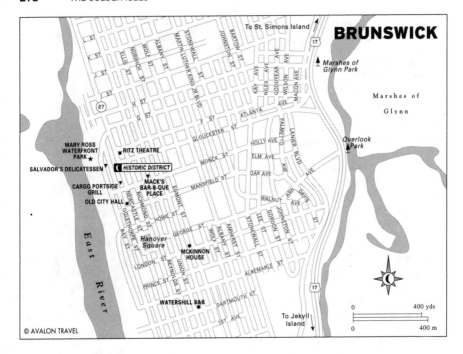

finest example of "carpenter Gothic" architecture in Georgia.

Mary Ross Waterfront Park

This downtown gathering place at Bay and Gloucester Streets also has economic importance as a center of local economic activity—for it's here where Brunswick's shrimp fleet is moored and the town's large port facilities begin. Unfortunately, nearby is a huge factory, dispensing its unpleasant odor over the waterfront 24/7.

In 1989 the park was dedicated to Mary Ross, member of a longtime Brunswick shrimping family and author of the popular Georgia history book *The Debatable Land.* While still a great read, sadly Ms. Ross was wrong when she wrote that the tabby ruins in the area were of Spanish origin. Devastated by the discovery that they actually dated from later and were of English construction, she vowed never to publish another word again.

At the entrance to the park is a huge and well-done model of a Liberty ship, like the thousands that were built in Brunswick during World War II.

Lover's Oak

At the intersection of Prince and Albany Streets, you'll find the Lover's Oak, a nearly 1,000-year-old tree. Local lore tells us that it's been a secret meeting place for young lovers for centuries (though one does wonder how much of a "secret" it actually could have been). It's about 13 feet in diameter and has 10 sprawling limbs.

Marshes of Glynn

Amid the light industrial sprawl of this area of the Golden Isles Parkway is the interesting little **Overlook Park,** just south of the visitors center on U.S. 17—a good, if loud, place for a picnic. From the park's picnic grounds or overlook you can see the fabled Marshes of Glynn

Lanier Oak near the fabled Marshes of Glynn

© JIM MOREKIS

which inspired Georgia poet Sidney Lanier to write his famous poem of the same title under the **Lanier Oak,** which is a little farther up the road in the median.

Hofwyl-Broadfield Plantation

South Carolina doesn't own the patent on well-preserved old rice plantations, as the Hofwyl-Broadfield Plantation (5556 Hwy. 17, 912/264-7333, www.gastateparks.org, Tues.–Sat. 9 A.M.–5 P.M., Sun. 2–5:30 P.M., last main house tour 4:45 P.M., $5), a short drive north of Brunswick, proves. With its old paddies along the gorgeous and relatively undeveloped Altamaha River estuary, the plantation's main home is an antebellum wonder, with an expansive porch and a nice house museum inside, with silver, a rice plantation model, and a slide show. There's also a nice nature trail.

William Brailsford of Charleston finished the plantation in 1807, which soon passed into the hands of the Troup family, who expanded the holdings to over 7,000 acres. Rice finally became financially unfeasible in the early 20th

century, and the plantation turned to dairy farming, a pursuit that lasted until World War II. Ophelia Troup Dent would finally will the site to the state of Georgia in 1973.

The best way to get there is by taking U.S. 17 north out of Brunswick until you see the signs; the plantation entrance is on your right.

ENTERTAINMENT AND EVENTS

The **Golden Isles Arts and Humanities Association** (1530 Newcastle St., 912/262-6934, www.goldenislesarts.org) is an umbrella organization for many arts activities in the Brunswick, Jekyll, and St. Simons area. They also manage the historic **Ritz Theatre** (1530 Newcastle St., 912/262-6934,) in downtown Brunswick, which offers a yearly performance season that's worth checking out if you have a free weekend night.

Nightlife

Brunswick's a conservative place with little bar scene to speak of. But a few miles

THE GOLDEN ISLES

IN THE FOOTSTEPS OF BARTRAM

The West has its stirring tale of Lewis and Clark, but the Southeast has its own fascinating – if somewhat less dramatic – tale of discovery, in the odyssey of William Bartram.

In March 1733, the 36-year-old Bartram – son of royal botanist John Bartram and definitely a chip off the old block – arrived in Savannah to begin what would become a four-year journey through eight Southern states and colonies. As Lewis and Clark would do in the following century, Bartram not only exhaustively documented his encounters with nature and with Native Americans, he made discoveries whose impact has stayed with us to this day.

Young "Willie," born near Philadelphia in 1739, had a talent for drawing and for plants, which of course thrilled his father, who wrote to a friend that "Botany and drawing is his darling delight." A failure at business, Bartram was happy to settle on a traveling lifestyle that mixed both his loves: art and flora. After accompanying his father on several early trips, Bartram set out on his own at the request of an old friend of his father's in England, Dr. John Fothergill, who paid Bartram 50 pounds per year plus expenses to send back specimens and drawings.

Though Bartram's quest would eventually move farther inland and encompass much of the modern American South, most of the first year was spent in coastal Georgia. After arriving in Savannah he moved southward, roughly paralleling modern US 17, to the now-dead town of Sunbury, through Midway and on to Darien, where he stayed at the plantation of Lachlan McIntosh on the great Altamaha River, which inspired Bartram to some of his most beautiful writing. Bartram also journeyed to Sapelo Island, Brunswick, St. Marys, and even into the great Okefenokee Swamp.

Using Savannah and Charleston as bases, Bartram mostly traveled alone, either by horse, by boat, or on foot. Word of his trip preceded him, and he was usually greeted warmly by local traders and Indian chiefs (except for one encounter with a hostile tribesman near the St. Marys River). In many places, he was the first white man seen since De Soto and the Spanish.

offshore is quite a different story, when the **Emerald Princess Dinner and Casino Cruises** (Gisco Point, 912/265-3558, www .emeraldprincesscasino.com, Mon.–Thurs. 7 P.M.–midnight, Fri.–Sat. 11 A.M.–4 P.M. and 7 P.M.–1 A.M., Sun. 1–6 P.M., $10) is operating. This is the classic gambling/party boat experience, with the action starting when the *Emerald Princess* slips into international waters and out of domestic gambling regulations. Ten bucks for the cruise gets you a light dinner. Drinks and chips, of course, are on you. No one under 21 allowed, and minimum and maximum bets vary by table. Reservations required.

To get to the dock, take U.S. 17 over the massive Sidney Lanier Bridge. Take a left onto the Jekyll Island Causeway and then an immediate left onto Gisco Point Drive. Follow signs into the parking lot.

Performing Arts

Though based in St. Simons Island, the **Coastal Symphony of Georgia** (912/634-2006, www.coastalsymphonyofgeorgia.org), under the baton of Vernon Humbert, plays many concerts in Brunswick during its season at different venues. Check the website for details.

The **Brunswick Community Concert Association** (912/638-5616, www.brunswick communityconcert.org, $25 adults, $5 students) brings an eclectic variety of high-quality national and regional musical acts to various venues around town.

The **Island Players** (1409 Newcastle St., 912/554-2034, www.theislandplayers.com, $20 adults, $5 students) bring some surprisingly hip comedies and dramas to their new space in the heart of downtown Brunswick.

The **C.A.P.E. Theater** (600 Mansfield St.,

His epic journey ended in late 1776, when Bartram gazed on his beloved Altamaha for the last time. Heading north and crossing the Savannah River south of Ebenezer, he proceeded to Charleston and from there to his hometown of Philadelphia – where he would remain for the rest of his days.

At its publication, his 1791 chronicle, *Travels Through North and South Carolina, Georgia, East and West Florida*, was hailed as "the most astounding verbal artifact of the early republic." In that unassuming yet timeless work, Bartram cemented his reputation as America's first native-born naturalist and practically invented the modern travelogue.

Thanks to the establishment of the William Bartram Trail in 1976, you can walk in his footsteps – or close to them, anyway, since historians are not sure of his route. The trail uses a rather liberal interpretation, including memorials, trails, and gardens, but many specific "heritage sites" in coastal Georgia have their own markers, as follows:

- River and Barnard Streets in Savannah to mark his disembarkation and the beginning of his trek

- LeConte-Woodmanston Plantation in Liberty County (Barrington Ferry Road south of Sandy Run Road near Riceborough)

- A mile and half south of the South Newport River off Highway 17

- St. Simon's Island on Frederica Road near the Fort Frederica entrance

- Off GA 275 at Old Ebenezer-Cemetery in Effingham County

Among the indigenous species Bartram was the first to notate are:

- Fraser Magnolia

- Gopher Tortoise

- Florida Sandhill Crane

- Flame Azalea

- Oakleaf Hydrangea

912/996-7740, www.capetheater.org, $10 adult, $5 children), short for Craft, Appreciation, Performance, and Education, is a community group that performs a mix of classics and musicals, generally in the First Presbyterian Church at Union and George Streets or on the second floor of Old City Hall for dinner theater. No reservations necessary unless you're attending a dinner theater show ($30 adults, $15 students).

The town's main dance group is **Invisions Dance Company,** which performs out of **Studio South** (1307 Grant St., 912/265-3255, www.studiosouthga.com).

Festivals and Events

Each Mother's Day at noon, parishioners of the local St. Francis Xavier Church hold the **Our Lady of Fatima Processional and Blessing of the Fleet** (www.brunswick.net), begun in 1938 by the local Portuguese fishing community. After the procession, at about 3 P.M. at Mary Ross Waterfront Park, comes the actual blessing of the shrimp-boat fleet.

Each Independence Day brings an **Old Fashioned Fourth of July Celebration** (www.brunswick.net) featuring games, free watermelon, and fireworks at Mary Ross Waterfront Park. Festivities start at about 7 P.M., with fireworks at about 9 P.M.

Foodies will enjoy the **Brunswick Stewbilee** ($9 adults, $4 children) the second Saturday in October 11:30 A.M.–3 P.M. Pro and amateur chefs match skills in creating the local signature dish and for the title of "Brunswick Stewmaster." There are also car shows, contests, displays, and much live music.

A popular ongoing event is the **Brunswick Farmer's Market,** happening every Tuesday, Thursday, and Saturday 7 A.M.–5 P.M. at Mary

THE GOLDEN ISLES

Ross Waterfront Park. Enjoy farm-fresh produce and assorted knick-knacks.

SHOPPING

Right in the heart of the bustle on Newcastle is a good indie bookstore, **Hattie's Books** (1531 Newcastle St., 912/554-8677, www.hattiesbooks .net, Mon–Fri. 10 A.M.–5:30 P.M., Sat. 10 A.M.–4 P.M.). Not only do they have a good selection of local and regional authors, but you can get a good cup of coffee, too.

Like Beaufort, South Carolina, Brunswick has made the art gallery a central component of its downtown revitalization, with nearly all of them on Newcastle Street.

Art Downtown (1422 Newcastle St., 912/ 262-0628, Tues.–Fri. 11 A.M.–6 P.M., Sat. 10 A.M.–4 P.M.) has an eclectic, funky mix of painting, sculpture, and pottery. Next door is **Artsy Studio** (1426 Newcastle St., 912/267-4738, Tues.–Sat. 10 A.M.–6 P.M.), with contemporary art somewhat on the traditional side but with more cutting-edge photography.

On the next block you'll find the eclectic **Kazuma Gallery** (1523 Newcastle St.,

912/279-0023, Mon–Fri. 10 A.M.–5:30 P.M., Sat. 10 A.M.–2 P.M.) as well as the **Ritz Theatre** (1530 Newcastle St., 912/262-6934, Tues.–Fri. 9 A.M.–5 P.M., Sat. 10 A.M.–2 P.M.), which has its own art gallery inside. Farther down is **The Gallery on Newcastle Street** (1626 Newcastle St., 912/554-0056, Thurs.–Sat. 11 A.M.–5 P.M.), showcasing the original oils of owner Janet Powers.

SPORTS AND RECREATION
Hiking, Biking, and Bird-Watching

As one of the Colonial Coast Birding Trail sites, **Hofwyl-Broadfield Plantation** (5556 Hwy. 17, 912/264-7333, www.gastateparks .org, Tues.–Sat. 9 A.M.–5 P.M., Sun. 2–5:30 P.M.) offers a great nature trail along the marsh. Clapper rails, marsh wrens, and a wide variety of warblers come through the site regularly.

Birders and hikers will also enjoy the **Earth Day Nature Trail** (One Conservation Wy., 912/264-7218), a self-guided, fully accessible walk where you can see such comparative rarities as the magnificent wood stork and

© JIM MOREKIS

Newcastle Street is the center of Brunswick social life and shopping.

other indigenous and migratory waterfowl. There are observation towers and binoculars available for checkout. To get there take U.S. 17 south through Brunswick. Just north of the big Sidney Lanier Bridge, turn left on Conservation Way and you'll see signage and come to a parking lot.

Just across the Brunswick River from town is **Blythe Island Regional Park** (6616 Blythe Island Hwy., 912/261-3805), an 1,100-acre public park with a campground, picnic area, and boat landing. The views are great, and it's big enough to do some decent biking and hiking. The best way there is to get back on I-95 and head south.

Another scenic park with a campground is **Altamaha Park of Glynn County** (1605 Altamaha Park Rd., 912/264-2342) northwest of Brunswick off U.S. 341, with 30 campsites and a boat ramp.

Golf

Compared to the more plentiful, high-dollar courses on the islands, golfing is reasonable in Brunswick. There are two main 18-hole public golf courses near the town: **Coastal Pines Golf Club** (1 Coastal Pines Circle, 912/261-0503, www.coastalpinesgolf.com, $47 green fees), open since 2001, and the older **Oak Grove Island Club** (126 Clipper Bay Rd., 800/780-8133, www.oakgroveisland golf.com, $49 green fees). (Green fees are averages and fluctuate with season and time.)

Kayaking and Boating

Most recreational adventurers in the area prefer to launch from St. Simons Island. The key public landing in Brunswick, however, is **Brunswick Landing Marina** (2429 Newcastle St., 912/262-9264). You can also put in at the public boat ramps at **Blythe Island Regional Park,** which is on the Brunswick River, or the **Altamaha Park of Glynn County** (1605 Altamaha Park Rd., 912/264-2342), on the Altamaha River slightly north.

For expert guided tours at a reasonable price, check out **South East Adventures** (1200 Glynn Ave./Hwy. 17, 912/265-5292, www

.southeastadventure.com), which has a dock right on the fabled "Marshes of Glynn."

ACCOMMODATIONS

In addition to the usual variety of chain hotels—most of which you should stay far away from—there are a some nice places in Brunswick to stay if you want to make it a base of operations, at very reasonable prices.

In the heart of Old Town in a gorgeous Victorian is the **McKinnon House** (1001 Egmont St., 912/261-9100, www.mckinnonhousebandb.com, $125), which had a cameo role in the film *Conrack*. Today this bed-and-breakfast is Jo Miller's labor of love, a three-suite affair with some plush interiors and an exterior that's one of Brunswick's most photographed spots.

Surprisingly affordable for its elegance, the **WatersHill Bed & Breakfast** (728 Union St., 912/264-4262, www.watershill .com, $100) serves a full breakfast and offers a choice of five themed suites, such as the French country Elliot Wynell Room or the large Mariana Mahlaney room way up in the restored attic.

If for some reason you'd rather opt for a standard chain place near the Interstate, your best bet is the **Holiday Inn Brunswick** (138 Glynco Pkwy., 877/477-5817, $100) off I-95 at Exit 38. It's a new facility with the latest amenities you'd expect in a big-box hotel, and there's a (pretty decent) restaurant attached—but no complimentary breakfast.

Without a doubt the most unique lodging in the area is the **Hostel in the Forest** (GA 82, 912/264-9738, $20, cash only), essentially a group of geodesic domes and whimsical treehouses a little ways off the highway. Formed over 30 years ago as an International Youth Hostel, the place initially gives off a hippie vibe, with an evening communal meal included in the price and a near-total ban on cell phones. But don't expect a wild time: No pets are allowed, the hostel discourages young children, and quiet time is strictly enforced at 11 P.M. It's an adventurous, peaceful, and very inexpensive place to stay, but be warned that there is no heating or cooling. To reach the hostel, take Exit 29 off I-95 and go west for two miles. Make a U-turn at the intersection at mile marker 11. Continue east on GA 82 for 0.5 mile. Look for a dirt road on the right with a gate and signage.

FOOD

For the most part, food comes in two flavors in Brunswick: barbecued and fried. A clear and notable exception is the relatively hip **(Cargo Portside Grill** (1423 Newcastle St., 912/267-7330, Tues.–Sat. 5:30–10 P.M., $20–30) in

the historic Elliot Building downtown. Chef Alix Kinagy draws in a respectable crowd of St. Simons residents over the bridge to sample his rack of lamb with a seared rosemary/garlic crust and sesame catfish.

The premiere barbecue in the Brunswick area is at the humble but nationally renowned **(Georgia Pig** (912/264-6664, Mon.–Thurs. 11 A.M.–7 P.M., Fri. and Sat. 11 A.M.–9 P.M., Sun. 11 A.M.–8 P.M., $6–10). Go over the South Brunswick River on I-95 and take Exit 29 onto U.S. 17 to find this out of the way, roadside classic in an unpretentious shack. It serves one of the

---

BRUNSWICK STEW

Of course, Virginians being Virginians, they'll insist that the distinctive Southern dish known as "Brunswick Stew" was named for Brunswick County, Virginia, in 1828, where a political rally featured stew made from squirrel meat. But all real Southern foodies know the dish is named for Brunswick, Georgia.

Hey, there's a plaque to prove it in downtown Brunswick – though it says the first pot was cooked on July 2, 1898, on St. Simons Island, not in Brunswick at all. However, I think we can all agree that "Brunswick Stew" rolls off the tongue much easier than "St. Simons Stew."

In any case, it seems likely that what we now know as Brunswick Stew is based on an old colonial recipe adapted from Native Americans that relied on the meat of small game – originally squirrel or rabbit but nowadays mostly chicken or pork – along with vegetables like corn, onions, and okra, simmered over an open fire. Today this tangy, thick, tomato-based delight is a typical accompaniment to barbecue along the Lowcountry and Georgia coasts, as well as a free-standing entrée on its own.

Done traditionally and correctly, a proper pot of Brunswick Stew is an involved kitchen project taking most of a day. But it's worth it! Here's a typical recipe from Glynn County, home of the famous Brunswick "Stewbilee" festival the second Saturday of October:

Sauce:
Melt ¼ cup butter over low heat, then add:

1 ¾ cups ketchup
¼ cup yellow mustard
¼ cup white vinegar
Blend until smooth, then add
½ tablespoon chopped garlic
1 teaspoon ground black pepper
½ teaspoon crushed red pepper
½ ounce Liquid Smoke
1 ounce Worcestershire sauce
1 ounce hot sauce
½ tablespoon fresh lemon juice
Blend until smooth, then add
¼ cup dark brown sugar
Stir constantly and simmer for 10 minutes, being careful not to boil. Set aside.

Stew:
Melt ¼ pound butter in a two-gallon pot, then add:
3 cups small diced potatoes
1 cup small diced onion
2 14.5-ounce cans chicken broth
1 pound baked chicken
8-10 ounces smoked pork
Bring to a boil, stirring until potatoes are near done, then add:
1 8.5-ounce can early peas
2 14.5-ounce cans stewed tomatoes
1 16-ounce can baby lima beans
¼ cup Liquid Smoke
1 14.5-ounce can creamed corn
Stir in sauce. Simmer slowly for two hours.
Makes one gallon of Brunswick Stew.

most sublime pulled-pork sandwiches in a tangy tomato-based sauce you'll encounter anywhere.

For good BBQ closer into town, try **Mack's Bar-Be-Que Place** (2809 Glynn Ave./U.S. 17, 912/264-0605, www.macksbbqplace.com, Mon.–Sat. 10:30 A.M.–9 P.M., $5–8), which also has an $8 "Country Buffet" Monday–Friday 11 A.M.–3 P.M.

Right off the riverfront you'll find a fun breakfast and lunch joint with early hours, **Salvador's Deli** (205 Gloucester St., 912/264-1543, Mon.–Fri. 6:30 A.M.–3 P.M., $5–10).

A nice and conveniently located place to get a good cup of coffee and a sweet treat downtown is **Daddy Cate's** (302 Gloucester St., 912/264-9363, Mon.–Fri. 7 A.M.–4:30 P.M., Sat. 8 A.M.–1:30 P.M.).

INFORMATION AND SERVICES

The **Brunswick/Golden Isles Visitor Center** (2000 Glynn Ave., 912/264-5337, daily 9 A.M.–5 P.M.) is at the intersection of U.S. 17 and the Torras Causeway to St. Simons Island.

It features the famous pot in which the first batch of Brunswick Stew was cooked over the bridge on St. Simons.

A downtown **information station** is in the Ritz Theatre (1530 Newcastle St., 912/262-6934, Tues.–Fri. 9 A.M.–5 P.M., Sat. 10 A.M.–2 P.M.).

The newspaper of record in town is the **Brunswick News** (www.thebrunswicknews .com).

The main **U.S. Postal Service office** in downtown Brunswick is at 805 Gloucester Street (912/280-1250).

GETTING THERE AND AROUND

Brunswick is directly off I-95. Take Exit 38 to the Golden Isles Parkway and take a right on U.S. 17. The quickest way to the historic district is to make a right onto Gloucester Street. Though plans and funding for a city-wide public transit system are pending, currently Brunswick has no public transportation to speak of.

Jekyll Island

Few places in the United States have as paradoxical a story as Jekyll Island. Once the playground of the world's richest people—whose indulgence allowed it to escape the overdevelopment that plagues nearby St. Simons—Jekyll then became a dedicated vacation area for Georgians of modest means, by order of the state legislature.

Today, it's somewhere in the middle—a great place for a relaxing, nature-oriented vacation, with some of the perks of luxury owing to its Gilded Age pedigree.

HISTORY

In prehistoric times, Jekyll was mainly a seasonal getaway for Native Americans. Indigenous tribes visited the area during the winter to enjoy its temperate weather and abundant shellfish. The Spanish also knew it

well, calling it *Isla de Las Ballenas* ("Island of the Whales") for the annual gathering of calving right whale families directly off the coast every winter—a mystical event that happens to this day.

After securing safe access to the island from the Creeks in 1733, Georgia's founder General James Oglethorpe gave the island its modern name, after his friend Sir Joseph Jekyll. The first English settler was Major William Horton in 1735, recipient of a land grant from the general, and the tabby ruins of one of Horton's homes remain today. A Frenchman, Christophe Du Bignon, purchased the island in 1800 and remained a leading figure.

Another mysterious event came in 1858, when Jekyll Island was the final port of entry for the infamous voyage of *The Wanderer,* the last American slave ship. After intercepting the ship and its contraband manifest of 409 African slaves—the importation of slaves having been banned in 1807—its owners and crew were put on trial in Savannah.

As a home away from home for America's richest industrialists in the late 1800s and early 1900s—such as J. P. Morgan, William Rockefeller, and William Vanderbilt—Jekyll Island was the unlikely seat of some of the most crucial events in modern American history. It was at the Jekyll Island Club that the Federal Reserve banking system was originated, in a secret convocation of investors and tycoons in 1910. Five years later, AT&T President Theodore Vail, on the grounds of the Club, would listen in on the first transcontinental phone call.

Jekyll's unspoiled beauty prompted the state legislature in 1947 to purchase the island and—ironically, considering the island's former history—declare it a totally accessible "playground" for Georgians of low to middle income (though a causeway wasn't completed until the mid-1950s). This stated public mission is why prices on Jekyll have stayed so low and development has stayed so well managed.

But a controversial redevelopment plan has been proposed that would introduce high-dollar resort-style development to parts of Jekyll for the first time since the days of J. P. Morgan and company. While the plan still guarantees that two-thirds of the island—currently administered on behalf of the state by the Jekyll Island Authority—will stay both undeveloped and publicly accessible, residents and conservationists alike worry about what the new development will mean for this magical barrier island known as "Georgia's Jewel."

ORIENTATION

You'll have to stop at the entrance gate and pay a $3 "parking fee" to gain access to this state-owned island. A friendly attendant will give you a map and newsletter and from there you're free to enjoy the whole island at your leisure.

As you dead-end into Beachview Drive, you're faced with a decision to turn either left or right. Most scenic and social activity is to

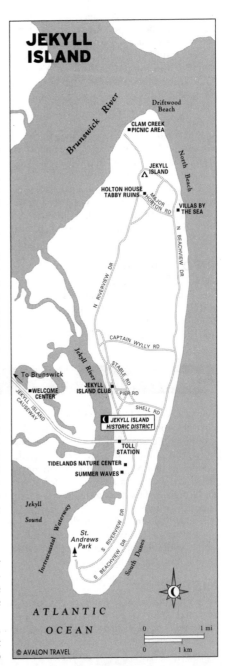

the north, with the left turn. For more peaceful beach-oriented activity with few services, turn right and head south. One historical reason for the lesser development at the south end is due to the fact that segregation laws were still in effect after the state's purchase of Jekyll in 1947. African American facilities were centered on the south end, while white activities went north.

SIGHTS
◖ Jekyll Island Historic District

A living link to one of the most glamorous eras of American history, the Jekyll Island Historic District is also one of the largest ongoing restoration projects in the southeastern United States. A visit to this 240-acre riverfront area is like stepping back in time to the Gilded Age, with croquet grounds, manicured gardens, and even ferry boats with names like the *Rockefeller* and the *J. P. Morgan.*

The Historic District essentially comprises the buildings and grounds of the old **Jekyll Island Club,** not only a full-service resort complex—consisting of the main building and several amazing "cottages" that are mansions in and of themselves—but a sort of living history exhibit chronicling that time when Jekyll was a gathering place for the world's richest and most influential people.

The Queen Anne–style main clubhouse, with its iconic turret, dates from 1886. But within a couple of years the club had already outgrown it, and the millionaires began building the ornate cottages on the grounds surrounding it. The Chicora cottage is gone, demolished after the supposedly accidental gunfire death of Edwin Gould in 1917, with only a hole in the ground remaining, but most of the others have been fully restored as lodgings. The most recent renovation was in 2000 for the most magnificent outbuilding, the 24-bedroom Crane Cottage, a Mediterranean villa that also hosts a fine restaurant.

The **Jekyll Island Museum** (100 Stable Rd., 912/635-4036, daily 9 A.M.–5 P.M., free), in the Historic District at the old Club stables, houses some good history exhibits. The

© JIM MOREKIS

the Jekyll Island Club and its croquet grounds

THE GOLDEN ISLES

JEKYLL ISLAND'S MILLIONAIRE'S CLUB

After the Civil War, as the Industrial Revolution gathered momentum seemingly everywhere but Georgia's Golden Isles, a couple of men decided to do something to break the foggy miasma of Reconstruction that had settled into the area, and make some money in the process.

In the late 1870s, John Eugene DuBignon and his brother-in-law Newton Finney came up with a plan to combine DuBignon's long family ties to Jekyll with Finney's extensive Wall Street connections in order to turn Jekyll into an exclusive winter hunting club. Their targeted clientele was a no-brainer: the newly minted mega-tycoons of America's Industrial Age.

Finney found 53 such elite millionaires willing to pony up to become charter members of the venture, dubbed the Jekyll Island Club. Among them were William Vanderbilt, J. P. Morgan, and Joseph Pulitzer. As part of the original business model, in 1886 Finney purchased the island from DuBignon for $125,000.

With the formal opening two years later began Jekyll Island's half-century as a premier playground for America's richest citizens, centered on the Victorian winter homes, called "cottages," built by each member and preserved today in the Historic District. While it was formed as a hunt club, the Jekyll Island Club welcomed the millionaires' families. In the 1920s, the focus began shifting to golf, and you can still play a portion of the historic course at the Club today.

By 1900, the Club's membership represented a sixth of the world's wealth. And the word "exclusive" has never been more appropriate: Non-members were not allowed to enjoy the facilities, regardless of social stature. Winston Churchill and even President McKinley were refused admission.

As the mega-rich are wont to do even today, these influential men often mixed business with pleasure. In 1910 secret meetings of the so-called "First Name Club" led to the development of the Aldrich Plan that laid the groundwork for the modern Federal Reserve System. Under assumed names, Senator Nelson Aldrich, Assistant Treasury Secretary A. Piatt Andrew, Banker's Trust Vice President Benjamin Strong, National City Bank President Frank Vanderlip, investment banker Paul Warburg, and J. P. Morgan partner Henry P. Davison came into the Club with the cover story of participating in a duck hunt.

Arriving by train at Brunswick, the stationmaster told them the cat was out of the bag and a gaggle of reporters had already gathered. But Davison took the stationmaster aside, saying, "Come out, old man, I will tell you a story." Returning a few minutes later, Davison told his colleagues, "That's all right. They won't give us away." What Davison's "story" was remains a mystery, but it must have been a pretty compelling one.

A few years later, AT&T president Theodore Vail, nursing a broken leg at his Mound Cottage on Jekyll, participated in the first transcontinental telephone call on January 25, 1915, between New York City, San Francisco, and the special line strung down the coast from New York and across Jekyll Sound to the Club grounds. Also on the line were the telephone's inventor Alexander Graham Bell, his assistant Thomas Watson, the mayors of New York and San Francisco, and President Woodrow Wilson himself.

The millionaires continued to frolic on Jekyll through the Great Depression, but worsening international economic conditions reduced membership, even though the cost of membership was lowered in 1933. The outbreak of World War II and the resulting drain of labor into the armed forces put a further cramp into the Club's workings, and it finally closed for good in 1942.

By the time prowling German U-boats began appearing off the Georgia coast, prompting island-wide blackouts, the Jekyll Island Club era already seemed like ancient history. The state would acquire the island after the war in 1947, turning the once-exclusive playground of millionaires into a playground for all the people.

Museum also provides a number of guided, themed tours (11 A.M., 1 P.M., 3 P.M., $16 adults, $8 for children 6–12) focusing on the Historic District, from the popular "Passport to the Century" (which includes entrance to two restored cottages) to "In the Service of Others" (focusing on the support staff of the golden age of the Jekyll Island Club). You can also purchase a guidebook for self-guided tours of the Historic District.

Georgia Sea Turtle Center

Within the grounds of the Historic District in a whimsically decorated building is the Georgia Sea Turtle Center (214 Stable Rd., 912/635-4444, www.georgiaseaturtlecenter .org, daily 10 A.M.–7 P.M., $6 adults, $4 children), which features interactive exhibits on these important marine creatures, for whom Jekyll Island is a major nesting ground. Helping to raise awareness about the need to protect the nesting areas of the big loggerheads that lay eggs on Jekyll each summer, the Sea Turtle Center also guides nighttime tours at 8:30 and 9:30 P.M. on the beach to explain about the animals and their habitat and hopefully to see some loggerheads in action. Walks begin in early June and end in August. These fill up fast, so make reservations in advance.

Driftwood Beach

Barrier islands like Jekyll are in a constant state of southward flux, as currents erode the north end and push sand down the beach to the south end. Hence the creation of Driftwood Beach, as the soil erodes from under the large trees, causing them to fall and settle into the sand. In addition to a naturalist's wonderland, it's also a starkly beautiful and strangely romantic spot.

The newsletter you get as you enter the island has a map with Driftwood Beach on it, but here's a tip: Drive north on Beachview until you see a pullover on your right immediately after the Villas By The Sea (there's no signage). Park and take the short trail through the maritime forest and you'll find yourself right there among the fallen trees and sand.

Horton House Tabby Ruins

Round the curve and go south on Riverview Drive, and you'll see the large frame of a two-story house on the left (east) side of the road. That is the ruins of the old Horton House, built by Jekyll's original English-speaking setter, William Horton. Horton's house has survived two wars, a couple of hurricanes, and a clumsy restoration in 1898 to its current state of preservation at the hands of the Jekyll Island Authority and various federal, state, and local partners.

His first house, also made of tabby, was burned by the Spanish during their retreat after losing the Battle of Bloody Marsh on nearby St. Simons Island. But the intrepid major rebuilt on the same spot in 1742, continuing to farm barley and indigo on the surrounding grounds as well as hosting Georgia's first brewery, ruins of which are nearby.

Frenchman Christophe Poulain Du Bignon would live in the Horton House for awhile after purchasing the island in the 1790s. Across the street from the house is the poignant little **Du Bignon Cemetery,** around which winds a nicely done pedestrian/bike path overlooking one of the most beautiful areas of marsh you'll see in all the Golden Isles.

ENTERTAINMENT AND EVENTS

There's no nightlife to speak of on Jekyll, it being intended for quiet, affordable daytime relaxation. The focus instead is on several annual events held at the **Jekyll Island Convention Center** (1 N. Beachview Dr., 912/635-3400), which as of this writing is imperiled by a development project.

In the beginning of the new year comes one of the area's most beloved and well-attended events, the **Jekyll Island Bluegrass Festival** (www.aandabluegrass.com). Many of the genre's biggest traditional names come to play at this casual, multi-day gathering. The focus here is on the music, not the trappings, so come prepared to enjoy wall-to-wall bluegrass, played by the best in the business. Keep in mind that during this weekend the island is awash in RVs from all over the country, so if you're camping you better make reservations.

The **Jekyll Island Beach Music Festival** (www.jekyllfest.com) in August seeks to perpetuate the favorite coastal tradition of beach music—think the Tams and the Drifters, not the Beach Boys or Jimmy Buffett—by bringing in the biggest names in that small but closely followed genre.

In September as the harvest comes in off the boats, the **Wild Georgia Shrimp and Grits Festival** (www.jekyllisland.com, free admission), seeks to promote the value of the Georgia shrimping industry by focusing on how good the little critters taste in various regional recipes.

SHOPPING

Nobody comes to Jekyll to shop. Other than a few schlocky spots clustered near the Convention Center as you first come on the island, shopping is limited to the cute, boutique **Historic District Shops,** housed in small, barn-like buildings off Stable Road in the Historic District right across the street from the History Museum. Shops include **Jekyll Island Trading Post** (912/635-2546), **Nature's Cottage** (912/635-3933), and **Santa's Christmas Shoppe** (912/635-3804).

SPORTS AND RECREATION
Hiking and Biking

Quite simply, Jekyll Island is a paradise for bicyclists and walkers, with a very well-developed and very safe system of paths totaling about 20 miles the entire circumference of the island, going by all major sights, including the Jekyll Island Club in the Historic District. In addition, walkers and bicyclists can enjoy much of the seven miles of beachfront at low tide.

Rent your bikes at **Jekyll Island Miniature Golf** (100 James Rd., 912/635-2648, daily 9 A.M.–8 P.M., $5.25/hr., $11.50/day). Take a left when you dead-end after the entrance gate, then another left.

Bird-Watching

The **Clam Creek Picnic Area** on the island's north end is on the Colonial Coast Birding Trail, and without even trying you will see a wide variety of wading birds and shorebirds. Shell collectors will also have a blast, as will those with a horticultural bent, who will marvel at the variety of species presented in the various ecosystems on the island, from beach to marsh hammock to maritime forest.

Golf and Tennis

True to Jekyll Island's intended role as a playground for Georgians of low-to-medium income, its golf and tennis facilities—all centrally located at the middle of the island—are quite reasonably priced.

The **Jekyll Island Golf Resort** (322 Captain Wylly Rd., 912/635-2368, www.jekyll island.com, $40–60 green fees) comprises the largest public golf resort in Georgia. A total of 63 holes on four courses—Pine Lakes, Indian Mound, Oleander, and Ocean Dunes (nine holes)—await. Check the website for "golf passport" packages that include local lodging.

The adjacent **Jekyll Island Tennis Center** (400 Captain Wylly Rd., 912/635-3154, www .gate.net/~jitc, $25/hr) boasts 13 courts, seven of them lighted, as well as a pro shop (daily 9 A.M.–6 P.M.).

If a different kind of golf is your thing, try **Jekyll Island Miniature Golf** (100 James Rd., 912/635-2648, Sun.–Thurs. 9 A.M.–8 P.M., Fri. and Sat. 9 A.M.–10 P.M., $6).

Fishing

Continuing north on Beachview Drive at the very top of the island is the well-done **Clam Creek Picnic Area** (daily dawn–dusk). This free facility on the Colonial Coast Birding Trail has a spacious fishing pier over the Jekyll River and a trailhead through the woods and out onto the beach. About a 20-minute walk on the sand gets you to Driftwood Beach from the other side.

A good local fishing charter company is Captain Vernon Reynolds' **Coastal Expeditions** (3202 E. 3rd St., 912/265-0392, www.coastalcharterfishing.com), departing from the Jekyll Harbor Marina. Half-day and full-day trips are available; call for rates.

© JIM MOREKIS

Jekyll Island boasts miles of uncrowded beaches.

Kayaking and Boating

Most kayaking activity in the area centers on St. Simons across the sound. But **Tidelands 4-H Nature Center** (100 Riverview Dr., 912/635-5032, www.tidelands4h.org) offers a variety of Jekyll-oriented guided kayak tours and also rents kayaks and canoes March–October.

Water Parks

Summer Waves (210 S. Riverview Dr., 912/635-2074, www.jekyllisland.com, Memorial Day–Labor Day, $19.95 adults, $15.95 for children under 48 inches tall) is just what the doctor ordered for kids with a surplus of energy. The 11-acre facility has a separate section for toddlers to splash around in, with the requisite more daring rides for the hard-charging preteens. Hours vary, so call ahead.

Horseback Riding and Tours

Victoria's Carriages and Trail (100 Stable Rd., 912/635-9500, Mon.–Sat. 11 A.M.–4 P.M.) offers numerous options, both on horseback as well as in a horse-drawn carriage. Carriage tours of the island depart every hour 11 A.M.–4 P.M. ($15 adults, $7 children). There's a night ride 6–8 P.M. ($38 per couple).

Horseback rides include a one-hour beach ride that leaves at 11 A.M., 1 P.M., and 3 P.M. ($55) and a sunset ride at 6:30 P.M. ($65) that lasts a little over an hour.

Victoria's is at the entrance to the Clam Creek Picnic Area on the north end of the island directly across the street from the Jekyll Island campground.

The **Tidelands 4-H Center** (912/635-5032) gives 1.5–2-hour Marsh Walks leaving Mondays at 9 A.M. from Clam Creek Picnic Area ($5 adults, $3 children), and Beach Walks ($5 adults, $3 children) leaving Wednesdays at 9 A.M. from the St. Andrews Picnic area and Fridays at 9 A.M. from South Dunes Picnic Area.

Captain Vernon Reynolds's **Coastal Expeditions** (3202 E. 3rd St., 912/265-0392, www.coastalcharterfishing.com, $24 adults, $10 children) provides dolphin tours

March–May Tuesday–Saturday at 1:30 P.M., and three trips daily June–August.

ACCOMMODATIONS
Under $150

While most bargain lodging on Jekyll is sadly sub-par, the old **Days Inn** (60 S. Beachview Dr., 912/635-9800, www.daysinnjekyll.com, $100) has seen a remodeling lately and is the best choice if budget is a concern (and you don't want to camp, that is). It has a good location on the south side of the island with nice ocean views.

$150-300

Lodging on Jekyll Island begins with the legendary 【 **Jekyll Island Club** (371 Riverview Dr., 800/535-9547, www.jekyllclub.com, $189–419), which is reasonably priced considering its history, postcard-perfect setting, and delightful rooms. Some of its 157 rooms and suites are available for under $200 a night, and even the finest, the Presidential Suite, tops out at about $420 in the high season of March–October.

While 60 rooms are in the main Club building, several outlying cottages, chief among them the Crane, Cherokee, and Sans Souci Cottages, are also available. All rates include use of the big outdoor pool overlooking the river, and a neat amenity is a choice of meal plans if you like ($86 per person for three meals a day, or $68 per person for breakfast and dinner).

Despite its auspicious beginnings, the Club has not been a total success story. The state tried to run it as a resort in the 1950s and '60s, but gave up in 1971. With Historic Landmark District status coming in 1978, restoration wasn't far behind, and the Club was first run as a Radisson. Now operated by Landmark, the Club is one of the "Historic Hotels of America" as ranked by the National Trust for Historic Preservation.

Keep in mind that not all the fixtures are original and the present interior design scheme was done with an eye to current commercial taste (those crusty old millionaires would never have gone for pastels).

A fun choice for families are the **Villas by the Sea** (1175 N. Beachview Dr., 866/375-7691,

Jekyll Island Campground is a great place to spend the night.

© JIM MOREKIS

www.jekyllislandga.com, $220), which are exactly that: one, two, or three-bedroom condo villas. Each one's individually owned, but you can opt for a maid service and there's also a central pool and bike rental.

Camping

One of the niftiest campgrounds in the entire area is the **Jekyll Island Campground** (197 Riverview Dr., 912/635-3021). It's a friendly place with an excellent location at the north end of the island—a short drive or bike ride from just about anything and directly across the street from the Clam Creek Picnic Area, with easy beach access. There are more than 200 sites, from tent to full-service pull-through RV sites. Tent sites are around $25 and RV sites are about $32. There's a two-night minimum on weekends and a three-night minimum on holiday and special event weekends. Reservations recommended.

FOOD

Cuisine offerings are few and far between on Jekyll. I'd suggest you patronize one of the three dining facilities at the **Jekyll Island Club** (371 Riverview Dr.), which are all open to the public. They're not only delicious, but pretty reasonable as well considering the swank setting.

My favorite is the (**Courtyard at Crane** (912/635-2400, lunch Sun.–Fri. 11 A.M.–4 P.M., Sat. 11 A.M.–2 P.M., dinner Sun.–Thurs. 5:30–9 P.M., $27–38). In the circa-1917, beautifully restored Crane Cottage, one of the old tycoon villas, the Courtyard offers *very* romantic evening dining (call for reservations) as well as tasty and stylish lunch dining, in the alfresco courtyard area or inside. The lunch menu—a great deal for the quality—is Mediterranean heavy, with wraps, sandwiches, and soups. The dinner menu moves more toward wine country casual chic, with a lot of pork, veal, and beef dishes to go with the requisite fresh seafood. As a plus, the coffee is great—not at all a given in Southern restaurants. Casual dress OK.

For a real and figurative taste of history, make a reservation at the **Grand Dining Room** (912/635-2400, breakfast Mon.–Sat. 7–11 A.M., Sun. 7–10 A.M., lunch Mon.–Sat. 11:30 A.M.–2 P.M., Sunday brunch 10:45 A.M.–2 P.M., dinner Mon.–Sun. 6–10 P.M., dinner $26–35), the Club's full-service restaurant. Focusing on Continental cuisine—ordered either à la carte or as a prix fixe "sunset dinner"—the Dining Room features a pianist each evening and for Sunday brunch. Jackets or collared shirts are required for men.

For a tasty breakfast, lunch, or dinner on the go and/or at odd hours, check out **Café Solterra** (912/635-2600, daily 7 A.M.–10 P.M.), great for deli-type food and equipped with Starbucks coffee.

There are two places for seaside dining and cocktails at the historic Jekyll Island Club Wharf. **Latitude 31** (1 Pier Rd., 912/635-3800, www.crossoverjekyll.com, Tues.–Sun. 5:30–10 P.M., $15–25, no reservations) is an upscale seafood-oriented fine-dining place, while the attached **Rah Bar** (Tues.–Sat. 11 A.M.–close, Sun. 1 P.M.–close, depending on weather) serves up oysters and shellfish in a very casual setting; try the Lowcountry boil or the crab legs.

INFORMATION AND SERVICES

The **Jekyll Island Visitor Center** (901 Downing Musgrove Cswy., 912/635-3636, daily 9 A.M.–5 P.M.) is on the long causeway along the marsh before you get to the island. Set in a charming little cottage it shares with the Georgia State Patrol, the Center has a nice gift shop and loads of brochures on the entire Golden Isles region. Don't hesitate to ask questions of the person taking your $3 entrance fee when you get to the island itself.

The **U.S. Postal Service** keeps an outpost at 18 South Beachview Drive (912/635-2625).

GETTING THERE AND AROUND

Jekyll Island is immediately south of Brunswick. Take Exit 38 off I-95 to the Golden Isles Parkway. Take a right onto U.S. 17 and keep going until you cross the huge Sidney

Lanier Bridge over the Brunswick River. Take an immediate left at the foot of the bridge onto the Downing Musgrove Cswy. (Jekyll Island Rd.). This long, scenic route over the beautiful marshes eventually takes you directly onto Jekyll, where you'll have to pay a $3 per vehicle fee to get onto the island.

Once on the island, most sites are on the north end (a left as you reach the dead-end at Beachview Dr.). The main circuit route around the island is Beachview Drive, which suitably enough changes into Riverview Drive as it rounds the bend to landward at the north end.

Many visitors choose to bicycle around the island once they're there, which is certainly the best way to experience both the sights and the beach itself at low tide.

St. Simons Island

Despite a certain and somewhat deserved reputation for aloof affluence, the truth is that St. Simons Island is also very visitor-friendly, and there's more to do here than meets the eye. Think of St. Simons—with a year-round population of about 13,000—as a smaller, less-polished Hilton Head and you've got the right idea. For those looking for island-style relaxation with no high-rise, cookie-cutter development—but still all the modern amenities and luxuries—St. Simons fits the bill perfectly.

HISTORY

St. Simons Island and its much smaller, symbiotic neighbor Sea Island (originally Long Island) were well known to Native Americans as a hunting and fishing ground. Eventually the Spanish would have two missions on St. Simons, one at the south end and one at the north end, as well as a town for non-converted native peoples called San Simon, which would eventually give the island its modern name.

A lasting European influence didn't come until 1736 with General James Oglethorpe's construction of Fort Frederica. The fort and surrounding town (also called Frederica) were a key base of operations for the British struggle to evict the Spanish from Georgia—which culminated in the decisive Battle of Bloody Marsh south of the fort—but fell into steep decline after the Spanish threat subsided.

In the years after American independence, St. Simons woke up from its slumber as acre after acre of virgin live oak was felled to make the massive timbers of new warships for the U.S. Navy, including the USS *Constitution*. In their place was planted a new crop—cotton. The island's antebellum plantations boomed to world-class heights of profit and prestige when the superior strain of the crop known as "Sea Island Cotton" came in the 1820s.

It's on St. Simons in 1803 that one of the most poignant chapters in the dark history of American slavery was written. In one of the first documented slave uprisings in North America, a group of slaves from the Igbo region of West Africa escaped custody and took over the ship that was transporting them to St. Simons from Savannah. But rather than do any further violence, immediately upon reaching shore on the west side of St. Simons, the slaves essentially committed mass suicide by walking into the swampy waters nearby, which forever after would be known as Ebo Landing (a corruption of the original Igbo).

The Civil War came to St. Simons in late 1861 with a Union blockade and invasion, leading Confederate troops to dynamite the lighthouse. Initially St. Simons was a sanctuary for freed slaves from the island's 14 massive plantations, and by late 1862 over 500 former slaves lived on St. Simons, including Susie King Taylor, who began a school for African American children. But in November of that year all former slaves were dispersed to Hilton Head and Fernandina, Florida.

St. Simons was chosen as one of the implementation sites of General William Sherman's Special Field Order No. 15, the famous "40 acres and a mule" order giving the Sea Islands of South Carolina and Georgia to freed slaves. However, after Sherman's order was quickly rescinded by President Andrew Johnson, life on St. Simons settled back into a disturbingly familiar pattern, with many local African Americans coming back to work the land as before—only as sharecroppers instead of slaves.

The next landmark development for St. Simons didn't come until the building of the first causeway in 1924, which led directly to the island's resort development by the mega-rich industrialist Howard Coffin, of Hudson Motors fame, who also owned nearby Sapelo Island to the north. By 1928, Coffin had completed the Sea Island Golf Club on the grounds of the old Retreat Plantation on the south end of St. Simons Island. He would move on to develop the famous Cloisters resort on Long Island (later Sea Island) itself.

ORIENTATION

Because it's only a short drive from downtown Brunswick on the Torras Causeway, St. Simons has much less of a remote feel than most other Georgia barrier islands, and is much more

GOLDEN ISLES ON THE PAGE

And now from the Vast of the Lord will
  the waters of sleep
Roll in on the souls of men,
But who will reveal to our waking ken
The forms that swim and the shapes
  that creep
Under the waters of sleep?
And I would I could know what swimmeth
  below when the tide comes in
On the length and the breath of the
  marvelous marshes of Glynn.

Sidney Lanier

Many authors have been inspired by their time in the Golden Isles, whether to pen flights of poetic fancy, page-turning novels, or politically-oriented chronicles. Here are a few of the most notable names:

- **Sidney Lanier:** The Macon, Georgia-born Lanier was a renowned linguist, mathematician, and legal scholar. Fighting as a Confederate during the Civil War, he was captured while commanding a blockade runner and taken to a POW camp in Maryland, where he came down with tuberculosis. After the war, he stayed at his brother-in-law's house in Brunswick to recuperate, and it was during that time

that he took up poetry, writing the famous "Marshes of Glynn," quoted above.

- **Eugenia Price:** Though not originally from St. Simons, Price remains the best-known local cultural figure, setting her "St. Simons Trilogy" there. After relocating on the island in 1965, she stayed there until her death in 1996. She's buried in the Christ Church cemetery on Frederica Road.

- **Tina McElroy Ansa:** Probably the most notable literary figure currently living on St. Simons Island is award-winning African American author Tina McElroy Ansa. Though few of her books deal with the Golden Isles region, they all deal with life in the South and Ansa is an ardent devotee of St. Simons and its relaxed, friendly ways.

- **Fanny Kemble:** In 1834, this renowned English actress married Georgia plantation heir Pierce Butler, who would become one of America's largest slave-owners. Horrified by the treatment of Butler's slaves at Butler Island just south of Darien, Georgia, Kemble penned one of the earliest anti-slavery chronicles, *Journal of a Residence on a Georgian Plantation in 1838-39*. Kemble's disagreement with her husband over slavery hastened their divorce in 1849.

THE GOLDEN ISLES

densely populated than any other Georgia island except for Tybee.

Most visitor-oriented activity on this 12-mile-long, heavily residential island about the size of Manhattan is clustered at the south end, where St. Simons Sound meets the Atlantic. The main reasons to travel north on the island are to golf or visit the historic site of Fort Frederica on the landward side.

The main roads to remember are Kings Way, which turns into Ocean Boulevard as it nears the active south end of the island, "the Village"; Demere Road (pronounced "DEMM-er-ee"), which loops west to east around the little island airport and then south, joining up with Ocean Boulevard down near the Lighthouse; Frederica Road, the dominant north–south artery; and Mallory Street, which runs north–south through the Village area and dead-ends at the Pier on St. Simons Sound. (You'll notice that Mallory Street is sometimes spelled "Mallery," which is actually the correct spelling of the avenue's namesake: Mallery King, child of Thomas King, owner of the historic Retreat Plantation.)

SIGHTS
◖ The Village
Think of "the Village" at the extreme south end of St. Simons as a mix of Tybee's downscale accessibility and Hilton Head's upscale exclusivity. This compact, bustling area only a few blocks long offers not only boutique shops and stylish cafés, but vintage stores and busking musicians. While visitors and residents here tend toward the affluent, they also tend not to be as flashy about it as some other locales. You'll find the vast majority of quality eating spots, as well as most quality lodging, here.

It's fun to meander down Mallory Drive, casually shopping or noshing, and then make your way out onto the short but fun **St. Simons Pier** to enjoy the breeze and occasional spray coming off the sound.

St. Simons Lighthouse Museum
Unlike many East Coast lighthouses, which tend to be in hard-to-reach places, anyone can walk right up to the St. Simons Lighthouse

the view from St. Simons Pier

© JIM MOREKIS

St. Simons Lighthouse Museum

Museum (101 12th St., 912/638-4666, www.stsimonslighthouse.org, Mon.–Sat. 10 A.M.–5 P.M., Sun. 1:30–5 P.M., $6 adults, $3 children). Once inside, you can enjoy the museum's exhibit and take the 129 steps up to the top of the 104-foot beacon—which is, unusually, still active—for a gorgeous view of the island and the ocean beyond. (The museum offers a "Family of Four" package admission—$25 for two adults and two children, as well as a combo ticket to the nearby Maritime Center for $10 adults, $5 children.)

The first lighthouse on the spot came about after planter John Couper sold this land, known as Couper's Point, to the government in 1804 for a dollar. This original beacon was destroyed by retreating Confederate troops in 1862 to hinder Union navigation on the coast. Traces of its foundations are near the current facility. The current lighthouse dates from 1872, built by Irishman Charles Cluskey, responsible for a lot of Greek Revival architecture

up and down the Georgia coast. Attached to the lighthouse is the oldest brick structure in Glynn County, the 1872 lighthouse keeper's cottage, now the museum and gift shop run by the Coastal Georgia Historical Society.

Maritime Center

A short walk from the lighthouse and likewise administered by the Coastal Georgia Historical Society, the Maritime Center (4201 First St., 912/638-4666, www.stsimonslighthouse.org, Mon.–Sat. 10 A.M.–5 P.M., Sun. 1:30–5 P.M., $6 adults, $3 children) is at the historic East Beach Coast Guard Station. Authorized by President Franklin Roosevelt in 1933 and completed in 1937 by the Works Progress Administration, the East Beach Station took part in military action in World War II, an episode chronicled in exhibits at the Maritime Center. On April 8, 1942, the German U-boat U-123 torpedoed and sank two cargo ships off the coast of St. Simons Island. The Coast Guardsmen of East Beach station mounted a full rescue effort, saving many crewmen of the merchant ships, including one ship's canine mascot.

With the increase in tourism to St. Simons in the late 20th century, the Coast Guard's job was made more difficult as traffic and development hindered the route from the station, where they kept watch, to their boathouse on the Frederica River on the other side of the island. The Coast Guard's tenure on East Beach ended after a fire in 1993 burned down their boathouse. Two years later the station was decommissioned and the Coasties moved to a new station in Brunswick.

The Maritime Center offers a "Family of Four" package admission—$25 for two adults and two children, as well as a combo ticket to the St. Simons Lighthouse for $10 adults, $5 children.

◖ Fort Frederica National Monument

The starkly beautiful, historically vital Fort Frederica National Monument (Frederica Rd., 912/638-3639, www.nps.gov/fofr, daily 9 A.M.–5 P.M., $3 adults, free for children

THE GOLDEN ISLES

under 15) lies on the landward side of the island, overlooking the key waterway of the Frederica River. Established by General James Oglethorpe in 1736 to protect Georgia's southern flank from the Spanish, the fort (as well as the village that sprang up around it, in which the Wesley brothers preached for a short time) was named for Frederick Louis, the Prince of Wales. The feminine "a" was added as a suffix to distinguish it from the older Fort Frederick in South Carolina.

Unlike the more imposing post-colonial installations, like Fort Pulaski on Tybee Island, Frederica is compact and easy to take in, and its tabby construction is more photogenic and pleasing to the eye. Examine the parapets of the sturdy little fortress and instantly see why this was such a strategic location, guarding the approach to the great Altamaha River. Take in the accompanying exhibits in the visitors center, including a 23-minute film every half-hour 9 A.M.–4 P.M. A park ranger also gives informative talks throughout the day.

Though the fort itself was not directly involved in a military clash, its garrison took part in the unsuccessful attack on St. Augustine, Florida in 1740 and was the force that swept south on St. Simons to decisively defeat the Spanish at Bloody Marsh two years later. With the ebbing of the Spanish threat, the need for a military presence on St. Simons subsided. By 1749 the fort was no longer active and the town of Frederica was largely destroyed in a disastrous fire in 1758. Fort Frederica became a National Monument in 1936 and was put on the National Register of Historic Places in 1966.

Bloody Marsh Battlefield

There's not a lot to see at the site of the Battle of Bloody Marsh (Frederica Rd., 912/638-3639, www.nps.gov/fofr, daily 8 A.M.–4 P.M., free), but—as with the similarly stirring site of Custer's Last Stand at the Little Bighorn—your imagination fills in the gaps, giving it perhaps more emotional impact than other, more substantial historic sites.

Essentially just a few interpretive signs overlooking a beautiful piece of salt marsh, the site is where British soldiers from nearby Fort Frederica ambushed a force of Spanish regulars on their way to besiege the fort. Frederica's garrison, the 42nd Regiment of Foot, was augmented by a company of tough Scottish Highlanders from Darien, Georgia who legend says attacked to the tune of bagpipes.

Though the battle wasn't actually that "bloody"—some accounts say the Spanish lost only seven men—the stout British presence convinced the Spanish to leave St. Simons a few days later, never again to project their once-potent military power that far north in America. You'll often hear it claimed that the Battle of Bloody Marsh is the reason we speak English instead of Spanish. That's certainly hyperbolic, but there's no doubt that had the battle gone the other way the course of American history would have been changed.

While the Battle of Bloody Marsh site is part of the National Park Service's Fort Frederica site, it's not at the same location. Get to the battlefield from the fort by taking Frederica Road south, and then a left (east) on Demere Road. The site is on your left as Demere veers right, in the 1800 block.

Christ Church

Just down the road from Fort Frederica is historic Christ Church (6329 Frederica Rd., 912/638-8683, www.christchurchfrederica .org, daily 2–5 P.M.). Though the first sanctuary dates from 1820, the original congregation at the now-defunct town of Frederica held services under the oaks at the site as early as 1736. The founder of Methodism, John Wesley, and his brother Charles both ministered to island residents during 1736 and 1737.

The original church was rendered unusable by Union occupation during the Civil War. A new church, the one you see today, was funded and built in 1883 by a local mill owner, Anson Dodge, as a memorial to his first wife. But Christ Church's claim to fame in modern culture is as the setting of local novelist Eugenia

Price's *The Beloved Invader,* the first work in her Georgia trilogy. The late Price, who died in 1996, is buried in the church cemetery.

Tours

St. Simons Island Trolley Tours (912/638-8954, www.stsimonstours.com, Apr., June, and July daily 11 A.M. and 1 P.M. , Jan.–Mar., May, Aug.–Dec. daily 11 A.M., $20 adults, $12 children 4–12, four and under free) offers just that, a ride around the island in comparative comfort.

For a more adventurous trek, book a dolphin tour from **Saint Simons Transit Company** (105 Marina Dr., 912/638-5678, www.stsimons transit.com), operating out of the Golden Isles Marina on little Lanier Island before you get on St. Simons itself. A dolphin tour will run you about $25 for adults and $10 for children; call for details and departure times.

ENTERTAINMENT AND EVENTS
Nightlife

St. Simons is far from Charleston's or Savannah's league when it comes to partying, but there is a fairly active nightlife scene, with a strong dose of island casual. Unlike some areas this far south on the Georgia coast, there's usually a sizeable contingent of young people out looking for a good time.

The island's premier club, **Rafters Blues and Raw Bar** (315½ Mallory St., 912/634-9755, www.raftersblues.com, Mon.–Sat. 4:30 P.M.–2 A.M.), known simply as "Rafters," brings in live music most every Thursday, Friday, and Saturday night, focusing on the best acts on the regional rock circuit.

A popular meeting-and-eating place is **Loco's Deli & Pub** (2463 Demere Rd., 912/634-2002, www.locosgrill.com, daily 11 A.M.–11 P.M.), which has a full menu heavy on burgers and finger food, along with live music on weekends. A similar blend of food, libation, and live music is at **Ziggy Mahoney's** (5514 Frederica Rd., 912/634-0999, Thurs.–Sat. 8 P.M.–2 A.M.).

Inside the Village Inn is the popular nightspot the **Village Pub** (500 Mallory St., 912/634-6056, www.villageinnandpub.com,

Rafters is the main music club in the village on St. Simons.

© JIM MOREKIS

Mon.–Sat. 5 P.M.–midnight, Sun. 5–10 P.M.). Slightly more upscale than most watering holes on the island, this is the best place for a quality martini or other premium cocktail.

Performing Arts

Because of its close proximity to Brunswick, a short drive over the bridge, St. Simons has a symbiotic relationship with that larger city in areas of art and culture.

Each summer beginning Memorial Day weekend and into September there are several "Jazz in the Park" concerts by regional artists. The shows are usually at 7–9 P.M. Sundays on the lawn of the St. Simons Lighthouse, and the beautiful setting and calming breeze is a delight. Admission is charged; bring a chair or blanket if you like.

Film

The island has its own multiplex, the **Island Cinemas 7** (44 Cinema Lane, 912/634-9100, www.georgiatheatrecompany.com).

SHOPPING

Most shopping on St. Simons is centered in the Village and is a typical beach town mix of hardware/tackle and casual clothing and souvenir stores. A funky highlight is **Beachview Books** (215 Mallory St., 912/638-7282, Mon.–Sat. 10:30 A.M.–5:30 P.M., Sun. 11:30 A.M.–3 P.M.), a rambling used bookstore with lots of regional and local goodies, including books by the late great local author Eugenia Price. The best antique shop in this part of town is **Village Mews** (504 Beachview Dr., 912/634-1235, Mon.–Sat. 10 A.M.–5 P.M.).

The closest thing to a mall is farther north on St. Simons at **Redfern Village** with some cute indie stores like **Beach Cottage Linens** (912/634-2000, Mon.–Fri. 10 A.M.–5:30 P.M., Sat. 10 A.M.–5 P.M.), **Thomas P. Dent Clothiers** (912/638-3118, Mon.–Sat. 9:30 A.M.–6 P.M.), and the craftsy **Rarebbits and Pieces** (912/638-2866, Mon.–Sat. 10 A.M.–5:30 P.M.). Redfern Village is on Frederica Road, one traffic light past the corner of Frederica and Demere.

SPORTS AND RECREATION
Beaches

Keep going from the pier past the lighthouse to find **Massengale Park** (daily dawn–dusk), with a playground, picnic tables, and restrooms right off the beach on the Atlantic side. The beach itself on St. Simons is underwhelming compared to some in these parts, but nonetheless it's easily accessible from the pier area and good for a romantic stroll if it's not high tide. There's a great playground, Neptune Park, right next to the pier overlooking the waterfront.

Kayaking and Boating

With its relatively sheltered landward side nestled in the marsh and an abundance of wildlife, St. Simons Island is an outstanding kayaking site, attracting connoisseurs from all over.

A good spot to put in on the Frederica River is the **Golden Isles Marina** (206 Marina Dr., 912/634-1128, www.gimarina.com), which is actually on little Lanier Island on the Torras Causeway right before you enter St. Simons proper. For a real adventure, put in at the ramp at the end of South Harrington Street off Frederica Road, which will take you out Village Creek on the seaward side of the island.

Undoubtedly the best kayaking outfitter and tour operator in this part of the Golden Isles is **SouthEast Adventure Outfitters** (313 Mallory St., 912/638-6732, www.southeast adventure.com, daily 10 A.M.–6 P.M.), which also has a location in nearby Brunswick. Michael Gowen and company offer an extensive range of guided tours all over the St. Simons marsh and sound area, as well as trips to undeveloped Little St. Simons Island to the north. Prices vary, so call or go to the website for information.

Another kayak tour operator is **Ocean Motion** (1300 Ocean Blvd., 912/638-5225, www.oceanmotion.biz).

Hiking and Biking

Like Jekyll Island, St. Simons is a great place for bicyclists. Bike paths go all over the island, and a special kick is riding on the beach almost the whole length of the island (but only at high tide!).

There are plenty of bike rental spots, with rates generally $15–20 per day depending on season. The best place to rent bikes is **Monkey Wrench Bicycles** (1700 Frederica Rd., 912/634-5551). Another good rental place is **Ocean Motion** (1300 Ocean Blvd., 912/638-5225, www.oceanmotion.biz).

You can rent another kind of pedal-power at **Wheel Fun Rentals** (532 Ocean Blvd., 912/634-0606), which deals in four-seat, pedaled carts with steering wheels.

Golf and Tennis

A popular place for both sports is the **Sea Palms Golf and Tennis Resort** (5445 Frederica Rd., 800/841-6268, www.seapalms.com, $70–80 green fees) in the middle of the island, with three nine-hole public courses and three clay courts.

The **Sea Island Golf Club** (100 Retreat Rd., 800/732-4752, www.seaisland.com, $185–260 green fees) on the old Retreat Plantation as you first come onto the island has two award-winning 18-hole courses: the Seaside and the Plantation.

Another public course is the 18-hole **Hampton Club** (100 Tabbystone Rd., 912/634-0255, www.hamptonclub.com, green fees $95) on the north side of the island, part of the King and Prince Beach and Golf Resort.

ACCOMMODATIONS
Under $150

You couldn't ask for a better location than the **St. Simons' Inn by the Lighthouse** (609 Beachview Dr., 912/638-1101, www.stsimonsinn.com, $134–199), which is indeed in the shadow of the historic lighthouse and right next to the hopping Village area. A so-called "condo-hotel," each of the standard and deluxe suites at the Inn are individually owned by off-site owners-however, each guest gets full maid service and a complimentary breakfast.

Another charming and reasonable place a stone's throw from the Village is **◖ Queens Court** (437 Kings Way, 912/638-8459,

$85–135), a traditional roadside motel from the late '40s, with modern upgrades including a nice outdoor pool in the central courtyard area. Despite its amazingly convenient location, you'll feel fairly secluded.

One of the most interesting lodgings in the Lowcountry and Georgia coast is **Epworth by the Sea** (100 Arthur J. Moore Dr., 912/638-8688, www.epworthbythesea.org, $90–100). This Methodist retreat in the center of the island boasts an entire complex of free-standing motels and lodges on its grounds, in various styles and configurations. Cafeteria-style meetings are the order of the day, and there are plenty of recreational activities on-site, including tennis, volleyball, baseball, football, soccer, and basketball. They also rent bikes, which is always a great way to get around St. Simons. Everyone loves the **Lovely Lane Chapel,** a picturesque sanctuary that's a favorite spot for weddings and holds worship services each Sunday at 8:45 A.M. (casual dress OK). Researchers can utilize the resources of the **Arthur J. Moore Methodist Museum and Library** (Tues.–Sat. 9 A.M.–4 P.M.).

$150-300

The most well-known lodging on St. Simons Island is the ◖ **King and Prince Beach and Golf Resort** (201 Arnold Rd., 800/342-0212, $249–320). Originally opened as a dance club in 1935, the King and Prince brings a swank, old-school glamour similar to the Jekyll Island Club (though less imposing). And like the Jekyll Island Club, the King and Prince is also designated one of the Historic Hotels of America.

Its nearly 200 rooms are spread out over a complex that includes several buildings, including the historic main building, beach villas, and free-standing guest houses. Some standard rooms can go for under $200 even in the spring high season. Winter rates for all rooms are appreciably lower, and represent a great bargain.

For a dining spot overlooking the sea, try the **Blue Dolphin** (lunch daily 11 A.M.–4 P.M., dinner daily 5–10 P.M., $15–30). The Resort's Hampton Club provides golf for guests and the public.

An interesting B&B on the island that's also within walking distance of most of the action on the south end is the 28-room **Village Inn & Pub** (500 Mallory St., 912/634-6056, www .villageinnandpub.com, $160–245), nestled among shady palm trees and live oaks. The Pub, a popular local hangout in a renovated 1930 cottage, is a nice plus.

Over $300

Affiliated with the Sea Island Resort, the **Lodge at Sea Island** (100 Retreat Ave., 912/638-3611, $650–2500) is actually on the south end of St. Simons Island on the old Retreat Plantation. Its grand assortment of 40 rooms and suites all have great views of either the Atlantic Ocean, the associated Plantation Course links, or both. Full butler service makes this an especially pampered and aristocratic stay.

FOOD

While the ambience at St. Simons has an up-scale feel, don't feel like you have to dress up to get a bite to eat—the emphasis is on relaxation and having a good time.

Breakfast and Brunch

◖ Dressner's Village Cafe (223 Mallory St., 912/634-1217, www.dressners.com, Mon.–Fri. 7:30 A.M.–7 P.M., Sat. and Sun. 8 A.M.–7 P.M., $5–10) right in the middle of the Village's bustle is one of the island's most popular places, but still with enough seats so you usually don't have to wait. Lunches are very good, with an awesome blackened grouper sandwich and great burgers. But breakfast all day is the real attraction here, and includes omelettes, steak and eggs, and a full range of griddle items.

Named for the birthday that the original three co-owners share, **Fourth of May Deli** (444 Ocean Blvd., 912/638-5444, breakfast daily 7 A.M.–1 P.M., lunch daily 11 A.M.–9 P.M., $8–20) is a deservedly popular breakfast and lunch place in the Village. Breakfast focuses on specialties like eggs Benedict and huevos rancheros, along with some fantastic breakfast burritos, a comparative rarity in the South. In addition to deli sandwiches, Fourth of May also has some mean seafood dishes.

Seafood

Despite its somewhat unappetizing name, **Mullet Bay** (512 Ocean Blvd., 912/634-9977, daily 11:30 A.M.–10 P.M., $7–18) in the Village is a favorite, good old-fashioned Southern seafood place, the kind where you get a big fried platter with two sides and hushpuppies.

A popular seafood place right in the action in the Village is **◖ Barbara Jean's** (214 Mallory St., 912/634-6500, www.barbarajeans .com, daily 11 A.M.–9 P.M., $7–20), which also has a great variety of imaginative veggie dishes to go along with its formidable seafood menu, including some excellent she-crab soup and crab cakes. They also have plenty of good landlubber treats for those not inclined to the marine critters.

Serving a host of seafood in your choice of style—grilled, blackened, steamed, or sautéed—**Crab Daddy's** (1217 Ocean Blvd., 912/634-1120, Sun.–Thurs. 5–10 P.M., Fri. and Sat. 5–10:30 P.M., $10–15) is a good, casual place for dinner.

Fine Dining

◖ J. Mac's Island Restaurant (407 Mallory St., 912/634-0403, www.jmacsisland restaurant.com, Tues.–Sat. 6–9 P.M., $20–30) is the Village's high-end restaurant, one that wouldn't be out of place in downtown Charleston or Savannah. Owner J. Mac Mason and head chef Connor Rankin conspire to bring a fresh take on Southern and seafood classics, with adventurous entr–es like seared "Creamsicle" marlin with jumbo asparagus and sweet corn puree–seared filet with gorgonzola and herb gratin.

Inside the King and Prince Resort, you'll find the old-school glory of the **Blue Dolphin** (201 Arnold Rd., 800/342-0212, lunch daily 11 A.M.–4 P.M., dinner daily 5–10 P.M., $15–30), redolent of the Great Gatsby era. The Blue Dolphin claims to be the only oceanfront dining on the island, and the views are certainly magnificent.

INFORMATION AND SERVICES

The **St. Simons Visitors Center** (530-B Beachview Dr., 912/638-9014, www.bgi vb.com, daily 9 A.M.–5 P.M.) is in the St. Simons Casino Building near Neptune Park and the Village.

The main newspaper in St. Simons is the **Brunswick News** (www.thebrunswick news.com).

The **U.S. Postal Service** (800/275-8777) has an office at 620 Beachview Drive.

GETTING THERE AND AROUND

Get to St. Simons through the gateway city of Brunswick. Take the Golden Isles Exit 38 off I-95, which will take you to the Golden Isles Parkway. Take a right onto U.S. 17 and look for the intersection with the Torras Causeway, a toll-free road which takes you the short distance onto St. Simons.

Immediately as you cross the Frederica River onto the island, look for a quick right onto Kings Way to take you directly to the Village area. Or you can take a quick left onto Demere Road to reach Frederica Road and the more northerly portion of the island, where you'll find Fort Frederica and Christ Church.

LITTLE ST. SIMONS ISLAND

This 10,000-acre, privately owned island, accessible only by water, is almost totally undeveloped—thanks to its salt-stressed trees, which discouraged timbering—and boasts seven miles of beautiful beaches.

All activity centers on the circa-1917 **(Lodge on Little St. Simons Island** (1000 Hampton Point Dr., 888/733-5774, www.little stsimonsisland.com, $950), named by *Condé Nast Traveler* as the top U.S. mainland resort in 2007. Within it lies the famed Hunting Lodge, where meals and cocktails are served. With 15

ultra-plush rooms and suites in an assortment of historic buildings, all set amid gorgeous natural beauty—there are five full-time naturalists on staff—the Lodge is a reminder of what St. Simons proper used to look like. Guest count is limited to 30 people.

Getting There and Around

Unless you enlist the aid of a local kayaking charter company, you have to be a guest of the Lodge to have access to Little St. Simons. The ferry, a 15-minute ride, leaves from a landing at the northern end of St. Simons at the end of Lawrence Road. Guests have full use of bicycles once on the island and can also request shuttle transportation just about anywhere.

SEA ISLAND

The only way to enjoy Sea Island—basically a tiny appendage of St. Simons facing the Atlantic Ocean—is to be a guest at **(The Sea Island Resort** (888/732-4752, www .seaisland.com, $700 and up). And guests visiting now are truly lucky; the legendary facility, routinely ranked as one of the best resorts on the planet, completed extensive renovations in 2008 and is back and better than ever.

The rooms at the Resort's premier lodging institution, **The Cloister,** nearly defy description—enveloped in Old World luxury, they also boast 21st-century technology. And the service at The Cloister is equally world-class, featuring 24-hour butler service in the finest European tradition.

There are hundreds of cottages for rental on Sea Island as well, all of which grant temporary membership in the Sea Island Club and full use of all its many amenities and services.

Getting There and Around

Get to Sea Island by taking Torras Causeway onto the island and then making a left onto Sea Island Causeway, which takes you all the way to the gate marking the only landward entrance to Sea Island.

THE GOLDEN ISLES

Darien and McIntosh County

It doesn't get near the attention or amount of visitors as Savannah to the north or the St. Simons/Jekyll area to the south, but the tiny town of Darien in McIntosh County, Georgia, has an interesting historic pedigree of its own—and is centrally located to some of the best treasures the Georgia coast has to offer, from the Harris Neck National Wildlife Refuge to the sea island of Sapelo.

HISTORY

Unlike Anglophilic Savannah to the north, the Darien area has had a distinctly Scottish flavor almost from the beginning (with the exception of the Spanish mission era, of which almost no trace remains). In 1736, Scottish Highlanders established a settlement at this area at the mouth of the Altamaha River at the bequest of General James Oglethorpe, who no doubt wanted the tough Scots protecting his southern border against the resurgent Spanish.

Though their colony was at the site of an earlier English effort, the abandoned Fort King George, they came up with a new name: Darien, honoring the failed 1697 settlement in Panama. Leading them was John McIntosh Mohr, who would go on to father several sons (who would become famous in their own right) and eventually lend his surname to the county in which Darien was contained.

The Scots brought a singularly populist sentiment to the New World. When Georgia planters lobbied to legalize slavery, which was outlawed by Oglethorpe, the Scots of Darien signed a petition against them in 1739—believed to be the first organized protest of slavery in America. The Darien settlers were also known for keeping more cordial relations with the Native Americans than the area's English settlements. Of course they were a frugal bunch, too, and The Bank of Darien was the largest bank south of Philadelphia in the early 1800s.

Unquestionably Darien's heyday was in that antebellum period, when for a brief time the town was the world's largest exporter of cotton, floated downriver on barges and shipped out through the port of Darien. A prosperous rice culture grew up around the Altamaha estuary as well, relying on the tidal flow of the area's acres and acres of marsh.

Almost none of this period remains, however, because on June 11, 1863, a force of mostly African American Union troops under the command of Colonel Robert G. Shaw (of the movie *Glory* fame) burned Darien to the ground, with all its homes and warehouses going up in smoke.

After the Civil War, lumber became the new cash crop, and Darien once again became a thriving seaport and lumber mill headquarters. Also, the late 1800s saw a new reliance on shrimping and oystering, industries that survive to this day (barely) despite the toll of overfishing and drought.

A different kind of industry prospered in the years after World War II. In those pre-Interstate days, U.S. 17 was the main route south to booming Florida. McIntosh County got a bad reputation for "clip joints," which would fleece gullible travelers with a variety of illegal schemes. This period is recounted in the bestseller *Praying for Sheetrock* by Melissa Fay Greene.

McIntosh County has cleaned up its act, but it's still one of the poorest counties in the United States. However, it is steadily growing more popular as an affordable place to build houses and for retirees.

SIGHTS
Darien Waterfront Park

Right where U.S. 17 crosses the Darien River find the **Darien Welcome Center** (corner U.S. 17 and Fort King George Dr., 912/437-6684, daily 9 A.M.–5 P.M.). From there it's a short walk down some steps to the newly refurbished little Darien Waterfront Park. This small but charming area on a beautiful bend of the Darien River—a tributary of the mighty

Altamaha just to the south—features some old tabby warehouse ruins, some of the only remnants of Darien's glory days as a major seaport and old enough to have century-old live oaks growing around them. To the east are the picturesque docks where the town shrimp boat fleet docks.

Vernon Square

Right around the corner from the Welcome Center on Washington Street is Vernon Square, a charming little nook of live oaks and Spanish moss that was the social center of Darien in the town's antebellum heyday. The Methodist Church on the square was built in 1843, damaged during the Civil War, then rebuilt in 1884 using materials from the first church. The nearby St. Andrews Episcopal Church, built in 1878, was once the site of the famous Bank of Darien.

◖ Harris Neck National Wildlife Refuge

In addition to being one of the single best sites in the South to view wading birds and waterfowl in their natural habitat, Harris Neck National Wildlife Refuge (912/832-4608, www.fws.gov/harrisneck, daily sunrise–sunset) also has something of a poignant backstory. Harris Neck was once home to a community of freed slaves who traced their identity back to the Mende people of Sierra Leone. For generations after the Civil War, they quietly struggled to eke out a living by farming the sandy soil, worn out by years of poor farming practices during the plantation era. But the land was taken by the federal government in World War II to build a U.S. Army Air Force base, primarily to train pilots on the P-40 Tomahawk fighter, the same plane used by the famed Flying Tigers.

After the war, the base was decommissioned and given to McIntosh County as a municipal airport. But the notoriously corrupt local government so mismanaged the facility that the feds once again took it over, eventually transferring it to the forerunner of the U.S. Fish and Wildlife Service. Now a nearly 3,000-acre nationally protected refuge, Harris Neck gets about 50,000 visitors a year to experience its mix of marsh, woods, and grassland ecosystems, and for its nearly matchless bird-watching.

Its former life as a military base has the plus of leaving behind a 15-mile system of good roads—including four-mile "wildlife drive"—on which visitors can travel quickly through the refuge. In the summer, look for egrets, herons, and wood storks nesting in rookeries. In the winter, waterfowl like mallards and teal flock to the brackish and freshwater pools. You can see painted buntings from late April until late September. Kayaks and canoes can put in at the little public boat ramp on the refuge.

To get there, take Exit 67 off of I-95 and go south on U.S. 17 about a mile, then east on Harris Neck Road (GA 131) for seven miles to the entrance gate on your left.

Fort King George State Historic Site

The oldest English settlement in what would become Georgia, Fort King George State Historic Site (1600 Wayne St., 912/437-4770, www.gastateparks.org/fortkinggeorge, Tues.–Sat. 9 A.M.–5 P.M., Sun. 2–5:30 P.M., $5 adults, $2.50 children) for a short time protected the Carolinas from attack, with its establishment in 1721 to its abandonment in 1727. Walking onto the site, with its restored, 40-foot-tall cypress blockhouse fort, shows you instantly why this place was so important: It guards a key bend in the wide Altamaha River, vital to any attempt to establish transportation and trade in the area.

In addition to chronicling the ill-fated English occupation of the area—plagued by insects, sickness, danger, and boredom—the site also has exhibits about other aspects of local history, including the Guale Indians, the Spanish missionary presence, and the era of the great sawmills. Nature lovers will enjoy the site as well, which offers gorgeous vistas of the marsh.

Fort King George holds regular reenactments, living history demonstrations, and

THE GOLDEN ISLES

cannon firings; go to the website for details. To get there, take U.S. 17 to the Darien River Bridge, and go east on Fort King George Drive. There's a bike route to the fort if you want to park in town.

Butler Island

South of Darien is the Altamaha River, Georgia's largest river (and only undammed one) and one of America's great estuarine habitats, with the second-largest watershed on the East Coast. It's a paradise for outdoors enthusiasts, one that amazed and delighted famed naturalist William Bartram on his journey here in the late 1700s. Over 30,000 ducks visit each year from mid-October through mid-April on this key stop on the Colonial Coast Birding Trail.

A great way to enjoy the river ecosystem is at the **Altamaha Waterfowl Management Area** (912/262-3173, http://georgiawildlife.dnr.state.ga.us). This was the site of Butler Island Plantation, one of America's largest and most successful tidewater plantations in the antebellum era. (The 75-foot brick chimney just off U.S. 17 is part of an old rice mill belonging to the plantation.)

In 1834, planter Pierce Butler II married English actress Fanny Kemble, who would go on to write one of the earliest anti-slavery chronicles, *Journal of a Residence on a Georgian Plantation in 1838–39*, about what she saw during her short stay at Butler Island. Just past the chimney is a large plantation house, which now houses offices of the Nature Conservancy. There's a picnic ground nearby.

The dominance of the plantation culture in this area is proved by the dikes and gates throughout the marsh, still plainly visible from the road. Many are still used by the Georgia Department of Natural Resources to maintain bird habitat. Birds you can see throughout the area include endangered wood storks, painted bunting, white ibis, all types of ducks, and even bald eagles.

Some of the best hiking and birding in the area is just south of the chimney on U.S. 17. Park on the east side of the road at an old dairy

This chimney off Highway 17 marks the old Butler Island Plantation.

barn and from there you'll find the trail head for a four-mile round-trip hike on the Billy Cullen Memorial Trail, which offers great bird-watching opportunities and interpretive signage. On the other side of U.S. 17 is the entrance to the Ansley Hodges Memorial, where a quarter-mile hike takes you to an observation tower. Be aware that hunting goes on near this area on some Saturdays during the year.

Kayaks and canoes can easily put in at the state-run landing at **Champney River Park** right there where U.S. 17 crosses the Champney River. There are a variety of fish camps up and down this entire riverine system, providing fairly easy launching and recovery.

Shellman Bluff

Just up U.S. 17 and northeast of Darien is the old oystering community of Shellman Bluff. It's notable not only the stunning views from the high bluff but for fresh seafood. Go to

Shellman's Fish Camp (912/832-4331) to put in for a kayak or canoe ride.

Smallest Church in North America

While several other churches claim that title, in any case fans of the devout and of roadside kitsch alike will enjoy the tiny little **Memory Park Christ Chapel** (U.S. 17, daily 24 hrs.). Built in 1949 by local grocer Agnes Harper, the church—which holds a dozen people, max—was intended as a round-the-clock travelers' sanctuary on what was then the main coastal road, U.S. 17. Upon her death, Mrs. Harper simply willed the church to Jesus Christ. The stained-glass windows are imported from England. Get there by taking Exit 67 off I-95 and south a short way on U.S. 17.

ACCOMMODATIONS

If you want to stay in McIntosh County, I strongly recommend booking one of the five charming rooms at **☾ Open Gates Bed and Breakfast** (301 Franklin St., 912/437-6985, www.opengatesbnb.com, $110). This lovingly restored and reasonably priced inn is on historic and relaxing Vernon Square in downtown Darien. Owners Kelly and Jeff Spratt are not only attentive innkeepers who rustle up a mean breakfast, they're also biologists who can hook you up with the best nature-oriented experiences and tours on this part of the coast.

FOOD

As you might expect, fresh seafood in a very casual atmosphere is the order of the day around here. The community of Shellman Bluff is the best pick, if you can deal with occasionally having to call for directions and to make sure they'll be open (there are few actual street addresses there and time is a fluid commodity). To get to Shellman Bluff, take the South Newport Exit 67 off I-95 and get on U.S. 17 south to Swinton Road. Take Swinton to Shellman Bluff Road. Follow signs for your destination, or call for directions.

Find **☾ Hunter's Café** (912/832-5771, lunch Mon.–Fri. 11 A.M.–2 P.M., dinner

Open Gates Bed and Breakfast in Darien

© JIM MOREKIS

5–10 P.M., Sat. and Sun. 7 A.M.–10 P.M., $10–20) and get anything that floats your boat—it's all perfect, and it's all fresh and local. Wild Georgia shrimp are a particular specialty.

Another Shellman Bluff favorite is **Speed's Kitchen** (912/832-4763, Thurs.–Sat. 5 P.M.–close, Sun. noon–close, $10–20), where people move anything but fast and the fried fish and crab-stuffed flounder are out of this world.

On the Darien waterfront, you'll find **Skipper's Fish Camp** (85 Screven St., 912/437-3579, www.skippersfishcamp.com, daily 11 A.M.–9 P.M., $15–25), which, as is typical for this area, also hosts a marina. Try the fried wild Georgia Shrimp, fresh from local waters.

South of Darien just off U.S. 17 on the Altamaha River, try **Mudcat Charlie's** (250 Rice Field Wy., 912/261-0055, daily 8 A.M.–2 P.M., $10–20), where fresh seafood is served in a friendly and very casual atmosphere, yes, right in the middle of a busy fish camp. Their specialty is a fine crab stew.

SAPELO ISLAND

Another of those amazing, undeveloped Georgia barrier islands that can only be reached by boat, Sapelo also shares with some of those islands a link to the Gilded Age.

History

The Spanish established a Franciscan mission on the north end of the island in the 1500s. Sapelo didn't become fully integrated into the Lowcountry plantation culture until its purchase by Thomas Spalding in the early 1800s. After the Civil War, many of the nearly 500 former slaves on the island remained, with a partnership of freedmen buying land as early as 1871.

Hudson Motors mogul Howard Coffin bought all of Sapelo, except for the African American communities, in 1912, building a palatial home and introducing a modern infrastructure. Among Coffin's visitors were two presidents, Calvin Coolidge and Herbert Hoover, and aviator Charles Lindbergh.

Coffin hit hard times in the Great

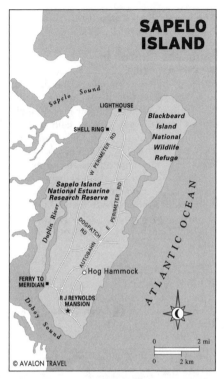

Depression and sold Sapelo to tobacco heir R. J. Reynolds in 1934, who consolidated the island's African Americans into the single Hog Hammock community. By the mid-1970s the Reynolds family had sold the island to the state, again with the exception of the 430 acres comprising Hog Hammock, with a little over 100 residents.

Today most of the island is administered for marine research purposes under the designation of **Sapelo Island National Estuarine Research Reserve** (www.sapelonerr.org).

Sights

Once on the island, you can take guided tours under the auspices of the Georgia Department of Natural Resources. Wednesdays 8:30 A.M.–12:30 P.M. is a tour of the **R. J. Reynolds Mansion** (www.reynoldsonsapelo.com) on the south end, and the rest of the island, including

Hog Hammock and the Long Tabby ruins. Saturdays 9 A.M.–1 P.M. is a tour of the historic **Sapelo Lighthouse** on the north end, and the rest of the island. June through Labor Day there's an extra lighthouse/island tour Fridays 8:30 A.M.–12:30 P.M. On the last Tuesday of the month March–October they do an extra-long day trip, 8:30 A.M.–3 P.M.

Tours are $10 adults, $6 children, free for those under age 6. Call 912/437-3224 for reservations. You can also arrange private tours.

Another key sight on Sapelo is a 4,500-year-old **Native American shell ring** on the north end, one of the oldest and best preserved anywhere.

Getting There
Visitors to Sapelo must embar on the ferry at the **Sapelo Island Visitors Center** (912/437-3224, www.sapelonerr.org, Tues.–Fri. 7:30 A.M.–5:30 P.M., Sat. 8 A.M.–5:30 P.M., Sun. 1:30–5 P.M., $10 adults, $6 ages 6–18) in little Meridian, Georgia, on GA 99 out of Darien. The visitors center actually has a nice nature hike of its own, and an auditorium where you can see an informative video. From there it's a half-hour trip over the Doboy Sound.

Keep in mind you must call in advance for reservations *before* showing up at the visitors center. I recommend calling at least a week in advance April–October.

ST. CATHERINE'S ISLAND
The interior of this beautiful island off the coast of Midway, Georgia, is off-limits to the public, but you can visit the beach up to the high-water mark by boat, enjoy its beautiful, unspoiled beaches, and spy on local wildlife. While that's about all you can do, it's important to know a little of the interesting background of this island.

Owned and administered by the St. Catherine's Island Foundation, it's unusual in that it has a 25-foot-high bluff on the northern end, an extraordinarily high geographic feature for a barrier island in this part of the world. Once central to the Spanish missionary effort on the Georgia coast, St. Catherine's was found to be home of over 400 graves of Christianized Native Americans (a large shell ring also exists on the island).

Declaration of Independence signer Button Gwinnett made a home here for a while until his death from a gunshot wound suffered in a duel in Savannah in 1777. After Sherman's famous "40 acres and a mule" order, a freed slave named Tunis Campbell was governor of the island, living in Gwinnett's home. But when the order was rescinded, all former slaves had to leave for the mainland.

In 1986, American Museum of Natural History archaeologist David Hurst Thomas began extensive research on Spanish artifacts left behind from the Santa Catalina de Guale mission, including foundations of living quarters, a kitchen, and a church—possibly the first Christian church in the modern-day United States. Today, however, the island, a National Historic Landmark, is better known as host to a New York Zoological Society project to recover injured or sick animals of endangered species and nurse them back to health for a possible return to the wild.

The closest marinas for the trip to the island's peaceful beaches are Shellman Fish Camp (912/832-4331) in McIntosh County and Halfmoon Marina (912/884-5819) in Liberty County.

BLACKBEARD ISLAND
While no one is positive if the namesake of Blackbeard Island actually landed here, the legends tell us he used it as a layover—even leaving some treasure here. Now federally administered as **Blackbeard Island National Wildlife Refuge** (912/652-4415, www.fws.gov/blackbeardisland), the island is accessible to the public by boat and gets about 10,000 visitors a year.

Plenty of hiking trails exist and the birdwatching is fantastic. It's also a major nesting ground for the endangered loggerhead turtle. Biking is permitted, but overnight camping is not.

For charters to Blackbeard, I recommend **SouthEast Adventures** (313 Mallory St., 912/638-6732) on St. Simons Island.

Cumberland Island and St. Marys

Actually comprising two islands—Great Cumberland and Little Cumberland—Cumberland Island National Seashore is the largest and one of the oldest of Georgia's barrier islands, and also one of its most remote and least developed. Currently administered by the National Park Service, it's accessible only by ferry or private boat.

Most visitors to Cumberland get there from the "gateway" town of St. Marys, Georgia, a nifty little fishing village that has so far managed to defy the increasing residential sprawl coming to the area.

ST. MARYS

Much like Brunswick to the north, the fishing town of St. Marys plays mostly a gateway role, in this case to the Cumberland Island National Seashore. That being said, it's a very friendly little waterfront community with undeniable charms of its own and a historic pedigree going back to the very beginnings of the nation.

History

As early as 1767, once the Spanish threat subsided, plans were made to establish a town in the area near the Florida border then known as Buttermilk Bluff. But it wasn't until 20 years later that a meeting was held on Cumberland Island to close the deal with Jacob Weed to purchase the tract—acquired by confiscation from two loyalist landowners—for the grand sum of $38.

The first influx of immigration to the area came as French Canadian refugees from Acadia (who would become known as Cajuns in Louisiana) came to St. Marys after being deported by the British. Another group of French-speakers came, fleeing Toussaint L'Ouverture's slave rebellion in Haiti.

During the colonial period, St. Marys was the southernmost U.S. city, and enjoyed not only importance as a seaport but was militarily important as well. Ironically, this strategic importance came into play more during America's conflict with Great Britain than with anything having to do with the Spanish.

In 1812 a British force took over Cumberland Island and St. Marys, with a contingent embarking up the river to track down the customs collection. However, in a bloody skirmish they were ambushed by American troops firing from the riverbanks. Though vowing to avenge their loss by burning down every building between the St. Marys and the Altamaha Rivers, the ensuing peace treaty ending the War of 1812 brought a ceasefire.

Unlike towns like Darien, which was put to the torch by Union troops, St. Marys was saved destruction in the Civil War. The lumber industry boomed after that conflict, as well as the local fishing and shrimping industry.

A hotel was built in 1916 (and hosted Marjorie Kinnan Rawlings, author of *The Yearlings*), but tourists didn't discover the area until the 1970s. It was also then that the U.S. Navy built the huge nuclear submarine base at Kings Bay, currently the area's largest employer, with almost 10,000 employees.

Development has increased in the area, with suburban sprawl beginning to cover the area like mushrooms after a heavy rain. Indeed, there's so much growth in the St. Marys/Camden County area that it's increasingly considered an outpost of the huge Jacksonville, Florida, metropolitan area to the south.

Orientation

Like Brunswick, the waterfront faces opposite the ocean and is instead oriented west toward a river, in this case the St. Marys River. Most activity in downtown St. Marys happens up and down Osborne Street, which perhaps not coincidentally is also how you get to the **Cumberland Island Visitor Center** (113 St. Marys St., 912/882-4335, daily 8 A.M.–4:30 P.M.) and from there board the *Cumberland Queen* for the trip to the island itself.

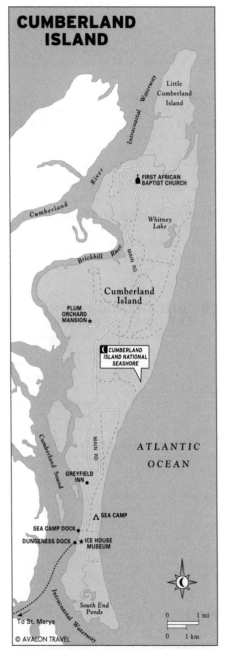

CUMBERLAND ISLAND

Little Cumberland Island

Intracoastal Waterway

River

Cumberland

★ FIRST AFRICAN BAPTIST CHURCH

Whitney Lake

Brickhill River

MAIN RD

Cumberland Island

PLUM ORCHARD MANSION ★

CUMBERLAND ISLAND NATIONAL SEASHORE

Cumberland Sound

MAIN RD

ATLANTIC OCEAN

GREYFIELD INN ●

▲ SEA CAMP

SEA CAMP DOCK ■
DUNGENESS DOCK ■ ★ ICE HOUSE MUSEUM

South End Ponds

0   1 mi
0   1 km

To St. Marys

Intracoastal Waterway

© AVALON TRAVEL

Sights

Tying the past to the present, it's only fitting that the home of the Kings Bay Submarine Base (which is not open to the public) has a museum dedicated to the "Silent Service." The **St. Marys Submarine Museum** (102 St. Marys St., 912/882-2782, www.stmarys-submuseum.com, Tues.–Sat. 10 A.M.–4 P.M., Sun. 1–5 P.M., $4 adults, $3 children) on the riverfront has a variety of exhibits honoring the contribution of American submariners. There's a neat interactive exhibit where you can look out of the genuine sub periscope that sticks out of the roof of the museum.

The most notable historic home in St. Marys is the **Orange Hall House Museum** (311 Osborne St., 912/576-3644, www.orangehall. org, Tues.–Sat. 9 A.M.–4 P.M., Sun. 1–4 P.M., $3 adults, $1 children). This beautiful Greek Revival home, circa 1830, survived the Civil War was the center of town social life during the Roaring Twenties, when it was owned by a succession of socialites from up north. The home is gorgeous inside and out, particularly during the holidays when it gets the full decorative treatment.

Events and Recreation

As a nod to its Cajun history, St. Marys hosts a heck of a **Mardi Gras Festival** each February, closing down six blocks of the riverfront for a parade. There's also live entertainment, vendors, and a costume ball.

For outdoor recreation near St. Marys, go to the **Crooked River State Park** (6222 Charlie Smith Sr. Hwy., 912/882-5256, www. gastateparks.org, daily office hours 8 A.M.– 10 P.M., Thurs. 8 A.M.–5 P.M.), which is not only a great place to put in for kayaking trips, including jaunts to Cumberland itself, but also has a wide range of lodging options as well.

A key stop on the Colonial Coast Birding Trail, Crooked River features its own nature center and is near a historic site just upriver, the tabby ruins of the McIntosh Sugar Works—actually a lumber mill from the early 1800s. The easiest way to get there is Exit 3 off I-95 and go about eight miles east.

THE GOLDEN ISLES

For renting kayaks or booking kayak and eco-tours, try **Up the Creek Xpeditions** (111 Osborne St., 912/882-0911, www.upthecreektours.com), which can take you all around the area including out to Cumberland Island.

Accommodations

Don't even think about staying at a chain hotel when you're in St. Marys. Stay at one of these cute historic inns for a song.

The most notable lodging for historic as well as economic value is the 18-room **Riverview Hotel** (105 Osborne St., 912/882-3242, www.riverviewhotelstmarys.com, under $100). This waterfront locale, like many old hotels in this area, has a great retro feel. It was built in the 1920s and has hosted such notables as author Marjorie Rawlings, John Rockefeller, poet Sidney Lanier, and Andrew Carnegie.

◖ **Emma's Bed and Breakfast** (300 West Conyers St., 912/882-4199, www.emmasbedandbreakfast.com, under $200) is situated on four beautiful acres in downtown St. Marys in a grand, Southern-style mansion with all the trappings and hospitality you'd expect.

You can also hang out on the veranda at the historic ◖ **Goodbread House** (209 Osborne St., 912/882-7490, www.goodbreadhouse.com, under $200), which offers rates below $100 in the off-season. The 1870 house features a stunning veranda and sumptuous interiors, including a classic dining room in which awesome breakfasts are served.

More outdoorsy visitors can stay at cottage, tent, or RV sites at **Crooked River State Park** (6222 Charlie Smith Sr. Hwy., 912/882-5256, www.gastateparks.org). There are 62 tent and RV sites (about $22) and 11 cottages ($85–110), as well as primitive camping ($25).

Food

St. Marys cannot compete in culinary sophistication with Charleston or Savannah, but it does have some of the freshest seafood around. One of the best places to eat seafood on the waterfront in St. Marys is at **Lang's Marina Restaurant** (307 W. St. Marys St., 912/882-4432, lunch Tues.–Fri. 11 A.M.–2 P.M., dinner

Wed.–Sat. 5–9 P.M., $15–20). The other premier seafood place is **Trolley's** (109 W. St. Marys St., 912/882-1525, Sun.–Thurs. 11 A.M.–9 P.M., Fri. and Sat. 11 A.M.–10 P.M., $15–20).

Information and Services

The **St. Marys Convention and Visitors Bureau** (406 Osborne St., 912/882-4000, www.stmaryswelcome.com) is a good source of information not only for the town but for Cumberland Island, though keep in mind that this is not actually where you catch the ferry to the island.

Getting There and Around

Take Exit 3 off I-95 to Kingsland-St. Marys Road (GA 40). This becomes Osborne Road, the main drag of St. Marys, as it gets closer into town. The road by the waterfront is St. Marys Street.

◖ CUMBERLAND ISLAND NATIONAL SEASHORE

Not only one of the richest estuarine environments in the world, Cumberland Island National Seashore (912/882-4335, www.nps.gov/cuis) is quite simply one of the most beautiful and romantic places on the planet, as everyone learned when the "it" couple of their day, John F. Kennedy Jr. and Carolyn Bessette were wed on the island in 1996. With more than 16 miles of gorgeous beach and an area of over 17,000 acres, there's no shortage of beauty either, and the island's already-remote feel is enhanced further by the efforts that have been taken to protect it from development.

Cumberland is far from pristine—it's been used for timbering and cotton, is dotted with evocative, abandoned ruins, and hosts a band of beautiful but voracious wild horses. But it is still a remarkable island paradise in a world where those kinds of locations are getting harder and harder to find.

History

Like modern-day Americans, the Timucuan Indians also revered this site, visiting it often for shellfish and for sassafras, a medicinal herb common on the island. Cumberland's size and great natural harbor made it a perfect base for Spanish friars, who established the first missionary on the island, San Pedro Mocama in 1587. In fact, the first Christian martyr in Georgia was created on Cumberland, when Father Pedro Martinez was killed by Indians.

As part of his effort to push the Spanish back into Florida for good, General James Oglethorpe established Fort William at the south end of Cumberland—the remains of which are now underwater—and a hunting lodge named Dungeness—an island place name which persists today. While land grants were made in the 1760s, they saw little follow-through, and by the time of naturalist William Bartram's visit in 1774 Cumberland Island was almost uninhabited.

But inevitably the Lowcountry planters' culture made its way down to Cumberland, which was soon the site of 15 thriving plantations and small farms. After the Revolution the heirs of one of its heroes, General Nathanael Greene, established Dungeness Plantation in 1802, its central building a now-gone tabby structure right on top of an ancient shell mound.

Actual military action wouldn't come to Cumberland until the War of 1812, when the British came in force and occupied the island for two months, using Dungeness as their headquarters. In the process they freed 1,500 slaves, who would then emigrate to various British colonies.

In 1818, Revolutionary War hero General "Lighthorse" Harry Lee—father of Robert E. Lee—arrived on Cumberland's shore, in failing health and determined to see the home of his old friend General Greene one last time. He died a month later and was buried there, his son returning later to erect a gravestone. Lighthorse Harry remained on Cumberland until 1913, when his remains were taken to Lexington, Virginia, to be beside those of his son. However, the gravestone on Cumberland remains to this day.

War—and another freeing of slaves—came again in the 1860s, when Union troops occupied the island. Though at war's end Cumberland was set aside as a home for freed African Americans—part of the famous and ill-fated "40 acres and a mule" proposal—politics intervened. Most of Cumberland's slaves were rounded up and taken to Amelia Island, Florida, though some settled at the north end (the "Settlement" area today).

As elsewhere on the Georgia coast, the Industrial Revolution came to Cumberland in the form of a vacation getaway for a mega-tycoon, in this case Thomas Carnegie, industrialist and brother of the better-known Andrew Carnegie of Carnegie Library fame. Carnegie built a new, even more grand Dungeness, which in a 1959 fire suffered the same fate as its predecessor.

Cumberland Island narrowly avoided becoming the next Hilton Head—literally—in 1969 when Hilton Head developer Charles Fraser bought the northern tip of the island and began bulldozing a runway. The dwindling but still influential Carnegies joined with the Georgia Conservancy to broker an agreement which resulted in dubbing Cumberland a National Seashore in 1972, saving it from further development. A $7.5 million gift from the Mellon Foundation enabled the purchase of Fraser's tract and the eventual incorporation of the island within the National Park system.

Sights

The ferry typically stops at two docks a short distance from each other, the Sea Camp dock and the Dungeness dock. At 4 P.M., Rangers offer a "Dockside" interpretive program at the Sea Camp. A short ways farther north at the Dungeness Dock, Rangers offer a "Dungeness Footsteps Tour" at 10 A.M. and 12:45 P.M., concentrating on the historic sites at the southern end of the island. Also at the Dungeness dock is the little **Ice House Museum** (912/882-4336, daily 9 A.M.–5 P.M., free) containing a range of exhibits on the island's history from Native American times to the present day.

Down near the docks are also where you'll find the stirring, almost spooky **Dungeness Ruins** and the nearby grave marker of Lighthorse Harry Lee. Controversy continues to this day as to the cause of the fire in 1866 that destroyed the old Dungeness home. Some say it was those freed slaves on the north end who lit the blaze, but others say it was the plantation's final owner, Robert Stafford, who did it out of spite after his former slaves refused to work for him after the war.

Moving north on the Main Road/Grand Avenue you come to **Greyfield Inn** (904/261-6408, www.greyfieldinn.com). Because it is a privately owned hotel, don't trespass through the grounds. A good ways farther north, just off the main road, you'll find the restored, rambling 20-room mansion **Plum Orchard,** another Carnegie legacy. Guided tours of Plum Orchard are available on the second and fourth Sunday of the month for $6 plus ferry fare; reserve a space at 912/882-4335.

At the very north end of the island, accessible only by foot or by bike, is the former freedmen's community simply known as **the Settlement,** featuring a small cemetery and the now world-famous **First African Baptist Church** (daily dawn–dusk)—a 1937 version of the 1893 original— a humble and rustic one-room church made of whitewashed logs in which the Kennedy/Bessette marriage took place.

Sports and Recreation
There are more than 50 miles of trails all over Cumberland, about 17 miles of nearly isolated beach to comb, and acres of maritime forest to explore—the latter an artifact of Cumberland's unusually-old age for a barrier island. Upon arrival, you might want to rent a bike at the **Sea Camp docks** (no reservations, arrange rentals on the ferry, $16 per day for adult bikes, $10 youth bikes, $20 overnight).

Shell-and-sharks-teeth collectors might want to explore south of Dungeness Beach as well as between the docks. Unlike some parks, you are allowed to take shells and fossils off the island.

Wildlife enthusiasts will be in heaven. More than 300 species of birds have been recorded on the island, which is also a favorite nesting ground for female loggerhead turtles in the late summer. Of course the most iconic image of Cumberland Island is its famous **wild horses,** a

WILD HORSES OF CUMBERLAND

Cumberland Island's famous wild horses are not actually direct descendants of the first horses brought to the island by Spanish and English settlers, though certainly feral horses have ranged the island for most of recorded history. The current population of 250 or so is actually descended from horses brought to the island by the Carnegie family in the 1920s.

Gorgeous and evocative though these magnificent animals are, they have a big appetite for vegetation and are frankly not the best thing for this sensitive barrier island ecosystem. But their beauty and visceral impact on the visitor is undeniable, which means the horses are likely to stay as long as nature will have them. And yes, these really are *wild* horses, meaning you shouldn't feed them even if they approach you for food, and you certainly won't be riding them.

free-roaming band of feral equines who traverse the island year-round, grazing as they please.

Accommodations
The only "civilized" lodging on Cumberland is the 13-room **Greyfield Inn** (main road and Grand Ave., 904/261-6408, www.greyfieldinn.com, $475), ranked by the American Inn Association as one of America's "Ten Most Romantic Inns." Opened in 1962 as a hotel, the Greyfield was originally built in 1900 as the home of the Carnegies. The rate includes meals, transportation, tours, and bike usage.

Many visitors opt to camp on Cumberland (reservations 877/860-6787, $4 per day, limit of up to seven nights) in one of three basic ways: at the **Sea Camp,** which has restrooms and shower facilities and permits fires; the remote **Stafford Beach,** a good hike from the docks and with no facilities; and pure wilderness camping farther north at **Hickory Hill, Yankee Paradise,** and **Brickman Bluff,** all of which are a multiple-mile hike away, do not permit fires, and have no facilities of any kind.

Reservations are needed for camping. *All* trash must be packed out on departure, as there are no refuse facilities on the island. Responsible alcohol consumption is limited to those 21 and over.

Getting There and Around

The most vital information about Cumberland is how to get ashore in the first place. Most visitors do this by purchasing a ticket on the *Cumberland Queen* at the **Cumberland Island Visitor Center** (113 St. Marys St., 912/882-4335, daily 8 A.M.–4:30 P.M., $17 adults, $12 children 12 and under, and $15 seniors) on the waterfront at St. Marys. The ferry ride is 45 minutes each way. Hours to call for reservations are Monday–Friday 10 A.M.–4 P.M.

The ferry does *not* transport pets, bicycles, kayaks, or cars. However, you can rent bikes at the Sea Camp docks once you're there. Every visitor to Cumberland over 16 years old must pay a $4 entry fee, including campers.

March 1–November 30, the ferry leaves St. Marys at 9 A.M. and 11:45 A.M., returning from Cumberland at 10:15 A.M. and 4:45 P.M. March 1–September 30, Wednesday–Saturday, there's an additional 2:45 P.M. departure from Cumberland back to St. Marys. December 1–February 28, the ferry does not operate on Tuesdays or Wednesdays, and there is no 2:45 P.M. departure from Cumberland.

One of the quirks of Cumberland, resulting from the unusual way in which it passed into federal hands, is the existence of some private property on which you mustn't trespass except where trails specifically allow it. Also, unlike the general public, these private landowners are allowed to use vehicles. For these reasons, it's best to make sure you have a map of the island, which you can get before you board the ferry at St. Marys.

There are no real stores and very few facilities on Cumberland. *Bring whatever you think you'll need,* whether it be food, water, medicine, suntan lotion, insect repellant, or otherwise.

The Okefenokee Swamp

Scientists often refer to Okefenokee as an "analogue," an accurate representation of a totally different epoch in earth's history. In this case it's the Carboniferous Period of about 350 million years ago, when the living plants were lush and green and the dead plants simmered in a slow-decaying peat that would one day end up as the oil that powers our entire civilization.

But for the casual visitor, Okefenokee might also be simply a wonderful place to get almost completely away from human influence and witness firsthand some of America's most interesting and gorgeous wildlife in its natural habitat. Despite the devastating wildfires of the spring of 2007—the largest the Southeast has seen in half a century, so large they were visible from space—the swamp has bounced back and is once again hosting visitors to experience its timeless beauty.

◖ OKEFENOKEE NATIONAL WILDLIFE REFUGE

It's nearly the size of Rhode Island and just a short drive off I-95, but the massive and endlessly fascinating Okefenokee National Wildlife Refuge (Route 2, Box 3330, 912/496-7836, www.fws.gov/okefenokee, Mar.–Oct. daily dawn–7:30 P.M., Nov.–Feb. daily dawn–5:30 P.M., $5 per vehicle) is of the lesser-visited national parks. Is it that very name "swamp" that keeps people away, with its connotations of fetid misery and lurking danger? Or simply its location out-of-sight and out-of-mind in South Georgia?

In any case, while it long ago entered the collective subconscious as a metaphor for the most untamed, darkly dangerous aspects of the American South—as well as the place where Pogo the Possum lived—the Okefenokee

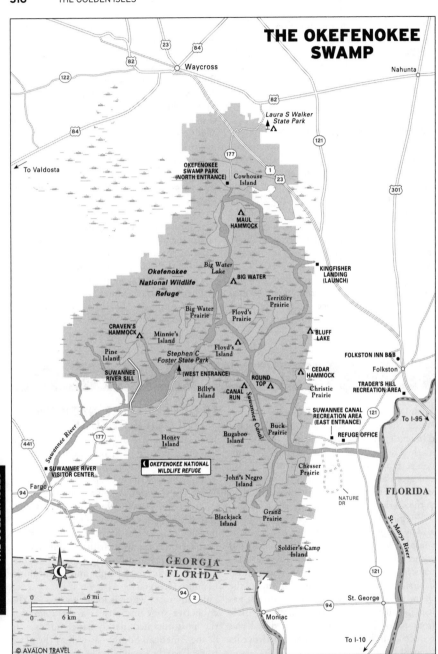

THE OKEFENOKEE SWAMP

Waycross

Nahunta

To Valdosta

Laura S Walker State Park

OKEFENOKEE SWAMP PARK (NORTH ENTRANCE)

Cowhouse Island

MAUL HAMMOCK

Okefenokee National Wildlife Refuge

KINGFISHER LANDING (LAUNCH)

Big Water Lake

BIG WATER

Territory Prairie

Big Water Prairie

Floyd's Prairie

CRAVEN'S HAMMOCK

Minnie's Island

BLUFF LAKE

FOLKSTON INN B&B

Floyd's Island

Pine Island

Stephen C Foster State Park

Folkston

SUWANNEE RIVER SILL

(WEST ENTRANCE)

CEDAR HAMMOCK

TRADER'S HILL RECREATION AREA

ROUND TOP

Christie Prairie

Billy's Island

CANAL RUN

SUWANNEE CANAL RECREATION AREA (EAST ENTRANCE)

To I-95

Buck Prairie

REFUGE OFFICE

Suwannee River

Honey Island

Bugaboo Island

☾ OKEFENOKEE NATIONAL WILDLIFE REFUGE

Chesser Prairie

NATURE DR

FLORIDA

SUWANNEE RIVER VISITOR CENTER

John's Negro Island

Fargo

St. Marys River

Grand Prairie

Blackjack Island

Soldier's Camp Island

GEORGIA FLORIDA

Moniac

St. George

To I-10

0   6 mi

0   6 km

© AVALON TRAVEL

THE GOLDEN ISLES

remains one of the most intriguing natural areas on the planet.

The nearby old rail town of Folkston is the gateway to the swamp for most visitors off of I-95, which is to say the bulk of them. In true Georgia fashion, the town is insular but friendly, slow but sincere.

History

The Okefenokee Swamp was created by an accident of geology. About 250,000 years ago, the Atlantic Ocean washed ashore about 70 miles farther inland from where it does today. Over time, a massive barrier island formed off this primeval Georgia coastline, running from Jesup, Georgia, south to what is now Starke, Florida.

When the ocean level dropped during the Pleistocene Era, this sandy island became a topographical feature known today as the Trail Ridge, its height effectively creating a basin to its west. Approximately 90 percent of the Okefenokee's water comes from rainfall into that basin, which drains slowly via the Suwannee and St. Mary's rivers.

Ordinarily, what the summer heat evaporates from the Okefenokee is more than replenished by rain, unless there's a severe drought like the one recently thatt caused the 2007 wildfires. But even the fires can't hold the swamp back. In fact, the Okefenokee is a fire ecosystem, meaning some plant species, like the cypress, depend on heat generated by wildfires to open their seedcones and perpetuate their lifecycle.

Because of constant rejuvenation by water and fire, biologists estimate that the oldest portion of this supposedly "ancient" swamp is actually no older than 7,000 years—the faintest blink of an eye in geological terms. Unlike Florida's Everglades, which actually comprise a single large and very slow-moving river—the Okefenokee is a true swamp.

Native Americans used the swamp as a hunting ground and gave us its current name, which means "Land of the Trembling Earth," a reference to the floating peat islands, called "houses," that dominate the landscape. The Spanish arrived about 1600, calling the swamp *Laguna de Oconi* (Lake Oconi), and establishing at least two missions in the area of two nearby Timucuan villages.

During the Seminole Wars of the 1830s, that tribe took refuge within the swamp for a time before continuing south into Florida. While trade had occurred on the outskirts for nearly a century before, it wasn't until the 1850s that the first white settlers set up camp inside the swamp itself.

It's a common mistake to call the Okefenokee "pristine," because like much of the heavily timbered and farmed southeastern coast, it is anything but. The swamp's ancient cypress stands and primordial longleaf pine forests were heavily harvested in the early 20th century. About 200 miles of old rail bed through the swamp still remain as a silent testament to the scope of that logging operation.

But the pace of logging gradually slowed to a stop, as the cost of the operation became prohibitive. In 1918, the Okefenokee Society was formed in nearby Waycross, Georgia, the first organized attempt to protect the habitat. In 1937, President Franklin Roosevelt brought the area within the federal wildlife refuge system.

In recent years, large deposits of titanium prompted several mining interests, including DuPont, to exercise rights in the area, to a great outcry from conservationists who worried that the intrusive 24-hour mining operations would destroy the swamp's habitat. However, a series of transactions involving the state and conservation trusts have, so far, resulted in halting those mining efforts.

Sights

Contrary to the popular image of a nasty, dank swamp, the Okefenokee is anything but a monoculture. It features a wide variety of ecosystems, from peat bogs to sandhills to blackgum and bay forests. Perhaps most surprising is the wide open vista of the swamp's many prairies or extended grasslands, 22 all told, which besides being stirring to the eye are also great places to see birds. So you see, not all of the Okefenokee is wet!

There is water aplenty here, though, with

© SONJA WALLEN

one of the Okefenokee Swamp's many prairies

over 60 named lakes and 120 miles of boating trails. And as you kayak or canoe on one of the water trails or on the old **Suwanee Canal** from the logging era, you'll notice the water's all very dark. This blackwater is not due to dirt or silt, but to natural tannic acid released into the water from the decaying vegetation that gave the swamp its name. While I don't recommend that you drink the water, it's actually very clean despite its color.

As you'd expect on a national wildlife refuge, the Okefenokee hosts a huge variety of animal life—more than 400 species of vertebrates, including over 200 varieties of birds and more than 60 types of reptiles. Birders get a special treat in late November/early December, when sandhill cranes come south to winter in the swamp. In January, their colonies are at their peak and the swamp echoes with their loud cries. Other common bird species you'll see are herons, egrets, and endangered wood storks and red-cockaded woodpeckers. The white ibis has seen a big spike in population in the refuge recently, as has the bald eagle.

A great place to see the sandhill cranes and other birds of the Okefenokee is to hike the three-quarter mile boardwalk out to the 50-foot **Chesser Island Observation Tower** on the eastern end of the swamp. You get there by driving or biking the eight-mile round-trip **Wildlife Drive,** which also takes you by the old **Chesser Homestead,** the remnants of one of the oldest settlements in the swamp. You can also hike out to Chesser; indeed there are many miles of hiking trails through the upland areas of the swamp near the East Entrance.

Probably the first creature one thinks of when one thinks of a swamp is the alligator. Certainly Okefenokee has plenty of them, and no one who has heard the roar of a male alligator break the quiet of the night will ever forget the experience. Most of the time, though, alligators are quite shy, and spotting them is an acquired skill. They often look like floating logs. Conversely, in warm weather you might see them out in the open, sunning themselves.

While no one can remember an incident of a gator attacking a human in the refuge, whatever you do, don't feed alligators in the wild. As a Fish and Wildlife ranger in Okefenokee once told me: "If a gator attacks a human, at some point in the past someone has fed that gator. Gators get used to being fed. Unfortunately, they can't tell the difference between the person and the food."

Believe it or not, the alligator is not even the top predator in the Okefenokee. That title belongs to the black bear. Biologists estimate that as many as 90 percent of alligator eggs laid in the refuge are eaten by the local black bear population. And as with the gators, please don't feed the bears.

Recreation and Accommodations

For most visitors, the best way to enjoy the Okefenokee is to book a guided tour through **Okefenokee Adventures** (866/843-7926, www.okefenokeeadventures.com), the designated concessionaire of the refuge. They offer a 90-minute guided boat tour ($16 adults, $10 children) that leaves each hour, and a 2.5-hour reservation-only sunset tour ($25 adults, $17 children) that takes you to see the gorgeous sunset over Chesser Prairie. Extended and/or custom tours, including multi-day wilderness excursions, are also available. They also rent bikes, canoes, and camping gear, and even run a decent little café where you can either sit down and have a meal or take it to go out on the trail.

It's possible to stay the night in the swamp, canoeing to one of the primitive camping "islands" in the middle of the refuge. You need to make reservations up to two months in advance, however, and you do this by calling **U.S. Fish and Wildlife** (912/496-3331, Mon.–Fri. 7–10 A.M.). A non-refundable fee of $10 per person (which also covers your entrance fee) must be received 16 days before you arrive (mailing address is Okefenokee National Wildlife Refuge, Route 2, Box 3330, Folkston, GA 31537). Campfires are allowed only at Canal Run and Floyds Island. A camp stove is required for cooking at all other shelters.

Privately owned canoes and boats with motors under 10 horsepower may put in with no launch fee, however you must sign in and out. No ATVs are allowed on the refuge, and bikes are allowed only on designated bike trails.

Keep in mind that some hunting goes on in the refuge at designated times. Pets must be leashed at all times.

At the **Stephen Foster State Park** (17515 Hwy. 177, 912/637-5274, fall and winter daily 7 A.M.–7 P.M., spring and summer daily 6:30 A.M.–8:30 P.M.), a.k.a., the **West Entrance,** near Fargo, Georgia, there are 66 tent sites ($24) and nine cottages ($100). Several miles away the state has just opened the new **Suwanee River Visitor Center** (912/637-5274, www.gastateparks.org, Wed.–Sun. 9 A.M.–5 P.M.), a "green" building featuring an orientation video and exhibits.

Getting There and Around

For the purposes of anyone using this book as a travel resource, the best way to access the Okefenokee—and the one I recommend—is the **East Entrance** (912/496-7836, www.fws.gov/okefenokee, Mar.–Oct. daily dawn–7:30 P.M., Nov.–Feb. daily dawn–5:30 P.M., $5 per vehicle), otherwise known as the **Suwanee Canal Recreation Area.** This is the main U.S. Fish and Wildlife Service entrance and the most convenient way to hike, rent boating and camping gear, and observe nature. The **Richard S. Bolt Visitor Center** (912/496-7836) has some cool nature exhibits and a surround-sound orientation video.

Get to the East Entrance by taking the Kingsland Exit 3 off I-95 to Georgia Highway 40 west. Go through Kingsland and into Folkston until it dead-ends. Take a right, then an immediate left onto Main Street. At the third light, make a left onto Okefenokee Drive (Hwy. 121 south).

Families with kids may want to drive a bit farther and hit the **North Entrance** at the privately run **Okefenokee Swamp Park** (US 1 south, 912/283-0583, www.okeswamp.com, daily 9 A.M.–5:30 P.M., $12 adults, $11 children 3–11) near Waycross, Georgia (fans of the old "Pogo Possum" will recall Waycross from the comic strip; and yes, there's a real "Fort Mudge" nearby). There you will find a more touristy vibe, with a reconstructed pioneer village, serpentarium, and animals in captivity.

From there you can take various guided tours for an additional fee. There's camping at the nearby but unaffiliated **Laura S. Walker State Park** (5653 Laura Walker Rd., 800/864-7275, www.gastateparks.org). Be aware the state park is not in the swamp and isn't very swampy.

Get to the North Entrance by taking Exit 6 off I-95 and go west on US 90 about 45 miles to GA 177 (Laura Walker Rd.). Go south through the state park; the Swamp Park is several miles from there.

If you really want that cypress-festooned, classic swamp look, take the long way around the Okefenokee to the **Stephen Foster State Park** (17515 Hwy. 177, 912/637-5274, fall and winter daily 7 A.M.–7 P.M., spring and summer daily 6:30 A.M.–8:30 P.M.), a.k.a., the **West Entrance,** near Fargo, Georgia. Guided tours are available.

Get to Stephen Foster State Park by taking Exit 3 off I-95 and take the signs to Folkston. Get on GA 121 south to St. George, and then go west on GA 94.

FOLKSTON

The chief attraction in Folkston, the little town right outside the refuge's East Entrance, is the excellent **❮ Inn at Folkston Bed and Breakfast** (509 W. Main St., 888/509-6246, www.innatfolkston.com, $120–170). There is nothing like coming back to its cozy Victorian charms after a long day out in the swamp. The four-room inn boasts an absolutely outstanding breakfast, an extensive reading library, and whirlpool tub.

A five-minute drive from the Inn is another Folkston claim to fame, the viewing depot for the **Folkston Funnel** (912/496-2536, www .folkston.com), a veritable train watcher's paradise. This is the spot where the big CSX double-track rail line—following the top of the ancient Trail Ridge—hosts 60 or more trains a day. Railroad buffs from all over the South congregate here, anticipating the next train by listening to their scanners. The first Saturday each April brings buffs together for the all-day "Folkston RailWatch."

BACKGROUND

The Land

GEOGRAPHY

The area covered by this book falls within the **Coastal Plain** region of the southeastern United States, which contains some of the most unique ecosystems in North America. It's a place where water is never far away and always features large in the daily lives, economy, and folkways of the region's people.

The ancient geography of the region determines the nature of the coast today, still in a profound state of flux from a variety of factors. Though it's hundreds of miles away, the Appalachian Mountain chain has a major influence on the southeastern coast. It's in Appalachia where so much of the coast's freshwater—in the form of rain—comes together and flows southeast—in the form of rivers—to the Atlantic Ocean.

Moving east, the next level down from the Appalachians is the **Piedmont** region (in South Carolina often called simply the Upstate). The Piedmont is a hilly area, the eroded remains of an ancient mountain chain now long gone. The Piedmont is largely forested, with generally poor, clay-heavy soil.

At the Piedmont's eastern edge is the **fall line,** so named because it's there where rivers make a drop toward the sea, generally becoming navigable. This slight but noticeable change in elevation—which actually marked

© JIM MOREKIS

Jekyll Island's Driftwood Beach highlights the effect of natural erosion on barrier islands.

the shoreline about 60 million years ago—not only encouraged trade, but has provided water power for mills for hundreds of years. Many inland cities of the region, like Macon, Georgia, and Columbia, South Carolina, trace their origin and commercial success to their strategic location on the fall line.

Around the fall line zone in the **Upper Coastal Plain** you can sometimes spot **sandhills,** usually only a few feet in elevation, generally thought to be the vestigial remains of primordial sand dunes and offshore sandbars. Well beyond the fall line and sometimes nearly invisible sandhills lies the **Lower Coastal Plain,** gradually built up over a 150 million-year span by sedimentary runoff from the Appalachian Mountains, then as high or even higher than the modern-day Himalayas.

The Coastal Plain was sea bottom for much of the earth's history, and in some eroded areas you can see dramatic proof of this in prehistoric shells, shark's teeth, and fossilized whale bones and oyster beds, often many miles inland. In some places, calcium from these ancient shells

has provided a lush home for distinct groups of unique plants, called **dijuncts.**

Sea level has fluctuated wildly with climate and geological changes through the eons. At various times over the last 50 million years, the Coastal Plain has submerged, surfaced, and submerged again. At the height of the last major Ice Age, when global sea levels were very low, the east coast of North America extended out nearly 100 miles farther than the present shoreline. (We now call this former coastal region the **continental shelf.**) The Coastal Plain has been in roughly its current form for about the last 15,000 years.

Rivers

Visitors from drier climates are sometimes shocked to see how huge the rivers can get in coastal Georgia and South Carolina, how wide and voluminous as they saunter to the sea, their seemingly slow speed belying the massive power they contain. Georgia and South Carolina's big **alluvial,** or sediment-bearing, rivers originate in the region of the Appalachian mountain chain. The headwaters of the Savannah River, for example, are near Tallulah Gorge in extreme north Georgia.

Some rivers form out of the confluence of smaller rivers, such as Georgia's mighty Altamaha, actually the child of the Ocmulgee and Oconee Rivers in the middle of the state. Others, like the Ashley and Cooper Rivers in South Carolina, originate much closer to the coast in the Piedmont.

The **blackwater river** is a particularly interesting Southern phenomenon, duplicated elsewhere only in South America and one example each in New York and Michigan. While alluvial rivers generally originate in highlands and carry with them a large amount of sediment, blackwater rivers originate in low-lying areas and move slowly toward the sea, carrying with them very little sediment.

Rather, their dark tea color comes from the tannic acid of decaying vegetation all along their banks, washed out by the slow, inexorable movement of the river toward the sea. While I don't necessarily recommend drinking it, despite its dirty color "blackwater" is for the most part remarkably clean and hygienic.

Blackwater courses featured prominently in this book are the Edisto River (the longest blackwater river in the world), Ebenezer Creek near Savannah, and Georgia's Suwannee River, which originates in the Okefenokee Swamp and empties in the Gulf of Mexico. Georgia's Altamaha River is a hybrid of sorts because it is partially fed by the blackwater Ohoopee River.

The Intracoastal Waterway

You'll often see its acronym ICW on signs—and sadly you'll probably hear the locals mispronounce it "Intercoastal Waterway"—but the casual visitor might actually find the Intracoastal Waterway difficult to spot. Relying on a natural network of interconnected estuaries and channels, combined with manmade **cuts,** the ICW often blends in rather subtly with the already extensive network of creeks and rivers in the area.

Mandated by Congress in 1919 and maintained by the U.S. Army Corps of Engineers, the Atlantic portion of the ICW runs from Key West to Boston and carries recreational and barge traffic away from the perils of offshore currents and weather. Even if they don't use it specifically, kayakers and boaters often find themselves on it at some point during their nautical adventures.

Estuaries

Most biologists will tell you that the Coastal Plain is where things get interesting. The place where a river interfaces with the ocean is called an estuary, and it's perhaps the most interesting place of all. Estuaries are heavily tidal in nature (indeed, the word derives from *aestus,* Latin for tide), and feature brackish water and heavy silt content.

Georgia typically has about a 6–8-foot tidal range, and the coastal ecosystem depends on this steady ebb and flow for life itself. At high tide, shellfish open and feed. At low tide, they literally clam up, keeping saltwater inside their shells until the next tide comes. Waterbirds and small mammals feed on shellfish and other animals at low tide, when their prey is exposed. High tide brings an influx of fish and nutrients from the sea, in turn drawing predators like dolphins, who often come into tidal creeks to feed.

An interesting regional feature of the estuaries is the **Carolina Bay,** elliptical depressions rich with biodiversity found all along the coast from Delaware to Florida. Named not for the water within them but for the proliferation of bay trees often found inside, Carolina Bays can be substantially older than the surrounding terrain, with many well over 25,000 years old.

It's the estuaries that form the most compelling and beautiful sanctuaries for the area's incredibly rich diversity of animal species. Many estuaries are contiguous with those of other rivers. (Charleston harbor, formed by the confluence of the Ashley and Cooper Rivers, is an excellent example of that phenomenon.)

For purposes of this book, key estuaries from north to south are: Cape Romaine, Charleston Harbor, ACE (Ashepoo, Edisto, Combahee) Basin, Beaufort River, May River, Calibogue

Sound, Savannah River, Wilmington River, Midway River, Altamaha River, and the Brunswick River.

Salt Marsh

All this water action in both directions—freshwater coming from inland, saltwater encroaching from the Atlantic—results in the phenomenon of the salt marsh, the single most recognizable and iconic geographic feature of the Georgia and South Carolina coast, also known simply as "wetlands." (Freshwater marshes are more rare, Florida's Everglades being perhaps the premier example.)

Far more than just a transitional zone between land and water, marsh is also nature's nursery. Plant and animal life in marshes tends to be not only diverse, but encompassing multitudes. Though you may not see its denizens easily, on close inspection you'll find the marsh absolutely teeming with creatures. Visually, the main identifying feature of a salt marsh is its distinctive, reed-like marsh grasses, adapted to survive in brackish water. Like estuaries, marshes and all life in them are heavily influenced by the tides, which bring in nutrients.

The marsh has also played a key role in human history as well, for it was here where the massive rice and indigo plantations grew their signature crops, aided by the natural ebb and flow of the tides. While most marsh you see will look quite undisturbed, very little of it could be called pristine. In the heyday of the rice plantations, much of the entire coastal salt marsh was crisscrossed by the canal-and-dike system of the rice paddies. You can still see evidence almost everywhere in the area if you look hard enough (the best time to look is right after takeoff or before landing in an airplane, since many approaches to regional airports take you over wetlands).

Anytime you see a low, straight ridge running through a marsh, that's likely the eroded, overgrown remnant of an old rice paddy dike. Kayakers occasionally find old wooden sluice gates on their paddles.

In the Lowcountry, you'll often hear the term **pluff mud.** This refers to the area's distinctive variety of soft, dark mud in the salt marsh, which often has an equally distinctive odor that locals love, but some visitors have a hard time getting used to. Extraordinarily rich in nutrients, pluff mud helped make rice such a successful crop in the marshes of the Lowcountry.

In addition to their huge role as wildlife incubators and sanctuaries, wetlands are also one of the most important natural protectors of the health of the coastal region. They serve as natural filters, cleansing runoff from the land of toxins and pollutants before it hits the ocean. They also help humans by serving as natural hurricane barriers, their porous nature helping to ease the brunt of the damaging storm surge.

Beaches and Barrier Islands

The often stunningly beautiful, broad beaches of Georgia and South Carolina—like Folly Beach, Sullivan's Island, Hunting Island, and Tybee Island—are almost all situated on barrier islands, long islands parallel to the shoreline and separated from the mainland by a sheltered body of water. Because they're formed by the deposit of sediment by offshore currents, they change shape over the years, with the general pattern of deposit going from north to south (i.e., the northern end will begin eroding first).

Most of the barrier islands are geologically quite young, only being formed within the last 25,000 years or so. One small barrier island off the coast of Savannah, Williamson Island, did not even exist 25 years ago.

Natural erosion, by current and by storm, combined with the accelerating effects of dredging for local port activity has quickened the decline of many barrier islands. Many beaches in the area are subject to a mitigation of erosion called **beach renourishment,** which generally involves redistributing dredged material closely offshore so that it will wash up on and around the beach.

As the name indicates, barrier islands are another of nature's safeguards against hurricane damage. Historically, the barrier islands have borne the vast bulk of the damage done by hurricanes in the region. Tybee Island near Savannah was completely under water in the hurricane of 1898. More recently, Sullivan's Island near Charleston was submerged by Hurricane Hugo. Like the marshes, barrier islands also help protect the mainland by absorbing the brunt of the storm's wind and surging water.

Though barrier islands are ephemeral by nature, they have played an important role in the area's geography from the beginning of time. In fact, nearly every major settlement on the Georgia coast today—including Savannah, Darien, and Brunswick—is built on the vestiges of massive barrier islands that once guarded a primordial shoreline many miles inland from the present one.

By far the largest of these ancient barrier islands, now on dry land, is the fabled **Trail Ridge,** which runs from Jesup, Georgia, to Starke, Florida. The Trail Ridge's height all along its distance made it a favorite route first for Native Americans and then for railroads, which still run along its crest today.

The Trail Ridge is such a dominant geographical feature even today that it's actually responsible for the formation of the Okefenokee Swamp. The Ridge effectively acts as a levee on the swamp's eastern side, preventing its drainage to the sea.

CLIMATE

One word comes to mind when one thinks about Southern climate: hot. That's the first word that occurs to Southerners as well, but virtually every survey of why residents are attracted to the area puts the climate at the top of the list. Go figure.

How hot is hot? The average high for July, the region's hottest month, in Savannah is about 92°F, in Charleston about 89°F. While that's nothing compared to Tucson or Death Valley, coupled with the region's notoriously high **humidity** it can have an altogether miserable effect.

Heat aside, there's no doubt that one of the most difficult things for an outsider to adjust to in the South is the humidity. The average annual humidity in Charleston and Savannah is about 55 percent in the afternoons and a whopping

85 percent in the mornings. The most humid months are August and September.

There is no real antidote to humidity—other than air conditioning, that is—though many film crews and other outside workers swear by the use of Sea Breeze astringent. If you and your traveling partner can deal with the strong minty odor, dampen a hand towel with the astringent, drape it across the back of your neck and go about your business.

Don't assume that because it's humid you shouldn't drink fluids. Just as in any hot climate, you should drink lots of water if you're going to be out in the Southern heat.

Technically the Georgia and South Carolina coasts are considered **subtropical.** During summer the famous high-pressure system called the **Bermuda High** settles over the entire southeastern United States, its rotating winds pushing aside most weather coming from the west. This can bring drought, as well as a certain sameness that afflicts the area during summer.

You'll no doubt grow to love the steady ocean breeze during the day all along the coast. But at night you may notice the wind changing direction and coming from inland. That's caused by the land cooling at night, and the wind rushing toward the warmer waters offshore.

This shift in wind current is mostly responsible for that sometimes awe-inspiring, sometimes just plain scary phenomenon of a typical Southern **thunderstorm.** Seemingly within the space of a few minutes on a particularly hot and still summer day, the afternoon is taken over by a rapidly moving stacked storm cloud called a **thunderhead,** which soon bursts open and pours an unbelievable amount of rain on whatever is unlucky enough to be beneath it, along with frequent, huge lightning strikes. Then, almost as quickly as it came on, the storm subsides and the sun comes back out again as if nothing happened.

August and September are by far the rainiest months in terms of rainfall, with averages well over six inches for each of those months. July is also quite wet, coming in at over five inches on average.

Winters here are pretty mild, but can seem much colder than they actually are because of the dampness in the air. The coldest month is January, with about a 58°F high for the month and a 42°F average low.

You're highly unlikely to encounter snow in the area, and if you do it will likely only be skimpy flurries that a resident of the Great Lakes region wouldn't even notice as snow. But don't let this lull you into a false sense of security. If such a tiny flurry were to hit, be aware that most people down here have no clue how to drive in rough weather and will not be prepared for even such a small amount of snowfall. Visitors from snow country are often surprised, sometimes bordering on shock, by how completely a Southern city will shut down when that once-in-a-decade few millimeters of snow finally hits.

Hurricanes

The major weather phenomenon for residents and visitors alike is definitely the mighty hurricane. These massive storms, with counterclockwise-rotating bands of clouds and winds pushing 200 miles per hour, are an ever-present danger to the southeast coast June–November of each year.

While the South Carolina coast has had its share of hurricane strikes, historically the Georgia coast has been relatively safe, if not immune, from major hurricane activity. In fact, as of this writing the last major storm to directly hit the Georgia coast was in 1898. Meteorologists chalk this up to the Georgia coast's relatively sheltered, concave position relative to the rest of the southeastern coastline, as well as prevailing pressure and wind patterns that tend to deflect the oncoming storms.

In any case, as most everyone is aware now from the horrific, well-documented damage from such killer storms as Hugo, Andrew, and Katrina, hurricanes are not to be trifled with. Old-fashioned, drunken "hurricane parties" are a thing of the past for the most part, the images of cataclysmic destruction everyone has seen on TV having long since eliminated any lingering romanticism about riding out the storm.

Tornadoes—especially those that come in the "back door" through the Gulf of Mexico and overland to the Georgia or Carolina coast—are a very present danger with hurricanes. As hurricanes die out overland, they can spawn literally dozens of tornadoes, which in many cases prove more destructive than the hurricanes that spawned them.

Local TV, websites, and print media can be counted on to give more than ample warning in the event a hurricane is approaching the area during your visit. Whatever you do, do not discount the warnings. It's not worth it. If the locals are preparing to leave, you should too.

Typically when a storm is likely to hit the area, there will first be a suggested evacuation. But if authorities determine there's an overwhelming likelihood of imminent hurricane damage, they will issue a **mandatory evacuation order.** What this means in practice that if you do choose to stay behind, you cannot count on any type of emergency services or help whatsoever.

Generally speaking, the most lethal element of a hurricane is not the wind but the **storm surge,** the wall of ocean water that the winds drive before them onto the coast. During Hurricane Hugo, Charleston's Battery was inundated with a storm surge of over 12 feet, with an amazing 20 feet reported farther north at Cape Romaine.

In the wake of such devastation, local governments have dramatically improved their once tepid disaster-response plans. For example, the large red traffic barriers you see stowed in their ready positions at many exits along I-16 in Georgia are a direct result of the chaos of the botched evacuation during Hurricane Floyd in 1999. Learning from that lesson, Georgia officials decided to make all four lanes of I-16 westbound in the event of a major evacuation, and those red barriers are there today to reroute traffic should they ever be needed.

ENVIRONMENTAL ISSUES

The coast of Georgia and South Carolina is currently experiencing a double whammy, environmentally speaking: Not only are its

THE NEW CHARLESTON GREEN

Most people know "Charleston Green" as a unique local color, the result of adding a few drops of yellow to post–Civil War surplus black paint. But these days the phrase might refer to all the environmentally friendly development in Charleston, which you might find surprising considering the city's location in one of the most conservative states in the country's most conservative region.

The most obvious example is the ambitious Navy Yard redevelopment, which seeks to re-purpose the closed-down facility. That project is part of a larger civic vision to re-imagine the entire 3,000-acre historic Noisette community of North Charleston, with an accompanying wetlands protection conservancy.

From its inception in 1902 at the command of President Theodore Roosevelt through the end of the Cold War, the Charleston Navy Yard was one of the city's biggest employers. Closed down in 1995 as part of a national base realignment plan, locals feared the worst.

But a 340-acre section, the **Navy Yard at Noisette** (www.navyyardsc.com), now hosts an intriguing mix of green-friendly design firms, small nonprofits, and commercial maritime companies. The activity centers on the restoration of three huge former naval warehouses at 7, 10, and 11 Storehouse Row. Nearby, on the way to where the CSS *Hunley* is currently being restored, is the big Powerhouse, once the electrical station for the whole yard and now envisioned as the center of a future entertainment/retail district.

In the meantime, the Navy Yard's no-frills retro look is so realistic that it has played host to scenes of the Lifetime TV series *Army Wives*.

Also in North Charleston, local retail chain Half Moon Outfitters recently completed a green-friendly warehouse facility in an old Piggly Wiggly Grocery store. The first LEED (Leadership in Energy and Environmental Design) Platinum certified building in South Carolina, the warehouse features solar panels, rainwater reservoirs, and locally harvested or salvaged interiors. There's also the LEED-certified North Charleston Elementary School, as well as North Charleston's adoption of a "Night Skies" ordinance to cut down on light pollution.

But North Charleston's far from the only place in town going green. On the peninsula, the historic meeting house of the Circular Congregation Church, which gave Meeting Street its name, has a green addition with geothermal heating and cooling, rainwater cisterns, and Charleston's first vegetative roof.

In addition to walking the historic byways of the Old Village of Mount Pleasant, architecture and design buffs might also want to check out the new 243-acre I'On (www.ionvillage .com) "neotraditional" planned community, a successful model for this type of pedestrian-friendly, New Urbanist development.

On adjacent Daniel Island, the developers of that island's 4,000 acre planned residential community recently were certified as an "Audubon Cooperative Sanctuary" for using wildlife-friendly techniques on its golf and recreational grounds.

Even ultra-upscale Kiawah Island has gone green in something other than golf – the fabled Kiawah bobcats are making a comeback, thanks to the efforts of the Kiawah Conservancy.

Why has Charleston proven so adept at moving forward? Locals chalk it up to two things: affluent, well-connected Charlestonians who want to maintain the area's quality of life, and the forward-thinking leadership of Mayor Joe Riley in Charleston and Mayor Keith Summey in North Charleston.

For many Charlestonians, however, the green movement manifests in simpler things: the pedestrian and bike lanes on the new Ravenel Bridge over the Cooper River, the thriving city recycling program, or the Sustainable Seafood Initiative, a partnership of local restaurants, universities, and conservation groups that brings only the freshest, most environmentally responsible dishes to your table when you dine out in Charleston.

distinctive wetlands extraordinarily sensitive to human interference, this is one of the most rapidly developing parts of the country. New and often-poorly planned subdivisions and resort communities are popping up all over the place. Vastly increased port activity, too, is taking a devastating toll on the salt marsh and surrounding barrier islands. Combine all that with the South's often skeptical attitude towards environmental activism, and you have a recipe for potential ecological disaster.

Thankfully, there are some bright spots. More and more communities are seeing the value of responsible planning and not greenlighting every new development sight unseen. Land trusts and other conservation organizations are growing in size, number, funding, and influence. The large number of marine biologists in these areas at various research and educational institutions means there's a wealth of education and talent available in advising local governments and citizens on how best to conserve the area's natural beauty.

Hilton Head Island is a longtime trendsetter for sustainable development, going back to the insistence of its original residential developer, Charles Fraser, that the Sea Pines development interfere as little as possible with the island's ecosystem. But of all the areas covered in this book, the city of Charleston and Charleston County are without a doubt leading the pack on environmental issues right now—perhaps because its wealth and comparatively large size mean it has so much more to lose if things go badly. Planners estimate the Charleston area will have to accommodate about 250,000 new residents over the next 25 years, and there's a clear consensus locally that the time to act is now.

One concrete step Charleston County has taken is devoting part of a new transportation sales tax to its new comprehensive greenbelt plan to help responsibly guide the next 25 years of development there. It calls for at least $12 million to go to preserving rural greenspace and nearly $2 million to conserve remaining urban greenspace.

Here's a closer look at some of the most urgent environmental issues facing the region today:

Marsh Dieback

The dominant species of marsh grass, *Spartina alterniflora* (pronounced Spar-TINE-uh) and *Juncus roemerianus* thrive in the typically brackish water of the coastal marsh estuaries, their structural presence helping to stem erosion of banks and dunes. While drought and blight have taken their toll on the grass, increased coastal development and continued channel deepening have also led to a steady creep of ocean saltwater further and further into remaining marsh stands.

Effects of Dredging

Port activity is economically vital—and becoming more so—to the coastal cities of Charleston, South Carolina, and to Savannah and Brunswick in Georgia. In addition, the submarine channel at Kings Bay Naval Base off St. Marys, Georgia, must be kept navigable. The downside of such large-scale industrial dredging is twofold:

1) The deeper the channel, the farther upstream salty ocean water pushes. This destroys freshwater and brackish habitats such as the salt marsh.

2) Deepening the channel increases both the volume and the velocity of the river, quickening erosion of the riverbanks.

The most heavily used shipping channels, Savannah and Charleston, leave behind visual evidence of the massive dredging required to keep them navigable for today's huge cargo vessels. All that silt and sand has to go somewhere. Some of it is deposited in **dredge spoil sites,** which from a distance look like huge, tightly packed earthworks. A notable example of such spoil sites is on Hutchinson Island, across the Savannah River from the Savannah waterfront.

The Paper Industry

Early in the 20th century, the Southeast's abundance of cheap, undeveloped land and plentiful, free water led to the establishment of massive pine tree farms to feed coastal pulp and paper mills. Chances are if you used a paper grocery bag recently, it was made in a paper mill in the South.

But in addition to making a whole lot of paper bags and providing lots of employment for residents through the decades, the paper industry also gave the area lots of air and water pollution, stressed local water supplies (it takes a lot of water to make paper from trees), and took away natural species diversity from the area by devoting so much acreage to a single crop, pine trees.

Currently the domestic paper industry is reeling from competition from cheaper Asian lumber stocks and paper mills. As a result, an interesting—and not altogether welcome—phenomenon has been the wholesale entering of Southeastern paper companies into the real estate business.

Discovering they can make a whole lot more money selling or developing tree farms for residential lots than making paper bags, pulp and paper companies are helping to drive overdevelopment in the region by encouraging development on their land rather than infill development closer to urban areas. So in the long run, the demise of the paper industry in the South may not prove the net advantage to the environment that was anticipated.

Aquifers

Unlike parts of the western U.S., where individuals can enforce private property rights to water, the South has generally held that the region's water is a publicly held resource. The upside of this is that everybody has equal claim to drinking water without regard to status or income or how long they've lived there. The downside is that industry also has the same free claim to the water that citizens do—and they use a heck of a lot more of it.

Currently most of the Georgia and South Carolina coasts get their water from aquifers, which are basically huge underground caverns made of limestone. Receiving **groundwater** drip by drip, century after century, from rainfall farther inland, the aquifers essentially act as massive, sterile warehouses for freshwater, accessible through wells.

The aquifers have human benefit only if their water remains fresh. Once saltwater from the ocean begins intruding into an aquifer, it doesn't take much to render all of it unfit for human consumption—forever. What keeps that freshwater fresh is natural water pressure, keeping the ocean at bay.

But nearly a century ago, paper mills began pumping millions and millions of gallons of water out of coastal aquifers. Combined with the dramatic rise in coastal residential development, that has decreased the natural water pressure of the aquifers, leading to measurable saltwater intrusion at several points under the coast.

Currently, local and state governments in both states are increasing their reliance on **surfacewater** (i.e., treated water from rivers and creeks) to relieve the strain on the underground aquifer system. But it's too soon to tell if that has contained the threat from saltwater intrusion.

Nuclear Energy

There are two nuclear power plants in and around the area covered in this book: Plant Hatch near Baxley, Georgia outside Savannah, and Plant Vogtle near Augusta, upriver from Savannah. Both are administered by the Southern Company, and both were built in the 1970s.

Looming upstream of the entire area is the massive, Cold War–era nuclear bomb plant Savannah River Site, near Aiken, South Carolina. Groundwater in the area has already shown measurable amounts of radiation from the site and activists have long warned of potential catastrophe from its aging infrastructure. On Christmas Day, 1991, Savannah citizens were alarmed by the announcement that an amount of radioactive tritium had accidentally been released from the plant into the Savannah River.

Air Pollution

Despite growing awareness of the issue, air pollution is still a big problem in the coastal region. Paper mills still operate, putting out their distinctive rotten-eggs odor, and auto emissions standards are notoriously lax in both Georgia and South Carolina.

The biggest culprit, though, are coal-powered electric plants, which are the norm throughout the region and which continue to pour large amounts of toxins into the atmosphere.

Mining

When you think mining you don't ordinarily think of the Southeastern United States. But large deposits of zircon (from which the artificial gem zirconium is made) and titanium (used to make titanium dioxide, the white pigment in suntan lotion and toothpaste) make portions of the coast vulnerable to large-scale 24-hour mining operations, which not only disrupt wildlife habitats but human activity as well because of their constant noise and light pollution.

In an encouraging note, a large titanium deposit right next to the Okefenokee Swamp will not be mined, thanks to a historic agreement. DuPont purchased 50-year mining rights to the deposit in the late 1990s, but public pressure persuaded them to forfeit those rights within a few years and donate much of the land to conservation.

Flora and Fauna

FLORA

Undoubtedly the most iconic plant life of the coastal region is the **Southern live oak** *(Quercus virginiana)*, the official state tree of Georgia. Named because of its evergreen nature, a live oak is technically any one of a number of evergreens in the *Quercus* genus, many of which reside on the Georgia and South Carolina coast, but in local practice almost always refers to the Southern live oak. Capable of living over 1,000 years and possessing wood of legendary resilience, the Southern live oak is one of nature's most magnificent creations. Though the timber value of live oaks has been well known since the earliest days of the American shipbuilding industry—when the oak dominated the entire coast inland of the marsh—their value as a canopy tree has finally been widely recognized by local and state governments as well.

Fittingly, the other iconic plant life of the coastal region grows on the branches of the live oak. Contrary to popular opinion, **Spanish moss** *(Tillandsia usnesides)* is neither Spanish nor moss. It's an air plant, a wholly indigenous cousin to the pineapple. Also contrary to folklore, Spanish moss is not a parasite nor does not harbor parasites while living on an oak tree—though it can after it has already fallen to the ground.

Also growing on the bark of a live oak, especially right after a rain shower, is the **resurrection fern** *(Polypodium polypodioides)*, which can stay dormant for amazingly long periods of time, only to spring back to life with the introduction of a little water.

You can find live oak, Spanish moss, and resurrection fern anywhere in the **maritime forest** ecosystem of coastal Georgia and South Carolina, a zone generally behind the **interdune meadows,** which is itself right behind the beach zone.

The oak may be Georgia's state tree, but far and away its most important commercial tree is the pine, used for paper, lumber, and turpentine. Rarely seen in the wild today due to tree farming, which has covered most of southern Georgia, the dominant species is now the **slash pine** *(Pinus elliottii)*, often seen in long rows on either side of rural highways. Before the introduction of large-scale monoculture tree farming, however, a rich variety of native pines flourished in the **upland forest** inland from the maritime forest, including **longleaf** *(Pinus palustris)* and **loblolly** *(Pinus taeda)* pines.

Right up there with live oaks and Spanish moss in terms of instant recognition would have to be the colorful, ubiquitous **azalea,** a flowering shrub of the *Rhododendron* genus. Over 10,000 varieties have been cultivated through the centuries, with quite a wide range of them on display during blooming season,

The live oak is an iconic image of the region.

March–April, on the Georgia and South Carolina coast (slightly earlier farther south, slightly later farther north).

The area's other great floral display comes from the **camellia** *(Camellia japonica)*, a large, cold-hardy evergreen shrub that flowers that generally bloom in late winter (January–March). An import from Asia, the southeastern coast's camellias are close cousins to *Camellia sinensis*, from which tea is made (and also an import).

Other colorful ornamentals of the area include the ancient and beautiful **Southern magnolia** *(Magnolia grandiflora)*, a native plant with distinctive large white flowers (evolved before the advent of bees); and the **flowering dogwood** *(Cornus florida)*, which for its very hard wood—great for daggers, hence its original name "dagwood"—is actually quite fragile.

An ornamental imported from Asia that has now become quite obnoxious in its aggressive invasiveness is the **mimosa** *(Albrizia julibrissin)*, which blooms March–August.

An indigenous bush with an interesting history is the **yaupon holly** *(Ilex vomitoria)*, from which coastal Native Americans made the famous "black drink." (Indeed, Ossabaw Island, Georgia, gets its name from a Native American phrase meaning "yaupon holly bushes place.") This bitter, caffeinated tea not only gave the tribes a buzz that helped them in spiritual quests, it was used for ritual purification and cleansing because it made them vomit copiously and loosened their bowels. However, holly tea in moderate amounts will have no noticeable effect other than a little caffeine boost, and the drink is still quaffed today in some rural areas of the coast.

Moving into watery areas, you'll find the remarkable **bald cypress** *(Taxodium distichum)*, a flood-resistant conifer recognizable by its tufted top, its great height (up to 130 feet), and its distinctive "knees," parts of the root that project above the waterline and which are believed to help stabilize the tree in lowland areas. Much prized for its beautiful, pest-resistant wood, great stands of ancient cypress once dominated the marsh along the coast; sadly, overharvesting and destruction of wetlands has made the magnificent sight of this ancient, dignified species much less common.

The acres of **smooth cordgrass** for which the Golden Isles are named are plants of the *Spartina alternaflora* species. (A cultivated cousin, *Spartina anglica*, is considered invasive.) Besides its simple natural beauty, *Spartina* is also a key food source for marsh denizens.

Playing a key environmental role on the coast are **sea oats** *(Uniola paniculata)*. This wispy, fast-growing perennial grass anchors sand dunes and hence is a protected species on the Georgia coast (it's a misdemeanor to pick them).

South Carolina isn't called the "Palmetto State" for nothing. Though palm varieties are not as common up here as in Florida, you'll definitely encounter several types along the Georgia and South Carolina coast. The **cabbage palm** *(Sabal palmetto)*, for which South Carolina is named, is the largest variety, up to 50–60 feet tall. Its "heart of palm" is an edible delicacy, which coastal Native Americans boiled in bear fat as porridge. In dunes and sandhills you'll find clumps of the low-lying **saw palmetto** *(Serenoa repens)*. The **bush palmetto** *(Sabal minor)* has distinctive fan-shaped branches. The common **Spanish bayonet** *(Yucca aloifolia)* looks like a palm, but it's actually a member of the agave family.

FAUNA
On the Land

Perhaps the most iconic land animal—or semi-land animal, anyway—of the Georgia and South Carolina coast is the legendary **American alligator** *(Alligator mississippiensis)*, the only species of crocodile native to the area. Contrary to their fierce reputation, locals know these massive reptiles, 6–12 feet long as adults, to be quite shy. If you come in the colder months you won't see one at all, since alligators require an outdoor temperature over 70°F to become active and feed. (Indeed, the appearance of alligators was once a well-known symbol of spring in the area.) Often all you'll see is a couple of eyebrow ridges sticking out of the water, and a gator lying still in a shallow creek can easily be mistaken for a floating log.

But should you see one or more gators basking in the sun—a favorite activity on warm days for these cold-blooded creatures—it's best to admire them from afar. A mother alligator, in particular, will destroy anything that comes near her nest. Despite the alligator's short, stubby legs, they run amazingly fast on land—faster than you, in fact.

If you're driving on a country road at night, be on the lookout for **white-tailed deer** *(Odocoileus virginianus)*, which, besides being quite beautiful, also pose a serious road hazard. Because coastal development has dramatically reduced the habitat—and therefore the numbers—of their natural predators, deer are very plentiful throughout the area and as you read this are hard at work devouring vast tracts of valuable vegetation. No one wants to hurt poor little Bambi, but the truth is that area hunters perform a valuable service by culling the local deer population, which is in no danger of extinction anytime soon.

The coast hosts fairly large populations of playful **river otter** *(Lutra Canadensis)*. Not to be confused with the larger sea otters off the West Coast, these fast-swimming members of the weasel family inhabit inland waterways and marshy areas, with dominant males sometimes ranging as much as 50 miles within a single waterway. As strict carnivores, usually of fish, otters are a key indicator of the health of their ecosystem. If they're thriving, water and habitat quality likely is pretty high. If they're not, something's going badly wrong.

While you're unlikely to encounter an otter, if you're camping you might easily run into the **raccoon** *(Procyon lotor)*, an exceedingly intelligent and crafty relative of the bear, sharing that larger animal's resourcefulness in stealing your food. Though nocturnal, raccoons will feed whenever food is available. Though raccoons can grow so accustomed to the human presence as to almost consider themselves part of the family, but resist the temptation to get close to them. Rabies is prevalent in the raccoon population and you should always, always keep your distance.

Another common campsite nuisance, the

opossum *(Didelphis virginiana)* is a shy, primitive creature that is much more easily discouraged. North America's only marsupial, an opossum's usual "defense" against predators is to play dead. That said, however, they have an immunity to snake venom and often feed on the reptiles, even the most poisonous ones.

Opossums are native to the area, but another similarly slow-witted, slow-moving creature is not: the **nine-banded armadillo** *(Dasypus novemcinctus)*. In centuries past, these armor-plated insect-eaters were mostly confined to Mexico, but are gradually working their way northward. Obsessive diggers, armadillos cause quite a bit of damage to crops and gardens. Sometimes jokingly called "'possum on the half shell," armadillo, like opossum, are frequent roadkill on Georgia and South Carolina highways.

While you're highly unlikely to actually see a **red fox** *(Vulpes vulpes)*, you might very well see their distinctive footprints in the mud of a marsh at low tide. These nocturnal hunters, a non-native species introduced by European settlers, range the coast seeking mice, squirrels, and rabbits.

Once fairly common in Georgia and South Carolina, the **black bear** *(Ursus americanus)* has suffered from hunting and habitat destruction. Of the regions in this book, the Okefenokee Swamp area is the only place in which you'll be close to one.

In the Water

Without a doubt the most magnificent denizen—if only part-time—of the southeastern coast is the **North American right whale** *(Eubalaena glacialis)*, which can approach 60 feet in length. Each year from December to March the mothers give birth to their calves and nurse them in the warm waters off the Georgia coast in an eons-old ritual. (In the summers they like to hang around the rich fishing grounds off the New England coast, though biologists still can't account for their whereabouts at other times of the year.) Their numbers were so abundant in past centuries that the Spanish name for Jekyll Island,

Georgia, was *Isla de las Ballenas* ("Island of the Whales"). Whaling and encounters with ship propellers have taken their toll, and numbers of this endangered species are dwindling fast now, with less than 500 estimated left in the world.

Another of humankind's aquatic cousins, the **Atlantic bottle-nosed dolphin** *(Ursiops truncates)*, is a well-known and frequent visitor to the coast, coming far upstream into creeks and rivers to feed. Children, adults, and experienced seamen alike all delight in encounters with the mammals, sociable creatures who travel in family units. When not occupied with feeding or mating activities—both of which can get surprisingly rowdy—dolphins show great curiosity about human visitors to their habitat. They will gather near boats, surfacing often with the distinctive chuffing sound of air coming from their blowholes. Occasionally they'll even lift their heads out of the water to have a look at you; consider yourself lucky indeed to have such a close encounter. Don't be fooled by their cuteness, however. Dolphins live life with gusto and aren't scared of much. They're voracious eaters of fish, amorous and energetic lovers, and will take on an encroaching shark in a heartbeat.

Another beloved part-time marine creature of the barrier islands of the Georgia and South Carolina coast is the **loggerhead turtle** *(Caretta caretta)*. Though the species prefers to stay well offshore the rest of the year, females weighing up to 300 pounds come out of the sea each May–July to dig a shallow hole in the dunes and lay over 100 leathery eggs, returning to the ocean and leaving the eggs to hatch on their own after two months. Interestingly, the mothers prefer to nest at the same spot on the same island year after year. After hatching, the baby turtles then make a dramatic, extremely dangerous (and extremely *slow* trek) to the safety of the waves, at the mercy of various predators. A series of dedicated research and conservation efforts, like the Caretta Project based on Wassaw Island, Georgia, are working hard to protect the loggerheads' traditional nursery grounds to ensure survival of this fascinating, loveable, and threatened species.

Of course the coastal waters and rivers are chock-a-block with fish. The most abundant and sought-after recreational species in the area is the **spotted sea trout** *(Cynoscion nebulosus)*, followed by the **red drum** *(Suaenops ocellatus)*. Local anglers also pursue many varieties of **bass, bream, sheepshead,** and **crappie.** It may sound strange to some accustomed to considering it a "trash" fish, but many types of **catfish** are not only plentiful here but are a common and well-regarded food source. Many species of **flounder** inhabit the silty bottoms of estuaries all along the coast. Farther offshore are game and sportfish like **marlin, swordfish, shark, grouper,** and **tuna.**

Each March, anglers jockey for position on coastal rivers for the yearly running of the **American shad** *(Alosa sapidissima)* upstream to spawn. This large (up to eight pounds), catfish-like species is a regional delicacy as a seasonal entrée, as well as for its tasty roe. There's a limit of eight shad per person per season.

One of the more interesting fish species in the area is the endangered **shortnose sturgeon** *(Acipenser brevirostrum)*. A fantastically ancient species that has evolved little in hundreds of millions of years, this small, freshwater fish is known to exist in the Altamaha, Savannah, and Ogeechee Rivers of Georgia and the estuaries of the ACE Basin in South Carolina. Traveling upriver to spawn in the winter, the sturgeons remain around the mouths of waterways the rest of the year, venturing near the ocean only sparingly.

Crustaceans and shellfish have been a key food staple in the area for thousands of years, with the massive shell middens of the coast being testament to Native Americans' healthy appetite for them. The beds of the local variant, the **eastern oyster** *(Crassostrea virginica)*, aren't what they used to be, due to overharvesting, water pollution, and disruption of habitat. In truth, most local restaurants import the little filter-feeders from the Gulf of Mexico these days. Oysters spawn May–August, hence the old folk wisdom about eating oysters only in

months with the letter "r," so as not to disrupt the breeding cycle.

Each year April–January, shrimp boats up and down the southeastern coast trawl for **shrimp,** most commercially viable in two local species, the white shrimp *(Penaeus setiferus)*, and the brown shrimp *(Penaeus aztecus)*. Shrimp are the most popular seafood item in the United States and account for hundreds of millions of dollars in revenue into the coastal economy. While consumption won't slow down anytime soon, the Georgia and South Carolina shrimping industries are facing serious threats, both from species decline due to pollution and overfishing and from competition from shrimp farms and the Asian shrimp industry.

Another important commercial crop is the **blue crab** *(Callinected sapidus)*, the species used in such Lowcountry delicacies as crab cakes. You'll often see floating markers bobbing up and down in rivers throughout the region. These signal the presence directly below of a crab trap, often of an amateur crabber.

A true living link to primordial times, the alien-looking **horseshoe crab** *(Limulus polyphemus)*, is frequently found on beaches of the coast during the spring mating season (it lives in deeper water the rest of the year). More closely related to scorpions and spiders than crabs, the horseshoe has evolved hardly a lick in hundreds of millions of years.

Any trip to a local salt marsh at low tide will likely uncover hundreds of **fiddler crabs** *(Uca pugilator* and *Uca pugnax)*, so-named for the way the males wave their single enlarged claws in the air to attract mates. (Their other, smaller claw is the one they actually eat with.) The fiddlers make distinctive burrows in the pluff mud for sanctuary during high tide, recognizable by the little balls of sediment at the entrances (the crabs spit out the balls after sifting through the sand for food).

One charming beach inhabitant, the **sand dollar** *(Mellita quinquiesperforata)*, has seen its numbers decline drastically due to being entirely too charming for its own good. Beachcombers are now asked to enjoy these flat little cousins to the sea urchin in their natural habitat and to refrain from taking them home. Besides, they start to smell bad when they dry out.

The **sea nettle** *(Chrysaora quinquecirrha)*, a less-than-charming beach inhabitant, is a jellyfish that stings thousands of people on the coast a year (though only for those with severe allergies are the stings potentially life-threatening). Stinging their prey before transporting it into their waiting mouths, the jellyfish also sting when disturbed or frightened. Most often, people are stung by stepping on the bodies of jellyfish washed up on the sand.

If you're stung by a jellyfish, don't panic. You'll probably experience a stinging rash for about half an hour. Locals say applying a little baking soda or vinegar helps cut the sting. (Some also swear fresh urine will do the trick, and I pass that tip along to you purely in the interest of thoroughness.)

In the Air

When enjoying the marshlands of the coast, consider yourself fortunate to see an endangered **wood stork** *(Mycteria americana)*, though their numbers are on the increase. The only storks to breed in North America, these graceful, long-lived birds (routinely living over 10 years) are usually seen on a low flight path across the marsh, though at some birding spots beginning in late summer you can find them at a **roost,** sometimes numbering over 100 birds. Resting at high tide, they fan out over the marsh to feed at low tide on foot. Old-timers sometimes call them "Spanish buzzards" or simply "the preacher."

Often confused with the wood stork is the gorgeous **white ibis** *(Eudocimus albus)*, distinguishable by its orange bill and black wingtips. Like the wood stork, the ibis is a communal bird that roosts in colonies.

Other similar-looking coastal denizens are the white-feathered **great egret** *(Ardea alba)* and **snowy egret** *(Egretta thula)*, the former distinguishable by its yellow bill and the latter by its black bill and the tuft of plumes on the back of its head.

Egrets are in the same family as herons. The most magnificent is the **great blue**

A wide variety of waterfowl live in the area or migrate through it.

© SOPHIA MOREKIS

heron *(Ardea herodias)*. Despite their imposing height—up to four feet tall—these waders are shy. Often you hear them rather than see them, a loud shriek of alarm that echoes over the marsh.

So how to tell the difference between all these wading birds at a glance? It's actually easiest when they're in flight. Egrets and herons fly with their necks tucked in, while storks and ibises fly with their necks extended.

Dozens of species of shorebirds comb the beaches, including **sandpipers, plovers,** and the wonderful and rare **American oystercatcher** *(Haematopus palliates)*, instantly recognizable for its prancing walk, dark brown back, stark white underside, and long, bright-orange bill.

Gulls and **terns** also hang out wherever there's water. They can frequently be seen swarming around incoming shrimp boats, attracted by the catch of little crustaceans.

The chief raptor of the salt marsh is the fish-eating **osprey** *(Pandion haliaetus)*. These large grayish birds of prey are similar to eagles but are adapted to a maritime environment, with a reversible outer toe on each talon (the better for catching wriggly fish) and closable nostrils so it can dive into the water after prey. Very common all along the coast, they like to build big nests on top of buoys and channel markers in addition to trees.

The **bald eagle** *(Haliaeetus leucocephalus)*, is making a comeback in the area, thanks to increased federal regulation and better education of trigger-happy locals. Apparently not as all-American as their bumper stickers might sometimes indicate, local farmers would often regard the national symbol as more of a nuisance and fire away anytime they saw one. Of course as we all should have learned in school, the bald eagle is not actually bald but has a head adorned with white feathers. Like the osprey, they prefer fish, but unlike the osprey will settle for rodents and rabbits.

Inland among the pines you'll find the most common area woodpecker, the huge **pileated woodpecker** *(Dryocopus pileatus)* with its huge crest. Less common is the smaller, more subtly marked **red-cockaded woodpecker** *(Picoides borealis)*. Once common in the vast primordial pine forests of the southeast, the species is now endangered, its last real refuge being the big tracts of relatively undisturbed land on military bases.

Insects

Down here they say that God invented bugs to keep the Yankees from completely taking over the South. And insects are probably the most unpleasant fact of life in the southeastern coastal region.

The list of annoying indigenous insects must begin with the infamous **sand gnat** *(Culicoides furens)*. This tiny and persistent nuisance, a member of the midge family, lacks the precision of the mosquito with its long proboscis. No, the sand gnat is more torture-master than surgeon, brutally gouging and digging away its victim's skin until it hits a source of blood. Most prevalent in the spring and fall, the sand gnat is drawn to its prey by the carbon dioxide trail of its breath.

While long sleeves and long pants are one way to keep gnats at bay, that causes its own discomfort because of the region's heat and humidity. The only real antidote to the sand gnat's assault—other than never breathing—is the Avon skin care product Skin So Soft, which has taken on a new and wholly unplanned life as the South's favorite anti-gnat lotion. Grow to like the scent, because the more of this stuff you lather on the better. And in calmer moments grow to appreciate the great contribution sand gnats make to the salt marsh ecosystem— as food for many species of birds and bats.

Running a close second to the sand gnat are the over three dozen species of highly aggressive **mosquito,** which breeds anywhere a few drops of water lie stagnant. Not surprisingly, massive populations blossom in the rainiest months, in late spring and late summer. Like the gnat, the mosquito—the biters are always female— homes in on its victim by trailing the plume of carbon dioxide exhaled in the breath.

More than just a biting nuisance, mosquitoes are now vectoring West Nile disease to the Lowcountry and Georgia coast, signaling a possibly dire threat to public health. Local governments in the region pour millions of dollars of taxpayer money into massive pesticide spraying programs from helicopters, planes, and trucks. While that certainly helps stem the tide, it by no means eliminates the mosquito population. (This is just as well, because like the sand gnat the mosquito is an important food source for many species, such as bats and dragonflies.)

Alas, Skin So Soft has little effect on the mosquito. Try over-the-counter sprays, anything smelling of citronella, and wearing long sleeves and long pants when weather permits.

But undoubtedly the most viscerally loathed of all pests on the Lowcountry and Georgia coasts is the so-called "palmetto bug," or **American cockroach** *(Periplaneta americana)*. These black, shiny, and sometimes grotesquely massive insects—up to two inches long—are living fossils, virtually unchanged over hundreds of millions of years. And perfectly adapted as they are to life in and among wet, decaying vegetation, they're unlikely to change a bit in 100 million more years.

While they spend most of their time crawling around, usually under rotting leaves and tree bark, the American cockroach can indeed fly—sort of. There are few more hilarious sights than a room full of people frantically trying to dodge a palmetto bug that has just clumsily launched itself off a high point on the wall. Because the cockroach doesn't know any better than you do where it's going, it can be a particularly bracing event—though the insect does not bite and poses few real health hazards.

Popular regional use of the term "palmetto bug" undoubtedly has its roots in a desire for polite Southern society to avoid using the ugly word "roach" and its connotations of filth and unclean environments. But the colloquialism actually has a basis in reality. Contrary to what anyone tells you, the natural habitat of the American cockroach—unlike its kitchen-dwelling, much-smaller cousin the German cockroach—is outdoors, often up in trees. They only come inside human dwellings when it's especially hot, especially cold, or especially dry outside. Like you, the palmetto bug is easily driven indoors by extreme temperatures and by thirst.

Other than visiting the Southeast during the winter, when the roaches go dormant, there's no convenient antidote for their presence. The best way to keep them out of your life is to stay away from decaying vegetation and keep doors and windows closed on especially hot nights.

History

BEFORE THE EUROPEANS

Based on studies of artifacts found throughout the state, anthropologists know the first humans arrived to the coasts of South Carolina and Georgia at least 13,000 years ago, at the tail end of the Ice Age. During this **Paleoindian Period,** sea levels were over 200 feet lower than present levels, and large mammals such as wooly mammoths, horses, and camels were hunted for food and skins.

However, rapidly increasing temperatures, rising sea levels, and efficient hunting techniques combined to quickly kill off these large mammals, relics of the Pleistocene Era, ushering in the **Archaic Period** of history in what's now the southeastern United States. Still hunter-gatherers, Archaic Period Indians began turning to small game such as deer, bear, and turkey, supplemented with fruit and nuts.

The latter part of the Archaic era saw more habitation on the coasts, with an increasing reliance on fish and shellfish for sustenance. It's during this time that the great **shell middens** of the Georgia and South Carolina coasts trace their origins. Basically serving as trash heaps for discarded oyster shells, as the middens grew in size they also took on a ceremonial status, often being used as sites for important rituals and meetings. Such sites are often called **shell rings,** and the largest yet found was over nine feet high and 300 feet in diameter.

Existing examples of shell rings are on Hilton Head Island, South Carolina, and St. Simons and Sapelo Islands in Georgia. The remains of a large shell midden are also on the nature trail at the Skidaway Island State Park in Savannah. Using ground-penetrating radar, archaeologists are finding more and more Archaic era shell middens and rings all the time.

The introduction of agriculture and improved pottery techniques about 3,000 years ago led to the **Woodland Period** of Native American settlement. Extended clan groups were much less migratory, establishing year-round communities of up to 50 people, who began the practice of clearing land to grow crops. The ancient shell middens of their forefathers were not abandoned, however, and were continually added onto.

Native Americans had been cremating or burying their dead for years, a practice which eventually gave rise to the construction of the first **mounds** during the Woodland Period. Essentially built-up earthworks sometimes marked with spiritual symbols, often in the form of animal shapes, mounds not only contained the remains of the deceased, but items like pottery to accompany the deceased into the afterlife.

Increased agriculture led to increased population, and with that population growth came competition over resources and a more formal notion of warfare. This period, from about A.D. 800–1600, is termed the **Mississippian Period.** It was the Mississippians who would be the first Native Americans in what's now the continental United States to encounter European explorers and settlers after Columbus. The Native Americans who would later be called **Creek Indians** were the direct descendants of the Mississippians in lineage, language, and lifestyle.

Native American social structure north of Mexico reached its apex with the Mississippians, who were not only prodigious mound builders but constructed elaborate wooden villages and evolved a top-down class system. The defensive palisades surrounding some of the villages attest to the increasingly martial nature of the tribes and their chieftains, or *micos.*

Described by later European accounts as a tall, proud people, the Mississippians often wore elaborate body art and, like the indigenous inhabitants of Central and South America, used the practice of **head shaping,** whereby an infant's skull was deliberately deformed into an elongated shape by tying the baby's head to a board for about a year.

The influence and mystique of the *micos* were so powerful to the Mississippians that the tribes and the areas they controlled were simply named after the chiefs themselves. What the earliest European visitors thought were Indian place names—for example, Guale in coastal Georgia, in the vicinity of modern-day St. Catherine's Island—were actually the names of the dominant *micos* in those areas.

By about A.D. 1400, however, change came to the Mississippian culture for reasons that are still not completely understood. In some areas, large chiefdoms began splintering into smaller subgroups, in an intriguing echo of the medieval feudal system going on concurrently in Europe. In other areas, however, the rise of a handful of über-*micos* subsumed smaller communities under their influence.

In either case, the result was the same: The landscape of the Southeast became less peopled, as many of the old villages, built around huge central mounds, were abandoned, some suddenly, as was the case with the community of the Irene Mound in Savannah (excavated and documented in the 1930s, but sadly plowed over for the city's expanding port facility).

As tensions and paranoia between the chiefdoms increased, the contested land between them became more and more dangerous for the poorly armed or poorly connected. Indeed, at the time of the Europeans' arrival much of the coastal area was more thinly inhabited than it had been for many decades.

THE SPANISH ARRIVE

The first known contact by Europeans on the southeastern coast came in 1521, roughly concurrent with Cortez's conquest of Mexico. A party of Spanish slavers, led by Francisco Cordillo, ventured to what's now Port Royal Sound, South Carolina, from Santo Domingo in the Caribbean. Naming the area Santa Elena, he kidnapped a few dozen Indian slaves and left, ranging as far north as the Cape Fear River in present-day North Carolina.

The first serious exploration of the coast came in 1526, when Lucas Vazquez de Ayllon and about 600 colonists made landfall at Winyah Bay in South Carolina, near present-day Georgetown. They didn't stay long, however, immediately moving down the coast and trying to set down roots in the Sapelo Sound area of modern-day Liberty County, Georgia.

That colony—called San Miguel de Gualdalpe—was the first European colony in America. (The continent's oldest continuously occupied settlement, St. Augustine, Florida, wasn't founded until 1565.) The colony also brought with it the seed of a future nation's dissolution: slaves from Africa. While San Felipe lasted only six weeks due to political tension and a slave uprising, conclusive artifacts from its brief life have been discovered in the area.

Hernando De Soto's infamous, ill-fated trek of 1539–1543 from Florida through southwest Georgia to Alabama (where De Soto died of a fever after four years of atrocities against any Indians in his path) did not find the gold he anticipated, nor did it enter the coastal region dealt with in this book. But De Soto's legacy was indeed soon felt there and throughout the Southeast, in the form of various diseases for which the Mississippian tribes had no immunity whatsoever: smallpox, typhus, influenza, measles, yellow fever, whooping cough, diphtheria, tuberculosis, bubonic plague.

While the barbaric cruelties of the Spanish certainly took their toll, far more damaging were these deadly diseases to a population totally unprepared for them. Within a few years, the Mississippian people—already in a state of internal decline—were losing huge percentages of their population to disease, echoing what had already happened on a massive scale to the indigenous tribes of the Caribbean after Christopher Columbus's expeditions.

As the viruses they introduced ran rampant, the Europeans themselves stayed away for a couple of decades after the ignominious end of De Soto's fruitless quest. During that quarter-century, the once-proud Mississippian culture continued to disintegrate, dwindling into a shadow of its former greatness. In all, disease would claim the lives of at least 80 percent of all indigenous inhabitants of the western hemisphere.

THE FRENCH MISADVENTURE

The next European presence around the Georgia and South Carolina coast was another ill-fated attempt, the establishment of Charlesfort in 1562 by French Huguenots under Jean Ribault on present-day Parris Island, South Carolina, in Port Royal Sound. Part of a covert effort by the Protestant French Admiral Coligny to send Huguenot colonizing missions around the globe, Ribault's crew of 150 first explored the mouth of the St. Johns River near present-day Jacksonville, Florida, before heading north to Port Royal.

After establishing Charlesfort, Ribault returned to France for supplies. In his absence, religious war had broken out in his home country, so Ribault sought sanctuary in England but was clapped in irons anyway. Meanwhile, most of Charlesfort's colonists grew so demoralized they joined another French expedition led by Rene Laudonniere at Fort Caroline on the St. Johns River. The remaining 27 built a ship to sail from Charlesfort back to France, 20 of whom survived the journey, which was cut short in the English Channel when they had to be rescued.

Ribault himself was dispatched to reinforce Fort Caroline, but was headed off by a contingent from the new Spanish fortified settlement at St. Augustine. The fate of the French presence on the southeast coast was sealed when not only did the Spanish take Fort Caroline, but a storm destroyed Ribault's reinforcing fleet. Ribault and all survivors were killed as soon as they came ashore.

To keep the French away for good and cement Spain's hold on this northernmost part of their province of La Florida, the Spanish built the fort of Santa Elena directly on top of Charlesfort. Both layers are currently being excavated and studied today.

THE MISSION ERA

With Spanish dominance of the region ensured for the near future, the lengthy mission era began. While it's rarely mentioned as a key part of U.S. history, the truth is that the Spanish missionary presence on the Georgia coast was longer and more comprehensive than its much more widely known counterpart in California.

St. Augustine's governor Pedro Menendez de Aviles—sharing "biscuits with honey" on the beach at St. Catherine's Island with a local *mico*—negotiated for the right to establish a system of Jesuit missions in two coastal chiefdoms: the Mocama on and around Cumberland Island, and the Guale (pronounced "wallie") to the north.

Those early missions, the first north of

Mexico, were largely unsuccessful. But a renewed, organized effort by the Franciscan Order came to fruition during the 1580s. Starting with Santa Catalina de Guale on St. Catherine's Island, missions were established all along the Georgia coast, from the mainland near St. Simons and Sapelo Islands, on the Altamaha, in the interior, and on all Georgia's barrier islands with the notable exception of Jekyll Island.

While the purpose of the missions was to convert as many Indians as possible to Christianity, they also served to further consolidate Spanish political control. It was a dicey proposition, as technically the mission friars served at the pleasure of the local chiefs. But the more savvy of the *micos* soon learned that cooperating with the militarily powerful Spanish—with the friars came soldiers to protect them—led to more influence and more supplies. Frequently it was the chiefs themselves who urged for more expansion of the Franciscan missions.

The looming invasion threat to St. Augustine from the great English adventurer and privateer Sir Francis Drake was a harbinger of trouble to come, as was a Guale uprising in 1597. The Spanish consolidated their positions near St. Augustine and Santa Elena on the Port Royal Sound was abandoned. As Spanish power waned, in 1629 Charles I of England laid formal claim to what's now the Carolinas, Georgia, and much of Florida, but made no effort to colonize the area.

Largely left to their own devices and facing an indigenous population dying off from disease, the missions in the Georgia interior nonetheless carried on in their vocation. A devastating Indian raid in 1661 on a mission at the mouth of the Altamaha River, possibly aided by the English, persuaded the Spanish to pull back the mission effort to the barrier islands. But even as late as 1667, right before the founding of Charles Town far to the north, there were 70 missions still extant in the old Guale kingdom.

Pirate raids and slave uprisings finished off the Georgia missions for good by 1684. By 1706

the Spanish mission effort in the southeast had fully retreated to St. Augustine. In an interesting postscript, 89 Native Americans—the sole surviving descendants of Spain's Georgia missions—evacuated to Cuba with the final Spanish exodus from Florida in 1763.

ENTER THE ENGLISH

With the native populations in steep decline due to disease and a wholesale retrenchment by European powers came a sort of vacuum to the southeastern coast. Into this vacuum came the first English-speaking settlers of South Carolina. The first attempt was an expedition by a Barbadian colonist, William Hilton, in 1663. While he didn't establish a new colony, he did leave behind his name on the most notable geographic feature he saw—Hilton Head Island.

In 1665 King Charles II gave a charter to eight **Lords Proprietors** to establish a colony in the area, generously to be named Carolina after the monarch himself. (One of the Proprietors, Lord Ashley Cooper, would see not one but both rivers in the Charleston area named after him.) Remarkably, none of the Proprietors ever set foot in the colony they established for their own profit.

Before their colony was even established, the Proprietors themselves set the stage for the vast human disaster that would eventually befall it. They encouraged slavery by promising that each colonist would receive 20 acres of land for every black male slave and 10 acres for every black female slave brought to the colony within the first year.

In 1666 explorer Robert Sandford officially claimed Carolina for the king, in a ceremony on modern-day Seabrook or Wadmalaw Island. The Proprietors then sent out a fleet of three ships from England, only one of which, the *Carolina,* would make it the whole way. After stops in the thriving English colonies of Barbados and Bermuda, the ship landed in Port Royal.

They were greeted without violence, but the fact that the local indigenous people spoke broken Spanish led the colonists to conclude that perhaps the site was too close to Spain's sphere of influence for comfort. A Kiawah chief, eager for allies against the fierce, slave-trading Westo tribe, invited the colonists north to settle instead.

So the colonists—148 of them, including three African slaves—moved 80 miles up the coast and in 1670 pitched camp on the Ashley River at a place they dubbed Albemarle Point after one of their lost ships. Living within the wooden palisades of the camp, the colonists farmed 10-acre plots outside the walls for sustenance.

The Native Americans of the area were of the large and influential Cusabo tribe of the Creeks, and are sometimes even today known as the **Settlement Indians.** Subtribes of the Cusabo whose names live on today in South Carolina geography were the Kiawah, Edisto, Wando, Stono, and Ashepoo.

A few years later some colonists from Barbados, which was beginning to suffer the effects of overpopulation, joined the Carolinians. The Barbadian influence, with an emphasis on large-scale slave labor and a caste system, would have an indelible imprint on the colony in years to come. Indeed, within a generation a majority of settlers in the new colony would be African slaves.

By 1680, however, Albemarle Point was feeling growing pains as well, and the Proprietors ordered the site moved to Oyster Point at the confluence of the Ashley and Cooper Rivers (the present-day Battery). Within a year Albemarle Point was completely abandoned, and the walled fortifications of Charles Town were built a few hundred yards up from Oyster Point on the banks of the Cooper River.

The original Anglican settlers were quickly joined by various **Dissenters,** among them French Huguenots, Quakers, Congregationalists, and Jews. A group of Scottish Presbyterians established the short-lived Stuart Town near Port Royal in 1684. Recognizing this diversity, the colony in 1697 granted religious liberty to all "except Papists." The Anglicans attempted a crackdown on Dissenters in 1704, but two years later Queen Anne stepped in and ensured religious freedom for all Carolinians (again with the exception of Roman Catholics, who wouldn't be a factor in the colony until after the American Revolution).

THE YEMASSEE WAR

Within 20 years the English presence had expanded throughout the Lowcountry to include the settlements of Port Royal and Beaufort. Charles Town became a thriving commercial center, dealing in deerskins with independent traders in the interior and with foreign concerns from England to South America. Its success was not without a backlash, as the local **Yemassee** tribe of the Creek Indians became increasingly disgruntled at the settlers' growing monopolies on deerskin and the slave trade.

Slavery was a sad and common fact of life from the earliest days of white settlement in the region. Indians were the most frequent early victims, with not only white settlers taking slaves from the tribes, but the tribes themselves conducting slaving raids on each other, often selling their hostages to eager colonists.

As rumors of war spread, on Good Friday, 1715, a delegation of six white Carolinians went to the Yemassee village of Pocataligo to address some of the tribe's grievances in the hopes of forestalling violence. Their effort was in vain, however, as Yemassee warriors murdered four of them in their sleep, the remaining two escaping to sound the alarm. The treacherous attack signaled the beginning of the two-year Yemassee War, which would claim the lives of nearly 10 percent of the colony's population and an unknown number of Native Americans—making it one of the bloodiest conflicts in American history.

Energized and ready for war, the Yemassee immediately attacked Charles Town itself, but killed about 90 of the 100 or so white traders in the interior, effectively ending all commerce in the area. As Charles Town began to swell with refugees from the hinterland, water and supplies began running low and the colony was in peril for its very existence.

After an initially poor performance by the

PIRATES OF THE SOUTH ATLANTIC

Pirates, along with their close cousins, slavers, were among the earliest explorers of the Atlantic seaboard of America, and other than Native American chiefs, were the only real authority in the area for decades. The creeks and barrier islands of the Georgia and Carolina coast provided important, hard-to-find sanctuaries off the regular pirate circuit down in the booty-laden Spanish Caribbean.

For most of us, pirate stories and movies are a form of escapism, in which the most unlikely scenarios happen with ease. But a real-life pirate story from the earliest days of the Charleston would almost seem too unbelievable even for Hollywood.

The encounter was at the hands of the infamous Edward Teach, a.k.a. Blackbeard. A tall, terrifying bully of a man, the legendary pirate also had a flair for the dramatic, as all proper pirates should. Given to twisting flaming wads of cloth into his beard when he attacked his prey, Blackbeard was also quite eccentric, as his Charleston escapade shows.

In May 1718, Blackbeard, driven northward from his usual hunting grounds in the Bahamas by a concerted effort from the British Navy, approached Charleston harbor in his flagship *Queen Anne's Revenge,* accompanied by three smaller vessels. He immediately seized several ships and kidnapped several leading citizens, including Councilman Samuel Wragg and his four-year-old son. He sent one captive ashore with the message that unless his demand was met, the heads of Wragg and son would soon be delivered to the colonial governor's doorstep.

Blackbeard's demand? A chest of medicine. For what purpose, we still aren't sure, but apparently it really was all he wanted. The medicines were delivered in short order and Blackbeard released his hostages and sailed north to Ocracoke Island, North Carolina, to enjoy a royal pardon he'd just received.

One of the pirates serving under Blackbeard during the Charleston escapade was Stede Bonnet, quite a contrasting figure in his debonair nature and posh finery. When Charleston's Colonel William Rhett – his house at 54 Hasell Street is still standing, the city's oldest – got wind that Bonnet and crew were still a-pirating off Cape Fear, North Carolina, he set out with a fleet to bring him to justice.

And that he did, bringing pirate and crew back to Charleston for a trial that almost didn't happen after Bonnet escaped from custody dressed as a woman (he was captured on Sullivan's Island). The dashing Bonnet actually garnered quite a bit of public sympathy – especially when he begged not to be hanged – but it wasn't enough to forestall the grim fate of the pirate and his crew: public execution at White Point, the bodies left to dangle as a warning to other buccaneers.

Another coastal menace, Richard Worley, was also hanged in Charleston. He supposedly was buried in a marshy creek downtown, where Meeting and Water Streets intersect today.

Though Savannah is home to the famous Pirate's House restaurant and got a major shout-out in Robert Louis Stevenson's *Treasure Island,* actual pirate history there is hard to nail down. There seems little doubt that a host of ne'er-do-wells made their way onto the rowdy Savannah waterfront, but the port's location nearly 20 miles upriver would have made it less-than-ideal territory for a true buccaneer, who always needed a fast getaway handy.

As for Blackbeard, his retirement plans were interrupted by a contingent of Virginians who tracked him down and killed him near Ocracoke. However, his legend lives to this day on Blackbeard Island, Georgia, a gorgeous, undeveloped barrier island that has changed little since the days when Mr. Teach himself allegedly stopped over between pirate raids.

The legends even say he left some treasure there, but don't try to look for it – Blackbeard Island is now a National Wildlife Refuge.

Carolina militia, a professional army—including armed African slaves—was raised. Well trained and well led, the new army more than held its own despite being outnumbered.

A key alliance with local Cherokees was all the advantage the colonists needed to turn the tide for good. While the Cherokee never received the overt military backing from the settlers that they sought, they did garner enough supplies and influence to convince their Creek rivals, the Yemassee, to begin the peace process. The war-weary settlers, eager to get back to life and to business, were eager to negotiate with them, offering goods as a sign of their earnest intent. By 1717 the Yemassee threat had subsided and trade in the region began flourishing anew.

No sooner had the Yemassee War ended, however, when a new threat emerged: the dread pirate Edward Teach, a.k.a. Blackbeard. Entering Charleston harbor in May 1718 with his flagship *Queen Anne's Revenge* and three other vessels, he promptly plundered five ships and began a full-scale blockade of the entire settlement. He took a number of prominent citizens hostage before finally departing northward.

SLAVERY

For the colonists, the Blackbeard episode was the final straw. Already disgusted by the lack of support from the Lords Proprietors during the Yemassee War, the humiliation of the pirate blockade was too much to take.

So to almost universal agreement in the colony, the settlers threw off the rule of the Proprietors and strenuously lobbied in 1719 to become a crown colony, an effort that came to final fruition in 1729. While this outward-looking and energetic Charlestown was originally built on the backs of merchants, with the introduction of the rice and indigo crops in the early 1700s it would increasingly be built on the backs of slaves.

For all the wealth gained through the planting of rice and cotton seeds, another seed was sown by the Lowcountry plantation culture. The area's total dependence on slave labor would soon lead to a disastrous war, a conflict

signaled for decades to those smart enough to read the signs.

By now Charleston and Savannah were firmly established as the key American ports for the importation of African slaves, with about 40 percent of the trade centered in Charleston alone. As a result, the black population of the coast outnumbered the white population by more than three-to-one. The very real fear of violent slave uprisings had great influence over not only politics, but day-to-day affairs.

These fears were eventually realized in the great **Stono Rebellion.** On September 9, 1739, 20 African American slaves led by an Angolan known only as Jemmy, met near the Stono River, 20 miles southwest of Charleston. Marching with a banner that read "Liberty," they seized guns from a store, killing the proprietors, with the eventual plan of marching all the way to Spanish Florida and sanctuary in the wilderness.

On the way they burned seven plantations and killed 20 more whites. A militia eventually caught up with them, killing 44 escaped slaves and losing 20 of their own. The prisoners were decapitated and had their heads spiked on every milepost between the spot of that final battle and Charleston.

Inspired by the rebellion, at least two other uprisings would take place over the next two years in South Carolina and Georgia. The result was not only a 10-year moratorium on slave importation into Charleston, but a severe crackdown on the education of slaves—a move that would have damaging implications for generations to come.

OGLETHORPE'S VISION

In 1729, Carolina was divided into north and south. In 1731, a colony to be known as Georgia, after the new English king, was carved out of the southern part of the Carolina land grant. A young English general, aristocrat, and humanitarian named James Edward Oglethorpe gathered together a group of Trustees—similar to Carolina's Lords Proprietors—to take advantage of that grant.

While Oglethorpe would go on to found

Georgia, his wasn't the first English presence. A military garrison was built Fort King George in modern-day Darien, Georgia, in 1721. A cypress blockhouse surrounded by palisaded earthworks, the fort defended the southern reaches of England's claim for seven years, braving attacks from the Spanish and Native Americans before being abandoned in 1728.

On February 12, 1733, after two stops in Beaufort and Charlestown, the ship *Anne* with its 114 passengers made its way to the highest bluff on the Savannah River. By the time of the English arrival on the banks of the Savannah River in 1733, the immediate area was controlled by the peaceful Yamacraw tribe, who had been encouraged by the powers-that-be in Charlestown to settle on this vacant land 12 miles up the river to serve as a buffer for the Spanish. Led by an elderly chief, or *mico*, named Tomochichi, the Yamacraw enjoyed the area's natural bounty of shellfish, fruit, nuts, and small game.

Ever the deft politician, Oglethorpe struck up a treaty and eventually a genuine friendship with Tomochichi. To the Yamacraw Oglethorpe was a rare bird indeed—a white man who behaved with honor and was true to his word. The tribe eagerly reciprocated by helping the settlers and pledging fealty to the British crown. Oglethorpe reported to the Trustees that Tomochichi personally requested "that we would Love and Protect their little Families."

In negotiations with local tribes using Mary Musgrove, a Creek-English settler in the area, as translator, the ever-persuasive Oglethorpe convinced the coastal Creek to cede to the crown all Georgia land to the Altamaha River "which our Nation hath not occasion for to use" in exchange for goods. The tribes also reserved the Georgia Sea Islands of Sapelo, Ossabaw, and St. Catherine's.

Oglethorpe's impact was felt farther down the Georgia coast, as St. Simons Island, Jekyll Island, Darien, and Brunswick were settled in rapid succession, and with them the entrenchment of the plantation system and widespread slave labor.

While the Trustees' utopian vision was largely economic in nature, like Carolina the Georgia colony also emphasized religious freedom. While to modern ears Charlestown's antipathy towards "papists" and Oglethorpe's original ban of Roman Catholics from Georgia might seem incompatible with this goal, the reason was a coldly pragmatic one for the time: England's two main global rivals, France and Spain, were both staunchly Catholic countries.

SPAIN VANQUISHED

Things heated up on the coast in 1739 with the so-called War of Jenkins' Ear, which despite its seemingly trivial beginnings over the humiliation of a British captain by Spanish privateers was actually a proxy struggle emblematic of the ongoing changes in the balance of power in Europe. A year later Oglethorpe had cobbled together a force of settlers, Indian allies, and Carolinians to reduce the Spanish fortress at St. Augustine, Florida.

The siege failed, and Oglethorpe retreated to St. Simon's Island to await the inevitable counterattack. In 1742, a massive Spanish force invaded the island but was eventually turned back for good with heavy casualties at the **Battle of Bloody Marsh.** That clash marked the end of Spanish overtures on England's colonies in America.

Though Oglethorpe returned to England a national hero, things fell apart in Savannah. The settlers became envious of the success of Charleston's slave-based rice economy and began wondering aloud why they couldn't also make use of free labor.

With Oglethorpe otherwise occupied in England, the Trustees of Georgia—who were becoming distant in more ways than just geographically from the new colony—gradually bowed to public pressure and relaxed the restrictions on slavery and rum. By 1753 the Trustees voted to return their charter to the crown, officially making Georgia the 13th and final colony of England in America.

With first the French and then the Spanish effectively shut off from the American East

Coast, the stage was set for an internal battle between England and its burgeoning colonies across the Atlantic.

REVOLUTION AND INDEPENDENCE

The population of the colonies swelled in the mid-1700s, not only from an influx of slaves but a corresponding flood of European immigrants, their arrival encouraged specifically to counter the rising black population.

The interior began filling up with Germans, Swiss, Scottish, and Irish settlers. Their subsequent demands for political representation led to tension between them and the coastal inhabitants, typically depicted through the years as an Upcountry vs. Lowcountry competition.

It's a persistent but inaccurate myth that the affluent elite on the southeastern coast were reluctant to break ties with England. While the Lowcountry's cultural and economic ties to England were certainly strong, the **Stamp Act** and the **Townshend Acts** combined to turn public sentiment against the mother country there as elsewhere in the colonies. South Carolinian planters like Christopher Gadsden, Henry Laurens, John Rutledge, and Arthur Middleton were early leaders in the movement for independence. Planters in what would be called Liberty County, Georgia, also strongly agitated for the cause. War broke out between the colonists and the British in New England, and soon made its way southward.

The British failed to take Charleston—the fourth-largest city in the colonies—in June 1776, an episode which gave South Carolina its "Palmetto State" moniker when Redcoat cannonballs bounced off the palm tree–lined walls of Fort Moultrie. The British under General Sir Henry Clinton successfully took the city, however, in 1780, holding it until 1782.

The British, under General Archibald Campbell, took Savannah in 1778. Royal Governor Sir James Wright returned from exile to Georgia to reclaim it for the crown, the only one of the colonies to be subsumed again into the British Empire. A polyglot force of colonists, Haitians, and Hessians attacked the British fortifications on the west side of Savannah in 1779, but were repulsed with horrific losses.

Though the area's two major cities were captured, the war raged on throughout the surrounding area. Indeed, throughout the Lowcountry fighting was as vicious as anything yet seen on the North American continent. With over 130 known military engagements occurring there, South Carolina sacrificed more men during the war than any other colony—including Massachusetts itself, "Cradle of the Revolution."

The struggle became a guerrilla war of colonists vs. the British as well as a civil war between patriots and loyalists, or **Tories.** Committing what would today undoubtedly be called war crimes, the British routinely burned homes, churches, and fields, and massacred civilians. Using Daufuskie Island as a base, British soldiers staged raids on Hilton Head plantations, looting, shooting, and burning.

In response, patriots of the Lowcountry bred a group of deadly guerilla soldiers under legendary leaders such as Francis Marion, "the Swamp Fox," and Thomas Sumter, "the Gamecock," who attacked the British in daring hit-and-run raids staged from the swamps and marshes. A covert group of patriots called the **Sons of Liberty** met clandestinely throughout the Lowcountry, plotting revolution over pints of ale. Sometimes their efforts transcended talk, however, and atrocities were committed against area loyalists.

In all, four South Carolinians signed the Declaration of Independence (Thomas Heyward Jr., Thomas Lynch Jr., Arthur Middleton, and Edward Rutledge), as did three Georgians (Button Gwinnett, Lyman Hall, and George Walton).

HIGH COTTON

True to form, the new nation wasted no time in asserting its economic strength. Rice planters from Georgetown north of Charleston on down to the Altamaha River in Georgia built on their already-impressive wealth, becoming America's richest men by far—with fortunes

ROBERT E. LEE AND SAVANNAH

That spot of spots! That place of places!! That city of cities!!!

Robert E. Lee on Savannah, in a letter to John Mackay

Before reluctantly surrendering his commission to serve the Confederacy, Robert E. Lee was a bright young up-and-comer with the U.S. Army Corps of Engineers. As a 22-year-old lieutenant, the multi-talented Virginian spent a year and a half in and around Savannah overseeing the construction of Fort Pulaski, named for the brave Polish count who lost his life in 1779's Siege of Savannah.

On his arrival in Savannah, construction was on hiatus due to the stifling summer heat. The handsome and dashing Lee made the most of his time off, making significant inroads into high Savannah society downtown. Lee was heartily welcomed into the home of his old West Point roommate John Mackay, whose three daughters adored him. The same was true of the two Minis daughters who lived nearby and also frequently had the young lieutenant over. (All this while Lee was conducting a long-distance courtship with his future wife back home in Virginia!)

Construction on Cockspur Island began in 1829 under Major Samuel Babcock, whose health problems soon forced Lee to take over. Most of Lee's work focused on draining and diking the marshy island and its blue clay soil, and much of his handiwork remains functional today. When Lee was reassigned in 1831, Lieutenant Joseph Mansfield completed construction of the fort in 1847. A mix of slave labor and paid artisans lived in a sprawling construction camp, but only brick structures remain, the wooden ones not surviving a series of hurricanes in subsequent years.

Fort Pulaski's construction was part of a broader initiative by President James Madison in the wake of the disastrous War of 1812, which dramatically revealed the shortcoming of U.S. coastal defense. Two hundred new forts were planned but by the beginning of the Civil War only 30 were complete. Based on state-of-the-art European design forged in the cauldron of the Napoleonic Wars, Fort Pulaski's thick masonry construction used 25 million bricks, many of them of the famous "Savannah Gray" variety handmade at the nearby Hermitage Plantation. At its unveiling, Fort Pulaski was considered to be invincible – indeed, perhaps the finest fortress ever made.

When Georgia seceded from the Union in January 1861, a small force of 134 Confederates immediately took control of two Savannah area fortifications, Fort Pulaski and Fort Jack-

---

built, of course, on the backs of the slaves working in their fields and paddies.

In 1786, a new crop was introduced that would only enhance the financial clout of the coastal region: cotton. A former loyalist colonel, Roger Kelsal, sent some seed from Anguilla in the West Indies to his friend James Spaulding, owner of a plantation on St. Simons Island, Georgia. This crop, soon to be known as **Sea Island cotton** and considered the best in the world, would eventually supplant rice as the crop of choice for coastal plantations. At the height of the Southern cotton boom in the early 1800s, a single Sea Island cotton harvest on a single plantation might go for $100,000—in 1820 money!

While Charleston was still by far the largest, most powerful, and most influential city on the southeastern coast of the United States, at the peak of the cotton craze Savannah was actually doing more business—a fact that grated to no end on the Holy City's entitled elite. Unlike Charleston, where the planters themselves dominated city life, in Savannah it was cotton brokers called **factors** who were the city's leading class.

It's during this time that most of the grand homes of downtown Savannah's Historic District were built. This boom period, fueled largely by cotton exports, was perhaps most iconically represented by the historic sailing of son. However, in early 1862 a Union sea-land force under General Quincy Gillmore came to covertly lay the groundwork for a siege of Fort Pulaski to ensure the success of Lincoln's naval blockade. (Besides being one of the North's most brilliant officers, Gillmore had a built-in advantage: Like Robert E. Lee, he also helped build the fort before the war.)

The siege would rely on several batteries secretly set up across the Savannah River. Some of the Union guns utilized new rifled chamber technology, which dramatically increased the muzzle velocity and penetrating power of their shells. The Union barrage began at 8:15 A.M. on April 10, 1862, and Fort Pulaski's walls immediately began to crumble under the withering Union fire. At least one shell struck a powder magazine, igniting an enormous explosion. After a mere 30 hours, Confederate General Charles Olmstead surrendered the "invincible" fortress.

But it was not only Fort Pulaski that was rendered obsolete – it was the whole concept of masonry fortification. From that point forward, military forts would rely on earthwork rather than brick to withstand artillery bombardment. In fact, the section of earthworks you see as you enter Fort Pulaski, the "demilune," was added after the Civil War – an ironic nod to the fort's own premature demise.

Fort Pulaski's new commander, General David Hunter, immediately issued an order freeing all local slaves and guaranteeing them a wage working at the fort. As the war dragged on over the next three years, a community of escaped slaves gradually grew on Cockspur Island, aided mostly by a former slave named March Haynes who ferried runaways from Savannah under cover of darkness.

The fort was occupied mostly by troops of the 48th New York Volunteers, who sometimes relieved the boredom of garrison duty by playing the brand-new game of baseball on the fort's vast, grassy parade ground. One of the first photographs of a baseball game was taken at Fort Pulaski in 1863.

Long after the war, Robert E. Lee paid a final visit to Savannah at age 63, accompanied by his daughter Agnes, to see his old comrade-in-arms General Joseph E. Johnston, who lived at 105 East Oglethorpe Avenue. During his stay in town, Lee slept at the Andrew Low house (Andrew's wife Mary was Jack Mackay's niece). Lee would die six months later.

Fort Pulaski is currently administered by the National Park Service, which maintains an excellent website at www.nps.gov detailing the rich history and fascinating archaeology of this, one of Savannah's great must-see sights.

the SS *Savannah* from Savannah to Liverpool in 29 days, the first transatlantic voyage by a steamship.

During the prosperous antebellum period, the economy of Charleston, Savannah, and surrounding areas was completely dependent on slave labor, but the cities themselves boasted large numbers of African Americans who were active in business and agriculture. For example, the vending stalls at the City Markets of both Charleston and Savannah were predominantly staffed by African American workers, some of them free blacks.

Despite the undeniable lack of equality, the racial apartheid typical of Reconstruction and the later Jim Crow era was generally not in evidence at this time. Working-class blacks and whites alike often frequented the same watering holes and lived in mixed neighborhoods, much to the consternation of the elite. Many churches of the South Carolina and Georgia coast had regular biracial attendance during this period. In fact, a strong case could be made that the area's churches are more segregated now than they were before the Civil War, with slavery in full swing.

SECESSION

Though much of the lead-in to the Civil War focused on whether or not slavery would be allowed in America's newest territories in the West, there's no doubt that all figurative roads eventually led to South Carolina. During Andrew Jackson's presidency in the 1820s, his vice president, South Carolina's John C. Calhoun, became a thorn in Jackson's side with his constant, aggressive advocacy for the concept of **nullification,** which Jackson strenuously rejected. In a nutshell, Calhoun said that if a state decided that the federal government wasn't treating it fairly—in this case with regards to tariffs that were hurting the cotton trade in the Palmetto State—it could simply nullify the federal law, superseding it with law of its own.

As the abolition movement gained steam in ensuing years and tensions over slavery rose, South Carolina Congressman Preston Brooks took things to the next level. On May 22, 1856, he beat fellow Senator Charles Sumner of Massachusetts nearly to death with his walking cane on the Senate floor. Sumner had just given a speech criticizing pro-slavery forces—including a relative of Brooks—and called slavery "a harlot." (In a show of support, South Carolinians sent Brooks dozens of new canes to replace the one he broke over Sumner's head.)

In 1860, the national convention of the Democratic Party, then the dominant force in U.S. politics, was held in—where else?—Charleston. Rancor over slavery and state's rights was so high that they couldn't agree on a single candidate to run to replace President James Buchanan. Reconvening in Maryland, the party split along sectional lines, with the northern wing backing Stephen A. Douglas. The southern wing, fervently desiring secession above all else, deliberately chose its own candidate, John Breckenridge, in order to split the Democratic vote and throw the election to Republican Abraham Lincoln, an outspoken opponent of the expansion of slavery.

During that so-called **Secession Winter** before Lincoln took office, seven states seceded from the union, first among them the Palmetto State, followed by Mississippi, Florida, Alabama, Georgia, Louisiana, and Texas.

CIVIL WAR

Five days after South Carolina's secession on Decemeber 21, 1860, U.S. Army Major Robert Anderson moved his garrison from Fort Moultrie in Charleston harbor to nearby Fort Sumter. Over the next few months and into the spring, Anderson would ignore many calls to surrender the fort and Confederate forces would prevent any Union resupply or reinforcement.

The stalemate was broken when the Confederates finally got their *causus belli* when a Union supply ship successfully ran the blockade and docked with supplies at Fort Sumter. Shortly before dawn on April 12, 1861, Confederate batteries around Charleston—ironically none of which were at the Battery itself—opened fire on Fort Sumter for 34 straight hours, until Anderson surrendered on April 13.

In a classic example of why you should always be careful what you wish for, the secessionists had been too clever by half in pushing for the election of Lincoln. Far from prodding the North to sue for peace, the fall of Fort Sumter instead caused the remaining states in the Union to rally around the previously unpopular tall man from Illinois. Lincoln's skillful—some would say cunning—management of the Fort Sumter standoff meant that from then on out, the South would bear history's blame for initiating the conflict that would claim over half a million American lives.

After Fort Sumter, the remaining four states of the Confederacy—Arkansas, Tennessee, North Carolina, and Virginia—seceded. The Old Dominion was the real prize for the secessionists, as Virginia had the South's only ironworks and by far the largest manufacturing base.

In November 1861, a massive Union invasion armada landed in Port Royal Sound in South Carolina, effectively taking the entire Lowcountry out of the war. The coast of Georgia was also blockaded, with Union forces using new rifled cannon in 1862 to quickly reduce Fort Pulaski at the mouth of the Savannah River.

Charleston, however, did host two battles in the conflict. The **Battle of Secessionville**

NATHANAEL GREENE AND MULBERRY GROVE

Like John Wesley, Nathanael Greene's time in Savannah was short and mostly unfortunate. Unlike Wesley, however, Greene never got a chance to leave and start anew.

One of the American Revolution's greatest heroes, Greene rose from the rank of private in the Continental Army to become George Washington's right-hand man. Ironically, this skillful soldier was born into a family of pacifist Quakers in Rhode Island in 1742.

As a brigadier general in the Rhode Island militia, Greene's innate military prowess caught Washington's eye during the siege of Boston, whereupon the future president gave Greene command of the entire southern theater of the fight for independence. While Greene never attempted the suicidal aim of taking on Lord Cornwallis's large and well-trained Southern contingent of British veterans, his guerrilla tactics did force the English contingent to divide and hence weaken itself.

It was Greene who sent General "Mad Anthony" Wayne in 1782 to finally free Savannah from the British, who resisted an earlier attempt to retake the city in 1779. In perhaps a nod to his Quaker roots, Greene insisted that no revenge be taken on Savannah's Loyalists, instead welcoming them into the new nation as partners.

As a reward for his service, Washington granted Greene a large estate on the banks of the Savannah River known as Mulberry Grove, primarily known to history as the place where Eli Whitney would later invent the cotton gin while serving as tutor to the Greene children. (Wayne would be awarded nearby Richmond Plantation.)

Mulberry Grove was less productive for Greene himself, however, who as a lifelong abolitionist refused to use slave labor on the plantation, and hence paid a steep financial price. The 44-year-old Greene spent less than a year at Mulberry Grove, mostly worrying about finances, when he caught sunstroke on a particularly brutal June day in 1786 and died shortly thereafter.

And there's where the real mystery begins. At some point Greene's remains were said to have been lost after a family vault in Colonial Cemetery was vandalized by Union troops. Almost a century passed until in 1900 the Society of the Cincinnati of Rhode Island appointed a search committee to find and properly inter the general's long-lost remains.

The remains were indeed found – right in the vault in Colonial Cemetery where they were supposed to have been, which you can see to this day. However, they were underneath someone else! After removing the coffin of one Robert Scott, excavators found "a mass of rotten wood and human bones mixed with sand," along with a rusty coffin plate reading:

Nathanael Greene,
Obit June 19, 1786
Age, 41 Years (sic)

So it was that in 1902, Greene's remains were finally put to rest under his monument in Johnson Square – dedicated to him by the Marquis de Lafayette 76 years earlier in 1825!

Sadly, all buildings at Mulberry Grove were razed by Sherman's troops in 1864, with only a few brick stairs and portions of foundation remaining. The area – visited not once but twice by George Washington after his friend's untimely death – entered industrial use in 1975 and is currently occupied by the Georgia Ports Authority. No full-scale archaeological dig has ever been done at the site, though the nonprofit Mulberry Grove Foundation (www.mulberrygrove.org) is working toward that as well as a plan to make part of the 2,200 acre parcel a wildlife preserve.

Greene's widow Catherine would go on to remarry and build another mostly vanished plantation, the famed Dungeness on Cumberland Island.

came in June 1862, when a Union force attempting to take Charleston was repulsed on James Island with heavy casualties.

The next battle, an unsuccessful Union landing on Morris Island in July 1863, was immortalized by the movie *Glory*. The 54th Massachusetts Regiment, an African American unit with white commanders, performed so gallantly in its failed assault on the Confederate Battery Wagner that it inspired the North and was cited by abolitionists as further proof that African Americans should be given freedom and full citizenship rights.

Another invasion attempt on Charleston would not come, but it was besieged and bombarded for nearly two years (devastation that was made even worse by a massive fire, unrelated to the shelling, which destroyed much of the city in 1861). Otherwise, the coast grew quiet as most of the Civil War raged in America's interior.

From Charleston to Brunswick, white Southerners evacuated the coastal cities and plantations for the hinterland, leaving behind only slaves to fend for themselves. In many coastal areas, African Americans and Union garrison troops settled into an awkward but peaceful coexistence. Many islands under Union control, such as Cockspur Island where Fort Pulaski sat, became endpoints in the Underground Railroad.

In Savannah, General William Sherman concluded his **March to the Sea** in Savannah in 1864, famously giving the city to Lincoln as a Christmas present. While staunch Confederates, city fathers were wise enough to know what would happen to their accumulated wealth and fine homes should they be foolhardy enough to resist Sherman's army of war-hardened veterans, most of them farm boys from the Midwest with a pronounced distaste for the "peculiar institution" of slavery.

The only military uncertainty left was in how badly Charleston, the "cradle of secession," would suffer for its sins. Historians and local wags have long debated why Sherman spared Charleston, the hated epicenter of the Civil War. Did he fall in love with the city

during his brief posting there as a young lieutenant? Did he *literally* fall in love there, with one of its legendarily beautiful and delicate local belles?

We may never know for sure, but it's likely that the Lowcountry's marshy, mucky terrain simply made it too difficult to move large numbers of men and supplies. So Sherman turned his terrifying, battle-hardened army inland toward the state capitol of Columbia, which would not be so lucky. Most of Charleston's once-great plantation homes, too, would be put to the torch.

For the African American population of Charleston and Savannah, however, it was not a time of sadness but the great Day of Jubilee. Soon after the Confederate surrender, black Charlestonians held one of the largest parades the city has ever seen, with one of the floats being a coffin bearing the sign, "Slavery is dead."

As for the place where it all began, a plucky Confederate garrison remained underground at Fort Sumter throughout the war, as the walls above them were literally pounded into dust by the long Union siege. The garrison quietly left the fort under cover of night on February 17, 1865.

Major Robert Anderson, who surrendered the fort at war's beginning, returned to Sumter in April 1865 to raise the same flag he'd lowered exactly four years earlier. Three thousand African Americans attended the ceremonies, including the son of Denmark Vesey himself. Later that same night, Abraham Lincoln was assassinated in Washington, D.C.

RECONSTRUCTION

A case could be made that slavery need not have led America into Civil War. The U.S. government had banned the importation of slaves long before, in 1808. The great powers of Europe would soon ban slavery altogether (Spain in 1811, France in 1826, and Britain in 1833). Visiting foreign dignitaries in the mid-1800s were often shocked to find the practice in full swing in the American South. Even Brazil, the world center of slavery, where four out of every 10 African slaves were brought (less than 5 percent came to the U.S.), would ban slavery in 1888.

Still, the die was cast, the war was fought, and everyone had to deal with the aftermath. For a brief time, Sherman's benevolent dictatorship on the coast held promise for an orderly post-war future. In 1865, he issued his sweeping "40 Acres and a Mule" order seeking dramatic economic restitution for coastal Georgia's free blacks. However, politics reared its ugly head in the wake of Lincoln's assassination and the order was rescinded, ushering in the chaotic Reconstruction era, echoes of which linger to this day.

Even as the trade in cotton and naval stores resumed to even greater heights than before, urban life and racial tension became more and more problematic. Urban population swelled as freed blacks from all over the depressed countryside rushed into the cities. As one, his name lost to history, famously said: "Freedom was free-er in Charleston."

It was at this time that the foundation for Jim Crow and its false promise of "separate but equal" was laid. Racial in origin, the Jim Crow laws also displayed a clear socio-economic bias as well; it was during Reconstruction that the practice evolved in some areas of wealthy whites walking on one side of the streets and poor whites and all blacks walking on the other side.

RECONCILIATION

The opening of the exclusive Jekyll Island Club in 1886 marked the coming of the effects of the Industrial Revolution to the Deep South and the rejuvenation of regional economies. In Savannah, the Telfair Academy of Arts and Sciences, the South's first art museum, opened that same year. The cotton trade built back to antebellum levels and the South was on the long road to recovery.

The Spanish-American War of 1898 was a major turning point for the South, being the first time since the Civil War that Americans were joined as one in patriotic unity. The southeastern coast felt this in particular, as it was a staging area for the invasion of Cuba.

President McKinley himself addressed the troops bivouacked in Savannah's Daffin Park, and Charlestonians cheered the exploits of their namesake heavy cruiser the USS *Charleston,* which played a key role in forcing the Spanish surrender of Guam.

Charleston would elect its first Irish American mayor, John Grace, in 1911, who would serve until 1923 (with a break in 1915–1919). Though it wouldn't open until 1929, the first Cooper River Bridge joining Charleston with Mount Pleasant was the child of the Grace administration, which is credited today for modernizing the Holy City's infrastructure (as well as tolerating high levels of vice during Prohibition) and making possible much of the civic gains to follow.

The arrival of the tiny but devastating boll weevil all but wiped out the cotton trade on the coast after the turn of the century, forcing the economy to diversify. Naval stores and lumbering were the order of the day at the advent of World War I, the combined patriotic effort for which did wonders in repairing the wounds of the Civil War, still vivid in many local memories.

A major legacy of World War I that still greatly influences life in the Lowcountry is the Marine Corps Recruiting Depot Parris Island, which began life as a small Marine camp in 1919.

RENAISSANCE AND DEPRESSION

In the Roaring Twenties, that boom period following World War I, both Charleston and Savannah entered the world stage and made some of their most significant cultural contributions to American life. The "Charleston" dance, originated on the streets of the Holy City and popularized in New York, would sweep the world. The Jenkins Orphanage Band, often credited with the dance, traveled the world, even playing at President Taft's inauguration.

In the visual arts, the "Charleston Renaissance" took off, specifically intended to introduce the Holy City to a wider audience. Key work included the Asian-influenced work of self-taught painter Alice Ravenel

Huger Smith and the etchings of Elizabeth O'Neill Verner. Edward Hopper was a visitor to Charleston during that time and produced several noted watercolors. The Gibbes Art Gallery, now the Gibbes Museum of Art, opened in 1905.

Recognizing the cultural importance of the city and its history, in 1920 socialite Susan Pringle Frost and other concerned Charlestonians formed the Preservation Society of Charleston, the oldest community-based historic preservation organization in America.

In 1924, lauded Charleston author DuBose Heyward wrote the locally set novel *Porgy.* With Heyward's cooperation, the book would soon be turned into the first American opera, *Porgy and Bess,* by George Gershwin, who labored over the composition in a cottage on Folly Beach. Ironically, *Porgy and Bess,* which premiered with an African American cast in New York in 1935, wouldn't be performed in its actual setting until 1970 because of segregation laws.

In Savannah, the Roaring Twenties coincided with the rise of Johnny Mercer, who began his theater career locally in the Town Theater Group. In 1925, Flannery O'Connor was born in Savannah, and the quirky, Gothic nature of the city would mark her later writing indelibly.

The Depression hit the South hard, but since wages and industry were already behind the national average, the economic damage wasn't as bad as elsewhere in the country. As elsewhere in the South, public works programs in President Franklin D. Roosevelt's New Deal helped not only to keep locals employed, but contributed greatly to the cultural and archaeological record of the area.

The Public Works of Art Project stimulated the visual arts, especially in Charleston, while the Georgia Writers Project published what is still one of the seminal oral histories of the Gullah/Geechee culture, *Drums and Shadows.* The Works Progress Administration renovated the old Dock Street Theatre in Charleston, and theatrical productions once again graced that historic stage. The Civilian Conservation Corps excavated and documented the great Irene Mound near Savannah and built much of the modern state park system in the area.

WORLD WAR II AND THE POSTWAR BOOM

With the attack on Pearl Harbor and the coming of World War II, life on the Georgia and South Carolina coast would never be the same. Military funding and facilities swarmed into the area, and populations and long-depressed living standards rose as a result. In many outlying Sea Islands of Georgia and South Carolina, electricity came for the first time.

The Charleston Navy Yard became the city's largest employer, and the city's population soared as workers swarmed in. The "Mighty Eighth" Air Force was founded and based in Savannah, and Camp Stewart, later Fort Stewart, was built in nearby Hinesville. In shipyards in Savannah and Brunswick, hundreds of Liberty ships were built to transport cargo to the citizens and allied armies of Europe.

America's post-war infatuation with the automobile—and its troublesome child, the suburb—brought exponential growth to the great cities of the coast. The first bridge to Hilton Head Island was built in 1956, leading to the first of many resort developments on the island, Sea Pines, in 1961.

With rising coastal populations came pressure to demolish more and more fine old buildings to put parking lots and high-rises in their place; a backlash grew among the cities' elites, aghast at the destruction of so much history. The immediate postwar era brought about the formation of both the Historic Charleston Foundation and the Historic Savannah Foundation, which began the financially and politically difficult work of protecting the historic districts from the wrecking ball of "progress." They weren't always successful, but the work of these organizations—mostly comprised of older women from the upper crust—laid the foundation for the successful coastal tourist industry to come, as well as preserving important American history for the ages.

CIVIL RIGHTS

The ugly racial violence that plagued so much of the country during the civil rights era didn't visit the cities of the Georgia and South Carolina coast. Whether due to the area's laid-back ambience or the fact that African Americans were simply too numerous there to be denied, cities like Charleston and Savannah experienced little real unrest during that time.

Contrary to popular opinion, the civil rights era wasn't just a blip in the 1960s. The gains of that decade were the fruits of efforts begun decades prior. Many of the efforts involved efforts to expand black suffrage. Though African Americans secured the nominal right to vote years before, primary contests were not under the jurisdiction of federal law. As a result, Democratic Party primary elections—the de facto general elections because of that party's total dominance in the South at the time—were effectively closed to African American voters. Savannah was at the forefront, and Ralph Mark Gilbert, pastor of the historic First African Baptist Church, launched one of the first black voter registration drives in the South.

In Charleston, the Democratic primary was opened to African Americans for the first time in 1947. In 1955, a successful black realtor, J. Arthur Brown, became head of the Charleston chapter of the NAACP and membership soared, bringing an increase in activism. In 1960, the Charleston Municipal Golf Course voluntarily integrated to avoid a court battle. Lunch counter sit-ins happened all over Charleston, successfully challenging the remaining segregation laws, all of which were eventually overturned.

Martin Luther King Jr. visited South Carolina in the late 1960s, speaking in Charleston in 1967 and helping reestablish the Penn Center on St. Helena Island as not only a cultural center, but a center of political activism as well. The hundred-day strike of hospital workers at the Medical University of South Carolina in 1969—right after King's assassination—got national attention and was the culmination of Charleston's struggle for civil rights.

By the end of the 1960s, the city councils of Charleston and Savannah had elected their first black aldermen, and the next phase in local history began.

A COAST REBORN

Without a doubt, the decade of the 1970s brought the seeds of the future success of the South Carolina and Georgia coasts. In Charleston, the historic tenure of Mayor Joe Riley began, and in Savannah came the election of a similarly influential and long-serving mayor, John P. Rousakis. The Irish American and the Greek American would break precedents and forge key alliances in both municipalities, reviving not only the local economies but the age-old rivalry between the two cities.

Beginning with downtown's Charleston Place, Riley embarked on a series of high-profile public works projects to reinvigorate the then-moribund Charleston historic area. King Street would soon follow. In the years 1970–1976, tourism in the Holy City would increase 60 percent. The resort industry, already established on Hilton Head, would hit Kiawah Island, Seabrook Island, and Isle of Palms with a vengeance.

In Savannah, Rousakis would renovate the then-seedy riverfront district, making it the centerpiece of the city's burgeoning tourist trade. The Savannah College of Art and Design (SCAD) opened in 1979 and began the process of renovating dozens of the city's historic buildings, a process that continues today.

The coast's combination of beautiful scenery and cheap labor proved irresistible to the movie and TV industry, which would begin filming many shows and films in the area in the 1970s and continuing on to this day. Beaufort, South Carolina, in particular, would emerge from its stately slumber as the star of several popular films, such as *The Great Santini* and *The Big Chill*.

Charleston received its first major challenge since the Civil War in 1989 when Hurricane Hugo—originally headed directly for Savannah—changed course at the last minute and slammed into the South Carolina coast just above Charleston. The Holy City, including many of its most historic locations, was massively damaged, with hardly a tree left standing.

However, in a testament to the toughness just beneath Charleston's genteel veneer, the city not only rebounded, but came back stronger. In perhaps typically mercantile fashion, Charlestonians used the devastation of Hugo as a reason to introduce a new round of residential construction to the entire area, particularly the surrounding islands.

The economic boom of the 1990s was particularly good to Charleston and Savannah, whose ports saw a huge dividend from increasing globalization. Also in the 1990s came the *Midnight in the Garden of Good and Evil* phenomenon, which would put Savannah—already on the upswing—on the tourist map for good.

Today Savannah's tourism business is healthier than ever, and Charleston is perennially ranked as one of America's top cities, both for visitors as well as for residents. Attracted by the coastal region, artists, writers, and entrepreneurs continue to flock, increasing the economic and social diversity of the area and taking it to new heights of livability.

Government and Economy

GOVERNMENT

Charleston, South Carolina, is run by the **strong mayor** form of municipal government, which means that the elected mayor, in Charleston's case Joe Riley, has extensive powers, including the ability to veto a measure approved by the city council. In practice this means that a mayor, for better or worse, is able to stamp the city with his or her own vision—Riley's influence can be seen in everything from the chichi Charleston Place to new low-income housing developments.

Savannah, Georgia, however, is run by the **council/manager** form of municipal government, in which the mayor is but one vote out of many on the city council. Day-to-day operations are in the hands of an appointed city manager who answers to the council. In practice this means a generally more professional and objective approach to the nuts-and-bolts of government, but an often-frustrating lack of accountability at the top.

Because of both states' strong rural roots, county governments are also very important, though becoming less so as urbanization continues and more areas consider city and county consolidation. In particular, county governments in Georgia hold great sway, in large part because there are so many of them! Visitors to the Peach State are often amazed at how small the counties are, and how many—159 in total. In practice this means that county governments hold a greater proportion of political power than in states where the counties are much larger in land area, like South Carolina.

Another important and long-parodied element of Southern political life is the power of the sheriff. Most sheriffs are elected officials in the South, and because they run the jails and serve the legal papers can and usually do amass a great deal of power in a political career. This is especially true in rural areas, where the sheriff is often the de facto "mayor."

Political Parties

For many decades, the South was completely dominated by the Democratic Party. Originally the party of slavery, segregation and Jim Crow, the Democratic Party began attracting Southern African American voters in the 1930s with the election of Franklin D. Roosevelt. The allegiance of black voters was further cemented in the Truman, Kennedy, and Johnson administrations.

The region would remain solidly Democratic until a backlash against the civil rights movement of the 1960s drove many white Southerners, ironically enough, into the party of Lincoln. This added racial element, so confounding to Americans from other parts of the country, remains just as potent today.

The default mode in the South is that white voters are massively Republican, and black voters massively Democratic. Since South Carolina is 69 percent white and Georgia 67 percent white, doing the math translates to an overwhelming Republican dominance. Both states have Republican governors—South Carolina's is Mark Sanford, Georgia's is Sonny Perdue—and the GOP controls all houses of both state's bicameral legislatures and accounts for all four of the states' U.S. senators.

However, the coastal areas covered in this book, with their large, predominantly Democratic African American populations, function somewhat separately from this realignment. For instance, in 2004 both South Carolina and Georgia gave 58 percent of their total vote to George W. Bush for president. But in Charleston County, Bush received a bare majority of 51 percent. In Chatham County, Georgia, where Savannah is located, Democrat John Kerry won with a plurality of 49.78 percent.

But don't make the mistake of assuming that local African Americans are particularly liberal because of their voting habits. Deeply religious and traditional in background and upbringing, African Americans in the area covered by this book are among the most socially conservative people in the region, even if their choice of political party does not always reflect that.

Intrastate Relations

A few years back a sociologist proposed, partially tongue-in-cheek, that since the coastal regions of the Southeast have more in common with each other than with residents of other parts of their own states, the borders should be realigned to reflect this demographic, cultural, and historic affiliation. Anyone who has spent time in the inland areas of South Carolina and Georgia will immediately recognize the basic truth in this proposal, however unlikely it is to actually happen.

The simple, easily observable fact is that Charleston, Beaufort, Savannah, and Brunswick have far more in common with each other than Charleston has with, say, Spartanburg, South Carolina, or Savannah has with Macon, Georgia. I don't know what you would name the state that resulted from the union of the coastal cities and towns, but I do know that the food would be awesome.

Georgia's largest city and capital is Atlanta, which is even farther removed—both physically and metaphysically—from Savannah than Columbia is from Charleston. Indeed, Savannah and Chatham County are considered so different from the rest of Georgia that old-timers still call Savannah the capital of the "State of Chatham."

ECONOMY

The coastal areas of South Carolina and Georgia are currently experiencing profound changes in economy and business. The rice crop moved offshore in the late 1800s and the center of the cotton trade moved to the Gulf states in the early 1900s. That left timber as the main cash crop all up and down the coast, specifically huge pine tree farms to feed the pulp and paper business.

For most of the 20th century, the largest employers along the coast were the massive, sulfur-smelling paper mills of companies like Union Camp and Georgia Pacific, which had as big an effect on the local environment as on its economy. But even that's changing, as Asian competition is driving paper companies to sell off their tracts for real estate development—not necessarily a more welcome scenario.

Since World War II, the U.S. Department of Defense has been a major employer and economic driver in the entire American South, and the Georgia and South Carolina coast is certainly no exception. Of the services, the U.S. Navy (which includes the Marines) is the dominant military presence in coastal South Carolina, employing over 16,000 military and civilian workers. Coastal Georgia tends to be more Army-dominated, focusing on the huge and vital Fort Stewart facility in Liberty

County. (An exception is the big Navy sub base at Kings Bay, Georgia.)

Despite the closing of the Charleston Naval Yard in the mid-1990s, the grounds now host the East Coast headquarters of SPAWAR (Space and Naval Warfare Systems Center), which provides high-tech engineering solutions for the Navy. Charleston also retains a large military presence in the Charleston Air Force Base near North Charleston, which hosts two airlift wings and employs about 6,000.

Farther down the coast, Beaufort, South Carolina, is home to the Naval Hospital Beaufort and the Marine Corps Air Station Beaufort and its six squadrons of FA-18 Hornets. On nearby Parris Island, is the legendary Marine Corps Recruit Depot Parris Island, which puts all new Marine recruits from east of the Mississippi River through rigorous basic training.

In the middle of southside Savannah sits Hunter Army Airfield, host to a battalion of U.S. Army Rangers. In nearby and largely rural Liberty County, Georgia, is the sprawling Fort Stewart, home base of the 3rd Infantry Division. Near the Florida border in St. Marys is the Naval Submarine Base Kings Bay, home port of eight Trident subs.

These defense facilities combine to bring billions of dollars into the local economy in payroll alone, not to mention the ancillary spending (home-buying, renting, etc.) that goes with it. However, the defense dollar has a downside: When large numbers of troops are deployed on repeat tours of duty, as with the war in Iraq, local economies suffer along with the troops' families.

Of course, tourism is also an important factor in the local economies of the area, particularly in seasonal, resort-oriented areas like Hilton Head, Kiawah, and Seabrook Islands. Though they have very diversified economies, Charleston and Savannah both increasingly rely on the tourist dollar as well. The Holy City in particular has a well-honed tourist infrastructure, bringing at least $5 billion a year into the local economy. Savannah's tourism industry, though growing, is still well behind Charleston's at less than $2 billion a year.

But even more than the tourist boom, by far the biggest economic news of modern times has been the exponential growth of local seaports. Of course the entire coast from Charleston to Brunswick has been dependent on maritime trade since its settlement. But from the 1990s on, the quickened pace of globalization has brought enormous investment, volume, and expansion to area port facilities.

Both the Charleston and Savannah ports experienced record volume in 2006–2007. After years of trying, the port of Savannah finally caught up with Charleston in 2007 to become not only the fastest-growing American port, but the fourth-busiest in the country.

Indeed, despite all other trends, manufacturing and industry remain the largest sectors of the economy in both Charleston and Savannah—due in no small part to the fact that both South Carolina and Georgia are "right to work" states with exceedingly low unionization rates.

Chatham County, Georgia, which contains Savannah, has over 250 manufacturing facilities, with the largest plants including Gulfstream Aerospace and International Paper. Charleston's major industrial employers are Verizon, Nucor, and the Vought aviation plant, which makes fuselages for the new Boeing 787.

Increasingly, however, higher education is more and more important to local economies, and will only continue to be so. For their size, Charleston and Savannah have impressive institutions of learning, almost all of which are growing in enrollment and endowment.

In Charleston, the Medical University of South Carolina is not only the city's largest employer but is growing in importance as a key national bioscience research center. In the liberal arts, the College of Charleston is becoming known for its excellence across the board, especially its nationally renowned music program. The American College of the Building Arts works to educate new generations of artisans, with some classes held at the Old City Jail downtown. Clemson University also has a strong agricultural research presence in Charleston.

The University of South Carolina Beaufort, on a beautiful campus near the historic downtown, is not only increasing its enrollment as the state's newest four-year facility, but has even opened a satellite campus in little Bluffton, South Carolina.

Savannah's higher education scene is best known for the Savannah College of Art and Design, a private institution that is the nation's largest art school and the downtown area's main restorer of old buildings. But another local institution worth mentioning is the rapidly growing Armstrong Atlantic State University, possibly the best education buy in the country. In addition, the University of Georgia maintains a strong marine research presence in Savannah at the Skidaway Institute of Oceanography, and the Georgia Institute of Technology has recently opened a satellite campus in Savannah's new high-tech corridor near the airport off I-95.

People and Culture

Contrary to how the region is portrayed in the media, the coast of Georgia and South Carolina from Charleston down to the Georgia/Florida border is hardly exclusive to natives with thick, flowery accents who still obsess over the Civil War and eat grits three meals a day. As you will quickly discover, the entire coastal area is heavily populated with transplants from other parts of the country, and in some areas you can actually go quite a long time without hearing even one of those Scarlett O'Hara accents.

Some of this is due to the region's increasing attractiveness to professionals and artists, drawn by the temperate climate, natural beauty, and business-friendly environment. Part of it is due to its increasing attractiveness

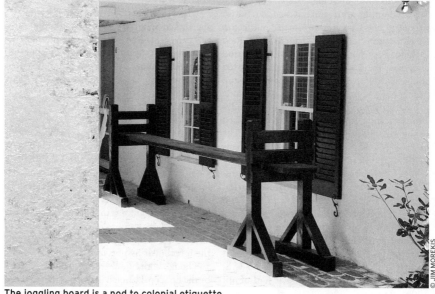

© JIM MOREKIS

The joggling board is a nod to colonial etiquette.

to retirees, most of them from the frigid Northeast. Indeed, in some places, chief among them Hilton Head, the most common accent is a New York or New Jersey one, and a Southern accent is rare.

In any case, don't make the common mistake of assuming you're coming to a place where footwear is optional and electricity is a recent development (though it's true that many of the islands didn't get electricity until the 1950s and '60s). Because so much new construction has gone on in the South in the last quarter-century or so, you might find some aspects of the infrastructure—specifically the roads and the electrical utilities—actually superior to where you came from.

POPULATION

The most solid numbers we have are from the 2000 census, unfortunately already several years old. When you see those figures keep in mind that many areas along the Georgia and South Carolina coast are experiencing double-digit population growth, though generally speaking, urban populations are staying steady or even declining in some cases.

For demographic purposes, Charleston is part of the Charleston/North Charleston Metropolitan Statistical Area (MSA), which includes Berkeley, Dorchester, and Charleston counties. In the 2000 census, it comprised about 550,000 people. The city of Charleston proper has a population of about 100,000.

The Hilton Head/Beaufort MSA includes Beaufort and Jasper counties and comprised about 142,000 people in the 2000 census. The town of Hilton Head had about 40,000 residents in 2000, and Beaufort had about 13,000.

The Savannah MSA, which includes Chatham, Bryan, and Effingham counties, numbered about 300,000 people in the 2000 census. The city of Savannah itself has a population of about 130,000.

The Brunswick MSA includes Brantley, Glynn, and McIntosh counties. Because it was first defined in 2003, there is no U.S. Census info yet, but in 2005 it had about 100,000 people.

Racial Makeup

Its legacy as the center of the U.S. slave trade and plantation culture means that the Charleston/Savannah region has a large African American population. The Charleston MSA had a 31 percent African American population in 2000, and the Savannah MSA had a 35 percent African American population in that census. In the cities proper, the black population is higher, about 35 percent in Charleston's case and nearly 60 percent in Savannah's.

One unfortunate legacy of the plantation era is the residual existence, even to this day, of a certain amount of de facto segregation. Visitors are often shocked to see how some residential areas from Charleston on down the Georgia coast even today still break sharply on racial lines—as do schools, with most public schools in the area being majority black and most private schools overwhelmingly white.

However, despite persistent media portrayals overt racism is extremely rare in the areas covered in this book. In the most remote areas an interracial couple might get some disapproving looks, but in any urban area of real size, hardly anyone will bat an eye.

The Hispanic population, as elsewhere in the United States, is growing rapidly, but statistics can be misleading. Though Hispanics are growing at a triple-digit clip in the region, they still remain under 3 percent of each state's population. Bilingual signage is becoming more common but is still quite rare.

RELIGION

The area from Charleston to Savannah is quite unusual in the Deep South for its wide variety of religious faiths. While South Carolina and Georgia remain overwhelmingly Protestant—at least three-quarters of all Christians in both states are members of some Protestant denomination, chief among them Southern Baptist and Methodist—Charleston and Savannah's cosmopolitan, polyglot histories have made them real melting pots of faith.

Though both cities were originally dominated by the Episcopal Church (known as the Anglican Church in England), from early on they were

VOODOO AND HOODOO

The spiritual system we know as voodoo – the word is a corruption of various West African spellings – came to the western hemisphere with the importation of slaves. Contrary to popular opinion, voodoo isn't a mere collection of primitive superstitions but is a clearly defined religion in its own right and is still the dominant religion of millions of West Africans.

Like many ancient belief systems, voodoo is based on the veneration of ancestors and the possibility of continued communication with them, and it's perhaps this characteristic that is responsible for so much misunderstanding. For example, up until fairly recently the African American Gullah and Geechee populations of the South Carolina and Georgia Sea Islands still had a common belief that the older slaves who were born in Africa could actually fly in spirit form back to the continent of their birth and back again.

While voodoo has always been unfairly sensationalized – the most notable recent example being the "voodoo priestess" Minerva in *Midnight in the Garden of Good and Evil* – it's not necessarily as malevolent in actual practice as in the overactive imaginations of writers and directors. For example, the stereotypical practice of sticking pins in dolls to bring pain to a living person actually has its roots in European and Native American folklore. But sensationalism sells, so you'll sometimes find such items being hawked to gullible tourists as "voodoo dolls."

Much of what the layperson thinks is voodoo is actually hoodoo, a body of folklore – not a religion – indigenous to the American South. Hoodoo combines elements of voodoo (communicating with the dead) and fundamentalist Christianity (extensive Scriptural references). In the United States, most African American voodoo tradition was long ago subsumed within Protestant Christianity, but the Gullah populations of the Sea Islands of South Carolina and Georgia still keep alive the old ways. In the Gullah/Geechee areas of the Georgia and Carolina Sea Islands, the word "conjure" is generally the preferred terminology for this hybrid belief system, which has good sides and bad sides and borrows liberally from African lore and Christian folkways.

The old Southern practice of painting shutters and doors blue to ward off evil comes from hoodoo, where the belief in ghosts, or "haints," is largely a byproduct of poorly understood Christianity (Mediterranean countries also use blue to keep evil at bay, and the word "haint" is of Scots-Irish origin). If you keep your eyes attuned, you can still see this particular shade of "haint blue" on rural and vernacular structures throughout the Lowcountry. (Were you to enter one of these homes, you would almost certainly find a horseshoe tacked over the front door as well.)

Another element of hoodoo that you can still encounter today is the role of the "root doctor," an expert at folk remedies who blends together various indigenous herbs and plants in order to produce a desired effect or result. In *Midnight in the Garden of Good and Evil*, this role belongs to the fabled Dr. Buzzard, who teaches Minerva everything she knows about "conjure work." However, a root doctor is not to be confused with a "gifted reader," a fortuneteller born with the talent to tell the future.

From the no-doubt embellished account in John Berendt's *Midnight,* scholars would put Minerva squarely into the category of root doctor or "conjurer" rather than the undeniably more compelling "voodoo priestess." They say Minerva (not her real name, according to Berendt) still lives today in Beaufort, South Carolina. But you won't see her while you're in the area – she shuns all publicity, and the people who know how to find her aren't talking.

SEPHARDIC JEWS

Visitors are sometimes surprised to discover that two of the oldest cities in the Anglo-Saxon Protestant South have rich and early histories of an active Jewish presence – specifically, **Sephardic** Jews (i.e., those with a Spanish or Portuguese background).

Contrary to modern political trends, Jews and Muslims on the Iberian Peninsula actually got along quite well while the Islamic Moors of North Africa dominated the area. But after Ferdinand and Isabella's completion of the Reconquista in that pivotal year of 1492 – also the date of Columbus's famous voyage – the Jews of Spain went from being respected citizens to persecuted pariahs nearly overnight. Five years later, Portugal followed suit, expelling all Jews on pain of death unless they became "New Christians," or *conversos*. As a result many fled for points beyond to practice their faith openly, whether to London or the Ottoman Empire or to Morocco.

A sizeable proportion of *conversos*, however, were actually so-called "crypto-Jews," who publicly practiced Roman Catholicism while secretly remaining devout Jews. Many synagogues of Sephardic origin today have their floors covered in sand to remember that dark time when Jewish congregations practiced their faith in basements covered with sand to muffle the sounds of their feet.

The diaspora of the Sephardic Jews, ironically, contributed greatly to the health of the global Jewish community, as skilled tradesmen, doctors, and men of letters spread out to Spanish, Portuguese, English, and Dutch colonies where the Inquisition had little sway. It was primarily from the ranks of this Sephardic diaspora that the Jewish settlers of the Lowcountry and Georgia coast came.

The first Jewish presence in Charleston was recorded in 1695, with Jews voting in local elections as early as 1702. Stimulated by the busy port trade of that city, the initially overwhelmingly Sephardic Charleston Jewish community quickly grew and prospered with the addition of **Ashkenazi,** or Eastern European, Jews in the late 1700s. By 1820, Charleston boasted the biggest American Jewish population in the United States.

Savannah's wasn't the first colonial town to host Jewish settlers, but the group of 42 Sephardic Jews who arrived five months after Oglethorpe's landing in 1733 was by far the largest contingent to travel to North America up to that time. All but eight of this core group were Spanish and Portuguese Jews who emigrated to London after spending years as "crypto-Jews" in their home countries.

Accepted without question by Oglethorpe, the Jews of Savannah quickly rose in power and influence. In fact, the first male white child born in Georgia was a Jewish boy, Philip "Uri" Minis.

In one of the great tales of the American melting pot, the assimilation of the Jews into Southern society was so complete that the Secretary of Stateof the Confederate States of America, Judah Benjamin, was a practicing Jew of Sephardic origin.

This assimilation also had a flip side, however, in that the Sephardic Jews were generally just as enthusiastic about owning slaves as any other white citizens of the area. In 1830, about 83 percent of Jewish households in Charleston had slaves, as compared to an almost-identical percentage of 87 percent of white Christian Charlestonians.

also havens for those of other faiths. Various types of Protestant offshoots soon arrived, such as the French Huguenots and Congregationalists in Charleston and the Scottish Presbyterians and German Salzburger Lutherans in the Savannah area. The seeds of Methodism and the "Great Awakening" were planted along the coast from Savannah up to Charleston.

Owing to vestigial prejudice from the European realpolitik of the founding era, the Roman Catholic presence on the coast was late in arriving, but once it came it was there to stay. Savannah, in particular, has by Southern standards quite a large Roman Catholic population, mostly due to the influx of Irish in the mid-1800s.

But most unusually of all for the deep South, Charleston and Savannah not only have large Jewish populations, but ones that have been key participants in the cities from the very first days of settlement. Sephardic Jews of primarily Portuguese descent were among the first settlers of both Charleston and Savannah, and kept up an energetic trade between the two cities for centuries afterward, continuing to the present day.

MANNERS

The prevalence and importance of good manners is the main thing to keep in mind about the South. While it's tempting for folks from more outwardly assertive parts of the world to take this as a sign of weakness, that would be a major mistake. Bottom line: Good manners will take you a long way here.

Southerners use manners, courtesy, and chivalry as a system of social interaction with one goal above all: to maintain the established order during times of stress. A relic from a time of extreme class stratification, etiquette and chivalry are ways to make sure that the elites are never threatened—and on the other hand, that even those on the lowest rungs of society are afforded at least a basic amount of dignity.

But as a practical matter, it's also true that Southerners of all classes, races, and backgrounds rely on the observation of manners

THE TO-GO CUP TRADITION

Arguably the single most civilized trait of Savannah, and certainly one of the things that most sets it apart, is the glorious old tradition of the "to-go cup." True to its history of hard-partying and general open-mindedness, Savannah, like New Orleans, allows you legally walk the streets downtown with an open container of your favorite adult beverage.

Of course, you have to be 21 and over, and the cup must be Styrofoam or plastic, never glass or metal, and less than 16 ounces. While there are boundaries to where to-go cups are legal, in practice this includes most all areas of the Historic District frequented by tourists. The quick and easy rule of thumb is keep your to-go cups north of Jones Street.

Every other election year, some local politician tries to get the church folk all riled up and proposes doing away with to-go cups in the interest of public safety. And he or she is inevitably shouted down by the outcry from the tourist-conscious Chamber of Commerce and from patriotic Savannahians defending their way of life.

Every downtown watering hole has stacks of cups at the bar for patrons to use. You can either ask the bartender for a to-go cup – alternately a "go cup" – or just reach out and grab one yourself. Don't be shy – it's the Savannah way.

as a way to sum up people quickly. To any Southerner, regardless of class or race, your use or neglect of basic manners and proper respect indicates how seriously they should take you—not in a socio-economic sense, but in the big picture overall.

The typical Southern sense of humor—equal parts irony, self-deprecation, and good-natured teasing—is part of the code. Southerners are loathe to criticize another individual directly, so often they'll instead take the opportunity to make an ironic joke. Self-deprecating humor is also much more common in the South than other areas of the country. Because of this, conversely you're also expected to be able to take a joke yourself without being too sensitive.

Another key element in Southern manners is the discussion of money—or rather, the non-discussion. Unlike some parts of the United States, in the South it's considered the height of rudeness to ask someone what their salary is or how much they paid for their house. Not that the subject is entirely taboo—far from it. You just have to know the code.

For example, rather than brag about how much or how little they paid for their home, a Southern head of household will instead take you on a guided tour of the grounds. Along the way they'll make sure to detail: A) all the work that was done; B) how grueling and unexpected it all was; and C) how hard it was to get the contractors to show up.

Depending on the circumstances, in the first segment, A), you were just told either that the head of the house is made of money and has a lot more of it to spend on renovating than you do, or they're brilliant negotiators who got the house for a song. In part B) you were told that you are not messing around with a lazy deadbeat here, but with someone who knows how to take care of themselves and can handle adversity with aplomb. And with part C) you were told that the head of the house knows the best contractors in town and can pay enough for them to actually show up, and if you play your cards right they might pass on their phone numbers to you with a personal recommendation.

See? Breaking the code is easy once you get the hang of it.

Etiquette

As we've seen, it's rude here to inquire about personal finances, along with the usual no-go areas of religion and politics. Here are some other specific etiquette tips:

Basics: Be liberal with "please" and "thank you," or conversely, "no thank you" if you want to decline a request or offering.

Eye contact: With the exception of elderly African Americans, eye contact is not only accepted in the South, it's encouraged. In fact, to avoid eye contact in the South means you're likely a shady character with something to hide.

Handshake: Men should always shake hands with a *very* firm, confident grip and appropriate eye contact. It's okay for women to offer a handshake in professional circles, but otherwise not required.

Chivalry: When men open doors for women here—and they will—it is not thought of as a patronizing gesture, but as a sign of respect. Accept graciously and walk through the door. Also, if a female of any age or appearance drops an object on the floor, don't be surprised if several nearby males jump to pick it up. This is considered appropriate behavior and not at all unusual.

The elderly: Senior citizens—or really anyone obviously older than you—should be called "sir" or "ma'am." Again, this is not a patronizing gesture in the South, but is considered a sign of respect. Also, in any situation where you're dealing with someone in the service industry, addressing them as "sir" or "ma'am" regardless of their age will get you far.

Bodily contact: Interestingly, though public displays of affection by romantic couples are generally frowned upon here, Southerners are otherwise pretty touchy-feely once they get to know you. Full-on body hugs are rare, but Southerners who are well acquainted often say hello or goodbye with a small hug.

Driving: With the exception of the Interstate perimeter highways around the larger cities, drivers in the South are generally less aggressive than in other regions. Cutting sharply in front of someone in traffic is taken as a personal offense. If you need to cut in front of someone, poke the nose of your car a little bit in that direction and wait for a car to slow down and wave you in front. Don't forget to wave back as a thank-you! Similarly, using a car horn can also be taken as a personal affront, so use your horn sparingly, if at all. In rural areas, don't be surprised to see the driver of an oncoming car offer a little wave. This is an old custom, sadly dying out. Just give a little wave back; they're trying to be friendly.

THE GUN CULTURE

One of the most misunderstood aspects of the South is the value the region places on the personal possession of firearms. No doubt, the Second Amendment to the U.S. Constitution ("A well regulated Militia, being necessary to the security of a free State, the right of the people to keep and bear Arms, shall not be infringed") is well known here and fiercely protected, at the governmental and at the grassroots level.

But while guns are indeed more casually accepted in everyday life in the South, the reason for this has less to do with personal safety than with the rural background of the region and its long history of hunting. If you're traveling U.S. 17, for example, from Charleston to I-95, and you see a pickup truck with a gun rack in the back containing one or more rifles or shotguns, this is not intended to be menacing or intimidating. Chances are the driver is a hunter, nothing more.

State laws do tend to be significantly more accommodating of gun owners here than in much of the rest of the country. It is legal to carry a concealed handgun in South Carolina and Georgia with the proper permit, and you need no permit at all to possess a weapon for self-defense. However, there are regulations regarding how a handgun must be conveyed in automobiles. Both states now have so-called "stand your ground" laws, whereby if you're in imminent lethal danger you do not have to first try to run away before resorting to deadly force to defend yourself.

ESSENTIALS

Getting There and Around

AIR

The most centrally located airport for the region covered in this book is **Savannah/Hilton Head International Airport** (400 Airways Ave., 912/964-0514, airport code SAV, www.savanna hairport.com) directly off I-95 at exit 104, about 20 minutes from downtown Savannah, a half-hour from Hilton Head Island, and less than two hours from Charleston. Airlines with routes into and out of SAV include AirTran (www.airtran.com), American Eagle (www .aa.com), Continental (www.continental.com), Delta (www.delta.com), Northwest Airlink (www.nwa.com), United Express (www.ual .com), and US Airways (www.airways.com).

Less convenient to the rest of the region because of its location well north of town is **Charleston International Airport** (5500 International Blvd., 843/767-1100, airport code CHS, www.chs-airport.com), served by AirTran (www.airtran.com), American Airlines (www.aa.com), Continental Airlines (www .continental.com), Delta (www.delta.com), Northwest Airlines (www.nwa.com), United Airlines (www.ual.com), and US Airways (www.usairways.com).

Many travelers to the region are using **Jacksonville International Airport** (2400 Yankee Clipper Dr., 904/741-4902, airport code JAX, www.jia.com) about 20 miles north

© SOPHIA MOREKIS

of Jacksonville, Florida. While it's a two-hour drive from Savannah, this airport's proximity to the attractions south of Savannah makes it attractive for some visitors, who can often find a good deal and make it worth their while to make the drive.

CAR

The main Interstate highway arteries into the region are the heavily traveled north/south I-95, the east/west I-26 coming into Charleston from Columbia, South Carolina, and the east/west I-16 coming into Savannah from Macon, Georgia. A common landmark road throughout the entire area covered by this book is U.S. 17, which used to be known as the Coastal Highway and which currently goes by a number of local incarnations as it winds its way down the coast, roughly paralleling I-95.

Charleston has a "perimeter" Interstate, I-526 (the Mark Clark Expressway), while Savannah as a much smaller version, I-516 (Lynes Parkway).

Rental Car

You don't have to have a car to enjoy Charleston and Savannah, but to really explore the areas surrounding those cities you'll need your own vehicle. Renting a car is easy and fairly inexpensive, as long as you play by the rules, which are simple. You need either a valid U.S. driver's license from any state or a valid International Driving License from your home country, and you must be at least 25 years old.

If you do not either purchase insurance coverage from the rental company or already have insurance coverage through the credit card you rent the car with, you will be 100 percent responsible for any damage caused to the car during your rental period. While purchasing insurance at the time of rental is by no means mandatory, it might be worth the extra expense just to have that peace of mind.

Some rental car locations are in cities proper, but the vast majority of outlets are in airports, so plan accordingly. The airport locations have the bonus of generally holding longer hours than their in-town counterparts.

TRAIN

Passenger rail service in the car-dominated United States is far behind other developed nations, both in quantity an quality. Charleston and Savannah are both served by the national rail system, Amtrak (www.amtrak.com), which is pretty good, if erratic at times—though it certainly pales in comparison with European rail transit. Both cities' Amtrak stations are in light industrial parts of town, nowhere near the major tourist centers. Charleston's station is at 4565 Gaynor Street (843/744-8263), while Savannah's is at 2611 Seaboard Coastline Drive (912/234-2611).

BOAT

One of the coolest things about the Charleston and Savannah area is the prevalence of the Intracoastal Waterway, a combined man-made/natural sheltered seaway going from Miami to Maine. Many boaters enjoy touring the coast by simply meandering up or down the Intracoastal, putting in at marinas along the way. There's a website for Intracoastal information at wwww.cruiseguides.com and a great resource of area marinas at www.marina mate.com.

Recreation

BEACHES

Some of the best beaches in America are in the region covered by this book. While the upscale amenities aren't always there and they aren't very surfer-friendly, the area's beaches are outstanding for anyone looking for a relaxing, scenic getaway.

By law, beaches in the United States are fully accessible to the public up to the high-tide mark during daylight hours, even if the beach fronts private property and even if the only means of public access is by boat. While certain seaside resorts have over the years attempted to make the dunes in front of their property exclusive to guests, this is actually illegal, though it can be hard to enforce.

On federally run National Wildlife Refuges, access is limited to daytime hours, from sunrise to sunset.

It is a misdemeanor to disturb the **sea oats,** those wispy, waving, wheat-like plants among the dunes. Their root system is vital to keeping the beach intact. Also never disturb a turtle nesting area, whether it is marked or not.

South Carolina

The barrier islands of the Palmetto State have seen more private development than their Georgia counterparts. Some Carolina islands, like Kiawah, Fripp, and Seabrook, are not even accessible unless you are a guest at their affiliated resorts, which of course means that the only way to visit the beaches there if you're not a guest is by boat, which I really don't advise.

Charleston-area beaches include **Folly Beach, Sullivan's Island,** and **Isle of Palms.** Folly Beach has a county recreation area with parking at **Folly Beach County Park.** Isle of Palms has a county recreation area with parking at **Isle of Palms County Park.**

Moving down the coast, some delightful

You can ride your horse on Hunting Island beaches.

© JIM MOREKIS

beaches are at **Edisto Island** and **Hunting Island,** which both feature state parks with lodging.

Hilton Head Island has about 12 miles of beautiful, family-friendly beaches, and while most of the island is devoted to private golf resorts, the beaches remain accessible to the general public at four convenient points with parking: **Driessen Beach Park, Coligny Beach Park, Alder Lane Beach Access,** and **Burkes Beach Road.**

Georgia

The main beach in Georgia is outside Savannah at **Tybee Island,** with full accessibility from end to end. The beach on the north end is smaller and quieter, while the south end is wider, windier, and more populated. There are public parking lots, but you can park at metered spots near the beach as well.

Farther south, a very good beach is at **Jekyll Island,** a largely undeveloped barrier island owned by the state. There are three picnic areas with parking, **Clam Creek, South Dunes,** and **St. Andrew.**

Nearby **St. Simons Island** does have a beach area, but it is comparatively narrow and small. Adjacent **Sea Island** is accessible only if you're a guest of the Sea Island Club.

The rest of Georgia's barrier islands are only accessible by ferry, charter, or private boat. Many outfitters will take you on a tour to barrier islands such as Wassaw or Sapelo; don't be shy about inquiring. The most gorgeous beach of all, perhaps anywhere, is at **Cumberland Island National Seashore.**

Surfing

By far the most popular surfing area in the region is the **Washout** at Charleston's Folly Beach. The key surf shop on Folly is **McKevlin's.** For Folly surf conditions, go to www.mckevlins.com or www.surfline.com.

The only other surfing of note in the area is on **Tybee Island's** south end near the Pier and Pavilion. The key surf shop on Tybee is **High Tide Surf Shop.** For a surf report go to www.hightidesurfshop.com.

ON THE WATER
Kayaking and Canoeing

Details for each destination are in their dedicated chapters. Some key kayaking/canoeing areas in the Charleston area are **Cape Romain National Wildlife Refuge, Shem Creek, Isle of Palms, Charleston Harbor,** and the **Stono River.** The best outfitter and tour operator in the area is **Coastal Expeditions.**

Farther south in the Lowcountry are the Ashepoo, Combahee, and Edisto blackwater rivers, which combine to form the **ACE Basin.** Next is **Port Royal Sound** near Beaufort. A good outfitter and tour operator in this area is **Carolina Heritage Outfitters.**

The Hilton Head/Bluffton area have good kayaking opportunities at Hilton Head's **Calibogue Creek** and Bluffton's **May River.** The best outfitter and tour operator here is **Outside Hilton Head.**

The Savannah area has rich kayaking/canoeing at Tybee Island, Skidaway Island, and the blackwater Ebenezer Creek. The best local outfitter and tour operator in this area is **Sea Kayak Georgia.**

© WWW.CHARLESTONCVB.COM

Kayaking resources are plentiful.

Farther south down the Georgia coast, the richest kayaking/canoeing area is in the **Altamaha River** estuary, a hybrid blackwater/alluvial river. Good kayaking can be found in the St. Simons Island area. The best outfitter and tour operator in the area is **SouthEast Adventures.**

Kayaking to Cumberland Island is a special experience; contact **Up the Creek Xpeditions** in St. Marys.

Fishing and Boating

Because of the large number of islands and wide area of salt marsh, life on the water is largely inseparable from life on the land in the Lowcountry and Georgia coast. Fishing and boating are very common pursuits here, with species of fish including spotted sea trout, channel bass, flounder, grouper, mackerel, sailfish, whiting, shark, amberjack, and tarpon. Farther inshore you'll find largemouth bass, bream, catfish, and crappie, among many more. While entire books can be and are devoted to each, here is an overview:

It's easy to fish on piers, lakes, and streams, but if you're over 16 years old you'll need to get a nonresident fishing license from the state. These are inexpensive and available in hardware stores, marinas, and tackle shops anywhere.

In Georgia, a regular license is $9, a one-day license $3.50. A separate license is required for trout fishing. Go to http://georgiawildlife.dnr .state.ga.us for more information or to purchase a license online.

In South Carolina, a nonresident seven-day license is $11. Go to www.dnr.sc.gov for more information or to purchase a license online.

The most popular places for casual anglers are the various public piers throughout the area. There are public fishing piers at Folly Beach, Hunting Island, Tybee Island, St. Simons Island, and Jekyll Island. Two nice little public docks are at the North Charleston Riverfront Park on the grounds of the old Charleston Navy Yard, and the Bluffton public landing on the May River. Many fishermen cast off of abandoned bridges unless signage dictates otherwise.

Fishing charters and marinas are ample throughout the region, for both inshore and offshore trips. Details for each destination are in their dedicated chapters.

ON THE LAND
Golf and Tennis

The first golf club in America was formed in Charleston, and that area has more than its share of fine courses. As far as quality is concerned, consensus pick for best course in South Carolina is definitely the Pete Dye–designed Ocean Course at the **Kiawah Island Golf Resort,** which is open to guests of the club. Coming in second would almost certainly be **Harbour Town** on Sea Pines Plantation in Hilton Head. Not coincidentally, both courses host PGA events.

In Georgia, the Ocean Forest Course at the **Sea Island Club** on Sea Island is a gem— though you must be a guest at the Club to play—as is the affiliated Seaside Course.

For value, go in the off-season, in the colder months, when prices are lowest. Not all courses close, and most are in great shape because of the reduced traffic.

The premier tennis facility in the area is the new **Family Circle Cup Tennis Center** on Daniel Island near Charleston, home of the eponymous women's event and some great public courts.

Other key tennis facilities are at the **King and Prince** on St. Simons and **Jekyll Island Tennis Center.**

Hiking and Biking

Due to the flat nature of the Lowcountry and Georgia coast, hiking and biking here is not very strenuous. However, the great natural beauty and prevalence of a rich range of plant and animal life make hiking and biking very rewarding experiences.

Probably the best trails can be found at state parks in the region, such as **Edisto Island State Park, Hunting Island State Park,** and **Skidaway Island State Park.**

Many National Wildlife Refuges in the area also feature excellent trails, such as **Pinckney**

© WWW.CHARLESTONCVB.COM

Some of the nation's best golfing is in the area.

Island NWR, Harris Neck NWR, and **Cape Romaine NWR.**

There are a couple of "rails to trails" projects that might appeal, the **James Island Trail** outside Charleston and the **McQueen Island Trail** on the way to Tybee Island outside Savannah.

Some areas are almost defined by the plethora of bike and pedestrian trails running nearly their entire length and breadth, such as Jekyll Island and Hilton Head Island.

Wide beaches, very conducive to biking on the sand, are one of the great pleasures of this area. Most bikes you rent in the area will have fat enough tires to do the job correctly. The best beach rides are on Sullivan's Island, Hilton Head Island, Jekyll Island, St. Simons Island, Cumberland Island, and Tybee Island.

Tips for Travelers

TRAVELING WITH CHILDREN

The Lowcountry and Georgia coast are very kid-friendly, with the possible exception of some B&Bs that are clearly not designed for younger children. If you have any doubts about this, feel free to inquire. Otherwise, there are no special precautions unique to this area.

There are no zoos per se in the area, but animal-lovers of all ages will enjoy **Charles Towne Landing** in Charleston and **Oatland Island Wildlife Center** in Savannah. Better still, take the kids on nature outings to the amazing National Wildlife Refuges in the area.

WOMEN TRAVELING ALONE

Women should take the same precautions they would take anywhere else. Many women traveling to this region have to adjust to the prevalence of traditional chivalry. In the South, if a man opens a door for you, it's considered a sign of respect, not condescension.

Another adjustment is the possible assumption that two or three women who go to a bar or tavern together might be there to invite male companionship. This misunderstanding can happen anywhere, but in some parts of the South it might be slightly more prevalent.

Being aware of it is the best defense, otherwise no other steps need to be taken.

ACCESS FOR TRAVELERS WITH DISABILITIES

While the vast majority of attractions and accommodations make every effort to comply with federal law regarding those with disabilities, as they're obliged to do, the very historic nature of this region means that some structures simply cannot be retrofitted for maximum accessibility. This is something you'll need to find out on a case-by-case basis, so call ahead.

The sites administered by the National Park Service in this book (Charles Pinckney National Historic Site, Fort Sumter, Fort Moultrie, Fort Pulaski, Fort Frederica, and Cumberland Island National Seashore) are as wheelchair-accessible as possible.

Some special shuttles are available. In Charleston, call the "Tel-A-Ride" service at 843/724-7420. A couple of cab companies in town to check out are **Express Cab Company** (843/577-8816) and **Flag A Cab** (842/554-1231). In Savannah, Chatham Area Transit (catchacat.org) runs a Teleride service at 912/354-6900.

For the visually impaired, in Charleston there's the **Association for the Blind** (1071 Morrison Dr., 843/723-6915, www.afb .org) and in Savannah there's the **Savannah Association for the Blind** (214 Drayton St., 912/236-4473).

Hearing disadvantaged persons can get assistance in Charleston at the Charleston Speech and Hearing Center (843/552-1212).

GAY AND LESBIAN TRAVELERS

Don't believe all the negative propaganda about the South. The truth is that the metropolitan areas of Charleston, Beaufort, and Savannah are tolerant of homosexuality, and gay and lesbian travelers shouldn't expect anything untoward to happen. Outside the metro areas, locals are less welcoming to gay men and lesbian women, although overt hostility is rare.

The best approach is to simply observe dominant Southern mores for anyone here, gay or straight. In a nutshell, that means keep public displays of affection and politics to a minimum. Southerners in general have a low opinion of anyone who flagrantly espouses a viewpoint too obviously or loudly.

For city-specific information, go to the relevant destination chapter under *Information and Services*.

SENIOR TRAVELERS

Both because of the large proportion of retirees in the region and because of the South's traditional respect for the elderly, the area is quite friendly to senior citizens. Many accommodations and attractions offer a slight senior discount, which can add up over the course of a trip. Always inquire *before* making a reservation, however, as checkout time is way too late.

TRAVELING WITH PETS

While the United States is very pet-friendly, that friendliness rarely extends to restaurants and other indoor locations. More and more accommodations are allowing pet owners to bring pets, often for an added fee, but please inquire *before* you arrive. In any case, keep your dog on a leash at all times. Some beaches in the area permit dog-walking at certain times of the year, but as a general rule keep dogs off of beaches unless you see signage saying otherwise.

Health and Safety

CRIME

While crime rates are indeed above national averages in many of the areas covered in this book, especially in inner city areas, incidents of crime in the more heavily trafficked tourist areas are no more common than anywhere else. In fact, these areas might be safer because of the amount of foot traffic and police attention.

By far the most common crime against visitors here is simple theft, primarily from cars. (Pickpocketing, thankfully, is quite rare in the United States). Always lock your car doors. Conversely, only leave them unlocked if you're absolutely comfortable living without whatever's inside at the time.

As a general rule, I try to lock valuables—such as CDs, a recent purchase, or my wife's purse—in the trunk. (Just make sure the "valet" button, allowing the trunk to be opened from the driver's area, is disabled.)

Should someone corner you and demand your wallet or purse, just give it to them. Unfortunately, the old advice to scream as loud as you can is no longer the deterrent it once was, and in fact may hasten aggressive action by the robber.

A very important general rule to remember is not to pull over for cars you do not recognize as law enforcement, no matter how urgently you might be asked to do so. This is not a common occurrence, but a possibility you should be aware of. A real police officer will know the correct steps to take to identify him or herself. If you find yourself having to guess, then do the safe thing and refuse to stop.

If you are the victim of a crime, *always call the police.* Law enforcement wants more information, not less, and the worst thing that can happen is you'll have an incident report in case you need to make an insurance claim for lost or stolen property.

Remember that in the United States as elsewhere, no good can come from a heated argument with a police officer. The place to prove a police officer wrong is in a court of law, perhaps with an attorney by your side, not at the scene.

For emergencies, always call 911.

AUTO ACCIDENTS

If you're in an auto accident, you're bound by law to wait for police to respond. Failure to do so can result in a "leaving the scene of an accident" charge, or worse.

In the old days, cars in accidents had to be left exactly where they came to rest until police gave permission to move or tow them. However, South Carolina and Georgia have recently loosened regulations so that if a car is blocking traffic as a result of an accident, the driver is allowed to move it enough to allow traffic to flow again. That is, if the car can be moved safely. If not, you're not required to move it out of the way.

Since it's illegal to drive in these states without auto insurance, I'll assume you have some. And because you're insured, the best course of action in a minor accident, where injuries are unlikely, is to patiently wait for the police and give them your side of the story. In my experience, police react negatively to people who are too quick to start making accusations against other people. After that, let the insurance companies deal with it. That's what they're there for.

If you suspect any injuries, call 911 immediately.

ILLEGAL DRUGS

Marijuana, heroin, methamphetamine, and cocaine and all its derivatives are illegal in the United States with only a very few, select exceptions, none of which apply to the areas covered by this book. The use of ecstasy and similar mood-elevators is also illegal. The penalties for illegal drug possession and use in South Carolina and Georgia are quite severe. Just stay away from them entirely.

ALCOHOL

The drinking age in the United States is 21. Most restaurants that serve alcoholic beverages allow those under 21 inside. Generally speaking, if only those over 21 are allowed inside, you will be greeted at the door by someone asking to see identification. These people are often poorly trained and anything other than a state driver's license may confuse them, so be forewarned.

Drunk driving is a problem on the highways of America, and South Carolina and Georgia are no exceptions. Always drive defensively, especially late at night, and obey all posted speed limits and road signs—and never assume the other driver will do the same. You may *never* drive with an opened alcoholic beverage in the car, even if it belongs to a passenger.

As far as retail purchase goes, in South Carolina you may only buy beer and wine on Sundays, not hard liquor. In most parts of Georgia, no alcoholic beverages are sold at the retail level on Sundays, other than in restaurants that also sell food.

GETTING SICK

Unlike most developed nations, the United States has no comprehensive national health care system (there are programs for the elderly and the poor). Visitors from other countries who need non-emergency medical attention are best served by going to free-standing medical clinics. The level of care is typically very good, but you'll be paying out of pocket for the service, unfortunately.

For emergencies, however, do not hesitate to go to the closest hospital emergency room, where generally the level of care is also quite good, especially for trauma. Worry about payment later. Emergency rooms in the United States are required to take true emergency cases whether or not the patient can pay for services.

Call 911 for ambulance service.

Pharmaceuticals

Unlike many European nations, antibiotics are available in the United States only on a prescription basis and are not available over the counter. Most cold, flu, and allergy remedies are available over the counter. While homeopathic remedies are gaining popularity in the United States, they are nowhere near as prevalent as in Europe.

Drugs with the active ingredient ephedrine are available in the United States without a prescription, but their purchase is often tightly regulated to cut down on the use of these products to make the illegal drug methamphetamine.

NOT GETTING SICK
Vaccinations

As of this writing, there are no vaccination requirements to enter the United States. Contact your embassy before coming to confirm this before arrival, however.

In the autumn, at the beginning of flu season, preventive influenza vaccinations, simply called "flu shots," often become available at easily accessible locations like clinics, health departments, and even supermarkets.

Humidity, Heat, and Sun

There is only one way to fight the South's high heat and humidity, and that's to drink lots of fluids. A surprising number of people each year refuse to take this advice and find themselves in various states of dehydration, some of which can land you in a hospital.

Remember: If you're thirsty, you're already suffering from dehydration. The thing to do is keep drinking fluids *before* you're thirsty, as a preventative action rather than a reaction.

Always use sunscreen, even on a cloudy day. If you do get a sunburn, get a pain relief product with aloe vera as an active ingredient. On extraordinarily sunny and hot summer days, don't even go outside between the hours of 10 A.M. and 2 P.M.

HAZARDS
Insects

Because of the recent increase in the mosquito-borne and often deadly West Nile virus, the most important step to take in staying healthy in the Lowcountry and Georgia coast—especially if you have small children—is to keep mosquito bites to a minimum. Do this with a combination of mosquito repellent and long sleeves and long pants, if possible. Not every mosquito bite will give you the virus; in fact, chances are quite slim that one will. But don't take the chance if you don't have to.

The second major step in avoiding insect nastiness is to steer clear of **fire ants,** whose large, gray or brown-dirt nests are quite common in this area. They attack instantly and in great numbers, with little or no provocation. They don't just bite, they inject you with poison from their stingers. In short, fire ants are not to be trifled with.

While the only real remedy is the preventative one of never coming in contact with them, should you find yourself being bitten by fire ants, the first thing is to stay calm. Take off your shoes and socks and get as many of the ants off you as you can. Unless you've had a truly large amount of bites—in which case you should seek medical help immediately—the best thing to do next is wash the area to get any venom off, and then disinfect with alcohol if you have any handy. Then a topical treatment such as calamine lotion or hydrocortisone is advised. A fire ant bite will leave a red pustule that lasts about a week. Try your best not to scratch it so that it won't get infected.

Outdoor activity, especially in woodsy, un-developed areas, may bring you in contact with another unpleasant indigenous creature, the tiny but obnoxious **chigger,** sometimes called the redbug. The bite of a chigger can't be felt, but the enzymes it leaves behind can lead to a very itchy little red spot. Contrary to folklore, putting fingernail polish on the itchy bite will not "suffocate" the chigger, because by this point the chigger itself is long gone. All you can do is get some topical itch or pain relief and go on with your life. The itching will eventually subside.

For **bee stings,** the best approach for those non-allergic to them is to immediately pull the stinger out, perhaps by scraping a credit card over the bite, and apply ice if possible.

A topical treatment such as hydrocortisone or calamine lotion is advised. In my experience the old folk remedy of tearing apart a cigarette and putting the tobacco leaves directly on the sting does indeed cut the pain. But that's not a medical opinion, so do with it what you will. A minor allergic reaction can be quelled by using an over-the-counter antihistamine. If the sting victim is severely allergic to bee stings, go to a hospital or call 911 for an ambulance.

Threats in the Water

While enjoying area beaches, a lot of visitors become inordinately worried about **shark attacks.** Every couple of summers there's a lot of hysteria about this, but the truth is that you're much more likely to slip and fall in a bathroom than you are to even come close to being bitten by a shark in these shallow Atlantic waters.

A far more common fate for area swimmers is to get stung by a **jellyfish,** or sea nettle. They can sting you in the water, but most often beachcombers are stung by stepping on beached jellyfish stranded on the sand by the tide.

If you get stung, don't panic; wash the area with saltwater, not freshwater, and apply vinegar or baking soda.

Lightning

The southeastern United States is home to some vicious, fast-moving thunderstorms, often with an amazing amount of electrical activity. Death by lightning strike occurs often in this region and is something that should be taken quite seriously. The general rule of thumb is if you're in the water, whether at the beach or in a swimming pool, and hear thunder, get out of the water immediately until the storm passes. If you're on dry land and see lightning flash a distance away, that's your cue to seek safety indoors. Whatever you do, do not play sports outside when lightning threatens.

Information and Services

TOURIST INFORMATION

Charleston

The main visitors center is the **Charleston Visitor Reception and Transportation Center** (375 Meeting St., 800/774-0006, www.charlestoncvb.com, Mon.–Fri. 8:30 A.M.–5 P.M.). Outlying visitors centers are the **Mt. Pleasant-Isle of Palms Visitor Center** (Johnnie Dodds Blvd., 843/853-8000, 9 A.M.–5:30 P.M.), and the **North Charleston Visitor Center** (4975-B Centre Pointe Dr., 843/853-8000, Mon.–Sat. 10 A.M.–5 P.M.).

Beaufort and the Lowcountry

The Beaufort **Visitors Information Center** is at 1006 Carteret St. (843/524-3163, www.beaufortsc.org, daily 9 A.M.–5:30 P.M.).

In Hilton Head, get information, book a room, get a tee time just as you come onto the island at the **Hilton Head Island Chamber of Commerce Welcome Center** (100 William Hilton Pkwy., 843/785-3673, www.hiltonheadisland.org, daily 9 A.M.–6 P.M.), in the same building as the Coastal Discovery Museum.

You'll find Bluffton's visitors center in the **Heyward House Historic Center** (70 Boundary St., 843/757-6293, www.heywardhouse.org, Mon.–Fri. 10 A.M.–3 P.M., Sat. 11 A.M.–2 P.M.).

Savannah

The main place for tourist information in Savannah is the downtown **Savannah Visitors Center** (301 MLK Jr. Blvd., 912/944-0455, Mon.–Fri. 8:30 A.M.–5 P.M., Sat., Sun. and holidays 9 A.M.–5 P.M.). The **Savannah Convention and Visitors Bureau** (101 E. Bay St., 877/728-2662, Mon.–Fri. 8:30 A.M.–5 P.M.) keeps an accurate and up-to-date list of lodgings at its website at www.savcvb.com.

Other visitors centers in the area include the **River Street Hospitality Center** (1 River St., 912/651-6662, daily 10 A.M.–10 P.M.), the **Tybee Island Visitor Center** (S. Campbell Ave. and Hwy. 80, 912/786-5444, daily 9 A.M.–5:30 P.M.), and the **Savannah Airport Visitor Center** (464 Airways Ave., 912/964-1109, daily 10 A.M.–6 P.M.).

The Golden Isles

The **Brunswick/Golden Isles Visitor Center** (2000 Glynn Ave., 912/264-5337, daily 9 A.M.–5 P.M.) is at the intersection of U.S. 17 and the Torras Causeway to St. Simons Island. A downtown information station is in Old City Hall, at the corner of Mansfield and Newcastle Streets (912/262-6934, daily 8 A.M.–5 P.M.).

The **Jekyll Island Visitor Center** (901 Downing Musgrove Cswy., 912/635-3636, daily 9 A.M.–5 P.M.) is before you get to the island, on the long causeway along the marsh. The **St. Simons Visitor Center** (530-B Beachview Dr., 912/638-9014, www.bgivb.com, daily 9 A.M.–5 P.M.), is in the St. Simons Casino Building near Neptune Park and the Village.

The **Darien Welcome Center** is at the corner of U.S. 17 and Fort King George Drive (912/437-6684, Mon.–Sat. 9 A.M.–5 P.M.). The **Sapelo Island Visitors Center** (912/437-3224, www.sapelonerr.org, Tues.–Fri. 7:30 A.M.–5:30 P.M., Sat. 8 A.M.–5:30 P.M., Sun. 1:30–5 P.M.) is actually not on Sapelo, but at the dock where you take the ferry, in Meridian, Georgia, on GA 99 out of Darien.

The **St. Marys Visitor Center** is located at 406 Osborne Street (912/882-4000, www.stmaryswelcome.com, Mon.–Sat. 9 A.M.–5 P.M., Sun. noon–5 P.M.).

Cumberland Island Visitors Center is at 113 St. Marys Street (912/882-4336, daily 8 A.M.–6 P.M.).

There are several entrances to the Okefenokee Swamp, with the closest thing to a visitors center being at the U.S. Fish and Wildlife Service's **Richard S. Bolt Visitor Center** (912/496-7836, daily 9 A.M.–5 P.M.) at the eastern entrance near Folkston, Georgia.

MONEY

Automated Teller Machines (ATMs) are available in all urban areas covered in this book. Be aware that if the ATM is not owned by your bank, not only will that ATM likely charge you a service fee, but your bank may charge you one as well.

While ATMs have made travelers checks less essential, travelers checks do have the important advantage of accessibility, as some rural and less-developed areas covered in this book have few-to-no ATMs. You can purchase travelers checks at just about any bank.

Establishments in the United States only accept the national currency (the U.S. dollar). To exchange foreign money, go to any bank.

Generally, establishments that accept credit cards will feature stickers on the front entrance with the logo of the particular cards they accept, though this is not a legal requirement. The use of debit cards has dramatically increased in the United States. Most retail establishments and many fast-food chains are now accepting them. Make sure you get a receipt whenever you use a credit card or a debit card.

MEDIA AND COMMUNICATIONS
Newspapers

The closest thing to a national newspaper in the United States is *USA Today*, which you will find at diverse locations from airports to gas stations. The national paper of record is the *New York Times*, which is available in larger urban areas but only rarely in outlying areas.

In Charleston, the paper of record is the *Post and Courier* (www.charleston.net). Its entertainment insert, *Preview*, comes out on Thursdays. The free alt-weekly is the decade-old *Charleston City Paper* (www.charlestoncitypaper.com), which comes out on Wednesdays and is the best place to find local music and arts listings. A particularly well-done and lively metro glossy is *Charleston Magazine* (www.charlestonmag.com), which comes out once a month.

In Beaufort, the daily newspaper of record is the *Beaufort Gazette* (www.beaufortgazette.com). An alternative weekly focusing mostly on the arts is *Lowcountry Weekly* (www.lcweekly.com). Hilton Head's paper of record is the *Island Packet* (www.islandpacket.com). A good Bluffton publication is *Bluffton Today* (www.blufftontoday.com).

In Savannah, the daily newspaper of record is the *Savannah Morning News* (912/525-0796, www.savannahnow.com). It puts out an entertainment insert on Thursdays called "Do." The independent free weekly newspaper in town is *Connect Savannah* (912/721-4350, www.connectsavannah.com), hitting stands each Wednesday.

The main paper in the much more sparsely populated Golden Isles region is the *Brunswick News* (www.thebrunswicknews.com), but many people read the newspaper of record of nearby Jacksonville, Florida, the *Florida Times-Union* (www.jacksonville.com).

Internet Access

Visitors from Europe and Asia are likely to be disappointed at the quality of Internet access in the United States, particularly the area covered in this book. Fiber optic lines are still a rarity, and while many hotels and B&Bs now offer in-room Internet access—some charge, some don't, make sure to ask ahead—the quality and speed of the connection might prove poor.

Wireless (Wi-Fi) networks also are less than impressive, though that situation continues to improve on a daily basis in coffeehouses, hotels, and airports. Unfortunately, many hot spots in private establishments are for rental only.

However, Charleston does have a municipal free Wi-Fi network. While Savannah does not yet have a city-wide Wi-Fi network, you can a list of free Savannah Wi-Fi hotspots at www.thecreativecoast.org/datainfo/hotspots.

Phones

Generally speaking, the United States is behind Europe and much of Asia in terms of cell phone technology. Unlike Europe, where "pay-as-you-go" refills are easy to find, most American cell phone users pay for monthly plans through a handful of providers.

Still, you should have no problem with cell

phone coverage in urban areas. Where it gets much less dependable is in rural areas and on beaches. Bottom line, don't depend on having cell service everywhere you go.

As with a regular landline, any time you face an emergency call 911 on your cell phone.

All phone numbers in the United States are seven digits preceded by a three-digit area code. You may have to dial a "1" before a phone number if it's a long-distance call, even within the same area code.

The area code for the part of South Carolina covered in this book is 843. The area code for the part of Georgia covered in this book is 912.

RESOURCES
Suggested Reading

NONFICTION
Georgia

Barrow, Elfrida De Renne and Laura Palmer Bell. *Anchored Yesterdays: The Log Book of Savannah's Voyage Across a Georgia Century in Ten Watches.* Athens, GA: University of Georgia Press, 2001. A re-issue of the whimsical 1923 classic, which provides a timeline of Savannah events written in the form of a ship's log.

Calonius, Erik. *The Wanderer: Last American Slave Ship and the Conspiracy That Set Its Sails.* New York, NY: St. Martin's Press, 2006. A page-turning tale of the last illegal slave shipment to land in the United States, on Jekyll Island, Georgia.

Fraser Jr., Walter J. *Savannah in the Old South.* Athens, GA: University of Georgia Press, 2005. An insightful and balanced history of Georgia's first city, from founding through Reconstruction.

Georgia Writers Project. *Drums and Shadows: Survival Studies Among the Georgia Coastal Negroes.* Athens, GA: University of Georgia Press, 1986. Arising from a government-funded research project during the Depression, this still ranks as one of the best oral histories ever assembled, using first-hand accounts from African American residents of Georgia's Sea Islands to paint a picture of a lifestyle gone by.

Greene, Melissa Fay. *Praying for Sheetrock.* New York, NY: Ballantine, 1992. In this modern classic, Greene explores the racism and corruption endemic in McIntosh County, Georgia, during the civil rights movement.

Kemble, Fannie. *Journal of a Residence on a Georgian Plantation in 1838–1839.* Athens, GA: University of Georgia Press, 1984. The groundbreaking anti-slavery account by a famed English actress of her stay with her husband on a rice plantation in McIntosh County, Georgia.

McCash, June Hall. *Jekyll Island's Early Years: From Prehistory Through Reconstruction.* Athens, GA: University of Georgia Press, 2005. For those interested in the lesser-known aspects of this beautiful barrier island's history.

Seabrook, Charles. *Cumberland Island: Strong Women, Wild Horses.* Winston-Salem, NC: John F. Blair, 2002. An even-handed journalistic look inside the tension between environmentalists and the residents of Cumberland Island.

Wood, Betty (ed.). *Mary Telfair to Mary Few: Selected Letters, 1802–1844.* Athens, GA: University of Georgia Press, 2007. The revealing, chatty letters of a great arts patron and member of a major Savannah slave-owning family, to her best friend who left the city and moved North because of her abolitionist leanings. We know that Mary Few replied, but her letters remain undiscovered.

South Carolina

D'Arcy David. *Civil War Walking Tours of the Lowcountry.* Altglen, PA: Schiffer Publishing, 2008. A quick-hitting, reader-friendly compendium of history-themed walking tours in Bluffton, Beaufort, Hilton Head, and Daufuskie.

Fraser Jr., Walter J. *Charleston! Charleston! The History of a Southern City.* Columbia, SC: University of South Carolina Press, 1991. Another typically well-written and balanced tome by this important regional historian.

Gessler, Diana Hollingsworth. *Very Charleston: A Celebration of History, Culture, and Lowcountry Charm.* Chapel Hill, NC: Algonquin Books, 2003. A quick, visually appealing insider's perspective with some wonderfully whimsical, cartoon-style illustrations.

Klein, Maury. *Days of Defiance: Sumter, Secession, and the Coming of the Civil War.* New York, NY: Vintage, 1999. A gripping and vivid account of the lead-up to war, with Charleston as the focal point.

Rogers Jr., George C. *Charleston in the Age of the Pinckneys,* Columbia, SC: University of South Carolina Press, 1980. This 1969 history is a classic of the genre.

Rosen, Robert. *A Short History of Charleston.* Columbia, SC: University of South Carolina Press, 1997. Quite simply the most concise, readable, and entertaining history of the Holy City I've found.

Woodward, C. Vann (ed.). *Mary Chestnut's Civil War.* New Haven, CT: Yale University Press, 1981. The Pulitzer Prize–winning classic compilation of the sardonically funny and quietly heartbreaking letters of Charleston's Mary Chestnut during the Civil War.

General Background

Aberjhani and Sandra West. *Encyclopedia of the Harlem Renaissance.* New York, NY: Checkmark Books, 2003. A brilliantly researched account of the great African American diaspora out of the South that eventually gave birth to the Charleston dance craze of the 1920s.

Lewis, Lloyd. *Sherman: Fighting Prophet.* Lincoln, NE: University of Nebraska Press, 1993. Though first published in 1932, this remains the most thorough, insightful, and well-written biography of General William Sherman in existence.

Lombardo, Bruce. *Chew Toy of the Gnat Gods: Reflections on the Wildlife of the Southeast Coast.* Marietta, GA: Cherokee Publishing, 2004. A biologist's entertaining look at the good, the bad, and the ugly of the coast's indigenous creatures.

Robinson, Sally Ann. *Gullah Home Cooking the Daufuskie Island Way.* Chapel Hill, NC: University of North Carolina Press, 2007. Subtitled "Smokin' Joe Butter Beans, Ol' 'Fuskie Fried Crab Rice, Sticky-Bush Blackberry Dumpling, and Other Sea Island Favorites," this cookbook by a native Daufuskie Islander features a foreword by Pat Conroy.

Stokes, Thomas L. *The Savannah.* Marietta, GA: Cherokee Publishing, 2007. This reissued classic is for those interested in a broader view of the influence of the key regional waterway. Features original sketches by Lamar Dodd, founder of the University of Georgia art school.

FICTION

Berendt, John. *Midnight in the Garden of Good and Evil.* New York, NY: Vintage, 1999. Well, not exactly fiction but far from completely true, nonetheless this modern classic definitely reads like a novel while remaining one of the unique and readable travelogues of recent times.

Conroy, Pat. *The Lords of Discipline.* New York, NY: Bantam, 1985. For all practical purposes set at the Citadel, this novel takes you behind the scenes of the notoriously insular Charleston military college.

Conroy, Pat. *The Water is Wide.* New York, NY: Bantam, 1987. Immortal account of Conroy's time teaching African American children in a two-room schoolhouse on "Yamacraw" (actually Daufuskie) Island.

Hervey, Harry. *The Damned Don't Cry.* Marietta, GA: Cherokee Publishing, 2003. The original *Midnight,* this bawdy 1939 potboiler takes you into the streets, shanties, drawing rooms, and boudoirs of real Savannahians during the Depression.

O'Connor, Flannery. *Flannery O'Connor: Collected Works.* Library of America, 1988. For a look into Savannah's conflicted, paradoxical soul, read anything by this native-born writer, so grounded in tradition yet so ahead of her time even to this day. This volume includes selected letters, an especially valuable (and entertaining) insight.

Internet Resources

RECREATION

South Carolina Department of Natural Resources
www.dnr.sc.gov

More than just a compendium of license and fee information—though there's certainly plenty of that—this site features a lot of practical advice on how best to enjoy South Carolina's great outdoors, whether you're an angler, a kayaker, a bird-watcher, a hiker, or a biker.

Georgia Department of Natural Resources
www.gadnr.org

Ditto for this site, which has lots of great information on the wildlife and geology of Georgia's beautiful and largely undeveloped barrier islands.

Charleston to Bermuda Boat Mapper
http://charthorizon.com/races/ 2007_charleston_bermuda/htdocs/

This cool site allows real-time tracking of all entrants in the 777-mile Charleston-to-Bermuda yacht race.

Coastal Bicycle Touring Club
www.cbtc.org

The clearinghouse for routes and rides by Savannah's most dedicated cyclists.

Georgia State Parks
www.gastateparks.org

Vital historical and visitor's information for Georgia's underrated network of historical state park sites along the coast, including camping reservations.

South Carolina State Parks
www.southcarolinaparks.com

Ditto for this site all about South Carolina's state parks.

Dozier's Waterway Guide
www.waterwayguide.com

A serious boater's guide to stops on the Intracoastal Waterway, with a lot of solid navigational information.

NATURE AND ENVIRONMENT

Francis Beidler Forest Blog
http://beidlerforest.blogspot.com

Informative blog by a nature expert with Francis Beidler Forest, a jointly owned conservation venture of the South Carolina Audubon Society and the Nature Conservancy.

Go Green Charleston
www.gogreencharleston.org

The latest environmental and sustainable living news in Charleston, with a lot of practical and fun visitors' information and links.

Green Drinks Savannah
www.greendrinkssavannah .moonfruit.com

Leave it to Savannah to make talking about the environment a cocktail-oriented pursuit. This site also has links to Green Drinks organizations in Beaufort, South Carolina, and St. Simons Island, Georgia.

Charleston Green Map
www.charlestongreenmap.org

A painstakingly compiled guide to green businesses, restaurants, and organizations in the Holy City.

Ocean Science
http://oceanscience.wordpress.com

A blog by the staff of Savannah's Skidaway Institute of Oceanography, focusing on barrier island ecology and the maritime environment.

Savannah Garden Diary
http://savannahgarden.net

Like the city itself, this is an eccentric but likeable blog about one woman's intimate exploration of gardening in Savannah.

FOOD

Charleston Chow
http://charlestonchow.blogspot.com

An unvarnished take on the local food and bev scene by a professional chef and former food critic for the Charleston *Post and Courier*.

Savannah Foodie
www.savannahfoodie.com

An insider's look at the Savannah restaurant scene, with an emphasis on breaking news.

HISTORY AND BACKGROUND

South Carolina Information Highway
www.sciway.net

An eclectic cornucopia of interesting South Carolina history and assorted background facts, which makes for an interesting Internet portal into all things Palmetto State.

New Georgia Encyclopedia
www.georgiaencyclopedia.org

A mother lode of concise, neutral, and well-written information on the natural and human history of Georgia from prehistory to the present.

Charleston Wiki Project
www.charlestonwiki.org

A Wikipedia just for Charleston, with a resident's point of view.

TOURISM INFORMATION

Charleston Convention and Visitors Bureau
www.charlestoncvb.com

This very professional and user-friendly tourism site is perhaps the best and most practical Internet portal for visitors to Charleston.

Citytrex.com
www.citytrex.com

Professionally produced downloadable MP3 walking tours covering Charleston, Beaufort, Savannah, and the Sea Islands of Georgia.

Index

A

ACE Basin: general discussion 22, 127; ACE Basin National Wildlife Refuge 155-156; birdwatching 144; recreation 120; shells 119; tours 143

African American history: Avery Research Center 53; Beach Institute 206; Cumberland Island 313; Darien 304; First African Baptist Church 191; Greene Square 195; Harris Neck National Wildlife Refuge 305; itinerary 16-19; Massie Heritage Center 210; Old Slave Mart 49; Oyotunji Village 151-152; Penn Center 148-150; Ralph Mark Gilbert Civil Rights Museum 211; roots of the "Charleston" 71; slavery 49, 343; St. Simons Island 294, 295; tours 72, 224; see also Gullah/Geechee history; specific place

African American Monument: 17, 187

Aiken-Rhett House: 13, 17, 54

air pollution: 329

airports: 10, 115, 262

air travel: 364-365

alcohol: 361, 371-372

Altamaha Park of Glynn County: 283

Altamaha River: 22, 306, 323

American Military Museum: 44

Andrew Low House Museum: 205

Angel Oak Park: 125

animals: 332-337

Ansa, Tina McElroy: 295

antiques: 85, 237, 238

aquariums: Aquarium Wharf 42; Cypress Gardens 123; South Carolina Aquarium 44; University of Georgia Marine Educational Center and Aquarium 218

aquifers: 329

archeological sites: Green's Shell Enclosure 155; Pinckney Island National Wildlife Refuge 160; Sapelo shell ring 309

architecture: Beaufort 131; Charleston 34-35; Preston, William Gibbons 188; Regency 200; tabby construction 150-151, 289; see also specific place

Armillary Sphere: 205

Armstrong House: 212

art galleries: Beaufort 141; Bluffton 173; Brunswick 282; Charleston 85; Hilton Head Island 165; Savannah 232, 237, 238

Arthur Ravenel, Jr. Bridge: 95

arts, the: Charleston 77-80; Savannah 229-232

Ashepoo River: 155

Asian Festival: 234

ATMs: 375

atomic bomb, missing: 222

Audubon-Newhall Preserve: 161

Auldbrass: 152

automobile accidents: 371

Avery Research Center: 16, 53

B

bald cypress trees: 124, 331

barbeques: 12

barrier islands: 324

Bartram, William: 280-281

baseball: 242-243

Bateaux: 156

Battery, the: 13, 32

Battlefield Park: 211

Battle Memorial Park: 212

Battle of Bloody Marsh: 298, 343

Battle of Secessionville: 84

Bay Street: 188

beaches: general discussion 324, 366-367; Charleston 91-92; Driftwood Beach 289; Hilton Head Island 165-166; Hunting Island 154; Little St. Simons Island 303; Seabrook Island 126; St. Catherine's Island 309; St. Simons Island 300

Beach Institute: 19, 206

Beacon Range Light: 196

Bear Island Wildlife Management Area: 144, 155

Beaufort: 131-156; accommodations 144-146; city layout 133; entertainment 137-141; food 146-148; history 131-133; maps 132; recreation 22, 142-144; shopping 141; sights 133-137; tourist information 374; transportation 148; trip planning 8

Beaufort Museum: 135

Beaufort National Cemetery: 17, 137

Beaufort Water Festival: 140

Beauregard, General: 55

beauty supplies: 87

Berendt, John: 15, 208

Berners Barnwell Sams House: 139

Bethel Methodist Church: 55

Bethesda Home for Boys: 218

beverages: 256, 361

biking: general discussion 368; Beaufort 143; Brunswick 282; Charleston 95; Edisto Beach State Park 119; Edisto Island 120; Hilton Head

Island 167; Jekyll Island 290; Savannah 244; Sea Pines Forest Preserve 161; St. Simons Island 300
Billie Burn Museum: 177
birds: 335
birdwatching: Beaufort 144; Blackbeard Island 309; Brunswick 282; Butler Island 306; Charleston 95; Crab Bank Heritage Preserve 92; Cumberland Island National Seashore 314; Harris Neck National Wildlife Refuge 305; Hilton Head Island 167; Hunting Island 154; Jekyll Island 290; Melon Bluff Nature and Heritage Preserve 265; Ossabaw Island 270; Pinckney Island National Wildlife Refuge 160; Savannah 244; Wassaw Island National Wildlife Refuge 268; Youmans Pond 265
Bistro Savannah: 21-23, 251
Blackbeard Island: 309
Black Heritage Festival: 232
blackwater rivers: 323
Blessing of the Fleet: 81
Bloody Marsh Battlefield: 298
Blues & BBQ Festival: 235
Bluffton: 172-177
Bluffton Oyster Company: 173
Blythe Island Regional Park: 283
boating: general discussion 365, 368; Beaufort 143; Charleston 93; Hilton Head Island 167; St. Simons Island 300
bobcats: 126
bogs: 161
Bonaventure Cemetery: 13, 23, 214-215
bookstores: 86, 141, 238, 282
Boone Hall Plantation: 67
boot camp: 154
Brighter Day Natural Foods: 23, 239
Broad Street: 32
Broughton Street: 197, 236
Brunswick: 275-285
Bryan County: 267
buggy tours: 72, 137, 224
Bull Island: 92, 95, 123
Butler Island: 306

C

Cabbage Row: 16, 39
Calhoun Mansion: 38
Calhoun Square: 209
camping: Beaufort 145; Charleston 102; Jekyll Island 293; Okefenokee National Wildlife Refuge 319, 320; Savannah 249; Tybee Island 219

Candler Oak: 212
canoeing: general discussion 367; Butler Island 306; Cypress Gardens 123; Little Tybee Island 240; Okefenokee National Wildlife Refuge 319
Cape Romaine National Wildlife Refuge: 22, 92, 95, 123-124
Capers Island Heritage Preserve: 92
Carnegie Library: 19, 213
Carolina Bay: 323
Carolopolis awards: 34
carriage tours: 72, 137, 224
car travel: 365
Cathedral of St. John the Baptist: 13, 204
Caw Caw Interpretive Center: 124
Celtic cross: 196, 197
cemeteries: Bonaventure Cemetery 13, 23, 214-215; Colonial Cemetery 203; DuBignon Cemetery 289; Laurel Grove Cemetery 216; Magnolia Cemetery 63; St. Catherine's Island 309; Zion Chapel of Ease Cemetery 160
Chalk on the Walk: 141
Chapels of Ease: 150, 155, 160
Charles II, King: 29
Charles Pinckney National Historic Site: 67
Charleston: 25-126; accommodations 97-102; architecture 34-35; city layout 31-32; earthquake 40-41; East Cooper 66-69; entertainment 73-85; farmers markets 113; festivals 80-85; food 102-113; French Quarter 45-50; Hampton Park 56-58; highlights 26; history 28, 29-30; maps 27, 33, 98, 118-119; North 62-66; recreation 22, 91-96; services 114-115; shopping 85-91; sights 32-72; tours 70-72; transportation 115-117; trip planning 8, 11-14, 30-31; visitors centers 114; waterfront 42-45
Charleston Battery: 96
Charleston dance: 71
Charleston Food & Wine Festival: 80
Charleston green: 34, 327
Charleston International Airport: 10, 115
Charleston International Antiques Show: 81
Charleston Museum: 54
Charleston Navy Yard: 63
Charleston Place: 88, 99
Charleston River Dogs: 96
Charleston Tea Plantation: 125
Charleston to Bermuda race: 44
Charles Towne Landing: 58
Chatham Artillery Guns: 188
Chazzfest: 84

Chesser Island Observation Tower: 318
children's activities: general discussion 369; Aquarium Wharf 42; Camp Fripp 155; Charles Towne Landing 58; Edisto Island Serpentarium 119; Oatland Island Wildlife Center 214; Seabrook Island 126; Southeastern Wildlife Exposition 80; Summer Waves 291; Waterfront Park 43; water parks 94, 291
Children's Museum of the Lowcountry: 55
chili cookoffs: 164
Chippewa Square: 202
Christ Church: 21, 298
Christ Episcopal Church: 192-193
Christmas: 85
Church of the Cross: 13, 172
cinemas: 80
Circular Congregational Church: 50
Citadel, the: 18, 56, 57
Citadel Bulldogs: 96
City Market: 188-191, 237, 245
civil rights movement: 211, 353
Civil War history: general discussion 18, 348; Battery, the 32; Charleston 28; Civil War Museum 267; Fort Pulaski National Monument 220; Fort Sumter 16, 18, 45; reenactments 84; Savannah 184; see also specific place
Civil War Museum: 267
Clam Creek Picnic Area: 14, 290
climate: 325-326
clothing: 10, 87, 236
Club One: 23, 228
Coastal Discovery Museum: 17, 160
Coastal Plain: 321
Cockspur Beacon: 221
Coffin, Howard: 308
Colbert, Stephen: 78
Coligny Circle: 164
College of Charleston: 53
colleges: 53, 189, 216, 357
Colonial Cemetery: 203
colonial history: 29, 338-341
Columbia Square: 195
Combahee River: 155
Confederate Museum: 52
Conroy, Pat: 15, 19, 134, 177
Cooper River Bridge Run: 81
cotton industry: 345-347
courtesy: 25
Courtyard at Crane: 23, 293
Crab Bank Heritage Preserve: 22, 92
crabs: 334

creole language: 176
crime: 371
Crooked River State Park: 311
cruises: 72, 225
CSS *Georgia*: 213
CSS *Hunley*: 18, 64, 65
cuisine: see Southern cooking
culture, the: 357-363
Cumberland Island National Seashore: 14, 23, 311, 312-315, 367
Cunningham House: 195
Cupcake: 20, 113
Cypress Gardens: 121

D

Daffin Park: 216
Daisy: 198-200
dance: 71, 77, 79, 229
Darien: 304-305
Darien Waterfront Park: 304
Daufuskie Island: 177
Deen, Paula: 189
DeSaussure House: 36
disabilities, travelers with: 370
diving: 93, 241
Dock Street Theatre: 48
dolphin tours: 161
Dorchester Academy and Museum: 265
double houses: 34
Drayton Hall: 13, 17, 18, 58
Drayton Tower: 202
Driftwood Beach: 14, 23, 289
drinks: 256, 361
drugs: 371
DuBignon, John Eugene: 288
DuBignon Cemetery: 289
Duke, Derek: 222
Dungeness Ruins: 313

E

Earth Day Nature Trail: 282
earthquake bolts: 34
earthquakes: 40-41
East Cooper: 66-69
Ebenezer Creek: 22, 240, 268, 323
economy: 355-357
ecotours: Cape Romaine National Wildlife Refuge 123-124; Charleston 72, 95; Edisto Island Tours 120; Melon Bluff Nature and Heritage Preserve 265; Savannah 225
Edgar Fripp House: 139
Edisto Beach State Park: 117
Edisto Island: 117-121, 367

Edisto Museum: 119
Edisto River: 155, 323
Edmonston-Alston House: 13, 36
8th Air Force: 217
Eliza Thompson House: 206, 247
Ellis Square: 190
Emmet Park: 197
English colonists: 340
environmental issues: general discussion
    326-330; Georgia Sea Turtle Center 289;
    "greening" Charleston 327; Kiawah Island
    Conservancy 126
estuaries: 323
etiquette: 25, 362
Evangelical Lutheran Church of the
    Ascension: 198

F
Factor's Walk: 188
Fall Festival: 235
fall line: 321
Fall Tours of Homes and Gardens: 84
Family Circle Cup: 81, 96
famous natives: 78
farmers markets: Brunswick 281; Charleston
    113; Savannah 239
Fashion Week, Charleston: 81
fauna: 332-337
Federal Courthouse and Post Office: 198
Federal Reserve, birthplace of the: 288
female travelers: 369
Festival of Houses and Gardens: 81
festivals: Beaufort 140; Brunswick 281;
    Charleston 80-85; Savannah 232-235; *see
    also specific place*
film: festivals 83, 140, 235; Hilton Head
    Island 163; industry 353; movie tours 224;
    Savannah 230-231; St. Simons Island 300
Finney, Newton: 288
firefighter's museum: 64
Firefly Café: 21, 254
First African Baptist Church: 17, 23, 191, 314
First Baptist Church: 203
fishing: general discussion 368; ACE Basin 120;
    Beaufort 143; Charleston 93; Folly Beach 70;
    Hilton Head Island 167; Hunting Island 154;
    Jekyll Island 290; Savannah 241; Sea Pines
    Forest Preserve 161
Flannery O'Connor Childhood Home: 205
flora: 330-332
Foley House: 21, 247
Folk Music Festival, Savannah: 235
Folkston: 320

Folkston Funnel: 320
Folly Beach: 69-70, 91, 112, 366
Food Fest: 163
Forces of Nature: 231
Ford, Henry: 267
Forrest Gump: 202, 218, 230
Forsyth Fountain: 213
Forsyth Park: 212-213
Fort Frederica National Monument: 297-298
Fort King George State Historic Site: 305
Fort McAllister: 18, 267
Fort Morris State Historic Site: 266
Fort Moultrie: 18, 68
Fort Pulaski National Monument: 13, 220, 346
Fort Stewart Museum: 266
Fort Sumter: 16, 18, 45
Four Corners of Law: 41
Fragrant Garden for the Blind: 213
Francis Beidler Forest: 96, 124
Francis Hext House: 139
Frank, Dorothea Benton: 15
Franklin Square: 190
French colonists: 339
French Huguenot Church: 46
French Quarter: 45-50, 104
French Quarter Inn: 97
Fripp Island: 155

G
gardens: Cypress Gardens 121; Festival of
    Houses and Gardens 81; Fragrant Garden for
    the Blind 213; Jekyll Island Historic District
    287; LeConte-Woodmanston Botanical
    Garden 265; Magnolia Plantation and
    Gardens 59-61; Mepkin Abbey Botanical
    Garden 121; Middleton Place Plantation
    61-62; NOGS Tour of Hidden Gardens 233;
    Phillip Simmons Garden 55; touring 81,
    84, 232, 233; Tour of Homes and Gardens
    (Savannah) 232; Trustees Garden 197; White
    Point Gardens 36
garden stores: 88
Gator: 230
gay resources: 115, 261, 370
gay scene: 77, 228
gear: 10
The General's Daughter: 231
geography: 321-325
geology: 321
Georgia Sea Turtle Center: 289
ghost tours: 71, 224
Gibbes Museum of Art: 50
The Gift: 231

Gingerbread Man: 231
Girl Scouts: 199
Glory: 230
Glynn County: 275-285
Gnats, Savannah Sand: 244
Golden Isles: 271-320; Brunswick 275-285; highlights 272; history 272-274; Jekyll Island 285-294; kayaking 22; maps 273; McIntosh County 304-315; Okefenokee National Wildlife Refuge 315-320; St. Marys 310-312; St. Simons Island 294-303; tourist information 374; trip planning 8, 274
golf: general discussion 368; Beaufort 144; Brunswick 283; Charleston 94; Edisto Island 120; Fripp Island 155; Hilton Head Island 168; Jekyll Island 290; Kiawah Island 125; Savannah 241-243; St. Simons Island 301; Verizon Heritage Classic Golf Tournament 163
government: 354-355
Governor's House Inn: 97
Grayson Stadium: 216, 244
Great Depression: 351
Greek Festival, Charleston: 83
Greek Festival, Savannah: 235
Green, Melissa Faye: 15
Greene, Nathanael: 349
Greene Square: 195
Green-Meldrim House: 18, 204
Green's Shell Enclosure: 160
Greyfield Inn: 314
Grove Plantation House: 155
Gullah Festival of South Carolina: 140
Gullah/Geechee history: general discussion 176; Beaufort 137; Hilton Head Island 159; Sapelo Island 19, 308; tours 162; voodoo 359
guns: 363

H

Hamilton-Turner Inn: 205
Hampton Park: 56-58, 110
Hang Fire: 23, 226
Harbour Town: 21, 161, 164
Harris Neck National Wildlife Refuge: 305
hazards: 372-373
health: 371-373
health stores: 87
heat exposure: 372
Henry C. Chambers Waterfront Park: 133-137
Hervey, Harry: 209
Heyward House Historic Center: 172
Heyward-Washington House: 39
"The Hiker" statue: 213

hiking: general discussion 368; Beaufort 143; Blackbeard Island 309; Brunswick 282; Butler Island 306; Caw Caw Interpretive Center 124; Charleston 95; Cumberland Island National Seashore 314; Cypress Gardens 123; Edisto Beach State Park 119; Harris Neck National Wildlife Refuge 305; Hilton Head Island 167; Jekyll Island 290; Melon Bluff Nature and Heritage Preserve 265; Pinckney Island National Wildlife Refuge 160; Savannah 243; Sea Pines Forest Preserve 161; St. Simons Island 300; Wassaw Island National Wildlife Refuge 268
Hilton Head International Airport: 10
Hilton Head Island: 156-177; accommodations 168-169; beaches 367; entertainment 162-164; food 169-171; history 158-159; maps 157; orientation 159; recreation 165-168; services 171; shopping 164; sights 160-162; transportation 172
Hilton Head National Golf Club: 168
Hilton Savannah DeSoto: 204
Historic District (Brunswick): 277
Historic District (Savannah): 191-212, 253-257
Historic Savannah Theatre: 202
history: 337-354; of the Charleston 71; civil rights movement 211, 353; colonial 338-341; cotton industry 345-347; Jekyll Island tycoon retreat 288; Oglethorpe, General James Edward 343-344; pre-European 337-338; secession 347-348; World War II 352; *see also* African American history; Civil War history; *specific place*
Hodgson Hall: 212
Hofwyn-Broadfield Plantation: 14, 279, 282
holidays: 9
Honey Horn: 155
hoodoo: 359
horseback riding: Jekyll Island 291; Seabrook Island 126; Sea Pines Forest Preserve 161
horses, wild: 314
Horton House Ruins: 14, 289
hospitality: 25
hospitals: 114, 260
Huguenots, French: 47
humidity: 325, 372
Hunter House: 23, 260
Hunting Island: 154, 367
Hunting Island State Park: 13, 21, 144, 145, 154
hurricanes: 326
Hyatt Regency Savannah: 187

I

Ice House Museum: 313
ice skating: 96
Il Cortile del Re: 20, 106
illness: 372
Independent Presbyterian Church: 203
Inn at Middleton Place: 60, 101
insects: 336, 372-373
Internet access: 375
Intracoastal Waterway: 323
I'on: 327
Irish Festival, Savannah: 232
Irish history: 196
ironwork: 35, 55
Isaiah Davenport House Museum: 195
islands, barrier: 324
Isle of Hope: 218
Isle of Palms: 68
Isle of Palms County Park: 91, 366
itineraries, sample: 11-23

J

Jackson, Shoeless Joe: 242-243
Jacksonville International Airport: 10
jazz: 84, 234
Jekyll Island: 285-294, 367
Jekyll Island Club: 288
Jekyll Island Club Hotel: 23, 287
Jekyll Island Historic District: 14, 287
Jenkins Orphanage: 71
Jen Library: 198
Jepson Center for the Arts: 201
Jerusalem Evangelical Lutheran Church: 268
jewelry: 88
Jewish Food Festival: 235
"Jingle Bells": 207
joggling boards: 34
John Mark Verdier House Museum: 135
John Rutledge House: 20, 100
Johns Island: 125
Johnson Square: 191
Jones, Noble: 217
Jones Street: 206
Joseph Johnson House: 139
Joseph Manigault House: 54
Joseph P. Riley Jr. Ballpark: 57
Judaism: 52, 360
Juliette Gordon Low Birthplace: 198

K

Kahal Kadosh Beth Elohim Reform Temple: 52
Kaleidoscope: 140

karaoke: 228
kayaking: general discussion 22, 367; ACE Basin 120; Beaufort 142; Bluffton 174; Butler Island 306; Cape Romaine National Wildlife Refuge 123-124; Charleston 92; Hilton Head Island 166; Jekyll Island 291; Little Tybee Island 240; Skidaway Narrows 240; St. Simons Island 300; tours 225
Kehoe House: 195, 247
Kemble, Fanny: 15, 295
Kiawah Island: 125
Kiawah Island Beachwalker Park: 92, 125
Kiawah Island Conservancy: 126
King Street: 11, 85, 108

L

Ladys Island Marina: 142
The Lady & Sons restaurant: 189
Lafayette Square: 204
La Fourchette: 20, 108
land, the: 321-330
Lanier, Sidney: 279, 295
Lanier Oak: 279
Laura S. Walker State Park: 320
Laurel Grove Cemetery: 216
Laurel Grove South: 19
LeConte-Woodmanston Botanical Garden: 265
Lee, Robert E.: 346-347
Legare Farms: 96, 125
The Legend of Bagger Vance: 231
lesbian resources: 261, 370
lesbian scene: 77, 228
Lewis Reeve Sams House: 139
Liberty County: 265
libraries: 115, 261
lighthouses: Beacon Range Light 196; Bloody Point Lighthouse 177; Cockspur Beacon 221; Harbour Town 161; Hunting Island 154; Morris Island Lighthouse 70; Sapelo Lighthouse 309; St. Simons Lighthouse Museum 296-297; Tybee Lighthouse 221
lightning: 373
literature: 15, 134, 295
Little St. Simons Island: 303
Little Tybee Island: 22, 240
loggerhead turtles: 289, 309, 314, 333
Lover's Oak: 278
Low, Juliette Gordon: 198-200, 205, 216
Lowcountry, the: Beaufort 131-156; ecosystem education 153; highlights 128; Hilton Head Island 156-177; kayaking 22; maps 129; romantic getaways 20-21; tourist information 374; trip planning 8, 130

Lowcountry boil: 147
Lowcountry Oyster Festival: 80-85
Lucas Theatre: 21, 194

M

Madison Square: 203
Magnolia Cemetery: 63
Magnolia Plantation and Gardens: 59-61
Mahoney-McGarvey House: 277
manners: 361-362
Mardi Gras: 311
Marine Corps Recruit Depot Parris Island: 153-154
Marine Memorial: 212
Marion Square: 11, 52
Maritime Center: 297
marshes: 155, 289, 298, 324, 328
Marshes of Glynn: 278
Marshlands: 139
Martin Luther King Jr. Boulevard: 210
Martus: 187
Mary Field School: 19, 177
Mary Rose Waterfront Park: 278
Massie Heritage Center: 19, 209
McIntosh County: 304-315
McQueen Island Trail: 244
Medal of Honor Memorial Museum: 66
media, the: 114, 375
medications: 372
Melon Bluff Nature and Heritage Preserve: 265
Memorial Day: 9
Memory Park Christ Chapel: 307
Menotti, Gian Carlo: 83
Mepkin Abbey: 121, 122
Mepkin Abbey Botanical Garden: 121
Mercer-Williams House Museum: 13, 206
Methodist Church: 192-193
Middleton Place Plantation: 13, 21, 61-62
Midnight in the Garden of Good and Evil: 178, 208-209, 212, 231
Midway: 264-265
Mighty Eighth Air Force Museum: 217
Miles Brewton House: 38
Milton Maxcy House: 138
mining: 330
Mistral: 20, 105
MOJA Arts Festival: 84
Monck's Corner: 121
Moncks Order: 122
money: 375
Monterey Square: 206
Moon River: 218
Morris Island Lighthouse: 70
Mount Pleasant: 111

movies: see film
Mulberry Grove: 349
music: Charleston 79; Gullah 176; Jekyll Island 289, 290; Savannah 228, 229, 233; shopping 87

N

Nathanael Greene Monument: 191
Nathanial Russell House: 37
Native American history: 68, 337-338, 341
Navy Yard at Noisette: 63, 327
Newcastle Street: 277
New Ebenezer: 268, 269
New Ebenezer Retreat and Conference Center: 268
newspapers: 375
nightlife: Beaufort 137; Brunswick 279; Charleston 73; Hilton Head Island 162-163; Savannah 226-229; St. Simons Island 299
North Beach: 244
North Charleston: 112
North Charleston and American LaFrance Fire Museum and Educational Center: 64
North Charleston Arts Festival: 82
nuclear energy: 329

O

Oaks, the: 139
Oatland Island Wildlife Center: 214
O'Conner, Flannery: 15, 205
Officer's Row: 222
Oglethorpe, General James Edward: 178, 182, 183, 343-344
Oglethorpe Square: 200
Okefenokee National Wildlife Refuge: 14, 315-320
Oktoberfest: 234
Old Bethel United Methodist Church: 55
Old Bluffton: 13, 172-173
Old Bluffton Historic District: 172
Old Chatham County Courthouse: 198
Old City Market: 11, 16, 51
Olde Pink House: 193, 255
Old Exchange: 42
Old Fort Jackson: 213
Old Fort (Savannah): 197
Old Powder Magazine: 49
Old Sheldon Church Ruins: 150
Old Slave Mart: 16, 49
Old Town Bluffton: 21, 172
Old Town Historic District (Brunswick): 14, 277
Old Village: 66
Oliver Sturgis House: 194

Orange Hall House Museum: 311
orphanage, first U.S.: 218
Osceola: 68
Ossabaw Island: 269-270
Overlook Park: 278
Owens-Thomas House: 13, 200
Oyotunji Village: 151
oysters: 36, 173, 334

P

packing: 10
Palmetto Trail: 95
paper industry: 328
Park Circle: 64
Parris Island: 153
Parris Island Museum: 154
Patriots Point Naval and Maritime Museum: 66
Penn Center: 13, 17, 148-150
Penn Center Heritage Days: 141
people, the: 196, 357-363
Pepper's Porch: 21, 175
performing arts: Beaufort 140; Brunswick
    280-281; Charleston 77-80; Hilton Head
    Island 163; Savannah 229-230; St. Simons
    Island 300
pets, traveling with: 370
pharmaceuticals: 372
Phillip Simmons Garden: 55
phone services: 375
piazzas: 34
Piccolo Spoleto: 83
Piedmont region: 321
Pierpont, James L.: 207
Pinckney, Charles: 67
Pinckney Island National Wildlife Refuge: 21,
    160, 167
Pinkie Masters: 23, 226
Pin Point, Georgia: 218
piracy: 342
pirate tours: 71
Plantation Days: 84
plantations: Boone Hall Plantation 67; Charleston
    Tea Plantation 125; Grove Plantation House
    155; Hofwyn-Broadfield Plantation 279;
    Magnolia Plantation and Gardens 59-61;
    Middleton Place Plantation 61-62
plantlife: 330-332
Plum Orchard: 314
Poetter Hall: 204
Pogo: 15
police: 114, 261
pollution: 329
Poor House and Hospital: 212

Porgy and Bess: 16, 39
Port Royal: 152
Port Royal Sound: 131
prairies: 317
Price, Eugenia: 279
Provost Dungeon: 42
pumpkin patches: 125

QR

quilting: 163
racial issues: 358
railroad museums: 211
railways: 320
Rainbow Row: 13, 37
Ralph Mark Gilbert Civil Rights Museum: 17, 211
Reconstruction: 350
recreation: 366-369
red wolves: 124
religion: general discussion 358; French
    Huguenots 47; Mepkin Abbey 122; Methodist
    Church 192-193; Salzburgers 269; Sephardic
    Jews 360; voodoo 359
rental cars: 365
Revolutionary War: general discussion 345;
    Charles Pinckney National Historic Site 67;
    Greene, Nathanael 349; Sunbury 266
Reynolds Square: 193
Richardson, Howard: 222
Richmond Hill: 267
right whales: 285, 333
Riley, Joseph P. "Joe": 90
Ritz Theatre: 277
Riverfront Park: 64
rivers: 322
River Street: 13, 185
R. J. Reynolds Mansion: 308
Robert Smalls House: 139
romantic getaways: 20-23
Roundhouse Railroad Museum: 211
Rousakis Plaza: 187

S

safety: 371-373
sailing: 44, 72
salt marshes: 324
Saltus River Grill: 21, 147
Salzburgers: 269
Sand Arts Festival: 234
Sands, the: 142, 153
San Miguel de Guadalpe: 274
Sapelo Island: 19, 308-309
Savannah: 178-270; accommodations 245-
    250; city layout 183; City Market 188-191;

day trips 264-270; entertainment 226-232; festivals 232-235; food 250-260; highlights 179; history 183-184, 346-347; maps 180, 186, 246; recreation 22, 240-244; services 260-262; shopping 236-239; sights 185-225; southside 217-219; tourist information 374; tours 223-225; transportation 262-263; trip planning 8, 11-14, 181; Tybee Island 219-223; Victorian District 212-213; waterfront 185-188; westside 216-217
Savannah College of Art and Design: 189
Savannah Cotton Exchange: 188
Savannah History Museum: 211
Savannah Music Festival: 233
Savannah National Wildlife Refuge: 240, 244
Savannah-Ogeechee River Canal: 217
Savannah Pride Festival: 262
Savannah State University: 216
Scottish Games: 234
Scottish heritage: 304
Scottish Rite Temple: 204
scuba diving: 93, 241
Seabrook Island: 126
Seabrook Village: 265
seafood: 12
seafood farming: 173
Sea Island: 294, 303, 367
Sea Pines Forest Preserve: 161
seaside getaways: 20-21
seasons, best travel: 9
sea turtles: 155, 160, 289
secession: 347-348
Second African Baptist Church: 17, 195
senior travelers: 370
Senti: 257
Sephardic Jews: 360
serpentariums: 119, 319
shark attacks: 373
Shellman Bluff: 306
shells: 119, 314
Shelter Cove: 164
Shem Creek: 92
Ships of the Sea Maritime Museum: 211
shoes: 88
shrimp: 140, 290, 334
Shrimp Festival, Beaufort: 140
Sidewalk Arts Festival: 233
Simmons, Phillip: 16, 55
single houses: 34
Skidaway Institute of Oceanography: 218
Skidaway Island: 218
Skidaway Island State Park: 218, 244
Skidaway Narrows: 22, 240

slavery: 49, 57, 343
society: 357-363
Soft Shell Crab Festival: 152
South Beach Marina: 165
South Carolina Aquarium: 44
South Carolina Stingrays: 96
Southeastern Wildlife Exposition: 80
Southern cooking: general discussion 12; Blues & BBQ Festival 235; Brunswick stew 284; Charleston 102-104, 107, 110; Chatham Artillery Punch 256; Lowcountry boil 147; Savannah 250, 253, 257, 259
Spanish-American War: 213
Spanish colonists: 338-340
spas: 177
Spiritline Cruises: 45
spoken word: 230
Spoleto Festival USA: 83
sporting goods stores: 88
sports: 96
Stamp Act: 345
St. Catherine's Island: 309
Stephen Foster State Park: 320
stew, Brunswick: 284
St. Helena's Episcopal Church: 136
St. John's Lutheran Church: 51
St. John's Reformed Episcopal Church: 55
St. Marys Submarine Museum: 311
St. Michael's Episcopal Church: 39
Stoney-Baynard Ruins: 161
Stono Rebellion: 343
storms: 326
St. Patrick's Day: 9, 181, 196, 233
St. Philip's Episcopal Church: 46
St. Simons Island: 22, 294-303, 367
St. Simons Lighthouse Museum: 296-297
St. Simons Pier: 296
Sullivan's Island: 15
Summerall Field: 57
Summer Waves: 291
Sunbury: 266
sun exposure: 372
surfing: 93, 241, 367
Suwanee Canal: 318
Suwanee River: 323
swamps: 124, 265, 315-320
Sweetgrass Cultural Arts Festival: 83

T

tabby construction: 150-151, 289
Tabernacle Baptist Church: 17, 136
tapas: 76
Taste of Beaufort: 140

Taste of Charleston: 84
telephone services: 375
Telfair Academy of Arts and Sciences: 201
Telfair Museum of Art: 13, 201
Telfair Square: 201
temperatures: 325-326
Temple Mickve Israel: 208
10 Storehouse Row: 64
tennis: general discussion 368; Charleston 94; Hilton Head Island 168; Jekyll Island 290; Savannah 243; Seabrook Island 126; St. Simons Island 301
theaters: Beaufort 140; Charleston 77; Historic Savannah Theatre 202; Lucas Theatre 194; Ritz Theatre 277; Savannah 229; Trustees Theatre 198
The Damned Don't Cry: 209
theft: 371
Thomas Fuller House: 138
thrift store shopping: 165
Thunderbolt: 215
thunderstorms: 325
"to go" cups: 361
tornadoes: 326
tourist industry: 356
tourist information: 374
tours: Beaufort 137, 138-139; Charleston 70-72; dolphin 161; Fort Sumter 45; garden 81, 84, 232, 233; Hilton Head Island 161; Jekyll Island 291; kayaking 92, 142; R. J. Reynolds Mansion 308; Savannah 223-225; St. Simons Island 299; Wassaw Island National Wildlife Refuge 269; *see also specific place*
Trail Ridge: 325
train travel: 365
transportation: 10, 364-365
Trinity United Methodist Church: 202
trip planning: 8-10
trolley tours: 223
Troup Square: 205
Trustees Garden: 197
tupelo trees: 124
turtle nesting: 155, 270, 309
Two Meeting Street: 20, 97
Tybee bomb: 222
Tybee Island: 219-223, 259, 367
Tybee Island Marine Science Center: 223
Tybee Lighthouse: 13, 221
Tybrisa: 223

UV

Union Baptist Church: 177
Unitarian Church: 51

Unitarian Universalist Church of Savannah: 206
University of Georgia Marine Educational Center and Aquarium: 218
vaccinations: 372
Vail, Theodore: 288
vegetation: 330-332
Verizon Heritage Classic Golf Tournament: 163
Victorian District (Savannah): 212-213, 238, 257-258
Vietnam War Memorial: 196
Village, the: 14, 296
Village at Wexford: 164
voodoo: 359

WXYZ

walking tours: 70-72, 224
Wallace, Paula: 189
Warren Lasch Conservation Center: 65
Warren Square: 195
Washington Square: 195
Washout: 93, 367
Wassaw Island National Wildlife Refuge: 268
Waterfront Park: 20, 43
water parks: 94, 291
water tours: 225
The Water is Wide: 19
The Waving Girl statue: 187
weather: 9, 10, 325-326
Wesley, John: 192-193
Wesley Monumental United Methodist Church: 210
West Ashley: 58-62, 110
West Broad St.: 210
Westside: 216
whales, right: 285, 333
White Point Gardens: 36
wildlife: 332-337
William Bull Sundial: 191
windsurfing: 94
WineFest: 163
wineries: 141
women, in the military: 56
women travelers: 369
World War II: 352
Wormsloe State Historic Site: 217
Wright Square: 198
Yemassee: 152
Yemassee War: 341
Yoruba Orisa culture: 152
Youmans Pond: 265
Zion Chapel of Ease Cemetery: 160
zoos: 58, 214

Map Index

Beaufort: 132
Beaufort and the Lowcountry: 129
Brunswick: 278
Brunswick and Glynn County: 276
Charleston Accommodations: 98
Charleston & Savannah: 2-3
Charleston and Vicinity: 27
Charleston Food: 103
Charleston Sights: 33
Cumberland Island: 311

Golden Isles, The: 273
Greater Charleston: 118-119
Hilton Head Island: 157
Jekyll Island: 286
Okefenokee Swamp, The: 316
Sapelo Island: 308
Savannah Accommodations and Food: 246
Savannah and Vicinity: 180
Savannah Sights: 186
Tybee Island: 219

Acknowledgments

I would like to thank the following good folks for their help on this project, in no particular order:

Savannah author Aberjhani for his insight into local African American history; Cathy Sakas of Grays Reef National Marine Sanctuary for her wisdom on the entire Georgia coast; Savannah journalist and diver Michael Jordan for his expertise in local waters; Fran and Amy with Half Moon Outfitters in Charleston for their tips on Lowcountry outdoor adventures; Dave Kyler with the Center for a Sustainable Coast on St. Simons for his tips on enjoying that island; Erin Coy and Katie Chapman with the Charleston Area Convention and Visitors Bureau; Erica Backus with the Savannah Convention and Visitors Bureau; Frank McIntosh with the Georgia Land Trust; Paul Medders with the Georgia Department of Natural Resources; John English, fellow Moon author and a former professor of mine at the University of Georgia; Elizabeth Hansen, Grace Fujimoto, and everyone else at Avalon Travel Publishing for making my first book such an enjoyable experience to work on; and my family for their unending support and encouragement.

Acknowledgment